0119921990 0

0317040797

Research in Psychology
Methods and Design

Third Edition

C. James Goodwin
Wheeling Jesuit University

John Wiley & Sons, Inc.

To Susan

ACQUISITIONS EDITOR   Ellen Schatz
MARKETING MANAGER   Bob Smith
SENIOR PRODUCTION EDITOR   Valerie A. Vargas
SENIOR DESIGNER   Harry Nolan
PHOTO EDITOR   Lisa Gee
PRODUCTION MANAGEMENT SERVICES   Hermitage Publishing Services

This book was set in Bembo by Hermitage Publishing Services and printed and bound by R. R. Donnelley & Sons. The cover was printed by Phoenix Color.

This book is printed on acid-free paper. ∞

Library of Congress Cataloging in Publication Data:

Goodwin, C. James
    Research in psychology: methods and design / C. James Goodwin.—3rd ed.
        p. cm.
    Includes bibliographical references and indexes.
    ISBN 0-471-39861-6 (cloth : alk. paper)
     1. Psychology—Research. 2. Psychology—Research—Methodology. 3. Psychology, Experimental. I. Title.
    BF76.5.G64 2001
    150'.7'2—dc21   2001033246

Printed in the United States of America

10   9   8   7   6   5   4   3   2

PREFACE

The Philosophy of the Text

In the process of preparing three editions of this text, I have been guided by several strong beliefs. First, I would like students to develop a clear sense of how experimental psychologists think. Thus, the student using this book will encounter thorough discussions of the nature of psychological science and how it differs from pseudoscience, the logic of scientific thinking, and the manner in which experimental psychologists (a) design their research, (b) carry it out, and (c) draw reasonable conclusions from it. Second, I want students to understand that psychologists use a variety of methods in their attempts to understand behavior. Although the book's main focus is on the experimental method, there is comprehensive treatment of numerous other research strategies. Third, because I believe that researchers must always be aware of the ethical dimensions of their research, I have placed the ethics chapter early in the book (Chapter 2) and I have included some additional discussion of ethics (Ethics Boxes) in *every* other chapter in the book. Fourth, because I have a love for psychology's history and believe that nobody can understand the present without knowing something of the past, I have incorporated some of the history of experimental psychology into the text. Recognizing that my text is for a methods course and not for a history course, however, I have only included historical information that illuminates important methodological concepts. Fifth, and perhaps most important, although I believe that doing psychological science is a joyful activity, it has been my experience that some students enter the course with a sense of dread. They believe it will be boring, difficult, and not especially relevant for them. To counter this, I have taken pains to write a student-friendly book that is appealing (lots of interesting descriptions of real research), understandable (clear writing in a conversational style), and valuable (a sharpening of important critical thinking skills).

The Organization of the Text

The book includes 12 chapters, an epilogue, and several useful appendices. By thoroughly explaining the scientific way of thinking and contrasting it with nonscientific and pseudoscientific thinking, the opening chapter lays the groundwork for all that follows. Chapter 2 is devoted to research ethics and concerns how the American Psychological Association's code of ethics is applied to research with both human and animal subjects; scientific fraud is also discussed. Chapter 3 examines the question of how ideas for research originate and explains the continually evolving relationship between theory and research. It also helps students learn to use psychology's most important electronic database—PsycINFO. Issues related to measuring behavior, sampling, and statistical analysis are the focus of Chapter 4, which leads up to four consecutive chapters on the experimental method, the Cadillac of research methods. There is a basic introduction to the experimental method (Chapter 5), a discussion of control problems in experimental research (Chapter 6), and two chapters devoted to experimental design (Chapters 7 and 8). Descriptions of other approaches to psychological research follow in subsequent chapters. These include correlational research (Chapter 9), quasi-experimental designs, applied research, and program evaluation (Chapter 10), research using "small N" designs (Chapter 11), and several varieties of descriptive research (Chapter 12). The appendices describe how to prepare the (in)famous APA-style research report, how to construct a survey, and how to carry out statistical analyses and draw conclusions about research outcomes. A final appendix provides feedback for the end-of-chapter self-tests and applications exercises.

At various points in the text, there are boxed sections of three general types. *Origins* boxes supply interesting information about the historical roots of experimental psychology and show how various research concepts and methods were created and have evolved over the years. *Classic Studies* boxes describe well-known experiments (e.g., the Bobo doll studies) that illustrate particular research designs and methodological issues. Finally, the above-mentioned *Ethics* boxes reflect my belief that a consideration of research ethics should occur in more than just a single chapter. The ethics boxes consider such topics as informed consent, the operation of participant pools, and the proper use of surveys.

It is not uncommon for methods texts to begin with simple descriptive methods (observation, survey, etc.), move through correlational and quasi-experimental methods, and eventually reach the experimental method. There is certainly some logic to this organizational scheme, but it is not the scheme I have chosen to use. Rather, when teaching the course some years ago, I was always disturbed by how late in the semester students were encountering such things as factorial designs—who wants to be figuring out interactions while they are still digesting their Thanksgiving dinner? I wanted to get to experiments sooner in the term because I wanted to be able to spend enough time on them if students ran into trouble. Also, because most of my labs used experimental designs, I wanted students to have some understanding of the studies they were running during the semester. So my chapter organization reflects the way I teach the course—I like to get to experiments as soon as possible. Reviewers of the text have been divided on the issue, with most liking the current organization, but some preferring to start with descriptive methods. I have been pleased to learn, however, that a number of reviewer/colleagues who like to begin the course with descriptive methods have been using my text anyway, and simply changing the chapter sequence to suit them. Thus, it is worth noting that the text is to some degree modular and can be taught using several different arrangements of chapters.

New to the Third Edition

The first two editions of *Research in Psychology* have been quite successful, and I believe a good book has been strengthened. In the third edition, in addition to some general rewriting for increased clarity throughout the text, these specific additions and changes occur:

- Responding to the concerns of my students, I have included some feedback for the Applications Exercises that are found at the end of each chapter. Appendix E helps students with about half of these exercise items, leaving the other half for instructors to assign as graded homework. Answers to all the exercises can be found in the Instructor's Manual.

- For the end-of-chapter reviews, I have eliminated the fill-in items and added short essay items instead, hoping to encourage a deeper level of conceptual understanding on the part of students.

- I have added chapter summaries and I now begin chapters with a preview and a set of learning objectives for the chapter.

- The description of pseudoscience (Chapter 1) has been improved by replacing the outdated biorhythms example with a more current examination of subliminal self-help tapes.

- A new section on special populations (e.g., children, prisoners) has been added to the ethics chapter.

- The Internet has had a dramatic effect on psychological scientists. Just one example concerns how psychologists conduct literature searches. The section of Chapter 3 dealing with online searching of PsycINFO has been rewritten to reflect the latest changes.

- Several of the case studies have been replaced with more recent and interesting examples (e.g., research on the alleged Mozart effect, a study on subliminal tapes that combines placebo and waiting list controls).

- Qualitative research procedures (e.g., focus groups) and issues related to the qualitative-quantitative distinction have been added at several points in the text.

- Stem and leaf displays and how to construct them have been added to the section on descriptive statistics (Chapter 4).

- Cross-cultural factors have been added to the discussion of external validity (Chapter 5).

- The descriptions of field studies, matching, and multiple regression have been elaborated.

- There is a new ethics box on practical tips for being an ethically competent experimenter (Chapter 8); ethics boxes on informed consent and participant pools have been elaborated.

- The description of multiple regression (Chapter 9) has been elaborated.
- The discussion of time series has been enlarged through the addition of several design variations (Chapter 10).
- A new case study on the changing criterion design has been added to Chapter 11.
- The Epilogue includes a new section summarizing the skills that students have learned in the course ("What I Learned in My Research Methods Course").
- Appendix A has a new section on tips for creating an effective poster presentation.

Pedagogical Aids

For the student, this text has several features designed to facilitate learning. Each chapter starts with a brief preview of what is to be found in the chapter and a set of learning objectives for the chapter. Chapters end with a summary of important points, followed by a set of review questions and applications exercises. The review includes multiple-choice questions (with feedback in Appendix E) and short essay questions. These sample test items are not just definitional; they ask students to apply some of the concepts learned in the chapter. The applications exercises include thought questions and problems to solve that require using the concepts learned in the chapter. Key terms and concepts appear in **boldfaced** print throughout the book and they are collected in a Glossary at the end of the book. To make it easier to find definitions of the boldfaced glossary terms, I have structured the Index so that the text page where a glossary term is first defined is boldfaced in the Subject Index. For example, the Subject Index includes the following:

counterbalancing, **191**–198, 218–222, 235, 262–265, 378

This indicates that (a) counterbalancing is a glossary term, because it has a boldfaced page number, and (b) page 191 is the page in the text where the term appears in boldface and is defined.

Supplemental Materials

- A major addition to the third edition project is a new combined Study Guide and Lab Manual. The study guide includes concept questions for students to answer as they work their way through chapters, sample objective test items (fill-ins, matching, multiple choice), and Applications Exercises similar to the ones found at the ends of chapters in the main text. The lab manual portion of the book includes detailed instructions and materials that enable students to complete simple data collection exercises (under supervision, of course) that illustrate various research methods.
- An Instructor's Manual can be downloaded from Wiley's website. It includes ideas for lecture elaborations, in-class active learning exercises, homework assignments, and a list of websites related to methodology.
- A password-protected Test Bank is also available from the website. Upon request, Wiley will mail a disk version of the Test Bank to adopters.

Acknowledgments

This project would not have been started, much less completed and evolved into a third edition, without the encouragement and support of many people, most notably my wife (Susan, a corporate auditor, good at keeping me on task yet willing to let me sneak out for an occasional guilt-free nine holes) and my children (Kerri, a fellow experimental psychologist and college professor, and Charles, a geologist-in-training and golfing buddy). The hundreds of students who have passed through my research methods course have been my principal source of inspiration in writing the book—during the years before I started writing it, many of them told me to stop complaining about the textbook being used and write my own. I would especially like to acknowledge Aimee Faso Wright, who was the leader of a group of students interested in cognitive mapping and was the senior author of the sample study on that topic in Appendix A. I'm delighted that she has become a Ph.D. pharmacologist.

To Darryl Bruce, my dissertation director, I owe a great debt. He first showed me just how exciting research in psychology can be during my grad school days in Tallahassee, and through our (almost) annual 3-hour APA breakfasts, he continues to be a mentor. I would also like to thank two of my colleagues in the Society for the Teaching of Psychology (APA's Division 2), Wayne Weiten and Steve Davis. At the very beginning of the project, both were instrumental in convincing me that I actually could write a text, and both continue to provide support, encouragement, and friendship.

Thanks go to the reviewers of this edition for their comments and suggestions: Professor William P. Smotherman, Binghamton University-SUNY; Professor Thomas Joiner, Florida Sate University; Professor Jason L. Hicks, Louisiana State University; Professor Margaret Ruddy, The College of New Jersey; Professor Jennifer Myers, University of Michigan; Professor Bradley H. Smith, University of South Carolina; Professor Allen Butt, Indiana State University.

Finally, the editors and production staff at John Wiley have continued to be superb, making the entire process a breeze (or at least much less onerous than I have any reason to expect) and continuing to pay for good meals at conventions. A special thanks goes to Ellen Schatz, Psychology Editor of the College Division at Wiley. She has been constantly supportive, gentle in her prodding, and wise beyond her years when making suggestions for improving the text.

CONTENTS

CHAPTER 7

Experimental Design I: Single-Factor Designs   213

CHAPTER 8

Experimental Design II: Factorial Designs   245

CHAPTER 9

Correlational Research   281

CHAPTER 10

Quasi-Experimental Designs and Applied Research   315

CHAPTER 11

Small N Designs   351

APPENDIX A
Communicating the Results of Research in Psychology 427

APPENDIX B
Developing Surveys for Research in Psychology 459

Summary of Case Studies

CHAPTER 1

Scientific Thinking in Psychology

Preview & Chapter Objectives

Welcome to what is perhaps the most important course you will take as an undergraduate student of psychology. This opening chapter begins by trying to convince you that a methods course is essential to your education, and then proceeds with an introduction to nonscientific, pseudoscientific, and scientific ways of thinking. Distinguishing science from pseudoscience is especially important for psychology, because much of what passes for "psychological truth" (e.g., the effectiveness of so-called subliminal self-help tapes) is the result of pseudoscience. The chapter closes with a discussion of the goals for a scientific psychology and brief descriptions of the work of two of experimental psychology's stars, Eleanor Gibson and B. F. Skinner. They both illustrate the enthusiasm that research psychologists show for their work. When you finish this chapter, you should be able to:

- Defend the importance of a research methods course.
- Explain how the overall purpose of a methods course differs from other courses in the psychology curriculum.
- Identify and evaluate nonscientific ways of knowing about things in the world.
- Describe the attributes of scientific thinking, as practiced by research psychologists.
- Recognize pseudoscience by identifying the four main features of pseudoscientific thinking.
- Describe the four main goals of research in psychology.

In the preface to his weighty two-volume *Principles of Physiological Psychology,* first published in 1874, the German physiologist Wilhelm Wundt boldly and unambiguously declared that his text represented "an attempt to mark out a new domain of *science*" (Wundt, 1874/1904; italics added). Shortly after publishing the book, Wundt established his now famous psychology laboratory at Leipzig, Germany, attracting students from all over Europe as well as from the United States. American universities soon established their own laboratories, about 20 of them by 1892 (Sokal, 1992). In that same year the American Psychological Association (APA) was founded, and before long it ratified a constitution identifying its purpose as "the advancement of Psychology as a *science.* Those who are eligible for membership are engaged in this work" (Cattell, 1895, p. 150; italics added). Thus for psychology's pioneers, both in Germany and in the United States, the "new psychology" was to be identified with science. It gradually forged an identity separate from those of physiology and philosophy to become the independent discipline it is today.

For the early psychologists, the new psychology was to be a science of mental life, the goal being to understand exactly how the mind was structured and/or how it enabled people to adapt to their environments. In order to study the mind scientifically, however, generally agreed-upon methods had to be developed and taught. Hence, students of the new psychology found themselves in laboratories learning the basic procedures for studying the mind. Indeed, one of psychology's most famous early texts was a two-volume (four if the instructor's manuals are included) laboratory manual published right after the turn of the twentieth century by the eminent experimental psychologist E. B. Titchener. The manuals were in use in lab courses well into the 1930s and were instrumental in training a generation of experimental psychologists (Tweney, 1987).

Although the particular methods have changed considerably over the years, today's psychology departments continue this long tradition of teaching the tools of the trade to psychology students. From the very beginning of psychology's history, then, teaching research methodology has been the heart and soul of the psychology curriculum. Of course, students tend to be suspicious of the argument that they should take the research methods course because "we've always done it that way." There should be other reasons to justify taking the course.

Why Take This Course?

The most obvious reason for taking a course in research methods is to begin the process of learning how to do research in psychology. My ideal scenario would be for you to become fascinated by research, decide that you would like to do some, get your feet wet as an undergraduate (e.g., collaborate with a professor and perhaps present your research at an undergraduate research conference), go to graduate school and complete a doctorate in psychology, begin a career as a productive researcher, and eventually be named recipient of the APA's annual award for "Distinguished Scientific Contributions"! Of course, I'm also a realist and know that most psychology majors have interests other than doing research, most do not go on to earn doctorates, most who earn doctorates do not become productive researchers, and very few productive scholars win prestigious APA awards. If you won't be a famous research psychologist some day, are there still reasons to take this course? Sure.

For one thing, a course in research methods provides a solid foundation for other psychology courses in more specific topic areas (social, cognitive, developmental, etc.). The difference between the methods course and these other courses is essentially the difference between process and content. The methods course teaches a process of acquiring knowledge that is then applied to all of the specific content areas represented by other courses in the psychology curriculum. A social psychology experiment in conformity might be worlds apart in subject matter from a cognitive psychology study on short-term memory, but their common bond is method—the way in which the knowledge about these phenomena is acquired. Fully understanding textbook descriptions of research in psychology is infinitely easier if you know something about the methods used to arrive at conclusions about behavior.

To illustrate, take a minute and look at one of your other psychology textbooks. Chances are that virtually every paragraph makes some assertion about behavior that either includes a specific description of a research study or at least makes reference to one. On my shelf, for example, is a social psychology text by Myers (1990) that includes the following description of a study about the effects of violent pornography on male aggression (Donnerstein, 1980). Myers wrote that the experimenter "showed 120 … men either a neutral, an erotic, or an aggressive-erotic (rape) film. Then the men, supposedly as part of another experiment, 'taught' a male or female confederate some nonsense syllables by choosing how much shock to administer for incorrect answers. The men who had watched the rape film administered markedly stronger shocks—but only toward female victims" (Myers, 1990, p. 393). While reading this description, someone unfamiliar with experimental design might get the general idea, but a researcher would also be registering that the study was at the very least a 2×3 between-subjects factorial design resulting in a type of interaction effect that takes precedence over any main effects; that the two independent variables (film type, victim gender) were both manipulated variables, thereby strengthening the causal interpretation of the results; and that the "victims" were not really shocked but were clued in to the purposes of the study (i.e., they were confederates).[1] Also, the thoughts "I wonder what would happen if there was more of a delay between viewing the film and the learning part of the study?" Or "I wonder how female subjects would react in a replication of the study?" might also float

---

[1] All of the jargon in this sentence will be part of your everyday vocabulary by the time you finish this course.

through the mind of someone in tune with the kind of "what do we do next?" thinking that accompanies knowledge of research methodology.

A third reason for taking experimental psychology is that even if you never collect a single piece of data after completing this course, knowledge of research methods will make you a more informed and critical consumer of information. We are continually exposed to claims about behavior from sources ranging from the people around us who are amateur psychologists (i.e., everyone) to media accounts ranging from the sublime (an account in a reputable magazine about research on the relationship between TV watching and aggressiveness) to the ridiculous (the tabloid headlines you read while waiting in line to pay for groceries). While the latter can be dismissed without much difficulty (for most people), the TV study might have been penned by a professional writer unaware of the important distinction between experimental and correlational research. Consequently, the article might describe a correlational study in cause-and-effect terms, a mistake you'll have no difficulty recognizing once you have finished Chapter 9. Another example might be a claim that while under hypnosis, people can be transported back to the moment of their birth, thereby gaining some great insight into the origins of their problems. What you will learn in Chapter 3 about what are called "parsimonious" explanations will make you suspicious about such a claim and enable you to think of several alternative explanations for the reports given by patients about their alleged birth experiences. Similarly, you will learn to become skeptical about the claims made by the "subliminal" tapes that your college bookstore probably sells.

Fourth, there is a very pragmatic reason for taking a methods course. Even if you have no desire to become a research psychologist, you might like to be a professional practitioner of psychology some day. Like researchers, practitioners must earn an advanced degree, preferably the doctorate. Even for future clinical psychologists, counselors, and school psychologists, graduate school almost certainly means doing some research, so a course in methodology is an obvious first step to learning the necessary skills. Furthermore, your chances of getting into any type of graduate program in the first place are improved significantly if you (a) did well in undergraduate research methods and statistics courses and (b) were involved in doing some research as an undergraduate. A study by Norcross, Hanych, and Terranova (1996), which examined the undergraduate courses most likely to be required for admission to graduate school, found that the methods course was ranked second, just behind statistics, while specific content courses (e.g., developmental and abnormal psychology) were not required by very many programs.[2]

Once you become a professional psychologist, your research skills will be invaluable. Even if you aren't an active researcher, you will need to keep up with the latest research in your area of expertise and you will need to be able to read research critically. Furthermore, good clinical work involves essentially the same kind of thinking that characterizes the laboratory scientist—hypotheses about a client's problems are created, tested by trying out various treatments, and the outcomes are systematically

---

[2] In an analysis of 1554 graduate programs, it was found that 85.2% "required" or "preferred" statistics. The percentages were 66.0% for the research methods course, 35.9% for "childhood/developmental," and 32.5% for "abnormal/psychopathology."

evaluated. Also, if you work for a social service agency, you may find yourself dealing with accreditation boards or funding sources and they will want to know if your psychological services are effective. As you will discover in Chapter 10, research evaluating program effectiveness touches the lives of most professional psychologists.

Not all psychology majors become professional psychologists, of course, yet a research methods course can help develop the kinds of skills that employers look for in bachelor's level job applicants. By the time you have completed this course, for example, you should be better at critical and analytical thinking, precise writing, and logical argument. In addition, you will know how to summarize and interpret empirical data, search for information in libraries and electronic databases, and present the results of your research in a clear and organized fashion. Your computer skills will also improve—you will either learn or increase your existing skill with some statistical software package (e.g., SPSS) and you might also become familiar with presentation software (e.g., PowerPoint).

Finally, a course in research methods introduces you to a particular type of thinking. As mentioned above, other psychology courses deal with specific content areas and concentrate on what is known about topic X. The methods course, however, focuses more on the process by which knowledge of X is acquired. That process is centered on scientific thinking, and it is deeply ingrained in all research psychologists. Before detailing the features of the scientific way of thinking, however, let me first describe some of the typical ways in which we arrive at our knowledge of the world.

Ways of Knowing

Take a moment and reflect on something that you believe to be true. It could be something as simple as the belief that it is better to water the garden in the morning rather than in the evening, or it could be something as profound as the belief in a personal God. How do we arrive at such beliefs?

In an 1877 essay called "The Fixation of Belief" (reprinted in Tomas, 1957), the American pragmatist philosopher Charles S. Peirce described four ways in which we achieve certainty in our beliefs—tenacity, authority, the a priori method, and the method of science. Peirce believed the first three methods were widespread but flawed and that science was the best way to achieve true knowledge.

Tenacity

Peirce's first method, **tenacity,** is an unquestioning faith in the truth of some matter that is stubbornly held, motivated by a fear of uncertainty. The person maintaining a belief tenaciously is impervious to contrary evidence and only pays attention to information supporting the belief. Peirce did not describe how these beliefs developed initially, except to say that they are usually simplistic and result from the "instinctive dislike of an undecided state of mind" (Tomas, 1957, p. 15). It is likely that these beliefs form when the individual hears some "truth" being continuously repeated, in the absence of contrary information. Thus, college students in the 1960s tenaciously believed in the idea of a generation gap and accepted as gospel the mantra "Don't trust anyone over the age of 30." (Of course, these same people are now in their 50s and deeply suspicious of anyone younger than 30.)

Tenaciously held beliefs will be of great comfort to the holder of them because they seem to provide certainty in an uncertain world, but they can be seriously flawed by personal bias. To a modern social psychologist, tenacity sounds very much like the phenomenon of **belief perseverance,** a closed-minded unwillingness to consider any evidence that is contrary to a strongly held belief (Anderson, Lepper, & Ross, 1980). To a true believer who "knows" that U.S. aircraft shot down a flying saucer and recovered dead aliens in Roswell, New Mexico, in 1947, any scientific evidence to the contrary will be ignored (or considered part of the cover-up). The tenacity phenomenon also contributes to the strength of prejudice; highly prejudiced people hold on to their biases tenaciously and cannot be persuaded otherwise. For the person convinced that all people on welfare are diabolically cheating the system, unwilling to work, and driving big cars, the long history of research by social scientists questioning this stereotype makes no impact whatsoever.

Authority

Peirce's second method of fixing belief is to follow **authority.** He was referring primarily to the authority of the state, which tries to "keep correct doctrines before the attention of the people, to reiterate them perpetually, and to teach them to the young" (Tomas, 1957, p. 16). More generally, however, the influence of authority is felt in a number of ways. As children we are influenced by and believe what our parents tell us (at least for a while), as students we generally accept the authority of textbooks and professors, as patients we take the pills prescribed for us by doctors and believe they will have beneficial effects, and so on. Of course, relying on the authority of others to fix our beliefs overlooks the fact that authorities can be wrong. Parents often pass along prejudices to their children, textbooks and professors are sometimes wrong or their knowledge is incomplete or biased, doctors can miss a diagnosis or prescribe the wrong medicine, and the fact that governmental authority is often misguided hardly needs elaboration.

On the other hand, we do learn important things from authority figures, especially those who are recognized as experts in particular fields. Thus, we read *Consumer Reports,* watch the Weather Channel, and (sometimes) pay attention when the medical community cautions us about our lack of exercise and poor eating habits. Also, it doesn't stretch the concept of authority to consider the giants in the arts and literature as authority figures who can teach us much about human behavior. Who can read Shakespeare or Dickens or Austen without gaining valuable insights about human nature?

Discourse and Logic

Peirce believed that tenacity and authority were seriously flawed as ways of knowing. They provide solace, and perhaps some occasional insights, but they very easily lead to error. His third method of "fixing belief" was an improvement over tenacity and authority but problematic in its own way. Peirce described it as the outcome of rational discussion between people with different ideas who "gradually develop beliefs in harmony with natural causes" (Tomas, 1957, p. 20). The beliefs that result from this process are said to be "agreeable to reason" (p. 20). This third approach, then, relies on the use of reason and a developing consensus among those debating the merits of one belief over another. Peirce called this the **a priori method** because it is based more on argument and logic than on direct experience. Beliefs are deducted from prior assumptions (a priori translates from the Latin as "from what comes before") according to the rules of logic. With just a hint of sarcasm, Peirce pointed out that the a priori method was favored by metaphysical philosophers who could reason eloquently to reach some truth, only to be contradicted by other philosophers who reasoned just as eloquently to the opposite truth (on the question of whether the mind and the body are one or two different essences, for instance). The result is that beliefs go in and out of fashion; in metaphysics, for instance, Peirce said that "the pendulum has swung backward and forward between a more material and a more spiritual philosophy, from the earliest times to the latest" (Tomas, 1957, p. 24).

Experience

Another important way of coming to know things was implied by Peirce in all three of the methods of fixing belief just described. This is **empiricism**—the process of learning things through direct observation or experience. You will see shortly that asking "empirical questions" is an important component of scientific thinking, and there is certainly truth in the old saying that "experience is the best teacher." Yet it can be dangerous to rely solely on one's experiences when trying to determine the truth of some matter. The difficulty is that our experiences are necessarily limited and our interpretations of our experiences can be influenced by a number of what social psychologists refer to as "social cognition biases." The belief perseverance mentioned in connection with tenacity is one of these biases. Others include the availability heuristic and the confirmation bias. The **availability heuristic** occurs when we experience unusual or very memorable events and then overestimate how often such events typically occur (Tversky & Kahneman, 1973). Thus, people who watch a lot of crime shows on TV overestimate their chances of being crime victims, and because spectacular plane crashes are given more attention in the media than car accidents, some people cannot believe that air travel is considerably safer than travel by automobile. The **confirmation bias** is a tendency to search out information that supports one's beliefs while ignoring contrary information (Wason & Johnson-Laird, 1972). For instance, persons believing in extrasensory perception (ESP) will keep close track of instances when they were "thinking about Mom, and then the phone rang and it was her!" Yet they ignore the far more numerous times when (a) they were thinking about Mom and she didn't call and (b) they weren't thinking about Mom and she did call. They also fail to recognize that if they talk to Mom about every 2 weeks, their frequency of "thinking about Mom" will increase near the end of the 2-week interval, thereby increasing the chances of a "hit." Experience can be an indispensable and reliable guide to life's difficulties, but we also need to be aware of its limits.

The availability heuristic and a confirmation bias can work together to distort the beliefs one develops from experience. A good example is when students change their answers on multiple-choice tests. Many students believe that the most frequent outcome of answer changing is that an initially correct answer will be changed to a wrong one. Students tend to hold that belief because when such an event does occur, it is very memorable (availability), perhaps making the difference between an A and a B. Once the belief starts to develop, it is strengthened whenever the same kind of change occurs (confirmation). Yet students tend to overlook cases when they change from one wrong multiple choice alternative to another wrong one and when they change from a wrong alternative to the correct one. It is only the memorable situation, changing from right to wrong, that damages their score. That such a belief in the effects of answer changing is erroneous can be inferred from studies showing that, in fact, the most likely outcome (about 58% of the time) is that a changed answer will go from wrong to correct. On the other hand, changing from the correct answer to a wrong one happens only about 20% of the time and the remaining 22% of outcomes are those in which the change is from one wrong answer to another (Benjamin, Cavell, & Shallenberger, 1984).

The Ways of Knowing and Science

The most reliable way to develop a belief, according to Peirce, is through the method of science. Its procedures allow us to know "real things, whose characters are entirely independent of our opinions about them" (Tomas, 1957, p. 25). That is, Peirce believed that the chief advantage of science lies in its objectivity, which he considered to be the opposite of subjectivity. That is, for Peirce, to be objective is to completely avoid any human bias or preconception. Before discussing scientific thinking in detail, however, it is important to point out that scientists are just as human as everyone else. They show tenacity, rely on authority, argue with each other in an a priori fashion, and learn from their experiences.

Concerning tenacity, scientists sometimes hold on to a pet theory or a favored methodology long after others have abandoned it, and they sometimes seem to be less than willing to entertain new ideas. Charles Darwin once wrote half seriously that it might be a good idea for scientists to die by age sixty, because after that age, they "would be sure to oppose all new doctrines" (cited in Boorstin, 1985, p. 468). On the other hand, the historian of science Thomas Kuhn (1970) has argued that refusing to give up on a theory, in the face of a few experiments questioning that theory's validity, can have the beneficial effect of ensuring that the theory receives a thorough evaluation. Thus, being a vigorous (tenacious) advocate for a theory can ensure that it will be pushed to its limits before being abandoned by the scientific community. The process by which theories are evaluated, evolve, and sometimes die will be elaborated in Chapter 3.

Research psychologists can also be susceptible to the influence of authority. The "authorities" are usually other scientists, and experts are certainly more likely to be reliable sources than not. Nonetheless, researchers know better than to assume automatically that something is true simply because a reputable scientist said it was true. Rather, scientists are normally guided by the motto engraved on the entrance to the headquarters of the British Royal Society—"Nullius en Verba"—which encourages them to "take nobody's word for it; see for yourself" (cited in Boorstin, 1985, p. 394). Of course, "seeing for yourself" also opens up the possibilities associated with the social cognition biases.

The a priori method is frequently found in science to the extent that scientists argue with each other, trying to reach a rational consensus on some issue, but often failing to do so (e.g., whether to use the computer as a useful metaphor for the brain). As you will see in Chapter 3, they also rely on the rules of logic and inductive/deductive reasoning to develop ideas for research and to evaluate research outcomes. But while scientific thinking includes elements of the ways of knowing described thus far, it has a number of distinct attributes. It is to these special features of scientific thinking that we now turn.

Attributes of Scientific Thinking in Psychology

The ways of thinking that characterize scientists in general and research psychologists in particular involve a number of interrelated assumptions and features. First, researchers assume that events in the world, including the world of human behavior, follow certain rules and are therefore orderly and predictable to a degree. That is, they make the assumptions of **determinism** and **discoverability:** events have causes, and these causes can be discovered by using scientific methods. This does not necessarily mean that events can be predicted with 100% certainty, however. It simply means that psychological phenomena occur with a regularity that is not random and that those regularities can be investigated successfully. Let us examine this assumption of determinism in greater detail.

Determinism

Students are often confused after reading that psychologists regard human behavior as "determined." They sometimes assume this means "predestined" or "predetermined." It doesn't. A believer in absolute predestination thinks that every event is determined ahead of time, perhaps by God, and develops a fatalistic belief that one can do little but accept life as it presents itself. However, the traditional concept of determinism contends simply that all events have causes. Some philosophers argue for a strict determinism, which holds that the causal structure of the universe enables the prediction of all events with 100% certainty, at least in principle. Others, however, influenced by 20th-century developments in physics, take a more moderate view that could be called probabilistic or **statistical determinism.** This approach argues that events can be predicted, but only with a probability greater than chance. Most research psychologists take this position.

Yet the concept of determinism, even the "less than 100%" variety, is troubling because it seems to require that we abandon our belief in free will. If every event is caused, so the argument goes, then how can one course of action be freely chosen over another? The psychologist would reply that if determinism is not true at least to some degree, how can we ever know anything about behavior? Imagine for a moment what it would be like if human behavior was completely unpredictable.

How could you decide whether to marry Ed or Ted? How could you decide whether or not to take a course from Professor Jones?

Of course, there are multiple factors influencing behavior, and it is difficult to know for sure what someone will do at any one moment. Nonetheless, behavior follows certain patterns and is clearly predictable. For example, because we know that children will often do things that work effectively for them, it is not hard to predict a tantrum in the toy department of a crowded store if that behavior has yielded toys for a child in that setting in the past. And because behavior learned in one setting tends to "generalize" to similar environments, it isn't hard to predict a tantrum in Wal-Mart for the child whose tantrums have worked effectively in Kmart.

Concerning the matter of free choice, the positivist philosopher of science Rudolph Carnap has argued that free choice is meaningless unless determinism is true, because choices should be made on some reasonable basis and there can be no such basis for a choice unless the world is lawful to a degree. According to Carnap, without "causal regularity, ... it is not possible to make a free choice at all. A choice involves a deliberate preference for one course of action over another. How could a choice possibly be made if the consequences of alternative courses of action could not be foreseen?" (1966, p. 220). In short, Carnap argued that the idea of free choice has no meaning unless determinism is in fact true! Thus, deciding between Ed and Ted as a marriage partner makes sense only if you know certain things that are predictable about them (e.g., Ed is more reliable). Deciding whether to take Professor Jones's course might hinge on her reputation for being predictably fair in treating students.

Most research psychologists believe that the issue about the existence of free will cannot be settled one way or the other by science. Rather, whether the choices we make in life are freely made or not is a philosophical matter, and our belief about free will must be arrived at through the use of reason (perhaps supplemented with tenacity and/or authority). However the issue is settled, it is clear to researchers that in order for choice to have any meaning for humans, events in the world must be somewhat predictable. Thus, when the psychologist investigates behavior and discovers regularities, this does not eliminate or even limit human freedom. Indeed, if Carnap is correct, such research may actually enhance our ability to choose by increasing our knowledge of the alternatives.

Objectivity

A second characteristic of scientific thinking, the attribute that Peirce found most appealing about science, is its relative **objectivity**. For Peirce, being objective meant eliminating such human factors as expectation and bias. The objective scientist was believed to be almost machine-like in the search for truth. Today, however, nobody believes that scientists can completely separate themselves from their already-existing attitudes and to be objective does not mean to be devoid of such normal human traits. Rather, an objective observation is simply one that can be verified by more than one observer. In science this usually takes the form of defining the terms and research procedures precisely enough so that any other person can repeat the study, presumably achieving the same observable outcome. This process of repeating a study to determine if its results occur reliably is called "replication" (see Chapter 3, pp. 93–94); as results are replicated, confidence in the reality of some psychological phenomenon is increased. On the other hand, questions are raised when results cannot be replicated. Outcomes that consistently fail to replicate are eventually discarded, which makes science a self-correcting discipline. As you will learn in the next chapter, a failure to replicate is also how scientific fraud is sometimes uncovered.

Of course, in order to repeat a study, one must know precisely what was done in the original one. This is accomplished by means of a prescribed set of rules for describing research projects. These rules are presented in great detail in the *Publication Manual of the American Psychological Association* (American Psychological Association, 1994), an invaluable resource for anyone reporting research results or writing any other type of psychology paper. Appendix A, a guide to writing a lab report in APA format, is based on the manual and provides a good introduction to writing the report.

Objectivity in psychological science has been a problem historically. When psychology first emerged as a new science, it defined itself as the "science of mental life" and one of its early methods was called **introspection.** This procedure varied considerably from one laboratory to another, but it was basically a form of self-report. Participants in an experiment would perform some task and then provide a description of their conscious experience of the task. To give you some sense of what introspection was actually like, read Box 1.1 before going any further. It provides an example of a verbatim introspective description in an experiment on attention, and it shows how introspective thinking was a part of the everyday cognition of early psychologists.

The problem with introspection was that although introspectors had to undergo rigorous training that attempted to eliminate the potential for bias in their self-observations, the method was fundamentally subjective (I cannot verify your introspections and you cannot verify mine). The problem motivated psychologists like John B. Watson to argue that if psychology was to be truly "scientific," it needed to measure something that was directly observable and could be verified objectively (i.e., by two or more observers). Behavior fit the bill for Watson, and his vigorous arguments that the basic data of psychology ought to be observable and measurable actions earned him the title of "founder of behaviorism" as a school of thought. Today, the term "behavior" can be found as part of psychology's definition in every introductory textbook of psychology.

With behavior as the data, then, the modern researcher investigating attention would not ask for detailed introspective accounts, as Dallenbach did in Box 1.1, but would design an experiment in which conclusions about attention could be drawn from some easily observed behavior in the Dallenbach task, such as the number of addition errors made while the subject was trying to keep track of the metronome activity. Presumably, two independent observers could agree on the number of errors that occurred in the task.

Data-Driven

A third attribute of scientific thinking in psychology is that researchers are **data-driven.** That is, they expect conclusions about behavior to be supported by the evidence of objective information gathered through some systematic procedure. For

Box 1.1

ORIGINS—A Taste of Introspection

The following introspective account is from a 1913 study by Karl Dallenbach dealing with the phenomenon of attention. Introspectors were instructed to listen to two metronomes set at different speeds and to count the number of beats between coincident beats (i.e., both metronomes hitting at the same instant). While counting, they were also asked to perform some other task, such as continuously adding numbers out loud. Needless to say, these tasks tested the limits of attention. After finishing a session, one introspector reported:

> The sounds of the metronomes, as a series of discontinuous clicks, were clear in consciousness only four or five times during the experiment, and they were especially bothersome at first. They were accompanied by strain sensations and unpleasantness. The rest of the experiment my attention was on the adding, which was composed of auditory images of the numbers, visual images of the numbers, sometimes on a dark gray scale which was directly ahead and about three feet in front of me. ... When these processes were clear in consciousness, the sounds of the metronomes were very vague or obscure. (Dallenbach, 1913, p. 467)

Notice that the introspector attempted to describe everything that happened in consciousness while performing the task, including sensory events ("strain"), emotion ("unpleasant"), and imagery, both auditory and visual. Also, the difficulty in keeping multiple tasks equally "clear in consciousness" led Dallenbach to conclude that attention was severely limited, a finding later rediscovered by more modern research on "selective" attention (e.g., Broadbent, 1958).

Scientific thinking does not disappear when the scientist leaves the lab. Thus, psychologists during the heyday of introspection often thought in introspectionist terms. In their letters to each other, for example, they would often reflect on some recent event by describing their conscious experience of it. For example, in a letter to Cornell's E. B. Titchener, Edmund Sanford of Clark University described an encounter with a violent thunderstorm in an introspective fashion. Sanford wrote that he had

> observed enough this summer to find that [he could not] find anything in it but organic and other sensations unpleasantly colored and, on the cognitive side, a cramp of apperception toward a small group of ideas related to the thing dreaded with certain resultants in instinctive act and thought. ... When the storm became imminent there would be cardiac and visceral symptoms to describe, etc. etc.—though when the thing was actually present these were as a general thing not so marked as in anticipation—i.e. as the storm approached. (Sanford, 1910)

instance, a claim made by a college admissions director that "this year's incoming class is better prepared than any in recent memory" (an annual claim at some schools) would compel the scientific thinker to respond, "Let's see the data for this year and the past few years," and "What do you mean by better prepared?" Furthermore, researchers try to judge whether the data given to support some claim are adequate for the claim to be made. Hence, if someone asserts that excessive TV watching reduces creativity in children, the scientist immediately begins to wonder about the type and amount of data collected (e.g., how was creativity measured, and how large was the data set?), the procedures used to collect the data, and the type of statistical analysis that was done.

This attitude can be detected easily in research psychologists; they even find themselves thinking about how data might bear on the problems they encounter in daily living. Even a neighbor's offhand observation about the tomato crop being better this year might generate in the researcher's mind a host of data-related questions to test the claim (How exactly did you count the tomatoes during the past 2 years? Did you measure the number picked per day or the number ripened per day? How did you define "ripe?"). Of course, there are certain hazards resulting from this kind of thinking, including a tendency for the neighbor to begin avoiding you. Sometimes the "driven" (as in compelled) part of the term "data-driven" seems to be the operative term!

A personification of this data-driven attitude taken to extremes can be found in the life of Sir Francis Galton, a 19th-century British jack-of-all-sciences, whose interests ranged from geography to meteorology to psychology. His importance for the topics of mental testing and correlational research will be examined in Chapter 9. Galton was positively obsessed with the idea of collecting data and making data-based conclusions. Thus, he once measured interest in various theater productions by counting the number of yawns that he could detect during performances; he studied association by counting the number of related ideas occurring to him on his morning walks; and he collected data on age-related hearing loss and species differences in hearing by inventing a device (the "Galton whistle") that could easily produce sounds of various pitches (Galton, 1883). Galton's most unusual attempt to draw a data-based conclusion was his controversial study on the "efficacy of prayer" (Galton, 1872). Like his half-cousin, Charles Darwin, Galton was skeptical about religion and decided to test the notion that prayers "worked." If prayers were effective, he reasoned, then sick people who pray should recover sooner than those who do not. Similarly, people who do a lot of praying for a living (i.e., the clergy) or who are the object of a great deal of prayer (i.e., the king and queen of England) should live longer than the general population. Galton also expected that ships carrying missionaries (with lots of folks back home praying for them) would be less likely to sink than other ships. None of these predictions proved to be true, however. For instance, by digging through biographical dictionaries, Galton found that eminent members of the clergy lived for an average of 66.42 years, while lawyers (presumably less likely to be the object of prayer) made it to a virtually identical average of 66.51 years (data from Forrest, 1974, p. 112). Galton was understandably criticized for his rather simplistic idea of the purpose of prayer, and his article on prayer was initially rejected (three times) as being "too terribly conclusive and offensive not to raise a hornet's nest" (cited in Forrest, 1974, p. 111), but the study certainly illustrates data-based thinking.

Empirical Questions

As mentioned earlier, empiricism is a term that refers to the process of learning things through direct observation or experience. **Empirical questions** are those that can be answered through the systematic observations and experiences that characterize scientific methodology. They are questions that are precise enough to allow specific predictions to be made. As you will see in Chapter 3, asking questions is the first step of any research project. How to develop a good empirical question will be one theme of that chapter.

We can begin to get an idea about what constitutes empirical questions, however, by contrasting them with questions that cannot be answered empirically. For example, recall that Peirce used the mind-body question to illustrate what he called the a priori method. Philosophers argued both sides of the question for many years (they're still at it!), and Peirce wasn't optimistic about the issue ever being resolved. Whether the mind and the body are two separate essences or one is simply not an empirical question. However, there are a number of empirical questions that can be asked that are related to this issue. For instance, it is possible to ask about the influence of mental activity (mind) on physical health (body) by asking the empirical question "What are the effects of psychological stress on the immune system?" Also, it is possible to look at the body's influence on mental states by asking how physical fatigue affects problem-solving ability in some task.

Although research psychologists believe that the scientific approach is the ideal way to answer questions, it is worth pointing out that there are many questions in our lives that science cannot answer adequately. These questions include such things as whether a deity exists or whether people are fundamentally good or evil. These are certainly important questions, but they cannot be answered scientifically. Of course, it is possible to investigate empirically such things as the specific factors that lead people to believe in a deity or that lead them to do good or bad things. Thus, potential empirical questions might include these:

> ✓ Does a belief in God increase with age (i.e., proximity to death)?
> ✓ Does helping behavior decline if the cost of helping outweighs the benefit?

To sum up, I would describe research psychologists as "skeptical optimists." They are open to new ideas and optimistic about using scientific methods to test these ideas, but at the same time they are tough-minded—they won't accept claims without data. Also, researchers are constantly thinking of ways to test ideas scientifically, they are confident that truth will emerge by asking and answering empirical questions, and they are willing (sometimes grudgingly) to alter their beliefs if the answers to their empirical questions are not what they expected.

Psychological Science and Pseudoscience

Because everyone is interested in human behavior, it is not surprising that many claims are made about its causes and inner workings. Many of those claims are based

FIGURE 1.1   The unfortunate popularity of pseudoscience.

on legitimate scientific inquiry, of course, following the rules of the game that you will learn about in this text and carried out by the skeptical optimists just described. That is, we know much about behavior as a result of relying on the kinds of thinking and the specific methods that characterize legitimate science. However, many claims are made in the name of psychological science using methods and ways of thinking that are not truly scientific but merely pseudoscientific ("pseudo-" is from the Greek word for "false"). In general, the term **pseudoscience** is applied to any field of inquiry that appears to use scientific methods and tries hard to give that impression, but is actually based on inadequate, unscientific methods and yields results that are generally false. The Sidney Harris cartoon in Figure 1.1 portrays an unfortunate truth about pseudoscience—its popular appeal. This appeal can also be seen in the high visibility of "psychic hotlines" and websites devoted to alleged psychic phenomena. What differentiates true science from pseudoscience, and what accounts for the popularity of pseudoscience?

Recognizing Pseudoscience

Those living in the late 19th century could send away to the New York firm of Fowler and Wells for a "Symbolic Head and Phrenological Map" for 10 cents. For another $1.25, the head and map would be accompanied by a copy of *How to Read*

Character: A New Illustrated Handbook of Phrenology and Physiognomy (Anonymous Advertisement, 1881). Thus equipped, people would then be in a position to measure character "scientifically" through an analysis of the shape of the skull.

Those living in the late 20th century could visit any one of several dozen websites and for about $30, order "subliminal" tapes promising to improve their lives. By merely listening to these tapes, one could apparently improve memory, lose weight, stop smoking, become a better sexual partner, improve self-esteem, become rich in the stock market, or even become a more proficient hunter of deer (buckblaster.com). Thus equipped, people would then be able to solve all of life's problems with minimal effort ("just relax, turn on the tape, and we'll do all the work for you").

As these examples suggest, people will pay for self-knowledge or self-improvement, especially if the methods appear to be scientific and are easy to implement and understand. Both 19th-century phrenology and the 20th-century subliminal self-help industry are pseudoscientific; there are important differences between the two, but in general they both serve to illustrate the main features of pseudoscience.

Associates with True Science

Pseudosciences do everything they can to associate themselves with legitimate science or give the appearance of being scientific. In some cases, the origins of a pseudoscience can be found in true science; in other instances, the pseudoscience confuses its concepts with genuine scientific ones. Phrenology illustrates the former, subliminal tapes the latter.

Phrenology originated in legitimate attempts to demonstrate that different parts of the brain had identifiably different functions, and it can be considered one of the first systematic theories about the localization of brain function (Bakan, 1966). It was created in the late 18th century by Franz Joseph Gall, a Viennese physician also known for his confirmation of the brain's contralaterality (the left side of the brain controls the right side of the body and vice versa). His belief in the relationship between personality and brain structure became known as "phrenology," the doctrine asserting that (a) different personality and intellectual attributes ("faculties") were associated with different parts of the brain, as illustrated in Figure 1.2, (b) particularly strong faculties resulted in larger brain areas, and (c) skull measurements yielded estimates of the relative strengths of faculties. By measuring skulls, then, one could identify personality and intelligence.

Phrenology remained popular into the early years of the 20th century, even though it had been discredited in a brilliant series of studies by the French physiologist Pierre Flourens by the mid-1800s (see Box 1.2). By the second half of the 19th century, despite being abandoned by scientists, phrenology as big business flourished: phrenological societies were formed, popular journals were established, and phrenological analysis was used for everything from choosing a career to hiring an honest servant. Even if a theory is discredited within the scientific community, then, it can still find favor with the public. This creates special problems for psychology as a science because it isn't difficult for virtually any type of theory about human behavior to have some popular appeal. The subliminal business is a good recent example.

Subliminal messages and their supposed influence on human behavior first achieved widespread notoriety in the 1950s when James Vicary, a marketing researcher, claimed that sales of popcorn and soda increased dramatically when sub-

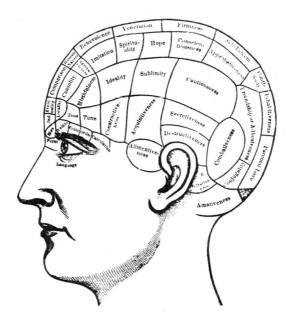

FIGURE 1.2   A skull showing the locations of the various faculties proposed by phrenologists.

Box 1.2

CLASSIC STUDIES—Disproving Phrenology

In 1846, a brief volume (144 pages) with the title *Phrenology Examined* appeared. Its author was Pierre Flourens (1794–1867), a distinguished French physiologist and surgeon known for demonstrating the role of the ear's semicircular canals in balance, for locating the respiratory center in the medulla oblongata, and for discovering the anesthetic properties of chloroform (Kruta, 1972). He was also phrenology's worst enemy. He certainly did not mince words, declaring:

> The entire doctrine of [phrenology] is contained in two fundamental propositions, of which the first is, that understanding resides exclusively in the brain, and the second, that each particular faculty of the understanding is provided in the brain with an organ proper to itself.
>
> Now, of these two propositions, there is certainly nothing new in the first one, and perhaps nothing true in the second one. (Flourens, 1846/1978, p. 18)

To disprove the phrenologists' claims, Flourens took an experimental approach to the problem of localization, using the method of "ablation." Although he did not create the procedure, he raised it to such a level of refinement that it is now associated with his name. Rather than wait for natural experiments to occur in the form of accidental brain damage, Flourens removed specific sections of the brain and observed the effects (ablation derives from the Latin words for "carry away" or "remove"). If the result of an ablation is an inability to see, then presumably the area of the removed portion has something to do with vision. Clearly, the method required animals as research subjects, and Flourens experimented on numerous species, ranging from dogs to pigeons.

Flourens' attack on phrenology consisted of showing that specific areas of the brain that were alleged to serve function X in fact served function Y, and that the cerebral cortex operated as an integrated whole rather than as a large collection of individual faculties located in specific places. One focus of his research was the cerebellum. To the phrenologists, this portion of the brain controlled sexual behavior and was the center of the faculty of "amativeness." In his celebrated *Outlines of Phrenology,* for instance, Johann G. Spurzheim (1832/1978) argued that sexuality "appears with the development of this part, and is in relation to its size. In children, for instance, the cerebellum is smaller than in adults, and in women and females generally it is less than in men and males" (p. 28). Apparently thinking of some anecdotal data, Spurzheim pointed out that sometimes the cerebellum "is of great magnitude in children, and then its special function, the propensity we treat of, appears in early life" (p. 28).

Flourens would have none of this. First, he ridiculed the circular logic of assigning "faculties" to a certain behavior and then explained that same behavior by pointing to the faculties:

> [W]hat sort of philosophy is that, that thinks to explain a fact by a word? You observe … a penchant in an animal, … a taste or talent in a man; *presto,* a particular faculty is produced for each one of the peculiarities, and you suppose the whole matter to be settled. You deceive yourself; your *faculty* is only a *word,*—it is the name of a fact,—and all the difficulty [of explanation] remains where it was before. (Flourens, 1846/1978, p. 39; italics in the original)

Flourens had little trouble ruling out the idea that the cerebellum had anything to do with sexual motivation. By carefully removing portions of the cerebellum, he showed that it was the center of motor coordination. Thus, pigeons deprived of the organ were unable to coordinate wing movements in order to fly, and dogs were unable to walk properly and were observed staggering, falling down, and bumping into objects they could normally avoid. Sexual motivation was unaffected, although damage to the cerebellum presumably would have made copulation awkward. Flourens also determined that the degree of abnormality in movement was directly proportional to the amount of cerebellum that he ablated.

With other animals, Flourens removed varying amounts of the cerebral cortex and found a similar relationship between the amount destroyed and the seriousness of the ensuing problem. He could find no indication of distinct functions residing in specific areas of the cortex, however, so he concluded that it operated as a whole and served the general functions of perception, intelligence, and will. Thus, pigeons without a cortex or with most of it removed seemed able to sense the world around them, but they showed no indication of being able to learn from their experiences or of understanding what they were sensing. They seemed unable to do anything except vegetate. The difference between a pigeon without a cerebellum and one without a cortex, then, was that the first bird would attempt to fly but could not manage to do so, while the second bird would not even think of trying.

Flourens effectively destroyed phrenology, but the issue of localization of function did not by any means disappear, and other physiologists soon demonstrated that the cortex had a greater degree of localization than Flourens was willing to grant. Paul Broca, for example, demonstrated that a relatively small area of the left frontal lobe of the cortex, later named for him, seemed to control the production of speech. For more on this issue of localization, take your department's courses in history and systems of psychology and physiological psychology.

liminal messages to "eat popcorn" and "drink Coca-Cola" were embedded in a film being shown at a theater in New Jersey. Presumably, while film-goers were watching the movie, their minds were being manipulated without their knowledge by the messages that were said to be below the threshold of conscious awareness, but accessible to the unconscious mind. Despite the lack of any independent verification of the increase in sales and the fact that Vicary later retracted his claim (Pratkanis, Eskenazi, & Greenwald, 1994), this episode continues to be reported by advocates of subliminal tapes as the "classic" example of the power of subliminal messages. Other reports of subliminal effects soon surfaced, summarized in several best-selling books by Wilson Key. In *Subliminal Seduction* (1973), for instance, Key claimed that advertisers regularly inserted below threshold sexual messages (e.g., genital-shaped ice cubes) to increase sales. The idea was that even though people would not consciously perceive the sex symbols, their unconscious would pick them up. The unconscious perception would produce some degree of arousal that would make the product somehow more attractive. The lack of any evidence to support the claims did not hurt sales of Key's books.

By the 1980s, subliminal self-help tapes began to appear on the market. By 1990, sales of these tapes reached $50 million annually (Beyerstein, 1993). Today, these tapes are readily available at numerous websites and you might even find them in your college bookstore. When playing one, the listener typically hears soothing music or nature sounds (e.g., ocean waves and the occasional seagull). Supposedly, subliminal messages such as "you can lose all the weight you'd like" are played at a volume too faint to be heard, but detected nonetheless by the unconscious mind. The unconscious then is said to influence the person's behavior in some unspecified fashion. Part of the tape's appeal is that the buyer is led to believe that dramatic self-improvement can be made with minimal effort: once the message is firmly in the unconscious, the individual will be driven by some powerful internal force.

Part of the marketing strategy for subliminal tapes is to convince potential buyers that the technology has a strong basis in established science. Indeed, there is a great deal of legitimate research on thresholds, some of it showing that certain behaviors can be influenced by stimuli that are below the threshold of conscious reporting. In studies of semantic priming, for example, participants are first shown a screen that contains a word (e.g., "infant"). The word is flashed very rapidly and is followed by a "masking" stimulus, which has the effect of making it virtually impossible for participants to verbally report the word just presented. That is, the word has been shown subliminally, below the threshold for conscious recognition. Participants next see a sequence of letters presented rapidly. Some form words, others don't, and the task is to respond as quickly as possible when a true word has been recognized. Researchers (e.g., Marcel, 1983) have consistently found that words (e.g., "child") that are semantically related to the subliminal word ("infant") are recognized more quickly than unrelated words (e.g., "chair"). "Child" will not be recognized more quickly than "chair" unless "infant" has been presented subliminally first. In short, the process of word recognition has been "primed" by the initial subliminal stimulus.

Any connection between this research on priming and the effects of subliminal tapes on behavior, however, is purely coincidental. It is a long way from having a small effect on word recognition to having a persuasive effect on the complex behaviors of people trying to lose weight. And as you might have guessed, research that evaluates the effects of subliminal tapes on behavior regularly shows that the tapes by themselves have no effect at all. Instead, any changes that occur are the result of other factors, such as the person's expectations about what should happen. A study by Greenwald, Spangenberg, Pratkanis, and Eskenazi (1991), for instance, cleverly demonstrated this expectancy effect. People were given subliminal tapes that were said to improve memory or enhance self-esteem. What the participants weren't told was that some of them were getting a self-esteem tape when they were told it was a memory tape and others who thought they were getting the memory tape in fact got the self-esteem tape. You might be able to guess what happened. Self-esteem increased for those given the self-esteem tape and told it was the self-esteem tape, but self-esteem also increased, by the same amount, for those given the memory tape but told it was a self-esteem tape. The same thing happened for those getting and expecting the memory tape—an equivalent improvement. In short, the only thing that mattered was what the participants expected to happen. If they expected enhanced self-esteem (or improved memory), their self-esteem (or memory) improved, regardless of which tape they actually heard.[3] Just as Flourens' research derailed phrenology, modern researchers have shown that subliminal self-help tapes are equally pseudoscientific.

Relies on Anecdotal Evidence

A second feature of pseudoscience, and one that helps explain its popularity, is the reliance on and uncritical acceptance of **anecdotal evidence,** specific instances that seem to provide evidence for some phenomenon. Thus, Gall's data consisted mostly of a catalogue of examples to support his theory: a thief with a large area of "acquisitiveness," a priest with an overdeveloped bump for "reverence," a prostitute with excessive "amativeness." Subliminal advocates use the same approach. Their literature is filled with testimonials from people who have dramatically improved their lives after using the tapes. In the area of weight loss, for example, where there is a long history of searching for a quick fix, reading about someone losing 20 pounds

---

[3] For another example of research questioning the effectiveness of subliminal tapes, refer to case study 10 in Chapter 7's discussion of control groups.

merely by lounging in the recliner and listening to tapes of seagulls can be irresistible. Anecdotal evidence has immediate appeal to the uncritical reader.

There is nothing wrong with accumulating evidence to support a theory; even anecdotal examples like the ones just mentioned are not automatically disqualified. The problem occurs when one relies exclusively on anecdotes or makes more of them than is warranted. The difficulty is that anecdotal evidence is selective; examples that don't fit are ignored (you might recognize this as another example of a confirmation bias). Hence, there may be some thieves with a particular skull shape, but in order to evaluate a specific relationship between skull configuration X and thievery, one must know (a) how many people who are thieves do not have configuration X and (b) how many people who have configuration X aren't thieves. Without having these two pieces of information, there is no way to determine if there is anything unusual about a particular thief or two with skull shape X. The identical problem occurs with subliminal tapes—advertisers aren't likely to report stories about people buying tapes and gaining weight.

One other reason to distrust a glowing testimonial is that it often results from a phenomenon familiar to social psychologists—**effort justification** (Aronson, 1999a). Following from Leon Festinger's theory of cognitive dissonance, the idea here is that after people expend significant effort, they feel compelled to convince themselves that the effort was worthwhile. After spending $30 on a subliminal tape and a few dozen hours listening to it, we don't like to think that we've thrown away hard-earned money and wasted valuable time. To reduce the discomfort associated with the possibility that we've been had, we convince ourselves that the investment of time and money was a good one.

Sidesteps Disproof

As you will learn in Chapter 3, one of the hallmarks of a good scientific theory is that it is stated precisely enough to be put to the sternest test of all—the test of disproof. That is, to be acceptable, a theory must be structured so that specific predictions can be made and experiments can yield outcomes counter to predictions. In pseudoscience this does not occur, even though on the surface it would seem that both phrenology and the effects of subliminals would be easy to disprove. Indeed, as far as the scientific community is concerned, disproof occurred for both.

Advocates of pseudosciences such as phrenology and subliminals have had to confront claims of disproof and the accompanying skepticism of legitimate scientists. Not all thieves have bumps in just the right places and not everyone listens to a tape and gets rich. Apologists respond to these threats rather creatively. Instead of allowing an apparent contradiction to hurt the theory, they sidestep the problem by rearranging the theory a bit or by adding some elements to accommodate the anomaly. Consequently, the apparent disproof winds up being touted as further evidence in support of the theory! For example, if a known pacifist nonetheless had a large area of destructiveness, a clever phrenologist would find even larger areas of cautiousness, benevolence, and reverence, and these would be said to offset the apparent violent tendencies. Likewise, when responding to a study showing that subliminal tapes have no measurable effects, defenders of subliminals might argue that tapes work through unconscious processes that are beyond the reach of conventional scientific methodology. That is, subliminals clearly work (after all, look at all our testimonials), and if science fails to find evidence to support the effects, there must be something wrong with the science. Furthermore, if someone fails to benefit from the tapes, they are probably experiencing some kind of unconscious motivational block. Thus, for pseudoscience, any possible outcome can be explained or, more accurately, explained away. Yet a theory that explains all possible outcomes fails as a theory because it can never make specific predictions. If a pacifist can have either a large or a small area of destructiveness, how can we predict whether someone will be a pacifist? Similarly, if a theory is said to be, by definition, beyond the reach of scientific disproof, on what rational basis can its effects be shown to be valid?

Another way that disproof is sidestepped by pseudoscience is that research reports in pseudoscientific areas are notoriously vague. One of science's important features is that its research results are public property, reported in books and journals that are available to anyone. More important, scientists describe their research with enough precision so that others can replicate the experiment if they wish. This does not happen with pseudoscience, where the research reports are usually vague or incomplete and, as seen above, heavily dependent on anecdotal support.

Reduces Complex Phenomena to Overly Simplistic Concepts

A final characteristic of pseudoscience worth noting is that these doctrines take what are actually very complicated phenomena (the causes of behavior and personality; the factors that bring about major life changes) and reduce them to simplistic concepts. This, of course, has great consumer appeal, especially in psychology. Trying to figure out and improve behavior is a universal human activity, and if the process can be simplified, either by measuring someone's head, listening to a tape, determining someone's astrological sign, or interpreting one's handwriting, then many people will be taken in by the apparent ease of the explanations. Please note that the actual simplicity of the explanatory concepts are masked by an apparent complexity of the measuring devices used in many of the pseudosciences. Thus, the phrenologists went through an elaborate set of skull measurements to measure faculties. Similarly, graphologists, alleged to be able to tell you all you need to know about yourself by analyzing your handwriting, often measure dozens of features of handwriting (e.g., slant angles).

In sum, then, pseudoscience is characterized by (a) a false association with true science, (b) a misuse of the rules of evidence by relying on anecdotal data, (c) a lack of specificity that avoids a true test of the theory, and (d) an oversimplification of complex processes. Perhaps because of our enormous interest in behavior, pseudoscientific approaches to psychology are not hard to find in any historical era, and many people seem to have difficulty seeing the inherent weaknesses in pseudoscientific doctrines. As you develop your skills as a scientific thinker by taking this research methods course, however, you should be able to distinguish valid psychological science from that which merely pretends to be.

The Goals of Research in Psychology

Scientific research in psychology has four interrelated goals. Researchers hope to develop complete descriptions of behaviors, to be able to make predictions about future behavior, and to be able to provide reasonable explanations of behavior. Furthermore, they assume that the knowledge derived from their research will be applied so as to benefit people, either directly or eventually.

Describing Behavior

To provide a good **description** in psychology is to identify regularly occurring sequences of events, including both stimuli or environmental events and responses or behavioral events. For example, a description of aggressive behavior in some primate species might include a list of the situations in which fighting is most likely to occur (e.g., over food), the types of threat signals that might precede actual combat (e.g., baring teeth), and the form of the fight itself (e.g., attacks directed at nonvital areas like shoulders and haunches). Description also involves classification, as when someone attempts to classify various forms of aggressive behavior (e.g., fighting vs. predation). Providing a clear, accurate description is an obvious yet essential first step in any scientific endeavor; without it, predictions cannot be made and explanations are meaningless.

Predicting Behavior

To say that behavior follows **laws** is to say that regular and predictable relationships exist between variables. The strength of these relationships allows **predictions** to be made with some degree of confidence. After describing numerous primate fights, for example, it might become clear that after two animals fight over food and one wins, the same two animals won't fight again. If they both spot a banana at the same time, the winner of the initial battle might display a threat gesture and the loser of that first fight will probably go away. If that series of events happened often enough, the researchers could make predictions about future encounters between these animals and, more generally, between animals who are winners and losers of fights.

Explaining Behavior

The third goal of the experimenter is **explanation.** To explain some behavior is to know what caused it to happen. The concept of causality is immensely complex, and its nature has occupied philosophers for centuries. Experimental psychologists recognize the tentative nature of explanations for behavior, but they are generally willing to conclude that X is causing Y to occur if they conduct an experiment in which they systematically vary X, control all outside factors that could affect the results, and observe that Y occurs with some probability greater than chance and that variations of Y can be predicted from the variations in X. That is, X and Y are said to "covary," or occur together, and because X occurs first, it is said to be the cause of Y. Furthermore, they will have confidence in the causal explanation to the extent that (a) the explanation makes sense with reference to some theory or some already existing sets of laws and (b) other possible explanations for Y occurring in the presence of X can be effectively ruled out. The process of theory building, and of how empirical research is derived from and affects the development of theory, will be elaborated in Chapter 3. For now, simply be aware that causality is a complicated process involving covariation, experimental control, a time sequence with cause preceding effect, a theoretical structure, and the ruling out of alternative explanations.

Controlling Behavior

This goal is sometimes controversial because it creates an unfair impression of psychologists deliberately and perhaps diabolically controlling other people's lives (Box 11.3 in Chapter 11 examines the issue in more detail). Actually, **control** refers simply to the various ways of applying those principles of behavior learned through psychological research. Psychologists assume that because of knowledge derived from the research they do, it is possible for people's lives to change for the better. Hence, research on the factors influencing depression enables therapists to help depressed people, research on aggression can help parents raise their children, and so on. This goal is seldom the immediate purpose of any particular study, but it is an underlying goal for all researchers.

A Passion for Research in Psychology (Part I)

This chapter began by listing a series of reasons why the experimental psychology course is essential for the student of psychology. Besides tradition and the obvious fact that the course is step 1 on the road to becoming a researcher in psychology, these reasons include helping you understand the content of other psychology courses better, making you a critical consumer of research information, improving your chances of getting into graduate school or getting a job, and giving you an appreciation of the attributes of scientific thinking. All this is fine, but in my opinion, the single most important reason to learn how to do research in psychology is that, simply put, doing research is great fun. It is challenging, frustrating at times, and the long hours in the lab can be tedious, but few researchers would exchange their careers for another. What could be more satisfying than getting an idea about behavior, putting it to the test of a research study, and having the results come out just as predicted? Who could not be thrilled about making some new discovery about behavior that might improve people's lives?

This attitude of seeing a research career as an ideal life is apparent in the final paragraph of a chapter written by the behaviorist E. C. Tolman for a series about various theoretical approaches to psychology. The chapter was among the last papers he wrote; it was published the year he died, 1959. After describing his famous theory of learning, Tolman concluded by saying, in part:

> The system [his theory] may well not stand up to any final canons of scientific procedure. But I do not much care. I have liked to think about psychology in ways that have proved congenial to me. Since all the sciences, and especially psychology, are still immersed in such tremendous realms of the uncertain and the unknown, the best that any individual scientist … can do seems to be to follow his own gleam and his own bent, however inadequate they may be. In fact, I suppose that actually this is what we all do. *In the end, the only sure criterion is to have fun. And I have had fun.* (Tolman, 1959, p. 152; italics added)

Let me wrap up this opening chapter with two brief examples of how experimental psychologists become almost obsessively devoted to their work and find great satisfaction in it.

Eleanor Gibson

On June 23, 1992, Eleanor Gibson was awarded the National Medal of Science by President George Bush (Figure 1.3). It is the highest honor a president can confer on a scientist. Gibson, then 82, was honored for a lifetime of research in developmental psychology, studying topics ranging from how we learn to read to how depth perception develops. She is perhaps best known to undergraduates for her "visual cliff" studies.

Gibson is a prototype of the devoted researcher who persevered even in the face of major obstacles. In her case the burden was sexism. This she discovered upon arrival at Yale University in 1935, eager to work in Robert M. Yerkes's primate lab (Yerkes was famous for his work in both comparative psychology and in mental testing). She was astounded by her first interview with him. As she later recalled, "He stood up, walked to the door, held it open, and said, 'I have no women in my laboratory'" (Gibson, 1980, p. 246).

Undaunted, Gibson eventually convinced the great behaviorist Clark Hull that she could be a scientist and finished her doctorate with him. Then in the late 1940s, she went to Cornell University with her husband, James Gibson (another famous name, this time in perception research). Eleanor labored there as an unpaid research associate for 16 years before being named professor.[4] It was during this period of uncertain status that she completed her work on perceptual development. A sense of her excitement about this research is evident from her description of how the visual cliff experiments first came about.

Briefly, the project evolved out of some perceptual development research with rats that she was doing with her Cornell colleague Richard Walk. They were both curious about depth perception. In the army, Walk had studied training programs for parachute jumpers, and at Cornell's "Behavior Farm," Gibson had observed newborn goats avoid falling from a raised platform. She also had a "long-standing aversion to cliffs, dating from a visit to the Grand Canyon" (Gibson, 1980, p. 258). With a lab assistant, Gibson

> hastily put together a contraption consisting of a sheet of glass held up by rods, with a piece of wallpaper under one side of it and nothing under the other side except the floor many feet below.
>
> A few rats left over from other experiments got the first try. ... We put a board about three inches wide across the division between the surface with flooring and the unlined glass, and put the rats on the board. Would they descend randomly to either side?
>
> What ensued was better than we had dared expect. All the rats descended on the side with textured paper under the glass. We quickly inserted some

---

[4]Cornell did not pay her a salary during this time, but she earned stipends via the many successful research grants that she wrote (e.g., the Rockefeller Foundation, National Science Foundation, U.S. Office of Education).

FIGURE 1.3   Eleanor Gibson receiving the National Medal of Science in 1992.

paper under the other side and tried them again. This time they went either way. We built some proper apparatus after that, with carefully controlled light-ing and so on. ... *It worked beautifully.* (Gibson, 1980, p. 259; italics added)

Gibson and Walk (1960) went on to test numerous species, including, of course, humans. The visual cliff studies, showing the unwillingness of 8-month-olds to cross the "deep side," even with Mom on the other side, are now familiar to any student of introductory psychology.

B. F. Skinner

If you ask students to name a famous psychologist other than Freud, many will say "B. F. Skinner" (Figure 1.4), who is perhaps psychology's most famous scientist. His work on operant conditioning created an entire subculture within experimental psychology called the "experimental analysis of behavior." Its philosophy will be explored in Chapter 11.

Skinner's three-volume autobiography provides a marvelous glimpse of his life and work. The following quote illustrates his almost childlike fascination with making a new discovery about behavior. It is from a period when Skinner had just completed his doctorate at Harvard and was staying on as a research fellow, sup-

FIGURE 1.4 B. F. Skinner as a young graduate student at Harvard, circa 1930.

ported by a grant from the National Research Council. In early 1932, he was studying a number of different conditioning phenomena, including experimental extinction. In his words:

> My first extinction curve showed up by accident. A rat was pressing the lever in an experiment on satiation when the pellet dispenser jammed. I was not there at the time, and when I returned *I found a beautiful curve.* The rat had gone on pressing although no pellets were received…
>
> The change was more orderly than the extinction of a salivary reflex in Pavlov's setting, and *I was terribly excited.* It was a Friday afternoon and there was no one in the laboratory whom I could tell. All that weekend I crossed streets with particular care and avoided all unnecessary risks to protect my discovery from loss through my accidental death. (Skinner, 1979, p. 95; italics added)

Note the use of the word "beauty" in both the Gibson and Skinner quotes. Gibson's visual cliff experiment "worked beautifully" and Skinner found a "beautiful curve." The language reflects the strong emotion that is often felt by research scientists engrossed in their work.

B. F. Skinner also had a healthy skepticism toward those (including most writers of research methods texts) who describe the scientific method as a series of specific steps to be completed. In an article chronicling how he eventually produced the apparatus associated with his name, the Skinner box, he articulated a number of informal "rules" of scientific conduct (Skinner, 1956). One of them captures the passion and curiosity of the best scientific thinkers: "When you run into something fascinating, drop everything else and study it" (p. 223).

Throughout the remainder of this book, you'll be learning the tools of the experimental psychology trade and will be reading about the work of other psychologists who are committed researchers in love with their work. My greatest hope is that by the end of this book, you will be hooked on research and want to contribute to our growing collection of knowledge about what makes people behave the way they do. And while I don't want you to ignore your other studies, I do hope that you will find research in psychology so fascinating that you will be tempted to "drop everything else and study it."

Chapter Summary

Why Take This Course?

The research methods course is at the core of the psychology curriculum. It should be taken by all psychology majors because it provides the foundation for doing research in psychology, serves as a basis for understanding other content courses in psychology, makes one a more critical consumer of information about behavior, is essential for admission to graduate studies, and teaches scientific thinking.

Ways of Knowing

Our knowledge of the world around us often derives from our experiences and how we interpret them, our reliance on the authority of others, and our use of reason. These sources of knowledge can be quite valuable, but they can also lead to error. Our experiences can be subject to cognitive biases (e.g., belief perseverance, availability heuristic, confirmation bias), authorities can be wrong, and while reason and logic are essential for critical thinking, reasonable arguments in the absence of empirical evidence can be unproductive in the search for truth. Research psychologists rely heavily on scientific thinking as a way of knowing and understanding behavior.

Attributes of Scientific Thinking in Psychology

Research psychologists assume that human behavior is lawful and predictable and that regularities in behavior can be discovered by using scientific methods. Researchers rely on observations that are said to be objective (i.e., can be verified by more than a single observer); historically, the emphasis on objectivity led to a shift from using introspection (a form of self-report) as a method to using methods that measured specific behaviors. Researchers also require conclusions about the causes of behavior to be data-based, and the questions asked (empirical questions) must be answerable through the use of scientific methods. Research psychologists are skeptical optimists—optimistic about discovering important things about behavior, but skeptical about claims made without solid empirical support.

Psychological Science and Pseudoscience

It is important to distinguish legitimate scientific inquiry from pseudoscience. The latter is characterized by a deliberate attempt to associate itself with true science, by relying on anecdotal evidence (e.g., glowing testimonials), by developing theories that are too vague to be adequately tested by scientific methods, and by a tendency to explain complicated phenomena with overly simplistic concepts. Nineteenth-century phrenology and 20th-century subliminal self-help audiotapes illustrate the characteristics of pseudoscience.

The Goals of Scientific Psychology

Research in psychology aims to provide clear and detailed descriptions of behavioral phenomena, to develop laws that enable scientists to predict behavior with some probability greater than chance, and to provide adequate explanations of the causes of behavior. The results of psychological research can also be applied to change behavior directly, which makes the control of behavior a fourth goal.

A Passion for Research in Psychology (Part I)

Psychological scientists tend to be intensely curious about behavior and passionate about their work. As a relatively young discipline, psychology has more questions than answers, so doing research in psychology can be enormously rewarding. The joy of doing research can be seen in the lives and work of famous psychologists such as Eleanor Gibson (the visual cliff studies) and B. F. Skinner (the discovery and promotion of operant conditioning).

Chapter Review

At the end of each chapter you will find two types of review materials: multiple choice and short essay questions. You should study the chapter thoroughly before attempting to answer them. Answers to the multiple choice items can be found in Appendix E. This appendix also provides references to the appropriate chapter page(s) for further information about the multiple choice questions.

Multiple Choice

1. What does it mean to say that scientific thinking includes the characteristic of objectivity?
   a. it means that true scientists never let human biases affect their work
   b. it refers to measurements that are made by some mechanical instrument, thereby eliminating human influence entirely
   c. it refers to observations that can be verified by two or more observers
   d. it refers to psychologists' near-obsession with the idea of answering questions by referring to data

2. John has a strong belief that people on welfare are content to receive "free money" and are not really interested in working. His tendency to pay special attention to and recall news stories about welfare fraud illustrates
   a. a confirmation bias
   b. his reliance on the authority of experts in forming his opinion
   c. the problem with introspection as a method in psychology
   d. an effort justification on his part

3. According to the text, there are four goals of scientific psychology. Which of the following activities falls under the category of "control"?
    a. accurately categorizing several varieties of schizophrenia
    b. establishing laws so that estimates can be made about what people will do in certain circumstances
    c. identifying the causes of aggression in young children
    d. using the results of eyewitness memory research to train police to interview witnesses more efficiently

4. All of the following are associated with pseudoscience except
    a. any possible outcome can be "explained" by the theory
    b. relatively simple phenomena are given extremely complex explanations
    c. a deliberate attempt is made to associate the pseudoscience with some normal scientific work
    d. there is a heavy reliance on anecdotal evidence

5. According to Kuhn, what is the consequence of a researcher's reluctance to give up on a theory?
    a. the researcher will be quickly recognized as a pseudoscientific fraud
    b. the theory won't be abandoned by the scientific community until it has been fully tested
    c. other researchers will become suspicious and the theory will be abandoned before it has been adequately tested
    d. the researcher's perseverance will pay off and others will be convinced

Short Essay

1. As ways of knowing, what are the shortcomings of tenacity, authority, and the a priori method?
2. Explain why it would be a good idea to take a research methods course prior to taking courses in such areas as social, abnormal, and cognitive psychology.
3. Research psychologists generally work on an assumption of statistical determinism. Explain what this means.
4. According to Carnap, determinism must exist in order for free choice to be possible. Explain the logic of his argument.
5. Using introspection to illustrate, explain how research psychologists use the term objectivity.
6. What is an empirical question? Give an example of an empirical question that would be of interest to someone studying religion and health.
7. Pseudosciences are criticized for relying on anecdotal evidence. What kind of evidence is this and why is it a problem?
8. Pseudosciences do what they can to appear scientific. How do those trying to sell you a subliminal self-help audiotape accomplish this?
9. Research in psychology is said to have four related goals. Describe them.
10. In order for research psychologists to feel confident that they have found a "cause" for some phenomenon, what conditions have to be met?

Applications Exercises

In addition to review exercises, the end of each chapter will include "applications" exercises. These will be problems and questions that encourage you to think like a research psychologist and to apply what you have learned in a particular chapter. For each chapter, in order to give you some feedback, I will provide answers to some of the items in Appendix E. Your instructor will have a complete set of answers to all of the exercises.

Exercise 1.1. Asking Empirical Questions

For each of the following nonempirical questions, think of an empirical question that would be related to the issue raised and lead to a potentially interesting scientific study.

1. Is God dead?
2. What is truth?
3. Are humans naturally good?
4. Are women morally superior to men?
5. What is beauty?
6. Is the mind a "blank slate" at birth or are we born with certain kinds of knowledge?

Exercise 1.2. Thinking Critically About an Old Saying

You have probably heard the old saying that "bad things come in threes." Use what you have learned about the various ways of knowing and about pseudoscientific thinking to explain how such a belief might be formed and why it is hard to convince a believer that there are problems with the saying. From what you have learned about scientific thinking, explain what needs to be made clearer in order to examine this theory more critically. That is, in order to determine if the saying is really true, what needs to be specified?

Exercise 1.3. Arriving at a Strong Belief

Consider people who have a strong belief in a personal God who, they believe, directs their daily lives. Using the various ways of knowing described in this chapter, explain how such a belief might form and be maintained.

Exercise 1.4. Graphology

You have probably seen full-page advertisements advocating the "science" of handwriting analysis. You might be asked to send in a sample of your handwriting, and for a fee, you will be sent a description of your personality. The basic idea behind graphology is that the way you form your letters is a reflection of the way you are. For example, a graphologist might report that you are shy or withdrawn if your writing is small and cramped.

a. Consider each of the main aspects of pseudoscience. How might each apply in the case of graphology?

b. Even though we have not begun to discuss research design, you probably have some sense of what an experiment is like. Design one that might be a true test of graphology's claim.

CHAPTER 2

Ethics in Psychological Research

Preview & Chapter Objectives

This second chapter will introduce you to a set of ethical principles formulated by the American Psychological Association (APA) that guide researchers in the planning, execution, and reporting of their research. The ethics code includes guidelines for psychological research that uses both human participants and animals.[1] The topic is presented early in the text because of its importance—ethical issues must be addressed at all stages of the research process. When you finish this chapter, you should be able to:

- Describe the origins of the ethics code and distinguish between its general principles and its specific standards.

---

[1] Humans are animals too, of course. When I use the term "animal research," I am referring to research with nonhuman animals.

- Describe the role of the Institutional Review Board (IRB) and what needs to be done to achieve IRB approval of research.
- Identify the essential features of a researcher's ethical responsibility when completing psychological research using human participants ranging from adults to members of special populations.
- Describe the arguments for and against the use of animals in psychological research.
- Identify the essential features of a researcher's ethical responsibility when completing psychological research using animal subjects.
- Identify the varieties of scientific fraud and understand why fraud sometimes occurs in science.

A system of **ethics** is a set of principles for behaving in a way that is morally correct. That is, to behave ethically is to do what is right. When conducting research in psychology, our ethical obligations encompass several areas. Research psychologists must (a) treat human research participants with respect and in a way that maintains their rights and dignity, (b) care for the welfare of animals when they are the subjects of research, and (c) be scrupulously honest in the treatment of data.

Before beginning to study the APA code of ethics, you should read Box 2.1, which describes one of psychology's best-known and most ethically infamous studies. The Little Albert experiment is often described as a pioneering investigation of how children develop fears, but it also serves well as a lesson in dubious ethical practice.

Box 2.1

CLASSIC STUDIES — Scaring Little Albert

The February 1920 issue of the *Journal of Experimental Psychology* contained a brief article called "Conditioned Emotional Reactions." Although it included several methodological weaknesses (Harris, 1979), it became one of psychology's best known and most frequently cited case studies. The authors were the arch-behaviorist John B. Watson and Rosalie Rayner, a graduate student of Watson's and soon to be his second wife. The study used just one participant, an 11-month-old boy given the pseudonym of Albert B. The purpose of the study was to see if Albert could be conditioned to be afraid.

The Little Albert study was part of Watson's project to study emotions. He already knew that infants are "naturally" afraid of little except loud noises and loss of support (he discovered this empirically, as shown in Figure 2.1). By early childhood, however, they develop a number of fears: of the dark, of spiders, of snakes, and so on. As a behaviorist, Watson believed these fears were the products of life's experiences, and he wanted to see if deliberately influencing events in a child's life could produce a learned fear.

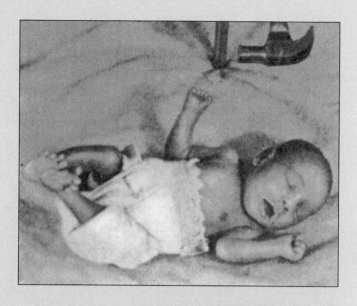

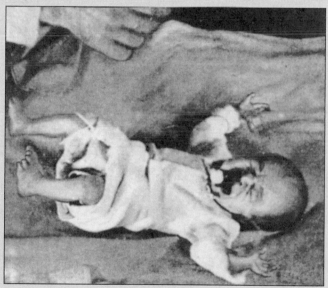

FIGURE 2.1 Stimuli producing fear in children, taken from films made by Watson of his infant research (including the Little Albert study); these stills were taken from the film, touched up, and reprinted by Watson in his *Psychological Care of Infant and Child* (1928). The top photo shows what happens when "[a] steel bar is struck with a hammer near [the infant's] head" (p. 26), while in the bottom photo, the infant reacts to having the "blanket upon which he is lying suddenly jerked" (p. 27), thereby producing loss of support.

In brief, Watson and Rayner first determined that Albert had no natural fear of a white rat, but would react with a strong fear response if a steel bar was struck with a hammer just behind his head (!). The procedure was to pair the loud noise with the rat. Here's what happened on the first trial:

> White rat suddenly taken from the basket and presented to Albert. He began to reach for rat with left hand. Just as his hand touched the animal the bar was struck immediately behind his head. The infant jumped violently and fell forward, burying his face in the mattress. (Watson & Rayner, 1920, p. 4)

After several trials, the loud noise was no longer needed; Albert had developed a powerful association and was terrified of the rat. Because of generalization to similar stimuli, he was also afraid of a rabbit, a fur coat, and cotton wool.

Of course, it is difficult to hold Watson and Rayner responsible for ethical guidelines that were published 33 years after they published the Little Albert study. It is clear, however, that they were aware that some persons might object to the study, that "a certain responsibility attaches to such a procedure" (Watson & Rayner, 1920, p. 3). They decided to proceed because Albert seemed to be a strong, healthy child, "on the whole stolid and unemotional. His stability was one of the principal reasons for using him.... We felt that we could do him relatively little harm by carrying out such experiments" (pp. 1–2). Watson and Rayner also justified the study by arguing that because such fears would be learned by Albert *anyway,* "as soon as [he] left the sheltered environment of the nursery for the rough and tumble of the home" (p. 3), he might as well learn them in a way that would advance science.

Although Watson and Rayner made no attempt to remove Albert's fear, Watson gave a talk at Vassar College several years later that inspired a student in the audience to make such an attempt. Mary Cover Jones was the listener, and she went on to demonstrate that a child's learned fears could be extinguished. Her successful elimination of the fear of a rabbit in a young boy (Jones, 1924) is often described as the pioneering use of a behavior therapy technique called systematic desensitization.

As you read about the APA ethical guidelines in this chapter, you should ask yourself whether the Little Albert study could be carried out today. If not, why not? If so, with what safeguards and changes in procedure?

Developing the APA Code of Ethics

Psychologists in the United States did not publish their first code of ethics until 1953 (APA, 1953). This 171-page document was the outcome of about 15 years of discussion within the APA, which created a temporary committee on Scientific and Professional Ethics in the late 1930s. The committee soon became a standing committee to investigate complaints of unethical behavior (usually concerned with the professional practice of psychology) that occasionally were brought to its attention. In 1948, this group recommended the creation of a formal code of ethics. Under the leadership of Nicholas Hobbs, a new committee on Ethical Standards for Psychology was formed and began what became a 5-year project (Hobbs, 1948).

TABLE 2.1 *General Principles of the APA Code of Ethics*

Principle A: Competence
- Psychologists "recognize the boundaries of their particular competencies and the limits of their expertise" and maintain competence through ongoing education.

Principle B: Integrity
- Psychologists are scrupulously honest in "the science, teaching, and practice of psychology" and are "honest, fair, and respectful of others."

Principle C: Professional and Scientific Responsibility
- Psychologists "uphold professional standards of conduct" and "accept appropriate responsibility for their behavior."

Principle D: Respect for People's Rights and Dignity
- Psychologists avoid treating people in a biased manner and respect their basic human rights "to privacy, confidentiality, self-determination, and autonomy."

Principle E: Concern for Others' Welfare
- Psychologists "seek to contribute to the welfare of those with whom they interact professionally" and do not "exploit or mislead other people during or after professional relationships."

Principle F: Social Responsibility
- Psychologists "apply and make public their knowledge of psychology in order to contribute to human welfare."

Source: APA (1992).

We have seen in Chapter 1 that psychologists are trained to think scientifically. What is noteworthy about the Hobbs committee is that, in keeping with psychology's penchant for relying on data before drawing conclusions, it opted for an empirical approach to forming the code. Using a procedure called the **critical incidents** technique, the committee surveyed the entire membership of the APA (there were about 7,500 members then), asking them to provide examples of "incidents" of unethical conduct that they knew about firsthand and "to indicate what [they] perceived as being the ethical issue involved" (APA, 1953, p. vi). The request yielded over 1,000 replies and included some incidents involving the conduct of research. The committee organized the replies into a series of several drafts that were published in *American Psychologist,* the Association's primary journal. The APA's Council of Directors accepted the final version in 1952 and published it the next year. Although it was concerned mainly with the professional practice of psychology, one of its sections was called "Ethical Standards in Research."

Over the years the code has been revised several times, most recently in 1992. Another revision is underway as this edition goes to press. It currently includes a set of 6 general principles, which are summarized briefly in Table 2.1, and 102 standards, clustered into the 8 general categories listed in Table 2.2. The general principles are "*aspirational* goals to guide psychologists toward the highest ideals of psychology," while the standards "set forth *enforceable* rules for conduct as psychologists" (APA, 1992, p. 1598; italics in the original). Hence, compared to the principles, the standards are designed to be more precise with regard to the behavior of the researcher, although as you read them, I suspect you will share the opinion of the social psychologist Joan Sieber (1994).

TABLE 2.2   *Categories of Ethical Standards in the 1992 Code*

Category	Sample Standards
1. General Standards [27]	1.02 Relationship of ethics and law 1.11 Sexual harassment 1.27 Referrals and fees
2. Evaluation, Assessment, or Intervention [10]	2.03 Test construction 2.05 Interpreting assessment results 2.08 Test scoring and interpretation services
3. Advertising and Other Public Statements [6]	3.01 Definition of public statements 3.04 Media presentations 3.06 In-person solicitation
4. Therapy [9]	4.02 Informed consent to therapy 4.05 Sexual intimacies with current patients or clients 4.09 Terminating the professional relationship
5. Privacy and Confidentiality [11]	5.02 Maintaining confidentiality 5.05 Disclosures 5.07 Confidential information in databases
6. Teaching, Training Supervision, Research and Publishing [26]	6.03 Accuracy and objectivity in teaching 6.06 Planning research 6.23 Publication credit
7. Forensic Activities [6]	7.02 Forensic assessments 7.04 Truthfulness and candor 7.06 Compliance with laws and rules
8. Resolving Ethical Issues [7]	8.02 Confronting ethical issues 8.05 Reporting ethical violations 8.06 Cooperating with ethics committees

Note: The number in brackets below each category refers to the total number of standards for each of these categories.

Note: The full text of all 102 standards can be found in the December 1992 issue of *American Psychologist* (Vol. 47, pp. 1597–1611).

She has criticized the current code for its lack of specificity, especially for those who conduct psychological research but are relatively new to the game (you and your fellow students, for instance). In this chapter, we'll examine the APA standards concerning research with both human and animal participants.[2]

Ethical Guidelines for Research with Humans

In the 1960s, one of the principles of the original code was elaborated into a separate code of ethics for research with human participants. An APA committee mod-

---

[2] Another useful source of information about the ethical treatment of human research participants is the Office of Research integrity in the Department of Health and Human Services. Its website is http://ori.dhhs,gov

eled on the Hobbs committee and headed by a former member of it, Stuart Cook, used the same critical incidents procedure and published an ethics code specifically for researchers in 1973 (APA, 1973); it was revised in 1982 (APA, 1982) and again as part of the general revision of 1992. It contains a number of standards that can be arranged conveniently into three general categories—those having to do with planning the study, those concerning the voluntary status of participants in the study, and those concerned with the treatment of those participating in research.

Planning the Study

All research on human behavior imposes some burden on those participating in the study. At a minimum, people are asked to spend time in an experiment when they could be doing something else. At the other extreme, they are sometimes placed in potentially harmful situations. In the name of psychological science, human **research participants**[3] have received electrical shocks, have been told they failed some apparently easy test, and have been embarrassed in any number of ways. That such experiences can be distressing is clearly illustrated in one of social psychology's most famous series of studies, the obedience research of Stanley Milgram (1963, 1974).

In the guise of a study on the effects of punishment on learning, Milgram induced volunteers to obey commands from an authority figure, the experimenter. Playing the role of teachers, participants were told to deliver what they thought were high-voltage shocks (no shocks were actually given) to another apparent volunteer (actually a professional actor) who was trying, without much success, to learn a sequence of word pairs. Milgram (1963) described one participant's experience as follows: "I observed a mature and initially poised businessman enter the laboratory smiling and confident. Within twenty minutes he was reduced to a switching, stuttering wreck, who was rapidly approaching a point of nervous collapse" (p. 377). As you might guess, Milgram's research has been controversial. He has been sharply criticized for exposing his volunteers to extreme levels of stress, for producing what could be long-term adverse effects on their self-esteem and dignity, and, because of the degree of deception involved, for destroying their trust in psychologists (Baumrind, 1964).

The basic dilemma faced by Milgram and every other researcher is to weigh the scientific value of the study being planned against the degree of intrusion on those contributing data to the study. On the one hand, experimental psychologists believe strongly in the need to conduct psychological research on a wide range of topics. Indeed, they believe that to fail to investigate some topic is to abdicate one's responsibility as a scientist. If the ultimate goal is to improve the human condition, and if knowledge about behavior is essential for this to occur, then it is obviously essential to learn as much as possible. On the other hand, as we've just seen, research can create discomfort for those participating in it, although very few studies come any-

---

[3] Until recently, research psychologists routinely used the term **subject** to refer to any research participant, human or animal, whose behavior was being measured in a study. This usage has changed, however, at least with regard to humans, and the APA now recommends the use of "research participant" or "participant" instead of "subject" on the grounds that the latter term is dehumanizing. It continues to be customary to refer to animals in research as "subjects," however.

where near the Milgram studies in terms of the level of stress experienced by participants. When planning a research study, then, the experimenter always faces the conflicting requirements of (a) producing meaningful research results that could ultimately increase our knowledge of behavior and (b) respecting the rights and welfare of the study's participants. Clearly, Milgram reached the conclusion that the potential value of his research outweighed the potential dangers of his procedures. He was motivated by questions about the Nazi Holocaust (Milgram was Jewish) and deeply concerned about the problem of obedience to authority. Did the Holocaust reflect some basic flaw in the German psyche? Or is the tendency to obey authority to be found in all of us, produced when the circumstances are right? These are important questions.

APA Standards 6.06 through 6.09 deal with the researcher's basic problem of planning a study in order to balance the need to discover the basic laws of behavior with the need to protect subjects. Here are the guidelines in the APA's language:

6.06. Planning Research

    a. Psychologists design, conduct, and report research in accordance with recognized standards of scientific competence and ethical research.

    b. Psychologists plan their research so as to minimize the possibility that results will be misleading.

    c. In planning research, psychologists consider its ethical acceptability under the Ethics Code. If an ethical issue is unclear, psychologists seek to resolve the issue through consultation with institutional review boards, animal care and use committees, peer consultations, and other proper mechanisms.

    d. Psychologists take reasonable steps to implement appropriate protections for the rights and welfare of human participants, other persons affected by the research, and the welfare of animal subjects.

6.07. Responsibility

    a. Psychologists conduct research competently and with due concern for the dignity and welfare of the participants.

    b. Psychologists are responsible for the ethical conduct of research conducted by them or others under their supervision and control.

    c. Researchers and assistants are permitted to perform only those tasks for which they are appropriately trained and prepared.

    d. As part of the process of development and implementation of research projects, psychologists consult those with expertise concerning any special population under investigation or most likely affected.

6.08. Compliance with Law and Standards

Psychologists plan and conduct research in a manner consistent with federal and state law and regulations, as well as professional standards governing the conduct of research, and particularly those standards governing research with human participants and animal subjects.

6.09. Institutional Approval

Psychologists obtain from host institutions or organizations appropriate approval prior to conducting research, and they provide accurate information about their research proposals. They conduct the research in accordance with the approved research protocol.

Standard 6.06 ensures that researchers appreciate the importance of making ethical considerations central to the original planning of the study. Right from the outset, the balance between the scientific importance of the study and the rights of the participants needs to be uppermost in the researcher's mind. Furthermore, the recommendation to seek advice (6.06.c) reflects the difficulty of making some of these decisions. This advice seeking usually takes the form of presenting the research plan to a committee, called the **Institutional Review Board (IRB).** This group consists of at least five people, usually faculty members from several departments and including at least one member of the outside community and one nonscientist (Department of Health and Human Services, 1983). IRBs have to be in place for any college or university receiving federal funds for research. They became especially prevalent in the late 1970s. Researchers seeking IRB approval typically respond to a series of survey-type questions (e.g., does the research involve monetary payment to participants?) and submit to the board a detailed description of research procedures, a statement about potential risks to participants and how they will be alleviated, and a sample "informed consent" form. Most IRBs distinguish between "expedited reviews," involving minimal risk, and "formal reviews," when there is greater potential risk to participants or when participants come from special populations (e.g., prisoners, children). Typically, only formal reviews involve the entire membership of an IRB.

IRBs provide an effective safeguard for participants, researchers, and universities, but they have been controversial at some schools for three reasons. One issue has been the extent to which IRBs should be judging the details of research procedures and designs (Kimmel, 1996). Researchers legitimately object to nonspecialists (e.g., philosophy professors) passing judgment on procedures they may not understand, such as the forms of counterbalancing you will learn about in Chapter 6. On the other hand, there are ethical implications of a poorly designed study. If it is flawed methodologically, its results will be worthless and the time of its participants wasted. At least one prominent researcher has suggested that IRBs should include method ology experts (Rosenthal, 1994). A second issue concerns the perception among some researchers that it is very difficult to win IRB approval of basic research. IRB members unfamiliar with some specific research area might fail to see the relevance of a proposed study in basic science, for instance, yet might be better able to "make sense of" an applied research study. It could be difficult for an IRB reader to see the need for a study examining several isolated variables on a recognition memory study done in the laboratory, using seemingly artificial materials. On the other hand, a study examining the ability to recognize people filmed on bank video cameras might appear to be more important and could gain IRB approval more easily. Third, some researchers complain that IRBs can be overzealous in their concern about the risk to participants, and that because there are no appeal procedures beyond the IRB, the board can exert coercive control over research. For instance, one researcher described by Kimmel (1996) was unable to obtain IRB approval for a study in which subjects had to detect tones of varying loudness. Despite the fact that no tone was louder than conversational speech, the IRB insisted that listening to the tones "entailed a slight risk to [participants'] welfare" (p. 279). The researcher refused to concede the point, argued with the IRB for 3 years, and then switched to animal research, stating that "the composition of animal welfare committees [was] a bit more reasonable" (p. 279). Obviously, not all IRBs are this arbitrary, but the lack of an appeal process is a legitimate problem.

Part of the planning stage for a study involves determining the degree of risk to be encountered by participants (implied in 6.06.d). Sometimes there is no risk at all, as when experiments observe public behavior and do not intervene in any way. At other times, volunteers may be "at risk" or "at minimal risk." The distinction is not razor sharp but is based on the degree to which the people being studied find themselves in situations similar to "those ordinarily encountered in daily life or during the performance of routine physical or psychological examinations or tests" (Department of Health and Human Services, 1983, p. 297). Hence, participants facing situations like those encountered in daily living that involve little or no stress are considered to be "at minimal risk." If the risks, physical or mental, are greater than that, participants are said to be "at risk." For instance, people would be at minimal risk in a sports psychology study investigating whether training in visual imagery techniques led to better athletic performance than the absence of such training. However, if that same study investigated whether the improvement due to training in imagery could be reduced by having participants ingest low or moderate doses of marijuana, the degree of risk would obviously be higher.

When there is minimal risk, IRB approval is usually routinely granted. However, when participants are "at risk," the experimenter must convince the IRB that the value of the study justifies the risk and that the study could not be completed in any other fashion, and must scrupulously follow the remaining guidelines to ensure that those contributing data are informed and well treated.

Standard 6.07 makes it clear that the ethical guidelines must be followed by all the researchers in a study, not just by the principal investigator, and that experimenters actually running the study must be properly trained. Although the principal investigator bears primary responsibility for any research project, everyone connected with the experiment must follow the guidelines and must be trained. This standard is especially relevant for you as a student researcher. Your instructor has the primary responsibility for any studies that you conduct in the research methods course, but you also bear an obligation to protect the people who serve in your research project. Also, before you collect any data, you should be given thorough instructions (6.07.c). Standard 6.07.d provides for research involving "special" populations. This applies to any category of participants not legally able to give consent, such as children or those who are mentally incapacitated. It can also refer to those who might feel coerced into volunteering to participate in research (e.g., prisoners). The problem of gaining consent with special populations will be considered shortly.

Standard 6.08 reminds researchers to be aware of laws or regulations pertaining to their projects. For instance, a few paragraphs earlier, you read about the concept of "risk" as applied to research participants, and you probably noticed a reference to a set of federal regulations from the Department of Health and Human Services. The mandating of IRBs in institutions receiving federal funds is another example of a regulation that researchers need to follow. Standard 6.09 is especially pertinent for researchers collecting data at a site that is different from their on-campus laboratory. A health psychologist, for instance, might be using a local wellness center as a location for studying adherence to an exercise program. Approval from the center would be needed before proceeding with the study.

Ensuring That Participants Are Volunteers

A second important consideration for researchers concerns the status of participants in the study and centers on the issues of informed consent, deception, and the right of people to withdraw from the study at any time. Standards 6.10 through 6.13 and Standard 6.15 are especially pertinent:

6.10. Research Responsibilities

Prior to conducting research (except research involving only anonymous surveys, naturalistic observations, or similar research), psychologists enter into an agreement with participants that clarifies the nature of the research and the responsibilities of both parties.

6.11. Informed Consent to Research

a. Psychologists use language that is reasonably understandable to research participants in obtaining their appropriate informed consent. Such informed consent is appropriately documented.

b. Using language that is reasonably understandable to participants, psychologists inform participants of the nature of the research; they inform participants that they are free to participate or to withdraw from the research; they explain the foreseeable consequences of declining or withdrawing; they inform participants of significant factors that may be expected to influence their willingness to participate (such as risks, discomfort, adverse effects, or limitations on confidentiality, except as provided in Standard 6.15, Deception in Research); and they explain other aspects about which the prospective participants inquire.

6.12. Dispensing with Informed Consent

Before determining that planned research (such as research involving only anonymous questionnaires, naturalistic observations, or certain kinds of archival research) does not require the informed consent of research participants, psychologists consider applicable regulations and IRB requirements, and they consult with colleagues as appropriate.

6.13. Informed Consent in Research Filming or Recording

Psychologists obtain informed consent from research participants prior to filming or recording them in any form, unless the research involves simply naturalistic observations in public places and it is not anticipated that the recordings will be used in a manner that could cause personal identification or harm.

6.15. Deception in Research

a. Psychologists do not conduct a study involving deception unless they have determined that the use of deceptive techniques is justified by the study's prospective scientific, educational, or applied value and that equally effective alternative procedures that do not use deception are not feasible.

b. Psychologists never deceive research participants about significant aspects that would affect their willingness to participate, such as physical risks, discomfort, or unpleasant emotional experiences.

c. Any other deception that is an integral feature of the design and conduct of an experiment must be explained to participants as early as feasible, preferably at the conclusion of their participation, but no later than at the conclusion of the research.

These standards can be considered together and center on the issues of informed consent and deception in psychological research. Standards 6.11, 6.12, and 6.13 describe the principle of **informed consent,** the notion that in deciding whether to participate in psychological research, human participants should be given enough information about the study to decide if they wish to volunteer. Participants experience **deception** (6.15) when they are not told complete details of the study at its outset or when they are misled about some of the procedures. How can these apparently contradictory concepts be reconciled?

One could argue that truly informed consent should never result in people being deceived about the purposes of the study. Some (e.g., Baumrind, 1985) have suggested eliminating deception in all psychology experiments, on the grounds that people in positions of trust (i.e., experimenters) should not be lying to others (i.e., participants). The outcome of deceptive research, she believes, is that participants could become mistrustful of experts and perhaps even cynical about the legitimacy of psychology as a science.

Several alternatives to deception have been suggested, including naturalistic observations and qualitative interview procedures. Greenberg (1967), for example, suggested using a simulation procedure in which people are told the complete purpose of a study ahead of time and are then asked to role-play someone who did not know the purpose ahead of time. Studies (e.g., Miller, 1972) evaluating this idea have not been very supportive, however. There is a difference between behaving naturally and acting the way you think you are supposed to act; consequently, it's not surprising that role-playing subjects and naive subjects behave differently. Furthermore, there is evidence that participants who are fully informed ahead of time about the purpose of an experiment behave differently from those who aren't informed. For instance, a study by Gardner (1978) looked at the effects of noise as a stressor for some subjects who were fully informed about the noise and others who weren't. The usual finding is that noise disrupts concentration and reduces performance on a variety of tasks, especially if the noise is unpredictable. Gardner, however, found that noise failed to have adverse effects on those who were first given complete information about the study, including the explicit direction that they could leave the study at any time. Apparently, the information increased the participants' *feeling of control* over the situation, and even the unpredictable noise didn't bother them; other research (e.g., Sherrod, Hage, Halpern, & Moore, 1977) has shown consistently that an increased perception of control over one's fate generally acts to reduce stress. Thus, fully informing participants in a study on the effects of unpredictable noise might produce an outcome that fails to discover the bad effects of such noise. In order to investigate fully the variables influencing the relationship between unpredictable noise as a stressor and performance on some tasks, it seems that some degree of deception is needed.

Milgram's obedience studies provide a further illustration of why psychologists sometimes withhold information about the true purpose of the study at the beginning of the experiment. We've seen that Milgram told his participants he was investigating the effects of punishment on learning. Teachers (the real participants) would try to teach a list of word pairs to a learner, believing they were shocking him for errors (see Figure 2.2). Milgram was not really interested in learning, of course. Rather, he wanted to know whether his volunteers would (a) continue to administer

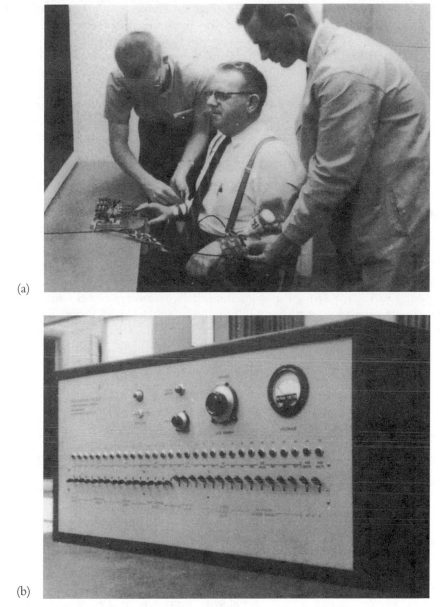

(a)

(b)

FIGURE 2.2 (a) The "learner" in Stanley Milgram's experiment being prepared for an experimental session; (b) the apparatus used by the "teacher" to (apparently) deliver shocks to the learner. From Milgram (1974).

apparent shocks of increasing voltage to a learner who was in obvious discomfort and clearly not learning much or (b) disobey the experimenter and stop the experiment at some point. The outcome: few people disobeyed orders. In the original study, 26 of 40 continued shocking the learner even when the voltage level reached 450 and *nobody* disobeyed until it reached 300 volts (Milgram, 1963)! If Milgram had informed his subjects that he was interested in seeing whether they would obey unreasonable commands, would the same results have occurred? Almost certainly not. Blind obedience to authority is not something that people value highly, so participants told ahead of time they are in a study of obedience will surely be less compliant than they otherwise might be. The key point is that researchers want participants to take the task seriously, to be thoroughly involved in the study, and to behave as naturally as possible. For that to happen, deception is sometimes necessary. Please keep in mind, of course, that the Milgram study is an extreme example of deception. In most research in psychology, deception involves the withholding of some information about the study rather than an elaborate cover story that misleads. That is, most deception research involves omitting some information in the consent process, rather than actively misleading participants about what they are to encounter (Fischman, 2000).

Standard 6.11.b makes it clear that volunteers, even after they have consented to participate in a study, should be aware that they can leave the experiment at any time without penalty. If an IRB had been operative when Milgram was planning his study, he clearly would have been asked to modify certain portions of his procedure. During the sequence of learning trials, for instance, if the teacher showed any hesitation about continuing to administer shocks (and almost all participants did), the experimenter said things like "The experiment requires that you continue" or "It is absolutely essential that you continue" (Milgram, 1963, p. 374). This certainly violates the "feel free to leave any time" provision of the code.

The most extraordinary instances of failure to obtain informed consent in research with human subjects occurred in Germany and its occupied territories during World War II, in medical research using concentration camp inmates as subjects. In the name of medical science, Nazi doctors and scientists such as Josef Mengele completed a series of horrific studies. To measure how long humans could survive, inmates were immersed in ice water, injected with gasoline, or deliberately exposed to infectious and deadly diseases, among other things. At their Nuremberg trials, the doctors defended their actions by arguing that voluntary consent didn't really exist in any medical research of the time and that the long-term importance of their research outweighed any adverse consequences to the participants. Their argument failed, they were convicted, and the presiding tribunal wrote what was called the Nuremberg Code. It became the basis for all subsequent codes of medical research ethics as well as the consent portion of the APA ethics code, establishing the principle that consent must be informed, competent, and voluntary, and that the person giving it must be able to comprehend the situation involved (Faden & Beauchamp, 1986).

Although the experiments performed on concentration camp victims are the most dramatic and appalling examples of consent violations, problems have occurred in the United States as well. See Box 2.2 for brief descriptions of three cases from the field of medical research, in which (a) severely retarded children were infected with hepatitis in order to study the development of the illness, (b) poor Southern black men with syphilis were left untreated for years and misinformed about their health, also for the purpose of learning more about the time course of the disease, and (c) Americans were given large doses of LSD without their knowledge.

Box 2.2

ETHICS—Historical Problems with Informed Consent

The research activities of doctors in the Third Reich are unprecedented in their callousness and cruelty. Nonetheless, there are cases in the United States of research projects that have provoked intensely critical reactions and have invited comparisons, albeit remote, to the Nazi doctors. Three famous examples are the Willowbrook hepatitis study, the Tuskegee syphilis study, and project MK-ULTRA.

At Willowbrook, an institution housing children with varying degrees of mental retardation, an experiment began in 1956 and continued into the 1970s in which approximately 1 in 10 new admissions was purposely infected with hepatitis. The parents were told of the procedure and agreed to it, but it was later shown that they might have felt pressured into giving consent. Also, the study violated the principle that research using the mentally disabled as subjects should not be done unless it "relates immediately to the etiology, pathogenesis, prevention, diagnosis, or treatment of mental disability itself" (Beauchamp & Childress, 1979, p. 182). The Willowbrook study was investigating hepatitis, not mental disability.

The study was initiated because hepatitis was rampant at the institution, partly due to a high proportion of severely retarded children who could not be toilet trained. At one point in the 1950s, there were 5,200 residents; of those, 3,800 had IQs lower than 20 and more than 3,000 were not toilet trained (Beauchamp & Childress, 1979). Even with the staff's best efforts, conditions were generally unsanitary and led to the spread of the disease. By deliberately infecting new admissions and placing them in a separate ward but not treating them, the researchers hoped to study the development of the disease under controlled conditions. Those in charge of the project defended it on the grounds that the children would almost certainly contract the disease anyway, so why not have them contract it in such a way that more could be learned about how to prevent it? Indeed, while the study has been legitimately criticized on consent grounds, it did contribute greatly to our knowledge of hepatitis and undoubtedly improved future treatment of the disease.

The Tuskegee study was designed to examine the physical deterioration of persons suffering from advanced syphilis (Jones, 1981). Beginning in the early 1930s, about 400 poor black men from the rural South were diagnosed with the disease and deliberately left untreated. They were never informed about the nature of the disease, nor were they told its name; doctors simply informed them that they had "bad blood." Also, local physicians were told of the study and agreed not to treat the men. Given the poverty of the participants, it was not difficult to induce (coerce?) them to visit the clinic periodically (free rides and a hot meal), where blood tests and other examinations were done. The project continued into the early 1970s, even though it was clear by the late 1940s that the subjects were dying at twice the rate of a control group and were developing significantly more medical complications (Faden & Beauchamp,

1986). Defenders of the study argued that when it began in the 1930s there was no effective treatment for the disease and little knowledge of it. Like Willowbrook, the Tuskegee study contributed to our knowledge of a serious disease, but was overshadowed by the consent violations.

While the chief investigators in both the Willowbrook and Tuskegee studies were misguided in their abuse of informed consent, they had a sincere desire to learn as much as possible about two devastating diseases, hepatitis and syphilis. The third example of a consent violation, unfortunately, lacked even the justification of an eventual medical benefit. This was a project launched by the Central Intelligence Agency (CIA), to expose unknowing human participants (usually soldiers) to the drug LSD in order to gauge the drug's ability to be useful as a weapon of war. The project was created in the early 1950s, in the context of the "cold war" between the United States and the Soviet Union. There was fear that the Communists were developing weapons that could alter minds, a concern heightened by reports of the so-called brainwashing of American POWs during the Korean War. Prompted in part by a false intelligence report that the Soviets were buying up the world's supply of LSD (Thomas, 1995), the CIA leadership approved a program to determine if LSD could be used to do such things as cause mental confusion in an enemy or render captured spies defenseless. Over a period of about 10 years, the CIA sponsored numerous studies on unwitting participants, often soldiers, but sometimes members of the general public. Soldiers signed consent forms, but the forms said nothing about the potential effects of the drug and were designed mostly to ensure that soldiers would not reveal their participation. That secrecy was important is clear from an internal CIA memo that read, in part,

> Precautions must be taken … to conceal these activities from the American public. … The knowledge that the Agency is engaging in unethical and illicit activities would have serious repercussions in political and diplomatic circles. (cited in Grose, 1994, p. 393)

What went on during MK-ULTRA? Projects included giving soldiers LSD then putting them in isolation, giving them the drug then performing a lie detection task, examining the effects of repeated doses (over 77 consecutive days in one case), and even surreptitiously giving the drug to men visiting prostitutes in a CIA-financed brothel, with agents observing behind two-way mirrors (Thomas, 1995). This latter study was code-named "Operation Midnight Climax."

At least two people died as part of MK-ULTRA and numerous others were adversely affected by it. Here is a typical case, as described in the 1994 Rockefeller Report, the result of a Congressional investigation into 50 years of CIA-sponsored biological experimentation:

> In 1957,——volunteered for a special program to test new military protective clothing. He was offered various incentives to participate in the program, including a liberal leave policy, family visitations, and superior living and recreational facilities. … During the 3 weeks of testing new clothing, he was given two or three water-size glasses of a liquid containing LSD to drink. Thereafter, Mr. —— developed erratic behavior and even attempted

suicide. He did not learn that he had received LSD as a human subject until 18 years later, as a result of congressional hearings in 1975. (Rockefeller Report, 1994)

The CIA did not bother to inform either Congress or the President about MK-ULTRA. The program ground to a halt in 1963, primarily because the studies did not yield information of military use. Congressional investigators discovered it in the mid-1970s and issued a full report and a rebuke (Grose, 1994).

Figure 2.3 on page 50 displays an example of a typical consent form for adult participants. Note that it has several features. Potential subjects agree to participate voluntarily after learning the general purpose of the study, the procedure, and the amount of time it will take. In addition, participants understand that full information about the study may not come right away, that they can leave the study at any time without penalty, that strict confidentiality will be upheld, and that if there are any lingering questions about the study or complaints to be made, there is a specific person to contact. Participants are also informed of any risk that might be encountered in the study. Lastly, participants confirm that effective debriefing occurs at the end of the study.

Informed Consent and Special Populations

One last point about informed consent, deception, and freedom to withdraw is that not all research participants are capable of giving consent, due to such factors as age or infirmity, and some persons might experience undue coercion to volunteer for research (e.g., prisoners). In these circumstances, additional procedures apply. For example, the Society for Research in Child Development (SRCD) follows a set of guidelines that build on and amplify some of the provisions of the code for adults. Thus, because children might not be able to fully understand a consent form, their parents or legal guardians are the ones giving consent. Nonetheless, unless the participants are infants, researchers remain obligated to inform the child about the study and to gain what is referred to as **assent** from the child. That is, researchers give the child as much information as possible in order to gauge whether the child is willing to participate. According to the SRCD code, assent occurs when "the child shows some form of agreement to participate without necessarily comprehending the full significance of the research necessary to give informed consent" (Society for Research in Child Development, 1996, p. 337). Assent also means that the researcher has a responsibility to monitor experiments with children and to stop the session if it appears that undue stress is being experienced. A parent may give informed consent for a study on the effects of TV violence on children's aggressive behavior, but the parent won't be in the room when the film is shown. It is up to the researcher to be sensitive enough to remove the child from the task at hand (and repair the damage) if the stress level is too high.

In addition to the assent provision, the SRCD code requires that additional consent be obtained from others who might be involved with the study in any way. For example, this would include teachers when a study includes their students. The code also

Procedure

- ✓ Experimenter describes the general nature of the study and asks the individual to consent to participate.
- ✓ Individual reads over the form, asks questions perhaps, then signs or doesn't sign.
- ✓ After debriefing, the participant signs the final part of the form.
- ✓ The participant is given a copy of the form.

An Experiment on Cognitive Mapping

The purpose of this research is to determine how accurately people can point to geographic locations. If you participate, you will be asked to move a compass-like object so that one arm of it points toward a series of locations. You will also be asked to indicate how confident you are about your decisions. The exercise will take approximately 15 minutes. The exact predictions that are being made in this study will be explained to you at the conclusion of your participation. If you have any questions or concerns about your participation or about the study in general, you may contact me as follows: _____

****

I have read the description of the experiment on cognitive mapping and I voluntarily agree to participate. I understand that I will be asked to point to the locations of a number of geographic places and that the full purpose of the study will be explained at the conclusion of my participation. I understand that I can quit the experiment at any time, without penalty, and that my participation and the record of my performance will be kept strictly confidential.

When the entire experiment has been completed [circle one]:

would   would not

like a brief summary of the overall results.

_____   _____
               Signature of participant   Date

****

At the end of the experiment, I was given a full explanation of the study and any questions that I had were answered adequately.

_____   _____
               Signature of participant   Date

FIGURE 2.3 A version of a consent form for research with human subjects.

cautions researchers about incentives that might be used, either to induce a willingness to participate, or as rewards for the tasks completed in the study. The rewards "must not unduly exceed the range of incentives that the child normally receives" (p. 337). Also, researchers should not use the potential rewards as an inducement to gain the child's assent; indeed, rewards should not even be mentioned until after the parents have given full informed consent (Scott-Jones, 2000). Finally, the SRCD code mirrors the provisions of the code for adults, but warns researchers to be even more vigilant in certain areas. These include the decisions about balancing scientific gain against risk to participants, the level of deception that can be justified, and the reporting of the study's results.

Additional provisions for the protection of participants exist with other special populations. Thus, legal guardians must give truly informed consent for research with people who are confined to institutions (e.g., the Willowbrook case). Second, it is imperative to ensure that participants do not feel coerced into volunteering for a study. This is a problem very difficult to avoid in such environments as prisons, because even with the best intentions of researchers, prisoners might not believe that their failure to volunteer won't cost them at some time in the future and perhaps even affect their future parole status. In general, researchers tend to rely on simple material rewards (e.g., money) and to make it clear to prisoners that their participation will not be noted in any way in their parole records (Diener & Crandall, 1978). As was the case for the SRCD code for research with children, the inducements to participate must be reasonable. Standard 6.14 of the APA ethics code concerns these related issues of inducement and coercion.

6.14. Offering Inducements for Research Participants

    a. In offering professional services as an inducement to obtain research participants, psychologists make clear the nature of the services, as well as the risks, obligations, and limitations.

    b. Psychologists do not offer excessive or inappropriate financial or other inducements to obtain research participants, particularly when it might tend to coerce participation.

A third issue with confined populations is confidentiality (Kimmel, 1996). While normal guidelines for disguising the identity of participants continue to apply, researchers might feel greater pressure to break confidentiality if some greater good is at stake (e.g., a prisoner participant reveals that he is about to kill another prisoner). Finally, as mentioned in Box 2.2 in the Willowbrook case, research with confined populations should provide knowledge that will in some way benefit that population.

Treating Participants Well

Several portions of the APA ethics code ensure that volunteers are treated fairly and with respect, that they receive complete information about the study at its conclusion, that any stress they encounter is relieved, and that their participation is kept in confidence. In the words of the guidelines:

6.18. Providing Participants with Information about the Study

    a. Psychologists provide a prompt opportunity for participants to obtain appropriate information about the nature, results, and conclusions of the research, and psychologists attempt to correct any misconceptions that participants may have.

b.   If scientific or humane values justify delaying or withholding this information, psychologists take reasonable measures to reduce the risk of harm.

6.19. Honoring Commitments

Psychologists take reasonable measures to honor all commitments they have made to research participants.

5.02. Maintaining Confidentiality

Psychologists have a primary obligation and take reasonable precautions to respect confidentiality rights of those with whom they work or consult, recognizing that confidentiality may be established by law, institutional rules, or professional or scientific relationships.

6.17. Minimizing Invasiveness

In conducting research, psychologists interfere with the participants or milieu from which data are collected only in a manner that is warranted by an appropriate research design and that is consistent with psychologists' roles as scientific investigators.

We have already seen that the experimental psychologist must make an estimate of the amount of risk to participants, with greater amounts of risk creating a greater burden to justify the study. This problem of risk and potential harm is addressed in the standard relating to deception (6.15) and once more in Standard 6.18, which makes it clear that responsibility does not end with the conclusion of the study. The researcher must attempt to alleviate any stress experienced during the experiment and follow up with participants to ensure their continued well-being. For instance, whatever one might think of the appropriateness of Milgram's study on obedience, he was clearly sensitive to the emotional health of his volunteers. After the study was completed, he sent participants a questionnaire about their experience (84% said they were glad they had participated) and a five-page report describing the results and their significance. He also did a 1-year follow-up study in which a psychiatrist examined 40 former participants and found "no evidence … of any traumatic reactions" (Milgram, 1974, p. 197).

Studies surveying research volunteers have found that fears of excessive harm in psychological research are exaggerated; participants seem to understand and accept the rationale for deception (Christensen, 1988; Fisher & Fryberg, 1994). One survey even found that college students were considerably more lenient than professional psychologists in their judgments about the ethical appropriateness of four hypothetical studies involving such things as experimentally produced stress and alterations of self-esteem (Sullivan & Deiker, 1973). For example, Table 2.3 shows how psychologists and students differed when asked about a study in which participants would be given a supposedly valid personality test and would then be told that "they had rather serious and deep-seated personality problems" (Sullivan & Deiker, 1973, p. 588). As you can see, the psychologists were more concerned than the students about the appropriateness of the study. Other research shows that objections about participating in psychological research seem to center more on concerns about being bored than being harmed (Coulter, 1986).

As mentioned in the earlier discussion of informed consent, when evaluating the problem of deception, it is important to keep in mind that the vast majority of psychological research involves tasks that are considerably less dramatic and decep-

TABLE **2.3**   *Responses of Psychologists and Students About the Ethical Acceptability of a Study Designed to Lower Self-Esteem*

Questions	Percent of Psychologists Answering "Yes"	Percent of Students Answering "Yes"
1. Would subjects volunteer if they knew the details of the study?	45	80
2. Is the deception unethical?	67	23
3. Are any other aspects unethical?	54	8
4. Was the deception justified?	32	84

Source: Sullivan & Deiker (1973, p. 589).

tive than self-esteem manipulations or procedures like Milgram's. In fact, in most studies involving deception, participants are not exposed to elaborate cover stories. Rather, the deception is often quite minor, involving such things as a memory task in which subjects studying and recalling a sequence of four or five word lists aren't told about a final recall of all the lists, as a way of controlling rehearsal. With the exception of some research in areas like social psychology, elaborate deceptions are the exception rather than the rule.

Standard 6.18 introduces the concept of **debriefing,** a postexperimental session in which all aspects of the research are thoroughly discussed with the participant. Debriefing serves two general purposes, referred to by Holmes (1976a, 1976b) as "dehoaxing" and "desensitizing." **Dehoaxing** means revealing the true purpose of the experiment to participants, and **desensitizing** refers to the process of reducing any stress or other negative feelings experienced in the session.

The amount of time spent debriefing depends on the complexity of the study, the presence and degree of deception, and the level of potential distress felt by participants. In a study involving deception, a debriefing session often begins by asking participants if they thought the study had a purpose other than the one initially described. This enables the experimenter to determine if the deception was effective; it also provides a lead-in, allowing the experimenter to reveal the true purpose of the study. It is also at this time that the experimenter tries to justify the deception (e.g., emphasizing the importance of getting one's true reactions) and begins to alleviate any stress involved. Participants "taken in" by the experiment's cover story are told that their behavior reflects the effectiveness of the cover story, not any personal weakness on their part. That is, people in many types of studies can be assured that the situation they experienced had powerful effects on their behavior, that their reactions don't reflect any individual inadequacies, and that others reacted similarly (Holmes, 1976b). In most cases, dehoaxing amounts to explaining the importance of eliciting natural behaviors and discussing the outcomes that the researcher expects.

One result of an effective debriefing is that skilled experimenters can better understand their current study and improve future ones. Participants can be asked for their ideas about revising the procedure in order to learn more about the problem being studied. In many cases, their descriptions of what they were thinking about during the experiment can be of immense help in interpreting the data and planning the next study.

A properly conducted debriefing can last longer than the experimental session itself. Several studies have shown that participants who are thoroughly debriefed evaluate the research experience positively. One study even showed that, compared to nondeceived subjects, those in deception studies actually rated their experiences higher in both enjoyment and educational value, apparently because the debriefing was more extensive (Smith & Richardson, 1983). The importance of leaving subjects with a good feeling about their research participation cannot be overstated. They have invested their time and their intellectual and emotional energy for us. We owe them a great deal.

We also owe them some privacy. Research participants should be assured (Standard 5.02) of complete confidentiality in the experiment. That is, they should be confident that their identities will not be known by anyone other than the experimenter and that only group or disguised data will be reported. The only exceptions to this occur in cases where researchers might be compelled by law to report certain things disclosed by participants (e.g., child abuse, a positive test for tuberculosis). In research that could involve such disclosure, researchers should word the consent form to make it clear that confidentiality could be limited (Folkman, 2000). The basic right to privacy is also the concern of Standard 6.17, which applies particularly to research outside of the laboratory that might affect people in daily living situations. We'll see in the next chapter, when laboratory and field research are compared, that concerns over invading the privacy of people going about their daily business keeps many researchers within the protected confines of the laboratory.

Ethical Guidelines for Research with Animals

As you recall from your course in general psychology, psychologists occasionally use animals as research subjects. Although some people have the impression that psychologists seem to study rats more than people, the truth is that animal research involves a relatively small proportion of the total research done in psychology—about 7–9% (Gallup & Suarez, 1985b). Nonetheless, many of psychology's important contributions to human welfare are based on a foundation of research with animals (Domjan & Purdy, 1995).

Animals are used in psychological research for several reasons. Methodologically, their environmental, genetic, and developmental histories can be easily controlled; ethically, most experimental psychologists take the position that, with certain safeguards in place, animals can be subjected to procedures that could not be used with humans. Consider Eleanor Gibson's visual cliff research again (Gibson & Walk, 1960). Thirty-six 6- to 14-month-old infants were placed in the middle of the apparatus, and although they were quite willing to crawl around on the "shallow" side, they hesitated to crawl onto the glass surface over the "deep" side. This shows that they were able to perceive depth and apparently were aware of some of its consequences. Does this mean that depth perception is innate? No, because these infants had 6 to 14 months of learning experience with distance perception. To control for this experience, it would be necessary to raise infants in complete visual isolation, a procedure that is obviously out of the question. Such a procedure *is* feasible with animals, however, in part because the isolation does not have to be long—animals develop the ability to move through their environments very quickly, sometimes in a matter of minutes. So Gibson and Walk tested a variety of species from rats to kittens to lambs, isolating them from birth until they could move around competently and then testing them on the visual cliff. They discovered that depth perception, at least as measured in the cliff apparatus, is built into the visual system for those species that rely on vision.

The Issue of Animal Rights

The use of animals in research is an emotional and controversial issue (not a new one, though—see Box 2.3). Animal rights activists have denounced the use of animals in studies ranging from medical research to cosmetics testing. In some cases, laboratories have been vandalized and animals released. During the 1980s, for example, animal rights extremists vandalized approximately 100 research facilities housing animals (Adler, 1992). The problem was severe enough to produce federal legislation, the Animal Enterprise Protection Act of 1992, specifically outlawing such vandalism and setting stiff penalties. Nonetheless, protests continued into the 1990s, organized by such groups as People for the Ethical Treatment of Animals (PETA) and the Animal Liberation Front (ALF), the latter identified as a terrorist organization by the FBI. In one instance, a prominent researcher in the area of drug abuse received death threats; her home and university phone numbers were widely circulated, resulting in harassing phone calls; and on Halloween, someone in a blackface mask appeared at her home and threatened to burn it down ("Animal Rights Activity Increases," 1997).

What is the case against the use of animals as research subjects? At the extreme, some argue that humans have no right to consider themselves superior to any other "sentient" species, that is, any species capable of experiencing pain (Singer, 1975). Animals are said to have the same basic rights to privacy, autonomy, and freedom from harm as humans and therefore cannot be subjugated by humans in any way, including participation in any form of research. Moderates among animal rights groups recognize the value of some medical research using animals, but reject other research on the grounds that researchers have inflicted needless pain and suffering when alternative approaches to research would yield essentially the same conclusions. This argument has been quite salutary in reducing unnecessary research on animals by the cosmetics industry, but it has been applied to research in psychology as well. Psychological research with animals has been described as needlessly repetitive and concerned with trivial problems that have no practical human benefit. Critics have suggested that instead of using animals in the laboratory, researchers could discover all they need to know about animal behavior by observing animals in their natural habitats, by substituting nonsentient for sentient animals, or by using computer simulations. How do research psychologists respond?

Using Animals in Psychological Research

Most psychologists flatly reject the argument that sentient animals have rights equal to those of humans. While granting that humans have a strong obligation to respect and

Box 2.3

ORIGINS—Antivivisection and the APA

Considering the high visibility of the animal research controversy, you might think it is a fairly recent development. Not so. Actually, it has a long history, as documented nicely by the comparative psychologist and historian Donald Dewsbury (1990).

The term "vivisection" derives from the Latin *vivus,* or "alive," and refers to surgical procedures on live animals, usually done for scientific purposes. The antivivisection movement developed in 19th-century England, where activists' efforts contributed to the passage of England's Cruelty to Animals Act in 1876, a code similar in spirit to modern APA guidelines for animals. The antivivisection movement quickly spread to the United States; the American Antivivisection Society was founded in 1883 in Philadelphia. Antivivisectionists and animal researchers (including physiologists and early experimental psychologists) engaged in the same arguments that are heard today, with claims of unspeakable torture on the one side and justifications on scientific grounds on the other.

One especially controversial series of studies concerned John B. Watson (again). In order to determine which senses were critical for maze learning, Watson did a series

DREAM OF THE MEDICAL VIVISECTIONIST CRANK WHO WANTONLY AND CRUELLY OPERATED ON RATS, TO SEE THE EFFECT, FROM A "SCIENTIFIC" VIEW-POINT, OF THE LOSS OF THE DIFFERENT SENSES.

FIGURE 2.4   Antivivisectionist cartoon of Watson on the operating table. From Dewsbury (1990).

of studies in which he surgically eliminated senses one at a time to examine the effects on rats in mazes (Watson, 1907). The study caused an outcry when it was reported in the *New York Times* on December 30, 1906, and Watson was satirized in the cartoon in Figure 2.4 (from Dewsbury, 1990).

The APA established its first code for regulating animal research in the 1920s, well before creating the code for research with humans. A committee chaired by Robert Yerkes was formed in 1924, and the following year the APA adopted its recommendations. The committee proposed that laboratories create an open door policy in which "any accredited member … of a humane society [could] be permitted to visit a laboratory to observe the care of animals and methods of experimentation" (Anderson, 1926, p. 125), that journals require authors to be clear about the use of humane procedures in their research, that psychologists defend the need for animal research, in both the classroom and publicly, and that the APA maintain a standing committee on "precautions in animal experimentation" (Anderson, 1926, p. 125).

protect nonhuman species, psychologists believe that humans can be distinguished from nonhumans because of our degree of awareness, our ability to develop culture and to understand history, and especially our ability to make moral judgments. Although animals are remarkable creatures capable of complex cognition, they are "incapable of being moral subjects, of acting rightly or wrongly in the moral sense, of having, discharging, or breaching duties and obligations" (Feinberg, 1974, p. 46). Of course, differentiating between human and nonhuman species does not by itself allow the use of the latter by the former. Psychologists argue, however, that the use of animals in research does not constitute exploitation. Rather, the net effect of such research is beneficial rather than costly, for both humans *and* for animals.

The most visible defender of animal research in psychology has been Neal Miller, a noted experimental psychologist. His research, on topics ranging from basic processes in conditioning and motivation to the principles underlying biofeedback, earned him the APA's Distinguished Scientific Contributions Award in 1959 and its Distinguished Professional Contributions Award in 1983. In "The Value of Behavioral Research on Animals" (1985), Miller argued that (a) animal activists grossly overstate the harm done to animals in psychological research, (b) animal research provides clear benefits for the well-being of humans, and (c) animals research clearly benefits animals as well. Concerning harm, Miller cited a study by Coile and Miller (1984) that examined 5 years' worth of published research in APA journals, a total of 608 studies, and found *no* instances of the forms of abuse claimed by activists. Also, examining the abuse claims shows that at least some of the alleged "abuse" may not be that at all, but merely seems to be because of the inflammatory language used. For instance, Coile and Miller cited several misleading statements from activist literature including: "[The animals] are deprived of food and water to suffer and die slowly from hunger and thirst" (Coile & Miller, 1984, p. 700). This evidently refers to the common laboratory practice in conditioning experiments of depriving animals of food for 24 hours. Animals then placed in a conditioning procedure are motivated to work for the food. Is this abuse? Perhaps not, considering that veterinarians recommend that most pets be fed just once a day (Gallup & Suarez, 1985a).

Miller argued that situations involving harm to animals during the research procedures are rare, used only when less painful alternatives cannot be used, and can be justified by the ultimate good that derives from the studies. This good applies both to humans and to animals, and the bulk of his 1985 article was an attempt to document the kinds of good that derive from animal studies. First, he argued that while the long history of animal conditioning research has taught us much about general principles of learning, it also has had direct application to human problems. An early example of this was a device developed and tested by Mowrer and Mowrer (1938) for treating enuresis (excessive and uncontrolled bedwetting) that was based explicitly on the classical conditioning work involving Pavlov's dogs. Teaching machines and several forms of behavior therapy are likewise grounded in conditioning principles. More recently, animal research has directly influenced the development of behavioral medicine—the application of behavioral principles to traditional medical practice. Disorders ranging from headaches to hypertension to the disabilities following strokes can be treated with behavioral procedures such as biofeedback.

Finally, Miller argued that animal research provides direct benefits to animals themselves. Medical research with animals has improved veterinary care dramatically, but behavioral research has also improved the welfare of various species. The study of animal behavior by research psychologists has led to the improvement of zoo environments, aided in nonchemical pest control, and discouraged coyote attacks on sheep by using taste avoidance conditioning as a substitute for lethal control. Behavioral research can even help preserve endangered species. Miller used the example of imprinting, the tendency for young ducklings and other species to follow the first stimulus that moves (usually the mother). Research on imprinting led to the procedure of exposing newly hatched condors to a puppet resembling an adult condor rather than to a normal human caretaker, thereby facilitating the bonding process for the incubator-raised bird and ultimately enhancing the survival of this threatened species.

One last point about using animals in psychological research is that despite the arguments of some animal rights groups, most people seem to think that animal research has value. Surveys of psychologists (Plous, 1996a) and psychology majors (Plous, 1996b), for instance, indicate that while there is considerable ambivalence about research in which animals experience pain and/or have to be put to death at the conclusion of the study, most psychologists and students of psychology believe that animal research in psychology is both justified and necessary. These views appear to be shared by students in general (Fulero & Kirkland, 1992; Gallup & Beckstead, 1988). Furthermore, the use of animals by research psychologists has not changed substantially in recent years as a consequence of pressure from animal rights groups. Although Gallup and Eddy (1990) reported that 14.7% of graduate programs that formerly had animal labs no longer have them, the decline was attributed more to changing research interests and cost rather than to pressure from animal rights protesters. Benedict and Stoloff (1991) found similar results among elite undergraduate colleges. More recently, in a survey of 110 undergraduate department chairpersons, Hull (1996) found virtually no change in their use of animal labs over a 5-year period; 47% reported using animals at the time of the survey, while 50% had used animals 5 years earlier. Hull's survey also revealed that departments using animals did not find APA and National Institutes of Health (NIH) guidelines difficult to follow and that the student response to the presence of an animal lab was mostly favorable. On the other hand, Plous (1996a) reported that strong support for animal research was higher among older than among younger psychologists, suggesting that animal research among psychologists, as well as animal labs for undergraduate psychology majors, may decline in the future.[4]

The APA Code for Animal Research

Standard 6.20 of the 1992 code sketches the ethical guidelines for animal use; the elements of the code are elaborated in an earlier document (APA, 1985). The guidelines deal with (a) the need to justify the study when the potential for harm exists, (b) the proper acquisition and care of animals, both during and after the study, and (c) the use of animals for educational rather than research purposes. The main theme is the issue of balancing the scientific justification for a particular project with the need to care humanely for the animals. Here are the highlights.

Justifying the Study

Just as the researcher studying humans must weigh the scientific value of the research against the degree of risk to the participants, the animal researcher must make the case that the "scientific purpose of the research [is] of sufficient potential significance as to outweigh any harm or distress to the animals used" (APA, 1985, p. 5). The "scientific purpose" of the study should fall within one of three categories. The research should "(a) increase knowledge of the processes underlying the evolution, development, maintenance, alteration, control, or biological significance of behavior, (b) increase understanding of the species under study, or (c) provide results that benefit the health or welfare of humans or other animals" (p. 4).

The longest section of the guidelines identifies the range of procedures that can be used. In general, researchers are told that their requirement for a strong justification increases with the degree of discomfort to be experienced by the animals. In addition, they are told that appetitive procedures (i.e., use of positive reinforcement) should be substituted for aversive procedures as much as possible, that less stressful procedures should be preferred to more stressful ones, and that surgical procedures require special care and expertise. Field research procedures should disturb the animals living in their natural habitat as little as possible.

Caring for the Animals

The research supervisor must be an expert in the care of the species of animals to be used, must carefully train all those who will be in contact with the animals, and must be fully aware of federal regulations about animal care. To further ensure proper care, a veterinarian must check the facilities twice annually and should be on call as a general consultant. The animals should be acquired from legitimate suppliers or bred in the laboratory. If wild animals are being studied, they must be trapped

---

[4] For more on this survey, refer to Chapter 12, where it is featured as a good example of survey research.

humanely. Analogous to the IRB for human research, there should be a "local institutional animal care and use committee" (APA, 1985, p. 4). Like an IRB, the animal use committee is composed of professors from several disciplines in addition to science, and includes someone from outside the university committee. A veterinarian must also be a member of the committee.

Once an experiment is over, alternatives to destroying the animals should be considered. However, euthanasia is sometimes necessary, "either as a requirement of the research, or because it constitutes the most humane form of disposition of an animal at the conclusion of the research" (APA, 1985, p. 8). In such cases, the process must be "accomplished in a humane manner, appropriate for the species, under anesthesia, or in such a way as to ensure immediate death, and in accordance with procedures approved by the institutional animal care and use committee" (p. 8).

Using Animals for Educational Purposes

The guidelines are designed primarily to aid researchers who use animals, but animals are often used educationally to demonstrate specific behaviors, to train students in animal research procedures, and to give students firsthand experience in studying such well-known phenomena as classical and operant conditioning. Unlike the research situation, however, the educational use of animals does not result directly in new knowledge. Consequently, the educator is urged to use fewer rather than more animals to accomplish a given purpose and to consider a variety of alternative procedures. For example, instead of demonstrating the same principle (e.g., shaping) to an introductory psychology class with a new rat each semester, the instructor might do it once and videotape the procedure for future classes.

Sometimes computer simulations of various phenomena can be substituted for live procedures; several excellent simulations of both classical and operant conditioning procedures exist. These simulations can be effective (and necessary in smaller schools that cannot keep up with federal regulations for the proper care of animals), but shaping a schematized rat to bar press is not quite the same as shaping a real rat. Students often experience a deep insight into the power of reinforcement contingencies when they witness them firsthand. Direct experiences with animals in undergraduate learning laboratories have motivated more than one student to become a research psychologist (Moses, 1991).

In summary, most psychologists defend the use of animals in behavioral research while recognizing the need to scrutinize closely the rationale for every animal study. Animal research has contributed mightily to our understanding of behavior and promises to help in the future search for solutions to AIDS, Alzheimer's disease, mental illness, and countless other human problems.

Scientific Fraud

There has been much discussion in recent years about fraud in science, with specific cases sparking debate about whether they represent just the occasional "bad apple" or, more ominously, the "tip of the iceberg." Obviously, scientists in general and research psychologists in particular are expected to be scrupulously honest in all

TABLE 2.4   *On Data Falsification and Plagiarism: Text of APA Standards*

Standard 6.21 Reporting of Results

(a) Psychologists do not fabricate data or falsify results in their publications.

(b) If psychologists discover significant errors in their published data, they take responsible steps to correct such errors in a correction, retraction, erratum, or other appropriate publication means.

Standard 6.22 Plagiarism

Psychologists do not present substantial portions or elements of another's work as their own, even if the other work or data source is cited occasionally.

Source: APA (1992).

their scientific activities. Principle B of the 1992 general code unambiguously states that psychologists "seek to promote integrity in the science, teaching, and practice of psychology" (APA, 1992). Furthermore, several of the specific standards of the 1992 code directly concern fraudulent research practices. This last section of the chapter addresses the following questions: What is scientific fraud? How prevalent is it, and how can it be detected? Why does it happen?

The *American Heritage Dictionary* (1971) defines fraud as "a deception deliberately practiced in order to secure unfair or unlawful gain" (p. 523). The two major types of fraud in science are (1) **plagiarism,** deliberately taking the ideas of someone else and claiming them as one's own and (2) **falsifying data.** In the 1992 code, plagiarism is specifically condemned in Standard 6.22, and data falsification receives similar treatment in Standard 6.21 (see Table 2.4 for the text of these standards). Plagiarism is a problem that can occur in all disciplines, but falsifying data is a problem that happens only in science; it will be the major focus here.

Data Falsification

If there is a mortal sin in science, it is the failure to be scrupulously honest in managing the data, the foundation stones on which the entire enterprise is built; if the foundation fails, all else collapses. Thus, the integrity of data is an issue of pivotal importance. This type of fraud can take several forms. First and most extreme, a scientist fails to collect any data at all and simply manufactures it. Second, some of the collected data are altered or omitted to make the overall results look better. Third, some data are collected, but "missing" data are guessed at and created in order to have a complete set of information. Fourth, an entire study is suppressed because its results fail to come out as expected. In each of these cases, the deception is deliberate and the scientist presumably "secures an unfair or unlawful gain" (e.g., publication).

The traditional view is that fraud is rare and easily detected because faked results won't be replicated (Hilgartner, 1990). That is, if a scientist produces a result with fraudulent data, the results won't represent some empirical truth. Other scientists, intrigued or surprised by this new finding, will try to reproduce it in their own labs and will fail to do so; the fraudulent findings will then be uncovered and eventually discarded. One hint of this kind of problem occurs if a researcher suspecting that something is odd asks to sees the raw data collected in the study in question. Scientists in psychology and other disciplines have a long history of being willing to share data and a refusal to do so would create suspicion about the "new" finding. That data sharing is a normal expectation is evident from the APA ethics code:

Standard 6.25

After research results are published, psychologists do not withhold the data on which their conclusions are based from other competent professionals who seek to verify the substantive claims through reanalysis and who intend to use such data only for that purpose, provided that the confidentiality of the participants can be protected and unless legal rights concerning proprietary data preclude their release.

In addition to failures to replicate findings, fraud may be detected (or at least suspected) during the normal peer review process. Whenever a research article is submitted for journal publication or a grant is submitted to an agency, it is reviewed by several experts, whose recommendations help determine whether the article will be published or the grant funded. Anything that seems odd probably will be detected by at least one of the reviewers. A third way of detecting fraud is when a researcher's collaborators suspect a problem. This happened in the 1980s in one of psychology's most notorious cases. In a series of studies that apparently made a breakthrough in the treatment of hyperactivity in retarded children, Stephen Breuning produced data showing that stimulant drugs could be more effective than antipsychotic drugs for treating the problem (Holden, 1987). However, a colleague suspected that the data were faked, a charge that was upheld after a 3-year investigation by the National Institute of Mental Health (NIMH), which had funded some of Breuning's research. In a plea bargain, Breuning pled guilty to two counts of submitting false data to NIMH; in exchange, NIMH dropped the charge that Breuning committed perjury during the investigation (Byrne, 1988).

One of the great strengths of science is the self-correction resulting from the replication process, peer reviews, and the honesty of colleagues. Indeed, this system has detected fraud numerous times, as in the Breuning case. But what if peers fail to notice something awry or what if some fraudulent result is consistent with other, nonfraudulent findings (i.e., it replicates)? If the bogus results fit with other legitimate research outcomes, there is little reason to question them and the fraud may go undetected for years. Something like this might have occurred in one of psychology's best-known cases of apparent fraud ("apparent" because the jury is still out).

The case involved one of Great Britain's most famous psychologists, Cyril Burt (1883–1971), a major player in the debate over the nature of intelligence. His twin studies are often cited as evidence for the idea that intelligence is mostly inherited from one's parents. One of Burt's results was that identical twins had virtually the same IQ score even if they were given up for adoption at birth and raised in different environments. His data went unchallenged for years and became assimilated into the literature on the heritability of intelligence. However, careful readers eventually noticed that in different publications describing the results with different numbers of twins, Burt kept reporting *exactly* the same statistical results (identical correlation coefficients). Such an outcome is highly unlikely mathematically. Detractors accused him of manufacturing the results to support his strong hereditarian beliefs, while defenders argued that he collected the data but became a forgetful and careless reporter with increasing age. It was also said in his defense that if he were intent on fraud, he surely would have done a better job of disguising it (e.g., making sure that the correlations were different). There is no question that something is odd about Burt's data, and even his defenders concede that much of the data have no scientific value. The question of how much was deliberate fraud and how much was oversight and/or sloppiness may never be determined, partly because after Burt's death, his housekeeper destroyed several chests containing notebooks and data (Kohn, 1986).

Analyzing the Burt affair has become a cottage industry (Green, 1992; Samelson, 1992), but for our purposes the point is that bad data, whether they result from error, oversight, or deliberate distortion, may fail to be noticed if they fit with other findings (i.e., if they are replicated elsewhere). This was the case with Burt; his data were quite similar to the findings from other twin studies (e.g., Bouchard & McGue, 1981).

It is worth mentioning that some commentators (e.g., Hilgartner, 1990) believe that while falsified data may go undetected because they replicate "good" data, they may not be detected for two other reasons as well. First, the sheer number of studies being published these days makes it easier for a bad study to slip through the cracks, especially if it isn't reporting some notable discovery that attracts widespread attention. Second, the reward system in science is structured so that new discoveries pay off, but scientists who spend their time "merely" replicating other work aren't seen as very creative. Consequently, the academic rewards elude them, and some questionable studies might escape the replication process.

The reward system is also believed to be part of the reason why fraud occurs in the first place. This brings us to the final question about fraud—why does it occur? Explanations range from individual (character weakness) to societal (a reflection of general moray decay in the late 20th century), with reasons relating to the academic reward system somewhere in the middle. Scientists who publish are promoted, tenured, win grants, and influence people. Sometimes the attendant "publish or perish" pressures overwhelm the individual and lead the researcher (or the researcher's assistants) to cut some corners. It might begin on a small scale—adding a few pieces of data to achieve the desired outcome—but expand over time.

What does this mean for you as a student researcher? At the very least, it means that you need to be compulsive about data. Follow procedures scrupulously and *never* succumb to the temptation to manufacture even a single piece of data. Likewise, never discard data from a participant unless there are clear procedures for doing so and these procedures are specified before the experiment begins (e.g., the participant doesn't follow instructions, the experimenter doesn't administer the procedure correctly). Finally, keep the raw data or, at the very least, the data summary sheets. Your best protection against a charge that your results seem unusual is your ability to produce the data on request.

The importance of being aware of the ethical implications of the research you're doing cannot be overstated. It is the reason for placing this chapter early in the text, and it won't be the last you'll hear of the topic. If you glance back at the Table of Contents, for instance, you will notice that each of the remaining chapters includes an "Ethics Box," which examines such topics as privacy in field research, recruiting participants, using surveys responsibly, and being an ethically competent experimenter. On the immediate horizon, however, is a chapter that considers the problem of how to begin developing ideas for research projects.

Chapter Summary

Developing the APA Code of Ethics

In keeping with psychology's habit of relying on data-based principles, the APA developed its initial ethics code empirically, using a critical incidents procedure. The code for research using human participants was first published in 1953 and has been revised periodically since then, most recently in 1992. It consists of general principles guiding the behavior of psychologists (e.g., concern for others' welfare) and specific standards of behavior, the violation of which can lead to censure (e.g., maintaining the confidentiality of research participants).

Ethical Guidelines for Research with Humans

The APA code for research with humans provides guidance for the researcher in planning and carrying out the study. Planning includes doing a cost/benefit analysis that weighs the degree of risk imposed on participants against the scientific value of the research. The code also requires that participants be given sufficient information to decide whether to participate (i.e., informed consent). Special care needs to be taken with children and with those who might feel coerced into participation (e.g., prisoners). Participants must be told that they are free to withdraw from the study without penalty and they must be assured of confidentiality. At the conclusion of their participation, they must receive a full debriefing. Institutional Review Boards (IRBs) have the responsibility for ensuring that research studies with human participants are conducted according to the ethics code. Certain forms of deception are acceptable in psychological research, but the researcher must convince an IRB that the legitimate goals of the study can only be met through deception.

Ethical Guidelines for Research with Animals

APA guidelines for research with animal subjects concern the care and humane treatment of animals used for psychological research, provide guidance in deciding about appropriate experimental procedures, and cover the use of animals both for research and for educational purposes. Although animal rights proponents have argued that animal research in psychology is inappropriate, most research psychologists argue that such research can benefit both humans and animals.

Scientific Fraud

Plagiarism, presenting the ideas of another as one's own, and data falsification, the manufacturing or altering of data, are the most serious forms of scientific fraud. Although data falsification is often discovered because of repeated failures to replicate unreliable findings, it may remain undetected because (a) the fraudulent findings are consistent with legitimate outcomes or (b) the sheer mass of published work precludes much replication. The academic reward system sometimes creates pressures that lead to scientific fraud.

Chapter Review

Multiple Choice

1. John Watson and Rosalie Rayner might have difficulty today if they presented a proposal for the Little Albert study to an IRB. Why?
   - a. studying emotions in 11-month-olds would not be acceptable because they cannot give assent
   - **b.** they would be proposing a potentially harmful procedure without making any provision to remedy the harm at the end of the study
   - c. they were using only a single subject, thereby limiting the generality of the study
   - d. the study would involve a violation of confidentiality, since Watson and Rayner revealed the child's name

2. As part of the informed consent procedure, participants are told
   - a. that the experiment will not include deception of any kind
   - b. that they can choose whether to participate or not, but once they agree to do so, they are obligated to complete the study
   - c. whether or not electrical shock will be used in the study
   - d. the general nature of the research unless deception is involved; if it is, they are told *nothing* about the study ahead of time

3. Studies on the use of deception in psychological research show that
   - a. it isn't needed; participants asked to role-play produce the same results as naive volunteers
   - b. students are more likely to judge a specific deception experiment to be unethical than are research psychologists
   - c. it is indeed harmful; most of Milgram's subjects needed counseling after going through the obedience study
   - d. participants fully informed about the purpose of a study often behave very differently from those not given full information

4. All of the following are included in the most recent APA code for the use of animals in research *except*
   - a. psychologists are no longer allowed to use animals for educational purposes only
   - b. pain is allowable if the value of the research outweighs the risk to the subjects
   - c. just as an IRB judges proposals for research with humans, there should be a similar group to evaluate animal research
   - d. if euthanasia is to occur after the research or as part of the design, it must be carried out painlessly

5. Which of the following is true about the fabrication of research data?
   - a. fraud will always be discovered in the end because the results of the fraudulent study will not be similar to those of legitimately conducted research
   - b. it is defined as making up all or most of the data for a study; altering just one or two data points does not constitute fraud

      c. it may remain undetected if it produces results similar to those of other studies

      d. it is quite rare, partly because the academic reward system is structured so that no real benefits result from the fabrication of data

Short Essay

1. Distinguish between the "general principles" of the APA ethics code and the "standards" of the code. Give an example of each.

2. Describe the role of the IRB and two reasons why they have been controversial.

3. Distinguish between "consent" and "assent" and explain how both concepts are important to research with children.

4. Describe the essential ingredients of an informed consent form to be used in research with adult participants.

5. Why is deception sometimes used in psychological research? How can the use of deception be reconciled with the concept of informed consent?

6. Describe the two main purposes of a debriefing session.

7. Which ethical principles were violated in (a) the Willowbrook study, (b) the Tuskegee study, and (c) MK–ULTRA?

8. Use the Gibson visual cliff study to illustrate why psychologists sometimes use nonhuman species as research subjects.

9. Describe the arguments for and against the use of nonhuman species in psychological research.

10. What are the essential features of the APA code for animal research?

11. Describe the ways in which data falsification are usually discovered.

12. Use the Burt case to illustrate why data falsification might be missed. What are two other reasons why this type of fraud might go undetected?

Applications Exercises

Exercise 2.1. Thinking Scientifically About Deception

From the standpoint of a research psychologist who is thinking scientifically, how would you design a study to evaluate the following claims that are sometimes made about deception? That is, what kinds of empirical data would you like to have to judge the truth of the claims?

1. Deception should never be used in psychological research because once people have been deceived in a study, they will no longer trust any psychologist.

2. Deception could be avoided by instructing subjects to "imagine" that they are in a deception study; they are then asked to behave as they think a typical person would behave.

3. Psychologists are just fooling themselves; most subjects see right through their deceptions.

Exercise 2.2. Recognizing Ethical Problems

Consider each of the following brief descriptions of actual research in social psychology. From the standpoint of the APA's code of ethics, which standards could cause problems with an IRB? Explain how you might defend each study to an IRB.

1. The effect of crowding on stress was investigated in a public men's room. A member of the research team followed a person into the bathroom and occupied either the urinal directly adjacent to the participant's or the next one down the line. Subjects of the observations were unaware that they were participating in a study. On the assumption that increased stress would affect urination, the amount of time it took for the participant to begin to urinate and the total time spent urinating were recorded by another researcher hidden in one of the stalls. As predicted, urination was more disrupted when the immediately adjacent urinal was occupied (Middlemist, Knowles, & Matter, 1976).

2. In a field experiment, a woman (who was actually part of the experiment) stood by her car on the side of the road. The car had a flat tire. To determine if modeling would affect the helping behavior of passing motorists, on some trials another woman with a flat tire was helped by a stopped motorist (all part of the staged event) about a quarter of a mile before the place where the woman waited for help. As expected, motorists were more likely to stop and help if they had just witnessed another person helping (Bryan & Test, 1967).

Exercise 2.3. Studying Obedience to Authority

Suppose you wanted to study obedience to authority today and planned to use a procedure similar to Milgram's. Part of your purpose is to see if his results will replicate 25 years after the original studies were done. How would you justify the study to an IRB and what changes would you have to make to Milgram's original procedure? Using the model presented in the chapter, write a consent form for your study.

Exercise 2.4. Avoiding Plagiarism

A student is writing a paper on lying and reads a book called *Telling Lies* by Paul Ekman (1985). The student comes across the following passage about a common situation in which someone is actually telling the truth but is very nervous and therefore appears to be lying:

> …Another equally important source of trouble, leading to disbelieving-the-truth mistakes, is the Othello error. This error occurs when the lie catcher fails to consider that a truthful person who is under stress may appear to be lying. … Truthful people may be afraid of being disbelieved, and their fear might be confused with the liar's detection apprehension…
>
> I have called this error after Othello because the death scene in Shakespeare's play is such an excellent and famous example of it… (Ekman, 1985, pp. 169–170)

The student's term paper on lying includes this paragraph:

> Disbelieving-the-truth mistakes are another kind of problem in the accurate detection of lying. Sometimes the person trying to catch someone else lying doesn't take into account that a truthful person under stress may seem to be lying. This is known as the Othello error. Thus, sometimes you could be telling the truth, yet afraid that nobody will believe you. As a result you would appear to be nervous about being detected.

When the paper is returned, the student is shocked to learn that the professor has made a charge of plagiarism and given the paper a failing grade. Why do you think this happened? How would you alter the paragraph so that a charge of plagiarism would not be made?

CHAPTER 3

Developing Ideas for Research in Psychology

Preview & Chapter Objectives

All research begins with a good question and this chapter is designed to help you develop such questions. The chapter begins by identifying a system for classifying research, then elaborates on a concept introduced in Chapter 1—the empirical question. You will then learn how research can develop from everyday observations of behavior, from theory, and from questions left unanswered by completed research. The chapter concludes with a discussion of PsycINFO, psychology's premier information database, and gives you some practical tips for using this electronic tool. When you finish this chapter, you should be able to:

- Distinguish between and identify the value of (a) basic and applied research, (b) laboratory and field research, and (c) qualitative and quantitative research.

- Understand how a good empirical question requires the use of operational definitions.

- Describe examples of research that develops from everyday observations and from serendipity.
- Describe the defining features of a theory in psychology and show how theories (a) lead to empirical research, (b) are influenced by the outcomes of research, and (c) need to be productive, parsimonious, and capable of falsification.
- Understand the importance of the "What's next?" question and the value of research that simultaneously replicates and extends prior research.
- Show how creative thinking works in science.
- Use PsycINFO to search for information about research in psychology.

As one of the requirements for this course, or perhaps as an independent project, you may be asked to develop an idea for a research project. You might react to this assignment with a feeling that the screen has gone blank, accompanied by a mounting sense of panic. Take heart—this chapter has come along just in time. When you finish it, you may not find ideas for research projects flowing freely into your mind, but you should at least have some good ideas about where to start. Before looking at the sources of ideas for research, however, let us categorize the varieties of psychological research.

Varieties of Psychological Research

Research in psychology can be classified in several ways. For example, one distinction can be made between basic and applied research. Research can also be categorized in terms of its setting and in terms of the relative emphasis on quantitative or qualitative analysis.

Basic versus Applied Research

Some research in psychology concerns describing, predicting, and explaining fundamental principles of behavior; this activity is referred to as **basic research.** On the other hand, **applied research** is so named because it has direct and immediate relevance to the solution of a real-world problem. To illustrate the distinction, consider memory research. A basic research study might investigate the organization of memory by having participants study a list of words, recall the list, study it again, recall it again, and so on through several trials (e.g., Tulving, 1966). The idea would be to see if the words gradually came to be recalled in the same groupings, thereby indicating how the words were being organized in participants' minds. The study would have no obvious practical application but would be done simply to learn more about the basic processes of memory organization. The results would presumably contribute to a developing body of knowledge about the inner workings of memory. An example of an applied research study in memory might be one concerned with eyewitness memory, in which participants would see a film of an accident and then later try to recall what they saw as accurately as possible (e.g., Loftus & Palmer, 1974). This study would have some obvious applicability to the problem of eyewitness testimony, an issue of importance to the legal system.

It is sometimes believed that applied research is more valuable than basic research because it seems to concern immediately relevant problems. It could be argued, however, that a major advantage of basic research is that the principles can potentially be used in a variety of applied situations. Nonetheless, basic research is a frequent target of politicians, who bluster about the misuse of tax dollars to fund research (through grants from federal agencies like the National Science Foundation) that doesn't seem very "useful" for anything. The charges are easy to make and tend to resonate with voters; after all, a major component of the American national character is the high value we place on the practical and the useful. Even those committed to a program of basic research recognize that grant funds are easier to obtain when the research appears to be useful. In an interview after being elected president of the American Psychological Society, for instance, the noted experimental psychologist Richard F. Thompson acknowledged that "[m]any of us who have been basic scientists have come to feel that to justify our existence we, too, have really got to try to develop applications to the problems of society" (Kent, 1994, p. 10).

Basic research will never be abandoned, of course. Much if not all applied research depends on a solid foundation of basic research; without this background, some applied projects would never be imagined, much less carried out. A good example is a study by Egeland (1975) on reading. The purpose of the experiment was to evaluate a method for training preschool children to differentiate letters that are similar (e.g., R and P). The method involved showing children cards like the ones in Figure 3.1. The task was to select each of the letters in the row of six that matched the single letter at the top of the card. Egeland highlighted the distinctive feature of the letter (e.g., the "\" in R distinguishes it from P) by printing it in red. With successive trials the red color was gradually faded to black. Compared to participants whose letters were printed all in black for every trial, the training group made fewer errors. They also performed better in a follow-up test a week later.

For our purposes, what is notable about the Egeland study is that the procedure is based on the idea that letter recognition is affected by the perception of individual components or features of the stimulus. At the time of Egeland's study, feature theory was the prevailing idea about how pattern recognition occurs, and there was a great deal of basic research investigating various aspects of the theory. For example, an early study by Neisser (1963) had participants scan arrays of letters like the

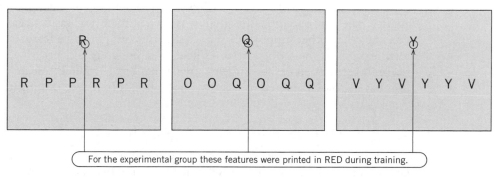

FIGURE 3.1 Stimulus card similar to that used by Egeland (1975).

```
1. Find the letter O:        2. Find the letter O:
     G  Q  Q  U                  A  X  A  N
     Q  S  G  G                  L  A  N  X
     U  Q  G  S                  X  X  N  L
     S  G  O  Q                  A  N  O  A
     U  Q  S  U                  L  L  X  A
     G  G  S  U                  A  L  A  N

3. Find the letter K:        4. Find the letter K:
     G  Q  Q  U                  A  X  A  N
     Q  S  G  G                  L  A  N  X
     U  Q  G  S                  X  X  N  L
     S  G  K  Q                  A  N  K  A
     U  Q  S  U                  L  L  X  A
     G  G  S  U                  A  L  A  N
```

FIGURE 3.2   Stimulus array from Neisser's (1963) study of feature detection.

ones in Figure 3.2. They were to respond as soon as they identified the target letter. As you can see from the arrays, Neisser varied the degree of similarity in the features making up the letters. The letter O took longer for participants to identify when embedded in the letters Q, U, S, and G than when embedded within X, A, N, and L, presumably because the O shares more features with letters like Q than with letters like X.

Although Egeland never mentioned the Neisser study or others like it in his study with preschoolers, it is clear that the solid foundation of research on feature theory played a role in developing the training program in reading. Furthermore, another completely different area of basic research also contributed to the idea for the training program. In animal conditioning research, procedures have been developed to produce what is called "errorless" discrimination training (e.g., Terrace, 1963), and it involves just the same kind of gradual stimulus change that occurred in the training program. This is a process repeated many times in psychological research. Basic researchers investigate some psychological phenomenon solely for the sake of learning about it, a body of knowledge is created, and that body serves as a foundation for applied research dealing with specific problems.

If it is true that basic research often leads to applications, it is also the case that applied research outcomes frequently have relevance for basic research, providing evidence that either supports or refutes theories. Supporting a feature theory of pattern recognition was not Egeland's goal, but the study did just that. Similarly, the research mentioned earlier on eyewitness memory is applied research, but its findings have also contributed to basic theories about the nature of long-term memory.

The Setting: Laboratory versus Field Research

Another way of classifying studies is by location. As is evident from the above labels, the distinction hinges on whether the study occurs inside or outside the lab.

Laboratory research allows the researcher greater control: conditions of the study can be specified more clearly, and participants can be selected and placed in conditions more systematically. On the other hand, in **field research** the research settings more closely match the situations encountered in daily living. Although field research is often applied research and laboratory research is often basic research, you should be aware that some basic research takes place in the field and some applied research takes place in the laboratory.

Laboratory research is sometimes criticized for being "artificial" and far removed from the situations encountered in everyday life. It is clear, however, that laboratory research has yielded important knowledge about behavior and a case can be made that there are more important considerations when judging the quality of research than mere similarity to daily living. Social psychologist Elliot Aronson (1999a), for example, makes a distinction between mundane and experimental realism. **Mundane realism** refers to how closely a study mirrors real-life experiences. **Experimental realism** concerns the extent to which a research study, which can occur either in the laboratory or in the field, "has an impact on the subjects, forces them to take the matter seriously, and involves them in the procedures" (p. 411). It is the experimental realism of the study that counts, according to Aronson. If participants are involved in the study and taking it seriously, then the researcher can draw valid conclusions about behavior. The Milgram experiments on obedience, discussed in the previous chapter, don't have much mundane realism—we are unlikely to find ourselves delivering electrical shocks to someone who fails to learn a word list. Milgram's volunteers were clearly involved, however, and his studies have strong experimental realism. We've seen that Milgram's research has been controversial, but there is no question that it shed important light on the factors influencing the general phenomenon of obedience to authority.

Proximity to real life is often considered to be a strength of field research, but there are other reasons for conducting research away from the lab. On the basis of their studies of cognitive functioning of children from India infected with intestinal parasites, for instance, Sternberg and Grigorenko (1999) argue that research in the field has several strengths. First, conditions in the field often cannot be duplicated in a laboratory. Sternberg and Grigorenko studied children living in cramped quarters in 113-degree heat, with the smell of excrement from open sewers almost overwhelming. Such conditions can hardly be created in a laboratory, if for no other reason than an IRB probably would not allow it. A second reason to do field research is to confirm the findings of laboratory studies and perhaps to correct misconceptions that might derive from the safe confines of a laboratory. A third reason is to make discoveries that could make an immediate difference in the lives of the people being studied. Fourth, although field research is ordinarily associated with applied research, it is also a good setting to do basic research. Sternberg and his colleagues have studied the effects of parasitic infections in numerous locations around the globe, and a major focus of their work is to test hypotheses derived from Sternberg's theories about the nature of intelligence.

Some researchers combine both laboratory and field research within a single series of studies and a good example is a project by Dutton and Aron (1974). They were interested in testing a hypothesis from a two-factor theory of romantic love: people experiencing strong physical arousal may sometimes misinterpret that arousal as love (the two factors in the theory are physiological arousal and a cognitive interpretation of the arousal). They created a situation in which male participants experienced different degrees of what normally would be considered fear and then were exposed to an attractive female. Dutton and Aron wanted to see if part of the arousal connected with fear would be misinterpreted as physical attraction for the female. In the field part of their study, they used two locations over a river in a national park in British Columbia, Canada. One was a swaying 450-foot-long suspension bridge featuring a 230-foot drop to the river (Figure 3.3). The other was a solid wooden bridge just 10 feet over the river. In both locations, attractive female confederates approached males and asked them for help with a psychology project on how scenic attractions could influence creativity. Agreeable participants were given a supposed test for creativity and were also given the female's phone number in case they had further questions about the project. Compared to males encountered on the "safe" bridge, which presumably aroused little fear, males on the suspension bridge had more sexual imagery in their test results and were more likely to call the female confederate.

These suspension bridge results came out as predicted from two-factor theory, but Dutton and Aron were rightly concerned that the results could have other interpretations. Perhaps the males who took the suspension bridge were just more adventurous than the other males who crossed on the safer bridge. To account for this possibility, two additional studies were carried out, one of them a laboratory study. Dutton and Aron recruited males for a study on the effects of electrical shock on learning. Also in the lab was an attractive female who appeared to be another participant but was actually an experimental confederate. The participants were led to believe that they would be experiencing either a strong or a mild shock, with the former expected to produce greater physiological arousal than the latter. This apparently happened because Dutton and Aron found that males in the strong shock con-

FIGURE 3.3   The suspension bridge used in Dutton and Aron's (1974) study of romance in high places.

dition were more physically attracted to the female than those expecting a weaker shock. Thus, the lab study reinforced the findings of the field study that males could misinterpret fear arousal as physical attraction. Together, the studies supported the two-factor theory of love.

The Dutton and Aron study shows that field research and laboratory research can yield similar results. To the extent that such an outcome occurs, it strengthens the argument that both types of research are important and necessary. But is the Dutton and Aron outcome an isolated event? Can it be said in general that the results of laboratory research mirror the results of field research? Apparently so, at least in some areas. Anderson, Lindsay, and Bushman (1999) examined several topics within social psychology and found a large collection (288 studies in all) of laboratory and field studies that investigated the same variables. For example, in the area of aggression, they matched up lab and field studies investigating the effects of anonymity on aggressive behavior. What they discovered was a high degree of correspondence between the results found in and outside of the lab. Such an outcome provides strong support for (a) laboratory researchers who tire of hearing about the "artificiality" of their studies and (b) field researchers who tire of hearing about how their studies lack the kinds of controls that enable firm conclusions to be drawn.

One final point about the decision on where to locate a study concerns ethics. Besides providing increased control, researchers often prefer the laboratory to the field because of problems with informed consent and privacy. In laboratory research, it is relatively easy to stick closely to the ethics code. In the field, however, it is difficult—often impossible—to provide informed consent and debriefing; in fact, in some situations the research procedures might be considered an invasion of privacy. Consequently, field studies can face a greater challenge from an IRB, and field researchers must show that the importance of their study justifies some of the risks involved. On the other hand, as seen in the Sternberg and Grigorenko (1999) example, IRBs might not allow the conditions of some field settings to be simulated in a laboratory. Before leaving this topic, please read Box 3.1, which considers privacy invasion in field research from a legal angle.

Quantitative versus Qualitative Research

Most research in psychology is quantitative in nature. That is, with **quantitative research,** the data are collected and presented in the form of numbers—average scores for different groups on some task, percentages of people who do one thing or another, and so on. In recent years, however, a number of research psychologists have begun doing what is known as **qualitative research,** sometimes borrowing techniques from sociologists and anthropologists. Qualitative research is not easily classified, but it often includes studies that collect detailed interview information, either from individuals or focus groups, it sometimes involves detailed case studies, and it sometimes involves basic observational studies. What these various forms of qualitative research have in common is that results are presented not as statistical summaries, but as analytical narratives that summarize the project. Of course, many studies combine quantitative and qualitative approaches, and a good example is a timely study by Walker (1996), who wondered if gender differences in the control of a TV remote control would affect the relationships of couples. Her primary method

Box 3.1

ETHICS—A Matter of Privacy

Unlike the laboratory situation, field research sometimes causes problems with informed consent, freedom to leave the study, debriefing, and invasion of privacy. An interesting study by Silverman (1975) illustrates why researchers are sometimes hesitant about doing field studies. He gave descriptions of 10 published field studies to two lawyers and asked them to judge whether the procedures might violate any laws or if there seemed to be any invasion of privacy. The procedures included having a confederate fall down in a subway car to see if anyone would help, leaving cars in different places to see if they would be vandalized, going to shoe stores and trying on many pairs of shoes, and asking for small amounts of money from passersby.

The two lawyers gave almost the *opposite* responses. Lawyer 1 believed that intent and a concern for the greater good were the key factors. The studies were designed for the ultimate good of increasing our knowledge of human behavior and not for the personal gain of the scientist. He believed that if charges were brought against the psychologist, the judge would "seek a balance between degree of annoyance and degree of legitimate purpose" (Silverman, 1975, p. 766). Lawyer 2, however, felt that in several of the studies there would be grounds not just for a civil suit on the part of individuals not wanting to be subjects of research (i.e., invasion of privacy), but for criminal action on the grounds of harassment, fraud, criminal trespass, and even disorderly conduct!

Silverman was disconcerted enough by the contrast in responses to bring the description of the subway helping behavior study to a judge for his considered opinion about whether civil or criminal charges could be brought. In general, the judge sided with lawyer 1, at least on the issue of criminal charges, but also pointed out that experiments in the field might have unforeseen consequences that could result in a negligence suit. In short, for the psychologist considering doing research in the field, there are some serious risks that don't occur in the laboratory.

By the way, you might be interested to know that lawyer 1, who didn't think the researcher would be in jeopardy, was a successful criminal lawyer accustomed to seeing his clients acquitted. Lawyer 2's specialty was in medical law; he usually "defended the legal rights of patients and subjects in medical practice and research" (Silverman, 1975, p. 767). In his mind, "research psychologists invading privacy" fell into the same category as "doctors harming patients."

was semistructured individual interviews with 72 people who comprised 36 couples. Some of the questions resulted in responses that were quantified; for instance, in response to a question about control over the remote when both partners were watching TV, women had control only 20% of the time. Most of the article, however, was a qualitative analysis, a narrative based on several open-ended questions in the interview, along with quotes from the interview to illustrate conclusions. Walker concluded, for example, that when both partners were watching TV, that men usually had control over what was being watched, and that in general, what should be a leisure activity could be a source of conflict instead. Research that is partly or wholly qualitative in nature will be described more fully in Chapter 10's discussion of program evaluation, and in Chapter 12's discussions on case studies, observational research, and interviewing.

Asking Empirical Questions

Whether a research project (a) concerns basic or applied problems or (b) occurs in the lab or the field, it always begins with a question. As you recall from Chapter 1, I referred to these as empirical questions. They have two important features: they must be answerable with data, and their terms must be precisely defined.

We saw in Chapter 1 that questions like "Are people good or evil?" and "Is there a personal God?" are interesting, and individuals can reach their own conclusions about them and perhaps convince others using Peirce's a priori method. However, the questions are not answerable with the evidence of empirical data. Of course, there are some questions related to good, evil, and religion that *are* empirical questions. These include:

✓ What is the relationship between belief in God and fear of death?
✓ Does belief in God influence the pain threshold of terminally ill patients?
✓ What is the effect of having an altruistic sibling on one's tendency to donate blood?

Notice that each of these questions allows data to be collected in some form. Before such data can be collected, however, these questions must be refined even further. This task can be referred to as "operationalizing" the terms in the question. The process of defining terms precisely is the second feature of an empirical question.

Operational Definitions

The term **operationism** originated in the 1920s in physics, with the publication of *The Logic of Modern Physics* (1927) by the Harvard physicist Percy Bridgman. Bridgman argued that the terminology of science must be totally objective and precise, and that all concepts should be defined in terms of a set of operations to be performed. These types of definitions came to be called **operational definitions.** The length of some object, for instance, could be defined operationally by a series of agreed-upon procedures. In Bridgman's words, the "concept of length is therefore fixed when the operations by which length is measured are fixed; that is, the concept of length involves as much as and nothing more than a set of operations" (Bridgman, 1927, p. 5).

Given the tendency of experimental psychologists to emulate the older sciences, it is not surprising that operationism was embraced by the psychological community when it first appeared. A strict operationism did not last very long in psychology, however, in part because equating a concept with a set of operations creates an arbitrary limitation on the concept. For psychologists the problem with operationism boiled down to how to accomplish it in practice when dealing with such complex psychological phenomena as aggression, creativity, depression, and so on. Among physicists it may not be difficult to agree on a set of operations for measuring the length of a line, but how does one operationalize a concept like "aggression"? Even if social psychologists can agree that the term refers to a behavior that reflects some intent to harm (Aronson, 1999a), exactly what behaviors are to be measured? In the aggression literature, the term has been operationalized as behaviors ranging from the delivery of electrical shocks to horn honking by car drivers to pressing a button that makes it hard for someone else to complete a task. Are these behaviors measuring the same phenomenon?

Despite this problem with the *strict* use of operational definitions, the concept has been of value to psychology by forcing researchers to define clearly the terms of their studies (Hilgard, 1987). This is especially important when you consider that most research in psychology concerns concepts that are open to numerous definitions. For instance, suppose a researcher is interested in the effects of hunger on maze learning. "Hunger" is a term that can mean several things and is not easily determined in a rat. How can you tell if a rat is hungry? The solution is to operationalize the term. You could define it operationally in terms of a procedure (not feeding the rat for 24 hours—it's reasonable to assume that the operation would produce hunger) or in terms of a behavior (creating a situation in which the rat has to work hard to earn food—it's reasonable to assume that a nonhungry rat wouldn't perform the task).

One important result of the precision resulting from operational definitions is that it allows an experiment to be repeated. As you know from Chapters 1 and 2, replication is an important feature of any scientific research. Also, research psychologists are not greatly troubled by the limitations imposed by having to define terms narrowly because in the long run the requirement for precision increases our confidence in the accuracy of theories about behavior. Psychologists use the concept of **converging operations,** which refers to the idea that our understanding of some behavioral phenomenon is increased when a series of investigations, all using slightly different operational definitions and experimental procedures, nonetheless converge on a common conclusion. Thus, if the results of several studies on the effects of hunger on maze learning reached the same conclusion, even though each used different operational definitions for hunger and for learning, then confidence would be high that a lawful relationship between hunger and maze learning had been established.

Developing precise empirical questions in psychology is a skill that takes some practice and involves a gradual narrowing from a broad topic to a specific question. These questions can have several different origins. They may evolve out of (a) everyday observations of behavior, (b) the need to solve a practical problem, (c) attempts to support or refute a theory, or (d) unanswered questions from a study just completed. Furthermore, researchers with some creative thinking skills are especially good at developing ideas for research.

Developing Research from Observations of Behavior and Serendipity

All of us have had the experience of observing behavior and wondering what caused it. Why does Norm get so angry when he misses a short putt, while Jeff, who misses just as many, shrugs it off and comments on how fortunate he is to be avoiding a committee meeting? Why is Grandpa able to recall vivid details of World War II yet unable to remember what he did yesterday? Why do some students eagerly volunteer to help tutor their peers, while others would not consider it? Why do some young children seem to be very outgoing, while others, perhaps in the same family, seem to be painfully shy? And on and on.

These same questions occur to experimental psychologists, and they are often the starting point for developing empirical questions. For Robert Sternberg, noted for his research on varieties of intelligence and the nature of human love, simple observations of daily life are his principal source of inspiration:

> All of my ideas (almost) come from watching people—myself, students I work with, my kids, my relationships with people, other people's relationships, and so on. … The point is that in psychology, there is no better data source than the people around you. I've never found books or lectures or labs as good as real experience for getting ideas. (R. J. Sternberg, personal communication, May 18, 1993)

One of psychology's most famous studies originated this way. The Russian psychologist Bluma Zeigarnik, a student of the famous German psychologist Kurt Lewin (see Chapter 8), gave her 164 research participants between 18 and 22 simple tasks, each requiring a few minutes to finish. They included such things as constructing a cardboard box, making a clay figure, completing puzzles, and performing arithmetic and other mental tasks. Each person was allowed to complete half of the tasks, but was interrupted and not allowed to finish the other half. To ensure that the interruption was clearly felt to be a disruption, Zeigarnik "always chose a time when the subject was most engrossed in his work" (1927/1967, p. 303). What she found was that the interrupted tasks were about twice as likely to be recalled as the uninterrupted ones. This phenomenon, that memory is better for incomplete rather than completed tasks, is today called the "Zeigarnik effect."

The idea for the study came from an activity well known to graduate students—sitting in a coffee shop talking about research. Lewin and his students often met informally for hours at a time at a cafe across the street from their laboratory in Berlin. The group couldn't help but notice that one of the waiters could remember what each student had ordered without writing it down. Soon after the bill was paid, however, the waiter had no memory of the orders. Could it be that before the bill was settled, the situation was "incomplete" and the waiter needed to keep the information in mind? Zeigarnik was intrigued, the study was designed, and the rest, as they say, is history.

A more modern example of observations leading to research comes from the social psychological research on helping behavior, which developed out of several well-publicized cases of failure to help. Most notable among them was the Kitty Genovese case in 1964, in which a woman was attacked several times and eventually murdered in New York City, in full view of at least 38 witnesses, none of whom even made an anonymous phone call to police. As John Darley, one of the leading researchers in the area of altruism and helping behavior, recalled later:

> Certainly the precipitating event for us all was the murder of a young lady in New York, the now famous Kitty Genovese case the *New York Times* picked up. A young lady was murdered, but sadly that's a rather typical incident. What was atypical was that thirty-eight people in her apartment building watched out their windows while this happened, and none of them did much in the way of helping. Bibb [Latané, Darley's co-worker] and I were having dinner together one night shortly thereafter. Everybody was talking about it and so were we. … We probably sketched out the experiments on a tablecloth that day. (Krupat, 1975, p. 257)

The Kitty Genovese case led Darley and Latané to conduct a series of experiments showing that unresponsive bystanders aren't simply uncaring; they often assume that someone else will help if there are other people around (Darley & Latané, 1968). The study of helping behavior is now well established, as you can tell by looking at any modern social psychology text, which invariably includes an entire chapter on the topic.

Serendipitous observations can also lead to research. **Serendipity,** the act of discovering something while looking for something else entirely, has been a source of numerous important events in the history of science. It can happen when a scientist is wrestling with a difficult research problem and some chance event accidentally provides the key, or it may occur when something goes wrong in an experiment, such as an apparatus failure. Skinner's experience with extinction curves following an apparatus breakdown, described in Chapter 1, is a good example of a serendipitous finding. Another involves the accidental discovery of feature detectors in the brain. This research was part of the basic research on feature detection, mentioned earlier in this chapter as the foundation upon which Egeland (1975) developed the idea for making features salient in order to teach reading. To examine the origins of the research that led eventually to a Nobel Prize for David Hubel and Torsten Wiesel, read Box 3.2.

Besides resulting from reflections of everyday behavior, research can also derive from specific problems that are in need of solution. This is especially true of applied research, the focus of Chapter 10. For now, an example will illustrate the point. To improve the ability of its students to survive their opening semester, a college creates a special seminar for freshman students. Empirically thinking administrators might establish an applied research project that compares a group of first-year students in an experimental seminar with a comparable group of other first-year students receiving the more typical freshman orientation. The research outcome would then influence decision making about the future of the program.

Developing Research from Theory

In Chapter 1 there was a brief discussion of the goals of scientific psychology; one of those goals was finding explanations for behavior. The process of developing

Box 3.2

ORIGINS—Serendipity and Edge Detectors

Some of the most important research in the second half of the 20th century on the physiology of the visual system was triggered by a serendipitous finding in the Harvard laboratory of David Hubel and Torsten Wiesel (Hubel & Wiesel, 1959). They were investigating the behavior of single neurons at various points in the visual pathway to see if the neurons could be made to fire in response to certain stimuli. Their experimental setup consisted of a screen on which various stimuli could be projected and seen by a cat with its head held stationary and an electrode implanted within a single cell of its visual system. (Even in the 1950s procedures were precise enough to isolate the activity of single neurons.)

Hubel and Wiesel were hoping the neuron would fire in response to black or white dots projected onto the cat's retina. Their first efforts were frustrating:

> The position of the microelectrode tip, relative to the cortex, was unusually stable, so much so that we were able to listen in on one cell for a period of about nine hours. We tried everything short of standing on our heads to get it to fire. (Hubel, 1988, p. 69)

Hubel and Wiesel persevered, eventually concentrating on one area of the retina. Oddly, passing the dot over that area sometimes produced neuron firing, but not reliably:

> After about five hours of struggle, we suddenly had the impression that the glass [slide] with the dot was occasionally producing a response, but the response seemed to have little to do with the dot. *Eventually we caught on: it was the sharp but faint shadow cast by the edge of the glass as we slid it into the slot that was doing the trick.* We soon convinced ourselves that the edge worked only when its shadow was swept across one small part of the retina and that the sweeping had to be done with the edge in one particular orientation. Most amazing was the contrast between the machine-gun discharge when the orientation of the stimulus was just right and the utter lack of a response if we changed the orientation or simply shined a bright flashlight into the cat's eyes. (Hubel, 1988, pp. 69–70; italics added)

The unexpected discovery that cells ("edge detectors") in the visual system were specialized to respond to edges and contours set at specific orientations was just the beginning. Hubel and Wiesel went on to develop an extensive research program identifying the types of stimuli that would trigger cells at all levels of the visual system; it won them the Nobel Prize in 1981. Their work also reflects the passion for doing research that was illustrated in Chapter 1 with the work of Gibson and Skinner. In discussing the years spent studying receptive fields for vision, roughly from 1950 to 1980, Hubel wrote:

> I count myself lucky to have been around in that era, a time of excitement and fun. Some of the experiments have been arduous, or so it has often seemed at 4:00 A.M., especially when everything has gone wrong. But 98 percent of the time the work is exhilarating. There is a special immediacy to neurophysiological experiments; we can see and hear a cell respond to the stimuli we use and often realize, right at the time, what the responses imply for brain function. (Hubel, 1988, p. vii)

these explanations is, in essence, the process of theory building and theory testing. In this section we'll look at what a theory is, the reciprocal relationship between theory construction and data collection, and how you can recognize useful theories.

The Nature of Theory

A **theory** in psychology is a set of logically consistent statements about some behavioral phenomenon that (a) best summarizes existing empirical knowledge of the phenomenon, (b) organizes this knowledge in the form of precise statements of relationships among variables (i.e., laws), (c) provides a tentative explanation for the phenomenon, and (d) serves as the basis for making predictions about behavior. These predictions are then tested with research. A theory is considered to be a working truth, subject to revision pending the outcome of empirical studies.

Theories differ in terms of their scope. Some aim to cover broad expanses of behavior and to be general theories—Erikson's stage theory of how our personality is developed and operates throughout the life span is an example. More frequently, however, a theory is more narrowly focused on some specific aspect of behavior. In social psychology, for instance, equity theory concerns how people relate to each other in terms of rewards, costs, and fairness; in abnormal psychology, learned helplessness theory attempts to account for psychological depression. Theories also differ in terms of their level of precision, with some being stated in precise mathematical terms and others described more simply as a set of logically connected statements.

As an example of how theories originate and evolve, and to illustrate several important features of theories, let's consider the learned helplessness example in more detail. This is a theory that developed out of animal learning research and has been applied to the human problem of depression. It is also another example of a serendipitous finding: the first experimental demonstration of learned helplessness occurred unexpectedly, the outcome of research with an entirely different purpose.

It occurred while two graduate students, Russell Leaf and Bruce Overmier, were working in the University of Pennsylvania lab of Richard Solomon (Peterson, Maier, & Seligman, 1993). They were testing predictions from a theory of avoidance conditioning, the details of which need not concern us. Basically, they wanted to transfer a classically conditioned response to an operant escape situation. First, they conditioned a dog to fear a tone by pairing the tone with a shock. This is a Pavlovian conditioning procedure in which a dog was restrained in a harness-like device called a "Pavlovian hammock." A tone was sounded and the animal was briefly shocked. Before long, the tone became a conditioned stimulus and the dog was afraid of it. After this initial conditioning, Overmier and Leaf placed the dog in a "shuttlebox," a two-sided chamber with a small half-wall in the middle. They planned to train the dog to jump from side A to side B when it was shocked on side A and to avoid the shock by jumping to the opposite side when it heard the tone that had been paired with the shock earlier. To their surprise, when the animal was shocked in side A, it did not respond as a dog normally does (i.e., by running around and eventually escaping the shock by jumping over the wall to side B). Rather, after some brief random activity in side A, the dog seemed to give up, passively accepting the shock, and often lying down on the grid and whimpering (Overmier & Leaf, 1965).

Another of Solomon's graduate students, Martin Seligman, became intrigued with the phenomenon after Overmier showed him one of the "helpless" dogs, and Seligman began examining the phenomenon more closely. What emerged was a series of studies identifying the conditions under which this odd behavior occurred. For instance, in the initial stages, when the animal is being shocked in the Pavlovian hammock, it struggles to escape but cannot, and eventually it gives up. Is the problem caused by the repeated shock itself or by the fact that the animal can do nothing about the shock (i.e., has no control over it)? To separate the effects of shock from the effects of a loss of control, Seligman and his colleagues ran several studies using what they called the "triadic" design (Seligman, 1975). Some dogs would receive uncontrollable shock, as before; others would receive just as much shock but would be able to turn off the shock by behaving in a certain way; and a third group would not be shocked at all.[1] The results were clear: only the animals experiencing uncontrollable shock developed the helpless behavior (Seligman, 1975). Other studies showed that the animal could be "immunized" against helplessness by first giving it experience with controllable shock before exposing it to uncontrollable shock (Seligman & Maier, 1967).

Seligman named the phenomenon "learned helplessness"—a learned unwillingness to avoid trauma after experiencing repeated failure to control unavoidable negative events (Seligman, 1975). In the Pavlovian hammock, the dog learned that shock could not be avoided, regardless of its efforts. It learned to stop trying. Seligman and his colleagues eventually extended their theory of learned helplessness into the realm of human psychopathology, specifically into the area of depression. It centered on the idea that depression was the result of someone's repeatedly experiencing unavoidable and uncontrollable aversive events. The theory's basic components were portrayed by Seligman (1975, p. 47) in the following way:

| Information about the contingency | → | Cognitive representation of the contingency (learning, expectation, perception, belief) | → | Behavior |

The process begins with the animal acquiring information (through experience) about the relationship (contingency) between its behavior under certain circum-

---

[1] You will learn more about this type of design, a "yoked" control group design, in Chapter 7.

stances and the outcomes of those behaviors. Seligman proposed that learned helplessness can develop when the animal learns that outcomes are unrelated to responses. That is, the animal experiences positive and negative outcomes in life, but its behaviors do not lead to these outcomes in any predictable way. This produces a "cognitive representation of the contingency." For example, the individual is said to develop an expectation that what it does and what subsequently happens are independent of each other. Thus, for the dog in the Pavlovian hammock, regardless of its varied efforts to escape the harness, it will be shocked. This expectation leads to the behavior of helplessness. In humans, Seligman proposed that psychological depression could be a form of learned helplessness—in the face of a long history of failure to control the outcomes in their lives, people may also give up.

The "expectation" in the theory is an example of what psychologists call a **construct.** This is a hypothetical factor that cannot be observed directly but is inferred from certain behaviors and assumed to follow from certain circumstances. The construct called "expectation" was central to Seligman's original theory, "the causal condition for the motivational, cognitive, and emotional debilitation that accompanies helplessness" (Seligman, 1975, p. 48). This expectation could be (a) inferred from the animal's behavior of failing to even attempt an escape and (b) assumed to follow from repeated experiences of having no control over events.

An important feature of any theory is its continual evolution in light of new data. No theory is ever complete, and as you will learn in a few pages, Seligman's was no exception. Its development nicely illustrates the reciprocal relationship between theory and data and demonstrates an important attribute of a good theory—its ability to make predictions that lead to new research. This requires some elaboration.

The Relationship Between Theory and Data

The move from theory to data involves the logical process of **deduction,** reasoning from a set of general statements toward the prediction of some specific event. With regard to theory, deduction takes the form of my (the scientist) reasoning that if my (general) theory is accurate, then I can predict that (specific) event X should occur with some probability greater than chance. The prediction about specific events that is derived this way from a theory is called a **hypothesis,** which in general can be considered an educated guess about what should happen under certain circumstances. These hypotheses lead to the design of a study, which produces results as predicted or fails to produce them. In the former case the theory is supported, and in the latter it is not. If it is supported by a large body of research, confidence is high that the theory is good; to put it another way, we could say that inductive support for the theory increases when individual experiments keep producing the results predicted by the theory. **Induction** is the logical process of reasoning from the specific (an individual experimental outcome) to the general (a theory).

Of course, experiments don't always come out as expected. The experiment might not be a good test of the hypothesis (e.g., bad choice of operational definitions for the variables being studied in an experiment), it might have some methodological flaws, or it might just be the odd experiment that just didn't work. Also, measurements of psychological phenomena are imperfect, so a failed experiment could be the result of some form of "measurement error" (more on this concept in the next chapter). Consequently, one unexpected result seldom calls a theory into question. If results repeatedly fail to support the theory, however, especially if they occur in different laboratories, confidence in it begins to wane and the theory may be discarded or, more likely, radically altered.

Note that in the previous two paragraphs I have avoided saying things like "a successful prediction 'proves' a theory to be true" and "a bad outcome 'disproves' a theory." This is because scientists hesitate to use the words "prove" and "disprove" when discussing theories and data, both on logical and on practical grounds.

On strictly logical grounds, it is impossible to prove a theory to be true, while it is possible to disprove a theory. To understand why requires a brief side trip to the rules of conditional ("if ... then") logic. Assume for the moment that all known crows are black. This statement can take the conditional form "If the bird is a crow, then it is certain that it will be black." Now suppose you see a bird that happens to be black. Can it be concluded that "therefore it must be a crow?" No, because other birds besides crows could be black. To conclude that it must be a crow is to commit the logical fallacy known as "affirming the consequent." The situation can be summarized as follows:

logical fallacy of affirming the consequent:
If the bird is a crow, then it will be black.
Here's a black bird.
Therefore, it must be a crow.

On the other hand, suppose you observe a yellow bird. Can you conclude that "therefore, it cannot be a crow"? Yes, because it has been asserted that all known crows are black. In conditional logic this conclusion is known as a "modus tollens." Thus:

logically correct modus tollens:
If the bird is a crow, then it will be black.
Here's a yellow bird.
Therefore, it cannot be a crow.

This distinction between affirming the consequent and a modus tollens can be applied directly to theory testing. The "If ... then" statement takes this form: "If theory X is true, then event Y can be expected to occur." Consider the learned helplessness theory again. Suppose I make this prediction: "If the learned helplessness theory of depression is true, then therapies that reduce depression in humans should also reduce helplessness behaviors in dogs." I then design a study in which some of the dogs conditioned to be helpless are given antidepressant drugs. My reasoning is that if these drugs help depressed humans, and if learned helplessness is the reason for depression, then drugs that work with depressed humans should work with helpless dogs. I run the study and discover that the treated dogs begin behaving normally (i.e., they are no longer helpless), an outcome that indeed occurred in a study like this by Porsolt, LePichon, and Jalfre (1977). If I now conclude that learned helplessness theory has been "proven" to be true, I am affirming the consequent:

> If the theory is true, then the antidepressants will work.
>
> The antidepressants worked.
>
> Therefore, the theory is true.

You can see that the conclusion about the theory being true (i.e., proven) cannot be made. The antidepressants may have worked for some reason having nothing to do with the learned helplessness theory. What can be said—and the careful scientist will never say more than this—is that the experiment "supports" or "is consistent with" the theory.

What if the antidepressants don't work and the animals show no lessening of the learned helplessness? On logical grounds, this would be a modus tollens and the theory could be considered not true (i.e., disproven):

> If the theory is true, then the antidepressants will work.
>
> The antidepressants didn't work.
>
> Therefore, the theory is not true.

Please note, however, my earlier comment that when discussing research results, scientists don't usually say things like "prove" and "disprove" on both logical and *practical* grounds. We've seen that to conclude that learned helplessness theory is proven because the drugs worked is to commit the fallacy of affirming the consequent. To conclude that the theory is disproven because the drugs failed to work might be technically correct (i.e., a modus tollens) but would be a most imprudent decision to make. As mentioned earlier, single experiments can fail to come out as predicted for any number of reasons, and to abandon a theory after just one problematic study is an outcome that simply never happens in science. Even strong disconfirming evidence, while it could have the effect of identifying some of the limits of the theory, probably won't have the effect of eliminating the theory entirely. Theories are indeed discarded, but only when scientists lose confidence in them, and this occurs only after predictions have been repeatedly disconfirmed in a number of laboratories and some competing theory begins to look more attractive.

Theories may be supported and theories may be discarded, but what happens most frequently is that they evolve as research accumulates. Leon Festinger, creator of one of psychology's more enduring theories, the theory of cognitive dissonance (see Chapter 12, Box 12.1), had this to say about the fate of theories: "One doesn't ask about theories, can I show that they are wrong or can I show that they are right, but rather one asks, how much of the empirical realm can it handle and how must it be modified and changed as it matures" (Festinger, 1999, p. 383). Evolution is exactly what happened in the learned helplessness case. A number of studies with human participants forced a reformulation of the theory to take additional cognitive factors into account (Abramson, Seligman, & Teasdale, 1978). For example, one feature of the new version is a construct called "explanatory style." Those experiencing failures who exhibit a pessimistic explanatory style are more likely to show learned helplessness effects than those who fail yet maintain optimistic styles. Pessimists "blame themselves and expect failure to recur over a longer period of time and in more situations" (Seligman & Schulman, 1986, p. 832). Optimists blame circumstances, not themselves, and although they may be just as deluded as pessimists, they don't get depressed.

Like the original learned helplessness theory, the revised version makes predictions that must be tested with data. An example is an interesting field study using life insurance sales agents (Seligman & Schulman, 1986), chosen in part because they experience failure much more often than success. The agents were evaluated with a questionnaire that measured explanatory style; the agents with optimistic styles were found to be more productive (i.e., sold 37% more policies over 2 years) and were about twice as likely to stay with the job than were more pessimistic agents.

Attributes of Good Theories

Some theories are judged by history to be more effective than others. Those judged to be good are characterized by several features. The most obvious one is **productivity**—good theories advance knowledge by generating a great deal of research, a trait that clearly can be applied to learned helplessness theory. Two other attributes of good theories, falsification and parsimony, require some elaboration.

Falsification

A popular misconception about theories in psychology is that the ultimate goal is to produce one that will be so good that it will explain every possible outcome. In fact, a theory that appears to explain everything is actually seriously flawed. To understand why, we need to look at an approach to testing theories first advocated by the philosopher of science Karl Popper (1959) and clearly implied in what you just read about proving and disproving theories.

According to Popper, science proceeds by setting up theories and then attempting to disprove or falsify them. Theories that are continually resistant to **falsification** are accepted as possibly true (with the emphasis on "possibly"). Recall my earlier comment that confidence in a theory increases as inductive support accumulates. This confidence never becomes absolute, however, because of the limits of induction. For example, 100 specific examples of birds could be found that would inductively support the conclusion "All birds can fly," yet it takes just a single non-flying bird (a kiwi, for example) to destroy the general conclusion. Similarly, 100 predictions derived from a theory could support a theory, but one disconfirmation could disprove it via modus tollens reasoning. Of course, we've already seen that on practical grounds, one disconfirmation will never lead to a wholesale abandonment of a theory. Nonetheless, Popper's argument suggests that disconfirmation carries greater weight than confirmation. At the very least, it requires that disconfirmations be investigated thoroughly.

If Popper is right, then theories have to be stated in such a way that the hypotheses derived from them are capable of disproof. That is, there must be some possible outcome to the experiment that could disprove the hypothesis. In practice, this requires the kind of precision in defining terms that was mentioned earlier, but it also requires that theories take the risk of being falsified.

As you recall from Chapter 1, one of the attributes of pseudoscience is its tendency to "sidestep disproof." This is just another way of saying the pseudoscientific theories fail the test of falsification. Phrenology illustrates the point, as you recall, by arranging the theory so that it could explain (more accurately, explain away) all possible anomalies, phrenologists managed to create the appearance of an infallible theory. In fact, by explaining everything, it failed to predict anything. Would a large area of "acquisitiveness" mean that a person would be a thief? According to phrenology, it might, but if the acquisitiveness was offset by a large area of "modesty," it might not. This isn't good enough.

A serious problem with Popper's falsification approach is that it fails to take into account the everyday psychology of doing research, in the sense that most researchers in the midst of their programs of research, like the phrenologists, develop a sense of ownership and tend to look for evidence in support of their theories. Unlike phrenologists and other pseudoscientists, however, real scientists clearly recognize the importance of falsification thinking. Even though researchers might hope to find support for their own theories, they are always trying to design experiments that can rule out one explanation or another.

A typical strategy is to take some phenomenon that might have several competing explanations for it and run a series of studies that systematically rules out one explanation at a time while providing support for a remaining explanation. In Seligman's learned helplessness studies, for example, the studies using the triadic design were designed to rule out the possibility that the helplessness effects were simply the result of the trauma associated with shock. With two groups of dogs receiving identical amounts of shock, the group able to control the shock showed no learned helplessness, while the group with no control became helpless. This outcome enabled Seligman to rule out (i.e., falsify) the idea that the helplessness effect was due only to the amount of shock received.

A famous historical example of a falsification strategy involves the investigation of a famous horse with alleged mathematical and reading abilities. Take a moment and read Box 3.3, which chronicles the case of Clever Hans, a horse with intellectual skills more apparent than real.

Parsimony

Besides being stated so as to be potentially falsified, good theories are **parsimonious.** This means, ideally, that they include the minimum number of constructs and assumptions that are necessary to explain the phenomenon adequately and predict future research outcomes. If two theories are equal in every way except that one is more parsimonious, then the simpler one is generally preferred.

In psychology, the idea originated with the late-19th-century British comparative psychologist Conwy Lloyd Morgan. He lived at a time when the theory of evolution was prompting naturalists to look for evidence of mental processes in animals (such as intelligence in horses like Clever Hans), hence supporting the Darwinian notion of continuity between species. This search produced a number of excessive claims, including the notion that moths approach candles because they are curious, that beavers show foresight and planning in their dam-building activities, and that ants are in the "habit of keeping domestic pets" (Romanes, 1886, p. 83). Morgan argued that animal behavior should be explained in the simplest terms possible. His famous statement, which came to be known as "Lloyd Morgan's Canon," was that "[i]n no case may we interpret an action as the outcome of the exercise of a higher psychical faculty, if it can be interpreted as the outcome of the exercise of one which stands lower in the psychological scale" (Morgan, 1903, p. 53). Instead of attributing reasoning to the dog that lifts a latch to get out of the yard, for example,

Box 3.3

CLASSIC STUDIES—Falsification and Der Kluge Hans

In Berlin at the turn of the 20th century, the best show in town, except perhaps for the just opened subway, could be found in the courtyard adjacent to a stable on Griebenow Street. There the spectator would encounter a horse (Figure 3.4) that appeared to have remarkable intellectual powers. When asked by his owner, Wilhelm von Osten, to multiply 4 by 4, the horse would tap his front hoof 16 times and stop. Adding, subtracting, multiplying, and dividing didn't challenge the remarkable animal, known to the German public as Clever (*Kluge* in German) Hans. Even fractions and decimals were no problem. When asked to add $\frac{2}{5}$ and $\frac{1}{2}$, the horse would tap out 9 for the numerator and 10 for the denominator (Sanford, 1914). The horse could also read and spell, using a system of tapping that translated letters into numbers.

FIGURE 3.4   Clever Hans at work.

If you've been developing your scientific thinking skills, I imagine you're a bit skeptical about this horse that read and did math better than some of your friends. Skeptics existed then too and one of them, Oskar Pfungst, provides us with a wonderful example of Popper's falsification strategy. Pfungst set out to see if he could rule out intelligence as an explanation for the behavior of the horse, while at the same time trying to find a more reasonable (i.e., parsimonious) explanation for what the horse was actually doing.

A special commission including scientists and animal trainers concluded that von Osten was not a fraud, but Pfungst suspected that the owner might be giving the animal some subtle cues about how to respond. He reasoned that if this was the case, then the horse would be correct only if the questioner knew the answer. And the horse's special skills in math might be related to the fact that von Osten was a mathematician.

To test the hypothesis that the horse would not know the answer unless the questioner did was easy. Pfungst simply set up several tests in which the questioner knew the correct answer sometimes but not at other times. For example, Pfungst had questioners hold up a card with a number on it. When the questioner was allowed to see the number before holding it up, the horse tapped out the number correctly 98% of the time. However, if the questioner was not allowed to look at the card before the horse did, Hans was correct only 8% of the time (Fernald, 1984). So much for mathematical ability. In a series of similar tests, Pfungst was able to rule out (falsify) the idea that Hans could use language.

Thus, Hans was clearly getting information about the correct answer from the person asking the question. How this occurred was still a puzzle that was eventually solved by Pfungst. To make a long story short, he was able to determine that the horse was responding to very slight visual cues from the questioner. Whenever someone asked a question, that person would bend forward very slightly or move his or her eyes down without being aware of it (perhaps glancing down at the horse's hoof to see if it would start tapping). Hans learned that the movement was a signal to begin responding. When Hans reached the correct answer, the person would straighten up or glance up, again just slightly and without awareness, but enough to signal Hans that it was time to stop.

The Clever Hans case illustrates two other points besides the falsification strategy of Pfungst. By showing that the horse's abilities were not due to a high level of intelligence but could be explained in terms of the simpler process of learning to respond to two sets of visual cues (when to start and when to stop), Pfungst provided a more *parsimonious* explanation of the horse's behavior. Secondly, if von Osten was giving subtle cues that influenced behavior, then perhaps experimenters in general might subtly influence the behavior of participants when the experimenter knows what the outcome will be. We'll return to this point in Chapter 6; it's an example of what is known as *experimenter bias*.

Morgan would explain the behavior more simply (i.e., more parsimoniously) as an example of trial and error learning. The dog tries many behaviors to get out of the yard, and eventually hits on one that works. That behavior gradually becomes strengthened with repeated success, and the animal has learned to escape.

In psychology a good illustration of parsimony is a comparison of Freudian and behaviorist theories about why 4-year-old boys imitate their fathers. The Freudian explanation requires acceptance of a large number of assumptions and constructs, including ideas about the unconscious control of behavior, infantile sexuality, Oedipal feelings, castration anxiety, repression, and identification with the aggressor. Briefly, the young boy is said to desire his mother sexually, but to fear being castrated by his father if the desire is discovered. Consequently, he represses the desire into the unconscious and identifies with the aggressive father. Learning theory simply assumes that (a) behaviors that are reinforced will tend to occur again in similar situations in the future and (b) parents are likely to notice and reinforce imitative behaviors. Learning theory is clearly more parsimonious than its Freudian counterpart in this instance, while still providing an adequate explanation and a basis for predicting further outcomes.

Developing Research from Other Research

To a large extent, this section on developing ideas for research is an extension of what was described earlier about the continuing relationship between theory and data, but research deriving from other research occurs even when theory development is not the prime focus. Sometimes researchers simply want to investigate some phenomenon in order to discover regular, predictable relationships between variables (i.e., to discover laws of behavior) and are not very concerned about theory building. Skinner's operant conditioning research (Chapter 11) falls into this category.

I believe the most common sources of ideas for research in psychology are unanswered questions from a study just completed. Psychologists do not conduct individual experiments that are separate from each other; they build **programs of research,** a series of interrelated studies. You won't find someone doing a study on helping behavior and then switching to do a study on aggression. Rather, researchers become involved in a specific area of investigation and conduct a series of investigations in that area that may last for years and may extend to many other researchers with an interest in the topic. The conclusion of one project invariably leads to another because while experiments answer some empirical questions, they also raise new ones. The research of Seligman and his colleagues and students on learned helplessness is a good example of a research program.

One unmistakable indication of how research leads to other research can be seen by scanning any issue of a recent psychology journal. Look at the authors of a specific publication; then look to see if those same names appear in the reference sections of the publication as authors of similar studies. As an illustration, in the first three issues of the *Journal of Experimental Psychology: Learning, Memory, and Cognition* for 1992, there are 52 different research articles. The authors of the articles reference other work by themselves in 48 of the 52 articles. Although some of this may be a normal human tendency to cite one's own work, for the most part it reflects the fact that researchers simply don't do single experiments—they establish systematic programs of interconnected experiments. Experiments lead to more experiments.

Research Teams and the "What's Next?" Question

If you asked research psychologists to describe their day-to-day existence, you would get a wide variety of answers, but one general principle would emerge: few researchers work by themselves. Rather, they assemble **research teams** within their laboratories. Typically, the team will include a senior researcher, Dr. X, several graduate students who are working for Dr. X, and perhaps one or two highly motivated undergraduates who have convinced Dr. X of their interest and willingness to work odd hours and perhaps clean animal cages. This team will have several experiments going on at once, and team members will spend long hours in the lab collecting data and analyzing them while drinking coffee. Also, they will often find themselves sitting around a table in the greasy spoon across the street, not unlike Lewin and his students, discussing research projects in various stages of completion (and drinking more coffee). When discussing completed projects, they will use what could be called "what's next?" thinking: given the outcome of this study, what should we do next? At some point in the conversation, someone will get an idea and ask the single most frequently heard question in conversations among research psychologists: "What do you think would happen if we did X?" The "X" refers to a rough idea for a study, and "what do you think would happen?" is a request for predictions about the outcome. The question will lead to a lively discussion in which the group will refine the idea or perhaps decide it is unworkable and think about the next "what's next?" question that comes up. If the idea is pursued, some procedure will be created, tried in the next few days in trial runs that are sometimes called **pilot studies,** refined further (additional coffee involved here), and eventually shaped into a tightly designed study that is then completed.

Once completed, then, a research study seldom stands by itself. Instead, its outcome almost always leads to another study, often designed to clarify some unanswered question of the first study. To illustrate, consider a series of two studies on face recognition by Burton, Wilson, Cowan, and Bruce (1999). In their initial study they wondered about participants' ability to recognize people shown in typical surveillance videos, where the visual quality is often poor. They compared participants who already knew the people on a video with others unfamiliar with the people on the tape. A third group consisted of police officers in training (presumably learning to be good at recognizing crooks on surveillance tapes of bank robberies). They found that participants relatively familiar with the people on the tape performed rather well on a recognition task, while those in the other two groups fared poorly. Given this outcome, and thinking along "what's next?" lines, Burton and his research team wondered about the basis for the accurate recognition when participants knew the people on the tapes. Was it the faces, the overall body shapes, or perhaps the way the people on the tapes walked? This question led to the obvious study, in which tapes were edited to obscure faces, bodies, or the gaits of the people on the video. They discovered that recognition performance was still quite good with body and gait obscured, but when viewers could not see the faces of those on the surveillance tape, accuracy disappeared. In short, the second study followed nicely from the first, and answered a question raised by the first study.

Thus research in psychology (a) usually involves a continuous series of interrelated studies, (b) is often a communal effort, combining the efforts of several people who are immersed in the same narrowly specialized research area, and (c) is very unstructured in its early stages. This lack of structure was noted some time ago by a panel of distinguished experimental psychologists brought together in 1958 by the Education and Training Board of the APA and charged with making recommendations about graduate training in experimental psychology. They described "the process of doing research—that is, of creating and building a science of psychology—[as] a rather informal, often illogical and sometimes messy-looking affair. It includes a great deal of floundering around in the empirical world, sometimes dignified by names like 'pilot studies' and 'exploratory research'" (Taylor, Garner, & Hunt, 1959, p. 169).

One fairly recent development in "what's next?" question-asking is the extension of the concept of a research team far beyond the confines of a single laboratory. In our computer age, it is quite common for researchers on different campuses to interact via e-mail. The digital conversations often include descriptions of a proposed method preceded by the famous question, "What do you think would happen if we did this?" Thus, while being separated by thousands of miles, researchers can nonetheless carry on the kind of informal discussion that leads to creative research. They can even drink coffee while communicating electronically.

Replication and Extension

Many studies that follow on the heels of completed studies will be similar enough to be considered replications but different enough so that they are not exact duplicates of prior research. In other words, they include both replication and extension. As research psychologists normally use the term, replication refers to a study that duplicates some or all of the procedures of some prior study. Extension, on the other hand, resembles a prior study and usually replicates part of it, but goes further and adds at least one new feature. Furthermore, in studies that are extensions, the term partial replication is often used to refer to that part of the study that replicates some portion of the earlier work. Sometimes the term "exact replication" or "direct replication" is used to describe a point-for-point duplication of some other study.

Exact replication was a procedure used in Pavlov's famous laboratory in Russia for training purposes. Whenever new workers came into the lab, their first experiment would be to replicate some previous study (Babkin, 1949). Thus, Pavlov had a continuous system of checking on results while new researchers developed the skills to carry on extensions of earlier findings. In general, however, exact replications seldom occur for the simple reason that researchers don't get promoted and tenured if all they do is repeat what someone else has done. Normally, exact replications occur only when serious questions are raised about some finding. For instance, if several researchers are trying to extend some finding and their studies include a partial replication that fails to come out as expected, it may be necessary to go back to the original study and do an exact replication to determine if the finding really was reliable. And as you recall from the previous chapter, failures to replicate sometimes lead to the discovery of scientific fraud.

A study by Marean, Werner, and Kuhl (1992) is a good example of how research can replicate and extend at the same time. These researchers were interested in whether infants as young as 2 months old could categorize different vowel sounds. The study was an extension of earlier work showing that 6-month-olds had this categorizing ability. Marean et al. wondered if the ability developed even earlier than age

6 months. Their study tested 2- and 3-month-old children, and as a partial replication of the earlier study, included 6-month-olds as well. Basically, the study showed that as early as 2 months, children showed different reactions to two different vowels spoken by the same person but did not react differently to two different persons speaking the same vowel. That is, they were discriminating by the general category of a vowel sound, not by the individual acoustic features of two different voices.

Creative Thinking in Science

One element of the research-generating process that has been implied several times in this chapter, but not dealt with directly, is scientific creativity. It is one thing to say that research can be generated from simple observations, from theory, or from the outcomes of other studies, but the jump from these sources of research ideas to the actual research study does not occur automatically. At some point, the experiment must be *created*. Sometimes the study follows logically from what preceded it and may be minimally creative, but at other times, a creative leap occurs.

Creative thinking in research design involves a process of recognizing meaningful connections between apparently unrelated ideas and seeing those connections as the key to developing the study. Such thinking does not occur in a vacuum, however, but rather in the context of some problem to be solved by a scientist with considerable knowledge of the problem at hand. As the famous biologist Louis Pasteur put it, "chance favors the prepared mind" (cited in Myers, 1992, p. 335). Thus, serendipity does not by itself produce the idea for a research study; the serendipitous event must be seen by the scientist immersed in a topic as the missing piece that solves the problem at hand. This is one reason why researchers work in teams—the presence of several minds increases the chances that someone will have an idea that someone else on the team will see as the missing piece to the puzzle.

To examine a specific example of scientific creativity, consider maze learning. Ask a psychologist to name famous pieces of research equipment, and mazes will be at or near the top of the list. Although the maze reached its peak of popularity in the period 1920–1940, it is still an important tool used to study such things as learning and spatial behavior. Credit for the first maze learning study with rats belongs to Willard Small of Clark University, who completed his studies near the end of the 19th century (Small, 1900).

How did Small get the idea of putting rats in mazes? Along with his laboratory colleague, Linus Kline, he was interested generally in rat behavior, in particular the rat's "home-finding tendencies." In a discussion with Edmund Sanford, director of Clark's lab, Kline described some tunnels he had observed "made by large feral rats to their nests under the porch of an old cabin. … These runways were from three to six inches below the surface of the ground and when exposed during excavation presented a veritable maze" (Miles, 1930, p. 331). The term "maze" apparently made a connection for Sanford, and he suggested that Kline build a maze himself. In particular, Sanford proposed using as a model the Hampton Court maze, England's most popular people-size labyrinth. At the time of their conversation, Sanford had just returned from a sabbatical in England and may have been at Hampton Court.

With other projects underway, Kline passed along the idea to Small, who built a 6- by 8-foot wire mesh maze, changing the Hampton Court maze's trapezoidal

(a)

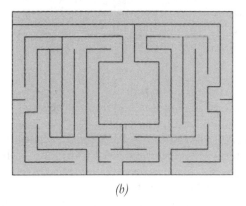

(b)

FIGURE 3.5 (a) The Hampton Court maze on a busy day. (b) Small's adaptation of the Hampton Court maze design for his pioneering study of maze learning in rats.

shape (Figure 3.5a) to rectangular (Figure 3.5b) but keeping the design the same. Small ran several studies examining how rats learned the maze; the Hampton design became common in the early decades of the 20th century and thus began a rats-in-mazes tradition that continues to the present day.[2]

---

[2] Incidentally, while critics sometimes refer to the maze as an example of the "artificiality" of laboratory research in psychology (i.e., no mundane reality for the rat), it is worth noting that Small's original intent in using the maze was not to create a sterile environment but one close to the rat's world, or, as Small (1900) put it, to create "as little difference as possible between the conditions of experiment and of ordinary experience" (p. 209).

The story is a good illustration of scientific creativity. Scientists (Kline and Small) knowledgeable in some research area (animal behavior) were wrestling with a difficult problem (how to study home finding in the rat). An offhand comment (Kline's recollections of rats tunneling under a porch) combined with Sanford's familiarity with the Hampton Court maze produced a link between seemingly unrelated events, and the problem was solved—the way to study a rat's home-finding tendencies was to create an apparatus modeled on a famous maze in England.

It is worth noting that while a thorough knowledge of one's field may be a prerequisite to creative thinking in science, the blade is double-edged; this knowledge can sometimes create rigid patterns of thinking that inhibit creativity. Scientists occasionally become so accustomed to a particular method or so comfortable with a particular theory that they fail to consider alternatives, thereby reducing the chances of making new discoveries. Consider maze learning again.

The maze has contributed a great deal to our understanding of basic learning processes, and its invention illustrates scientific creativity at its best. However, the apparatus has also led to many dead ends, so to speak. Once established as a standard apparatus, the maze occasionally hindered creativity, leading researchers to narrow the focus of their work to situations that were relevant to mazes but perhaps to little else. The phenomenon of "centrifugal swing" is an example. Investigated heavily in the 1920s and 1930s, it was said to be a tendency for an animal to emerge from one turn in a maze (presumably at high speed) and swing by centrifugal force to the far wall. This would then influence the direction of its next turn. This swing was contrasted with a "forward-moving tendency." Dozens of studies attempted to tease out the factors that would produce either a swing or a forward move (e.g., Schneirla, 1929). The studies were elegantly designed and they no doubt helped develop the research skills of a number of experimental psychologists, but the research had no importance beyond the maze apparatus itself and shed no light on fundamental learning processes.

Perhaps the famous behaviorist E. C. Tolman was only half serious when he closed his 1937 APA presidential address by professing that "everything important in psychology … can be investigated in essence through the … analysis of the determiners of rat behavior at a choice-point in a maze" (cited in Hilgard, 1978, p. 364). His comment, however, shows how apparatus can shape scientific thinking. The origins of scientific equipment like mazes may reveal creative thinking at its best (e.g., Sanford's idea to use the Hampton Court maze), but innovation can be dampened once an apparatus or a research procedure becomes established. A thorough knowledge of mazes and maze learning can help the researcher develop creative studies, but this same knowledge can hinder creativity as well.

Reviewing the Literature

Research projects do not develop in a vacuum. The psychologists involved in a program of research are thoroughly familiar, not just with the work of their own lab, but also with the work done in other labs doing similar research. Those deriving experiments from theory are likewise familiar with the research concerning the theory in question. Even the experimenter who gets an idea for a study after making a casual observation often makes that observation within the context of some related knowledge or some problem at hand. How is one's knowledge of the literature acquired? Computerized databases provide a good starting point.

Computerized Database Searches

Chances are that you have already used an electronic database to search for information in your school's library. Some common ones are Info Trac, Academic Abstracts, and Medline. In psychology, the APA's PsycINFO Services provides a variety of search tools. Some are in book form, but most are accessed electronically. The primary database, from which all the others are derived, is called PsycINFO. It includes references to journal articles, doctoral dissertations, technical reports, books, and book chapters. It includes entries dating back to 1887, the year when American psychology's first journal, the *American Journal of Psychology,* was founded. It covers literature published in more than 45 countries and over 1,300 journals. Every month about 5,500 new items are added to the database. For the most up-to-date information, you should check out PsycINFO's website: www.apa.org/psycinfo

As a student, you will find PsycINFO in one of two forms. Your library might subscribe to a service that provides the database in a CD-ROM format (this used to be called PsycLIT). More likely, and more convenient for you, your library might have a license to offer PsycINFO on your campus network, through some service such as EBSCOhost. The best way to learn the mechanics of using PsycINFO is to sit at a terminal and experiment, perhaps starting by working your way through the "help" screens. The APA also publishes various guides, and the librarians can assist you as well. Your best help, however, will probably come from experienced junior or senior psychology majors. They will be able to show you how to broaden or narrow your searches and give you tips on how to search most efficiently.

Once your search has produced specific research articles, you can ask PsycINFO to show you the "records" for them. These can then be printed or downloaded to your disk. Figure 3.6 shows you what a typical PsycINFO record for a journal article looks like (you should recognize the article as one featured prominently earlier in this chapter). As you can see, each record includes several important categories of information. These categories are called "fields," and they include, among other things, the article's title and its author(s), all the needed reference information (journal, volume, page numbers), an abstract of the article, and descriptors (terms that can be used to search further). Reading the abstracts will tell you whether the article is especially relevant for you; if so, you can then find the article itself in your library's journal collection or acquire it through your library's interlibrary loan procedures.

Search Tips

Experience is the best teacher of PsycINFO, but there are some guidelines that can help you become a proficient user. First, if you are unsure about the best terms to use when starting a search, use the Thesaurus, which is built directly into PsycINFO and found by clicking on "subject search." The Thesaurus is an electronic version of a book published by APA *(Thesaurus of Psychological Index Terms)* that provides exten-

Title:	Effects of errorless training on teaching children to discriminate letters of the alphabet.
Author(s):	Egeland, Byron
Affiliation:	U Minnesota, School Psychology Training Program
Source:	Journal of Applied Psychology. Vol 60(4), Aug (1975), (pp. 533–536).
ISSN/ISBN:	0021–9010
Language:	English
Abstract:	108 preschool 4–5 yr olds were taught to discriminate letters of the alphabet by either (a) an errorless-training approach in which the obvious cue used during training highlighted the distinctive feature of the letter to be discriminated, (b) errorless-training approach in which the obvious cue did not highlight the distinctive feature, or (c) the traditional reinforcement-extinction approach. The first errorless-training group made fewer errors during training as compared to the reinforcement-extinction group. On both an immediate and a delayed posttest, the first errorless-training group made significantly fewer errors compared to the other two groups; this indicates that errorless training is effective, provided that the distinctive feature of the letter to be discriminated is highlighted during training. ((c) 1999 APA/PsycINFO, all rights reserved)
Key Phrase:	errorless training with vs without distinctive feature highlighted vs traditional reinforcement-extinction approach; discrimination of letters of alphabet; 4–5 yr olds
Subjects:	Teaching-methods; errors-; Letters-alphabet; visual-discrimination; stimulus-salience; preschool-age-children
Classification:	2300 Human Experimental Psychology
Population:	Human
Age Group:	Preschool Age (2–5 yrs); Childhood (birth-12 yrs)
Release Date:	19751001
Database:	PsycINFO 1967-Current

FIGURE 3.6   A sample PsycINFO record for the study by Egeland (1975) on training children to discriminate letters.

sive cross–referencing of specific terms that are used as key words when searching. For example, if you ask the Thesaurus to find the topic "schizophrenia," you will be shown a number of potential search terms that are "related to" schizophrenia (e.g., anhedonia), "broader than" schizophrenia (e.g., psychosis), and "narrower than" schizophrenia (e.g., hebephrenic schizophrenia). Clicking directly on these terms will begin a search. The Thesaurus will also tell you when the term was first introduced into the database (1967 for schizophrenia), and that such terms as "chronic schizophrenia" are not search descriptor names used by PsycINFO (schizophrenia is "used for" it instead). If you had typed in that term when initiating a search, you would have been told that chronic schizophrenia was discontinued as a search term in 1988 and to "use schizophrenia" instead.

In addition to searching for specific terms, PsycINFO gives you the opportunity to search by author, and by specific journals. You can also choose a "publication type" search, a wonderful device for focusing on specific types of articles and books. One of my interests is the history of psychology, for example, and I can now search specifically for "obituaries." Other publications types that can be chosen include "longitudinal studies," "experimental replications," "literature review," and "meta analysis."

A good search strategy is to begin with the most recent years and work backward in time. In addition to starting with relatively new research, this approach will help you to narrow a search. So if you search under "cognitive maps" you will find more than 100 articles, but if you ask for cognitive maps *and* articles published in the year 2001, you will just retrieve perhaps a dozen. Also, searching under "publication type" for "literature review" or "meta analysis" is a good tip. These kinds of articles summarize the results of many other articles. Their references sections alone will have great value in your search. Be especially primed to notice articles in the journal *Psychological Bulletin* and chapters in the book series *Annual Review of Psychology*. Both publish long literature reviews that are potential gold mines because they also contain extensive reference lists. Once you begin finding good articles on your topic of choice, you can use the reference sections of the actual articles as a means of further search. From these references you might pick up some new search terms and you can identify names of researchers who seem to publish a lot on the topic.

Another search tip is to use the "and" function to narrow the search and to use the truncation function to avoid narrowing it too much. For example, suppose you are taking social psychology and looking for articles on altruism, our tendency to help others in need. Furthermore, suppose you want to examine altruism from the standpoint of evolutionary psychology. If you just ask PsycINFO to find records with the word "altruism" in them, you will retrieve too many records. The search I just completed to illustrate this point yielded 1,797 records (by the time you read this the number will be much higher). When I asked PsycINFO to search for "altruism AND evolutionary psychology," however, only four records were produced. That is a much more manageable number, of course, but it might occur to you that there must be more than four articles dealing with this topic. There are. By asking for "evolutionary psychology," though, I eliminated records that included just the terms "evolution" or "evolutionary." To solve the problem, the evolutionary term could be "truncated" (i.e., shortened). This is done by using only the first few key letters and adding an asterisk. For example, using "evol★" will retrieve all the terms that begin with those four letters, including evolutionary, evolution, evolved, and evolving. When I asked for "altruism and evol★," 178 records appeared. This is better than four, but still too many to begin looking at them one at a time. My next strategy was to start with the most recent years. So I asked for "altruism and evol★" for the years 1995 through 1999, and that produced 37 records. That's a nice convenient number to begin looking at the actual records and abstracts.

As you become proficient in using PsycINFO, you will begin to identify useful information about your topic of interest. As you begin to read some of this information, and perhaps talk it over with other students or professors, you will start to know the literature (see Table 3.1 for some tips on how to read a research article effectively). This knowledge, in turn, will put you in a better position to develop ideas for research and to formulate them as empirical questions. With a good empirical question in hand, you are ready to begin designing a study that will provide some answers to that question. The problem of design will be dealt with shortly. First, however, it is necessary to introduce you to some of the basics about the data that you will be collecting to help answer your empirical questions.

TABLE 3.1   *Getting the Most Out of Reading Journal Articles*

At some point in your research methods course, perhaps as part of an assignment to complete a literature review, you will find yourself reading research articles that have been published in one of the psychology journals. It is important to keep in mind that journal articles were not written for an undergraduate audience; rather, they are aimed at other professional researchers. Hence, they can be very hard to read. Here are some tips to make the task easier:

- Get as much as you can out of the Abstract. This is an overall summary of the research and probably the easiest section of the paper to read and understand; so read it several times.
- In the opening paragraph or two of the Introduction, look for a general statement of the problem being studied. By the way, this part of the paper will not have a label called "Introduction," but it will include everything between the Abstract and the section labeled "Method."
- Near the end of the Introduction, probably in the final paragraph, look for explicit statements of the hypothesis or hypotheses being tested in the study. These hypotheses will emerge out of the problem statement and the research questions raised by the studies that will have been described in the middle part of the Introduction. Write down the hypotheses and keep them in mind as you continue reading.
- In the Method section, pay careful attention to the description of the procedure and experimental design. Try to place yourself in the role of a participant and develop a clear idea of what the participants had to do in the study. If it's an experimental study, write down the independent and dependent variables (you've seen these terms in your general psychology course and you'll learn much more about them in Chapter 5).
- The Results section might be especially difficult, because it will include some statistical information and symbols that might seem quite foreign. A good Results section will have a clear verbal description of what the results were, however, and the graphs and tables should be helpful. In a well-written Results section, you should be able to understand the gist of what happened in the study without looking at a single number or symbol.
- The last main part of the article is the Discussion section. It often begins by summarizing the main results, so if the Results section is Greek to you, there's still hope. The main purpose of the Discussion section is to explain the results with reference to the original hypotheses, so the writer will be making connections back to the Introduction. A final thing to look for in the Discussion is a description of what research should be done next (the "What's Next? Question). The Discussion section of an article is a great source of ideas for new research.

Chapter Summary

Varieties of Psychological Research

Basic research in psychology aims to discover fundamental principles of behavior, while applied research is undertaken with specific practical problems in mind. Both basic and applied research can take place either in the laboratory or in a field setting. Laboratory research allows greater control, but field research more closely approximates real-life situations. Research that involves participants in the procedures (i.e., has experimental reality), even if it places people in situations far removed from everyday living, can yield important information about behavior. Most research in psychology is quantitative in nature, involving numerical data subjected to statistical analysis, but recent years have seen an increase in what is called qualitative research (e.g., content analysis of structured interviews).

Asking Empirical Questions

The initial step in any research project is to formulate an empirical question—one that can be answered with the evidence of objective data. Empirical questions include terms that are defined precisely enough (i.e., operationally) to allow replication to occur. Several studies on the same topic might use different operational definitions of terms, yet might converge on the same general conclusion about behavior (e.g., hunger levels influence the rate of maze learning).

Developing Research from Observations and Serendipity

Some research ideas derive from reflection on everyday observations, especially of events that are unusual enough to attract one's attention. Specific problems to be solved also lead to research; much of the applied research in general and program evaluation research in particular develops this way. Sometimes we observe events that occur unexpectedly or accidentally. Serendipity is the act of discovering something by accident; serendipitous events often yield ideas for further research. The discovery of edge detectors is an example.

Developing Research from Theory

Theories summarize and organize existing knowledge, provide a basis for making predictions, and provide a working explanation about some phenomenon. There is a reciprocal relationship between theory building and research. Empirical questions can be deduced from theory and these questions lead to experiments. The conclusions of the completed experiments then either support or fail to support the theory. Theories cannot be proven to be true, although they can be disproven, at least in principle. Actually, however, a theory is discarded only after a consensus develops that it is consistently failing to make good predictions. In most cases, theories evolve to take into account the accumulating knowledge about some phenomenon. Theories in psychology are useful to the extent that they generate research that increases our understanding of behavior. Also, good theories are parsimonious and stated precisely enough to be falsified by well-designed research.

Developing Research from Other Research

Researchers in psychology seldom think in terms of isolated experiments. Instead, they produce programs of research, series of interrelated experiments within a specific area. They continually use the results of experiments as starting points for the next experiment. Research programs often include studies that involve replications of existing findings, along with extensions into new areas.

Creative Thinking in Science

Scientific creativity occurs when researchers make connections among ideas or events that most people see as being unrelated. The creative scientist is knowledgeable in a particular research area and is prepared to notice the relevance of apparently unrelated events to the problem at hand.

Reviewing the Literature

Empirical questions occur more frequently to the investigator who knows the research literature in a particular area. Most searching is done electronically using such tools as PsycINFO.

Chapter Review

Multiple Choice

1. Compared with field research, which of the following is true about laboratory research?
   a. laboratory research achieves greater mundane realism
   b. to achieve experimental realism, the study has to be conducted in the laboratory
   c. laboratory research achieves a greater degree of control over the conditions of the experiment
   d. it is more difficult to gain informed consent in laboratory research than in field research

2. What is the advantage of using operational definitions?
   a. they force researchers in different labs to use exactly the same definition for a given psychological construct
   b. they facilitate the replication process
   c. they increase the study's mundane reality
   d. none of the above—because of disagreement about how to define constructs, operational definitions are seldom used

3. One of the predictions from learned helplessness theory is that if animals have prior experience with successful escape, they will be less likely to show the typical helplessness behavior after they encounter inescapable shock. Suppose you did a study to test this idea, and sure enough, the dogs with prior successful escapes didn't show subsequent helplessness. What can be concluded?
   a. the theory has received deductive support
   b. the theory has been proven to be true
   c. the theory has received inductive support
   d. the theory has not been supported

4. Study 1 compares 2- and 4-month-old children on a perceptual task. Study 2 uses the same task and compares four groups of children ages 2, 4, 6, and 8 months. The second study
   a. has greater experimental reality than the first one
   b. is an example of a converging operation
   c. is a good example of replication and extension
   d. is redundant—there's no need to include the first two groups (ages 2 and 4 months)

5. The saying "chance favors the prepared mind" makes it clear that
   a. creative scientists are also highly knowledgeable about their area

    b.   whether someone is a creative scientist is more or less a matter of luck (chance)

    c.   the most creative thinkers are those who are unfamiliar with the topic being studied

    d.   serendipitous events happen only for the most experienced researchers

Short Essay

1. Why is the Egeland study on reading an example of applied research and the Neisser study on letter identification an example of basic research?

2. What are the comparative advantages and disadvantages of research completed in and out of the laboratory?

3. In the Dutton and Aron study of romance in "high places," why did the researchers believe it was necessary to complete a second laboratory study, given the results of their field study?

4. Give three different operational definitions of hunger and explain why research using all three could result in what is called converging operations.

5. What is a theory in psychology and what are the attributes of good theories?

6. Use learned helplessness theory to illustrate the reciprocal relationship between theory and data. Be sure to work the terms deduction, induction, and hypothesis into your answer.

7. Explain why you are unlikely to hear scientists say that a theory has been *proven* to be true.

8. Explain how the Clever Hans study illustrates the importance of (a) a falsification strategy, and (b) the use of parsimonious explanations.

9. What are pilot studies and what purpose do they serve?

10. Use the origins of maze learning to illustrate the process of creative thinking in science.

Applications Exercises

Exercise 3.1.—What's Next?

Recall the basic finding of Milgram's study on obedience. Adult males regularly obeyed commands to shock a "learner" in the room next door for errors made by the learner on a verbal learning task. More than half of the participants increased the shock level all the way to 450 volts. Pretend that you are part of Milgram's research team and this first study has been completed.

1. Given the results, what would you do in the next study?

2. What do you think would happen (i.e., what would the hypothesis be)?

Think of at least three different variations on the procedure that could increase our knowledge of the factors influencing obedience.

Exercise 3.2.—Creating Operational Definitions

Create two different operational definitions for each of the following psychological constructs.

1. frustration
2. shyness
3. anxiety
4. sense of direction

Exercise 3.3.—Confirmation Bias

We have seen in this chapter that one strategy used by scientists is to arrive at some empirical conclusion by ruling out or *falsifying* alternative explanations. But this strategy is difficult to develop, as the following exercise from Wason and Johnson-Laird (1972, pp. 172–173) shows. Try it.

> Imagine that you are holding four cards and each has a letter printed on one side and a number printed on the other. As you look at the cards, this is what you see:
>
> E   K   4   7
>
> You must decide which cards have to be turned over in order to determine whether the following rule is true or not:
>
> *If a card has a vowel on one side, then it has an even number on the other side.*
>
> Which cards would you turn over? (Hint: think in falsification terms—which cards, if turned over, would falsify the statement?)

Exercise 3.4.—Searching PsycINFO

Using PsycINFO find records for any five of the articles referenced in this chapter. For each of the five articles, (a) find another article by the same author, and (b) find another article on the same topic that was published within the last three years.

CHAPTER 4

Measurement, Sampling, and Data Analysis

Preview & Chapter Objectives

In this chapter we begin to take a close look at data. Specifically, we will examine the wide range of events measured in psychological research, the factors determining whether these measures are of any value, the so-called scales of measurement, and the methods for selecting the individuals who will provide these behavioral measures through their participation in a study. The chapter also introduces (and, for some of you I hope, reviews) the important distinction between descriptive and inferential statistics, and considers the logic of hypothesis testing. When you finish this chapter, you should be able to:

- Understand the relationship between a construct (e.g., visual imagery) and a measurable behavior (e.g., reaction time).
- Distinguish between the reliability of a behavioral measure and several forms of the measure's validity.

- Identify the defining features of nominal, ordinal, interval, and ratio scales, and know when each is to be used.
- Describe three varieties of probability sampling (simple random, stratified, cluster) and know when each is used.
- Understand when probability sampling is needed and why most research in psychology uses nonprobability sampling.
- Summarize data effectively using measures of central tendency (e.g., mean), measures of variability (e.g., standard deviation), and visual displays (e.g., stem and leaf displays).
- Understand the logic of hypothesis testing and what is involved in making an inferential analysis of data.

You know from Chapter 1 that research psychologists are "data driven," insisting that conclusions about behavior be based on data collected via scientific methods. Deciding precisely which behaviors to measure, how to take the measurements, and how to make sense of the resulting collection of numbers is no simple task. This chapter just begins our discussion of the relationship between data and psychological knowledge.

What to Measure—Varieties of Behavior

The variety of behaviors measured by experimental psychologists is virtually unlimited. What gets measured ranges from overt behaviors such as running through a maze to verbal reports by means of questionnaires to recordings of physiological activity while performing some task. To illustrate the rich variety of behaviors measured in psychological research, consider these examples.

1. A study on "Span of Apprehension in Schizophrenic Patients as a Function of Distractor Masking and Laterality" (Elkins, Cromwell, & Asarnow, 1992) investigated attention span limitations in schizophrenic patients. Compared with nonschizophrenic controls, they did poorly when asked to identify target letters appearing in an array of distracting letters. The behavior measured was whether or not they could accurately name the target letters in different circumstances.

2. A study on "Differential Calculation Abilities in Young Children from Middle- and Low-Income Families" (Jordan, Huttenlocher, & Levine, 1992) tested these children on a variety of math problems and found that children from middle-income families outperformed those from low-income families when problems were presented verbally but that the two groups performed the same on nonverbal problems. Two different behaviors were measured: the children's responses to the math problems and the strategies they used. The children were observed solving the problems, and scorers recorded whether the behaviors included such strategies as counting on fingers.

3. A study on "Perceived Social Support, Social Skills, and Quality of Relationships in Bulimic Women" (Grissett & Norvell, 1992) gave bulimic and nonbu-

limic women a battery of self-report tests to complete. The behaviors measured were their responses to these surveys (e.g., the Perceived Support Scale). Participants were also put into a brief conversation that was taped with a confederate and rated by observers. The women's verbal and nonverbal behaviors during the conversation were scored on a measure of "social effectiveness." Bulimic women did not believe they received much social support, and they were not rated very highly on social effectiveness.

4. A study asking "Does a Cognitive Map Guide Choices in a Radial-Arm Maze?" (Brown, 1992) answered "maybe not." Radial-arm mazes, which feature a central platform and alleyways radiating from it in all directions, are among the more popular modern mazes. They are often used to study a rat's spatial memory (cognitive map), and the study by Brown investigated the rats' ability to avoid traveling down already-visited pathways. The behaviors measured were "macrochoices," operationally defined as occurring whenever a rat so much as stuck its nose into a pathway, and "microchoices," defined as orienting toward a pathway but not going down it (all this confirmed by videotape from a camera looking down on the maze).

Developing Measures from Constructs

From these examples you can see that researchers measure behavior in many ways. But how do they decide what to measure? Where do they get the idea to measure calculation strategies by observing finger counting, microchoices by observing bodily orientation, or attention by seeing which letters are selected from an array?

In part, they know what to measure because they know the literature in their area of expertise, and so they know what measures are typically used by other investigators. They also develop ideas for new measures by modifying commonly used measures. Finally, they develop measures out of the process of refining the constructs of interest in the study. Let me elaborate.

When a researcher is planning a study, one of the first decisions is to define the constructs to be used in the project as precisely as possible. Sound familiar? It should because we are talking about operational definitions again. Part of the design for any study involves taking the constructs of interest, which by definition are not directly observable, and deciding which behaviors will adequately reflect those constructs. In the previous examples, each researcher was faced with the task of taking some phenomenon and turning it into a manageable experiment by carefully defining the constructs in terms of measurable behaviors. Table 4.1 summarizes the four previously-mentioned studies in terms of the constructs studied and how they were operationalized into specific behaviors.

One thing you may notice is that none of these constructs (attention, calculation ability, etc.) are directly observable—each must be inferred from the measures used to investigate it. This process is repeated over and over again in psychology and allows the research psychologist to ask some empirical questions that might seem impossible to answer at first glance. Let's consider in greater detail two specific examples of procedures frequently used to investigate questions that might seem difficult, if not impossible, to answer empirically:

TABLE 4.1   *Sample Constructs and How They Are Measured*

Construct	Behavior to Measure the Construct
Attention span	Letter identification accuracy
Calculation ability	Number of problems done correctly
Perceived social support	Score on self-report test
Social effectiveness	Observer ratings of social interaction
Rat macrochoice	Entering arm of radial maze or not
Rat microchoice	Orienting toward arm of radial maze

Do preverbal infants understand the concept of gravity?

Can you demonstrate that people use visual images?

The measures used to study these seemingly nonempirical questions are as simple as recording (a) how long an infant looks at something and (b) how long it takes people to make decisions. Read on.

Case Study 1—Habituation

Do infants have a concept of gravity? How could you ever find out? You cannot ask them directly, of course, but the question can be asked indirectly via a technique in which the amount of time a baby spends looking at different stimuli is measured. This so-called habituation procedure involves showing an infant the same stimulus over and over again and then changing to a new stimulus. From other research it is known that infants prefer novelty (Spelke, 1985), so if the same stimulus is presented repeatedly, they lose interest (i.e., they stop looking). The term "habituation" is defined as a gradual decrease in responding to repeated stimuli. If a new stimulus is presented *and* it is recognized as something new or unusual, the infant will increase the time spent looking at it. So if looking time in response to stimuli decreases and then suddenly increases, you can infer that the infant has noticed something new.

With this in mind, consider a delightful study by Kim and Spelke (1992). They compared 5- and 7-month-olds and concluded that some type of basic understanding of gravity develops during that period of infancy. The infants were first shown repeated film clips of balls rolling up or down inclined planes, as depicted in the top two frames of Figure 4.1. During the habituation trials, some infants saw a ball rolling down the plane while speeding up (condition 1), while others saw the ball rolling up the plane while slowing down (condition 2). These events reflect the natural effects of gravity on balls rolling down and up hills. After habituation occurred (i.e., looking time decreased significantly after repeated trials), the infants encountered either a "natural test event" (middle frames) or an "unnatural test event" (lower frames). Notice that the natural test event differs from the habituation event in two ways: direction and speed. Hence, if an infant experienced downward motion and the ball speeding up during habituation, this same infant saw upward motion and the ball slowing down during the natural event. On the other hand, the unnatural event differs in just one way: direction. The infant experiencing downward motion and the ball speeding up during habituation would see the ball moving in a different direction during the unnatural event, but the speed would be the same (i.e.,

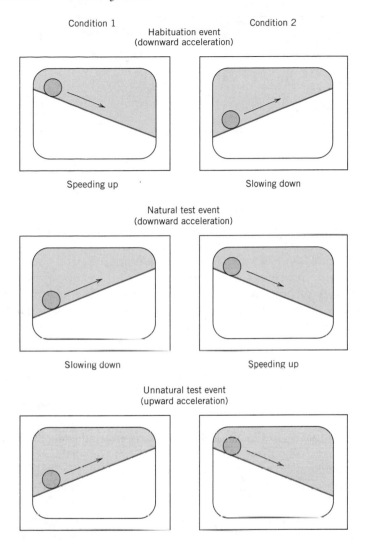

FIGURE 4.1 Stimulus items from Kim and Spelke's (1992) habituation study.

accelerating). In terms of how much one of the test events differed from the habituation event, it seems reasonable to expect the infants to perceive the natural event as novel (two factors changed) and to look longer at it than at the unnatural one (one factor changed). Indeed, the 5-month-old infants did just that. The 7-month-olds, however, looked at the *unnatural* event more, presumably because it violated what gravity dictates, whereas the natural event continued to be consistent with the law of gravity displayed in the habituation events. Hence, the younger infants noticed changes in the total number of stimulus dimensions, while the older ones noticed changes violating the law of gravity. From the measures of preferential looking, then, Kim and Spelke concluded that the infants, at least the 7-month-olds, possessed an understanding of the concept of gravity.

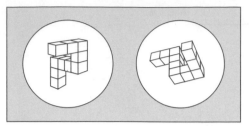 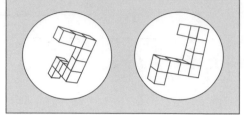

FIGURE 4.2 Stimulus items from Shepard and Metzler's (1971) mental rotation studies.

Case Study 2—Reaction Time

Do we use visual images as part of our cognitive processing? How could you find out? Of course, you could ask, but if someone says, "Yes, I'm using images," how could you be sure about what the person was doing? That is, you would be confronting the same problem that brought about the demise of introspection as a method—its lack of objectivity. You could, however, ask people to perform some task that would produce one type of behavior if images were being used and a different type of behavior if images weren't being used. That was the strategy behind a well-known series of studies by Shepard and his colleagues of what is termed "mental rotation."

Look at the two pairs of geometric objects in Figure 4.2. Could each right-hand object of each pair be the same as the left-hand object, but merely rotated to a different position? Or is it a different configuration altogether? How did you decide? Shepard and Metzler (1971) asked participants to make these decisions but went one step further and recorded *how long it took* for them to decide. Their rationale was that if participants solve these problems by taking the left-hand object and turning its image mentally until it overlaps the right-hand object, then the rotation process will take a certain amount of time. Furthermore, the more mental rotation required to reach the overlap point, the more time the process should take. I think you can see where this is going. Shepard and Metzler systematically varied the degree of rotation and found that as the angle increased, so did the amount of time needed to make the decision. From these measures of reaction time, then, they inferred that mental imagery was occurring.

Reaction time is one of psychology's oldest and most enduring methods, but the rationale for its use has changed over the years. For more on its origins and evolution as a tried-and-true method in experimental psychology, see Box 4.1.

Evaluating Measures

How can you tell if some measure of behavior is good? What accounts for the confidence with which psychologists use such things as preferential looking, reaction time, IQ tests, surveys of perceived social support, and so on? To answer the question requires a discussion of two key factors: reliability and validity.

Box 4.1

ORIGINS—Reaction Time: From Mental Chronometry to Mental Rotation

The use of reaction time in psychology can be traced to the work of F. C. Donders, a Dutch physiologist, who argued that times for mental events could be determined by calculating the differences between the reaction times for different kinds of tasks (Boring, 1950). His idea ushered in a flood of research on what became known as "mental chronometry." Researchers would measure the time for a simple reaction (SRT): a single response made as quickly as possible after perceiving a single stimulus, a red light for instance. The task could then be complicated by displaying one of two stimuli and telling the person to respond to only one of them. This was called discrimination reaction time (DRT) because the person first had to discriminate between the two stimuli, such as a red and a green light, and then respond. DRT includes SRT plus the mental event of "discrimination," so subtracting SRT from DRT was believed to produce the time for the mental event of discrimination:

$$DRT = SRT + discrimination$$
$$\therefore discrimination = DRT - SRT$$

The procedure could be elaborated even more, with additional mental events subtracted out, and it generated a great deal of excitement at the end of the 19th century because psychology was trying to establish itself as a science, and what could be more scientific than to have mental events measured to the fraction of a second? The procedure was especially popular in Wundt's laboratory at Leipzig and was quickly imported to the United States, as you can see from Figure 4.3, which shows a reaction time experiment in progress at Clark University in the early 1890s.

Unfortunately, it soon became apparent that serious problems existed with the procedure. In particular, some reaction times were faster than predicted from the complication logic, others slower. Oswald Külpe, one of Wundt's students, pointed out the fatal flaw—mental events don't combine in a simple additive fashion to form more complicated events. Rather, a complex mental event has a quality all its own that is more than the sum of simpler events.

Although Külpe's arguments effectively ended mental chronometry, and reaction time as a method declined in use during the heyday of behaviorism (roughly 1930–1950), it has subsequently enjoyed a resurgence in several areas of cognitive psychology. The idea is no longer to measure the precise times of mental events but to test predictions from cognitive theories. The mental rotation studies are a good example. Shepard predicted that if mental rotation occurs in the minds of participants, then this mental activity should take a certain amount of time (Shepard & Metzler, 1971). Larger degrees of rotation should take greater amounts of time, and as you've seen, this indeed occurred.

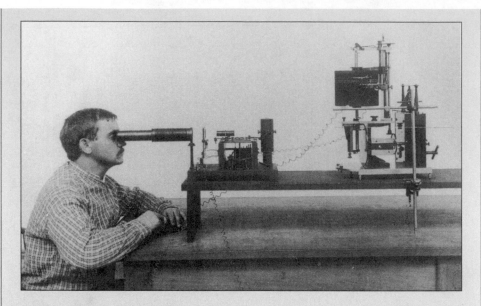

FIGURE 4.3 Reaction time study in progress at Clark University, circa 1892. The response will be made by releasing a telegraph key with the right hand as quickly as possible when the stimulus is seen through the tube.

Reliability

In general, a measure of behavior is said to be **reliable** if its results are repeatable when the behaviors are remeasured. Reaction time is a good example; its high reliability is one reason for its popularity over the years. Someone responding to a red light in .18 second on one trial will almost certainly respond with just about the same speed on other trials, and practically all of the trials will be in the general vicinity of .18 second. Similarly, scores on the Graduate Record Exam (GRE) are reasonably reliable. Someone with a combined score of 850 on the GRE general test would probably score close to that a second time and would be very unlikely to reach a score like 1350.

From these two examples, you can see why reliability is essential in any measure. Without it, there is no way of determining what a score on a particular measure *means*. Presumably, in reaction time you're trying to determine how fast someone is. If the reaction times vary wildly, there is no way to answer the question. Likewise, if GRE scores bounced 400 or 500 points from one testing session to another, the numbers would be of no use whatsoever to graduate schools because they would have no way of estimating the student's real score.

A behavioral measure's reliability is a function of the amount of **measurement error** present. If there is a great deal of error, reliability is low, and vice versa. No behavioral measure is perfectly reliable, so some degree of measurement error occurs with all measurement. That is, every measure is some combination of a hypothetical true score plus some measurement error. Ideally, measurement error is low enough so that the observed score is close to the true score.

The reaction time procedure provides a good illustration of how measurement error works and how it affects reliability. As in the previous example, suppose a person takes .18 second on a reaction time trial. Is this the true measure of speed? Probably not, a conclusion easily reached when you notice that for the following five trials this same person's reaction times are:

.16 sec .15 sec .19 sec .17 sec .19 sec

These scores vary because some degree of measurement error contributes to each trial. This error is caused by several possible factors, some of which operate randomly from trial to trial. For example, on a particular trial the person might respond faster than the true score by guessing that the stimulus was about to be presented or slower because of a momentary lapse of attention. Also, some systematic amount of error could occur if, for example, the experimenter signaled the participants to get ready just before turning on the stimulus and the amount of time between the ready signal and the stimulus was constant. Then the participants could learn to anticipate the stimulus and produce reaction times that would be systematically faster than true ones.

Despite the presence of a small degree of measurement error, the above scores do cluster together pretty well, and the reaction times certainly would be judged more reliable than if the scores following the .18 second one were these:

.11 sec .25 sec .19 sec .09 sec .31 sec

With scores ranging from less than a tenth of a second to nearly a third of a second, it is difficult to say what the person's real speed is.

When scores are reliable, then, the researcher can assign some meaning to their magnitude. Reliability also allows the researcher to make more meaningful comparisons with other sets of scores. For example, comparing the first set of scores (.16, .15, etc.) with the ones below reveals a clear difference in basic speed of response:

.23 sec .26 sec .21 sec .22 sec .24 sec

It is probably fair to say that this second person is a bit slower than the person described earlier.

There are ways of calculating reliability, but this is seldom done in experimental research. Rather, confidence in the reliability of a measure develops over time, a benefit of the replication process. For example, the habituation and reaction time procedures have been used often enough and yielded consistent enough results for researchers to be highly confident about their reliability.

Reliability *is* assessed more formally in research that evaluates the adequacy of any type of psychological test. These are instruments designed to measure such constructs as personality factors, abilities (e.g., IQ), and attitudes. They are usually paper-and-pencil tests in which a person responds to questions or statements of some kind. In the study mentioned earlier on bulimia, participants filled out several of these measures, including one called the Perceived Support Scale. Analyses designed to establish the reliability of this kind of test require the use of correlational procedures.

For example, the test could be given on two occasions and the similarity of the two sets of results could be determined. Unless dramatic changes are taking place in the participant's life, the scores on two measurements with the Perceived Support Scale should be similar. The degree of similarity is expressed in terms of a correlation (high similarity = strong correlation). The specifics of this kind of analysis, especially as it relates to the whole area of psychological testing, will be explained more fully in Chapter 9.

Validity

A behavioral measure is said to be **valid** if it measures what it has been designed to measure. A measure of perceived social support should truly measure the amount of support that people believe they have and should not measure some different construct. A test of intelligence should truly measure intelligence and not something else.

Sometimes a measure is assumed to have a degree of validity simply because it makes sense. As a measure of intelligence, a test with problems requiring some thinking makes more sense than a test in which people have to ride a bicycle accurately between two white lines. That is, problem solving and reasoning have more face validity as measures of intelligence than does bike riding (which has face validity as a measure of balance). Of course, face validity is not sufficient by itself; a test can seem to make sense and still not be a valid test. Most of the surveys found in popular magazines fit into this category.

A more critical test of validity is called **criterion validity**, which concerns whether the measure (a) can accurately forecast some future behavior or (b) is meaningfully related to some other measure of behavior. For a test to be useful as an IQ test, for example, it should (a) do a reasonably good job of predicting how well a child will do in school and (b) produce results similar to those produced by other known measures of intelligent behavior. It is called "criterion" validity because the measure in question is related to some outcome or criterion. In the examples just used, the criterion variables would be (a) future grades in school and (b) scores on an already established test for intelligence. As with reliability estimates, criterion validity research is correlational in nature and occurs primarily in research on psychological testing. You'll see it again in Chapter 9.

Another type of validity, **construct validity**, is especially relevant to experimental research. It concerns two issues at the same time: whether the construct being measured by a particular instrument is a valid construct and whether the particular instrument is the best one for measuring it. Construct validity is closely tied to the nature of theory, the deduction of research hypotheses from theory, and the evaluation of theories following the outcomes of research. As such, construct validity is never established or destroyed with a single study and is never proven for the same reason that theories are never proven. Rather, confidence in construct validity accumulates gradually and inductively as research produces supportive results.

As we've seen, psychology is loaded with constructs that cannot be observed directly—things like hunger, anxiety, intelligence, depression, perceived social support, attention span, and so on. Because these constructs are hypothetical, their presence can only be inferred from the measures designed for them. Research measuring a construct in a particular way that yields predictable research outcomes serves to validate both the construct itself and the tool used to measure it.

Case Study 3—Construct Validity

As a concrete example of how construct validity builds, consider a series of studies by the personality psychologist Walter Mischel and his colleagues. Mischel was interested in the problem of impatience in children. That is, children sometimes want things right now; they have difficulty waiting. Mischel devised a construct he called "delay of gratification" and set about trying to develop an adequate measure of it. The research program he developed showed both that delay of gratification is valid as a construct that fits into a general cognitive–social learning theory of personality and that the measures he developed were good ones.

One simple measure devised by Mischel was to ask children to choose between a small reward that was available immediately and a larger reward that would only be given to them after a delay. Mischel reasoned that if the inability to delay gratification was characteristic of young children, then older children should be more willing to wait for the larger reward than younger ones. This led to the obvious study (cited in Mischel, 1981) in which children completed a brief task and then were told:

> I would like to give each of you a piece of candy, but I don't have enough of these (indicating the larger, more preferred reinforcement) with me today. So you can either get this one (indicating the smaller, less preferred reinforcement) right now, today, or, if you want to, you can wait for this one (indicating), which I will bring back next Wednesday [one week later]. (Mischel, 1981, pp. 164–165)

The results confirmed Mischel's prediction: the immediate (but small) reward was chosen by 81% of 7-year-olds, 48% of 8-year-olds, and 20% of 9-year-olds.

Of course, this one study was not sufficient to establish delay of gratification as a valid construct; nor did it establish Mischel's measure as a valid tool. So he continued developing a series of studies, exploring the ways in which the evolving construct related to other already established constructs. For instance, he found that children willing to delay gratification were also more emotionally mature, more achievement oriented, less likely to be delinquent, and more likely to be socially responsible (Mischel, 1981). Thus, delay of gratification became accepted as a valid construct because of the accumulated research that came out as expected.

Reliability and Validity

For a measure to be of any value in psychological research, it must have some degree of both reliability and validity. Reliability is important because it enables one to have some confidence that the measure taken is close to the true measure. Validity is important because it tells you if the measure actually measures what you hope it does. Note that validity assumes reliability, but the converse is not true. Measures can be reliable but not valid; valid measures must be reliable, however.

A simple example illustrates this. In Chapter 1 you learned something about 19th-century phrenology, a popular theory claiming that you could measure a person's "faculties" by examining skull contour. From the present discussion of reliability, you should recognize that phrenological measures of the skull were indeed highly reliable—the distance between a point 2 inches above your left ear and 2 inches above your right ear will not change very much if measured on two separate occasions. However, to say that the measure is an indication of the faculty of "destructiveness" is quite another matter. We know the skull contour measurement is not a valid measure of destructiveness because it doesn't make much sense to us today (face validity), fails to predict aggressive behavior (criterion validity), and does not fit well with other research on constructs relating to destructiveness, such as impulsiveness, or with research on brain function (construct validity).

The issues of reliability and validity have ethical implications, especially when measures are used to make decisions about people's lives. Students are accepted or not accepted into college or graduate school, job applicants are hired or not hired, and people are given a psychiatric diagnosis and treatment, all on the basis of measurements of ability or behavior. If you were applying for a job and your score on some test was to be the determining factor, you would be justifiably upset to learn that the test was neither very reliable nor valid.

One final point. The concept of validity has been discussed in the context of measurement here. As you will see in the next chapter, however, measures of psychological constructs are not the only things judged to be valid or not. Validity also extends more broadly to the entire research project being undertaken. Strictly in the context of measurement, validity concerns whether the tool being used measures what it is supposed to measure. In the broader realm of the entire research project, validity concerns whether the experiment has been properly conducted and whether the hypothesis in question has been properly tested.

Scales of Measurement

Whenever a behavior is measured, numbers are assigned to it in some fashion. We say that someone responded in 3.5 seconds, scored 120 on an IQ test, or finished third best in a maze test. We also talk of placing X number of individuals into categories as a consequence of what they do or of some characteristic they possess. These examples illustrate four different ways of assigning numbers to events, that is, four different **measurement scales.** A clear understanding of these scales is an important prelude to a discussion of statistics because the type of measurement scale being used dictates the appropriate statistical analyses to be completed. Confusion over measurement scales is also behind the problem experienced by Dilbert in Figure 4.4.

Nominal Scales

Sometimes the number we assign to events serves only to classify them into one group or another. When this happens, we are using what is called a **nominal scale** of measurement. In this case, the numbers assigned mean no more than a category label (e.g., 15 males, 25 females). Studies using these scales typically assign people to categories and count the number of people falling into each category. We use nominal scales when we ask empirical questions like these:

FIGURE 4.4 Problems with scales of measurement.

✓ Comparing male and female joggers, who is more likely to run during the morning and who is more likely to run in the evening?

✓ If you divide mentally disturbed people into those who are shy and those who are outgoing, will introverts be more likely to be suffering from anxiety disorders than extroverts?

✓ If you divide people into those expecting to experience severe shock and those not expecting it, will it affect their "affiliative" tendency?

This last example was the empirical question asked in a well-known experiment in social psychology by Stanley Schachter (1959). He told half of the female participants that the experiment they were about to begin would measure their physiological reactions to intense electrical shock; the remaining women were told the shocks would be very mild and feel like a tickling sensation. After informing the women in each group about the forthcoming shock, Schachter told them to wait for 10 minutes while the equipment was set up and asked whether they preferred to wait by themselves or with others (no preference was a third option). How they answered this question was Schachter's real interest, and the study ended after the participants expressed their preference.

Schachter was investigating the effects of anxiety on a construct called "affiliation" (the tendency to want to be with others). The results? Those expecting severe shock preferred to wait with others, while those expecting mild shock generally showed no preference. The study illustrates the use of a nominal scale because Schachter organized the data by counting the number of people who fell into six different categories, depending on (a) what kind of shock they were expecting and (b) how they responded to the key question. The number of people (called a "frequency count") in each of these categories can be seen in Table 4.2. The data are also converted into percentages, a common procedure when using nominal data.

Ordinal Scales

Ordinal scales of measurement are basically sets of rankings. College transcripts, for example, usually list a student's general class rank: 1st, 2nd, 3rd, 50th, and so on. From these rankings you can infer that one student had higher grades than another.

TABLE 4.2   *Using Nominal Scales: Schachter's Study of Affiliation*

	Number of People Expressing These Preferences		
	Wait Alone	**Wait with Others**	**Don't Care**
Those expecting severe shock	3 (9%)	20 (63%)	9 (23%)
Those expecting mild shock	2 (7%)	10 (33%)	18 (60%)

Source: Schachter (1959).

Relative position is the only thing you know, however, Ed, Fred, and Ted would be ranked 1, 2, and 3 in each of the following cases, even though Ed is clearly superior to Fred and Ted only in the second case:

Case 1	Case 2
Ed's GPA = 4.0	Ed's GPA = 4.0
Fred's GPA = 3.9	Fred's GPA = 3.6
Ted's GPA = 3.8	Ted's GPA = 3.5

Studies using ordinal scales ask questions like these:

✓ If a child ranks five toys and is given the one ranked third, will the ranking for that toy go up or down after the child has played with it for a week?

✓ Do students rank textbook authors in the sciences and in the humanities differently when they are told the gender of the writers?

✓ How do young and old people rank 10 movies that vary in the levels of sex and aggression found in them?

A good example of the use of an ordinal scale is a study by Korn, Davis, and Davis (1991). Historians of psychology and department chairpersons were asked to list, in rank order from 1 to 10, the psychologists they considered to be most important. Two sets of rankings were solicited: one for the top 10 of "all time" and the second for a "contemporary" top 10. The returns were then summarized to yield a picture of eminence in psychology. Who topped the chart? B. F. Skinner was considered the most eminent contemporary psychologist by both historians and chairpersons. Chairpersons also ranked Skinner first for all time; historians, who tended to select psychologists from earlier periods for their all time list, dropped Skinner to eighth place and put Wundt on top.

Interval Scales

Most research in psychology uses interval or ratio scales of measurement. Interval scales extend the idea of rank order to include the concept of equal intervals between the events that are ordered. Research using psychological tests of personality, attitude, and ability are the most common examples of studies usually considered to involve interval scales. Scores on intelligence tests, for example, are usually assumed to be arranged this way. Someone with an IQ of 120 is believed to be more intelligent (granting, for the sake of illustration, that IQ measures intelligence in some way) than someone else with an IQ of 110. Furthermore—and this is the defining feature of an interval scale—the difference in intelligence between people with IQs of 120 and 110 is assumed to be the same as the difference between people with IQs of 110 and 100. In other words, each single point of increase in an IQ score is believed to represent the same amount of increase in intelligence—the intervals are equal. Note the word "assumed," however; some psychologists prefer to consider IQ (and scores on most personality tests as well) to be an example of an ordinal scale, arguing that it is difficult, if not impossible, to be sure about the equal-interval assumption in this case. Most accept the inclusion of IQ as an example of an interval scale, though, partly for a practical reason: psychologists prefer to use interval and ratio scales generally because data on those scales allow more sophisticated statistical analyses.

The brief description earlier of the study of bulimia used several measures (e.g., Perceived Social Support Scale) that illustrate interval scales. Also, take a look at Box 4.2, which describes a classic set of studies in which interval scales were used in an attempt to show that our body type influences the kind of person we are.

Box 4.2

CLASSIC STUDIES—Measuring Somatotypes: When 7-1-1 Met 1-1-7

You have already learned that phrenologists speculated about the relationship between some physical characteristic (skull contour) and what a person was like. Phrenology seems almost quaint to us today, but the idea of a relationship between physical characteristics and personality has been an enduring one. A more systematic attempt to explore the connection was made by William Sheldon (1940, 1942).

What is striking about Sheldon's work is the attempt to define physique in terms of a precise scale of measurement. After examining about 4,000 photos of naked college men, he and his research team developed a system of classifying physique in terms of three 7-point interval scales. Each scale reflected the degree to which the men displayed three ideal body types: endomorphy (fat), mesomorphy (muscular), and ectomorphy (thin). Everyone was assumed to have some degree of each of the physiques, with one of them usually predominant. Thus, an extremely round person might be labeled a 7-1-1, while a very thin person would be a 1-1-7, and Arnold Schwarzenegger would be a 1-7-1. A 4-4-4 would be a perfectly balanced person. The set of numbers applied to a particular man was called his "somatotype."

After measuring somatotypes, Sheldon set out to measure personality types. These he believed also fell into three categories that could be measured on 7-point interval scales that would summarize the results of several personality tests. He labeled the categories "viscerotonia," "somatotonia," and "cerebrotonia." Generally, viscerotonics were sociable, fun-loving, slow-moving, even-tempered, and very interested in food. Somatotonics were aggressive, self-centered, and risk-taking, and cerebrotonics were shy and secretive, preferred to be alone, and tended to pursue intellectual tasks.

Sheldon's final step was to see if somatotypes related to personality types. You will not be surprised to learn that these pairs occurred together most often:

endomorph—viscerotonia

mesomorph—somatotonia

ectomorph—cerebrotonics

Sheldon believed that body type caused the individual to develop a certain personality, but critics pointed out that the relationships were not that strong and could be accounted for in several ways. Being an endomorph could cause someone to like food, but couldn't a strong liking for food create an endomorph?

The issues surrounding Sheldon's work were complex, and his theory has been generally discredited, but for our purposes, the study is a classic example of trying to quantify human character and relate it to what the person looks like on some measurable scale of physique, in this case an interval scale. Incidentally, you might have noticed the absence of gender-neutral language in this description of Sheldon's work, with personal pronouns like "his" and "him" being used. This is because Sheldon studied only males. Why? Recall that his procedure involved examining photographs of 4,000 naked men. Apparently he gave some thought to replicating the study with women but demurred because of "conventional sanctions against the necessary photographing of nude female [college students]" (Bavelas, 1978). You'll be reading about "convenience" samples in this chapter; some samples are more convenient than others.

It is important to note that with interval scales, a score of zero is simply another point on the scale — it does not mean an absence of the quantity being measured. The standard example is temperature. Zero degrees does not mean an absence of temperature; it is simply a point on the scale that means "put your sweater on." Likewise, if there is a test of shyness with scores ranging from 0 to 20, a score of 0 is simply the lowest point on the scale and does not imply the complete absence of shyness.

Ratio Scales

In a **ratio scale**, the concepts of order and equal interval are carried over from ordinal and interval scales, but in addition, the ratio scale has a *true zero point*. That is, for ratio scores, a score of zero means the complete absence of the attribute being measured. For instance, an error score of zero, attained by a rat running a maze, means the absence of any wrong turns. Ratio scales are typically found in studies using physical measures like height, weight, and time. The case studies earlier in this chapter on habituation and reaction time both illustrate the use of a ratio scale.

Who to Measure—Sampling

In addition to deciding which measures to use when doing research in psychology, the investigator must decide who will be asked to participate and have their behaviors measured. Two general approaches are taken: probability sampling and nonprobability sampling.

Probability Sampling

This strategy is used whenever the goal is to learn something specific about an identifiable group of individuals. As a group, those individuals are called a **population;** any subgroup of them is called a **sample.** Sometimes it is possible to study all members of a population. For example, if you wanted to learn the attitudes of all the people in your experimental psychology class about the issue of animal experimentation, and did not wish to generalize beyond that class, you could survey everyone in the class. In this case, the size of the population would be the size of your class. As you might guess, however, the population of interest to a researcher is usually much too large for every member in it to be tested. Hence, a subset of that population, a sample, must be selected.

Even though the entire population might not be tested in a study, the researcher wishes to draw conclusions about this broader group, not just about the sample. Thus, it is important for the sample to reflect the attributes of the population as a whole. When this happens, the sample is said to be **representative;** if it doesn't happen, the sample is said to be **biased** in some fashion. If you want to investigate student perceptions of college life, it would be a serious mistake to select people from a list that included only those living in college residence halls. Because off-campus residents and commuter students might have very different attitudes from on-campus residents, the results of your survey would be biased in favor of the latter (you'll be learning more about survey research procedures in Chapter 12).

Perhaps the most famous historical example of biased sampling occurred during political polling in the presidential election of 1936. As it had been doing with reasonable success for several previous elections, the magazine *Literary Digest* tried to predict the election outcome by sending out about 10 million simulated ballots to subscribers, to others selected from a sample of phone books from around the country, and to others from motor vehicle registration information (Sprinthall, 2000). Close to 25% (almost 2.5 million) of the ballots were returned to the magazine; of these respondents, 57% preferred the Republican candidate, Alf Landon, and 40% chose the incumbent president, Franklin Roosevelt. In the actual election, Roosevelt won in a landslide with more than 60% of the vote. Can you guess why the sample was biased?

Although the editors of *Literary Digest* were aware that their own subscribers tended to be upper middle class and Republican, they thought they were broadening the sample and making it more representative by adding people chosen from phone books and car registration data. In fact, they were simply selecting more Republicans. In the midst of the Great Depression, practically the only people who could afford phones and cars were members of the upper middle and upper classes, who were more likely to be Republicans than Democrats. So in the survey the magazine actually was asking Republicans how they were going to cast their votes.

You might have noticed another flaw in the *Literary Digest* survey. A large number of ballots were returned, and the magazine was quite confident in its prediction of a Landon victory because the data reflected the views of a substantial number of people—about 2.5 million. Note, however, that not only does the total represent only one-fourth of the ballots originally sent out, but the returns were from those who *chose* to send them back. So those responding to the survey tended to be not just Republicans, but Republicans who wished to make their views known (in light of which the 57% preferring Landon actually looks rather small, don't you think?).

This **self-selection, problem** is common in surveys that appear in popular magazines and in requests by people like Ann Landers for readers to let her know about some issue. A survey will appear; then, a month or so later, the results of those who returned the survey will be reported, usually in a way implying that the results are valid. The person reporting the survey will try to impress you with the total number of returns rather than the representativeness of the sample. An example of this ploy is a report on female sexuality (Hite, 1987) that claimed, among other things, that more than 90% of married women felt emotionally abused in their relationships. When criticized because the survey was sent only to a select group of women's organizations and that only 4.5% of 100,000 people returned the survey, the author simply pointed out that 4,500 people were enough for her (just as 2.5 million people were enough for *Literary Digest*).

As a scientific thinker, you should be very skeptical about claims made on the basis of these kinds of sampling procedures. The lesson, of course, is that if you want to make a statement about a specific population with some accuracy, you must use a sample that represents that population and you must select the sample directly, not rely simply on who decides to return the survey.

Random Sampling

The most fundamental type of probability sampling is to take a **simple random sample.** In essence, all this means is that each member of the population has an equal chance of being selected as a member of the sample. To select a random sample of 100 students from your school, for instance, you could place all their names in a large hat and pick out 100. In actual practice, the procedure is a bit more sophisticated than this, however, usually involving a random number table such as the one found in Appendix D. To learn the essence of the procedure, work through the example in Table 4.3, which shows you how to use random numbers to select a sample of 5 individuals from a population of 20.

Simple random sampling is often an effective, practical way to create a representative sample. It is sometimes the method of choice for ethical reasons as well. In situations in which only a small group can receive some benefit or must incur some cost and there is no other reasonable basis for decision making, random sampling is the fairest method to use. A famous example occurred in 1969 in the midst of the Vietnam War, when a draft lottery system was established. For obvious reasons of fairness, each of the 365 days of the year was to have an equal probability of being selected first, second, third, and so on. Unfortunately, the actual procedure had some

TABLE 4.3 *Selecting a Random Sample Using a Table of Random Numbers*

Task: Select a random sample of 5 individuals from a population of 20 individuals.

Step 1.   Assign numbers from 01 to 20 to the individuals who make up your population.

Step 2.   Go to a table of random numbers. Here's a portion of one:

```
2  2  1  7  6  8  6  5  8  4  6  8  9  5
1  9  3  6  1  7  5  9  4  6  1  3  7  9
1  6  7  7  2  3  0  2  7  7  0  9  6  1
7  8  0  3  7  6  7  1  6  1  2  0  4  4
0  3  2  8  1  2  2  6  0  8  7  3  3  7
```

Step 3.   Pick a spot to begin searching through the table. This can be anywhere; just be sure that you don't begin any two searches in the same place. Let's suppose you begin with the top number in the third column. It's a 1. You will need to consider pairs of numbers together because the population consists of people numbered 01 through 20. Hence you must use the 1 and the 7 next to it as your starting point.

Step 4.   Your search for a sample of five begins with number 17, which falls within the range of 01 to 20. The first person in your sample, therefore, is person 17.

Step 5.   Continue down the double column until you've found five individuals with numbers between 01 and 20. Here's the table again, with the spacing between columns arranged to make it easier to detect pairs of numbers. The five selected numbers are underlined, the section of the table that needed to be searched is boldfaced, and arrows indicate the direction of search.

```
2  2  1  7  6  8  6  5  8  4  6  8  9  5
1  9  3  6  1  7  5  9  4  6  1  3  7  9
1  6  7  7  2  3  0  2  7  7  0  9  6  1
7  8  0  3  7  6  7  1  6  1  2  0  4  4
0  3  2  8  1  2  2  6  0  8  7  3  3  7
```

Thus the sample consists of population members numbered 17, 3, 12, 2, and 8. Notice that numbers larger than 20 (e.g., 36) are bypassed and if a number repeats itself (17), it is not selected twice.

bias (Kolata, 1986). Capsules, one for every day of the year, were placed in a large drum one month at a time. The January capsules went in first, then the February ones, and so on. The drum was rotated to mix the capsules, but apparently this did not succeed completely because when the dates were drawn, those capsules entering the drum last tended to be the first to be picked. This was not a good time to have a birthday in December.

There are two problems with simple random sampling. First, there may be some systematic features of the population that you might like to have reflected in your sample. Second, the procedure may be impractical if the population is extremely large. How could you get a list of everyone in the United States in order to select a simple random sample of Americans? The first problem is solved by using stratified sampling; cluster sampling solves the second difficulty.

Stratified Sampling

Suppose you wanted to measure the attitudes about abortion on your campus and the school's population is 5,000, of whom 4,000 are women. You decide to sample 100 students. If you take a simple random sample, there are probably going to be more women than men in your sample, but the proportions in the sample won't match those in the population precisely. Your goal is to make the sample truly representative of the population, and on a question like abortion, there might be important differences of opinion between males and females. Therefore, if your sample happens to be overrepresented with males, it might not truly portray campus attitudes. In a situation like this, it would be a good idea to decide ahead of time that if 80% of the population is female, then exactly 80% of the sample will also be female. That is, just as the population has these two layers (or "strata"), so should the sample.

In a **stratified sample,** then, the *proportions* of important subgroups in the population are represented precisely in the sample. In the above example, 80 females would be randomly sampled from the list of females, and 20 males would be selected from the list of males.

Note that some judgment is required here: the researcher has to decide just how many layers to use. In the case of the abortion survey, males and females were sampled in proportion to their overall numbers. Should each of the four undergraduate classes be proportionately represented also? What about Protestants and Catholics? What about left- and right-handers? Obviously, the researcher has to draw the line somewhere. Some characteristics (religion) are more critical than others (handedness) in deciding how to stratify the sample. Based on what has occurred in prior research or the goals of the current study, it's up to the researcher to use some good sense.

Cluster Sampling

Stratified sampling is an effective procedure, but it still doesn't solve the problem of trying to sample from a huge population, when it is often impossible to acquire a complete list of individuals in the population. **Cluster sampling,** a procedure frequently used by national polling organizations, solves the problem. With this approach the researcher randomly selects a cluster of people all having some feature in common. A campus survey at a large university might be done this way. If a researcher wanted a cross-section of students and stratified sampling was not feasible, an alternative would be to get a list of required "core" classes. Each class would be a cluster and would include students from a variety of majors. If 40 core classes were being offered, the researcher might randomly select 10 of them and then administer the survey to all students in each of the selected classes.

If the selected clusters are too large, the researcher can sample a smaller cluster within the larger one. Suppose you wanted to find out how students liked living in the high-rise dorms on your campus, which you've defined operationally as any dorm with eight floors or more. Suppose 15 of these buildings exist on your campus, housing a total of 6,000 students. Using cluster sampling, you could first select six of the buildings (each building = a cluster), and then, for each building, randomly select three floors and sample all of the residents (about 40 per floor, let's say) of the selected floors in the selected dorms. This would give you an overall sample size of 720 (40 × 3 × 6). Notice that you also could combine some elements of stratified sampling here. If 10 of the dorms house women and men live in the remaining 5, you might select your first cluster to reflect these proportions: 4 female dorms and 2 male dorms.

Nonprobability Sampling

From what you've just read, you might think that a failure to use probability sampling results in an inferior study. This is certainly the case if the goal of the project is to describe specific features of a defined population accurately by investigating just a segment of it. However, most research in experimental psychology is not like this. Rather, the goal is usually to study relationships between variables: using imagery improves memory; observing aggression leads to aggression; as the number of bystanders increases, helping behavior decreases; and so on. Of course, the hope is that the results of these studies will extend beyond the people participating in them, but the researcher assumes that if the relationship studied is a powerful one, it will occur for most individuals within a particular population, regardless of how they are chosen. Naturally, whether this assumption turns out to be true depends on the normal processes of replication and extension discussed in Chapter 3. So in a study on the capacity limits of short-term memory in adults, it is not necessary to select a random sample: virtually any group of reasonably fluent adults will do.

Convenience Sampling

This is the most frequent (and, yes, the most convenient) type of nonprobability sampling. In a **convenience sample,** the researcher simply requests volunteers from a group of available people who meet the general requirements of the study. Most typically they are college freshmen and sophomores from the "subject pool"—general psychology students being asked to participate in a study or two: you might have been in that boat yourself once. (For more on the ethics of subject pools, see Box 5.2.)

Sometimes the convenience sampling approach is taken but a specific type of person is recruited for the study (this is sometimes called "purposive" sampling). For instance, when Stanley Milgram first recruited participants for his obedience studies, he placed ads in the local newspaper asking for volunteers. He deliberately (i.e., purposively) avoided using college students because he was concerned that they might be "too homogeneous a group … [he] wanted a wide range of individuals drawn from a broad spectrum of class backgrounds" (Milgram, 1974, p. 14). He could have tried a more sophisticated stratified or cluster sampling approach, but even if he had, there was no guarantee that the people he selected would be willing to come into the lab. Besides the fact that not all research needs a sample that is precisely representative of a population, Milgram's procedure shows that nonprobability sampling is often chosen for practical reasons.

FIGURE 4.5   A common perception of statistics.

Statistical Analysis

The first sentence in a well-known self-help book called *The Road Less Traveled* (Peck, 1978) is "Life is difficult" (p. 15). This is a belief that seems to be shared by many students taking a course in statistics, who readily identify with the character in Figure 4.5. I won't try to convince you that doing statistics compares with lying on a Florida beach in February, but I hope you'll come to see that part of the excitement of doing research in psychology is completing an analysis of the data you've painstakingly collected and finding out whether or not something *actually* seemed to happen in the study. I've seen mature, responsible adults holding their breath while waiting for the results of a statistical analysis to appear, then being reduced to anguish or raised to ecstasy moments after looking at the magic numbers in front of them. So if you develop a passion for doing research in psychology, much of your emotion will be invested in dealing with the subtleties of statistical analysis.

My goal here is to introduce you to statistical thinking and to the kinds of statistical analysis that you'll encounter when doing research in psychology. Ideally, you have already taken a course in statistics. If not, you should take one as soon as possible, especially if you have any desire to go to graduate school in psychology. Believe it or not, when graduate schools list the courses that they especially look for in applicants to their programs, the statistics course is number 1, just ahead of research methods (refer back to the 1996 survey by Norcross, Hanych, & Terranova, described in Chapter 1, p. 4). I'll be covering some of the essentials of statistical analysis, but there is no substitute for a full course (or two).

You will find information about how to decide on the appropriate statistical analysis and how to actually carry out some of the more common procedures in Appendix C. You also will find some discussion of statistical topics popping up at regular intervals throughout the rest of the book for the simple reason that designing research in psychology cannot be separated from the analysis of that research. In this chapter, you will learn about the difference between descriptive and inferential statistics and about the logic of hypothesis testing.

Descriptive and Inferential Statistics

The most fundamental distinction between types of statistics is between those called "descriptive" and those referred to as "inferential." The difference parallels what you learned earlier about samples and populations. Simply put, **descriptive statistics** summarize the data collected from the sample of participants participating in your study, and **inferential statistics** allow you to draw conclusions about your data that can be applied to the broader population.

Descriptive Statistics

In essence, descriptive statistical procedures enable you to turn a large pile of numbers that cannot be comprehended at a glance into a very small set of numbers that can be more easily understood. Descriptive statistics include measures of central tendency, variability, and association, presented both numerically and visually (e.g., in graphs). In this chapter, we'll consider the more common procedures for measuring central tendency and variability. Measures of association (coefficients of correlation) will be covered in Chapter 9.

To illustrate measures of central tendency and variability, consider some sample data from a hypothetical memory study in which 20 people study and then try to recall a list of 25 words. Each number in the data set below represents the number of words recalled by each of the 20 participants.

16	18	19	19
17	19	15	21
14	16	15	17
17	20	17	15
18	17	18	18

You can easily see that communicating the results of this study requires something more than just showing someone this pile of 20 numbers. Instead, you could try to identify a *typical* score or what is called a "measure of central tendency." The most common measure of central tendency used by research psychologists is the *mean,* or average, which is found simply by adding the scores together and dividing by the total number of scores. Thus:

$$\bar{X} = \frac{\Sigma X}{n}$$

where

$$\bar{X} = \text{the mean (pronunced "ex-bar")}$$
$$\Sigma X = \text{the sum of the individual scores}$$
$$n = \text{the number of scores in the sample}$$

For the memory data:

$$\bar{X} = \frac{\Sigma X}{n} = (16 + 17 + 14 + \ldots 18)/20 = 346/20 = 17.30$$

Two other measures of central tendency are the median and the mode. The **median** is the score in the exact middle of a set of scores. Half of the scores will be higher and half will be lower than the median. To determine the median by hand, the first step is to arrange the scores in sequence, from the lowest to the highest score. For the memory data, this produces:

14 15 15 15 16 16 17 17 17 17 17 18 18 18 18 19 19 19 20 21

⇑

The next step is to determine the **median location,** the place in the sequence of scores where the median will lie (Howell, 1997). It is determined by the formula:

$$\text{median location} = \frac{n + 1}{2}$$

For the memory data, the median location is $(20 + 1)/2 = 10.5$, which means that it falls midway (.5) between the 10th and the 11th number in the sequence. Counting from left to right, you can see that the 10th number is a 17 and the 11th number is also a 17 (I've marked this point in the sequence above with an ⇑). The median is an average of the two numbers on either side of the median location, 17 in this case. It is the exact middle of the set of scores—there are 10 scores on either side of it.

The median is sometimes used when a set of scores includes one or two that are very different from the rest; in this situation, the mean gives a distorted view of the typical score. For instance, suppose the IQ scores of the five teachers in your psychology department were 93, 81, 81, 95, and 200 (the last probably that of the person teaching the research methods course). The mean IQ score, which happens to be 110 (you should check this), gives a false impression that the psychology faculty as a whole is well above average. The median gives a better estimate of a typical IQ in this case. Thus, the median location is equal to $(5 + 1)/2 = 3$, and with the scores lined up in sequence, the third number is 93:

81   81   **93**   95   200

⇑

Clearly, the median IQ of 93 is a much better indication of the typical intellectual capacity to be found in this hypothetical psychology department.

The **mode** is the score occurring most frequently in a set of scores. It is 81 in the above example. The mode for the hypothetical memory scores is the same as the median—17 occurs five times, more often than any of the other scores. Because there are no unusually high or low scores in the memory data set, the mean (17.3), median (17), and mode (17) are quite close to each other, and each gives a good idea of central tendency.

Measures of central tendency are obviously needed to summarize data. Less obvious but equally important, the amount of variability in any set of scores needs to be described. Suppose you are the pro at a local country club, ready to begin giving lessons to one group of five golfers at 8:00 and another group at 9:00. You measure their ability by determining their normal score for nine holes. Here's the data:

8:00 group:　50　52　58　46　54

9:00 group:　36　62　50　72　40

Notice that the mean is the same for both sets of golfers: 260/5 = 52 strokes. The pro will have plenty to say to each member of both groups. The second group, however, creates much more of a problem. The scores there go from 36 (quite good) to 72 (ouch!). In the 8:00 group, however, the scores are generally close to each other—all five are at about the same ability level. Clearly, before starting the lessons, the pro would like to know more than the mean score for the group.

The simplest and crudest measure of variability is the **range**—the difference between the high and low scores of a group. For memory data presented earlier, the range is 7 (21–14). For the golf lesson example, the 8:00 group has a range of 12 (58–46), while the range for the 9:00 class is a whopping 36 (72–36). The range provides a rough estimate of variability, but it doesn't tell you any more than the difference between the most extreme scores. A more comprehensive measure of variability, the one used most often when reporting summary data, is the standard deviation.

The **standard deviation** for a set of sample scores is a measure of the average amount by which the scores in the sample distribution deviate from the mean score. Two methods for calculating the size of a standard deviation are shown in Table 4.4. The first follows directly from the definition and gives you a better understanding of the meaning of a standard deviation; the second is a computational formula, easier to complete with a calculator. For the scores in the hypothetical memory study, one standard deviation is equal to 1.81 words. For the golf lesson example, the standard deviation for the 8:00 class is 4.47 strokes, while the one for the 9:00 group is 15.03 strokes.

A final measure of variability is the **variance**, which is the number calculated during the standard deviation calculation just prior to taking the square root (3.27 for the memory scores). This number is seldom reported when listing descriptive statistics because it represents the units of measurement squared (e.g., "words recalled squared"). It is, however, the central feature of perhaps the most common inferential procedure found in psychology—the "analysis of variance," described in Chapters 7 and 8 and detailed in Appendix C.

Measures of central tendency and variability are universal features of any description of data, but researchers also like to examine the entire set of scores in some useful way. Just looking at the set of data doesn't help, but there are other ways to organize the scores so that they present a visual image that is meaningful. One way to accomplish this is by creating what is called a **histogram**. This is a graph that shows the number of times each score occurs or, if there is a large number of scores, how often scores within a fixed range occur. The first step is to create a **frequency distribution,** a table that records the number of times that each score occurs. The frequency distribution of scores for the memory study looks like this:

TABLE 4.4 *Calculating Standard Deviations*

If you are using a statistics package like SPSS or SAS, standard deviations will be printed out as part of almost any analysis you do. Likewise, most calculators include some basic statistical functions, and the standard deviation will be one of them. Thus, you may avoid having to do the calculation. However, you may have a cheap calculator or a concerned professor (or both) who shares my belief that doing these things by hand provides a better grasp of their meaning. So here goes.

There are two ways to calculate a standard deviation. The first uses what is called a "deviation formula." Working through it gives you the best insight into the nature of a standard deviation, which by definition is an approximate measure of the average amount that each score deviates from the mean. Here's how to do it for the 20 memory scores:

Step 1.   Calculate the mean score:

$$\bar{X} = \Sigma X/n = \textbf{17.3}$$

Step 2.   Calculate deviation scores, square each one, and add them up. Each deviation score (small x) is found by substracting the mean from each individual score (big X). That is, $x = X - \bar{X}$. Squaring gets rid of the negative numbers.

X	$\bar{X}$	x	x^2
16	17.3	−1.3	1.69
17	17.3	−0.3	0.09
14	17.3	−3.3	10.89
...	...	...	...
18	17.3	−0.7	0.49
			$\Sigma x^2 = \textbf{62.20}$

Step 3.   Calculate the standard deviation (*SD*).

$$SD = \sqrt{\Sigma x^2/(n-1)}$$
$$= \sqrt{62.2/(20-1)}$$
$$= \sqrt{3.27}$$
$$= \textbf{1.81}$$

The deviation formula works fine but is a bit awkward for the calculator. A simpler method is to use what is called a computational formula, which is mathematically identical to the deviation formula. The formula is:

$$SD = \sqrt{\frac{\Sigma X^2 - \dfrac{(\Sigma X)^2}{n}}{n-1}}$$

and the calculation goes like this:

Step 1.   Calculate ΣX^2 and $(\Sigma X)^2$.

$$\Sigma X^2 = 16^2 + 17^2 + 14^2 + \ldots 18^2$$
$$= 256 + 289 + 196 + \ldots 324$$
$$= \textbf{6048}$$
$$(\Sigma X)^2 = (16 + 17 + 14 + \ldots 18)^2$$
$$= 346^2$$
$$= \textbf{119,716}$$

TABLE 4.4   *Calculating Standard Deviations* (continued)

Step 2.   Calculate $\Sigma X^2 - (\Sigma X)^2/n$
                                 $= 6048 - (119,716)/20$
                                 $= 6048 - 5985.80$
                                 $= \mathbf{62.2}$

Step 3.   Divide the result of step 2 by $(n - 1)$
                                 $= 62.2/19$
                                 $= \mathbf{3.27}$

Step 4.   To get the standard deviation, take the square root of the result of step 3:
                                 $SD = \sqrt{3.27}$
                                 $SD = \mathbf{1.81}$

score	frequency	frequency as asterisks
14	1	★
15	3	★★★
16	2	★★
17	5	★★★★★
18	4	★★★★
19	3	★★★
20	1	★
21	1	★

Plotting the histogram is easy once this table of frequencies has been created. Simply place the actual score values on the X-axis of a graph and the frequency of occurrence on the Y-axis; then place the bars appropriately. The result should look like Figure 4.6. Notice that taking the pattern of asterisks from the frequency distribution and rotating it 90° results in the equivalent of Figure 4.6.

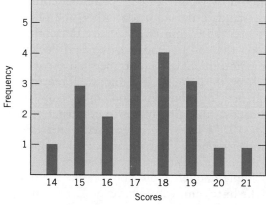

FIGURE 4.6   A histogram of scores on a memory test.

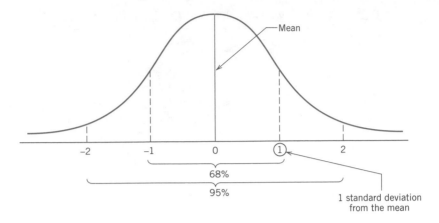

FIGURE 4.7   The normal curve.

Another thing to note about the histogram is that it bulges somewhat near the middle and is relatively flat at each end. This is a distribution of scores that roughly approximates what would happen if you created a histogram for the entire population, not just for the 20 people in the sample described here. Such a population distribution is the familiar bell-shaped curve known as the **normal curve** or normal distribution. You've seen it before; it looks like the one in Figure 4.7.

The normal curve is a frequency distribution just like one for the memory scores, except that instead of being an *actual* (or "empirical") distribution of sample scores, it is a *hypothetical* (or "theoretical") distribution of what all the scores in the population would be like if everyone was tested. The mean score, as well as the median and the mode, is in the exact middle of a normal distribution. A key point in statistical analysis is that if empirical distributions of scores resemble the normal distribution, then the mathematical properties of the normal distribution can be used to draw conclusions about the empirical distribution.

In the normal curve in Figure 4.7, notice that I have marked two standard deviations on either side of the mean. From the mathematical properties of the curve, it is possible to know that about two-thirds or 68% of all the scores in a population of scores fall within a single standard deviation on either side of the mean. Furthermore, about 95% of all scores fall within two standard deviations on either side of the mean. Obviously, scores that fall beyond two standard deviations are rare; they occur only 5% of the time. You might even describe such events as significant, as in "statistically significant." Keep this concept in mind; we'll return to it shortly.

In addition to frequency distributions and histograms, another common approach to displaying a data set meaningfully is to construct what is called a **stem and leaf display** (Tukey, 1977). They are often used when there is such a wide range of scores that a simple frequency distribution and histogram would be cumbersome. For example, if you gave 20 persons a test for shyness and the scores ranged from 10 to 70, a simple frequency distribution like the one for the memory data would be huge and the histogram would have an *X*-axis a mile long. The problem can be solved by grouping the data into intervals (10–19, 20–29, 30–39, etc.). Each bar on a histogram would reflect the number of scores within that interval. Note, however, that grouping the data in this manner means losing some of the information. If there were six people in the shyness example who scored between 30 and 39, all you would see would be the one bar representing a frequency of six, and you wouldn't know what each of those six people scored. With a stem and leaf display, you would be able to know this information. Here's how the stem and leaf display works. Suppose the shyness scores for the 20 people are as follows (I've bold-faced the six people in the range from 30–39):

49	22	**33**	46
36	64	**39**	41
41	68	43	61
36	47	**32**	49
43	67	**37**	43

In the stem and leaf display with two-digit numbers, the "leaf" will be the smaller digit (the ones digit) and the "stem" will be the larger digit (the tens digit). Thus, for the first number, 49, the stem is 4 and the leaf is 9. For a 36, the stem is 3 and the leaf is 6. To organize the stems and leafs into the display, the first step is to arrange the numbers in ascending order, as you would when looking for the median (30–39 again boldfaced). Hence:

22 **32 33 36 36 37 39** 41 41 43 43 43 46 47 49 49 61 64 67 68

Then list the stems in a left-hand column and the leaves corresponding to each stem in a right-hand column, like this:

Stems	Leaves
2	2
3	**236679**
4	113336799
5	
6	1478

If you rotate the stem and leaf display 90° and imagine filling in the leaf numbers to create bars, you would have the equivalent of a histogram for grouped data. Notice the advantage of a stem and leaf display over a normal histogram, however. For example, in the range 30–39, the histogram would show a single bar that reached to the level of six on the Y-axis. On the stem and leaf, however, you not only see the "height" of the scores in the range, you can also examine the actual scores. Stem and leaf displays also enable you to spot scores that seem to be relatively far removed from other scores. In the above example, the absence of any scores on the 50s is immediately evident, and the four scores in the 60s stand out as somewhat removed from the other data.

In articles describing research outcomes, descriptive statistics are reported three ways. First, if there are just a few numbers to report (e.g., means and standard deviations for the two groups in an experiment), they are sometimes worked into the narrative description of the results. Second, the means and standard deviations might be presented in a table, and third, they might be reported in the visual form of a graph. Descriptions of how to construct tables and graphs that conform to the guidelines of the APA can be found in the sample research report in Appendix A, and Chapters 7 and 8 include some information on graph making. Also, take a look at Box 4.3, which makes it clear that statistical analysis and graph making have an ethical dimension.

Box 4.3

ETHICS—Lying with Statistics

We've all been exposed to deceptive and unethical use of statistical information. Although politicians might be the worst offenders, with authors of aspirin commercials perhaps a close second, statistics are abused frequently enough that most people tend to be skeptical about them, and you often hear people say things like "Statistics don't really tell you anything useful—you can make them do anything you'd like." Is this really true?

Certainly there are decisions to be made about how to present data and what conclusions to draw from them. You can be reasonably confident that articles published in reputable journals, having gone through a tough peer review process, are reporting statistical analyses that lead to defensible conclusions. What you need to be careful about are the uses of statistics in the broader public arena or by people determined to convince you of the truth of their tenaciously held beliefs.

Being informed about the proper use of statistics will enable you to identify these questionable statistical practices. Some things to be careful about were first described in Darrell Huff's delightful *How to Lie with Statistics* (1954). It begins with a famous quote attributed to the British politician Benjamin Disraeli that sums up a common perception of statistics: "There are lies, damned lies, and statistics" (p. 2).

Here's an example of how to lie with statistics that relates specifically to the visual portrayal of data—graphs. Suppose you read about a study of reaction time comparing males and females that includes the following graph (Figure 4.8).

This is a type of graph that Huff called a "Gee Whiz" graph, for obvious reasons: when you first look at it, you find yourself saying, "Gee whiz, what a big difference!" The problem, however, is that the difference has been grossly exaggerated by fiddling with the vertical or *Y*-axis. You'll notice it is not labeled. If it were, the labels might look like the left-hand graph in Figure 4.9. More reasonable labeling of the *Y*-axis yields the graph on the right, which gives you a more truthful picture of what a statistical analysis would probably confirm—that no significant difference exists.

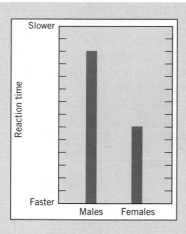

FIGURE 4.8 A bar graph showing hypothetical male and female reaction time differences with an unlabeled Y-axis.

The moral is obvious: beware the Y-axis. Be especially skeptical about graphs that seem to show large differences with a Y-axis that is not labeled at all, labeled ambiguously, or labeled in very tiny gradations.

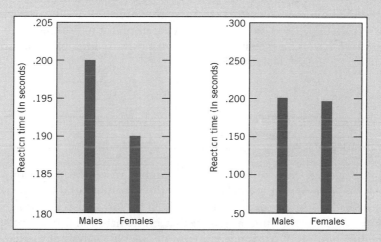

FIGURE 4.9 Bar graphs showing (a) a repeat of Figure 4.8, with the Y-axis labeled and (b) the same data as in Figure 4.8, but with the Y-axis realistically labeled.

Inferential Statistics

Like most people, researchers need to be liked and admired by others. One way to accomplish this goal is to produce interesting research outcomes, results that apply beyond the data collected in the study. That is, although a study looks at merely a small *sample* of all the data that could be collected, the researcher's hope is to arrive at a conclusion that will apply to the wider *population*. After all, the idea of the whole research enterprise is to arrive at general laws of behavior.

To illustrate what an inferential analysis tries to accomplish, let's consider a hypothetical maze-learning study comparing rats fed immediately after reaching the end of a complicated maze with rats fed 10 seconds after reaching the end of the maze. Thus, the empirical question is whether immediate reinforcement enhances maze learning. Suppose the following results occurred for five rats in each group. Each score is the number of trials it takes for the rat to learn the maze; learning is operationally defined as two consecutive errorless runs through the maze.

Rat #	Immediate Food	Rat #	Delayed Food
1	12	6	19
2	13	7	20
3	16	8	16
4	11	9	18
5	14	10	15

Notice that the scores within each column are not all the same, a result of slight differences between the five rats in each group and perhaps some other random factors. Despite the lack of absolute uniformity, however, it appears that the rats given immediate reinforcement learned the maze faster (i.e., on fewer trials).

Of course, we need more than a general impression resulting from a quick glance at the numbers. The first step is to calculate some descriptive statistics, such as the mean and standard deviation. They are:

	Immediate	Delayed
Mean	13.2	17.6
Standard deviation	1.9	2.1

On the average then, at least for this sample, maze learning required more trials when the food reward was delayed. Also, the variability of the scores within each set, as reflected in the standard deviations, is fairly low and is about the same for both groups. Can we conclude *in general* that immediate reinforcement speeds up maze learning? Not yet. What is needed is an inferential analysis of the data, which in this case involves hypothesis testing.[1]

Hypothesis Testing

The first step in testing hypotheses is to make the assumption that there is no difference in performance between the different conditions that you are studying, in this case between immediate and delayed rewards. This assumption is called the **null hypothesis** (null = nothing), symbolized H_0 and pronounced "h sub oh." The research hypoth-

---

[1] A second category of inferential analysis is called "estimation"; it involves estimating population values from individual sample scores.

esis, the outcome you are *hoping* to find (fewer learning trials for rats receiving immediate reward) so that you can win friends and influence people, is called the **alternative hypothesis** or H_1. Thus in your study, you hope to be able to disprove or reject H_0, thereby supporting (not proving) H_1, the hypothesis close to your heart.

If this language sounds odd to you, think of it as analogous to what happens in a court of law. There, the accused person is presumed innocent. That is, the assumption is that the defendant has done nothing (null–thing). The job of the prosecution is to convince the jury of the alternative hypothesis, namely, that the defendant committed the crime. Like the prosecutor, the researcher must show that something indeed happened, namely, that the reinforcement delay influenced learning in the case being examined here.

There can be only two outcomes to an inferential analysis. The differences you find between the two groups of rats could be due to some genuine, real, honest-to-goodness effect or they could be due to chance. That is, the sample differences might mirror a true difference or they might not. Hence, an inferential statistical analysis yields only two results—you can either reject H_0 or fail to reject it. Failing to reject H_0 means that any differences you've found (and studies almost always find some differences between groups) were most likely chance differences—you have failed to find a genuine effect that can be generalized beyond your sample. Rejecting H_0 means that you believe that an effect truly happened in your study and that the results can be generalized. In the maze example, rejecting H_0, that is, finding a statistically significant difference, means that it really does seem to be general rule that immediate reinforcement aids maze learning.

The researcher's hypothesis (H_1) is never proven to be true in an absolute sense, just as defendants are never *absolutely* proven guilty: guilt is said to be proven only beyond a reasonable doubt. Thus, H_0 can only be rejected (and at the same time H_1 supported) with some degree of confidence, which is set by what is called the **alpha (α) level.** Technically, alpha refers to the probability of obtaining your particular results if H_0 is really true. By convention, alpha is set at .05 ($\alpha = .05$), but it can be set at other levels as well (e.g., $\alpha = .01$). If H_0 is rejected when alpha equals .05, it means that you believe the probability is very low (5 out of 100) that your research outcome is the result of chance factors. If it is not due to chance, then it must be due to something else, namely (you hope) the phenomenon you are studying, immediacy of reinforcement in this case.

The choice of .05 relates to the earlier discussion of the characteristics of the normal curve. Remember that for a normal distribution of scores, the probability that a given score will be more than two standard deviations from the mean is low, 5% or less. Such an event is rare. Similarly, when comparing two sets of scores, as in the maze study, one asks about the probability of the obtained difference between the means occurring if the truth was that no real difference existed (i.e., if H_0 is true). If that probability is low enough, we reject H_0 and decide that some real difference must be occurring. The "low enough" is the probability of 5%, or .05. Another way to put it is to say that the obtained difference between the means would be so unexpected (i.e., rare) if H_0 were true that we just cannot believe that H_0 is true. We believe that something else happened (e.g., reinforcement delay really does slow down learning), so we reject H_0 and conclude that a "statistically significant" difference exists between groups.

Type I and Type II Errors

Clear from the previous example is the fact that when you decide whether or not to reject H_0, you could be wrong. Actually, there are two kinds of errors you could make. First, you might reject H_0 and support H_1, get all excited about making some new breakthrough discovery, but be wrong. Rejecting H_0 when it is in fact true is called a **Type I error.** The chance of this happening is equal to the value of alpha, normally .05. That is, setting alpha at .05 and rejecting H_0 means that there is a 5% chance of making a Type I error—a 5% chance of thinking you have a real effect but being wrong. Type I errors are sometimes suspected when a result fails several attempts at replication.

The other kind of mistake you could make is called a **Type II error.** This happens when you fail to reject H_0 but you are wrong. That is, you don't find a significant effect in your study, naturally feel depressed about it, but are in error. There really is a true effect in the population; you just haven't found it in the sample you studied. Type II errors sometimes occur when the measurements used aren't very reliable or aren't sensitive enough to detect differences between conditions. As you will see in Chapter 10, this sometimes happens in program evaluation research. A program might indeed have a significant but small effect on those in it, but the measures used are too weak to pick up this subtle effect.

Table 4.5 summarizes the four possible outcomes of an inferential statistical analysis comparing two conditions of an experiment. As you can see, correct decisions result from rejecting H_0 when it is false and not rejecting H_0 when it is true. Erroneously rejecting H_0 produces a Type I error; a failure to reject H_0 when H_0 is false is a Type II error. If it makes it easier to understand the terminology, you can make the following substitutions in Table 4.5:

TABLE 4.5   *Statistical Decision Making: Four Possible Outcomes of a Study Comparing Two Conditions, X and Y*

		The True State of Affairs	
		H_0 **is true:** There should be no difference between X and Y	H_0 **is false:** There really is a difference between X and Y
Your Statistical Decision	**Fail to reject H_0:** In my study, I found no significant difference between X and Y, so I cannot reject H_0	Correct decision	Type II error
	RejectH_0: In my study, I found a significant difference between X and Y, so I reject H_0	Type I error	Correct decision (experimenter heaven)

For "Fail to Reject H_0," substitute:

— "You did the study, you went through all the proper analyses, and what you came up with was zilch, nothing, zippo, no significant differences, and yes, you have good reason to be distraught, especially if this is your senior thesis project!"

For "Reject H_0," substitute:

— "You did the study, you went through all the proper analyses, and the difference came out significant at the .05 level, and yes, your life now has meaning and you'll be able to impress your friends and especially your thesis director because you went through all this work and you *actually found something!*"

For "H_0 is true," substitute:

— "Regardless of what might have occurred in your study, no real difference exists."

For "H_0 is false," substitute:

— "Regardless of what might have occurred in your study, a real difference does exist."

With the substitutions in mind, correct decisions mean either that (a) no real difference exists, which is okay because you didn't find one anyway or (b) a real difference exists and you found it (experimenter heaven). A Type I error means there's no real difference, but you think there is because of the results of your particular study. A Type II error means there really is a difference, but you missed it in your study.

Inferential Analysis

An inferential statistical decision to reject or not reject the null hypothesis in a study like the maze-learning study depends on analyzing two general types of variability in the data. The first refers to the differences in the "number of trials to reach criterion" scores for the two groups of rats. These differences are caused by some combination of (a) systematic variance and (b) error variance. **Systematic variance** is the result of some identifiable factor, either the variable of interest (reinforcement delay) or some factor that you've failed to control adequately.[2] **Error variance** is nonsystematic variability due to individual differences between the rats in the two groups and any number of random, unpredictable effects that might have occurred during the study. Error variance also occurs within each group, also as a result of individual differences and other random effects, and accounts for the differences found there. Mathematically, many inferential analyses will calculate some form of ratio that takes this form:

$$\text{Inferential statistic} = \frac{\text{Variability between conditions (systematic + error)}}{\text{Variability within each condition(error)}}$$

---

[2] These uncontrolled factors, called "confounds," will be examined in depth in the next chapter.

The ideal outcome is to find that variability between conditions is huge and variability within each condition is relatively small.

As you can see, this outcome seems to occur for our hypothetical maze data. The differences between the two conditions are substantial—it takes longer for the rats with delayed reinforcement to learn the maze (17.6 > 13.2), while the scores within each condition cluster fairly close together, as reflected in the small standard deviations (2.1 and 1.9). The particular inferential test you would probably use in this case is called a "*t* test for independent groups," a procedure familiar to you if you have taken a basic course in statistics. Appendix C describes how you would actually do this test.

Power and Effect Size

As a researcher, one hopes to be able to reject the null hypothesis when it is in fact false (the "experimenter heaven" cell of Table 4.5). The probability of this happening is referred to as the **power** of the statistical test. Power is affected by the alpha level, the size of the treatment effect, and especially, the sample size. This latter attribute is directly under the experimenter's control, and researchers sometimes perform a "power analysis" at the outset of a study to help them make decisions about the best sample size for their study. Students are often frustrated when their study "doesn't come out" (i.e., no significant differences), an outcome that often results from nothing more than a small sample size. That is, power was low and their outcome might possibly be a Type II error—something indeed might have happened in their study, but they failed to detect it. In general, Type II errors and power are inversely related. The greater the power, the less likely it is that a Type II error will occur, and vice versa. The other side of the coin is that a huge sample size might produce a result that is statistically significant, but relatively meaningless. That is, a tiny but statistically significant difference between groups might have little practical importance in a study with huge numbers of participants.[3] For instance, it would be possible to complete a maze study, find a 1-second difference in average running time, and have that difference significant at the .05 level if a sufficiently large number of rats were used in each group. Such a difference, however, would be practically meaningless. On the other hand, a moderately sized effect found with a relatively small sample size, could be more important.

These types of outcomes have made researchers more interested in reporting what is called the **effect size,** the amount of variability in the dependent variable that can be accounted for or attributed to the independent variable (Cohen, 1988). That is, effect size refers to the relative magnitude of the differences between the various conditions of an experiment, with sample size taken into account. Several "effect size indices" have been developed in recent years, one of which (Cohen's *d*) is illustrated in Appendix C. The important point for now is that hypothesis testing and effect size determination can be seen as complementary. Hypothesis testing gives us an indication that some type of reliable effect

---

[3] Note the word "might." It is also possible that a very small effect could have great practical importance. For example, Rosenthal and Rosnow (1991) report the example of the relationship between taking aspirin and avoiding a heart attack. It is a very small effect—taking aspirin reduces the heart attack rate by a mere 3% or so—yet for an at-risk population of around 1 million, the 3% reduction would produce 30,000 fewer heart attacks per year.

occurred in our study, while effect size tells us the magnitude of that effect. That is, hypothesis testing answers a "yes-no" question, while an effect size calculation answers a "how much?" question.

Armed with some of the basic tools psychologists use to think about data, you are now ready to tackle the first of three chapters dealing with the experimental method, psychology's most powerful tool for trying to understand the intricacies of behavior and mental processes. We'll begin with a general introduction to the experimental method and then consider some control problems that occur with such research; third, we'll examine the features of the most common types of experimental designs.

Chapter Summary

What to Measure – Varieties of Behavior

The behaviors measured in psychological research range from overt actions to self-reports to physiological recordings; the measures chosen for a particular study will depend on the manner in which the study's constructs are operationally defined. In many areas of psychological research, standard measures have developed over the years (e.g., preferential looking, reaction time).

Evaluating Measures

High-quality measures of behavior are both reliable and valid. To be reliable is to be repeatable and low in measurement error. Measures are valid if they actually measure what they are supposed to measure. Confidence in validity increases if a measure makes sense (face validity) and predicts future outcomes well (criterion validity). Construct validity accrues when a research program investigating relationships between the construct being measured and related phenomena results in consistent, predictable outcomes.

Scales of Measurement

Data for psychological research can be classified into four different scales of measurement: nominal, ordinal, interval, and ratio. In a nominal scale, numbers are category labels and the frequency of scores per category is the main interest. Ordinal scales occur when events are placed in rank order. Both interval and ratio scales assume equal intervals between quantitatively increasing scores; only ratio scales have a true zero point, however. Traditionally, psychologists have preferred to rely on interval and ratio scales because of the wider range of statistical analyses available when these scales are used.

Who to Measure—Sampling

If the goal of research is to learn something about a specific population, then the sample selected for study should be representative of that population and should be formed through some type of probability sampling. In simple random sampling, every member of the population has an equal chance of being selected. Stratified sampling assures that important subgroups in the population are represented proportionally in the sample. Cluster sampling is used when it is impossible to know all the members of the population. For most research in psychology, the goal is not to estimate a population value, but to identify systematic relationships among variables, and nonprobability sampling is both customary and adequate. Most psychological research uses convenience sampling, a form of nonprobability sampling.

Statistical Analysis

Statistical analysis in psychology is an essential tool for understanding the meaning of research outcomes. Descriptive statistics are calculated for the sample of participants in a particular study. They provide a summary of results and include measures of central tendency (e.g., mean, median, mode) and variability (range, standard deviation, variance). Data can be presented visually via graphical representation (e.g., histogram, stem and leaf display). Inferential statistics allow decisions about whether the results of a study are due to chance factors or appear to reflect some genuine relationship that can be applied to the larger population. The goal of an inferential analysis is to reject the hypothesis of no difference (i.e., the null hypothesis) when a true difference indeed occurs. A Type I error happens when the null hypothesis is rejected but should not have been, and a Type II error occurs when a true effect exists, but no significant difference is found in the study. Information about the magnitude of some research outcome comes from determining effect size.

Chapter Review

Multiple Choice

1. Reaction time methodology developed in the 19th century in the context of the mental chronometry experiments. In such a study, if simple reaction time (SRT) took .24 second and discrimination reaction time (DRT) took .29 second, what was concluded about the time for the mental event of discrimination?
    a. it took .29 second
    b. it took .29 + .24 second, or .53 second
    c. it took .29 − .24 second, or .05 second
    d. it cannot be calculated unless SRT > DRT

2. Which of the following is true about the reliability of a measure?
    a. a measure is reliable if it seems to make sense as a measure of some construct (e.g., problem solving seems reasonable as a measure of intelligence)
    b. if the measure being used for a construct is reliable, then similar results will occur if the measurement is taken a second time
    c. the higher the measurement error, the higher the reliability
    d. the phrenologist's skull measurements would score low on a test for reliability

3. A researcher developing a measure of shyness determines that students scoring high on the measure also score high for introversion on a well-known introversion–extraversion scale. The outcome *best* illustrates
    a. face validity
    b. criterion validity
    c. reliability
    d. construct validity

4. What is the advantage of cluster sampling over simple random sampling and stratified sampling?
   a. unlike the others, cluster sampling is an example of probability sampling
   b. with cluster sampling, it is not necessary to begin with a complete list of the population
   c. cluster sampling allows you to represent subgroups of the population (e.g., males and females) accurately
   d. cluster sampling is the only one that could be called "convenience" sampling

5. Which of the following measurement scales is accurately paired with an example?
   a. interval—numbers assigned to houses as street addresses
   b. ratio—temperature in Celsius
   c. nominal—how long babies look at novel stimuli
   d. ordinal—a college student deciding that professor X is the toughest grader, professor Y is next, and so on

Short Essay

1. Describe the logic behind Donders' "mental chronometry" research. What was the basic flaw?

2. Define reliability and explain why phrenological measurements would have been highly reliable.

3. Describe how you would determine (a) the face validity and (b) the criterion validity of some test.

4. Use delay of gratification as an example to illustrate how construct validity is determined.

5. Describe the essential difference between descriptive and inferential statistics.

6. Distinguish between means, medians, and modes, and explain when a median is a better descriptor of central tendency than a mean.

7. Describe the purpose of a stem and leaf display and why it can be better than a histogram for displaying a set of scores.

8. In measurement scale terms, explain the Dilbert cartoon in Figure 4.4.

9. Describe the basic logic of hypothesis testing and distinguish between Type I and Type II errors.

10. What is effect size and how does its calculation complement hypothesis testing?

Applications Exercises

Exercise 4.1.—Sampling

1. Use the table of random numbers in Appendix D to select a simple random sample of students from your experimental psychology class; your instructor will provide a class list and indicate the sample size.

2. Repeat the exercise but select a stratified sample that reflects the male–female proportions of your experimental psychology class.

Exercise 4.2.—Scales of Measurement

For each of the following studies, indicate which scale of measurement is being used for the behavior being measured.

1. Sally wishes to discover whether the children of Republicans and Democrats are more likely to major in the sciences, humanities, or business.

2. Fred decides to investigate whether rats that have learned one maze will learn a second one more quickly than naive rats.

3. Jim hypothesizes that children will rank different TV shows higher if they are in color but that adults' rankings won't be affected by color.

4. Nancy believes that somatotype changes with age, so she proposes to use Sheldon's scale to measure somatotypes for a group of people on their 10th, 15th, and 20th birthdays.

5. Susan is interested in helping behavior and believes that whether or not someone helps will be influenced by weather—the chances of someone helping will be greater on sunny than on cloudy days.

6. John wishes to determine which of five new varieties of beer will be liked best (i.e., recognized as number 1) by the patrons of his bar.

7. Ellen is interested in how students perceive the safety of various campus buildings. She asks a sample of students to arrange a deck of cards in a pile, each containing the name of a campus building, with the safest building on top and the least safe building on the bottom.

8. Pat believes that those with an obsessive–compulsive disorder will make fewer formatting errors on APA-style lab reports than those without the disorder.

Exercise 4.3.—H_0, H_1, Type I Errors, and Type II Errors

For each of the following studies, (a) identify the null hypothesis, (b) make your best guess about the alternative hypothesis—that is, what you would expect to happen in this study, (c) describe a research outcome that would be a Type I error, and (d) describe an outcome that would be a Type II error.

1. In a study of how well people can detect lying, male and female participants will try to detect deception in films of females lying in some parts of the film and telling the truth in other parts.

2. In a perception study, infants will be habituated to slides of normal faces and then shown faces with slight irregularities to see if they can detect the differences.

3. Depressed and nondepressed patients will be asked to predict how they will do in negotiating a human maze.

4. Some atheletes will be given training in a new imaging procedure that they are to use just prior to shooting foul shots; they will be compared with other athletes not given any special training.

Exercise 4.4.—Descriptive Statistics

For the hypothetical maze-learning study, which compared immediate with delayed rewards, calculate the mean, median, range, variance, and standard deviation for each group.

Exercise 4.5.—Inferential Statistics

Following the example in Appendix C, complete the appropriate *t* test for the same maze-learning study. What do you conclude? Do the rats learn faster if given immediate rewards?

CHAPTER 5

Introduction to Experimental Research

Preview & Chapter Objectives

The middle four chapters of this text, Chapters 5 through 8, concern the design of experiments. The first half of Chapter 5 outlines the essential features of an experiment—varying some factor of interest (the independent variable), controlling all other factors (extraneous variables), and measuring the outcome (dependent variables). In the second part of this chapter, you will learn how the validity of a study can be affected by how well it is designed. When you finish this chapter, you should be able to:

- Define a manipulated independent variable and identify examples of situational, task, and instructional variables.
- Distinguish between experimental and control groups.
- Recognize the presence of confounding variables in an experiment and understand why confounding creates problems for interpreting the results of an experiment.

- Distinguish independent from dependent variables, given a description of an experiment.
- Distinguish between manipulated and subject variables and understand the interpretation problems that accompany the use of subject variables.
- Recognize the factors that can reduce the statistical conclusion validity and the construct validity of an experiment.
- Describe the various ways in which an experiment's external validity can be reduced.
- Describe and be able to recognize the various threats to an experiment's internal validity.
- Understand the ethical guidelines for running a "participant pool."

When Robert Sessions Woodworth finally published his *Experimental Psychology* in 1938, the book's contents were already well known among psychologists. As early as 1909, Woodworth was giving his Columbia University students copies of a mimeographed handout called "Problems and Methods in Psychology," and a companion handout called "Laboratory Manual: Experiments in Memory, etc." appeared in 1912. By 1920, the manuscript filled 285 pages and was called "A Textbook of Experimental Psychology." After a 1932 revision, still in mimeograph form, the book finally was published in 1938. By then Woodworth's students were using it to teach their own students, and it was so widely known that the publisher's announcement of its publication said simply, "The Bible Is Out" (Winston, 1990).

The so-called Columbia bible was encyclopedic, with more than 823 pages of text and another 36 pages of references. After an introductory chapter, it was organized into 29 different research topics such as "memory," "maze learning," "reaction time," "association," "hearing," "the perception of color," and "thinking." Students wading through the text would learn about the methods used in each content area, and they would also learn virtually everything there was to know in 1938 about each topic.

The impact of the Columbia bible on the teaching of experimental psychology has been incalculable. Indeed, the teaching of experimental psychology today, and to some degree the structure of the book you're now reading, are largely cast in the mold set by Woodworth. In particular, he took the term "experiment," until then loosely defined as virtually any type of empirical research, and gave it the definition it has today. In particular, he contrasted it with correlational research, a distinction now taken for granted.

The defining feature of the experimental method was the manipulation of what Woodworth called an "independent variable," which would affect what he called the "dependent variable." In his words, the experimenter "holds all the conditions constant except for one factor which is his 'experimental factor' or his 'independent variable.' The observed effect is the 'dependent variable' which in a psychological experiment is some characteristic of behavior or reported experience" (Woodworth, 1938, p. 2). Although the terms were not invented by Woodworth, he was the first to use them as they are used today.

While the experimental method manipulates independent variables, the correlational method, according to Woodworth, "[m]easures two or more characteristics of the same individuals [and] computes the correlation of these characteristics. This method ... has no 'independent variable' but treats all the measured variables alike" (Woodworth, 1938, p. 3). You will learn more about correlational research in Chapter 9. In this and the next three chapters, however, the focus will be mostly on the experimental method, the researcher's most powerful tool for identifying cause-and-effect relationships.

Essential Features of Experimental Research

Since the time of Woodworth, psychologists have thought of an **experiment** as a systematic research study in which the investigator directly varies some factor (or factors), holds all else constant, and observes the results of the systematic variation. The factors under the control of the experimenter are called independent variables, the variables being held constant are referred to as extraneous variables, and the behaviors measured are the dependent variables. Let's consider each of these in more detail.

Establishing Independent Variables

Any experiment can be described as a study that investigates the effect of X on Y. X is Woodworth's **independent variable:** it is the factor of interest to the experimenter, the one that is being studied to see if it will influence behavior. It is sometimes called a "manipulated" factor because the experimenter has complete control over it and is creating the situations that research participants will encounter in the study. As you will see below, the concept of an independent variable can also be stretched to cover to what are called nonmanipulated or subject variables, but for now, let us consider only those independent variables that are under the experimenter's total control.

Independent variables must have a minimum of two *levels*. That is, at the very least, an experiment involves a comparison between two situations (or *conditions*). For example, suppose a researcher is interested in the effects of different dosages of marijuana on reaction time. In such a study, there have to be at least two different dosage levels in order to make a comparison. This study would be described as an experiment with "amount of marijuana" as the independent variable and "dosage 1" and "dosage 2" as the two levels of the independent variable. Of course, independent variables can have more than two levels. In fact, there are distinct advantages to adding levels beyond the minimum of two, as you will see in Chapter 7 on experimental design.

Experimental research can be either basic or applied in its goals, and it can be conducted either in the laboratory or in the field (see Chapter 3 for an elaboration of these distinctions). Experiments that take place in the field are sometimes called **field experiments.** The term **field research** is a broader term for any empirical research outside of the laboratory, including both experimental studies and studies using nonexperimental methods.

Varieties of Independent Variables

The range of factors that can be used as independent variables is limited only by the creative thinking ability of the researcher. However, independent variables that are manipulated in a study tend to fall into three somewhat overlapping categories: situational variables, task variables, and instructional variables.

Situational variables refer to different features in the environment that participants might encounter. For example, in a helping behavior study, the researcher interested in studying the effect of the number of bystanders on the chances of help being offered might create a situation in which participants encounter a person in need of help. Sometimes the participant is alone with the person needing aid; at other times the participant and the victim are accompanied by a group of either three or six bystanders. In this case, the situational independent variable would be the number of potential helpers on the scene besides the participant, and the levels would be zero, three, and six bystanders.

Sometimes experimenters vary the type of task performed by participants. One way to manipulate **task variables** is to give groups of participants different kinds of problems to solve. For instance, research on the psychology of reasoning often involves giving participants different kinds of logical problems to determine the kinds of errors people tend to make. Similarly, mazes can differ in the degree of complexity, different types of illusions could be presented in a perception study, and so on.

Instructional variables are manipulated by asking different groups of participants to perform a particular task in different ways. For example, participants in a memory task who are all shown the same list of words might be given different instructions about how to memorize the list. Some might be told to form visual images of the words, others might be told to form associations between adjacent pairs of words, and still others might be told simply to repeat each word three times as it is presented.

Of course, it is possible to combine several types of independent variables in a single study. A study of the effects of crowding, task difficulty, and motivation on problem-solving ability could have participants placed in either a large or a small room, thereby manipulating crowding through the situational variable of room size. Some participants in each type of room could be given difficult crossword puzzles to solve and others less difficult ones; this illustrates a task variable. Finally, an instructional variable could manipulate motivation by telling participants that they will earn either $1 or $5 for completing the puzzles.

Control Groups

In some experiments, the independent variable is whether or not some treatment is administered. The levels of the independent variable in this case are essentially 1 and 0; some participants get the treatment and others don't. In a study of the effects of TV violence on children's aggressive behavior, for instance, some children might be shown a violent TV program, while others don't get to see it. The term **experimental group** is used as a label for the first situation, in which the treatment is present. Those in the second type of condition, in which treatment is withheld, are said to be in the **control group.** Ideally, the participants in a control group are identical to the experimental group participants in all ways except that they do not get the experimental treatment.

In essence, the control group provides a baseline measure against which the experimental group's behavior can be compared. Think of it this way: control group = comparison group. You will learn about several specialized types of control groups in Chapter 7, the first of two chapters dealing with experimental design.

Controlling Extraneous Variables

The second feature of the experimental method is that the researcher tries to control what are called **extraneous variables.** These are any uncontrolled factors that are not of interest to the researcher but which might influence the behavior being studied. As long as these are held constant, they present no danger to the study. If they are not adequately controlled, however, they might influence the behavior being measured in some systematic way. The result is called confounding. A **confound** is any uncontrolled extraneous variable that "covaries" with the independent variable and could provide an alternative explanation of the results. That is, a confounding variable changes at the same time that an independent variable changes (i.e., they "covary") and consequently, its effect cannot be separated from the effect of the independent variable. Hence, when a study has a confound, the results could be due to the effects of *either* the confounding variable, the independent variable, or some combination of the two, and there is no way to decide among these alternatives.

To illustrate some obvious confounding, consider a verbal learning experiment in which a researcher wants to show that students who try to learn a large amount of material all at once don't do as well as those who spread their learning over several sessions. That is, massed practice (cramming?) is predicted to be inferior to distributed practice. Three groups of students are selected, and each is given the same five chapters in a general psychology text to learn. Participants in the first group are given 3 hours on Monday to study the material. Participants in the second group are given 3 hours on Monday and 3 hours on Tuesday, and those in the final group get 3 hours each on Monday, Tuesday, and Wednesday. On Friday, all of the groups are tested on the material (see Table 5.1 for the design). The results show that Group 3 scores the highest, followed by Group 2. Group 1 does not do well at all, and the researcher concludes that distributed practice is superior to massed practice. Do you agree with this conclusion?

You probably don't because there are at least two serious confounds in this study, both easy to spot. The participants certainly differ in how their practice is distributed (1, 2, or 3 days), but they *also* differ in how much total practice they get (3, 6, or 9 hours). This is a perfect example of a confound—it is impossible to tell if the results are due to one factor (distribution of practice) or the other (total practice hours); the two factors covary perfectly. The way to describe this situation is to say that "distribution of practice is confounded with total study hours." The second confound is perhaps less obvious but is equally problematic. It concerns the retention interval. The test is on Friday for everyone, but different amounts of time have elapsed between study and test for each group. Perhaps Group 3 did the best because they studied the material most recently and forgot the least amount. In this experiment, then, distribution of practice is confounded both with total study hours and with retention interval. Each confound by itself could account for the results, and the factors may also have interacted with each other in some way to provide yet another interpretation.

TABLE 5.1   *Confounding in a Hypothetical Distribution of Practice Experiment*

	Monday	Tuesday	Wednesday	Thursday	Friday
Group 1	3	—	—	—	Exam
Group 2	3	3	—	—	Exam
Group 3	3	3	3	—	Exam

Note: The 3 in each cell equals the number of hours spent studying five chapters of a general psychology text.

Look at Table 5.2, which gives you a convenient way to identify confounds. In the first column are the levels of the independent variable and in the final column are the results. The middle columns are extraneous variables that should be held constant through the use of appropriate controls (next chapter). If they are not kept constant (as is the case here), then a confound exists. As you can see, the results could be explained by the variation in any of the first three columns, either individually or in some combination. To correct the confound problem in this case, you need to ensure that the middle two columns are constant instead of variable.

In the Applications Exercises at the end of the chapter you will be identifying confounds. You'll find the task easier if you fit the problems into the Table 5.2 format. Take a minute and redesign the distributed practice study. How would you eliminate the confounding from these extraneous variables?

Learning to be aware of potential confounding factors and building appropriate ways to control for them is one of the scientific thinking skills that is most difficult to develop. Not all confounds are as obvious as the massed/distributed practice example. We'll encounter the problem often in the remaining chapters and address it again shortly in the context of a discussion of what is called the internal validity of a study.

Measuring Dependent Variables

The third part of any experiment is measuring some behavior that is presumably being influenced by the independent variable. The term **dependent variable** is used to describe those behaviors that are the measured outcomes of experiments. If,

TABLE 5.2   *Identifying Confounds*

Levels of IV Distribution of Practice	EV 1 Study Hours	EV 2 Retention Interval	DV Retention Test Performance
1 day	3 hours	3 days	Lousy
2 days	6 hours	2 days	Average
3 days	9 hours	1 day	Great

IV = independent variable.
EV = extraneous variable.
DV = dependent variable

as mentioned earlier, an experiment can be described as the effect of X on Y and X is the independent variable, then Y is the dependent variable. In a study of the effects of TV violence on children's aggressiveness, the dependent variable would be some measure of aggressiveness. In the marijuana and reaction time study, it would be a measure of reaction time. In the distribution of practice study, it would be a measure of exam performance.

The credibility of any experiment and its chances of discovering anything of value depend partly on the decisions made about what behaviors to measure as dependent variables. We've already seen that empirical questions cannot be answered unless the terms are defined with some precision. You might take a minute and review the section on asking empirical questions in Chapter 3. It will remind you about the concept of operational definition. When designing an experiment, one key component concerns the operational definitions for the behaviors to be measured as dependent variables. Unless the behaviors are defined precisely, replication is impossible.

One final point. It is important to realize that a particular construct could be either an independent, an extraneous, or a dependent variable, depending on the research problem at hand. An experiment might manipulate a particular construct as an independent variable, try to control it as an extraneous factor, or measure it as a dependent variable. Consider the construct of anxiety, for instance. It could be a manipulated independent variable by telling participants that they will be experiencing shocks that will be either moderate or painful and then asking participants if they prefer to wait by themselves or with others. Anxiety could also be a factor that needs to be held constant in some experiments. For instance, if you wanted to evaluate the effects of a public speaking workshop on the ability of students to deliver a brief speech, you wouldn't want to videotape the students in one group without taping those in the other group as well. If everyone is taped, then the level of anxiety created by that factor is held constant for everyone. Finally, anxiety could be a dependent variable in a study of the effects of different types of exams (e.g., multiple choice vs. essay) on the perceived test anxiety of students during final exam week. Some physiological measures of anxiety might be used in this case. Anxiety could also be considered a personality characteristic, with some people having more of it than others; this last possibility leads to the next topic.

Manipulated versus Subject Variables

Up to this point, the term independent variable has meant some factor manipulated directly by the researcher. An experiment compares one condition created by and under the control of the experimenter with another. However, in many studies, comparisons are also made between groups of people who differ from each other in ways other than those manufactured by the person designing the study. These comparisons are made between factors that are referred to variously as ex post facto variables, natural group variables, nonmanipulated variables, or **subject variables,** which is the term I will use most often. They refer to already existing characteristics of the individuals participating in the study, such as gender, age, intelligence, physical or psychiatric disorder, and any personality attribute you can name. When using subject variables in a study, the researcher cannot manipulate them directly but must *select* people for the different conditions by virtue of the characteristics they already have.

To illustrate the differences between manipulated and subject variables, consider a hypothetical study of the effects of anxiety on human maze learning. You could *manipulate* anxiety directly by creating a situation in which one group is made anxious (told they'll be performing in front of a large audience perhaps), while a second group is not (no audience). In that study, any person who volunteers could potentially wind up in one group or the other. To do the study using a *subject* variable, on the other hand, you could select two groups differing in their characteristic levels of anxiety and ask each to try the maze. The first group would be those who were anxious types of people (as determined ahead of time by a personality test for anxiety proneness). The second group would include more relaxed types of people. Notice the major difference between this situation and one involving a manipulated variable. With anxiety as a subject variable, volunteers coming into the study cannot be placed into either of the conditions (anxious-all-the-time-Fred cannot be put into the low-anxiety group), but must be in one group or the other, depending on attributes they *already* possess prior to entering the study.

Some researchers, true to Woodworth's original use of the term, prefer to reserve the term independent variable for those variables directly manipulated by the experimenter. Others are willing to include subject variables as examples of a particular type of independent variable on the grounds that the experimenter has some degree of control over them by virtue of the decisions involved in selecting them in the first place. I take this latter position and will use the term independent variable in the broader sense. However, whether this term is used broadly (manipulated + subject) or narrowly (manipulated only) is not important, providing you understand the difference between a manipulated and a nonmanipulated or subject variable.

Case Study 4—Using Subject Variables

Schneider and Bjorkland (1992) provide a nice example of a study that investigated several subject variables at the same time. The study also illustrates the processes of replication and extension (see Chapter 3). The researchers were interested in how memory performance would be influenced by (a) expertise in some specific domain and (b) general aptitude. Earlier studies focused on expertise alone, but in this study, an "important extension of the original design concerned the consideration of children's aptitude levels" (p. 462). Hence, there were two main subject variables.[1] The first was level of expertise regarding the game of soccer, and it included two levels—expert and novice. The second was general aptitude, as determined by a "cognitive ability test." As is often the case when using subject variables, two different sessions were needed to complete the study, one to assess subject variables in order to form separate groups and a second to run the experiment itself. In the first session of this study, a large group of second and fourth graders were given the cognitive ability test and a 10-item test that measured level of soccer knowledge. On

---

[1] Actually, there were three others: gender, interest in soccer, and grade level, but we'll just focus on the two major ones.

the basis of their scores on these tests, they were selected for part two of the study and placed into four main groups: soccer expert–high aptitude, soccer expert–low aptitude, soccer novice–high aptitude, and soccer novice–low aptitude.

In the second session, they tried their hands at a sort-recall task: given a collection of terms, they were told to sort them into categories and then, shortly thereafter, to recall them. They did this twice, once for a soccer-related list of items and once for items unrelated to soccer (half completed the tasks in this sequence, the other half in the opposite order—a technique called counterbalancing, to be discussed in the next chapter). The results were complicated, but the main ones were that high-aptitude children generally outperformed low-aptitude children, regardless of soccer expertise level and for both types of list. Looking at expertise by itself, however, the results were that soccer experts outperformed novices, but only on the soccer-related task. Thus, on the soccer list, experts recalled 62% of the information, while novices recalled only 44%. On the nonsoccer list, however, the two groups scored about the same: 52% for the soccer experts and 48% for the novices.

Only a study using *manipulated* independent variables can be called an experiment in the strictest sense of the term; it is sometimes called a "true" experiment (which sounds a bit pretentious and carries the unfortunate implication that other studies are "false"). Studies using independent variables that are *subject* variables are occasionally called ex post facto studies or quasi experiments ("quasi" meaning "to some degree" here).[2] Sometimes (often, actually) studies will include both manipulated and subject independent variables. Being aware of the presence of subject variables is important because they affect the kinds of conclusions that can be drawn from the study's results.

Drawing Conclusions When Using Subject Variables

Put a little asterisk next to this section—it is extremely important. Recall from Chapter 1 that one of the goals of research in psychology is to discover explanations for behavior. That is, we wish to know what caused some behavior to occur. Simply put, with manipulated variables, conclusions about the causes of behavior can be made; with subject variables, they cannot. The reason has to do with the amount of control held by the experimenter in each case.

With manipulated variables, the experiment can meet the criteria listed in Chapter 1 for demonstrating causality. The independent variable precedes the dependent variable, covaries with it, and, assuming that no confounds are present, can be considered the most reasonable explanation for the results. In other words, if you vary some factor and successfully hold all else constant, the results can *only* be attributed to the factor varied. In a confound-free experimental study with two groups, these groups will be essentially equal to each other (i.e., any differences will be random ones) in all ways except for the manipulated factor.

When using subject variables, however, the experimenter can also vary some factor (i.e., select participants having certain characteristics) but cannot hold all else constant. Selecting participants who are high or low on some definition of anxiety

---

[2] The term quasi-experimental design is actually a broader designation referring to any type of design in which participants cannot be randomly assigned to the groups being studied (Cook & Campbell, 1979). These designs are often found in applied research and are elaborated in Chapter 10.

proneness does not guarantee that the two groups will be equivalent in other ways. In fact, they might be different from each other in several ways (in self-confidence perhaps) that could influence the outcome of the study. When a difference between the groups occurs in this type of study, we cannot say that the differences were *caused* by the subject variable. In terms of the conditions for causality, while we can say that the independent variable precedes the dependent variable and covaries with it, we cannot eliminate alternative explanations for the relationship because certain extraneous factors cannot be controlled. When subject variables are present, all we can say is that the groups performed differently on the dependent measure.

An example from social psychology might help to clarify the distinction. Suppose you were interested in altruistic behavior and wanted to see how it was affected by the construct of "self-esteem." The study could be done in two ways. First, you could manipulate self-esteem directly by first giving participants a personality test. By providing different kinds of false feedback about the results of the test, both positive and negative, self-esteem could be raised or lowered temporarily. The participants could then be asked to do some volunteer work to see if those feeling good about themselves would be more likely to help.[3] A second way to do this study is to give participants a reliable and valid personality test for level of self-esteem and select those who score in the upper 25% and lower 25% on the measure as the participants for the two groups. Self-esteem in this case is a subject variable—half of the participants will be low self-esteem types, while the other half will be high self-esteem types. As in the first study, these two groups of people could be asked about volunteering.

In the first study, differences in volunteering can be traced *directly* to the self-esteem manipulation. If all other factors are properly controlled, the temporary feeling of increased or decreased self-esteem is the *only* thing that could have produced the differences in helping. In the second study, however, you cannot say that high self-esteem is the direct cause of the helping behavior; what you can say is that people with high self-esteem are more likely to help than those with low self-esteem. All you can do is to speculate about the reasons why this might be true because these participants may differ from each other in other ways unknown to you. For instance, high self-esteem types of people might have had prior experience in volunteering, and this experience might have had the joint effect of raising or strengthening their self-esteem and increasing the chances that they will volunteer in the future. Or they might have greater expertise in the specific volunteering tasks (e.g., public speaking skills). As you will see in Chapter 9, this difficulty in interpretation is exactly the problem encountered when trying to draw conclusions from correlational research.

Returning for a moment to the Schneider and Bjorkland (1992) study, which featured the subject variables of soccer expertise and general aptitude, the authors were careful to avoid drawing conclusions about causality. The word "cause" never appears in their article, and the descriptions of results are always in the form "this group scored higher than this other group."

Before moving on to the discussion of the validity of experimental research, read Box 5.1. It identifies the variables in a classic study that you probably recall from your

---

[3] Manipulating self-esteem raises ethical questions that were considered in a study by Sullivan and Deiker (1973). See Chapter 2, p. 52.

Box 5.1

CLASSIC STUDIES—Bobo Dolls and Aggression

Ask any student who has just completed a course in child, social, or personality psychology (perhaps even general psychology) to tell you about the Bobo doll studies. The response will be immediate recognition and a brief description along the lines of "Oh, yes, the studies showing that children will punch out an inflated doll if they see an adult doing it." A description of one of these studies is a good way to clarify further the differences between independent, extraneous, and dependent variables. The study was published by Albert Bandura and his colleagues in 1963 and is entitled "Imitation of Film-Mediated Aggressive Models" (Bandura, Ross, & Ross, 1963).

Establishing independent variables

The study included both manipulated and subject variables. The major manipulated variable was the type of experience that preceded the opportunity for aggression. There were four levels, including three experimental groups and a control group.

Experimental group 1: real-life aggression (children directly observed an adult model aggressing against the Bobo doll)

Experimental group 2: human film aggression (children observed a film of an adult model aggressing against Bobo)

Experimental group 3: cartoon film aggression (children observed a cartoon of "Herman the Cat" aggressing against a cartoon Bobo)

Control group: no exposure to aggressive models

The nonmanipulated independent variable (subject variable) was gender. Male and female students from the Stanford University Nursery School (mean age = 52 months) were the participants in the study. (Actually, there was also another manipulated variable; participants in groups 1 and 2 were exposed to either a same-gender or opposite-gender model.) The basic procedure of the experiment was to expose the children to some type of aggressive model (or not, for the control group), and then put them into a room full of toys (including Bobo), thereby giving them the opportunity to be aggressive themselves.

Controlling extraneous variables

Several possible confounds were nicely avoided. First, in groups 1 and 2, the adults aggressed against a *5-foot* Bobo doll. When given a chance to pummel Bobo themselves, the children were put into a room with a *3-foot* Bobo doll. This kept the size relationship between person and doll approximately constant. Second, participants in all four groups were mildly frustrated before being given a chance to aggress. They were allowed to play for a few minutes with some very attractive toys and then were told by the experimenter that the toys were special and were being reserved for some other children. Thus, for *all* the children there was an approximately equivalent increase in their degree of emotional arousal just prior to the time when they were given the opportunity to be aggressive. Any differences in aggressiveness, then, could be attributed to the imitative effects and not to any emotional differences between the groups.

Measuring dependent variables

Several different measures of aggression were used in this study. Aggressive responses were categorized as imitative, partially imitative, or nonimitative, depending on how closely they matched the model's behavior. For example, the operational definition of imitative aggressive behaviors included striking the doll with a wooden mallet, punching it in the nose, and kicking it. Partially imitative behaviors included hitting something else with the mallet and sitting on the doll but not hitting it. Nonimitative aggression included shooting darts from an available dart gun at targets other than Bobo and acting aggressively toward other objects in the room.

Briefly, the results of the study were that children in groups 1, 2, and 3 showed significantly more aggression than those in the control group, but the same amount of overall aggression occurred regardless of the type of modeling. Also, boys were more aggressive than girls in all conditions; some gender differences also occurred in the form of the aggression: girls "were more inclined than boys to sit on the Bobo doll but [unlike the boys] refrained from punching it" (Bandura et al., 1963, p. 9). Figure 5.1 summarizes the results.

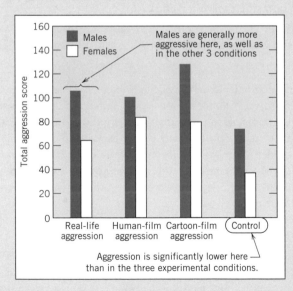

FIGURE 5.1 Data from Bandura, Ross, and Ross's Bobo study (1963) of the effects of imitation on aggression.

general psychology course—one of the so-called Bobo experiments that first investigated imitative aggression. Working through the example will help you apply your knowledge of independent, extraneous, and dependent variables and will allow you to see how manipulated and subject variables are often encountered in the same study.

The Validity of Experimental Research

Chapter 4 introduced the concept of validity in the context of measurement. The term also applies to experiments as a whole. Just as a measure is valid if it measures what it is supposed to measure, psychological research is said to be valid if it provides the understanding about behavior that it is supposed to provide. This section of the chapter introduces four different types of validity, following the scheme outlined by Cook and Campbell (1979) for research in field settings but applicable to any research in psychology. The four types of validity are statistical conclusion validity, construct validity (again), external validity, and internal validity.

Statistical Conclusion Validity

The previous chapter introduced you to the use of statistics in psychology. In particular, you learned about measurement scales, the basic distinction between descriptive and inferential statistics, and the basics of hypothesis testing. **Statistical conclusion validity** concerns the extent to which the researcher uses statistics properly and draws the appropriate conclusions from the statistical analysis.

The statistical validity of a study can be reduced in several ways. First, researchers might do the wrong analysis or violate some of the assumptions required for performing a particular analysis. For instance, the data for a study might be arranged on an ordinal scale, thereby requiring the use of a particular type of statistical procedure. The researcher, however, mistakenly uses an analysis that is appropriate only for interval or ratio data. Second, the researcher might selectively report some analyses that came out as predicted but might not report others (guess which ones?), a practice that borders on fraud (see Chapter 2). The third example of a factor that reduces the statistical validity of a study concerns the reliability of the measures used. If the dependent measures are not reliable, there will be a great deal of error variability, which reduces the chances of finding a significant effect. If a true effect exists (i.e., the null hypothesis should be rejected) but low reliability results in a failure to find it, the outcome would be a Type II error.

The careful researcher plans the statistical analysis at the same time that the experimental design is being planned. In fact, no experiment should ever be designed without thought being given to how the data will be analyzed.

Construct Validity

The previous chapter described construct validity in the context of measuring psychological constructs: it refers jointly to whether a test truly measures some hypothetical construct (e.g., delay of gratification) and whether the construct truly exists. In experimental research, **construct validity** has a related but slightly different meaning: it refers to the adequacy of the definitions for both the independent and dependent variables used in the study. In a study of the effects of TV violence on children's aggression, questions about construct validity could be (a) whether the programs chosen by the experimenter are the best choices to contrast violent with nonviolent television programming and (b) whether the measures of aggression used are the best ones that could be chosen. If the study used violent cartoon characters (e.g., Elmer Fudd shooting at Bugs Bunny) compared to nonviolent characters (e.g., Winnie the Pooh), someone might argue that children's aggressive behavior is unaffected by fantasy; hence, a more valid manipulation of the independent variable called "level of filmed violence" would involve showing children realistic films of people that varied in the amount of violence portrayed.

Similarly, someone might criticize the appropriateness of a measure of aggression used in a particular study. This in fact has been a problem in research on aggression. For rather obvious ethical reasons, you cannot design a study that results in participants punching each other's lights out. Instead, aggression has been defined operationally in a variety of ways, some of which might seem to you to be more valid (e.g., angered participants believing they are delivering shocks to another person) than others (e.g., horn honking by frustrated drivers). As was true for the discussion of construct validity in the previous chapter when the emphasis was on valid measurement, the validity of the choices about exactly how to define independent and dependent variables develops over time as accumulated research fits into a coherent (and converging) pattern.

External Validity

Experimental psychologists have been criticized for knowing a great deal about college sophomores and white rats and very little about anything else. This is in essence a criticism of **external validity,** the degree to which research findings generalize beyond the specific context of the experiment being conducted. For research to achieve the highest degree of external validity, its results should generalize in three ways—to other populations, to other environments, and to other times.

Other Populations

The comment about rats and sophomores fits here. As we've seen in Chapter 2, part of the debate over the appropriateness of animal research has to do with how well this research provides explanations that are relevant for human behavior. Concerning sophomores, recall that Milgram deliberately avoided using college students and selected adults from the general population as subjects for his obedience studies. The same cannot be said of most social psychologists, however. A survey by Sears (1986) of research in social psychology found that 75% of the research published in 1980 in that field used undergraduates. When Sears repeated the survey for research published in 1985, the number was 74%. Sears argued that the characteristics of college students as a population could very well bias the general conclusions about social phenomena. Compared to the general population, for instance, college students are more able cognitively, more self-centered, more susceptible to social influence, and more likely to change their attitudes on issues. To the extent that research investigates issues related to those features, results from students might not generalize to other groups, according to Sears. He suggested that researchers expand their database and replicate important findings on a variety of populations. However, he also pointed out that many research areas (e.g., perception) produce outcomes relatively unaffected by the special characteristics of college students, and there is no question that students exist in large numbers and provide the classic example of a convenience sample (Chapter 4). Some special ethical considerations apply to this group, as outlined in Box 5.2.

Box 5.2

ETHICS—Recruiting Participants: Everyone's in the Pool

Most research psychologists are employed by colleges and universities and consequently find themselves surrounded by an available supply of potential human guinea pigs. Because students may not readily volunteer to participate in studies, most university psychology departments establish what is called the subject pool or more recently, the participant pool. The term refers to a group of students, typically those enrolled in introductory psychology classes, who are asked to participate in research as part of a course requirement. If you are a student at a large university, you have probably had the experience of "volunteering" for two or three experiments in order to avoid losing points or acquiring a grade of "Incomplete" for the course. At a large university, if 800 students take general psychology each semester and each student signs up for three studies, that makes 2,400 participants available to researchers.

Subject pools are convenient for researchers in search of participants, and they are defended on the grounds that research participation is part of the educational process (Kimmel, 1996). Ideally, students can acquire deeper insights into the research process by participating in experiments and learning something about the psychological phenomena being investigated. To maintain its "voluntary" nature, students are given the opportunity to complete the requirement with alternatives other than direct research participation. Problems exist, however. Critics argue that participant pools are not really voluntary, that alternative activities (e.g., writing papers) are often so onerous that students are effectively compelled to be research participants, and that the experience is more likely to be tedious and meaningless than educational (Korn, 1988). There is research to support such concern. A study by Sieber and Saks (1989) found evidence that 89% of 366 departments surveyed had pools that failed to meet at least one of the APA's recommendations (page 162). Nonetheless, many departments try to make the research experience educational for students. For example, during debriefing for a memory experiment, the participant/student could be told how the study relates to the information in Chapter X of the text being used in the introductory course. Many departments also include creative alternative activities. These include having nonparticipating students (a) observe ongoing studies and record their observations, (b) participate "behind the scenes" in a faculty member's project (e.g., by coding data), (c) participate in some community volunteering effort, or (d) attend a research presentation by a visiting scholar (Kimmel, 1996). Some studies have shown that students generally find participation valuable, especially if researchers make an explicit attempt to tie their participation to the education occurring in the general psychology course (e.g., Landrum & Chastain, 1999; Leak, 1981).

The APA (1982, pp. 47–48) has provided some explicit guidelines about recruiting students as research participants, the main points being these:

- ✓ students should be aware of the requirement before signing up for the course;
- ✓ students should get a thorough description of the requirement on the first day of class, including a clear description of alternative activities if they opt not to serve as research participants;
- ✓ alternative activities must equal research participation in time and effort and, like participation, must have some educational value;
- ✓ all proposals for research using participant pools must have prior IRB approval;
- ✓ special effort must be made to treat students courteously;
- ✓ there must be a clear and simple procedure for students to complain about mistreatment without their course grade being affected;
- ✓ all other aspects of the APA ethics code must be rigorously followed; and
- ✓ the department must have a mechanism in place to provide periodic review of participant pool policies.

The "college sophomore problem" is only one example of a concern over generalizing to other groups. Another has to do with gender. Some of psychology's most famous research has been limited by using only males (or, less frequently, only females) but drawing conclusions as if they apply to everyone. Perhaps the best-known example is Lawrence Kohlberg's research on children's moral development. Kohlberg (1963) asked adolescent boys (aged 10–16) to read and respond to brief accounts of various moral dilemmas. On the basis of the boys' responses, Kohlberg developed a six-stage theory of moral development that became a fixture in developmental psychology texts. At the most advanced stage, the person acts according to a set of universal principles based on preserving justice and individual rights.

Kohlberg's theory has been criticized on external validity grounds. For example, Carol Gilligan (1982) argued that Kohlberg's model overlooks important gender differences in thinking patterns and in how moral decisions are made. Males may come to place the highest value on individual rights, but females tend to value the preservation of relationships. Hence, females responding to some of Kohlberg's moral dilemmas might not seem to be as advanced morally as males, but this is due to a biasing of the entire model because Kohlberg sampled only males, according to Gilligan.

Research psychologists also are careful about generalizing results from one culture to another. For example, "individualist" cultures are said to emphasize the unique person over the group, and personal responsibility and initiative are valued. On the other hand, the group is more important than the individual in "collectivist" cultures (Triandis, 1995). Research conclusions based just on one culture might not be universally applied. To take just one example, most children in the United States are taught to place great value on personal achievement. In Japan, on the other hand, children learn that if they stand out from the crowd, they might diminish the value of others in the group; individual achievement is not as valuable. One study found that personal achievement was associated with positive emotions for American students, but with *negative* emotions for Japanese students (Kitayama, Markus, Matsumoto, & Norasakkunkit, 1997). To conclude that feeling good about achievement is a universal human trait would be a mistake. Does this mean that all research in psychology should make cross-cultural comparisons? No, of course not. It just means that conclusions sometimes need to be drawn cautiously, and with reference to the group studied in the research project.

Other Environments

Besides generalizing to other types of individuals, externally valid results are applicable to other stimulus settings. This problem is the basis for the occasional criticism of laboratory research mentioned in Chapter 3–it is sometimes said to be artificial and too far removed from real life. Recall from the discussion of basic and applied research (pp. 72–73) that the laboratory researcher's response to criticisms about artificiality is to use Aronson's concept of experimental reality. The important thing is that people be involved in the study; mundane reality is secondary.

Nonetheless, important developments in many subareas of psychology have resulted from attempts to study psychological phenomena in real-life settings. A good example concerns the history of research on human memory. For much of the 20th century, memory research occurred largely in the laboratory, where countless college sophomores memorized seemingly endless lists of words, nonsense syllables, strings of digits, and so on. The research created a comprehensive body of knowledge about basic memory processes and that is important, but whether the principles discovered in the lab generalized to real-life memory situations was not clear. Change occurred in the 1970s, led by Cornell's Ulric Neisser. In *Cognition and Reality* (1976), he argued that the laboratory tradition in cognitive psychology, while producing important results, nonetheless had failed to yield enough useful information about information processing in real-world contexts. He called for more research concerning what he referred to as **ecological validity**—research with relevance for the everyday cognitive activities of people trying to adapt to their environment. Experimental psychologists, Neisser urged, "must make a greater effort to understand cognition as it occurs in the ordinary environment and in the context of natural purposeful activity. This would not mean an end to laboratory experiments, but a commitment to the study of variables that are ecologically important rather than those that are easily manageable" (p. 7).

Neisser's call to arms was embraced by many (but not all, of course) cognitive researchers, and the 1980s and 1990s saw increased study of such topics as eyewitness memory (e.g., Loftus, 1979) and the long-term recall of subjects learned in school, such as Spanish (e.g., Bahrick, 1984). Neisser himself completed an interesting analysis of the memory of John Dean (Neisser, 1981), the White House chief counsel who blew the whistle on President Richard Nixon's attempted cover-up of illegal activities in the Watergate scandal of the early 1970s. Dean's testimony before Congress precipitated the scandal and led to Nixon's resignation. Dean's 245-page account was so detailed that some reporters referred to him as a human tape recorder. Of course, it was later revealed that the Oval office meetings described by Dean were also tape-recorded by the White House. Comparing the tapes with Dean's testimony gave Neisser a perfect opportunity to evaluate Dean's supposedly photographic memory, which turned out to be not so photographic after all—he recalled the general topics of the meetings reasonably well but missed a lot of the details. The important point for external validity is that Neisser's study is a good illustration of how our knowledge of memory can be enriched by studying phenomena outside of the normal laboratory environment.

Other Times

The third way in which external validity is sometimes questioned has to do with the longevity of results. Some of the most famous experiments in the history of psychology are the conformity studies done by Solomon Asch in the 1950s (e.g., Asch, 1956). These experiments were completed during a historical period when conservative values were dominant in the United States, the "red menace" of the Soviet Union was a force to be concerned about, and conformity and obedience to authority were valued in society. In that context, Asch found that college students were remarkably susceptible to conformity pressures. Would the same be true today? Would the factors that Asch found to influence conformity (e.g., group consensus) operate in the same way now? In general, research concerned with more fundamental processes (e.g., cognition) stands the test of time better than research involving social factors that may be embedded in some historical context.

In summary, the external validity of some research finding increases as it applies to other people, places, and times. But must researchers design studies that include many different groups of people, take place in several settings, and get repeated every decade? Of course not. External validity is not determined by an individual research project. Rather, this is another case demonstrating the importance of the processes of replication and extension. For the researcher designing a particular study, the considerations of external validity pale compared to the importance of our next topic.

Internal Validity

The final type of experimental validity described by Cook and Campbell (1979) is called **internal validity**—the degree to which an experiment is methodologically sound and confound-free. In an internally valid study, the researcher feels confident that the results, as measured by the dependent variable, are directly associated with the independent variable and are not the result of some other, uncontrolled factor. In a study with confounding factors, as we've already seen in the massed/distributed practice example, the results will be uninterpretable. The outcome could be the result of the independent variable, the confounding variable(s), or some combination of both, and there is no clear way to decide between the different interpretations.

Threats to Internal Validity

Any uncontrolled extraneous factor can reduce a study's internal validity, but there are a number of problems that require special notice (Cook & Campbell, 1979). These so-called threats to internal validity are especially dangerous when control groups are absent, a problem that sometimes occurs in program evaluation research (Chapter 10). Many of these threats occur in studies that extend over a period of time during which several measures are taken. For example, participants might receive a pretest, an experimental treatment of some kind, and then a posttest. Ideally, the treatment should produce some positive effect that can be assessed by observing changes from the pretest to the posttest. A second general type of threat occurs when comparisons are made between groups that are said to be "nonequivalent." These so-called subject selection problems can interact with the other threats.

Pre-Post Studies

Do students learn general psychology better if the course is self-paced and computerized? If a college institutes a program to reduce test anxiety, can it be shown that it works? If you train people in various mnemonic strategies, will it improve their memories? These are all empirical questions that ask whether people will change as the result of some experience (a course, a program, memory training). To judge whether change occurred, one typical procedure is to evaluate people prior to the experience with what is known as a **pretest.** Then after the experience, some **posttest** measure is taken. The ideal outcome for the examples I've just described is that on the posttest, people (a) know general psychology better than they did at the outset, (b) are less anxious in test taking than they were before, or (c) show improvement in their memory. The typical research design compares experimental and control groups, with the latter not experiencing the treatment:

| Experimental:: | pretest | *treatment* | posttest |
| Control:: | pretest | | posttest |

In the absence of a proper control group, there are several threats to the internal validity of research using pretests. Suppose we are trying to evaluate the effectiveness of a college's program to help students who suffer from test anxiety (i.e., they have decent study skills and seem to know the material, but they are so anxious during exams that they don't perform well on them). During orientation, first-year students fill out several questionnaires, including one that serves as a pretest for test anxiety. Let's assume that the scores can range from 20 to 100, with higher scores indicating greater anxiety. Incoming students who score high are asked to participate in the college's test anxiety program, which includes relaxation training, study skills training, and other techniques. Three months later they are assessed again for test anxiety, and the results look like this:

pretest   *treatment*   posttest

90   70

Thus, the average pretest score of those selected for the program is 90, and the average posttest score is 70. Assuming that the difference is statistically significant, what would you conclude? Did the treatment program work? Was the change due to the treatment or could other factors have been involved? I hope you can see that there are several ways of interpreting this outcome. Read on.

History and Maturation

Sometimes an event occurs between pre- and posttesting that produces large changes unrelated to the treatment program; when this happens, the study is confounded by the threat of **history.** For example, suppose the college in the previous example decided that grades are counterproductive to learning and that all courses would henceforth be graded on a pass/fail basis. Furthermore, suppose this decision came after the pretest for test anxiety and in the middle of the treatment program for reducing anxiety. The posttest might show a huge drop in anxiety, but this result could very likely be due to the historical event of the college's change in grading policy rather than to the program. Wouldn't you be a little more relaxed about this research methods course if grades weren't an issue?

In a similar fashion, the program for test anxiety involves first-year students at the very start of their college careers, so pre-post changes could also be the result of a general **maturation** of these students as they become accustomed to college life. As you probably recall, the first semester of college is a time of great change in one's life. Maturation is always a concern whenever a study extends over some period of time.

Notice that if a control group is used, the experimenter can account for the effects of both history and maturation. These effects can be ruled out and the test anxiety program deemed effective if these results occurred:

	pretest	*treatment*	posttest
Experimental::	90		70
Control::	pretest		posttest
	90		90

On the other hand, either history or maturation or both would have to be considered as explanations for the changes in the experimental group if the control group scores also dropped to 70 on the posttest.

Regression

To regress is to go back, in this case in the direction of a mean score. Hence the phenomenon I'm about to describe is sometimes called **regression to the mean.** In essence it refers to the fact that if score 1 is an extreme score, then score 2 will be closer to whatever the mean for the larger set of scores is. This is because, for a large set of scores, most will cluster around the mean and only a few will be far removed from the mean (i.e., extreme scores). Imagine you are selecting some score randomly from the

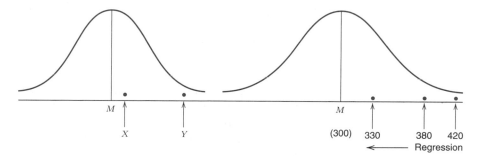

FIGURE 5.2 Regression to the mean.

normal distribution in Figure 5.2. Most of the scores center on the mean, so if you make a random selection, you'll most likely choose a score near the mean (X on the left-hand side of Figure 5.2). However, suppose you just happen to select one that is far removed from the mean (i.e., an extreme score—Y). If you then choose again, are you most likely to pick:

a. the exact same extreme score again?
b. a score even more extreme than the first one?
c. a score less extreme (i.e., closer to the mean) than the first one?

My guess is that you've chosen alternative "c," which means that you understand the basic concept of regression to the mean. To take a more concrete example (refer to the right-hand side of Figure 5.2), suppose you know that on the average (based on several hundred throws), Ted can throw a baseball 300 feet. Then he throws one 380 feet. If you are betting on his *next* throw, where would you put your money?

a. 380 feet
b. 420 feet
c. 330 feet

Again, I imagine you've chosen "c," further convincing yourself that you get the idea of the regression phenomenon. But what does this have to do with our pretest–posttest study?

In a number of pre–post studies, people are selected for some treatment because they've made an extreme score on the pretest. Thus, in the test anxiety study, participants were picked because on the pretest they scored very high for anxiety. On the posttest their anxiety scores might improve, but the improvement could be a regression effect rather than the result of the memory improvement program. Once again, a control group of equivalent high-anxiety participants would enable the researcher to spot a possible regression effect. For instance, the following outcome would suggest that some regression might be involved,[4] but the program nonetheless had an effect over and above regression. Can you see why this is so?

---

[4] Notice that the sentence reads "might be involved," not "must be involved." This is because it is also possible that the control group's change from 90 to 80 could be due to one of the other threats. Regression would be suspected if these other threats could be ruled out.

Experimental::	pretest	*treatment*	posttest
	90		70
Control::	pretest		posttest
	90		80

Regression effects can cause a number of problems and were probably the culprit in some early studies that erroneously questioned the effectiveness of the well-known Head Start program. That particular example will be taken up in Chapter 10 as an example of some of the problems involved in assessing large-scale, federally supported programs.

Testing and Instrumentation

Testing is considered to be a threat to internal validity when the mere fact of taking the pretest has an effect on posttest scores. There could be a practice effect of repeated testing or some aspects of the pretest could sensitize participants to something about the program. For example, if the treatment program is a self-paced, computerized general psychology course, the pretest would be some test of knowledge. Participants might be sensitized by the pretest to topics about which they seem to know nothing; they could then pay more attention to those topics during the course and do better on the posttest as a result.

Instrumentation is a problem when there are changes in the measurement instrument from pretest to posttest. In the self-paced general psychology course mentioned earlier, the pretest and posttest wouldn't be the same but would presumably be equivalent in level of difficulty. However, if the posttest happened to be easier, it would produce improvement that was more apparent than real. Instrumentation is sometimes a problem when the measurement tool involves observations. Those doing the observing might get better at it with practice, making the posttest instrument essentially different (more accurate in this case) from the pretest instrument.

Like the problems of history, maturation, and regression, the possible confounds of testing and instrumentation can be accounted for by including a control group. The only exception is that in the case of pretest sensitization, the experimental group might have a slight advantage over the control group on the posttest because the knowledge gained from the pretest might enable the experimental participants to focus on specific weaknesses during the treatment phase, while the control participants would not have that opportunity.

Evaluating Pretests—The Solomon Design

Sometimes the effects of pretesting itself can be evaluated using a design called the Solomon four-group design (Solomon, 1949). It looks like this:

Experimental 1::	pretest	*treatment*	posttest
Experimental 2::		*treatment*	posttest
Control 1::	pretest		posttest
Control 2::			posttest

Comparing the two experimental groups allows one to determine if the pretest is interacting with the treatment to produce changes in the posttest. Similarly, comparing the control groups tests whether the pretest by itself affects posttest performance. The ideal outcome of a Solomon design to evaluate the test anxiety program would be as follows:

	pretest	treatment	posttest
Experimental 1::	90	*treatment*	70
Experimental 2::		*treatment*	posttest 70
Control 1::	pretest 90		posttest 90
Control 2::			posttest 90

On the other hand, an outcome suggesting that the low anxiety on the posttest was due to a pretesting effect would be this:

	pretest	treatment	posttest
Experimental 1::	90	*treatment*	70
Experimental 2::		*treatment*	posttest 90
Control 1::	pretest 90		posttest 70
Control 2::			posttest 90

The Solomon design provides a nice way to evaluate the effects of pretesting but is rather costly to implement. Compared to the simple experimental plus control group design, more volunteers will be needed and two separate treatment programs might have to be run.

Participant Problems

Threats to internal validity can also arise from concerns over the individuals participating in the study. In particular, Cook and Campbell (1979) identified two problems.

Subject Selection Effects

One of the defining features of an experimental study with a manipulated independent variable is that participants in the different conditions are equivalent to each other except for the independent variable. In the next chapter you will learn how these equivalent groups are formed through random assignment and matching. If groups are not equivalent, then **subject selection** effects might occur. For example, suppose two sections of a general psychology course are being offered and a researcher wants to compare a traditional lecture course with the one combining lecture and discussion groups. School policy (a) prevents the researcher from randomly assigning students to the two courses and (b) requires full disclosure of the nature of the courses. Thus, students can sign up for either section. You can see the difficulty here. If students in the lecture plus discussion course outperform students in the straight lecture course, what caused the difference? Was it the nature of the course (the discussion element) or was it something about the students who *chose* that course? Maybe they were more articulate (hence interested in discussion) than those in the straight lecture course. In short, there is a confound due to the selection of subjects for the two groups being compared.

Selection effects can also interact with other threats to internal validity. For example, in a study with two groups, some historical event might affect one group but not the other. This would be referred to as a history × selection confound (read as "history by selection"). Similarly, two groups might mature at different rates, respond to testing at different rates, be influenced by instrumentation in different ways, or show different degrees of regression.

One of psychology's classic studies is (unfortunately) a good example of a selection effect. Now known as the "ulcers in executive monkeys" study, it was a pioneering investigation in the area of health psychology. For a close examination of this methodologically flawed (and ethically dubious) experiment and its aftermath, read Box 5.3.

Box 5.3

CLASSIC STUDIES—Selection Problems and Executive Monkeys

The April 1958 issue of the magazine *Scientific American* included an attention-getting article called "Ulcers in 'Executive' Monkeys." It described several studies by Joseph V. Brady of the Walter Reed Army Institute of Research. Motivated partly by an Army study showing a relationship between gastric secretion by soldiers during a physical exam and the subsequent development of ulcers, Brady set out to investigate the relationship between emotionality and physical disorder by studying emotional behavior in rhesus monkeys. Much to his chagrin, many of his animals died, and autopsies revealed that most of them suffered from ulcers. In particular, those with ulcers tended to be animals in an avoidance conditioning procedure in which the monkeys were kept in restraining chairs and could respond only by pressing a lever to escape from or avoid electric shock to the feet.

Brady reasoned that the ulcers could have resulted either from the repeated shock or from the stress associated with being in an avoidance conditioning procedure. Using good falsification thinking, he set up an experiment to rule out the possibility that shock alone caused the ulcers. He did this by putting two monkeys in adjoining restraint chairs. One monkey, the "executive" (note the obvious reference to the stereotype of the hard-driving, stressed-out business executive), could avoid the shocks that were programmed to occur every 20 seconds by pressing a lever at any time during the interval. For the control monkey, the lever didn't work and it was shocked every time the executive monkey let the 20 seconds go by and was shocked.

Thus, both monkeys were shocked equally often, but only one monkey had the ability to control the shocks. These contingencies were in effect for 6 hours followed by a 6-hour rest period. In a 24-hour period, then, the monkeys had two 6-hour work sessions and two 6-hour rest sessions (the monkeys never left the restraining chairs, however).

Twenty-three days later (!) the executive monkey died and was found to have an ulcer. No ulcers were found in the control monkey. Brady then replicated the experiment with a second pair of monkeys and found the same result. He eventually reported data on four pairs of animals (Brady, Porter, Conrad, & Mason, 1958), concluding that the psychological stress of being in command, not just of one's own fate but also of that of a subordinate, could lead to health problems, ulcers in this case. Can you see why the Army funded this research?

The study was widely reported in introductory psychology texts, and its publication in *Scientific American* gave it an even broader audience. However, a close examination of Brady's procedure showed that a subject selection confound had occurred. Specifically, Brady did not place the monkeys randomly in the two groups. Rather, all eight of them started out as executives in the sense that they were pretested on how quickly they would learn the avoidance conditioning procedure. Those responding most quickly were placed in the executive condition for the experiment proper. Although Brady didn't know it at the time, animals differ in their characteristic levels of emotionality and the more emotional ones respond most quickly to shock. Thus, he unwittingly placed highly emotional (e.g., ulcer-prone) animals in the executive condition and more laid-back animals in the control condition.

The first to point out this problem was Weiss (1968), whose better-controlled studies with rats (e.g., Weiss, 1977) produced results the *opposite* of Brady's. As you will learn from the discussion in Chapter 7 of yoked control groups, Weiss found that those with control over the shock in fact developed *fewer* ulcers than those with no control over the shocks.

One final aspect of the Brady research that probably occurred to you is that a modern-day animal subjects committee would require substantial changes in his procedures. Studying the relationship between stress and physical disease is vital, but it can be studied without the draconian procedure of keeping rhesus monkeys tightly restrained and relatively immobile for weeks at a time.

Attrition

Participants do not always complete the experiment they begin. Some studies may last for a relatively long period of time and people move away, lose interest, and even die. In some studies, participants may become uncomfortable and exercise their right to be released from further testing. Hence, for any number of reasons, there may be 100 participants at the start of the study and only 60 at the end. This problem sometimes is called subject mortality, but I'll avoid the unfortunate connotations of that term and use the term **attrition** instead. Attrition is a problem because, if particular types of people are more likely to drop out than others, then the group finishing the study is on average made up of different types of people than is the group that started the study. In essence, then, this is similar to the selection problem because the result is that the group beginning the study is not equivalent to the group completing the study. Note that one way to test for differences between those continuing a study and those leaving is to look at the pretest scores or other attributes at the outset of the study for both groups. If "attriters" and "continuers" are indistinguishable at the start of the study, then overall conclusions at the end of the study are strengthened, even with the loss through attrition.

This concludes our introduction to the experimental method. The next three chapters will elaborate—Chapter 6 begins by distinguishing between-subjects designs from within-subjects (or repeated measures) designs and describes a number of control problems in experimental research. In particular, it looks at the problems of creating equivalent groups in between-subjects designs, controlling for sequence effects in within-subjects designs, and the biasing effects that result from the fact that both experimenters and participants are humans. Chapters 7 and 8 look at a variety of research designs, ranging from those with a single independent variable (Chapter 7) to those with multiple independent variables, which are known as factorial designs (Chapter 8).

Chapter Summary

Essential Features of Experimental Research

An experiment in psychology involves establishing independent variables, controlling extraneous variables, and measuring dependent variables. Independent variables refer to the creation of experimental conditions or comparisons that are under the direct control of the researcher. Manipulated independent variables can involve placing participants in different situations, assigning them different tasks, or giving them different instructions. Extraneous variables are factors that are not of interest to the researcher; failure to control them leads to a problem called confounding. When a confound exists, the results could be due to the independent variable or they could be due to the confounding variable. Dependent variables are the behaviors that are measured in the study; they must be defined precisely (operationally).

Manipulated versus Subject Variables

Some research in psychology compares groups of participants who differ from each other in some way before the experiment begins (e.g., gender, age, introversion). When this occurs, the independent variable of interest in the study is said to be selected by the experimenter rather than manipulated directly, and it is called a subject variable. Research in psychology frequently includes both manipulated and subject variables. In a well-controlled study, conclusions about cause and effect can be drawn when using manipulated variables but not when using subject variables.

The Validity of Experimental Research

There are four ways in which psychological research can be considered valid. Valid research uses statistical analysis properly (statistical conclusion validity), defines independent and dependent variables meaningfully (construct validity), generalizes its results beyond the particular experiment just completed (external validity), and is free of confounding variables (internal validity).

Threats to Internal Validity

The internal validity of an experiment can be threatened by a number of factors. History, maturation, regression, testing, and instrumentation are confounding factors especially likely to occur in poorly controlled studies that include comparisons between pretests and posttests. Selection problems can occur when comparisons are made between groups of individuals that are nonequivalent before the study begins (e.g., Brady's ulcers in executive monkeys study). Selection problems also can interact with the other threats to internal validity. In experiments extending over time, attrition can result in a type of selection problem—the small group remaining at the conclusion of the study could be systematically different from the larger group that started the study.

Chapter Review

Multiple Choice

1. Schachter's study of how people expecting severe shock prefer to wait with others, described in Chapter 4 as an example using a nominal scale, might be criticized because all the participants were female. This would be a criticism of the study's
    a. construct validity
    b. external validity
    c. internal validity
    d. ecological validity

2. One year prior to their retirement, 50 people volunteer for an exercise program to reduce hypertension. One year after their retirement, all 50 people remain in the program and their blood pressure is down. It is difficult to interpret these data because of what threat to internal validity?
    a. attrition
    b. subject selection
    c. instrumentation
    d. history

3. In a memory study, a researcher wishes to show that using visual imagery enhances recall. Some participants are told to create images, and others are told to repeat each word two times. Because forming images takes longer than repeating, those in the imagery group are shown the words at a slower presentation rate (4 seconds per item) than those in the repetition group (2 seconds per item). Which of the following is true about this study?
    a. presentation rate is confounded with the instructional independent variable
    b. presentation rate is the independent variable
    c. it has internal validity but lacks external validity
    d. it is a nicely designed study with an instructional variable as the manipulated independent variable

4. Which of the following is true of the famous Bobo doll study?
    a. all of the independent variables were manipulated
    b. the researchers controlled the "Bobo" factor by using the same inflatable doll for both the adults and the children

     c. children imitated the models only when the models were portrayed as cartoons

     d. the manipulated independent variable was an example of a situational variable

5. For an experimental group in a program to reduce anxiety, the mean pretest score is 79 (maximum = 100) and the mean posttest score is significantly lower: 68. This change was most likely the result of

     a. regression

     b. maturation

     c. program effectiveness

     d. any of the above (or some combination) could have brought about the change

Short Essays

1. With anxiety as an example, illustrate the difference between independent variables that are (a) manipulated variables and (b) subject variables.

2. Use examples to show the differences between situational, task, and instructional independent variables.

3. What is a confound and why does the presence of one make it difficult to interpret the results of a study?

4. When a study uses subject variables, it is said that causal conclusions cannot be drawn. Why?

5. Describe the circumstances that could reduce the statistical conclusion validity of an experiment.

6. Describe three types of circumstances in which external validity can be reduced.

7. Distinguish between the internal and external validity of a study.

8. Explain how the presence of a control group can help reduce the various threats to internal validity. Use either history, maturation, or regression as a specific example.

9. Explain how the Solomon design can be used to evaluate the effects of pretesting participants.

10. Use the Brady study of "ulcers in executive monkeys" to illustrate subject selection effects.

Applications Exercises

Exercise 5.1.—Identifying Variables

For each of the following, identify the independent variable(s), the levels of the independent variable(s), and the dependent variable(s). For independent variables, identify whether they are manipulated variables or nonmanipulated subject variables. For dependent variables, indicate the scale of measurement being used.

1. In a cognitive mapping study, first-year students are compared with seniors in their ability to point accurately to campus buildings. Some of the buildings are in the center of the campus along well-traveled routes; other buildings are on the periphery of the campus. Participants are asked to indicate (on a scale of 1 to 10) how confident they are about their pointing, and the amount of error (in degrees) in their pointing is recorded.

2. In a study of the effectiveness of a new drug in treating depression, some patients receive the drug while others only think they are receiving it. A third group is not treated. After the program is completed, participants complete the Beck Depression Inventory and are rated on depression (10-point scale) by trained observers.

3. In a Pavlovian conditioning study, hungry animals are conditioned to salivate to the sound of a tone by pairing the tone with food. For some animals, the tone is turned on and then off again before the food is presented. For others, the tone remains on until the food is presented. For still others, the food precedes the tone. Experimenters record when salivation first begins and how much saliva accumulates for a fixed time interval.

4. In a study of developmental psycholinguistics, 2-, 3-, and 4-year-old children are shown dolls and asked to act out several scenes to determine if they can use certain grammatical rules. Sometimes each child is asked to act out a scene in the active voice (Ernie hit Bert); at other times, each child acts out a scene in the passive voice (Ernie was hit by Bert). Children are judged by whether or not they act out the scene accurately (two possible scores) and by how quickly they begin acting out the scene.

5. In a study of maze learning, some rats are fed after reaching the end of the maze during the course of 30 trials; others aren't fed at all; still others are not fed for the first 15 trials but are fed for each of the 15 trials thereafter; a final group is fed for the first 15 trials and not fed for the last 15. The researcher makes note of any errors (wrong turns) made and how long it takes the animal to reach the goal.

6. In a helping behavior study, passersby in a mall are approached by a student who is either well dressed or shabbily dressed. The student asks for directions to either the public restroom or the nearby Kmart. Nearby, an experimenter records whether or not people provide any help.

Exercise 5.2.—Spot the Confound(s)

For each of the following, identify the independent and dependent variables, the levels of each independent variable, and find at least one extraneous variable that has not been adequately controlled (i.e., that is creating a confound). Use the format illustrated in Table 5.2.

1. A testing company is trying to determine if a new type of driver (club 1) will drive a golf ball greater distances than three competing brands (clubs 2–4). Twenty male golf pros are recruited. Each golfer hits 50 balls with club 1, then 50 more with 2, then 50 with 3, then 50 with 4. To add realism, the experiment

takes place over the first four holes of an actual golf course—the first set of 50 balls is hit from the first tee, the second 50 from the second tee, and so on. The first four holes are all 380–400 yards in length, and each is a par 4 hole.

2. A researcher is interested in the ability of schizophrenic patients to judge different time durations. It is hypothesized that loud noise will adversely affect their judgments. Participants are tested two ways. In the "quiet" condition, some participants are tested in a small soundproof room that is used for hearing tests. Those in the "noisy" condition are tested in a nurse's office where a stereo is playing music at a constant (and loud) volume. Because of scheduling problems, locked-ward (i.e., slightly more dangerous) patients are available for testing *only* on Monday and open-ward (i.e., slightly less dangerous) patients are available for testing *only* on Thursday. Furthermore, hearing tests are scheduled for Thursdays, so the soundproof room is available only on Monday.

3. An experimenter is interested in whether memory can be improved if people use visual imagery. Participants (all females) are placed in one of two groups—some are trained in imagery techniques, others are trained to use rote repetition. The imagery group is given a list of 20 concrete nouns (for which it is easier to form images than abstract nouns) to study, and the other group is given 20 abstract words (ones that are especially easy to pronounce, so repetition will be easy), matched with the concrete words for frequency of general usage. To match the method of presentation with the method of study, participants in the imagery group are shown the words visually (on a computer screen). To control for any "compu-phobia," rote participants also sit at the computer terminal, but the computer is programmed to read the lists to them. After hearing their respective word lists, participants have 60 seconds to recall as many words as they can in any order that occurs to them.

4. A social psychologist is interested in helping behavior and happens to know two male graduate students who would be happy to assist. The first (Ned) is generally well dressed, but the second (Ted) doesn't care much about appearances. An experiment is designed in which passersby in a mall will be approached by a student who is either well-dressed Ned or shabbily dressed Ted. All of the testing sessions occur between 8 and 9 o'clock in the evening, with Ned working on Monday and Ted working on Friday. The student will approach a shopper and ask for a quarter for a cup of coffee. Nearby, the experimenter will record whether or not people give money.

Exercise 5.3.—Operational Definitions (Again)

In Chapter 3, you first learned about operational definitions and completed an exercise on the operational definitions of some familiar constructs used in psychological research. In this exercise, you are to play the role of an experimenter designing a study. For each of the four hypotheses:

(a) identify the independent variable(s), decide how many levels of the independent variable(s) you would like to use, and identify the levels;

(b) identify the dependent variable in each study; and

(c)   create operational definitions for your independent and dependent variables.

1.   People will be more likely to offer help to someone in need if the situation unambiguously calls for help.

2.   Ability to concentrate on a task deteriorates when people feel crowded.

3.   Good bowlers improve their performance in the presence of an audience, while average bowlers do worse.

4.   Animals learn a difficult maze best when they are moderately aroused. They do poorly in difficult mazes when their arousal is low or high. When the maze is easy, performance improves steadily from low to moderate to high arousal.

CHAPTER 6

Control Problems in Experimental Research

Preview & Chapter Objectives

In Chapter 5 you learned the essentials of the experimental method—manipulating an independent variable, controlling everything else, and measuring the dependent variable. In this chapter we will begin by examining two general types of experimental design, one in which different groups of participants contribute data for different levels of the independent variable (between-subjects design) and one in which the same participants contribute data to all the levels of the independent variable (within-subjects design). As you are about to learn, there are special advantages associated with each approach, but there are also problems that have to be carefully controlled—the problem of equivalent groups for between-subjects designs and problems of sequence for within-subjects designs. The last third of the chapter addresses the issue of bias and the ways of controlling it. When you finish this chapter, you should be able to:

- Discriminate between-subjects designs from within-subjects designs.
- Understand how random assignment can solve the equivalent groups problem in between-subjects designs.

179

- Understand when matching should be used instead of random assignment in order to produce equivalent groups.
- Distinguish between progressive and carryover effects in within-subjects designs and understand why counterbalancing normally works better with the former than with the latter.
- Describe the various forms of counterbalancing for situations in which participants are tested once per condition and more than once per condition.
- Describe the specific types of between- and within-subjects designs that occur in research in developmental psychology and understand the problems associated with each.
- Describe how experimenter bias can occur and how it can be controlled.
- Describe how participant bias can occur and how it can be controlled.

In his landmark experimental psychology text, just after introducing his now famous distinction between independent and dependent variables, R. S. Woodworth emphasized the importance of control in experimental research. As he put it, "[w]hether one or more independent variables are used, it remains essential that all other conditions be constant. Otherwise you cannot connect the effect observed with any definite cause. The psychologist must expect to encounter difficulties in meeting this requirement…" (Woodworth, 1938, p. 3). Some of these difficulties we've already seen. The general problem of confounding and the specific threats to internal validity discussed in the previous chapter are basically problems of controlling extraneous factors. In this chapter, we'll look at some other aspects of maintaining control: the problem of creating equivalent groups in experiments involving separate groups of participants, the problem of sequence effects in experiments in which participants are tested several times, and problems resulting from bias.

Recall that an independent variable must have a minimum of two levels. At the very least, an experiment will compare condition A with condition B. Those who participate in the study might be placed in level A, level B, or both. If they receive either A *or* B but not both, the design is a **between-subjects design,** so named because the comparison of levels A and B will be a contrast *between* two different groups of individuals. On the other hand, if each participant receives both levels A *and* B, you could say that both levels exist *within* each individual; hence, this design is called a **within-subjects design** (or sometimes, a repeated-measures design). Let's examine each approach.

Between-Subjects Designs

Between-subjects designs are sometimes used because they must be used. If the independent variable is a subject variable, for instance, there is usually no choice. A study comparing introverts with extroverts requires two different groups of people. Unless the researcher could round up some multiple personalities who were introverted in one personality and extroverted in another, there is no alternative but to compare two different groups. One of the few times a subject variable won't be a between-subject variable is when behaviors occurring at two different ages are being compared and the same persons are studied at two different times in their lives. Another possibility is when marital status is the subject variable, and the same people are studied before and after a marriage or a divorce. Most of the time, however, using a subject variable means that a between-subjects design will be used.

Using a between-subjects design is unavoidable in some studies that use certain manipulated independent variables. That is, it is sometimes the case that when subjects participate in one level of an independent variable, the experience gained there will make it impossible for them to participate in other levels. This often happens in social psychological research and in research involving deception. Consider an experiment on the effects of the physical attractiveness of a defendant on recommended sentence length by Sigall and Ostrove (1975). They gave college students descriptions of a crime and asked them to recommend a jail sentence for the woman convicted of it. There were two separate between-subjects manipulated independent variables. One was the type of crime—either a burglary in which "Barbara Helm" broke into a neighbor's apartment and stole $2,200 or a swindle in which Barbara "ingratiated herself to a middle-aged bachelor and induced him to invest $2,200 in a nonexistent corporation" (Sigall & Ostrove, 1975, p. 412). The other manipulated variable was Barbara's attractiveness. Some participants saw a photo of her in which she was very attractive, others saw a photo of an unattractive Barbara (the same woman posed for both photos), and a control group did not see any photo. The interesting result was that when the crime was burglary, attractiveness paid off for the defendant. Attractive Barbara got a *lighter* sentence on average (2.8 years) than unattractive (5.2) or control (5.1) Barbara. However, the opposite happened when the crime was swindling. Apparently thinking that Barbara was using her good looks to commit the crime, participants gave attractive Barbara a harsher sentence (5.5 years) than the unattractive (4.4) or control (4.4) woman.

You can see why it was necessary to run this study with between-subjects variables. For those participating in the Attractive-Barbara-Swindle condition, for example, the experience would certainly affect them and make it impossible for them to "start fresh" in, say, the Unattractive-Barbara-Burglary condition. In some studies, participating in one condition makes it impossible for the same person to be in a second condition. Sometimes, it is essential that each condition include naive participants.

While the advantage of a between-subjects design is that each participant enters the study fresh, and naive with respect to the procedures to be tested, the prime disadvantage is that large numbers of individuals may need to be recruited, tested, and debriefed. Hence, the researcher invests a great deal of energy in this type of design. My doctoral dissertation on memory involved five different experiments requiring between-subjects factors; more than 600 students trudged in and out of my lab before the project was finished!

Another disadvantage of between-subjects designs is that differences between the conditions could be due to the independent variables, but they might also be due to differences between the two groups. To deal with this potential confound, deliberate steps must be taken to create what are called **equivalent groups.** These are groups that are equal to each other in all important ways except for the levels of the independent variable. The number of equivalent groups in a between-subjects study corresponds exactly to the number of different conditions in the study, with one group of subjects tested in each condition.

The Problem of Creating Equivalent Groups

There are two common techniques for creating equivalent groups in a between-subjects experiment. The ideal approach is to use random assignment. A second strategy is to use matching.

Random Assignment

First, be sure you understand that random assignment and random selection are not the same thing. Random selection, described in Chapter 4, is a procedure for getting volunteers to come into your study. Random assignment is a method for placing these participants, once selected, into the different groups. When **random assignment** is used, every person volunteering for the study has an equal chance of being placed in each of the groups to be formed.

The goal of random assignment is to take individual difference factors that could bias the study and spread them evenly throughout the different groups. Suppose you're comparing two presentation rates in a memory study. Further suppose that anxious participants won't do as well on memory tasks as nonanxious participants, but you are unaware of that fact. Some participants are shown the words at a rate of 2 seconds per word; others at 4 seconds per word. The prediction is that recall will be better for the 4-second group. Here's some hypothetical data that such a study might produce. Each number refers to the number of words recalled out of a list of 30. After each participant number, I've placed an "A" or an "R" in parentheses as a way of telling you which participants are anxious and which are relaxed. Data for the anxious people are shaded.

Participant	2–Second Rate	Participant	4–Second Rate
S1(R)	16	S9 (R)	23
S2(R)	15	S10 (R)	19
S3(R)	16	S11 (R)	19
S4(R)	18	S12 (R)	20
S5(R)	20	S13 (R)	25
S6(A)	10	S14 (A)	16
S7(A)	12	S15 (A)	14
S8(A)	13	S16 (A)	16
M	**15.00**	**M**	**19.00**
SD	**3.25**	**SD**	**3.70**

If you look carefully at these data, you'll see that the three anxious participants in each group did worse than their five relaxed peers. However, because there is an equal number of anxious participants in each group, the dampening effect of anxiety on recall is about the same for both groups. Thus, the main comparison of interest, the difference in presentation rates (the 4-second rate yields better recall, 19.15), is preserved.

Random assignment won't guarantee placing an equal number of anxious participants in each group, but in general the procedure has the effect of spreading potentially confounding factors evenly throughout the different groups. This is especially true when large numbers of individuals are being assigned to each group. In fact, the greater the number of participants involved, the greater the chance that random assignment will work to create equivalent groups. If groups are equivalent and if all else is adequately controlled, then you are in that enviable position of being able to say that your independent variable was responsible if you find differences between your groups.

You might think the actual process of random assignment would be fairly simple—just use a table of random numbers to assign each arriving participant to a group or, in the case of a two-group study, flip a coin. Unfortunately, however, the result of such a procedure is that your groups will almost certainly contain different numbers of people. In the worst-case scenario, imagine you are doing a study using 20 participants divided into two groups of 10. You decide to flip a coin as each volunteer arrives: heads, they're in group A; tails, group B. But what if the coin comes up heads all 20 times?

To complete a random assignment of participants to conditions in a way that guarantees an equal number of participants per group, a researcher can use **block randomization,** a procedure ensuring that each condition of the study has a participant randomly assigned to it before any condition is repeated a second time. Each "block" contains all the conditions of the study in a randomized order. Table 6.1 shows you how this could be accomplished by hand, although in actual practice researchers often rely on a simple computer program to generate a sequence of conditions meeting the requirements of block randomization.

Matching

When only a small number of participants is available for your experiment, random assignment can sometimes fail to create equivalent groups. The following example shows you how this might happen. Let's take the same study of the effect of presentation rate on memory used earlier and assume that the data you examined reflect an outcome in which random assignment happened to work. That is, there was an exact balance of five relaxed and three anxious people in each group. However, it is *possible* that random assignment could place all six of the anxious participants in *one* of the groups. This is unlikely, but it could occur (just as it's remotely possible for a perfectly fair coin to come up heads 10 times in a row). If it did, this might happen:[1]

---

[1] This same pattern of results could occur if an experimenter failed to randomly assign and naively tested the first eight people to sign up in the 2-second rate group and the next eight people in the other group. It is conceivable that the more anxious students would delay volunteering to participate, increasing the chances of them being placed in the 4-second group.

TABLE 6.1   *Block Randomization*

As a procedure for creating equivalent groups, block randomization forms blocks containing each of the conditions in the study. Within each block, the conditions are randomly arranged. Here's how it would work in a study comparing the effectiveness of four different presentation rates on memory for a word list.

Step 1.   Decide how many participants you would like to test. If you wish to test an equal number per condition, the number must be a multiple of the total number of conditions (four in this case). Let's say you need 80 participants, 20 for each presentation rate.

Step 2.   Designate the four conditions by the numbers 1, 2, 3, and 4. Each block is defined as some random sequence of those four numbers.

Step 3.   Go to a table of random numbers and work your way down the columns or across the rows looking for the numbers 1–4. Select each of the numbers once before selecting any of them a second time. For example, suppose a portion of the random numbers table looked like this and you began with the second row, reading across:

$$2\ 2\ 1\ 7\ 6\ 8\ 6\ 5\ 8\ 4\ 6\ 8\ 9\ 5$$
$$\rightarrow\quad \underline{1}\ 9\ \underline{3}\ 6\ 1\ 7\ 5\ 9\ \underline{4}\ 6\ 1\ \underline{3}\ 7\ 9$$
$$1\ 6\ 7\ 7\ \underline{2}\ \underline{3}\ 0\ \underline{2}\ 7\ 7\ 0\ 9\ 6\ \underline{1}$$
$$7\ 8\ 0\ \underline{3}\ 7\ 6\ 7\ \underline{1}\ 6\ 1\ \underline{2}\ 0\ \underline{4}\ 4$$
$$0\ \underline{3}\ \underline{2}\ \underline{8}\ \underline{1}\ \underline{2}\ 2\ 6\ 0\ 8\ 7\ \underline{3}\ 3\ 7$$

I've underlined the sequence of random numbers you would select in this case. Thus, your first block would be 1–3–4–2. The 1, 3, and 4 are determined by the table; once those three numbers are selected, the fourth number has to be a 2, so there's no need to look for it in the table. The second block is 1–3–2–4, the third is 3–2–1–4, and so on. You'll need to select 20 blocks of four in order to cover the total of 80 participants.

Step 4.   Create a master sheet with all of the sequences on it.* As each participant completes the experiment, cross off one of the 80 letters on the master sheet. After you've transformed the numbers from the random number table back to the letters designating the four conditions of the experiment, a portion of the master sheet might look like this after the first six participants have been tested.

block 1.   ~~1 3 4 2~~
block 2.   ~~1 3~~ 2 4
block 3.   3 2 1 4
         •   •
         •   •
         •   •
block 20.   2 4 3 1

---

* Never test a single participant until you have set up a master sheet that identifies exactly how each one is to be treated.

Participant	2-Second Rate	Participant	4-Second Rate
S1(R)	15	S9 (R)	23
S2(R)	17	S10 (R)	20
S3(R)	16	S11 (A)	16
S4(R)	18	S12 (A)	14
S5(R)	20	S13 (A)	16
S6(R)	17	S14 (A)	16
S7(R)	18	S15 (A)	14
S8(R)	15	S16 (A)	17
M	**17.00**	**M**	**17.00**
SD	**1.69**	**SD**	**3.07**

This outcome, of course, is totally different from the first example. Instead of concluding that recall was better for a slower presentation rate (as in the earlier example), the researcher in this case could not reject the null hypothesis (17 = 17) and would wonder what happened. After all, participants were randomly assigned, and the researcher's prediction about better recall for a slower presentation rate certainly makes sense. So what went wrong?

What happened was that random assignment inadvertently created two decidedly nonequivalent groups—one made up entirely of relaxed people and one mostly including anxious people. A 4-second rate probably does produce better recall, but the true difference was wiped out in this study because the mean for the 2-second group was inflated by the relatively high scores of the relaxed participants and the 4-second group's mean was suppressed because of the anxiety effect. Another way of saying this is that the failure of random assignment to create equivalent groups probably led to a Type II error (presentation rate really does affect recall; this study just failed to find the effect). To repeat what was mentioned above, the chance of random assignment working to create equivalent groups increases as sample size increases.

To deal with the problem of equivalent groups in a situation like this, a matching procedure could be used. In **matching,** participants are grouped together on some trait such as anxiety level, and then distributed randomly to the different groups in the experiment. In the memory study, "anxiety level" would be called a **matching variable.** Individuals in the memory experiment would be given some reliable and valid measure of anxiety, those with similar scores would be paired together, and one person in each pair would be randomly assigned to the 2-second rate and the other would be put into the 4-second rate. As an illustration of exactly how to accomplish matching in a two-group experiment, work through the example in Table 6.2.

Matching often is used when the number *(N)* of participants is small, and random assignment is therefore risky and might yield nonequivalent groups. In order to undertake matching, however, two important conditions have to be in place. First, you must have good reason to believe that the matching variable will have a predictable effect on the outcome of the study. That is, you must be confident that the matching variable is correlated with the dependent variable. This was the case in our

TABLE 6.2   *How to Use a Matching Procedure*

In a study on problem solving requiring two different groups, a researcher is concerned that a participant's academic skills may correlate highly with performance on the problems to be used in the experiment. The participants are college students, so the researcher decides to match the two groups on grade point average (GPA). That is, deliberate steps will be taken to ensure that the two groups are equivalent to each other in academic ability, as reflected in their average GPAs. Here's how it is done:

Step 1. Get a score for each person on the matching variable. That's easy in this case because it simply means retrieving GPA data from the Registrar (with the students' consent, of course). In other cases of matching, the matching variable must be determined by pretesting participants on the variable; this can mean bringing participants to the lab twice, which can be inconvenient (another reason why researchers like random assignment). Suppose there will be 10 volunteers (Ss) in the study, 5 per group. Here are their GPAs:

S1:	3.24	S6:	2.45
S2:	3.91	S7:	3.85
S3:	2.71	S8:	3.12
S4:	2.05	S9:	2.91
S5:	2.62	S10:	2.21

Step 2. Arrange the GPAs in ascending order:

S4:	2.05	S9:	2.91
S10:	2.21	S8:	3.12
S6:	2.45	S1:	3.24
S5:	2.62	S7:	3.85
S3:	2.71	S2:	3.91

Step 3. Create 5 pairs of scores, with each pair consisting of quantitatively adjacent GPA scores.

Pair 1:   2.05 and 2.21
Pair 2:   2.45 and 2.62
Pair 3:   2.71 and 2.91
Pair 4:   3.12 and 3.24
Pair 5:   3.85 and 3.91

Step 4. For each pair, randomly assign one participant to Group 1 and the other to Group 2. Here's one possible outcome:

	Group 1	Group 2
	2.05	2.21
	2.62	2.45
	2.91	2.71
	3.12	3.24
	3.85	3.91
mean GPA:	**2.91**	**2.90**

Now the study can proceed with some assurance that the two groups will be equivalent to each other (2.91 is virtually the same as 2.90) in terms of academic ability.

Note. If more than two groups are being tested, the matching procedure is the same up to and including step 2. In step 3, instead of creating pairs of scores, the researcher creates clusters equal to the number of groups needed. Then in step 4, the participants in each cluster are randomly assigned to the multiple groups.

hypothetical memory study—anxiety clearly reduced recall. When there is a high correlation between the matching variable and the dependent variable, the statistical techniques for evaluating matched-groups designs are sensitive to differences between the groups. On the other hand, if matching is done when there is a low correlation between the matching variable and the dependent variable, the chances of finding a true difference between groups declines. So it is important to be careful when picking matching variables.

A second important condition for matching is that there must be some reasonable way of measuring or identifying participants on the matching variable. In some studies, participants must be tested on the matching variable first, then assigned to groups, then put through the experimental procedure. Depending on the circumstances, this might require bringing participants into the lab on two separate occasions, which can create logistical problems. Also, the initial testing on the matching variable might give participants an indication of the study's purpose, thereby introducing some bias into the study. The simplest matching situations occur when the matching variables are constructs that can be determined without directly testing the participants (e.g., grade point average scores from school records), or by matching on the dependent variable itself. That is, in a memory study, participants could be given an initial memory test, then matched on their performance and assigned to 2-second and 4-second groups. Their pre-existing memory ability would thereby be under control and the differences in performance could be attributed to the presentation rate.

In the Chapter 4 discussion of stratified sampling, I pointed out that researchers using the procedure face the problem of how many strata to use. Matching creates a similar dilemma for the investigator. In a memory study, should I match the groups for anxiety level? What about intelligence level? What about education level? You can see that some judgment is required here, for matching is difficult to accomplish with more than one matching variable, and often results in having to eliminate participants because matches sometimes cannot be made. The problem of deciding on and measuring matching variables is one reason research psychologists often prefer to make the effort to recruit enough volunteers to use random assignment, even when they might suspect that some extraneous variable correlates with the dependent variable. In memory research, for instance, researchers are seldom concerned about their anxiety levels, intelligence, or education level. They simply make the groups large enough, and assume that random assignment will distribute these potentially confounding factors evenly throughout the conditions of the study.

Within-Subjects Designs

As mentioned at the start of the chapter, each participant is exposed to each level of the independent variable in a within-subjects design. Because everyone in this type of study is measured several times, you will sometimes see this procedure described as a "repeated-measures" design (e.g., see Chapter 7). One practical advantage of this design should be obvious—fewer people need to be recruited. If you have a study comparing two conditions and you want to test 20 people in condition 1, you'll need to recruit 40 people for a between-subjects study but only 20 for a within-subjects study.

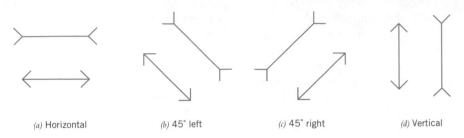

(a) Horizontal   *(b)* 45° left   *(c)* 45° right   *(d)* Vertical

FIGURE 6.1   Set of four Müller-Lyer illusions: horizontal, 45° left, 45° right, vertical.

Within–subjects designs are sometimes the only reasonable choice. In experiments in such areas as physiological psychology and sensation and perception, comparisons often are made between conditions that require just a brief amount of time to test but might demand extensive preparation. For example, a perceptual study using the Müller-Lyer illusion might vary the orientations of the lines to see if the illusion is especially strong when presented vertically (see Figure 6.1). The task might involve showing the illusion on a computer screen and asking the participant to press a certain key that changes the length of one of the lines. Participants are told to adjust the two lines until they seem to be the same length. Any one trial might take no more than 5 seconds, so it would be absurd to make the "illusion orientation" variable a between-subjects factor and use someone for a fraction of a minute. Instead, it makes more sense to make the orientation variable a within-subjects factor and give each participant a sequence of trials to cover all levels of the variable (and perhaps duplicate each level several times). And unlike the attractive/unattractive Barbara Helm study, serving in one condition would not make it impossible to serve in another.

A within-subjects design might also be necessary when volunteers are scarce because the entire population of interest is small. Studying astronauts or people with special expertise (e.g., world-class chess players) are just two examples. Of course, there are times when even with a limited population, the design may require a between-subjects manipulation. Evaluating the effects of a new form of therapy for those suffering from a rare form of psychopathology might require comparing those in therapy with others in a control group not being treated.

Besides convenience, another advantage of within-subjects designs is that they eliminate the equivalent groups problem that occurs with between-subjects designs. Recall from Chapter 4 that an inferential statistical analysis comparing two groups examines the variability between experimental conditions with the variability within each condition. Variability between conditions could be due to (a) the independent variable, (b) other systematic variance resulting from confounding, and/or (c) nonsystematic error variance. A significant portion of the error variance in a between-subjects design results from individual differences between subjects in the different groups. But in a within-subjects design any between-condition individual difference variance disappears. Let's look at a concrete example.

Suppose you are comparing two golf balls for distance. You recruit 10 professional golfers and randomly assign them to two groups of 5. After warming up, each golfer hits one ball or the other. Here are the results:

Pros in the First Group	Golf Ball 1	Pros in the Second Group	Golf Ball 2
Pro 1	255	Pro 6	269
Pro 2	261	Pro 7	266
Pro 3	248	Pro 8	260
Pro 4	256	Pro 9	273
Pro 5	245	Pro 10	257
M	**253.00**	**M**	**265.00**
SD	**6.44**	**SD**	**6.52**

There are several things to note here. First, there is some variability within each group, as reflected in the standard deviation for each group. This is error variance due to individual differences within each group and to other random factors. Second, there is apparently an overall difference between the groups. The pros in the second group hit their ball farther than the pros in the first group. Why? Three possibilities:

a. chance: perhaps this is not a statistically significant difference, and even if it is, there's a 5% chance that it is a Type I error if the null hypothesis is true.
b. the golf ball: perhaps the brand of golf ball hit by the second group simply goes farther (this, of course, is the research hypothesis).
c. individual differences: maybe the golfers in the second group are stronger or more skilled.

The chances of the third possibility's being a major problem are reduced by the procedures for creating equivalent groups described earlier. Using random assignment or matching allows you to be reasonably sure that the second group of golfers is approximately equal to the first group in ability, strength, and so on. Despite that, however, it is still possible that *some* of the difference between these groups can be traced back to the individual differences between the two groups. This problem simply does not occur in a within-subjects design. Suppose you repeated the study but used just the first five golfers, and each pro hits ball 1, and then ball 2. Now the table looks like this:

Pros in the First Group	Golf Ball 1	Golf Ball 2
Pro 1	255	269
Pro 2	261	266
Pro 3	248	260
Pro 4	256	273
Pro 5	245	257
M	**253.00**	**265.00**
SD	**6.44**	**6.52**

Of the three possible explanations for the differences in the first set of data, explanation 3 can be eliminated for the second set. In the first set, the difference in the first row between the 255 and the 269 could be due to chance, the difference between the balls, or individual differences between pro 1 and pro 6. In the second set there is no second group of golfers, so the third possibility is gone. Thus, in a within-subjects design, individual differences are eliminated from the estimate of the amount of variability between conditions. Statistically, this means that in a within-subjects design, an inferential analysis will be more sensitive to small differences between means than will be the case for a between-subjects design.

But wait. Are you completely satisfied that in the second case, the differences between the first set of scores and the second set could *only* be due to (a) chance factors and/or (b) the superiority of the second ball? Are you thinking that perhaps pro 1 actually changed in some way between hitting ball 1 and hitting ball 2? Although it's unlikely that the golfer will add 20 pounds of muscle between swings, what if some kind of practice or warm-up effect was operating? Or perhaps the pro detected a slight malfunction in his swing at ball 1 and corrected it for ball 2. Or perhaps the wind changed. In short, with a within-subjects design, a major problem is that once a participant has completed the first part of a study, the experience or altered circumstances could influence performance in later parts of the study. The problem is referred to as a **sequence** or **order effect,** and it can operate in several ways.

First, trial 1 might affect the participant in some way so that performance on trial 2 is steadily improved, as in the example of a practice effect. On the other hand, sometimes repeated trials produce gradual fatigue or boredom and performance steadily declines from trial to trial. These two effects can both be referred to as **progressive effects** because it is assumed that performance changes steadily (progressively) from trial to trial. Also, some particular sequences might produce effects that are different from those of other sequences, what could be called a **carryover effect.** Thus, in a study with two basic conditions, experiencing condition A before B might affect the person much differently than experiencing B before A. For example, suppose you were studying the effects of noise on a card sorting task using a within-subjects design. Participants have to sort the cards into several categories under some time pressure. In condition A, they have to sort the cards while distracting noises come from the next room and these noises are presented randomly and are therefore unpredictable. In condition B, the same total amount of noise occurs; however, it is not randomly presented but instead occurs in predictable patterns. If you put the people in condition A first, then in B, they will probably do poorly in A (most people do). This poor performance might discourage them and carry over to condition B. They should do better in B, but as soon as the noise begins, they might say to themselves, "Here we go again," and perhaps not try as hard. On the other hand, if you run condition B first, with the predictable noise, your volunteers might do reasonably well (most people do), and some of the confidence might carry over to the second part of the study. When they encounter condition A, they might do better than you would ordinarily expect. Thus, performance in condition A might be much worse in the sequence A–B than in the sequence B–A, and a similar problem would occur for condition B. In short, the sequence in which the conditions are presented, independent of any practice or fatigue effects, might influence the study's outcome. In studies where carryover effects might be suspected, researchers often switch to a between-subjects design. Indeed, studies comparing predictable and unpredictable noise typically put people in two different groups. Between-subjects are not always the best choice, however, so it is important to know how to control for sequence effects in a within-subjects design.

The Problem of Controlling Sequence Effects

The typical way to control sequence effects is to use more than one sequence, a strategy known as **counterbalancing.** As will be elaborated below, the procedure works better for progressive effects than for carryover effects. There are two general categories of counterbalancing, depending on whether participants are tested in each experimental condition just one time or are tested more than once per condition.

Testing Once Per Condition

In some experiments, participants will be tested in each of the conditions but tested only once per condition. Consider, for example, an interesting study by Reynolds (1992) on the ability of chess players to recognize the level of expertise in other chess players. He recruited 15 chess players with different degrees of expertise from various clubs in New York City and asked them to look at six different chess games that were said to be in progress (i.e., about 20 moves into the game). On each trial, the players examined the board of an in-progress game (they were told to assume that the pair of players of each game were of equal ability) and estimated the skill level of the players according to a standard rating system. The games were deliberately set up to reflect different levels of player expertise. Reynolds found that the more skilled of the 15 players made more accurate estimates of the ability reflected in the board setups they examined than did the less skilled players.

You'll recognize the design of the Reynolds study as including a within-subjects variable. Each of the 15 participants examined all six games. Also, you can see that it made sense for each game to be evaluated just one time by each player. Hence Reynolds was faced with the question of how to control for any sequence effects that might be present. He certainly didn't want all 15 participants to see the six games in exactly the same order. How might he have proceeded?

Complete Counterbalancing

Whenever participants are tested once per condition in a within-subjects design, one solution to the sequence problem is to use **complete counterbalancing.** This means that every possible sequence will be used at least once. The total number of sequences needed can be determined by calculating $X!$, where X is the number of conditions, and "!" stands for the mathematical calculation of a factorial. For example, if a study has three conditions, there are six possible sequences that can be used:

$$3! = 3 \times 2 \times 1 = 6$$

The six sequences in a study with conditions A, B, and C would be:

A B C   B A C
A C B   C A B
B C A   C B A

The problem with complete counterbalancing is that as the number of conditions increases, the possible sequences that will be needed increases exponentially. There are 6 sequences needed for three conditions, but simply adding a fourth condition creates a need for 24 sequences ($4 \times 3 \times 2 \times 1$). As you can guess, complete counterbalancing was not possible in Reynolds' study unless he recruited many more than 15 chess players as participants. In fact, with six different games (i.e., conditions), he would need to find 6! or 720 players to cover all the possible sequences. Clearly, a different strategy was used in this case.

Partial Counterbalancing

Whenever a subset of the total number of sequences is used, the result is called **partial counterbalancing.** This was Reynolds' solution; he simply took a random sample of the 720 possible sequences by ensuring that "the order of presentation [was] randomized for each subject" (Reynolds, 1992, p. 411). Sampling from the population of sequences is a common strategy whenever there are fewer participants available than possible sequences or when there are a fairly large number of conditions.

Reynolds sampled from the total number of sequences, but he could have chosen another approach that is used frequently—the balanced **Latin square.** This device gets its name from an ancient Roman puzzle about arranging Latin letters in a matrix so that each letter appears only once in each row and each column (Kirk, 1968). The Latin square strategy is more sophisticated than simply choosing a random subset of the whole. With a perfectly balanced Latin square, you are assured that (a) every condition of the study occurs equally often in every sequential position and (b) every condition precedes and follows every other condition exactly once. Work through Table 6.3 to see how to construct the following 6×6 Latin square. Think of each letter as one of the six games inspected by Reynolds' chess players.

A B F C E D
B **C** A D F E
C D B E **A** F
D E C F B **A**
E F D **A** C **B**
F **A** E B D C

I've boldfaced condition **A** (game A) to show you how the square meets the two requirements listed in the preceding paragraph. First, condition A occurs in each of the six sequential positions (first in the first row, third in the second row, etc.). Second, A is followed by each of the other letters exactly one time. From the top row to the bottom, (1) A is followed by each of the other letters exactly one time. From the top row to the bottom, (1) A is followed by B, D, F, nothing, C and E and (2) A is preceded by nothing, C, E, B, D, and F. The same is true for each of the other letters. To use the 6×6 Latin square, one randomly assigns each of the six conditions of the experiment (six different chess games for Reynolds) to one of the six letters, A through F.

TABLE 6.3　　*Building a Balanced Latin Square*

In a balanced Latin square, every condition of the study occurs equally often in every sequential position, and every condition precedes and follows every other condition exactly once. Here's how to build a 6 × 6 square.

Step 1.　Build the first row. It is fixed according to this general rule:
　　A B "X" C "X–1" D "X–2" E, "X–3," F, etc.
　　where A refers to the first condition of the study and "X" refers to the letter symbolizing the final condition of the experiment. To build the 6 × 6 square, this first row would substitute:
　　　X = the sixth letter of the alphabet → F
　　　X–1 = the fifth letter → E
　　Therefore, the first row would be
　　　A　B　**F** (subbing for "X")　C　**E** (subbing for "X 1")　D

Step 2.　Build the second row. Directly below each letter of row 1, place in row 2 the letter that is next in the alphabet. The only exception is the F. Under that letter, return to the first of the six letters and place the letter A. Thus:
　　　A　B　F　C　E　D
　　　B　C　A　D　F　E

Step 3.　Build the remaining four rows following the step 2 rule. Thus, the final 6 × 6 square is:
　　　A　B　F　C　E　D
　　　B　C　A　D　F　E
　　　C　D　B　E　A　F
　　　D　E　C　F　B　A
　　　E　F　D　A　C　B
　　　F　A　E　B　D　C

Step 4.　Take the six conditions of the study and randomly assign them to the letters A through F to determine the actual sequence of conditions for each row. Assign an equal number of participants to each row.

When using Latin squares, it is necessary for the number of participants to be equal to or be a multiple of the number of rows in the square. The fact the Reynolds had 15 participants in his study tells you that he didn't use a Latin square. If he added three more chess players, giving him an N of 18, he could have randomly assigned three players to each of the six rows of the square (3 × 6 = 18).

Testing More Than Once per Condition

In the Reynolds study, there was no particular reason to ask the chess players to look at any of the six games more than once. Similarly, if participants in a memory experiment are asked to study and recall four lists of words, with the order of the lists determined by a 4 × 4 Latin square, they will seldom be asked to study and recall any particular list a second time unless the researcher is specifically interested in the effects of repeated trials on memory. However, in many studies it is reasonable, even necessary, for participants to experience each condition more than one time. This often happens in research in sensation and perception for instance. A look back at Figure 6.1 provides an example.

Suppose you were conducting a study in which you wanted to see if participants would be more affected by the illusion when it was presented vertically than when shown horizontally or at a 45° angle. Four conditions of the study are assigned to the letters A–D:

> A = horizontal
> B = 45° to the left
> C = 45° to the right
> D = vertical

Participants in the study are shown the illusion on a computer screen and have to make adjustments to the lengths of the parallel lines until they perceive that the lines are equal. The four conditions could be presented to people according to one of two basic procedures.

Reverse Counterbalancing

When using **reverse counterbalancing,** the experimenter simply presents the conditions in one order, then presents them again in the reverse order. In the illusion case, the order would be A–B–C–D, then D–C–B–A. If the researcher desires to have the participant perform the task more than twice per condition, and this is common in perception research, this sequence could be repeated as many times as necessary. Hence, if you wanted each participant to adjust each of the four illusions of Figure 6.1 eight separate times, and you decided to use reverse counterbalancing, participants would see the illusions in this sequence:

A–B–C–D — D–C–B–A — A–B–C–D — D–C–B–A — A–B–C–D — D–C–B–A
— A–B–C–D — D–C–B–A

Reverse counterbalancing was used in one of psychology's most famous studies, completed in the 1930s by J. Ridley Stroop. You've probably tried the Stroop task yourself—when shown color names printed in the wrong colors, you were asked to name the color rather than read the word. That is, when shown the word "RED" printed in blue ink, the correct response is "blue" not "red." Stroop's study is a classic example of a particular type of design described in the next chapter, so you will be learning more about his work when you encounter Box 7.1.[2]

Block Randomization

A second way to present a sequence of conditions when each condition is presented more than once is to use **block randomization,** the same procedure outlined earlier in the context of how to assign participants randomly to groups in a between-

---

[2] Although reverse counterbalancing normally occurs when participants are tested more than once per condition, the principle can also be applied in a within-subjects design in which participants see each condition only once. Thus, if a within-subjects study has six different conditions, each tested only once per person, half the participants would get the sequence A–B–C–D–E–F, while the remaining participants would get the reverse order (F–E–D–C–B–A).

subjects experiment. The basic rule is that every condition occurs once before any condition is repeated a second time. Within each block, the order of conditions is randomized. This strategy eliminates the possibility that participants can predict what is coming next, a problem that can occur with reverse counterbalancing.

To use the illusions example again (Figure 6.1), participants would encounter all four conditions in a randomized order, then all four again but in a block with a new randomized order, and so on for as many blocks of four as needed. A reverse counterbalancing order would look like this:

$$A–B–C–D \quad D–C–B–A$$

A block randomization procedure might produce either of these two sequences (among others):

$$B\ C\ D\ A \quad C\ A\ D\ B \quad or \quad C\ A\ B\ D \quad A\ B\ D\ C$$

To give you a sense of how block randomization works in an actual within-subjects experiment employing many trials, consider the following auditory perception study by Carello, Anderson, & Kunkler-Peck (1998).

Case Study 5—Counterbalancing with Block Randomization

Our ability to localize sound has been known for a long time: under normal circumstances, we are quite adept at identifying the location from which a sound originates. What interested Carello and her research team was whether people could identify something about the physical size of an object simply by hearing it drop on the floor. She devised the apparatus pictured in Figure 6.2 to examine the question. Participants heard a wooden dowel hit the floor, then tried to judge its length. They made their response by adjusting the distance between the edge of the desk they were sitting at and a movable vertical surface during a "trial," which was defined as having the same dowel dropped five times in a row from a given height. During the five drops, participants were encouraged to move the wall back and forth until they were comfortable with their decision about the dowel's size. In the first of two experiments, the within-subjects independent variable was the length of the dowel and there were seven levels (30, 45, 60, 75, 90, 105, and 120 cm). Each participant judged dowel length three times for each dowel. Naturally the researchers counterbalanced the order of presenting the different dowel lengths and the procedure they used was block randomization. That is, each of the seven lengths was tested in one random order, then in a second random order, then in a third. Note again an important feature of this block randomization procedure—each dowel length was tested once before being tested for a second time and each was tested twice before being tested a third time.

Although you might think this length-judging task would be very difficult, the participants performed remarkably well. They did even better in a second experiment that replicated the first except that the seven dowel lengths were smaller (from 10 to 40 cm) than in experiment 1 (30 to 120 cm). There are two other features of these experiments worth noting. First, they are a good example of the typical strategy in perception research—within-subjects designs requiring few participants and using many trials. Eight students participated in experiment 1 and six performed in experiment 2, and each person performed the task 21 times. Second, recall the Chapter 3 discussion

FIGURE 6.2   The experimental setup for Carello, Anderson, and Kunkler-Peck (1998). After hearing a rod drop, participants adjusted the distance between the edge of their desk and the vertical surface facing them to match what they perceived to be the length of the rod.

of pilot studies (p. 92). Their purpose is to try out procedures and make slight adjustments if problems become apparent. Something similar happened in this research, although experiment 1 was not really a pilot study. One of the aspects of the experiment 1 procedure did lead to a change in experiment 2, however. In experiment 1, the dowels were dropped onto the floor. In experiment 2, they were dropped onto an elevated surface. Why? As Carello, Anderson, and Kunkler-Peck (1998) described it, the reason was a very practical one (and, reading between the lines, one for which the graduate student collecting the data was thankful). The change in procedure helped "to reduce the back and knee strain on the experimenter" (p. 212).

Problems with Counterbalancing

The various counterbalancing procedures help reduce sequence effects, but some may do so imperfectly because counterbalancing assumes that sequential effects are linear and this may not always be true, especially for carryover effects. To see why this can be a problem, consider the following hypothetical example.

Suppose you were doing a human maze-learning experiment comparing two types of mazes like those in Figure 6.3, a sequential maze (a) requiring a series of left–right turns and a more spatial arrangement (b) like the Hampton Court maze. In a study with mazes like these, you would be blindfolded and told to work your way through the maze by moving a stylus or a golf tee (which works quite well, actually) through the grooves that make up the pathways.

In the study, assume that a within-subjects design is being used. Half of the participants learn maze A followed by maze B; the remainder learns B, then A. This procedure would be complete counterbalancing. Assuming that the entire session lasts an hour and that participants become tired or bored as the time passes, performance on the second maze might suffer. But it is reasonable to assume that this increase in boredom over the hour is a progressive effect, a *linear* change from trial to trial. Hence, counterbalancing, which results in each maze being tested first and second an equal number of times, will balance out the effects of boredom. Let's say that boredom adds three errors to a typical score and that maze B (producing an average of 15 errors) is harder than maze A (with an average of 10 errors). For the sequences A→B and B→A, this might happen:

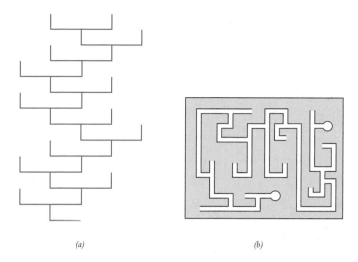

(a)   *(b)*

FIGURE 6.3   Human stylus mazes of two types: a sequential maze (a) and a spatial maze (b).

	Errors Due To:		
	Difficulty	**Boredom**	**Total**
Maze A then	10	0	**10**
Maze B	15	+3	**18**
Maze B then	15	0	**15**
Maze A	10	+3	**13**

With the two sequences combined, boredom contributes equally to mazes A and B and its effect washes out. The overall error scores are an average of 11.5 for maze A [(10 + 13)/2] and 16.5 [(18 + 15)/2)] for the more difficult maze B.

On the other hand, as mentioned earlier, carryover effects can create problems that counterbalancing might not cure. Suppose, for example, that solving maze A gives people an insight about solving mazes in general, but the same insight does *not* result when solving maze B. If this happened, then in the sequence A→B, learning A first will produce a great deal of positive transfer that carries over to maze B. On the other hand, learning B first will not produce much if any positive transfer to A in the sequence B→A. Another way of saying this is that the two sequences produce **asymmetric transfer** (Poulton, 1982). That is, one sequence produces a particular outcome that is not matched by the counterbalanced sequence. In the maze example, let's assume that learning A first has the effect of making B very easy; specifically, it reduces the total errors in B by 10. On the other hand, learning B first produces no transfer to A. Thus:

	Errors Due To:			
	Difficulty	**Transfer**	**Boredom**	**Total**
Maze A then	10	—	—	**10**
Maze B	15	−10	+3	**18**
Maze B then	15	—	—	**15**
Maze A	10	0	+3	**13**

With the two sequences combined, the boredom effect still balances out, but the asymmetric transfer effect doesn't. The final error scores are an average of 11.5 for *both* maze A [(10 + 13)/2] and the supposedly more difficult maze B [(8 + 15)/2]. The transfer problem would result in a finding of no difference between the mazes, undoubtedly an unpleasant surprise for the researcher. If one suspects asymmetric transfer, it is wise to switch to a between-subjects design if such a change is feasible.

Control Problems in Developmental Research

As you have learned, the researcher must weigh several factors when deciding whether to use a between-subjects design or a within-subjects design. There are some additional considerations for researchers in developmental psychology, where two specific varieties of these designs occur. These methods are known as cross-sectional and longitudinal designs.

You've seen these terms before if you have taken a course in developmental or child psychology. Research in these areas includes age as the prime variable—after all, the name of the game in developmental psychology is to discover how we change as we grow older. A **cross-sectional study** takes a between-subjects approach. A cross-sectional study comparing the language performance of 3-, 4-, and 5-year-old children would use three different groups of children. A **longitudinal study,** on the other hand, studies a single group over a period of time; it takes a within-subjects or repeated-measures approach. The same language study would measure language behavior in a group of 3-year-olds, then study these same children when they turned 4 and 5.

The obvious advantage of the cross-sectional approach to the experiment on language is time; such a study might take a month to complete. If done as a longitudinal study, it would take 3 years. However, a potentially serious difficulty with some cross-sectional studies is a special form of the problem of nonequivalent groups and involves what are known as **cohort effects.** A cohort is a group of people born at about the same time. If you are studying three age groups, they differ not just simply in chronological age but also in terms of the environments in which they were raised. The problem is not especially noticeable when comparing 3-, 4-, and 5-year-olds, but what if you're interested in whether intelligence declines with age and decide to compare groups aged 30, 50, and 70? You might indeed find a decline with age, but does it mean that intelligence gradually decreases with age, or might the differences relate to the very different life histories of the three groups? For example, the 70-year-olds went to school during the Great Depression, the 50-year-olds were educated during the post–World War II boom, and the 30-year-olds were raised on TV. These factors could bias the results. Indeed, this outcome has occurred. Early research on the effects of age on IQ suggested that significant declines occurred, but these studies were cross-sectional (e.g., Miles, 1933). Subsequent longitudinal studies revealed a very different pattern (Schaie, 1988). For example, verbal abilities show very little decline, especially if the person remains verbally active (moral: use it or lose it).

While cohort effects can plague cross-sectional studies, longitudinal studies also have problems, most notably with attrition. If a large number of participants drop out of the study, the group completing it may be very different from the group starting it. Referring to the age and IQ example, if people stay healthy, they may remain more interested in the intellectual life than if they are sick all the time. If they are chronically ill, they may die before a study is completed, leaving a group that may be generally more intelligent than the group starting the study. There are also potential ethical problems in longitudinal studies. As people develop and mature, they might change their attitudes about their willingness to participate. Most researchers doing longitudinal research recognize that informed consent is an ongoing process, not a one-time event. Ethically sensitive researchers will periodically renew the consent process in long-term studies, perhaps every few years (Fischman, 2000).

In trying to balance cohort and attrition problems, some researchers use a strategy that combines cross-sectional with longitudinal studies. For instance, a series of studies by K. Warner Schaie (1983), known as the Seattle Longitudinal Study, selected a new cohort every seven years (starting in the 1950s) and retested cohorts every seven years. This reduces the magnitude of any cohort effect by using groups differing by seven years of age and reduces the problem of attrition by adding new participants at regular intervals. Any one particular cohort might have a high rate of attrition, but with a lot of cohorts, at least some of the groups remain relatively intact for an extended period of time.

The length of the Seattle project is impressive, but the world's record for perseverance in a repeated-measures study occurred in what is arguably the most famous longitudinal study of all time. Before continuing, read Box 6.1, which chronicles the epic tale of Lewis Terman's study of gifted children.

Problems with Biasing

Because human beings are always the experimenters and usually the participants in psychology research, there is the chance that the results of a study could be influenced by some "bias," a preconceived expectation about what is to happen in an experiment. These biases take several forms but fall into two broad categories: those affecting experimenters and those affecting research participants. These two forms of bias often interact.

Box 6.1

CLASSIC STUDIES—The Record for Repeated Measure

In 1921, the psychologist Lewis Terman (1877–1956) began what became the longest-running repeated-measures design in the history of psychology. A precocious child himself, Terman was always interested in studying gifted children. His doctoral dissertation, supervised by Edmund Sanford at Clark University in 1905, was his first serious investigation of giftedness; he compared bright and dull local school children to see which tests might best distinguish between them (Minton, 1987). This early interest in giftedness and mental testing foreshadowed Terman's two main contributions to psychology. First, he took the intelligence test created by Alfred Binet of France and transformed it into the still popular Stanford-Binet IQ test. Second, he began a longitudinal study of gifted children that was still going strong long after Terman himself died.

Terman was motivated by the belief, shared by most mental testers of his day, that America should become a meritocracy. That is, he believed that positions of leadership should be held by those most *able* to lead. You can see how this belief led to his interests in IQ and giftedness. To bring about a meritocracy, there must be ways to recognize (i.e., measure) talent and nurture it.

Unlike his dissertation, which studied just 14 children, Terman's longitudinal study of gifted children was a mammoth undertaking. Through a variety of screening procedures, he recruited 1,470 children (824 boys and 646 girls). Most were in elementary school, but a sample of 444 were in junior or senior high school (sample numbers from Minton, 1988). Their average IQ score was 150, which put the group roughly in the top 1% of the population. Each child was given an extensive battery of tests and questionnaires by the team of graduate students assembled by Terman. By the time the initial testing was complete, each child had a file of about 100 pages long (Minton, 1988)! The results of the first analysis of the group were published in more than 600 pages as the *Mental and Physical Traits of a Thousand Gifted Children* (Terman, 1925).

Terman intended to do just a brief follow-up study, but the project took on a life of its own. The sample was retested in the late 1920s (Burks, Jensen, & Terman, 1930), and additional follow-up studies during Terman's lifetime were published 25 (Terman & Oden, 1947) and 35 (Terman & Oden, 1959) years after the initial testing. Following Terman's death, the project was taken over by Robert Sears, a member of the gifted group and a well-known psychologist in his own right. In the Foreword to the 35-year follow-up, Sears wrote: "On actuarial grounds, there is considerable likelihood that the last of Terman's Gifted Children will not have yielded his last report to the files before the year 2010!" (Terman & Oden, 1959, p. ix). Between 1960 and 1986, Sears produced five additional follow-up studies of the group, and he was working on a book-length study of the group as they aged when he died in 1989 (Cronbach, Hastorf, Hilgard, & Maccoby, 1990). The book was eventually published as *The Gifted Group in Later Maturity* (Holahan, Sears, & Cronbach, 1995).

There are three points worth making about this mega-longitudinal study. First, Terman's work shattered the stereotype of the gifted child as someone who was brilliant but socially retarded and prone to burnout early in life. Rather, the members of his group as a whole were both brilliant and well adjusted and they became successful as they matured. By the time they reached maturity, "the group had produced thousands of scientific papers, 60 nonfiction books, 33 novels, 375 short stories, 230 patents, and numerous radio and television shows, works of art, and musical compositions" (Hothersall, 1990, p. 353). Second, the data collected by Terman's team continue to be a source of rich archival information for modern researchers. For instance, studies have been published on the careers of the gifted females in Terman's group (Tomlinson-Keasy, 1990), and on the predictors of longevity in the group (Friedman et al., 1995). Third, Terman's follow-up studies are incredible from the methodological standpoint of a longitudinal study's typical nemesis—attrition. The following figures (taken from Minton, 1988) are the percentage of living participants who participated in the first three follow-ups:

After 10 years: 92%

After 25 years: 98%

After 35 years: 93%

These are remarkably high numbers and reflect the intense loyalty that Terman and his group had for each other. Members of the group referred to themselves as "Termites," and some even wore termite jewelry (Hothersall, 1990). Terman corresponded with hundreds of his participants and genuinely cared for his special people. After all, the group represented the type of person Terman believed held the key to America's future.

Experimenter Bias

The Clever Hans case (Box 3.3, pp. 89–90) is often used to illustrate the influence of **experimenter bias** on the outcome of some study. Hans's trainer, knowing the outcome to the question "What is 3 times 3?", sent subtle head-nodding cues that were read by the apparently intelligent horse. Similarly, experimenters testing hypotheses sometimes may inadvertently do something that leads participants to behave in ways that confirm the hypothesis. Although the stereotype of the scientist is that of an absolutely objective, dispassionate, even mechanical person, we've seen that researchers in fact become rather emotionally involved in their research. It's not difficult to see how a desire to confirm some strongly held hypothesis might lead an unway experimenter to behave in such a way as to influence the outcome of the study.

For one thing, biased experimenters might treat the research participants in the various conditions differently. One procedure demonstrating this was developed by Robert Rosenthal. Participants in some of his studies (e.g., Rosenthal & Fode, 1963a) were shown a set of photographs of faces and asked to make some judgment about the people pictured in them. For example, they might be asked to rate each photo on how successful the person seemed to be, with the interval scale ranging from −10 (total failure) to +10 (totally successful). All participants saw the same photos and made the same judgments. The independent variable was experimenter expectancy. Some experimenters were led to believe that most people would give people the benefit of the doubt and rate the pictures positively; other experimenters were told to expect negative ratings. Interestingly enough, the experimenter's expectancies typically produced effects on the participants' rating behavior, even though the pictures were identical for both groups. How can this be?

According to Rosenthal (1966), experimenters innocently communicate their expectancies in a number of subtle ways. For instance, on the person perception task, the experimenter holds up a picture while the participant rates it. If the experimenter is expecting a "+8" and the person says "−9", how might the experimenter act—with a slight frown perhaps? How might the participant read the frown? Might he or she try a "+7" on the next trial to see if this could elicit a smile or a nod from the experimenter? In general, could it be that experimenters in this situation, without even being aware of it, are subtly shaping the responses of their participants? Does this remind you of Clever Hans?

Rosenthal has even shown that experimenter expectancies can be communicated to subjects in animal research. For instance, rats learn mazes faster for experimenters who *think* their animals have been bred for maze-running ability than for those expecting their rats to be "maze-dull" (Rosenthal & Fode, 1963b). The rats, of course, are randomly assigned to the experimenters and are equal in ability. The key factor here seems to be that experimenters expecting their rats to be "maze-bright" treat them better; for example, they handle them more, a behavior known to affect learning.

It should be noted that some of the Rosenthal research has been criticized on statistical grounds and for interpreting the results as being due to expectancy when they may have been due to something else. For example, Barber (1976) raised questions about the statistical conclusion validity of some of Rosenthal's work. In at least one study, according to Barber, 3 of 20 experimenters reversed the expectancy, getting data the opposite of the expectancies created for them. Rosenthal omitted these experimenters from the analysis and obtained a significant difference for the remaining 17 experimenters. With all 20 experimenters included in the analysis, however, the difference disappeared. Barber also contends that in the animal studies, some of the results occurred because experimenters simply fudged the data (e.g., misrecording maze errors). Another difficulty with the Rosenthal studies is that his procedures don't match what normally occurs in experiments; most experimenters test all the participants in all conditions of the experiment, not just those participating in one of the conditions. Hence Rosenthal's results might overestimate the amount of biasing that occurs.

Despite these reservations, the experimenter expectancy effect cannot be ignored; it has been replicated in a variety of situations and by many researchers other than Rosenthal and his colleagues (e.g., Word, Zanna, & Cooper, 1974). Furthermore, experimenters can be shown to influence the outcomes of studies in ways other than through their expectations. The behavior of participants can be affected by the experimenter's race and gender, as well as by demeanor, friendliness, and overall attitude (Adair, 1973). An example of the latter is a study by Fraysse and Desprels-Fraysse (1990), who found that preschoolers' performance on a cognitive classification task could be influenced by experimenter attitude. The children performed significantly better with "caring" than with "indifferent" experimenters.

Controlling for Experimenter Bias

It is probably impossible to eliminate experimenter effects completely. Experimenters cannot be turned into machines. However, one strategy to reduce bias is to mechanize procedures as much as possible. For instance, it's not hard to remove a frowning or smiling experimenter from the person perception task. With modern computer technology, participants could be shown photos on a screen and asked to make their responses with a key press while the experimenter is in a different room entirely.

Similarly, procedures for testing animals automatically have been available since the 1920s, even to the extent of eliminating human handling completely. E. C. Tolman didn't wait for computers to come along before inventing "a self-recording maze with an automatic delivery table" (Tolman, Tryon, & Jeffries, 1929). The "delivery table" was so called because it "automatically delivers each rat into the entrance of the maze and 'collects' him at the end without the mediation of the experimenter. Objectivity of scoring is insured by the use of a device which automatically records his path through the maze" (Tryon, 1929, p. 73). Today such automation is routine. Recall from Chapter 4 the study of rats in the radial maze, in which rat "macrochoices" and "microchoices" were verified by videotaping each animal's performance and defining those two constructs in terms of easily verifiable behaviors (Brown, 1992). Furthermore, computers make it easy to present instructions and stimuli to participants while also keeping track of data.

A second approach to controlling for experimenter bias is to use what is called a **double-blind** procedure. This means simply that experimenters are kept in the dark (blind) about what to expect of participants in a particular testing session. Neither the experimenters nor the participants know which condition is being tested, hence the designation "double." A double blind can be accomplished when the principal investigator sets up the experiment but a colleague (usually a graduate student) actually collects the data. Double blinds are not always possible of course, as illustrated by the Dutton and Aron (1974) study you read about in Chapter 3. As you recall, female experimenters arranged to encounter men either on a suspension bridge swaying 230 feet over a river or on a solid bridge 10 feet over the same river. It would be a bit difficult to prevent those experimenters from knowing which condition of the study was being tested! On the other hand, many studies lend themselves to a procedure in which experimenters are blind to which condition is in effect. In a study comparing genuine maze-bright and maze-dull rats, it's easy to prevent experimenters from knowing which rats are being tested. In fact, in that particular case, the experimenters testing the rats probably wouldn't even know that the study had to do with rat intelligence.

Participant Bias

People participating in psychological research also cannot be expected to respond like machines. They are humans who *know* they are in an experiment. Presumably they have been told about the general nature of the research during the informed consent process, but in deception studies they also know they haven't been told everything. Furthermore, even if there is no deception in a study, participants may not believe it—after all, they are in a "psychology experiment," and aren't psychologists always trying to "psychoanalyze" people? In short, **participant bias** can occur in several ways, depending on what participants are expecting and what they believe their role should be in the study. When behavior is affected by the knowledge that one is in an experiment and is therefore important to the study's success, the phenomenon is sometimes called the **Hawthorne effect** after a famous series of studies of worker productivity. To understand the origins of this term, you should read Box 6.2 before continuing. You may be surprised to learn that most historians believe the Hawthorne effect has been misnamed and that the data of the original study were seriously distorted for political reasons.

Box 6.2

ORIGINS—Productivity at Western Electric

The research that led to naming the so-called Hawthorne effect took place at the Western Electric Plant in Hawthorne, Illinois, over a period of about 10 years, from 1924 to 1933. According to the traditional account, the purpose of the study was to investigate the factors influencing worker productivity. Numerous experiments were completed, but the most famous series became known as the Relay Assembly Test Room study.

In the Relay Assembly experiment, six female workers were selected from a larger group in the plant. Their job was to assemble relays for the phone company. Five workers did the actual assembly, and the sixth supplied them with parts. The assembly was a time-consuming, labor-intensive, repetitive job requiring the assembly of some 35 parts per relay. Western Electric produced about 7 million relays a year (Gillespie, 1988), so naturally they were interested in making workers as productive as possible.

The first series of relay studies extended from May 1927 through September 1928 (Gillespie, 1988). During that time, several workplace variables were studied (and confounded with each other, actually). At various times there were changes in the scheduling of rest periods, total hours of work, and bonuses paid for certain levels of production. The standard account has it that productivity for this small group quickly reached high levels and stayed there even when working conditions were worsened. The example always mentioned concerned the infamous "12th test period" when workers were informed that the work week would increase from 42 to 48 hours per week, and that rest periods and free lunches would be discontinued. Virtually all textbooks describe the results somewhat like this:

[N]o matter what changes were made—whether there were many or few rest periods, whether the workday was made longer or shorter, and so on—the women tended to produce more and more telephone relays. (Elmes, Kantowitz, & Roediger, 1992, p. 205)

Supposedly, the workers remained productive because they believed they were a special group and the focus of attention—they were part of an experiment. This is the origin of the concept called the Hawthorne Effect, the tendency for performance to be affected because people know they are being studied. The effect may be genuine, but whether it truly happened at Western Electric is uncertain.

A close look at what actually happened reveals some interesting alternative explanations. First, although accounts of the study typically emphasize how delighted the women were to be in this special testing room, the fact is that of the five original assemblers, two had to be removed from the room for insubordination and low output. One was said to have "gone Bolshevik" (Bramel & Friend, 1981). (Remember, the Soviet Union was brand new in the 1920s and the "red menace" was a threat to industrial America, resulting in things like a fear of labor unions.) Of the two replacements, one was especially talented and enthusiastic and quickly became the group leader. She apparently was selected because she "held the record as the fastest relay-assembler in the regular department" (Gillespie, 1988, p. 122). Her efforts contributed mightily to the high level of productivity.

A second problem with interpreting the relay data is a statistical problem. In the famous 12th period, productivity was recorded as output per week rather than output per hour, yet workers were putting in an extra 6 hours per week compared to the previous test period. If the more appropriate output per hour is used, productivity actually *declined* slightly (Bramel & Friend, 1981). Also, the women were apparently angry about the change, but afraid to complain lest they be removed from the test room, thereby losing bonus money. Lastly, it could have been that in some of the Hawthorne experiments, increased worker productivity could have been simply the result of feedback about performance, along with rewards for productivity (Parsons, 1974).

Historians argue that events must be understood within their entire political/economic/institutional context, and the Hawthorne studies are no exception. Painting a glossy picture of workers unaffected by specific working conditions and more concerned with being considered special ushered in the human relations movement in industry and led corporations to emphasize the humane management of employees in order to create one big happy family of labor and management. However, such a picture also helps to maintain power at the level of management and impede efforts at unionization, which some historians (e.g., Bramel & Friend, 1981) believe were the true motives behind the studies completed at Western Electric.

Most research participants, in the spirit of trying to help the experimenter and contribute meaningful results, take on the role of the **good subject,** first described by Orne (1962). There are exceptions, of course, but in general participants tend to be very cooperative, to the point of persevering through repetitive and boring tasks, all in the name of psychological science. Furthermore, if participants can figure out the hypothesis, they may try to behave in such a way that confirms it. Orne used the term **demand characteristics** to refer to those aspects of the study that reveal the hypotheses being tested. If these features are too obvious to participants, they no longer act naturally and it becomes difficult to interpret the results. Did participants behave as they normally would or did they come to understand the hypothesis and behave so as to make it come true?

Orne demonstrated how demand characteristics can influence a study's outcome by recruiting students for a so-called sensory deprivation experiment (Orne & Scheibe, 1964). He assumed that participants told they were in such an experiment would expect the experience to be stressful and might respond accordingly. This indeed occurred. Participants who sat for 4 hours in a small but comfortable room showed signs of stress *only* if (a) they signed a form releasing the experimenter from any liability in case anything happened to them and (b) the room included a "panic button" that could be pressed if they felt too stressed by the deprivation. Control participants were given no release form to sign, no panic button to press, and no expectation that their senses were being deprived. They did not react adversely.

The possibility that demand characteristics are operating has an impact on decisions about whether to opt for between- or within-subject designs. Participants serving in all the conditions of a study have a greater opportunity to figure out the hypothesis(es). Hence, demand characteristics are potentially more troublesome in within-subject designs than in between-subjects designs. For both types of designs, demand characteristics are especially devastating if they affect some conditions but not others, thereby introducing a confound.

Besides being good subjects (i.e., trying to confirm the hypothesis), participants wish to be perceived as competent, creative, emotionally stable, and so on. The belief that they are being evaluated in the experiment produces what Rosenberg (1969) called **evaluation apprehension.** Participants want to be evaluated positively, so they may behave as they think the ideal person should behave. This concern over how one is going to look and the desire to help the experimenter often leads to the same behavior among participants, but sometimes the desire to create a favorable impression and the desire to be a good subject conflict. For example, in a helping behavior study, astute participants might guess that they are in the condition of the study designed to reduce the chances that help will be offered. On the other hand, altruism is a valued, even heroic, behavior. The pressure to be a good subject and support the hypothesis pulls the participant toward nonhelping, but evaluation apprehension makes the individual want to help. At least one study has suggested that when faced with the option of confirming the hypothesis and being evaluated positively, the latter is the more powerful motivator (Rosnow, Goodstadt, Suls, & Gitter, 1973).

Controlling for Participant Bias

The primary strategy for controlling participant bias is to reduce demand characteristics to the minimum. One way of accomplishing this, of course, is through deception. As we've seen in Chapter 2, the primary purpose of deception is to induce participants to behave more naturally than they otherwise might. A second strategy, normally found in drug studies, is to use a placebo control group (see Chapter 7). This procedure allows for a comparison between those actually getting some treatment (e.g., a drug) and those who think they are getting the treatment but aren't. If the people in both groups behave identically, the effects can be attributed to participant expectations of the treatment's effects.

A second way to check for the presence of demand characteristics is to do what is sometimes called a **manipulation check.** This can be accomplished during debriefing by asking participants in a deception study to indicate what they believe the true hypothesis to be (the "good subject" might feign ignorance though). It can also be done during the study. Sometimes a random subset of participants in each condition is stopped in the middle of an experiment and asked about the clarity of the instructions, what they think is going on, and so on. Manipulation checks are also used to see if some procedure is producing the effect it is supposed to produce. For example, if some procedure is supposed to make people feel anxious (e.g., telling participants to expect shock), a sample of participants might be stopped in the middle of the study and assessed for level of anxiety.

A final way of avoiding demand characteristics is to conduct field research. If participants are unaware that they are in a study, they are unlikely to spend any time thinking about research hypotheses and reacting to demand characteristics. Of course, field studies have problems of their own, as you recall from the discussion of informed consent in Chapter 2 and of privacy invasion in Box 3.1 (p. 76).

Although I stated earlier that most research participants play the role of "good subjects," this is not uniformly true, and some differences exist between those who truly volunteer and are interested in the experiment and those who are more reluctant volunteers and less interested. For instance, true volunteers tend to be slightly more intelligent and to have a higher need for social approval (Adair, 1973). Differences between volunteers and nonvolunteers can be a problem when college students are asked to serve as participants as part of a course requirement; some students are more enthusiastic volunteers than others. Furthermore, a "semester effect" can be operating. The true volunteers, those really interested in participating, sign up earlier in the semester than the reluctant volunteers. Therefore, if you ran a study with two groups, and Group 1 was tested in the first half of the semester and Group 2 in the second half, the differences found could be due to the independent variable, but they also could be due to differences between the true volunteers who sign up first and the reluctant volunteers who wait as long as they can. Can you think of a way to control for this problem? If the concept "block randomization" occurs to you, and you say to yourself "this will distribute the conditions of the study equally throughout the duration of the semester," then you've accomplished something in this chapter. Well done.

To close out the chapter, read Box 6.3, which concerns the ethical obligations of those participating in psychological research. The list of responsibilities you'll find there is based on the assumption that research should be a collaborative effort between experimenters and participants. We've seen that experimenters must follow the APA ethics code. In Box 6.3 you'll learn that participants have some responsibilities too.

In the last two chapters you have learned about the essential features of experimental research and some of the control problems that must be faced by those who wish to do research in psychology. We've now completed the necessary groundwork for introducing the various kinds of experimental designs used to test the effects of independent variables. So, let the designs begin!

Chapter Summary

Between-Subjects Designs

In between-subjects designs, individuals participate in just one of the experiment's conditions; hence, each condition in the study involves a different group

Box 6.3

ETHICS—Research Participants Have Responsibilities Too

The APA ethics code spells out the responsibilities that researchers have to those who participate in their experiments. Participants have a right to expect that the guidelines will be followed, and if not, there should be a clear process for registering complaints. But what about the participants? What are their obligations?

An article by James Korn in the journal *Teaching of Psychology* (1988) outlines the basic rights that college students have when they participate in research, but it also lists the responsibilities of those who volunteer. They include:

✓ being responsible about scheduling by showing up for their appointments with researchers and arriving on time;

✓ being cooperative and acting professionally by giving their best and most honest effort;

✓ listening carefully to the experimenter during the informed consent and instructions phases and asking questions if they are not sure what to do;

✓ respecting any request by the researcher to avoid discussing the research with others until all the data have been collected; and

✓ being active during the debriefing process by helping the researcher understand the phenomenon being studied.

The assumption underlying this list is that research should be a collaborative effort between experimenters and participants. Korn's suggestion that participants take a more assertive role in making research more collaborative is a welcome one. This assertiveness, however, must be accompanied by enlightened experimenting that values and probes for the insights that participants have about what might be going on in a study. An experimenter who simply "runs a subject" and records the data is ignoring valuable information.

of participants. Such a design is usually necessary when subject variables (e.g., gender) are being studied or when being in one condition of the experiment changes participants in ways that make it impossible for them to be in another condition. With between-subjects designs, the main difficulty is creating groups that are essentially equivalent to each other on all factors except for the independent variable.

The Problem of Creating Equivalent Groups

The preferred method of creating equivalent groups in between-subjects designs is random assignment. Random assignment has the effect of spreading unforeseen confounding factors evenly throughout the different groups, thereby eliminating their damaging influence. The chance of random assignment working effectively increases as the number of participants per group increases. If few participants are available, if some factor (e.g., intelligence) correlates highly with the dependent variable, and if that factor can be assessed without difficulty before the experiment begins, then equivalent groups can be formed by using a matching procedure.

Within-Subject Designs

When each individual participates in all of the study's conditions, the study is using a within-subjects or repeated-measures design. For these designs, participating in one condition might affect how participants behave in other conditions. That is, sequence or order effects can occur, both of which can produce confounded results if not controlled. Sequence effects include progressive effects (they gradually accumulate, as in fatigue) and carryover effects (one sequence of conditions might produce effects different from another sequence).

The Problem of Controlling Sequence Effects

Sequence effects are controlled by various counterbalancing procedures, all of which ensure that the different conditions are tested in more than one sequence. When participants serve in each condition of the study just once, complete (all possible sequences used) or partial (a sample of different sequences or a Latin square) counterbalancing will be used. When participants serve in each condition more than once, reverse counterbalancing or block randomization can be used. Asymmetric transfer can occur when carryover effects are present; such transfer reduces the effectiveness of counterbalancing.

Control Problems in Developmental Research

In developmental psychology, the major independent variable is age, a subject variable. If age is studied between subjects, the design is referred to as a cross-sectional design. It has the advantage of efficiency, but cohort effects can occur, a special form of the problem of nonequivalent groups. If age is a within-subjects variable, the design is called a longitudinal design and attrition can be a problem. The two designs can be combined by selecting new cohorts every few years and testing each cohort longitudinally.

Problems with Biasing

The results of research in psychology can be biased by experimenter expectancy effects. These can lead the experimenter to treat participants in various conditions in different ways, making the results impossible to interpret. Such effects can be reduced by automating the procedures and by using double-blind control procedures. Participant bias also occurs. Participants might confirm the researcher's hypothesis if demand characteristics suggest to them the true purpose of a study or they might behave in unusual ways simply because they know they are in an experiment. Demand characteristics are usually controlled through varying degrees of deception and the extent of participant bias can be evaluated through the use of a manipulation check.

Chapter Review

Multiple Choice

1. The primary advantage of between–subjects designs over within–subjects designs is that between–subjects designs
   a. require fewer participants
   b. avoid, by definition, the problem of equivalent groups
   c. reduce the amount of error variance between conditions
   d. avoid, by definition, the problem of sequence effects

2. Which of the following is true about block randomization?
   a. it is used as a procedure to accomplish matching
   b. it is another term for a Latin square
   c. in a between–subjects study, it can be used to ensure equal numbers of participants per group
   d. in a within–subjects study, it is the name of the procedure for accomplishing complete counterbalancing

3. As a technique for creating equivalent groups, when is matching preferred over random assignment?
   a. any time a large number of research participants is available
   b. whenever a potential confound exists
   c. whenever a measurable extraneous variable is known to correlate with the dependent variable
   d. whenever strong demand characteristics are present

4. When asymmetric transfer effects occur
   a. counterbalancing may not be successful in eliminating sequence effects
   b. partial rather than complete counterbalancing must be used
   c. complete counterbalancing must be used
   d. matching must be used, rather than random assignment

5. Experimenter expectancy effects
   a. have been found in research with human participants but not in animal research
   b. can be reduced by automating the procedure as much as possible
   c. won't occur as long as participants are unaware of the hypothesis being tested
   d. have never been replicated after Rosenthal's research, so they probably aren't a real problem

Short Essay

1. Under what circumstances would a between-subjects design be preferred over a within-subjects design?
2. Under what circumstances would a within-subjects design be preferred over a between-subjects design?
3. How does random selection differ from random assignment and what is the purpose of the latter?
4. As a means of creating equivalent groups, when is matching most likely to be used?
5. Distinguish between progressive effects and carryover effects and explain why counterbalancing might be more successful with the former than the latter.
6. In a taste test, Joan is asked to evaluate four dry white wines for taste: wines A, B, C, and D. In what sequence would they be tasted if (a) reverse counterbalancing or (b) block randomization were being used? How many sequences would be required if the researcher used complete counterbalancing?
7. What are the defining features of a Latin square and when is one likely to be used?
8. What specific control problems exist in developmental psychology with (a) cross-sectional studies and (b) longitudinal studies?
9. Describe an example of a study that illustrates experimenter bias. How might such bias be controlled?
10. What are demand characteristics and how might they be controlled?

Applications Exercises

Exercise 6.1.—Between-Subject or Within-Subject?

Think of a study that might test each of the following hypotheses. In particular, indicate whether you think the independent variable should be a between- or a within-subjects variable or whether either approach would be reasonable. Explain your decision in each case.

1. A neuroscientist hypothesizes that damage to the primary visual cortex is permanent in older animals.
2. A sensory psychologist predicts that it is easier to distinguish slightly different shades of gray under daylight than under fluorescent light.
3. A clinical psychologist thinks that phobias are best cured by repeatedly exposing the person to the feared object and not allowing the person to escape until the person realizes that the object really is harmless.
4. A developmental psychologist predicts cultural differences in moral development.
5. A social psychologist believes people will solve problems more creatively when in groups than when alone.

6. A cognitive psychologist hypothesizes that spaced practice of verbal information will lead to greater retention than massed practice.

7. A clinician hypothesizes that people with an obsessive–compulsive disorder will be easier to hypnotize than people with a phobic disorder.

Exercise 6.2.–Constructing a Balanced Latin Square

A memory researcher wishes to compare long-term memory for a series of word lists as a function of whether the person initially studies either four lists or eight lists. Help the investigator in the planning stages of this project by constructing the two needed Latin squares, using the procedure outlined in Table 6.3.

Exercise 6.3.—Using Block Randomization

An experimenter wishes to test the hypothesis that victim status will influence how people judge a rapist. Participants are given a description of an assault and are asked to recommend a sentence for the attacker who has been found guilty. Victim status is manipulated by telling the different groups that the 21-year-old victim was a prostitute, a pregnant mother of two, a college student without sexual experience, or just a 21-year-old woman (control group). Five participants will be tested per group. Use a block randomization procedure to assign participants to the four groups, and produce a sheet that lists what condition each of the 20 participants will encounter.

Exercise 6.4.—Random Assignment and Matching

A researcher is investigating the relative effectiveness of two different weight loss programs. Participants will be assigned to the two groups and to a waiting list control group. To ensure that the people in one group aren't significantly heavier than those in any other group at the start of the study, it is decided to match the three groups on their starting weights. Here are the weights for the 15 participants in pounds.

156	167	183	170	145
143	152	145	181	162
175	159	169	174	161

First, use a matching procedure to form equivalent groups. Then reassign participants using random assignment (consider each column a "block" and use block randomization to place equal numbers of participants in each group). Compare these two approaches by calculating two sets of mean weights for the three groups, one for each method of creating equivalent groups. Compare your results to those of the rest of the class. What do you conclude about matching and random assignment?

CHAPTER 7

Experimental Design I: Single-Factor Designs

Preview & Chapter Objectives

Chapters 5 and 6 have set the stage for this and the following chapter. In Chapter 5, I introduced you to the experimental method; distinguished independent, extraneous, and dependent variables; considered the problem of confounding; and discussed several factors relating to the validity of psychology experiments. Chapter 6 compared between-subjects and within-subjects designs, described the basic techniques of control associated with each (e.g., random assignment, counterbalancing), and dealt with the problems of bias in psychological research. With the stage now ready, this and the next chapter can be considered a playbill—a listing and description of the various experimental designs that yield the productions that constitute experimental research in psychology. This chapter considers designs that feature single independent variables with two or more levels. Adding independent variables creates factorial designs, the subject of Chapter 8. When you finish this chapter, you should be able to:

- Identify the four varieties of single-factor designs: independent groups, matched groups, nonequivalent groups, repeated measures.
- Know when to use a *t* test for independent groups and when to use a *t* test for dependent groups.
- Understand the logic behind the use of the three special types of control groups: placebo, waiting list, and yoked.
- Understand the ethical issues involved with the use of control groups.
- Explain the two different reasons for using more than two levels of an independent variable.
- Decide when to use a bar graph to present data and when to use a line graph.
- Understand why multiple *t* tests are inappropriate and a 1-way ANOVA is appropriate when analyzing data from single-factor, multilevel studies.

In Chapter 3's discussion of scientific creativity (p. 94), I used the origins of maze learning research as an example. Small's research, using a modified version of the Hampton Court maze, was just the first of a flood of studies on maze learning that appeared in the first two decades of the 20th century. Most of the early research aimed to determine which of the rat's senses was critical to the learning process. You might recall from Chapter 2 (Box 2.3, p. 56) that John Watson ran into trouble with antivivisectionists for doing a series of studies in which he surgically eliminated one sense after another, and discovered that maze learning was not hampered even if rats were deprived of most of their senses. He concluded that rats rely on their muscle or kinesthetic sense to learn and recall the maze. In effect, the rat learns to take so many steps, then turn right, and so on. To test his kinesthesis idea directly, he completed a simple yet elegant study with his University of Chicago colleague Harvey Carr (Carr & Watson, 1908). After one group of rats learned a complicated maze, Carr and Watson removed a middle section of the maze structure, thereby making certain portions of the maze shorter than before. They predicted that rats trained on the longer maze might literally run into the walls when the maze was shortened. Sure enough, in a description of one of the rats, Carr and Watson noted that it "ran into [the wall] with all her strength. Was badly staggered and did not recover normal conduct until she had gone [another] 9 feet" (p. 39). A second group of rats was trained on the shorter maze, and then tested on the longer one. These rats behaved similarly, often turning too soon and running into the side wall of an alley, apparently expecting to find a turn there. Long after he left academia, John Watson remembered this study as one of his most important. Subsequent research on maze learning questioned the kinesthesis hypothesis, but the important point here is that good research does not require immensely complex research designs. In some cases, two groups will do just fine.

Single Factor—Two Levels

As you can see from the decision tree in Figure 7.1, there are four basic designs involving one independent variable that has two levels, and they result from a series of decisions about the independent variable being investigated. First, this variable

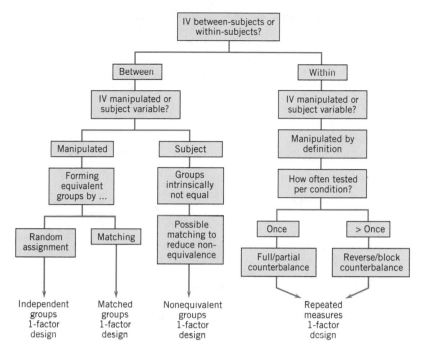

FIGURE 7.1 Decision tree—single-factor designs.

can be tested between or within subjects. If it is tested between subjects, it could be either a manipulated or a subject variable. If the independent variable is manipulated, the design will be called either an **independent groups design** if simple random assignment is used to create equivalent groups or a **matched groups design** if matching followed by random assignment is needed. As you recall from Chapter 6, decisions about matching have to do with sample size and the need to be especially careful about extraneous variables that are highly correlated with the dependent variable. If a subject variable is being investigated, the groups are composed of different categories of individuals (e.g., male/female, introverted/extroverted, liberal/conservative). The design is sometimes called an "ex post facto" design because the groups are formed "after the fact" of their already-existing subject characteristics; it has also been referred to as a "natural groups" design and as a **nonequivalent groups design,** the term I will use. Because groups are made up of different types of individuals in this kind of design, researchers using them often try to reduce the nonequivalence as much as possible by matching the groups on a variety of factors. For instance, a nonequivalent groups study comparing males and females might ensure that the participants in each group are about the same age and from the same socioeconomic class.

The final single-factor design is a **repeated-measures design,** used when the independent variable is tested within subjects. That is, each participant in the study experiences each level of the independent variable (i.e., is measured repeatedly). The major attributes of each of the four main types of designs are summarized in Table 7.1. Let's look at some specific examples.

TABLE 7.1   *Attributes of Four Single-Factor Designs*

Type of Design	Minimum Levels of Independent Variable?	Independent Variable Between or Within?	Independent Variable Type?	Creating Equivalent Groups
Independent groups	2	between	manipulated	random assignment
Matched groups	2	between	manipulated	matching
Nonequivalent groups	2	between	subject	matching may reduce nonequivalence
Repeated measures	2	within	manipulated	n/a

Between-Subjects, Single-Factor Designs

Single-factor studies using only two levels are not as common as you might think. Most researchers prefer to use more complex designs, which usually produce more elaborate and more intriguing outcomes. Also, few journal editors are impressed with single-factor, two-level designs. Nonetheless, there is a certain beauty in simplicity, and nothing could be simpler than a study comparing just two conditions. The following are case examples of three such experiments.

Case Study 6—Independent Groups

An example of an independent groups design using a single factor with two levels is a well-known study by Blakemore and Cooper (1970). They were interested in the effects of experience on the development of the visual system. Two-week-old cats were randomly assigned to the two levels of a manipulated independent variable that could be called "visual environment." The cats were to be raised in a setting dominated by either horizontal or vertical stripes. I think you can see why this had to be a between-subjects rather than a within-subjects design; it wouldn't make sense to raise a kitten in a vertical environment and *then* in a horizontal environment. In studies like this one, participants experiencing one level of the independent variable are in essence "used up"; the experience makes it impossible for them to "start over" in the experiment's other condition.

Figure 7.2 shows Blakemore and Cooper's sketch of the apparatus for the "vertical" condition. The cat is standing on Plexiglas, and the stripes extend above and below the surface. The wide collar around the cat's neck keeps the animal visually focused on the walls of the chamber. Over a period of several months, the cats were exposed to either the vertical or the horizontal world for 5 hours per day; they were kept in a darkened environment otherwise.

At the end of the study, Blakemore and Cooper tested the animals both behaviorally and by measuring the activity of neurons in their visual cortex. In general, the cats recovered quickly from the deprivation. After "10 h[ours] of normal vision they … would jump with ease from a chair to the floor" (Blakemore & Cooper, 1970, p. 477). However, the cats raised in a vertical environment apparently could

FIGURE 7.2 Apparatus for Blakemore and Cooper's (1970) experiment on the effects of experiencing only horizontal or vertical environments.

not perceive horizontal events very well; likewise, horizontally raised cats had problems with vertical stimuli:

> The differences were most marked when two kittens, one horizontally and the other vertically experienced, were tested simultaneously with a long black or white rod. If this was held vertically and shaken, the one cat would follow it and play with it. Now if it was held horizontally the other cat was attracted and its fellow ignored it. (Blakemore & Cooper, 1970, p. 478)

Obviously, early experience can profoundly affect how the brain develops.

Case Study 7—Matched Groups

Old movies sometimes feature attempts to extract information from a hero who has been locked up, perhaps tortured, and deprived of sleep for 2 or 3 days. Can sleep deprivation affect the responses to interrogation questions? That was the empirical question asked by Blagrove (1996) in an interesting study using a matched groups design. More specifically, he wanted to know if sleep-deprived people would be influenced by misleading questions. He recruited college students for three separate studies, each involving two groups—some participants were sleep deprived and others weren't. The sleep-deprived students spent their time in the laboratory, kept awake for 21 straight hours in the first two studies and 43 hours in the third. Close monitoring by "20 shifts of research assistants" (p. 50) ensured that they remained awake. Nondeprived students were allowed to sleep at home. The matching variable was "self-reported habitual sleep durations" (p. 50). Blagrove wanted to make sure that the typical length of sleep was held constant for the two groups to "control for sleep length related group differences in personality and sleep-stage characteristics"

(p. 50). So the average self-reported sleep times for the two groups were 8.4 and 8.5 hours for the first study, 8.3 and 8.1 for the second, and 8.4 and 8.1 for the third.

All participants in the study were given a standardized suggestibility test in which they listened to a story and then responded to leading questions about it (i.e., questions that could not be directly answered from information given in the story). After responding, they were given negative feedback about their responses and then questioned again to see if they changed any answers. In general, they were more influenced by the leading questions and more likely to change their answers after being sleep deprived, especially in the third study, in which the sleep deprivation lasted for 43 hours. And using the matching procedure, to ensure that the groups were similar in their typical sleeping patterns, made it possible to attribute the group differences to sleep deprivation.

Case Study 8—Nonequivalent Groups

Stimulated perhaps by Terman's mega-longitudinal study of gifted children (see Box 6.1, pp. 200–201), considerable research over the years has attempted to shed light on the gifted child. A study by Knepper, Obrzut, and Copeland (1983) asked whether gifted children might be adept at social and emotional problem solving, in addition to their normal advantages over average children in cognitive problem solving. Their experiment nicely illustrates a nonequivalent groups design. The independent variable was a subject variable, degree of giftedness, and two levels were compared, gifted (operationally defined as IQ = 130 or higher) and average (IQ between 90 and 110) students. The mean IQs for the groups were 136.9 and 102.9, respectively. A specific matching procedure was not used, but age was controlled by using only sixth graders. All were given a test called the Means-Ends Problem Solving Test, which measures the quality of solutions to interpersonal (social) and intrapersonal (emotional) problems. The gifted children indeed outperformed the average children on these tests of social and emotional problem solving, a finding consistent with Terman's conclusion that gifted children are not just "brains," but also have some social skills.

One important caution. Recall from Chapter 5 (pp. 155–156) that conclusions about cause and effect cannot be drawn when subject variables are involved. Thus, it would be inappropriate to say that giftedness somehow caused an increase in the ability to solve and emotional problems. All that can be said is that the gifted and nongifted children differed in how well they solved such tasks.

Within-Subjects, Single-Factor Designs

As you already know, any within-subjects design (a) requires fewer participants, (b) is more sensitive to small differences between means, and (c) typically uses counterbalancing to control for sequence problems. A within-subjects design with a single independent variable and two levels will counterbalance in one of two ways. If subjects participate in each condition just once, complete counterbalancing will be used. Half of the participants will experience condition A then B, and the rest will get B then A. If participants are tested more than once per condition, reverse counterbalancing (ABBA) can be used. This route was taken by J. Ridley Stroop in the first two of three studies he reported in 1935. This study is high on anyone's "top 10 classic studies" list. For a close look at it (and to learn more about swastikas than you probably know at the moment), read Box 7.1 before continuing.

Another counterbalancing strategy for a study with just two conditions, when each condition is being tested many times, is simply to alternate the conditions (ABAB…). Such an approach was taken in the following case study.

Box 7.1

CLASSIC STUDIES—Psychology's Most Widely Replicated Finding?

Reverse counterbalancing was the strategy used in a study first published in 1935 by J. Ridley Stroop. The study is so well known that the phenomenon it first demonstrated is now called the "Stroop effect." In an article accompanying a 1992 reprinting of the original paper, Colin MacLeod called the Stroop effect the "gold standard" of measures of attention, and opened his essay by writing that

> it would be virtually impossible to find anyone in cognitive psychology who does not have at least a passing acquaintance with the Stroop effect. Indeed, this generalization could probably be extended to all those who have taken a standard introductory course, where the Stroop task is an almost inevitable demonstration. (MacLeod, 1992, p. 12)

MacLeod went on to state that the Stroop effect is one of psychology's most widely replicated and most frequently cited findings. What did Stroop do?

The original study summarized three experiments, completed by Stroop as his doctoral dissertation. We'll focus on the first two because they each illustrate a within-subjects design with one independent variable, tested at two levels, and using reverse counterbalancing. In the first experiment, 14 males and 56 females performed two tasks. Both involved reading the names of colors. Stroop (1992, p. 16) called one of the conditions RCNb ("**R**eading **C**olor **N**ames printed in **b**lack"). Participants read 100 color names (e.g., GREEN) printed in black ink as quickly and accurately as they could. The second condition Stroop (1992, p. 16) called RCNd ("**R**eading **C**olor **N**ames where the color of the print and the word are **d**ifferent"). In this case the 100 color names were printed in colored ink, but the colors of the ink did not match the color name (e.g., the word GREEN was printed in red ink). The subjects' task was to read the word (e.g., the correct response is "green").

As a good researcher, Stroop was aware of the problems with sequence effects, so he used reverse counterbalancing (ABBA) to deal with the problem. After subdividing each of the stimulus lists into two sets of 50 items, Stroop gave some participants the sequence RCNb–RCNd–RCNd–RCNb, and an equal number of participants the sequence RCNd–RCNb–RCNb–RCNd. Thus, each subject read a total of 200 color names.

Stroop's experiment 1 found *no difference* in performance between the RCNb and RCNd conditions. The average amount of time to read 100 words of each type was 41.0 seconds and 43.3 seconds, respectively. Reading the color names in the RCNd condition, then, was unaffected by having the words printed in contrasting colors.

It was in experiment 2 that Stroop found the huge difference that eventually made his name so well known. Using the same basic design, this time the response was *naming the colors* rather than reading color names. In one condition, NC ("**N**aming **C**olor test"), participants named the colors of square color patches. In the second and key condition, NCWd ("**N**aming **C**olor of **W**ord test where the color of the print and the word are **d**ifferent"), participants saw the same material as in the RCNd condition of experiment 1, but this time, instead of reading the color name, they were to name the color in which the word was printed. If the letters of the word GREEN were printed in red ink, the correct response this time would be "red," not "green." Participants in 1935 had the same difficulty experienced by people today. Because reading is such an overlearned and automatic process, it interferes with the color naming, resulting in errors and slower reading times. Stroop found that the average color naming times were 63.3 seconds for condition NC and a whopping 110.3 seconds for the NCWd condition. I've taken the four different outcomes, reported by Stroop in the form of tables, and drawn a bar graph of them in Figure 7.3. As you can see, the Stroop effect is a robust phenomenon.

I mentioned earlier that Stroop actually completed three experiments for his dissertation. The third demonstrated that participants could improve on the NCWd task (the classic Stroop task) if given practice. An interesting aspect of this final study was that in the place of square color patches on the NC test, Stroop substituted color patches in the shape of swastikas, which "made it possible to print the NC test in shades which more nearly match[ed] those in the NCWd test" (Stroop, 1992, p. 18). The swastika is an ancient religious symbol formed by bending the arms of a traditional Greek cross (+). Ironically, Stroop's study was published the same year (1935) that the swastika became officially adopted as the symbol for Nazi Germany.

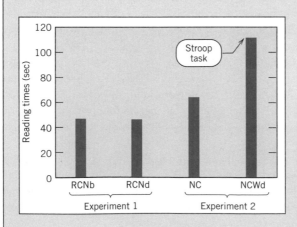

FIGURE 7.3 Combined data from the first two experiments of the original Stroop study (1935).

FIGURE 7.4 Apparatus used in Lee and Aronson's (1974) moving-room study.

Case Study 9—Repeated Measures

In a study of motion perception and balance, Lee and Aronson (1974) tested some predictions from a theory of perception proposed by James Gibson, mentioned briefly in Chapter 1 as the husband of Eleanor Gibson. In particular, they were interested in how we maintain our balance in a moving environment. Children aged 13 to 16 months were placed in the apparatus pictured in Figure 7.4. When an infant was facing the back wall, the experimenter could move the walls and ceiling either forward or backward.

It was hypothesized that moving the room forward (Figure 7.5.a) would create an "optic flow pattern" identical to the one produced if the infant's head was moving backward (Figure 7.5.b). This, in turn, would trigger a compensating tilt forward by the child. If so, then moving the room forward should cause the infant to lean forward or perhaps fall forward (Figure 7.5.c). Just the opposite was predicted when the room was moved backward.

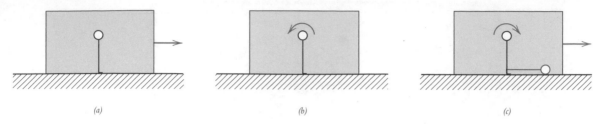

(a)   (b)   (c)

FIGURE 7.5   Predicted effects of moving the room forward in Lee and Aronson's (1974) experiment.

Unlike the study with the cats raised either in a vertical or a horizontal world, there is no reason why Lee and Aronson's infants could not experience both experimental conditions: the room moving forward or backward. Hence, a within-subjects approach was taken: the design was a single-factor repeated-measures design. The independent variable was the direction of the room's movement, either forward or backward, and the infants' body lean or falling was measured as the dependent variable. Twenty repeated trials were completed per subject, with the room's movement alternating from trial to trial. For some children, the alternating sequences began with the room moving forward; for others, the room moved backward on their first trial. Seven participants were tested, ranging in age from 13 to 16 months, but three of them became distressed and for them the experiment was terminated. The responses of the remaining four participants were recorded by three observers (why would more than one observer be needed?). Some loss of balance in the predicted direction occurred on 82% of the trials. Loss of balance was categorized by the observers as a sway (26% of the trials), a stagger (23%), or a fall (33%—ouch!).

One drawback to a counterbalancing procedure that simply alternates between conditions A and B is that subjects can easily predict what condition is about to occur. However, Lee and Aronson correctly decided that this problem was unlikely to influence their results, given the ages of their participants. Another reason for their choice of counterbalancing was practical: with the infants remaining in the moving room throughout the experimental session, once the room had been moved in one direction, the next trial had to be a movement in the opposite direction.

Analyzing Single-Factor, Two-Level Designs

To determine whether the differences found between the two conditions of a two-level design are significant or due simply to chance, some form of inferential statistical analysis is required. When interval or ratio scales of measurement are used in the experiment, the most common approach is to use one of two varieties of the *t* test, a procedure mentioned near the end of Chapter 4 and described in more detail in Appendix C. Other techniques are required when nominal or ordinal scales of measurement are used.

There are two forms of the *t* test. The first is called a **test for independent groups,** and as the name implies, it is used when the two groups of participants are completely independent of each other. This occurs (a) whenever participants in the study are randomly assigned to the groups or (b) if the variable being studied is a subject variable (e.g., males vs. females). If the independent variable is a within-subjects factor, or if two separate groups of people are formed in such a way that some relationship exists between them (e.g., participants in group A are matched on intelligence with participants in group B), a *t* **test for dependent groups** (sometimes called a *t* test for correlated groups) is used. For the four single-factor designs just considered, the following *t* tests would be appropriate:

- *t* test for independent groups
  - independent groups design
  - nonequivalent groups design
- *t* test for dependent groups
  - matched groups design
  - repeated-measures design

In essence, the *t* test examines the difference between the two mean scores and determines (with some probability) whether this difference is larger than expected by chance factors alone. If it is larger, and if potential confounds can be ruled out, then the researcher can conclude with a high probability that the differences are real, get the study published, and perhaps get promoted. See Appendix C for step-by-step instructions on how to carry out both varieties of *t* tests, as well as an accompanying analysis of effect size.

Control Group Designs

I introduced the basic distinction between experimental groups and control groups in Chapter 5 (p. 150). Experimental groups receive some treatment, while those in the control group do not. To expand the logic to repeated-measures designs, which do not have different groups, a parallel distinction can be made between experimental conditions and control conditions. Besides the typical control group situation in which a group is left untreated, there are three other specific types of control groups worth describing: placebo controls, waiting list controls, and yoked controls.

Placebo Control Groups

A "placebo" is a substance that appears to have a specific effect but in fact is pharmacologically inactive. Sometimes patients will feel better when given a placebo but told it is drug X, simply because they believe the drug will make them better. In research, members of a **placebo control group** are led to believe they are receiving some treatment when in fact they aren't. You can see why this would be necessary. Suppose you wished to determine if alcohol slows down reaction time. If you used a simple experimental group that was given alcohol and a second group that received nothing to drink, then gave both groups a reaction time test, the reactions might be slower for the first group. Can you conclude that alcohol slows reaction time? No—participants might hold the general belief that alcohol will slow them down, and their reactions might be subtly influenced by that knowledge. To solve this biasing problem, you should include a group given a drink that seems to be alcoholic (and cannot be distinguished in taste from the true alcoholic drink) but is not. This group is the placebo control group. Should you eliminate the straight control group (no drinks at all)? Probably not—these individuals yield a simple baseline measure of reaction time. If you use all three groups and get these average reaction times:

experimental group: .32 seconds

placebo control: .22 seconds

straight control: .16 seconds

you could conclude that what people expect about the effects of alcohol slows reaction time somewhat (from .16 to .22) but that alcohol by itself also has an effect beyond people's expectations (.22 to .32).

An example of a study with both a placebo control group and a straight control group examined the effects of parasitic infection on various cognitive and motor skills in Jamaican children (Sternberg, Powell, McGrane, & Grantham-McGregor, 1997). Fourth and fifth graders with mild infections were randomly assigned (after matching for gender) to a drug treatment group and a placebo group. A third (nonequivalent) group of children did not have infections. The drug effectively eliminated the infection and was administered to the placebo children immediately after the end of the study, but the infection's consequences lingered. Compared to the untreated, uninfected controls, children in both the drug group and the placebo group did poorly on several cognitive tasks. Hence, while the drug might have an important medical effect, it did little to improve the cognitive deficits that accompany the illness. Because the children lived in an environment where parasitic infections are commonplace, Sternberg et al. recommended that a program of cognitive remediation be added to the medical intervention.

Waiting List Control Groups

Waiting list control groups are often used in research designed to assess the effectiveness of some program (Chapter 10) or in studies on the effects of psychotherapy. In this design, the participants in the experimental group are in a program because they are experiencing some type of problem that the program is supposed to alleviate. For instance, a study by Miller and DiPilato (1983) evaluated the effectiveness of two forms of therapy (relaxation and desensitization) to treat clients who suffered from nightmares. They wanted to include a no-treatment control, but to ensure that the clients in all three groups were generally equivalent to each other, the control group subjects also had to be nightmare sufferers. Those assigned to the waiting list were assured that they would be helped, and after the study ended they were given treatment equivalent to that experienced by the experimental groups.

Giving the waiting list participants an opportunity to benefit from some therapy procedure provides an important protection for participant welfare, but it also creates pressures on the researcher to use this control procedure only for therapies or programs of relatively brief duration. In fact, some might argue that it is unethical to put people into a waiting list control group because they won't receive the program's benefits right away. This issue can be especially problematic when research

Box 7.2

ETHICS—Who's in the Control Group?

In a study on human memory in which an experimental group gets special instructions to use visual imagery while a control group is just told to learn the word lists, the question of who is assigned to the control group does not create an ethical dilemma. However, things are not so simple when an experiment is designed to evaluate a program or treatment that, if effective, would clearly benefit people, perhaps even by prolonging their lives. For example, in a well-known study of the effects of personal control on health (Langer & Rodin, 1976), some nursing home residents were given increased control over their daily planning, while control group residents had their daily planning done for them (for the most part) by the nursing staff. On the average, residents in the first group were healthier, mentally and physically, and were more likely to be alive when the authors came back and did an 18-month follow-up study (Rodin & Langer, 1977). If you discovered that one of your relatives had been assigned to the control group, do you think you would be concerned?

In a similar vein, there has been some controversy over the assignment of participants to control groups in studies with cancer patients (Adler, 1992). The research concerned the effects of support groups on the psychological well being and physical health of women with breast cancer. The findings indicated that women in support groups recovered more quickly and even lived longer than women not placed in these groups (i.e., they are in the control group). Some researchers argued that the results did not reflect the benefits of support groups as much as the harm done to those in the control group who might feel left out or rejected. This could create stress, and it is known that stress can harm the immune system, leading to a host of health-related problems. So is there some truth to Figure 7.6? Can being in a control group kill you?

Defenders of the control group approach to evaluating programs make three strong arguments. First, they point out that hindsight is usually perfect. It is easy after the fact to say that "a program as effective as this one ought to be available to everyone." The problem is that *before* the fact it is not so obvious that a program would be effective. The only way to tell is to do the study. Prior to Langer and Rodin's nursing home study, for example, one easily could have predicted that the experimental subjects would be unnecessarily stressed by the added responsibility of caring for themselves and drop like flies. Similarly, those defending the cancer studies point out that when these studies began, few women expressed any preference about their assignment to either an experimental or a control group, and some actually preferred to avoid the support groups (Adler, 1992). Hence, it was not likely that control group participants really felt left out or deprived.

Second, researchers point out that in research evaluating a new treatment or program, the comparison is seldom between the new treatment and no treatment; it is usually between the new treatment and the current treatment. So for control group members, available services are not really being withheld; they are receiving the normal services. Furthermore, once the study has demonstrated some positive effect of

FIGURE 7.6   Potential consequences of being assigned to the control group?

the experimental treatment, members of the control groups are typically given the opportunity to be treated.

   Third, treatments cost money, and it is certainly worthwhile to spend the bucks on the best treatment. That cannot be determined without well-designed research on program effectiveness, however. In the long run, then, programs with empirically demonstrated effectiveness serve the general good and may in many cases save or prolong lives.

evaluates life-influencing programs. Read Box 7.2 for an examination of this issue and a defense of the use of control groups in research.

   Remember the Chapter 1 discussion of pseudoscience, as illustrated with the case of subliminal self-help audiotapes? As we saw, there is ample research indicating that any positive effects of these tapes are the result of what people expect to happen. Testing expectancy often involves the use of placebo controls, but consider the following case study, which effectively combines both placebos and waiting lists to yield a new interpretation of what these tapes accomplish.

Case Study 10—Using Both Placebo and Waiting List Control Groups

One of the favorite markets for the subliminal self-help audiotape business is in the area of weight loss. Americans in particular try to lose weight by trying an unending variety of techniques, from fad diets to surgery. People are especially willing to try something when minimal effort is involved, and this is a defining feature of subliminal tapes—just pop in a tape and pretty soon your unconscious will be directing your behavior so that weight loss will be inevitable. In a study that creatively combined a placebo control and a waiting list control, Merickle and Skanes (1992) evaluated the effectiveness of these self-help weight loss tapes. Forty-seven adult females were recruited through newspaper ads and randomly assigned to one of three groups. The experimental group participants ($N = 15$) were given a commercial subliminal self-help tape that was supposed to help listeners lose weight. Those in the placebo control group ($N = 15$) thought they were getting a subliminal tape designed for weight loss, but in fact were given one designed to relieve dental anxiety (the researchers had a sense of humor). The two tapes were indistinguishable to ordinary listeners. A third group, the waiting list control ($N = 17$), was told "that the maximum number of subjects was currently participating in the study and that ... they had to be placed on a waiting list" (p. 774). Those in the experimental and placebo groups were told to listen to their tapes for 1 to 3 hours per day and participants in all three groups were weighed weekly for five weeks. The results? Those in the experimental group lost a modest amount of weight, but the *same* amount was also lost by the placebo control group. This is the typical outcome with this type of study, indicating that the subliminal tapes have no effect by themselves. The interesting outcome, however, was that the waiting list group also lost weight, about the same amount as the other two groups. This led Merickle and Skanes to conclude that subliminal tapes do not produce their results simply because of a placebo effect. If this had been true, the placebo group participants, believing their mind was being altered, would have lost weight, but the waiting list group folks, not yet in possession of the tapes, would not have lost any weight. Their outcome led the authors to argue that the effect of the tapes was to focus a person's attention on the problem at hand, in this case weight loss. The subjects in all three groups, "may have lost weight simply because participation in the study increased the likelihood that they would attend to and think about weight-related issues during the course of the study" (p. 776). In this study, then, the waiting list group had the effect of evaluating the strength of the placebo effect and providing an alternative explanation for the apparent success of subliminal tapes. Also, although the authors didn't mention it, the study's outcome also sounds suspiciously like a Hawthorne effect, which you learned about in Chapter 6 (p. 204).

One final point worth mentioning about this study is that the second author, Heather Skanes, was the experimenter throughout the study and the first author, Philip Merickle, arranged the tape labels. Thus, he was the only one who knew who was getting the weight loss tape (experimental group) and who was getting the dental anxiety tape (placebo group). That is, the authors built a nice double-blind control into their study.

Yoked Control Groups

A third type of control group is the **yoked control group.** It is used when participants in the experimental group, for one reason or another, participate for varying amounts of time or are subjected to different types of events in the study. Each member of the control group is matched or "yoked" to a member of the experimental

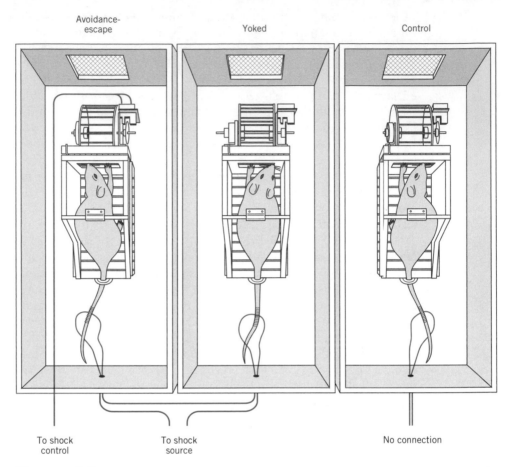

Avoidance-escape   Yoked   Control

To shock control   To shock source   No connection

FIGURE 7.7 The experimental setup of the Weiss (1968) study, illustrating the use of a yoked control group.

group so that for the groups as a whole, the time spent participating or the types of events encountered is kept constant. A specific case example will clarify the concept.

Case Study 11—Yoked Controls and Stress

A good example of a yoked control group is a study by Weiss (1968) on the relationship between control of stress and health. Experimental rats were exposed to occasional mild shocks to their tails, which they could turn off (i.e., control) or avoid altogether by rotating a small wheel with their paws (Figure 7.7). A control group of rats was never shocked. Rats in the middle position of the apparatus were in the yoked control group. Each rat in this group was yoked to (paired with) a rat in the experimental group so that it received the exact same number of shocks but could not control them. On a given trial, a tone would sound, which could be heard by all three animals. The rat in the experimental group then had 10 seconds to turn the wheel. If it failed to do so, it received a mild shock to its tail, and the yoked rat also received a shock (regardless of what it happened to be doing at the time). Thus, the rats in the experimental and yoked control groups received exactly the same degree of aversiveness (i.e., same number of shocks), but they differed in whether they had control over the situation. Weiss concluded that having control over the shock helped the rats avoid some of the unhealthy consequences of stress. The yoked rats were more likely to develop ulcers and to lose weight, while rats in the experimental group and the unshocked rats were relatively unaffected by their experience.

You might recognize the Weiss design. It was also used by Seligman's research team in their studies on learned helplessness. If you look back to the discussion of theory in Chapter 3 (pp. 82–84), you will find a description of a yoked control procedure in Seligman's triadic design, although I didn't use the term "yoked" at that point (except in a footnote). Another example of a yoked control was the Brady study of ulcers in executive monkeys, the focus of Box 5.3 (pp. 170–171). In fact, Weiss's study was designed in part to correct for the methodological deficiencies (i.e., subject selection problems) in Brady's research (Weiss, 1977).

Single Factor—More Than Two Levels

When experiments include a single independent variable, using two levels is the exception rather than the rule. Most single-factor studies use three or more levels; for that reason, they often are called **single-factor multilevel designs.** As was true for two-level designs, these include both between- and within-subjects designs and can be of the same four types: independent groups, matched groups, nonequivalent groups, and repeated measures.

Between-Subjects, Multilevel Designs

A distinct advantage of multilevel designs is that they enable the researcher to discover **nonlinear effects.** To take a simple between-subjects example, suppose you were interested in the effects of caffeine dosage on reaction time. You set up an experiment that compares two dosage levels (1 mg and 3 mg), get the results in Figure 7.8, and conclude that as a stimulant, caffeine speeds up reaction time. As the dosage increases, reaction time quickens in a straight-line (i.e., linear) fashion.

Now suppose another researcher does this study but uses a multilevel design that includes four dosages (1 mg, 2 mg, 3 mg, and 4 mg)—an example of replicating (1 mg and 3 mg) and extending (2 mg and 4 mg) your finding. The study might produce the results in Figure 7.9.

This outcome replicates your results for the 1-mg and 3-mg conditions exactly, but the overall pattern for the four conditions calls your conclusion into serious question. Instead of caffeine simply reducing reaction time, the conclusion now would be that (a) adding caffeine quickens reaction time, but only after a level of 2 mg is reached and (b) caffeine reduces reaction time only up to a point; after 3 mg, caffeine begins to slow down reaction time. That is, the outcome is no longer a simple linear result but rather a nonlinear one. In general, then, the advantage of multi-

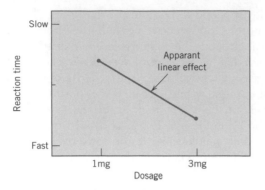

FIGURE 7.8 Hypothetical effects of caffeine on reaction time—two levels.

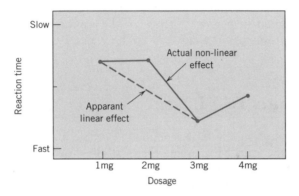

FIGURE 7.9 Hypothetical effects of caffeine on reaction time—four levels.

level designs is that they are more informative and often provide for more interesting outcomes than two-level designs.

One of psychology's most famous graphs illustrates a nonlinear effect. It shows how the passage of time influences the rate of forgetting and yields some insight into the common feeling one gets two days after an exam—"I don't remember anything!" The curve comes from the pioneering memory research of Hermann Ebbinghaus, as described briefly in Box 7.3.

In addition to identifying nonlinear relationships, single-factor multilevel designs can also test for specific alternative hypotheses and perhaps rule them out. This is a strategy you will recognize from the discussion in Chapter 3 (pp. 87–88) of the merits of *falsification*. A perfect example is a study by Bransford and Johnson (1972).

Case Study 12—Multilevel Independent Groups

Cognitive psychologists interested in how we comprehend new information have shown that understanding new ideas is easier if they are placed in some context. For example, understanding a textbook chapter is easier if you first read a preview and set of objectives, as I hope you have already discovered as you have been using this text. The Bransford and Johnson study illustrates these context effects. In their study, participants were asked to comprehend this paragraph. Try it yourself:

> If the balloons popped, the sound wouldn't be able to carry, since everything would be too far away from the correct floor. A closed window would also

Box 7.3

ORIGINS—Nonlinear Results: The Ebbinghaus Forgetting Curve

The 19th-century German psychologist Hermann Ebbinghaus (1850–1909) is justifiably famous for his pioneering research on memory and forgetting. At a time when psychology was in its infancy and "how to do psychological research" guides did not exist, Ebbinghaus managed to complete an extended series of studies that set a standard for precision and methodological rigor. His purpose was to examine the formation of associations in the mind, and his first task was to find materials that were devoid of associations. His solution, considered one the best examples of creativity in scientific psychology, was to string together sequences of consonants, vowels, and consonants. These CVCs are more widely known as nonsense syllables; Ebbinghaus created about 2,300 of them. For several years, showing either tremendous perseverance or a complete lack of any social life, Ebbinghaus spent hours at a time memorizing and trying to recall various lists of these CVCs. Yes, he was the only participant. He systematically varied such factors as the number of syllables per list, the number of study trials per list, and whether the study trials were crammed together or spaced out. He published his results in a small monograph called *Memory: A Contribution to Experimental Psychology* (1885/1964).

In his most famous study, the one resulting in a nonlinear outcome, Ebbinghaus examined the time course of forgetting. His empirical question was this: Once some material has been memorized, how much of that memory persists after varying amounts of time? His procedure was to first commit to memory eight 13-item lists of nonsense syllables, then wait for some period of time, then attempt to relearn the lists. His time intervals were 20 minutes, 1 hour, 9 hours, 1 day, 2 days, 6 days, and 31 days. Ebbinghaus recorded the total time for both the original learning of the eight lists and the relearning of the lists. Original learning minus relearning yielded a measure of "savings," which was converted to a percentage by dividing by the time of original learning. Thus, if the original learning took 20 minutes and relearning took 5 minutes, 15 minutes or 75% (15/20 × 100) of the original learning time was saved.

His results, which you can probably find in the memory chapter of your general psychology text, are shown in Figure 7.10. As you can see, recall declined with the passage of time, but the decline was not a steady or linear one. Clearly, it is a nonlinear effect. Forgetting occurs very rapidly at first, but then the rate of forgetting slows down. Thus, after a mere 20 minutes, only about 60% (58.2, actually) of the original learning had been saved. At the other end of the curve, there wasn't much difference between an interval of a week (25.4% saved) and a month (21.1%).

From the standpoint of methodological control, there are several other interesting things about the Ebbinghaus research. To ensure a constant presentation rate, for example, Ebbinghaus set a metronome to 150 beats per minute and read each CVC exactly on one of the beats. He also tried to study the lists in the same environment and at about the same time of day, and to use no memorization technique except pure repetition. Also, he worked only when sufficiently motivated so that he could "keep the attention concentrated on the tiresome task and its purpose" (Ebbinghaus, 1885/1964, p. 25).

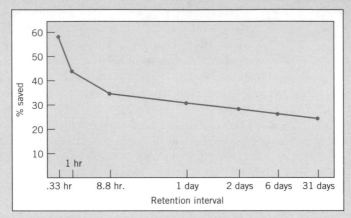

FIGURE 7.10   The Ebbinghaus forgetting curve—a non-linear outcome

prevent the sound from carrying, since most buildings tend to be well insulated. Since the whole operation depends on a steady flow of electricity, a break in the middle of the wire would also cause problems. Of course, the fellow could shout, but the human voice is not loud enough to carry that far. An additional problem is that a string could break on the instrument. Then there could be no accompaniment to the message. It is clear that the best situation would involve less distance. Then there would be fewer potential problems. With face to face contact, the least number of things could go wrong. (Bransford & Johnson, 1972, p. 392)

I imagine your reaction to this passage is "Huh?"—a response shared by many of the participants in the original study. However, Bransford and Johnson found that comprehension could be improved by adding some context. Here's what they did.

They designed a single-factor independent groups study with five levels of the independent variable. Participants randomly assigned to a control group were asked to do what I just asked of you. They read the paragraph and tried to recall as much as they could of the 14 idea units included in it. They recalled an uninspiring average of 3.6 ideas. A second group read the story twice to see if recall might improve with simple repetition. It didn't—they recalled 3.8 ideas. A third group was first given a look at the cartoon in Figure 7.11a. Then they read and tried to recall the paragraph. They recalled 8.0 ideas out of 14. Clearly, the cartoon gave these participants an overall context within which to comprehend the sentences of the para-

FIGURE 7.11 Cartoon providing (a) context and (b) partial context for Bransford and Johnson's (1972) study.

graph. But is it necessary to see the cartoon *first,* before reading the passage? Yes. The fourth condition of the study had participants read the paragraph, *then* see the cartoon, then recall the paragraph. They recalled 3.6 ideas, just like the control group. Finally, the fifth group was given a partial context. Before reading the passage, they saw the cartoon in Figure 7.11b. It contains all the elements of 7.11a, but rearranged. Participants in this group recalled an average of 4.0 ideas. In graph form, the results looked like Figure 7.12.

Considering just two groups, "No Context-1 Repetition" and "Context Before," this study is reasonably interesting, showing a simple improvement in comprehension by adding some context in the form of the cartoon. However, adding the other conditions makes it a *really* interesting study by ruling out (i.e., falsifying) some alternative factors that might be thought to improve recall. Thus, context improves our understanding of something but *only* if that context occurs first. Because pre-

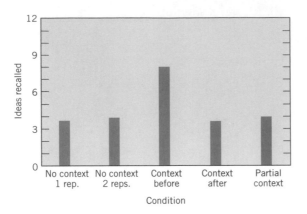

FIGURE 7.12 Data for the five conditions of Bransford and Johnson's study in bar graph form.

senting the context after the reading doesn't help, it can be inferred that context improves recall by facilitating the initial processing of the information, not just its subsequent retrieval. Also, the argument that simple repetition would improve performance can be ruled out—doubling the repetitions didn't improve performance. Lastly, it isn't enough just to present all the individual elements of the story (as in the partial context condition)—the elements have to be arranged in a way that relates meaningfully to the material to be recalled.

Within-Subjects, Multilevel Designs

Whereas a single-factor repeated-measures design with two levels has limited counterbalancing options, going beyond two levels makes all the counterbalancing options available. If each condition is tested just once per subject, then both full and partial counterbalancing procedures are available. And when each condition is tested several times per subject, both reverse and block randomization procedures can be used. In the following case study, each condition was tested just once and a Latin square was used to accomplish counterbalancing.

Case Study 13—Multilevel Repeated Measures

Can listening to Mozart make you smarter? Some people apparently think so, and the phenomenon has been dubbed the "Mozart Effect." Despite the lack of any consistent evidence to support the idea, it has been promoted to parents as a way to give their children an edge in the IQ wars. As you might guess, there's even a Mozart Effect website (www.mozarteffect.com) that features a variety of tapes and books for sale. In true pseudoscience fashion, the site argues for the phenomenon's effectiveness through the use of testimonials and anecdotal evidence. In a description of one of the tapes for sale on the website, which features Mozart's violin concertos, the website claims that listening to the concertos will "increase verbal, emotional and spatial intelligence, improve concentration and memory, and strengthen intuitive thinking skills," and that the "high frequencies of the violins exercise the ears so the stimulation to the brain is balanced by the wonderful harmonies" (whatever that means). So what is the basis for these extraordinary claims?

The origin appears to be a brief study published in 1993 in the journal *Nature,* in which the researchers evidently showed that listening to 10 minutes of Mozart could produce a short-term (i.e., the effect didn't last) increase in spatial reasoning ability among college students (Rauscher, Shaw, & Key, 1993). Cognitive psychologists were skeptical of even this short-term effect and numerous unsuccessful attempts were made to replicate the finding. One such study was completed by Steele, Ball, and Runk (1997).

Steele and his colleagues included three conditions in their study: listening to Mozart for 10 minutes, listening to a recording of soothing environmental sounds (e.g., a gentle rainstorm) for 10 minutes, and not listening to anything—sitting quietly for 10 minutes and trying to relax. All 36 participants were tested in each of the three conditions, making this a within-subjects, multilevel design. Although complete counterbalancing would have been easy to implement (six different sequences of conditions, six participants randomly assigned to each sequence), the authors chose to use a 3 × 3 Latin square, with 12 participants randomly assigned to each row of the square. To avoid the bias that might result if participants thought they were evaluating the Mozart effect, they were "told that the experiment concerned the effect of relaxation on recall" (Steele et al., 1997, p. 1181). The memory task was a reversed digit span procedure: given a stimulus such as "6-8-3-1-7," the correct response would be "7-1-3-8-6." On a given trial, participants would listen to Mozart, listen to gentle rainfall, or sit quietly, then be given three consecutive digit span tasks. Each digit span included 9 numbers, presented in a random order. Thus, a score from 0 to 27 could be earned.

The study did produce some statistically significant findings, but none that would comfort those marketing the Mozart effect tapes. The average number of digits correctly recalled was virtually identical for all three conditions: 18.53 for the Mozart tape, 18.50 for the gentle rain tape, and 18.72 for the control condition. There was a significant practice effect, however. Regardless of the order in which the conditions were presented, participants improved from the first set of digit span tests to the third set. From the first to the third, the averages were 15.64, 19.14, and 20.97. So, should people play Mozart tapes for their children? Of course—it's wonderful music. Will it make them smarter? Apparently not, although it could make them enjoy classical music, an outcome of value by itself.

Presenting the Data

One decision to be made when reporting the results of any research study is how to present the data. There are three choices. First, the numbers can be presented in sentence form, an approach that might be fine for reporting the results of experimental studies with just two or three levels (e.g., the Mozart example) but makes for tedious reading as the amount of data increases. You might have noticed this when reading about the results of the five conditions of the Bransford and Johnson (1972) study. A second approach is to construct a table of results. A table for the Bransford and Johnson study might look like Table 7.2.

A third way to present the data is in the form of a graph, which would portray the Bransford and Johnson study as you've already observed in Figure 7.12. Notice that in an experimental study, a graph always places the dependent variable on the

TABLE 7.2   *The Bransford and Johnson (1972) Data in Table Format*

Table 1: *Mean Number of Idea Units Recalled as a Function of Different Learning and Recall Contexts*

Condition	Mean Score	Standard Deviation
No context 1 repetition	3.60	.64
No context 2 repetitions	3.80	.79
Context before	8.00	.65
Context after	3.60	.75
Partial context	4.00	.60

Note: The maximum score is 14.

vertical *(Y)* axis and the independent variable on the horizontal *(X)* axis. The situation becomes a bit more complicated when more than one independent variable is used, as you will see in the next chapter. Regardless of the number of independent variables, however, the dependent variable always goes on the vertical axis.

Deciding between tables and figures is often a matter of the researcher's preference. Graphs can be especially striking if there are large differences to report or if interactions occur (Chapter 8). Tables are often preferred when there is so much data that a graph would be uninterpretable or when the researcher wishes to inform the reader of the precise values of the means; they may have to be guessed at with a graph. One rule you can certainly apply is that you should never present the same data in both table and graph form. In general, you should present data in such a way that the results you have worked so hard to obtain are shown most clearly.

Types of Graphs

Notice that I have presented the Bransford and Johnson data in the form of a bar graph. Why not present it as a line graph, as in Figure 7.13? Bad idea. The problem concerns the nature of the construct being used as the independent variable and whether its underlying dimension is continuous. A **continuous variable** is one for which a number of intermediate values exist. That is, the variable exists on a continuum. An example might be the dosage level of a drug. In a study comparing 3 mg, 5 mg, and 7 mg of some drug, dosage is a continuous variable. Presumably, we also could use 4-mg or 6-mg dosages if there was a good reason for doing so. For continuous independent variables, it is appropriate to use a line graph to portray the results. That is, because it is reasonable to interpolate between the points of the graph to guess what the effects of intermediate values might be, the line can be used for estimating these in-between effects. Thus, in the drug study, a graph could look like Figure 7.14, and the researcher would be on reasonably solid ground in pre-

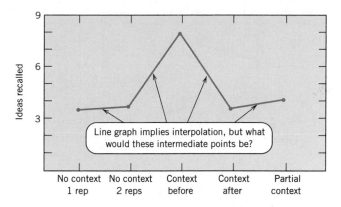

FIGURE 7.13 Bransford and Johnson data inappropriately drawn as a line graph.

dicting the effects of intermediate values of the drug, as illustrated by the point marked with an asterisk in Figure 7.15.

Of course, interpolation can be problematic if a study uses two levels of the independent variable, the two levels are far apart, and the relationship is actually nonlinear. Thus, in a drug study comparing 2-mg and 10-mg dosages that produce the solid line in Figure 7.16, interpolating the effects of a 5-mg dosage would produce a large error if the true curve looked like the dotted line. This study would be a good candidate for a single-factor multilevel design.

The situation is different if the independent variable is a **discrete variable,** in which each level represents a distinct category and no intermediate points can occur. In this case no interpolation can be done, and to connect the points with a line is to imply the existence of these intermediate points when in fact they don't exist. So when using discrete variables, as in the Bransford and Johnson study (Figure 7.12), a bar graph is normally used. The basic rule is this:

If continuous: line graph preferred, bar graph acceptable

If discrete: bar graphs preferred, line graph inappropriate

In general, then, bar graphs can be used for both continuous and discrete data, but line graphs should only be used for continuous data. Refer back to Box 4.3 for

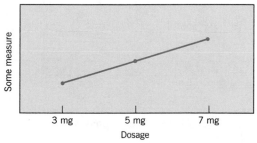

FIGURE 7.14 Appropriate use of a line graph with a continuous variable such as a drug's dosage level.

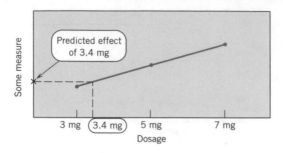

FIGURE 7.15 Interpolating between the points of a line graph.

a reminder about the ethics of presenting the data. It is easy to mislead the uninformed consumer of research by doing such things as altering the distances on the *Y*-axis. Your responsibility as a researcher is to present your results honestly in a way that best illustrates the true outcome of the study.

Analyzing Single-Factor, Multilevel Designs

We have seen that in the case of single-factor, two-level designs with the dependent variable measured on an interval or ratio scale, the null hypothesis can be tested with an inferential statistic called the *t* test. For a multilevel design such as the Bransford and Johnson study, you might think the analysis would be a simple matter of completing a series of *t* tests between all of the possible pairs of conditions (e.g., context before vs. context after). Unfortunately, things aren't quite that simple. The difficulty is that completing multiple *t* tests increases the risks of making a Type I error. That is, the more *t* tests you calculate, the greater are the chances of having one accidentally yield significant differences. In the Bransford and Johnson study, you would have to complete 10 different *t* tests to cover all the pairs of conditions.

The chances of making at least one Type I error when doing multiple *t* tests can be estimated by using this formula:

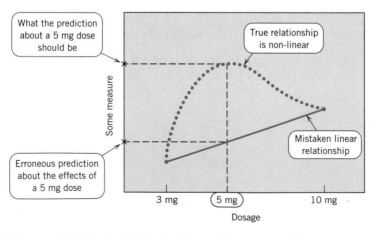

FIGURE 7.16 Problems with interpolation when there is a non-linear effect and a wide range between

$$1 - (1-\text{alpha})^c$$
where c = the number of comparisons being made

Thus, if all the possible t tests are completed in the Bransford and Johnson study, there is a very good chance (4 out of 10) of making at least one Type I error:

$$1 - (1-.05)^{10} = 1 - (.95)^{10} = 1 - .60 = .40$$

To avoid the problem of multiple t tests in single-factor designs, researchers use a procedure called a 1-way analysis of variance or 1-way **ANOVA** (**AN**alysis **Of VA**riance). The "1-way" means one independent variable. In essence, a 1-way ANOVA tests for the presence of some "overall" significance that could exist somewhere among the various levels of the independent variable. Hence, in a study with three levels, the null hypothesis is "level 1 = level 2 = level 3." Rejecting the null hypothesis does not identify exactly which of the "='s" is really "≠," however. To determine precisely where the significance lies requires what is called "subsequent testing" or "post hoc (after the fact) analysis." In a study with three levels, subsequent testing would analyze each of the three pairs of comparisons, but only after the overall ANOVA has indicated that some significance exists. If the ANOVA does not find any significance, subsequent testing is normally not done, unless some specific predictions about particular pairs of conditions were made ahead of time. Appendix C shows a 1-way ANOVA, followed by a common post hoc test called a "Tukey's HSD test."

The 1-way ANOVA yields an "F score" or an "F ratio." Like the score from a t test, the F score examines to what extent the obtained mean differences could be due to chance or are the result of some other factor (presumably the independent variable). The ANOVA is a basic tool widely used by experimental psychologists, and if you aren't already familiar with its operation from taking a statistics course, you should work through the examples in Appendix C. You should also be aware that even though t tests are normally used when the independent variable has just two levels, a 1-way ANOVA also could be used in that situation. Actually, the t test can be considered a special case of the ANOVA, used when there is a single independent variable with just two levels.

The designs in this chapter have in common the presence of a single independent variable. In Chapter 8, you will encounter the next logical step—designs with more than one independent variable. These are called "factorial designs."

Chapter Summary

Single Factor—Two Levels

The simplest experimental designs have a single independent variable with two levels of that variable. These designs can include between-subjects variables or within-subjects variables. Between-subjects variables can be directly manipulated or they can be selected as subject factors. If manipulated, participants can be randomly assigned to groups (independent groups design) or matched on some potentially confounding variable, then randomly assigned (matched groups design). If a subject variable is used, the design is a nonequivalent groups design. Single-factor designs using a within-subjects variable are sometimes called repeated-measures designs (e.g., the famous Stroop studies). Studies using two levels of the independent variable are normally evaluated statistically with t tests (assuming interval or ratio data).

Control Group Designs

In control group designs, there is at least one condition in which the experimental treatment is absent. Varieties of control groups include placebo controls, often found in drug research; waiting list controls, found in research on the effectiveness of some type of program or therapy; and yoked controls, in which control group participants are carefully matched to treatment group participants on some factor requiring precise control.

Single Factor—More Than Two Levels

When only two levels of some experimental variable are compared, the results always will appear to be linear because a graph of the results will have only two points. Some relationships are nonlinear, however (e.g., the Ebbinghaus forgetting curve), and they can be discovered by adding more than two levels to an independent variable. Adding levels can also function as a way to test and perhaps rule out (falsify) alternative hypotheses. Like the two-level case, these multilevel designs can be either between- or within-subjects designs. Results may be presented visually through the use of bar graphs when the independent variable is a discrete variable or with a line graph if the variable is continuous. Studies using more than two levels of an independent variable are normally evaluated statistically with a 1-way analysis of variance or "ANOVA" (assuming interval or ratio data).

Chapter Review

Multiple Choice

1. Children in four different age groups (5, 7, 9, and 11 years) are tested on the Stroop task (using only the key condition that Stroop called NCWd) in order to see if experience in reading affects performance on the task (presumably, older children have more experience reading). How would you describe the design?
   a. independent groups, one-factor, multilevel
   b. single-factor, repeated–measures
   c. nonequivalent groups, one-factor, multilevel
   d. matched groups, one-factor, two-level

2. What do all single-factor, repeated-measures designs have in common?
   a. they will always have a control group
   b. participants will be tested in each condition of the study and will always be tested more than once per condition
   c. matching will be the preferred method of creating equivalent groups
   d. every participant will be tested in each of the conditions of the study

3. The case study examining the effects of sleep deprivation on being influenced by leading questions illustrated which design?
   a. within-subjects, multilevel
   b. independent groups

c. ~~matched groups~~

d. nonequivalent groups

4. The essential feature of a yoked control group is that
   a. its members receive a placebo
   b. ~~what happens to its members is determined by what happens to members of the experimental group~~
   c. compared to experimental group members, its members receive a slightly smaller amount of the independent variable
   d. it is used whenever the researcher wishes to uncover nonlinear effects

5. Suppose you tried to replicate the Ebbinghaus memory research. It takes you 20 minutes to learn a list of CVCs on Monday and 15 minutes to relearn the list on Tuesday. What is your savings score?
   a. 25%
   b. 75%
   c. 5%
   d. cannot be determined without knowing how many items were on the list

Short Essay

1. Consider independent groups designs, matched groups designs, and nonequivalent groups designs. What do they all have in common and how do they differ?

2. In the case study that compared sleep-deprived persons with those not so deprived, why was a matched group design used, instead of an independent groups design, and what was the matching variable?

3. Describe the Stroop effect and the experimental design used by Stroop.

4. Describe the two varieties of two sample *t* tests and with reference to the designs in the first part of the chapter (single factor—two levels), explain when each is used.

5. Use the example of the effects of alcohol on reaction time to explain the usefulness of a placebo control group.

6. Use the subliminal tapes study to illustrate the usefulness of a waiting list control group.

7. Use the Weiss study of the effects of control on stress to explain what is meant by a yoked control group.

8. Use the hypothetical caffeine and reaction time study to illustrate how multi-level designs can produce nonlinear effects.

9. Use the Bransford and Johnson experiment on the effects of context on memory to illustrate the advantage of having more than two levels of an independent variable.

10. Describe when it is best to use (a) a line graph, and (b) a bar graph. Explain why a line graph would be inappropriate in a study comparing the reaction times of males and females.

Applications Exercises

Exercise 7.1.—Identifying Designs

For each of the following descriptions of studies, identify the independent and dependent variables involved and the nature of the independent variable (between-subjects or within-subjects; manipulated or subject variable), and name the experimental design being used.

1. In a study of how bulimia affects the perception of body size, a group of bulimic women and a group of same-age nonbulimic women are asked to examine a graded series of drawings of women of different sizes and to indicate which size best matches the way they think they look.

2. College students in a cognitive mapping study are asked to use a direction finder to point accurately to three unseen locations that differ in distance from the laboratory. One is a nearby campus location, one is a nearby city, and the third is a distant city.

3. Three groups of preschoolers (50 per group, assigned randomly) are in a study of task perseverance in which the size of the delay of reward is varied. The children in all three groups are given a difficult puzzle and told to work on it as long as they would like. One group is told that as payment they will be given $5 at the end of the session. The second group will get the $5 after two days from the end of the session, and the third will get the money after 4 days.

4. To examine whether crowding affects problem-solving performance, participants are placed in either a large or a small room while attempting to solve a set of word puzzles. Before assigning participants to the two conditions, the researcher takes a measure of their verbal intelligence to ensure that the average verbal IQ of the groups is equivalent.

Exercise 7.2.—Outcomes

For each of the following studies, decide whether to illustrate the described outcomes with a line graph or a bar graph; then create graphs that accurately portray the outcomes.

1. In a study of the effects of marijuana on immediate memory for a 30-item word list, participants are randomly assigned to either an experimental group, a placebo control group, or a straight control group.

   Outcome A. Marijuana impairs recall, while expectations about marijuana have no effect on recall.

   Outcome B. Marijuana impairs recall, but expectations about marijuana also reduce recall performance.

   Outcome C. The apparently adverse effect of marijuana on recall can be attributed entirely to placebo effects.

2. A researcher uses a reliable and valid test to assess the autonomy levels of three groups of first-year female college students after they have been in college for

2 months. Someone with a high level of autonomy has the ability to function well without help from others, that is, to be independent. One group (R300) is made up of resident students whose homes are 300 miles or more from campus; the second group includes resident students whose homes are less than 100 miles from campus (R100); the third group includes commuter students (C).

Outcome A. Commuter students are more autonomous than resident students.

Outcome B. The farther one's home is from the campus, the more autonomous that person is likely to be.

Outcome C. Commuters and R300 students are both very autonomous, while R100 students are not.

3. Animals learn a maze and, in the process of so doing, errors (i.e., wrong turns) are recorded. When they reach the goal box on each trial, they are rewarded with food. For one group of rats, the food is delivered immediately after they reach the goal (0 delay). For a second group, the food appears 5 seconds after they reach the goal (5-second delay).

Outcome A. Reinforcement delay hinders learning.

Outcome B. Reinforcement delay has no effect on learning.

4. Basketball players shoot three sets of 20 foul shots under three different levels of arousal—low, moderate, and high. Under low arousal, every missed free throw means they have to run a lap around the court (i.e., it is a minimal penalty, not likely to cause arousal). Moderate arousal means two laps per miss and high arousal means four laps per miss (i.e., enough of a penalty to create high arousal, perhaps in the form of anxiety). It is a repeated-measures design; assume proper counterbalancing.

Outcome A. There is a linear relationship between arousal and performance; as arousal increases, performance declines.

Outcome B. There is a nonlinear relationship between arousal and performance; performance is good only for moderate arousal.

CHAPTER 8

Experimental Design II: Factorial Designs

Preview & Chapter Objectives

Chapter 7 introduced you to some basic experimental designs—those involving a single independent variable, with either two or more levels being compared. The next logical step is to increase the number of independent variables. When that happens, the result is a factorial design, the focus of this chapter. When you complete this chapter, you should be able to:

- Describe factorial designs using a standardized notation system (2 × 2, 3 × 5, etc.).

- Place data accurately into a factorial matrix.

- Understand what is meant by a main effect and know how to determine if one exists.

- Understand what is meant by an interaction effect and know how to determine if one exists.

- Identify the varieties of factorials that correspond to the single-factor designs of Chapter 7 (independent groups, matched groups, nonequivalent groups, repeated measures).
- Identify a mixed design and understand why counterbalancing is not always necessary in such a design.
- Identify a P × E factorial, recognize its historical connection to Kurt Lewin and understand what it means when such a design produces main effects and interactions.
- Calculate the number of participants needed to complete each of the factorial varieties.
- Know how to be an ethically competent experimenter.

As you have been working your way through this research methods course, you have probably noticed that experimental psychologists sometimes seem to have a language of their own. They talk about operationalizing constructs, building stem and leaf displays, and eliminating confounds, and when they talk about regression they are not discussing Freud. You haven't seen anything yet. After this chapter, you'll be able to say things like this: "It was a two by three mixed factorial that produced one main effect for the repeated measures variable plus an interaction." Let's start with the basics.

Factorial Essentials

Suppose you are interested in memory and wish to find out if recall can be improved by training people to use visual imagery while memorizing a list of words. You could create a simple two-group experiment in which some people are trained to use visual imagery techniques while memorizing the words and some are told to use rote repetition. Suppose you also wonder about how memory is affected by a word list's presentation rate. Again, you could do a simple two-group study. Some participants see the lists at the rate of 2 seconds per word, others at 4 seconds per word. With a factorial design, *both* of these studies can be done as part of the same experiment.

By definition, a **factorial design** involves any study with more than one independent variable (also referred to as a "factor"). In principle this could involve dozens of variables, but in practice these designs usually involve two or three factors, or sometimes four. Let's stay with the memory example as a way of introducing a notation system for describing factorials.

Identifying Factorial Designs

First, a factorial is described with a numbering system that simultaneously identifies the number of independent variables and the number of levels of each variable. Thus a 2 × 3 (read this as "two by three") factorial design has two independent variables; the first has two levels, the second has three. A 3 × 4 × 5 factorial has three independent variables, with three, four, and five levels, respectively. The memory study would be a 2 × 2 design, with two levels of the "type of training" independent variable (imagery and rote repetition) and two levels of the "presentation rate" independent variable (2 and 4 seconds per item).

Second, the conditions to be tested in a factorial study can be identified by looking at all possible combinations of the different levels of each independent variable. In the memory study, this produces a display called a **factorial matrix,** which looks like this:

Presentation rate

		2-sec/word	4-sec/word
	Imagery	imagery/2 sec	imagery/4 sec
Type of training	Rote	rote/2 sec	rote/4 sec

Before going on, there's something you should note very carefully. Up to this point in the book, I have been using the concepts "conditions of the experiment" and "levels of the independent variable" as if they meant the same thing. These concepts indeed are interchangeable in single-factor experiments. In factorials, however, this is no longer the case. In all experimental designs, the term "levels" refers to the number of levels of the independent variable. In factorial designs, the term "conditions" equals the number of cells in the matrix like the one you just examined. Hence, the 2 × 2 memory study has *two* independent variables, each with *two* levels. It has *four* different conditions, however, one for each of the four cells. The number of conditions in any factorial can be determined simply by calculating the product of the numbers in the notation system. A 3 × 3 design has 9 conditions; a 2 × 2 × 4 design has 16.

You can visualize a generalized 2 × 2 factorial matrix this way:

Factor **B**

		Level **B1**	Level **B2**
	Level **A1**	condition **A1B1**	condition **A1B2**
Factor **A**	Level **A2**	condition **A2B1**	condition **A2B2**

It's important to be clear about this labeling system because when you are using a computerized statistics package, this is the language you will probably encounter. If the computer asks you for the data from cell A2B1 and you enter the data from cell A1B2 by mistake, the analysis will proceed and give you a nice printout, but the results will be wrong. Obviously, it is essential to enter the data in the proper cells. You will encounter this labeling system if you work your way through the 2-way ANOVA in Appendix C.

Table 8.1 shows you how this system of laying out factorials and labeling the cells works with a 2 × 4 and a 2 × 2 × 2 design. Ignore the matrices with shaded cells for the moment; those will make sense after you finish reading the next section.

TABLE 8.1   *Sample Factorial Designs*

1. **2 × 4** factorial:

	B1	B2	B3	B4
A1	A1B1	A1B2	A1B3	A1B4
A2	A2B1	A2B2	A2B3	A2B4

Testing for the main effect of A (i.e., comparing A1 and A2)

	B1	B2	B3	B4
A1	A1B1	A1B2	A1B3	A1B4
A2	A2B1	A2B2	A2B3	A2B4

Testing for the main effect of B (i.e., comparing B1, B2, B3, and B4)

	B1	B2	B3	B4
A1	A1B1	A1B2	A1B3	A1B4
A2	A2B1	A2B2	A2B3	A2B4

2. A **2 × 2 × 2** factorial:

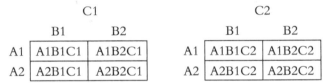

	C1			C2	
	B1	B2		B1	B2
A1	A1B1C1	A1B2C1	A1	A1B1C2	A1B2C2
A2	A2B1C1	A2B2C1	A2	A2B1C2	A2B2C2

Testing for the main effect of A (i.e., comparing A1 and A2)

	C1			C2	
	B1	B2		B1	B2
A1	A1B1C1	A1B2C1	A1	A1B1C2	A1B2C2
A2	A2B1C1	A2B2C1	A2	A2B1C2	A2B2C2

Testing for the main effect of B (i.e., comparing B1 and B2)

	C1			C2	
	B1	B2		B1	B2
A1	A1B1C1	A1B2C1	A1	A1B1C2	A1B2C2
A2	A2B1C1	A2B2C1	A2	A2B1C2	A2B2C2

Testing for the main effect of C (i.e., comparing C1 and C2)

	C1			C2	
	B1	B2		B1	B2
A1	A1B1C1	A1B2C1	A1	A1B1C2	A1B2C2
A2	A2B1C1	A2B2C1	A2	A2B1C2	A2B2C2

Outcomes—Main Effects and Interactions

In factorial studies, two kinds of results occur—main effects and interactions. Main effects refer to the overall influence of the independent variables, while interactions examine whether the variables combine to form a more complex result. Let's examine each in more detail.

Main Effects

In the memory experiment we've been using as a model, the researcher is interested in the effects of two independent variables: type of training and presentation rate. In factorial designs, the term **main effect** is used to describe the overall effect of a particular independent variable. So in a study with two independent variables, such as a 2 × 2 factorial, there can be at most two main effects. Determining the main effect of one factor involves using the data for all levels of the other factor(s). In the memory study, this can be illustrated as follows. The main effect of type of training is determined by combining the data for both presentation rates. Hence, all of the information in the lightly shaded cells (imagery) would be combined and compared with the combined data in the heavily shaded cells (rote):

		Presentation rate (B)	
		2-sec/word B1	4-sec/word B2
	Imagery A1	imagery/2 sec A1B1	imagery/4 sec A1B2
Type of training (A)			
	Rote A2	rote/2 sec A2B1	rote/4 sec A2B2

Similarly, the main effect of presentation rate is determined by combining the data for both types of training. In the following matrix, the effect of presentation rate would be evaluated by comparing all of the information in the lightly shaded cells (2 sec/item) with all the data in the heavily shaded cells (4 sec/item):

		Presentation rate (B)	
		2-sec/word B1	4-sec/word B2
	Imagery A1	imagery/2 sec A1B1	imagery/4 sec A1B2
Type of training (A)			
	Rote A2	rote/2 sec A2B1	rote/4 sec A2B2

If you now take a second look at the shaded matrices in Table 8.1, you'll see that I have indicated which cells combine during the various main effects analyses for the 2×4 and the $2 \times 2 \times 2$ designs.

Let's consider some hypothetical data that might be collected in a memory experiment like the example we've been using. Assume there are 25 participants in each condition (cell) and their task is to memorize a list of 30 words. The average number of words recalled for each of the four conditions might look like this:

Presentation rate

	2–sec/word	4–sec/word
Imagery	17	23
Rote	12	18

Type of training

Does imagery training produce better recall than rote repetition? That is, is there a main effect of type of training? The way to find out is to compare all the "imagery" data with all the "rote" data. Specifically, this involves calculating what are called "row means." The "imagery" row mean is **20** words [(17+23)/2 = 40/2 = 20], and the "rote" row mean is **15** words [(12+18)/2 = 30/2 = 15]. When asking if there is a main effect of training type, the question is: "Is the difference between the means of 20 and 15 statistically significant or due to chance?"

In the same fashion, calculating column means allows us to see if there is a main effect of presentation rate. For the 2 sec/item column, the mean is **14.5** words; it is **20.5** words for the 4 sec/item row (you should check this). Putting all of this together yields this outcome:

Presentation rate

	2–sec/word	4–sec/word	Overall
Imagery	17	23	**20.0**
Rote	12	18	**15.0**
Overall	**14.5**	**20.5**	

For these data, then, it appears that imagery improves memory (20 > 15) and that recall is higher if the words are presented at a slower rate (20.5 > 14.5). That is, there seem to be two main effects here (of course, it takes an ANOVA to make a judgment about whether the differences are significant or due to chance). For a real example of a study that produced a strong main effect, consider this case study of how visual imagery can enhance memory.

Case Study 14—A Significant Main Effect

The hypothetical example that I've been using, in which visual imagery is used to improve memory, wasn't just pulled out of thin air. Researchers in cognitive psychology have known for some time that recall performance can be improved by using imagery when memorizing. A study by Wollen, Weber, and Lowry (1972) tried to evaluate separately two factors that might contribute to imagery's usefulness. Some prior research had suggested that memory is better if the memorizer uses bizarre rather than normal images, presumably on the grounds that something really unusual will stand out in one's mind. Other research demonstrated that memory could be enhanced if images for items to be remembered could be combined into a single image. Wollen et al. used a factorial design to examine both the bizarreness factor and the combination factor.[1] Participants were given word pairs to study. For example, one pair was "piano-cigar." During recall, their task was to respond "cigar" when given the word "piano."

During presentation of the word pairs, participants were shown one of four different sets of drawings, including the ones in Figure 8.1, for the piano-cigar pair. As you can see, two of the images are combined and two are not, and two of the images are unusual (i.e., bizarre) and two are not. The mean number of pairs recalled in the four conditions of this 2 × 2 independent groups factorial showed a strong main effect for the combination factor, but no significant effect for the bizarreness factor (maximum score = 9):

	Bizarre	Normal	Overall
Combined	6.67	6.60	**6.64**
Not combined	3.05	3.50	**3.28**
Overall	**4.86**	**5.05**	

In this study at least, bizarreness didn't matter—overall memory performance was virtually the same whether the images were bizarre (4.86 out of 9) or not (5.05). On the other hand, combining the images produced a large effect. Memory was much better when the images were combined (6.64) than when they were not (3.28). In bar graph form, these same results are shown in Figure 8.2.

Interactions

Main effects are important outcomes in factorial designs, but the distinct advantage of factorials over single-factor designs lies in their potential to show interactive

---

[1] They also tested a third factor that they called "relevance." Some of the word pairs were accompanied by images depicting the words, as in Figure 8.1, while other word pairs were shown with irrelevant images. Recall was better in the relevant condition.

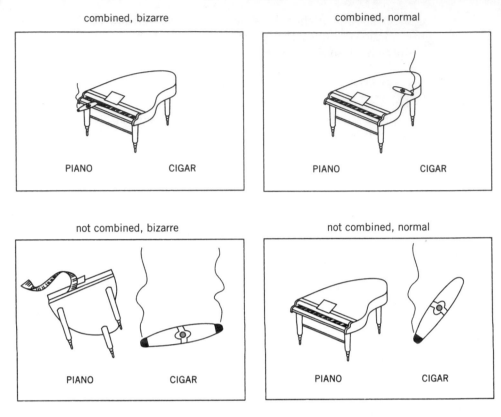

FIGURE 8.1   Sample stimulus materials from the imagery study by Wollen et al. (1972).

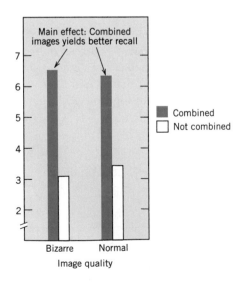

FIGURE 8.2   Bar graph showing a main effect for combined images, no main effect for bizarreness of the images, and no interaction.

(Constructed from data in Wollen et al., 1972)

effects. In a factorial design, an **interaction** is said to occur when the effect of one independent variable depends on the level of another independent variable. This is a moderately difficult concept to grasp, but it is of immense importance because interactions often provide the most interesting results in a factorial study. To start, consider a simple example. Suppose I believe that general psychology is best taught as a laboratory self-discovery course rather than as a straight lecture course, but I also wonder if this is generally true or true only for certain kinds of students. Perhaps science majors would especially benefit from the laboratory approach. To test the idea, I need to compare a lab with a lecture version of general psychology, but I also need to compare different types of students, perhaps science majors and humanities majors. This calls for a 2 × 2 design that would look like this:

		Course type	
		Lab emphasis	Lecture emphasis
Student's major	Science	Science students in a lab course	Science students in a lecture course
	Humanities	Humanities students in a lab course	Humanities students in a lecture course

In a study like this, the dependent variable would be some measure of learning; let's use a score from 1 to 100 on a standardized test of knowledge of general psychology, given during final exam week. Suppose these results occurred:

	Lab emphasis	Lecture emphasis
Science	80	70
Humanities	70	80

Are there any main effects here? No—all the row and column means are the same: 75. So did nothing at all happen in this study? No—something clearly happened. Specifically, the science students did better in the lab course, but the humanities students did better in the lecture course. Or to put it in terms of the definition of an interaction, the effect of one variable (course type) depended on the level of the other variable (major). Hence, even if no main effects occur, an interaction can occur and produce an interesting outcome.

This teaching example also highlights the distinct advantage of factorial designs over single-factor designs. Suppose you completed the study as a single-factor, two-level design, comparing lab with lecture versions of general psychology. You would probably use a matched group design, and use student GPA and perhaps major as matching variables. In effect, you might end up with the same people who were in the factorial example. However, by running it as a single-factor design, your results would be:

Lab course: 75   Lecture course: 75

and you might conclude that it doesn't matter whether general psychology includes a lab or not. With the factorial design, however, you know that the lab indeed matters, but only for certain types of students. In short, factorial designs can be more informative than single-factor designs. To further illustrate the concept of interactions, consider the outcome of the following case study.

Case Study 15—An Interaction with No Main Effects

There has been considerable research indicating that people remember something best if they are in the same location or context where they learned it in the first place. You might have experienced this if you were able to find your lost keys after putting yourself, either mentally or physically, back in the place where you last remembered seeing them.

The study winning the prize for the most creative test of this context-dependent learning hypothesis was carried out by Godden and Baddeley (1975). They used a 2 × 2 factorial in which participants learned a list of 36 words in one setting, then recalled the list in either the same setting or a different one. What makes the experiment creative is the choice of settings. Members of a diving club were the participants, and they learned the lists either on the shore of a beach or in the water at a depth of 20 feet! The first independent variable was the location where learning took place, and the two levels were "on land" and "under water." The second variable was where recall occurred, and it also had the two levels of land and sea. Hence, there were four conditions to the study:

1. learn on land—recall on land
2. learn on land—recall underwater
3. learn underwater—recall on land
4. learn underwater—recall underwater

All divers eventually participated in all four conditions, making this a repeated-measures factorial design. The results, expressed as the average number of words recalled per list, were as follows:

		Where they recalled		
		On land	Underwater	Overall
Where they learned	On land	13.5	8.6	**11.1**
	Underwater	8.4	14.4	**9.9**
	Overall	**11.0**	**10.0**	

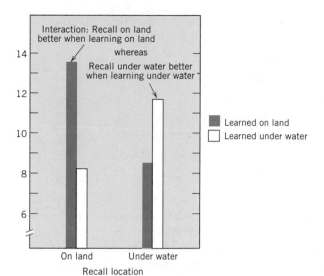

FIGURE 8.3 Bar graph showing an interaction between study and recall locations.

(Constructed from data in Godden & Baddeley, 1975)

This outcome is similar to the pattern found in the hypothetical study about ways of teaching general psychology to science and humanities students. Row and column means are virtually identical, indicating an absence of significant main effects. Thus, for the experiment as a whole, where the lists were learned didn't matter (i.e., 11.1 is not significantly different from 9.9), and where they were recalled was likewise irrelevant (i.e., 11.0 doesn't differ from 10.0). But examining the four individual cell means shows that an interaction clearly occurred. When the divers learned on land, they recalled well on land (13.5) but poorly underwater (8.6); when they learned under water, they recalled poorly on land (8.4) but did well when recalling while submerged (11.4). That is, learning was best when the learning context matched the recall context. Figure 8.3 presents the data in bar graph form.

You might be interested in some of the control procedures developed for this study. The divers had difficulty hearing the tape-recorded words through the "diver underwater communication" gear because of the noise produced by their breathing, so they had to learn to hold their breath for periods of 6 seconds at a time while the words were presented in clusters of three. Four-second "breathing" intervals occurred between the clusters of three words. To keep list presentation conditions constant, the same procedures were simulated when the lists were presented on land. Also, all testing took place after divers had completed their normal diving routines for the day. Thus "subjects began each session in roughly the same state, that is, wet and cold" (Godden & Baddeley, 1975, p. 327). If you're wondering about the "cold," thinking perhaps that the British researchers must have had the good sense to run this study in the Bahamas, the answer is that no, they weren't *that* creative (or well funded). The study was conducted on the west coast of *Scotland*.

Combinations of Main Effects and Interactions

The example of context-dependent memory illustrates one type of outcome in a factorial design (an interaction, but no main effects), but there are many patterns of results that could occur. In a simple 2 × 2 design, for instance, there are eight possibilities:

1. a main effect for factor A only
2. a main effect for factor B only
3. main effects for A and B only
4. a main effect for A plus an interaction
5. a main effect for B plus an interaction
6. main effects for both A and B plus an interaction
7. an interaction only, no main effects
8. no main effects, no interaction

Let's briefly consider several of these outcomes in the context of the earlier hypothetical experiment on imagery training and presentation rate. For each of the following examples, I have created some data that might result from the study on the effects of imagery instructions and presentation rate on memory for a 30-word list, translated the data into a graph, and given a verbal description of the results. I haven't tried to create all of the eight possibilities listed above; rather, the following examples illustrate outcomes that might actually occur in this type of study.

1. Imagery instructions improve recall, regardless of presentation rate, which doesn't affect recall. That is, there is a main effect for factor A (imagery instructions) but no main effect for presentation rate (B). This graph should remind you of the graph for case study 12 (Figure 8.2), except that the graph below is a line graph instead of a bar graph.

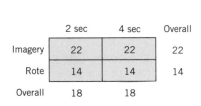

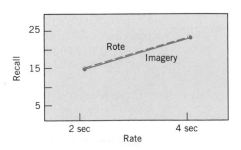

	2 sec	4 sec	Overall
Imagery	22	22	22
Rote	14	14	14
Overall	18	18	

2. Recall is better with slower rates of presentation, but the imagery instructions were not effective in improving recall. That is, there is a main effect for factor B (presentation rate) only.

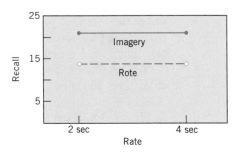

	2 sec	4 sec	Overall
Imagery	14	22	18
Rote	14	22	18
Overall	14	22	

3. Recall is better with slower rates of presentation; in addition, the imagery instructions were effective in improving recall. In this case, then, main effects for both factors occur. This is the outcome most likely to occur if you actually completed this study.

	2 sec	4 sec	Overall
Imagery	18	22	20
Rote	14	18	16
Overall	16	20	

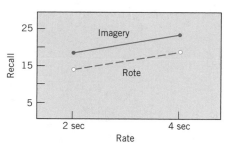

4. At the 2-second presentation rate, imagery training clearly improves recall (i.e., from 12 to 28); however, at the 4-second rate, recall is almost perfect, regardless of how subjects are trained. That is, there is an interaction between type of training and presentation rate. In this case, the interaction may have been influenced by what is called a **ceiling effect,** a result in which the scores for different conditions are all so close to the maximum (30 words in this example) that no difference could occur.[2] Here, the imagery group recalls just about all the words, regardless of presentation rate. To test for the presence of a ceiling effect, you could replicate the study with 50–item word lists and see if performance improves for the imagery/4-second group.

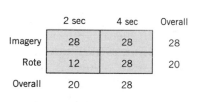

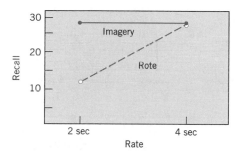

	2 sec	4 sec	Overall
Imagery	28	28	28
Rote	12	28	20
Overall	20	28	

You may be wondering about the obvious main effects that occur in this example. Surely the row (20 and 28) and column (also 20 and 28) means indicate significant overall effects for both factors. Technically, yes, the analysis probably would yield statistically significant main effects in this example, but this is a good illustration of the fact that interactions usually take precedence over main effects when interpreting the results. In this particular case, the main effects aren't really meaningful; the statement that imagery yields a general improvement in recall is not quite accurate. Rather, it only seems to improve recall at the faster presentation rate. Likewise, concluding that 4 seconds per

---

[2] It is also possible for the scores in two conditions to be equal because they couldn't get any lower. Yes, these are called *floor effects.*

item produces better recall than 2 seconds per item is misleading—it's only true for the rote groups. Hence, the interaction is the key finding here. In any factorial study, if both main effects and interactions occur, the interactions should be interpreted first.

5. This is not to say that main effects never matter when an interaction exists. Consider this last example:

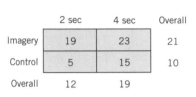

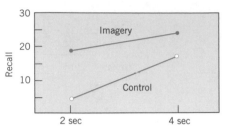

In this case, imagery training generally improves recall (i.e., there's a main effect for A: 21 > 10). Also, a slower presentation rate improves recall for both groups (i.e., a main effect for B also: 19 > 12). Both of these outcomes are worth reporting. What the interaction shows is that slowing the presentation rate improves recall somewhat for the imagery group (23 is a bit better than 19) but improves recall considerably for the control group (15 is a lot better than 5). Another way of describing the interaction is to say that at the fast rate, the imagery training is especially effective (19 is a lot better than 5). At the slower rate, imagery training still yields better recall, but not by as much as the slow rate (23 is somewhat better than 15).

From examining these graphs, you might have noticed a standard feature of interactions. In general, if the lines on the graph are parallel to each other, then no interaction is present. If the lines are nonparallel, however, an interaction probably exists. Of course, this rule about parallel and nonparallel lines is only a general guideline. Whether an interaction exists (in essence, whether the lines are sufficiently nonparallel) is a statistical decision, to be determined by the analysis of variance.

Identifying interactions by examining whether lines are parallel or not is easier with line graphs than with bar graphs. Hence, the guideline mentioned in Chapter 7 about line graphs being used only with continuous variables is sometimes ignored if the key finding is an interaction. For example, a study by Keltner, Ellsworth, and Edwards (1993) showed that when participants were asked to estimate the likelihood of some bad event (e.g., a car accident) occurring, there was an interaction between the emotion they were experiencing during the experiment and whether the hypothetical event was said to be caused by a person or by circumstances. When participants were feeling sad, they believed that events produced by circumstances (e.g., wet roads) were more likely to occur than events produced by individual actions (e.g., poor driving). When participants were angry, however, the opposite happened. As you can see from Figure 8.4, a line graph was drawn even though the X-axis uses a discrete variable. Keltner et al. (1993) probably wanted to show the interaction as clearly as possible, so they ignored the guideline about discrete variables. To repeat a point made earlier, when presenting any data, the overriding concern is to make one's hard-earned results as clear as possible to the reader.

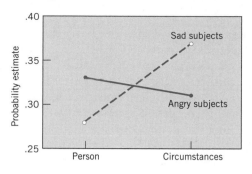

FIGURE 8.4 Using a line graph to highlight an interaction.

(From Keltner et al., 1993)

Before we turn to a system for categorizing the different types of factorial designs, you should read Box 8.1. It describes one of psychology's most famous experiments, a classic study supporting the idea that between the time you last study for an exam and the time you take the exam, you should be sleeping. It was completed in the early 1920s, a time when the term "factorial design" was not even in the vocabulary of experimental psychology and a time when analysis of variance, the statistical tool most frequently used to analyze factorials, was just being conceptualized. Yet the study illustrates the kind of thinking that leads to factorial studies—the desire to examine more than one independent variable at the same time.

Box 8.1

CLASSIC STUDIES—To Sleep, Perchance to Recall

As you now know, the major attraction of factorial designs is their ability to simultaneously examine the effects of two or more independent variables, as well as the interacting effects of these variables. Although the term "factorial design" and the statistical tools to analyze factorials were not used widely until after World War II (see Box 8.3), attempts to study more than one variable at a time occurred well before that time. A classic example is a study by John Jenkins and Karl Dallenbach, first reported as part of a series of studies from Cornell University in 1924. The Jenkins and Dallenbach (1924) study still appears in many general psychology books as the standard example of "retroactive interference"—the tendency for memory to be hindered if other mental activities intervene between the time of study and the time of recall. In essence, the study was a 2 × 4 repeated-measures factorial. The "2" was whether or not activities intervened between learning and a recall test, and the "4" referred to four different retention intervals; recall was tested either 1, 2, 4, or 8 hours after initial learning. What made the study interesting (and eventually, famous) was the factor with two levels. The study's participants spent the intervening time either awake and doing normal student behaviors, or asleep in Cornell's psychology lab. The prediction, that being asleep would produce lesser amounts of retroactive interference, and therefore better recall, was supported.

A close examination of the study illustrates some of the attributes of typical 1920s-era research and also shows that experimenters were just as careful about issues of control then as they are now. First, as you will learn in Chapter 10, research in psychology's early years often featured very few participants. In contrast to what typically happens in memory research today, using many participants and summarizing data statistically, early studies were more likely to include just one, two, or three participants and report the data for each—additional participants served the purpose of replication. This happened in the Jenkins and Dallenbach (1924) study; there were just two participants (referred to as "Observers" or "Os", another typical convention of the time), both seniors at Cornell. When using small numbers of participants, researchers tried to get as much out of them as they could, and the result in this case was what we would call a repeated-measures study today. That is, both students contributed data to all eight cells of a 2 × 4 design. Specifically, the plan was to have each student learn and recall lists eight different times in each of the eight conditions—a total of 64 separate trials (scheduling problems resulted in a failure to complete two of the waking trials for one student and one of the waking trials for the other student). If you are beginning to think that the study was a major undertaking for the two Cornell seniors, you're right. During the course of the study, the two students and Dallenbach, who served as experimenter, "lived in the laboratory during the course of the experiments" (p. 606) in a makeshift dorm room. Except when the students were "indisposed," tests were made every day and every night between April 14, 1923, and June 7. I'm not sure when Cornell's graduation was that year, but I don't imagine too many seniors today would be willing to give up their last month and a half of college to science!

As good researchers, Jenkins and Dallenbach (1924) were concerned about experimental control, and they used many of the procedures you've been learning about in this course. For instance, they used 10-item lists of nonsense syllables (consonant–vowel–consonant stimuli), presented one syllable at a time, and the participants read them aloud during the study trials, until one perfect recitation occurred (i.e., their operational definition of learning). To ensure a consistent pronunciation of the syllables, half the vowels in each list had dashes placed on top of them, indicating that they were to be pronounced as "long" vowels; unmarked vowels were pronounced as "short" vowels. To avoid a potential confound of having long and short vowels presented in some systematic fashion, the "marks were distributed irregularly, but were so arranged that the long and short vowels occurred equally often in the various positions within the series" (p. 606). In short, the researchers used counterbalancing to control the sequence of long and short vowels in the lists. They also used counterbalancing to avoid sequence effects in the presentation of the different retention intervals—"[t]he time-intervals between learning and reproduction were varied at haphazard" (p. 607). Times for learning the lists were kept constant. For the "awake" condition, students learned their lists between 8 and 10 in the morning, then went about their normal business as students, then returned to the lab for recall after 1, 2, 4, or 8 hours. For the "asleep" condition, lists were studied between 11:30 at night and 1 in the morning. Students then went to bed, and were awakened for recall by Dallenbach 1, 2, 4, or 8 hours later. There was one potential confound in the study—on the awake trials, the students were told when to return to the lab for recall (i.e., they knew the retention interval), but during the asleep trials, students did not know when they would be awakened. Jenkins and Dallenbach were aware of the problem, considered alternatives, but decided their procedure was adequate.

   The results? Figure 8.5 is a reproduction of the graph in the article, showing the data for each student. Each data point is an average of the eight (usually) trials for each condition of the study. Several things are clear. First, both students behaved similarly. Second, and this was the big finding, there was a big advantage for recall after sleeping, compared with recall after being awake. Third, there appears to be a hint of an interaction. As Jenkins and Dallenbach described it: "The curves of the waking experiments take the familiar form: a sharp decline which becomes progressively flatter. The form of the curves of the sleep experiments, however, is very different: after a small initial decline, the curves flatten and a high and constant level is thenceforth maintained" (1924, p. 610).

   There was one other intriguing outcome of the study, one never reported in textbook accounts. As the experiment progressed, it became increasingly difficult for Dallenbach to

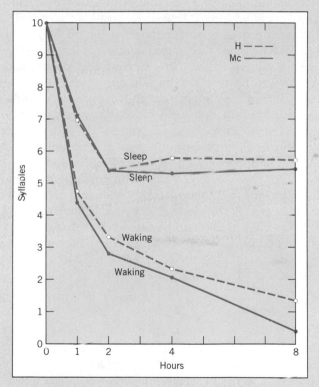

FIGURE 8.5 The Jenkins and Dallenbach study on retroactive interference, showing data for both of the Cornell students who participated, L. R. Hodell (H) and J. S. McGrew (Mc). Keep in mind that the study was completed long before an ethics code would have deleted the participants' names.

(From Jenkins & Dallenbach, 1924)

wake the students (no mention of whether Dallenbach had trouble getting up at all hours of the night). It was also hard for Dallenbach to "know when they were awake. The Os would leave their beds, go into the next room, give their reproductions, and the next morning say that they remembered nothing of it" (Jenkins & Dallenbach, 1924, p. 607)! At the time, a semi-asleep state was thought to be similar to hypnosis, so Jenkins and Dallenbach rounded up another student and replicated part of the study, but instead of having the student sleep for varying amounts of time, they had the student learn and recall the lists at different retention intervals while hypnotized. They found recall to be virtually perfect for all the intervals, an early hint at what later came to be called "state-dependent learning" by cognitive psychologists.

Varieties of Factorial Designs

Like the decision tree in Figure 7.1 for single-factor designs, Figure 8.6 shows you the decisions involved in arriving at one of six possible factorial designs. You'll recognize that four of the designs mirror those in Figure 7.1, but two designs are unique to factorials. First, while the independent variable must be either a between-subjects or a within-subjects variable in a single-factor design, both types of variables can be present in a factorial design. When this happens, the design is called a **mixed factorial design.** In a mixed design, at least one variable must be tested between subjects, and at least one must be tested within subjects. Second, some between-subjects factorials include both a manipulated independent variable and a subject variable. Because these designs can yield an interaction between the type of person in the study and the environment created in the study, they can be called **P × E factorial designs,** or "Person by Environment designs," with "environment" defined broadly to include any manipulated independent variable. A further distinction can be made within P × E designs, depending on whether the manipulated variable is a between-subjects or a within-subjects factor. If the latter is the case, the P × E design could be called a P × E mixed factorial. Figures 8.7 and 8.8 show the decisions to be made when using mixed and P × E designs. Let's examine each of them in more detail.

Mixed Factorial Designs

In Chapter 6, you learned that when independent variables are between-subjects variables, creating equivalent groups can be a problem and procedures like random assignment can help solve the problem. Similarly, when independent variables are within-subjects variables, a difficulty arises because of potential sequence effects and counterbalancing is the normal solution. Thus, in a mixed design, the researcher usually gets to deal with both the problems of equivalent groups and the problems of sequence effects. Not always though—there is one type of mixed design where counterbalancing is not used because sequence effects are the outcome of interest. For example, in learning and memory research, "trials" is a frequently encountered within-subjects independent variable. Counterbalancing makes no sense in this case

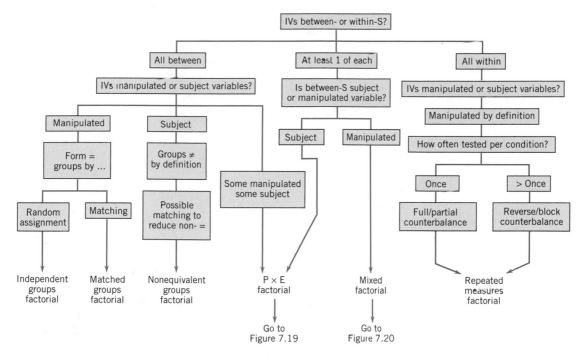

FIGURE 8.6 Decision tree—factorial designs.

because one purpose of the study will be to show sequential changes from trial to trial. The following two case studies show mixed designs, one requiring counterbalancing and one in which trials is the repeated measure.

Case Study 16—A Mixed Factorial with Counterbalancing

Riskind and Maddux (1993), perhaps as a consequence of seeing too many bad horror movies involving spiders, were interested in how people manage their emotions in

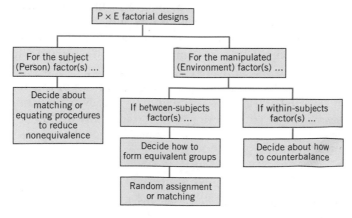

FIGURE 8.7 Decisions to be made with a P × E design.

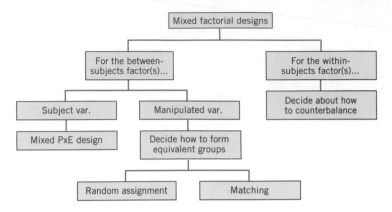

FIGURE 8.8   Decisions to be made with mixed designs.

frightening circumstances. They created a 2 × 2 mixed factorial design in which they manipulated self-efficacy and "looming." Self-efficacy refers to a person's sense of competence in dealing with life's problems and is normally used in research as a subject variable. In this study, however, the feeling of self-efficacy was manipulated by the experimenters. Participants were told to visualize a situation in which they were sitting in a chair in a small room that also contained a tarantula. In the High Self-Efficacy situation, they were instructed to imagine that the door to the room was unlocked, that they were free to move around, and that they had a magazine available to swat the spider if necessary. Participants randomly assigned to the Low Self-Efficacy condition, however, were told to imagine that they were tied securely to the chair, that the door was locked, and that the newspaper was out of reach. While visualizing these circumstances, participants saw films of spiders that were either (a) stationary or moving away from them or (b) moving toward them (i.e., looming). This second variable was a repeated-measures one, and it was presented in a counterbalanced order (unfortunately, the authors didn't report exactly which counterbalancing procedure they used). The dependent variable was a self-reported assessment of fear.

The outcome, portrayed in Figure 8.9 in both factorial matrix and graph form, is a good example of how interactions are often more important than main effects. As you can see, differences occurred for both row and column means, and both main effects were statistically significant. More important, however, there was an interaction between the factors. A large amount of fear (4.50) occurred when the situation of a bad horror movie was simulated (looming spider plus low self-efficacy), while the film viewers reported only moderate to low amounts of fear in the other three conditions (2.24, 2.64, 2.73). Thus, for high self-efficacy participants, fear was fairly low regardless of the relative motion of the spider. On the other hand, for those experiencing low self-efficacy, the amount of fear was clearly affected by whether the spider was looming or not.

Case Study 17—A Mixed Factorial without Counterbalancing

A good example of the situation in which "trials" is the within-subjects factor in a mixed design is a memory procedure called "release from PI" (Wickens, Born, &

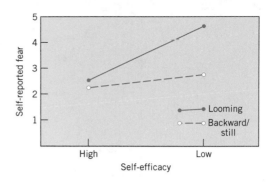

FIGURE 8.9 The interactive effects of looming and self-efficacy on fear.

(From Riskind & Maddux, 1993)

Allen, 1963). PI, or proactive interference, is a phenomenon in which the learning and recall of new information is hindered by the prior learning of old information. You might have experienced this if you found it difficult to remember a new phone number because your old one kept coming to mind. The amount of interference is expected to be especially great if the old information is similar to the new information. One way to test the idea that strength of PI is a function of item similarity is to have participants study and recall a sequence of stimulus items that are similar, then switch to a different type of stimulus item. Presumably, PI should build up from trial to trial for the similar items, then "release" when the stimulus type changes. Behaviorally, this means that recall accuracy should gradually decrease while PI is accumulating, then increase again once the release occurs.

Release from PI research normally uses words or nonsense syllables as stimuli, but a study by Gunter, Berry, and Clifford (1981) took a different and more applied approach: they used items from television news shows in a series of experiments. We'll consider their experiment 1, which serves as a nice illustration of a mixed factorial design without counterbalancing.

Participants were told they would be seeing clips from a televised news broadcast and would then be tested on the content of the news items. On each trial, they saw a sequence of three stories, then worked on a distractor task (a crossword puzzle) for a minute, then tried to recall as much as they could about the stories. Each participant experienced four such trials. Half of them were randomly assigned to the release from PI condition; they went through three trials in which all the news was from a single general category (e.g., domestic political events) and a fourth ("release") trial with news from a different category (e.g., foreign political events). The remaining participants were in a control group; all four of their trials were from the same category. Thus the design was a 2 (release/no release) × 4 (trials) mixed factorial design. Whether or not participants were in the release condition was the between-subjects factor, and trials was the repeated-measures or within-subjects factor.

Figure 8.10 shows the results. That PI was operating is clear from the control group's recall scores; they steadily declined. Release from PI also occurred, as is evident from the recall scores of the experimental group.

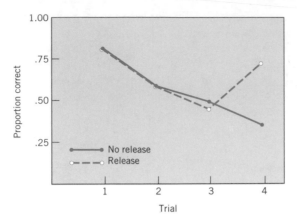

FIGURE 8.10   Release from PI.

(Data from Gunter et al., 1981)

One of the control features of this study is worth noting. A possible problem was that performance on the release trial might have gone up simply because the foreign news items were easier to recall than the domestic items. To eliminate this possibility, half of the participants in the release group saw three domestic trials followed by a foreign trial; the other half saw three foreign trials followed by a domestic trial. Likewise, in the control group, half saw four domestic trials and the remainder saw four foreign trials. The order made no difference to the results.[3]

Factorials with Subject and Manipulated Variables: P × E Designs

Chapter 5 introduced the concept of a subject variable—some already existing attribute of an individual such as age, gender, or some personality characteristic. You also learned to be cautious about drawing conclusions when subject variables are involved. Assuming proper control, causal conclusions can be drawn with manipulated independent variables, but with subject variables such conclusions cannot be drawn. P × E designs include both subject (the "P") and manipulated (the "E") variables. Causal conclusions can be drawn if a significant main effect occurs for the manipulated "Environmental" factor, but they cannot be drawn when a main effect occurs for the subject variable or "Person" factor, and they also cannot be drawn if an interaction occurs. Despite this limitation, designs including both subject and manipulated variables are popular, in part because they combine the two research traditions identified by Woodworth in his famous "Columbia bible" (see the opening paragraphs of Chapter 5). The correlational tradition is associated with the study of individual differences, and the subject variable or the "P" factor in the P × E design looks specifically at these differences. A significant main effect for this factor shows that two different *types* of individuals perform differently on whatever behavior is being measured as the dependent variable. The experimental tradition, on the other hand, is concerned with identifying general laws of behavior that apply to

---

[3] Calling the design a 2 × 4 design emphasizes the two important variables, but technically, this was a 2 × 2 × 4 mixed design, with the second "2" being the between-subjects factor of news category, foreign or domestic.

some degree to everyone, regardless of individual differences. Hence, finding a significant main effect for the manipulated or the "E" factor in a P × E design indicates that the situational factor is powerful enough to influence the behavior of many different kinds of persons. Consider a hypothetical example that compares introverts and extroverts (the "P" variable) and asks participants to solve problems in either a small, crowded room or a large, uncrowded room (the "E" variable). Suppose you get results like this (DV = number of problems solved):

	Small room	Large room
Introverts	12	12
Extroverts	18	18

In this case, there would be a main effect for personality type, no main effect for environment, and no interaction. Extroverts clearly outperformed introverts (18 > 12), regardless of whether they worked in crowded conditions or not. The researcher would have discovered an important way in which individuals differ, and the differences extend to more than one kind of environment.

A very different conclusion would be drawn from this outcome:

	Small room	Large room
Introverts	12	18
Extroverts	12	18

This yields a main effect for the environmental factor, no main effect for personality type, and no interaction. Now it is the environment (room size) that produced the powerful effect (18 > 12), and this effect extended beyond just a single type of individual; regardless of personality type, performance deteriorated under crowded conditions. Thus, finding a significant main effect for the "P" factor indicates that powerful personality differences occur, while finding a significant main effect for the "E" factor shows the power of some environmental influence to go beyond just one type of person. Of course, another result could be two main effects, indicating that each factor is important.

The most interesting outcome of a P × E design, however, is an interaction. When this occurs, it shows that for one type of individual, changes in the environment have one kind of effect, while for another type of individual, the same environmental changes have a different effect. Staying with the introvert/extrovert example, suppose this happened:

	Small room	Large room
Introverts	18	12
Extroverts	12	18

In this case, neither main effect would be significant, but an interaction clearly occurred. One thing happened for introverts, and something different occurred for extroverts. Specifically, introverts performed much better in the small than in the large room, while extroverts did much better in the large room than in the small one.

Factorial designs that include both subject variables and manipulated variables are popular in educational research and in research on the effectiveness of psychotherapy (Smith & Sechrest, 1991). In both areas, the importance of finding significant interactions is indicated by the fact that such designs are sometimes called **ATI designs,** or "Aptitude-Treatment Interaction designs." As you might guess, the "aptitude" refers to the nonmanipulated subject (person) variable and the "treatment" refers to the manipulated, environmental variable. An example from psychotherapy research is a study by Abramovitz, Abramovitz, Roback, and Jackson (1974). Their "P" variable was locus of control. Those with an external locus generally believe that external events exert control over their lives, while internals believe that what happens to them is a consequence of their own decisions and actions. In the study, externals did well in therapy that was more directive in providing guidance for them, but they did poorly in nondirective therapy, which places more responsibility for progress on the client. For internals, the opposite was true: They did best in the nondirective therapy and not too well in directive therapy.

ATIs in educational research usually occur when the aptitude or person factor is a learning style variable and the treatment or environmental factor is some aspect of instruction. For example, Figure 8.11 shows the outcome of some educational research reported by Valerie Shute, a leading authority on ATI designs (Shute, 1994). The study compared two educational strategies for teaching basic principles of electricity: rule induction and rule application. Participants were randomly assigned to one strategy or the other. The subject variable was whether learners scored high or low on a measure of "exploratory" behavior. The graph shows that those scoring high on exploratory behavior performed better in a rule induction setting, where

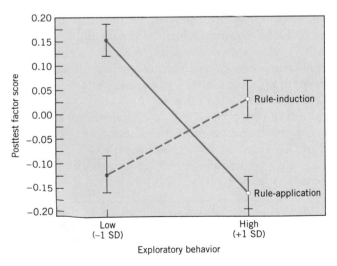

FIGURE 8.11   A P × E interaction between level of exploratory behavior and type of learning environment.

(From Shute, 1994)

they were asked to do more work on their own, while those scoring low on exploratory behavior performed better in a rule application environment, where the educational procedures were more structured for them.

P × E factorial designs are also very popular in personality research and in health psychology. The following case study is a good example of a study from health psychology that also examines a personality factor.

Case Study 18—A Factorial Design with a P × E Interaction

Over the past 25 years or so, there has been considerable interest in the personality features of those with a so-called Type A behavior pattern (Friedman & Rosenman, 1974). Type A individuals are competitive, achievement oriented, and compulsive about many things, including time (they are often early, never late). They try to do many things at once and seem to have a very high energy level. More ominously, Type A's who combine these traits with a generally hostile attitude tend to develop coronary heart disease. That is, under certain circumstances, a Type A behavior pattern can be decidedly unhealthy.

Research on Type A behavior often uses a P × E factorial design. The "P" (subject) variable is the behavior pattern—Type A or its antithesis, the more laid-back Type B. Selection of participants for each of these groups is determined by scores on some test for the Type A/B patterns. The "E" variable is some factor manipulated by the experimenter. For example, in a study by Holmes, McGilley, and Houston (1984), Type A and B college students were differentiated by their scores on a student version of the Jenkins Activity Survey, a test frequently used in research on Type A behavior patterns. A total of 394 students took the test, and the researchers recruited 30 high scorers and 30 low scorers. Participants in these two groups then were randomly assigned to one of three tasks that differed in how challenging they were. Hence the manipulated independent variable was task difficulty. The task was a "digit span" procedure, borrowed from an IQ test, in which participants listened to a sequence of numbers (e.g., 3–4–8) and had to repeat them in reverse order (8–4–3). The three levels of difficulty were defined in terms of the number of digits read to participants during the six trials completed by each of them: two, five, or seven. Arousal during the task, operationally defined in terms of several physiological measures, including systolic blood pressure, was the dependent variable.

Figure 8.12 shows the P × E interaction that occurred. Arousal for Type A's and B's did not differ on easy and moderate tasks, but on very difficult tasks, systolic pressure continued to increase for the A's but leveled off for the B's. That is, compared to Type B's, Type A's showed significantly elevated systolic blood pressure, but only on really challenging tasks. There was no overall main effect for personality type, but there was a main effect for task difficulty, as you can detect from the generally increasing blood pressure as the task became more difficult. In sum, the study showed that "differences in arousal … between Type A and Type B persons are most likely to emerge at high levels of challenge" (Holmes et al., 1984, p. 1326), a finding consistent with the highly competitive, achievement focus of Type A persons.

By the way, those advocating the use of P × E designs can trace their partiality to the work of Kurt Lewin (1890–1947), a pioneer in social and child psychology. The central theme guiding Lewin's work was that a full understanding of behavior

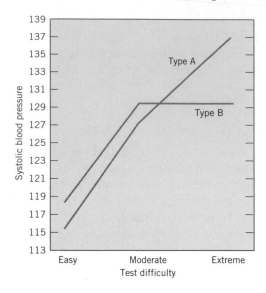

FIGURE 8.12 A P × E interaction: Type A versus Type B personalities and level of task difficulty.

(From Holmes et al., 1984)

required studying both the person's attributes and the environment in which the person operated. He expressed this idea in terms of the well-known formula, $B = f(P, E)$—**B**ehavior is a joint **f**unction of the **P**erson and the **E**nvironment (Goodwin, 1999). P × E factorial designs, which derive their name from Lewin's formula, are perfectly suited for discovering the kinds of interactive relationships that Lewin believed characterized human behavior.[4]

Recruiting Participants for Factorial Designs

It should be evident from the definitions of the varieties of factorials that the number of participants needed could vary considerably, depending on the design. If you need 5 participants to fill one of the cells in the 2 × 2 factorial, for example, the total number of people to be recruited could be 5, 10, or 20. Figure 8.13 shows you why. In Figure 8.13a, both variables are tested between subjects and 5 different participants will be needed per cell, for a total of 20. In Figure 8.13b, both variables are tested within subjects, making the design a repeated-measures factorial. The same five individuals will contribute data to each of the four cells. In a mixed design, Figure 8.13c, one of the variables is tested between subjects and the other is tested within subjects. Thus, 5 participants will participate in two cells and 5 will participate in the other two cells, a total of 10.

Knowing how many participants to recruit for an experimental leads naturally to the question of how to treat the people who arrive at your experiment. Box 8.2 provides a hands-on, practical guide to being an ethical researcher.

---

[4] One unfortunate implication of Lewin's choice of the label "P" is the implication that a P × E design involves human participants only. Yet it is quite common for such a design to be used with animal subjects (a study in which the subject variable is the gender of the primates being tested for instance).

(a) For a 2 × 2 design with four different groups and five participants per cell—20 subjects needed

S1	S11
S2	S12
S3	S13
S4	S14
S5	S15
S6	S16
S7	S17
S8	S18
S9	S19
S10	S20

(a)

(b) For a 2 × 2 repeated—measures design with five participants per cell—five subjects needed

S1	S1
S2	S2
S3	S3
S4	S4
S5	S5
S1	S1
S2	S2
S3	S3
S4	S4
S5	S5

(b)

(c) For a 2 × 2 mixed design with five participants per cell—10 subjects needed

S1	S1
S2	S2
S3	S3
S4	S4
S5	S5
S6	S6
S7	S7
S8	S8
S9	S9
S10	S10

(c)

FIGURE 8.13 Participant requirements in factorial designs.

Box 8.2

ETHICS—On Being a Competent and Ethical Researcher

You learned about the APA code of ethics in Chapter 2, and you have been encountering Ethics boxes in each of the subsequent chapters. Although you should have a pretty good sense of what the ethical requirements of a study are (consent, debriefing, etc.), you might not be quite sure how to put this into actual practice. Hence, this might be a good time to give you a list of practical tips for being an ethically responsible experimenter. Here goes.

✓ Don't just get to your session on time—be early enough to have all the materials organized and ready to go when your participants arrive.

✓ Always treat the people who volunteer for your study with the same courtesy and respect that you would hope to receive if the roles were reversed. Greet them when they show up at the lab and thank them for signing up and coming to the session. They might be a bit apprehensive about what will happen to them in a "psychology" experiment, so your first task is to put them at ease, while at the same time maintaining your professional role as the person in charge of the session. Always remember that they are doing you a favor—the reverse is not true. Smile often.

✓ Start the session with the informed consent form and don't convey the attitude that this is a time-consuming technicality that has to be completed before the important part starts. Instead, make it clear that you want your participants to have a clear idea of what they are about to do. If they don't ask questions while reading the consent form, be sure to ask them if they have any questions when they finish reading. Make sure there are two copies of the signed consent form—one for them to take with them and one for your records.

✓ It is a good idea to write out the "Instructions to Participants" ahead of time. Depending on the study, you can read them the instructions, or give them the instructions to read. If it isn't necessary to have elaborate written instructions, at least have a list with you that includes the key points of the instructions about the procedure.

✓ Before you test any "real" participants, practice playing the role of experimenter a few times with friends or lab partners. Go through the whole experimental procedure—think of it as a dress rehearsal and an opportunity to iron out any problems with the procedure.

✓ Be alert to any signs of distress in participants during the session. Depending on the constraints of the procedure, this could mean halting the study and discarding their data, but their welfare is more important than your data. Also, you're not a professional counselor—if they seem disturbed by their participation, gently refer them to your course instructor.

✓ Prepare the debriefing carefully. As a student experimenter, you probably won't be running studies involving elaborate deceptions or producing high levels of stress, but you will be responsible for making this an educational experience for your participants. Hence, you should work hard on a simplified description of what the study hopes to discover and you should give them the chance to suggest improvements in the procedure or ideas for the next study. So don't rush the debriefing or give a cursory description that gives the impression that you hope they will just leave. And if they seem to want to leave without any debriefing (some will), don't let them. Debriefing is an important part of your responsibility as a researcher and an educator. (Of course, if they say, "I thought you said we could leave any time," there's not much you can do!)

✓ Before they go, remind them that the information on the consent form gives them names of people to contact about the study. Give them a rough idea of when the study will be completed and when they can expect to hear about the overall results. Also, ask them not to discuss the experiment with others who might be participants. **Leakage,** a tendency for participants to tell others about the studies they've completed, can be a serious problem, especially at small schools (see Box 6.3, p. 208, for more on the responsibilities of research participants). If you have been good to them throughout the session, however, that increases the chances of their cooperation in this regard.

✓ As they are leaving, be sure to thank them for their time and effort and be sure you are smiling as they go out the door. Remember that some of the students you test will be undecided about a major and perhaps thinking about psychology; their participation in your study could enhance their interest.

Analyzing Factorial Designs

We've already seen that multilevel, single-factor designs are analyzed with a 1-way ANOVA. Similarly, factorial designs using interval or ratio data are analyzed with N-way ANOVAs, with N referring to the number of independent variables involved. Hence, a 2 × 3 factorial would be analyzed by a 2-way ANOVA and a 2 × 2 × 4 by a 3-way ANOVA.

When doing a 1-way ANOVA, just one *F*-ratio is calculated. Then there may be subsequent testing if the *F* is significant. For a factorial design, however, more than one *F*-ratio will be calculated. Specifically, there will be an *F* for each possible main effect and for each possible interaction. For example, in the 2 × 2 design investigating the effects of imagery training and presentation rate on memory, an *F*-ratio will be calculated to examine the possibility of a main effect for type of training, another for the main effect of presentation rate, and a third for the potential interaction between the two (see Appendix C for an example of a 2 × 2 ANOVA). In an A × B × C factorial, there will be *seven F*-ratios calculated: three for the main effects of A, B, and C, three more for the 2-way interaction effects of A × B, B × C, and A × C, plus one for the 3-way interaction, A × B × C. Subsequent testing may occur with factorial ANOVAs as well as with 1-way ANOVAs. For example, in a 2 × 3 ANOVA, a significant *F* for the factor with three levels would trigger a subsequent analysis (e.g., Tukey's HSD—see Appendix C) that compared the overall performance of levels 1 and 2, 1 and 3, and 2 and 3.

Before closing this chapter, let me make one final point about factorials and the analysis of variance. You've been looking at many factorial matrices in this chapter. They might vaguely remind you of farming. If so, it's no accident, as you can discover by reading Box 8.3, which tells you a bit about Sir Ronald Fisher, who invented the analysis of variance.

Box 8.3

ORIGINS—Factorials Down on the Farm

Imagine that you're in a small plane flying over Kansas. Looking out the window, you see mile after mile of farms, with their fields laid out in blocks. The pattern might remind you of the 2 × 2 and 3 × 3 factorial matrices that you've just encountered in this chapter. This is because factorial designs and the ANOVA procedures for analyzing them were first developed in the context of agricultural research, devised by Sir Ronald Fisher. The empirical question was, "What are the best possible conditions or combinations of conditions for raising crop X?"

Ronald Aylmer Fisher (1890–1962) was one of Great Britain's best-known statisticians, equal in rank to the great Karl Pearson, who invented the correlation measure we now call "Pearson's *r*" (next chapter). Fisher created statistical procedures useful in testing predictions about genetics, but he is perhaps best known among research psychologists for creating the analysis of variance, which yields the *F*-ratios that allow one to decide about the null hypothesis in experimental research. You can easily guess what the "F" represents.

For about a 15-year period beginning in 1920, Fisher worked at an experimental agricultural station at Rothamsted, England. While there, he was involved in research investigating the effects on crop yield of such variables as fertilizer type, rainfall level, different planting sequences, and different genetic strains of various crops. He published articles with titles like "Studies in Crop Variation. VI. Experiments on the Response of the Potato to Potash and Nitrogen" (Kendall, 1970, p. 447). In the process, he invented analysis of variance as a way of analyzing the data. He especially emphasized the importance of using factorial designs, "for with separate [single-factor] experiments we should obtain no light whatever on the possible *interactions* of the different ingredients" (Fisher, 1935/1951, p. 95, italics added). In the real world of agriculture, crop yields resulted from complex combinations of factors, and studying one factor at a time wouldn't allow a thorough evaluation of those interactive effects.

A simple 2×2 design for one of Fisher's experiments, with each block representing how a small square of land was treated, might look like Figure 8.14. As with any factorial, this design allows one to evaluate main effects (of fertilizer and type of wheat in this case), as well as the interaction of the two factors. In the example in Figure 8.14, if we assume that the shaded field produces significantly more wheat than the other three (which equal each other), then we would say that an interaction clearly occurred—the fertilizer was effective, but only for one specific strain of wheat.

Fisher first published his work on ANOVA in book form in 1925 (a year after Jenkins and Dallenbach published their classic sleep and memory study), as part of a larger text on statistics (Fisher, 1925). His most famous work on ANOVA, which combined a discussion of statistics and research methodology, appeared 10 years later as *The Design of Experiments* (Fisher, 1935/1951). ANOVA techniques and factorial designs were slow to catch on in the United States, but by the early 1950s, they had become institutionalized as a dominant statistical tool for experimental psychologists (Rucci & Tweney, 1980).

	Experimental fertilizer	No experimental fertilizer
Wheat: genetic strain I	Wheat field A	Wheat field B
Wheat: genetic strain II	Wheat field C	Wheat field D

FIGURE 8.14 An agricultural interaction.

This completes our two-chapter sequence about experimental designs. It's a pair of chapters (along with Chapters 5 and 6) sure to require more than one reading and much practice with designs before you'll feel confident about your ability to use "experimental psychologist language" fluently and to create a methodologically sound experiment that is a good test of your hypothesis. Next up is a closer look at another research tradition, in which the emphasis is not on examining differences, but in examining degrees of association between measured variables.

Chapter Summary

Factorial Essentials

Factorial designs examine the effects of more than one independent variable. Factorials are identified with a notation system that identifies the number of independent variables, the number of levels of each variable, and the total number of conditions. For example, a 2×3 ("2 by 3") factorial has two independent variables, the first with two levels and the second with three levels, and six different conditions (2 times 3).

Outcomes—Main Effects and Interactions

The overall influence of an independent variable in a factorial study is called a main effect. There are two possible main effects in a 2×3 design, one for the factor with two levels and one for the factor with three levels. The main advantage of a factorial design over studies with a single independent variable is that factorials allow for the possibility of discovering interactions between the factors. In an interaction, the influence of one independent variable differs for the different levels of the other independent variable. The outcomes of factorial studies can include significant main effects, interactions, both, or neither.

Varieties of Factorial Designs

All of the independent variables in a factorial design can be between-subjects factors or all can be within-subjects factors. Between-subjects factorial designs can include independent groups, matched groups, or nonequivalent groups. Within-subjects factorials are also called repeated-measures factorial designs. A mixed factorial design includes at least one factor of each type (between and within). Factorials with at least one manipulated variable and at least one subject variable allow for the discovery of Person $\times$ Environment (P $\times$ E) interactions. When these interactions occur, they show how stimulus situations affect one type of person one way and a second type of person another way. A main effect for the P factor (i.e., subject variable) indicates important differences between types of individuals that exist in several environments. A main effect for the E factor (i.e., manipulated variable) indicates important environmental influences that exist for several types of persons. In educational research and research on the effectiveness of psychotherapy, these interactions between persons and environments are sometimes called Aptitude-Treatment-Interactions (ATIs).

Chapter Review

Multiple Choice

1. A researcher predicts that introverts will do better on a problem-solving task if they do it by themselves rather than in front of an audience. Extroverts, however, are expected to do better with an audience than alone. The researcher
   a. is predicting a main effect for the audience variable
   b. is using a mixed factorial design

     c. expects an interaction effect to occur
     d. is using two manipulated variables

2. A 3 × 3 mixed factorial design uses five people in cell A1B1. How many people need to be recruited for this study?
     a. 5
     b. 10
     c. 45
     d. 15

3. A 2 × 3 × 5 factorial design has
     a. 10 different independent variables
     b. 25 different conditions
     c. 3 different independent variables
     d. a maximum of 30 main effects

4. A 2 × 2 mixed factorial design will always include
     a. two subject variables
     b. a between-subjects factor and a within-subjects factor
     c. a within-subjects variable and a repeated-measures variable
     d. one manipulated variable and one subject variable

5. In a maze-learning experiment, 30 rats are tested with the lights on and 30 more with the lights off. Also, within each of the two groups, 10 rats receive reinforcement as soon as they reach the goal, 10 others are reinforced 5 seconds after they reach the goal, and the remaining 10 are fed 10 seconds after reaching the goal. What can you say about this design?
     a. both independent variables are subject factors
     b. it is best described as a 2 × 2 independent groups design
     c. it is best described as a 2 × 3 mixed design
     d. six different conditions are being tested

Short Essay

1. In the context of a factorial design, distinguish between the concepts of "levels" and "conditions."

2. What is meant by a main effect? In terms of the contents of a factorial matrix, how does one go about determining if a main effect has occurred?

3. Use the Godden and Baddeley study (Scottish diving club) to illustrate the fact that important results can occur in a study, even if no main effects occur.

4. In a study with both main effects and an interaction, explain why the interaction must be interpreted first, and the statistically significant main effects might have little meaning for the overall outcome of the study.

5. What is a ceiling effect? If one occurs, how might the method be adjusted to eliminate the effect?

6. Distinguish between a mixed factorial design and a P × E design.

7. Use the introvert/extrovert and room size example to show how P × E designs can discover important ways in which (a) individuals differ and (b) situations can be more powerful than individual differences.

8. Mixed factorial designs may or may not involve counterbalancing. Explain.

9. Describe the basic research design and the general outcome of Jenkins and Dallenbach's famous study on sleep and memory.

10. What is meant by the concept of leakage and how might it be prevented?

Applications Exercises

Exercise 8.1.—Identifying Designs

For each of the following descriptions of studies, identify the independent and dependent variables involved, the levels of the independent variable, and the nature of each independent variable (between-subjects or within-subjects; manipulated or subject variables). Identify the measurement scale for each dependent variable. Also, describe the number of independent variables and levels of each by using the factorial notation system (e.g., 2 × 3), and use Figure 8.6 to identify the experimental design.

1. On the basis of scores on the Jenkins Activity Survey, three groups of participants are identified: Type A, Type B, and intermediate. An equal number of participants in each group is given one of two tasks to perform. One of the tasks is to sit quietly in a small room and estimate, in the absence of a clock, when 2 full minutes have elapsed. The second task is to make the same estimate, except that while in the small room, the participant is playing a handheld video game.

2. College students in a cognitive mapping study are asked to use a direction finder to point accurately to three unseen locations that differ in distance from the lab. One is a nearby campus location, one is a nearby city, and the third is a distant city. Half of the participants perform the task in a windowless room with a compass indicating the direction of north. The remaining participants perform the task in the same room without a compass.

3. In a study of touch sensitivity, two-point thresholds are measured on 10 different skin locations for an equal number of blind and sighted adults. Half of the participants perform the task in the morning and half in the evening.

4. Three groups of preschoolers are put into a study of delay of gratification in which the size of the delay is varied. Children in all three groups complete a puzzle task. One group is told that as payment they can have a dollar now or three dollars tomorrow. The second group chooses between a dollar now or three dollars two days from now, and the third group chooses between a dollar now or three dollars three days from now. For each of the three groups, half the children solve an easy puzzle and half solve a difficult puzzle. The groups are formed in such a way that the average parents' income is the same for children in each group.

5. In a study of visual illusions and size perception, participants adjust a dial that alters one of two stimuli. The goal is to make the two stimuli appear to be equal in size, and the size of the error in this judgment is measured on each trial. Each participant completes 40 trials. On half of the trials, the pairs of stimuli are in color; on the other half, they are in black and white. For both the colored and

the black-and-white stimuli, half are presented at a distance of 10 feet from the participant and half are presented 20 feet away.

6. In a study of reading comprehension, sixth-grade students read a short story about baseball. The students are divided into two groups based on their knowledge of baseball. Within each group, half of the students are high scorers on a test of verbal IQ, while the remaining students are low scorers.

Exercise 8.2.—Main Effects and Interactions

For each of the following studies:

a. identify the independent variables, and the levels of each, and the dependent variable

b. place the data into the correct cells of a factorial matrix

c. determine if main effects and/or interactions exist

d. give a verbal description of the study's outcome

e. draw a graph of the results

For the purposes of the exercise, assume that a difference of "2" between any of the row or column or cell means is a significant difference.

1. A researcher is interested in the effects of ambiguity and number of bystanders on helping behavior. Participants fill out a questionnaire in a room with zero or two other people who appear to be other subjects but aren't. The experimenter distributes the questionnaire and then goes into the room next door. After 5 minutes there is a loud crash, possibly caused by the experimenter falling. For half of the participants, the experimenter unambiguously calls out that he has fallen, is hurt, and needs help. For the remaining participants, the situation is more ambiguous—the experimenter says nothing after the apparent fall. Twenty participants are tested in each condition, and the experimenter records how long it takes (in seconds) before a participant offers help.

0 bystanders, ambiguous	24
2 bystanders, ambiguous	38
0 bystanders, unambiguous	14
2 bystanders, unambiguous	14

2. A researcher interested in maze learning hypothesizes that maze learning can be influenced by the size of the reinforcer and by the delay in reinforcement. Animals are given 40 learning trials in a maze, and the number of errors per trial is recorded. There are six conditions. At the end of the maze there is

   a. a 10-mg food pellet, and it is given to the animal immediately, or

   b. a 10-mg food pellet, but the animal has to wait 10 seconds in the goal box before the food is given, or

   c. a 10-mg food pellet, but the animal has to wait 20 seconds in the goal box before the food is given, or

   d. a 20-mg food pellet, and it is given to the animal immediately, or

   e.   a 20-mg food pellet, but the animal has to wait 10 seconds in the goal box before the food is given, or

   f.   a 20-mg food pellet, but the animal has to wait 20 seconds in the goal box before the food is given.

The average number of errors for animals in the six groups are:

1: 10   2: 40   3: 45   4: 5   5: 35   6: 40

Exercise 8.3.—Estimating Participant Needs

For each of the following, use the available information to determine how many research participants will be needed to complete the study (hint: one of these is unanswerable without more information):

1.   a 3 × 3 mixed factorial; cell A1B1 needs 10 participants.
2.   a 2 × 3 repeated–measures factorial; cell A1B1 needs 20 participants.
3.   a 2 × 2 × 2 independent groups factorial; cell A1B1C1 needs 5 participants.
4.   a 2 × 4 mixed factorial; cell A1B1 needs 8 participants.

9

Preview & Chapter Objectives

You have just finished a four-chapter sequence that concentrated on the experimental method in psychology. Four chapters remain, each dealing with a slightly different research tradition. In this chapter, you will encounter correlational research, an approach that focuses on examining relationships among variables. You will see that caution is needed to interpret correlational research and that correlational studies can be useful when psychologists try to make predictions about behavior. When you finish this chapter, you should be able to:

- Understand the origins of correlational research in the work of Francis Galton and recognize the significance of Cronbach's "two disciplines" address.

- Distinguish between positive and negative bivariate correlations, create scatterplots to illustrate them, and recognize the factors that can influence the size of correlation coefficients (e.g., range restriction).

- Calculate a coefficient of determination (r^2) and interpret its meaning.
- Understand how a regression analysis accomplishes the goal of prediction.
- Understand how directionality can make it difficult to interpret correlations and how a cross-lagged panel correlation can help with the directionality problem.
- Understand the third variable problem and how such variables can be evaluated through a partial correlation procedure.
- Describe the research situations in which correlational research is likely to be used.
- Describe the logic of the multivariate procedures of multiple regression and factor analysis.

Remember Robert Woodworth and the "Columbia bible," his precedent-setting text in experimental psychology (Chapter 5's opening paragraphs)? The book institutionalized the distinction we routinely make today between independent and dependent variables in experimental studies. The second distinction made by Woodworth, between experimental and correlational methods, likewise has had a profound effect on research in psychology. The experimental method manipulates variables, according to Woodworth, while the correlational method "[m]easur[es] two or more characteristics of the same individual [and] computes the correlation of these characteristics. ..." (Woodworth, 1938, p. 3). Woodworth took pains to assure the reader that these two research strategies were of equal value. The correlational method was "[t]o be distinguished from the experimental method, [but] standing on a par with it in value, rather than above or below. ..." (Woodworth, 1938, p. 3). After making this assertion, however, Woodworth referred the reader elsewhere for information about correlational research and devoted the remaining 820 pages of his text to research illustrating the experimental method. The reader could be excused for thinking that correlational research was not quite as important as experimental research.

Psychology's Two Disciplines

The Woodworth text began a process of separation that led eventually to Lee Cronbach's 1957 presidential address to the American Psychological Association, entitled "The Two Disciplines of Scientific Psychology" (Cronbach, 1957). As you can guess, the two disciplines were correlational and experimental psychology. According to Cronbach, correlational psychology is concerned with investigating the relationships between naturally occurring variables and with studying individual differences. The experimental psychologist is not usually interested in individual differences, however, but rather with minimizing or controlling these differences in order to show that some stimulus factor influences every individual's behavior in some predictable way to some measurable degree. The correlationist observes variables and relates them; the experimentalist manipulates variables and observes the outcome. The correlationist looks for ways in which people differ from each other; the experimentalist looks for general laws that apply to everyone.

Cronbach was concerned that correlational psychology held second-class status in scientific psychology and expressed the belief that it was time for a synthesis to occur, for both approaches to be valued equally by advocates of each, and for research to encompass both strategies. As he put it:

It is not enough for each discipline to borrow from the other. Correlational psychology studies only variance among organisms; experimental psychology studies only variance among treatments. A united discipline will study both of these, but it will also be concerned with the otherwise neglected *interactions between organismic variables and treatment variables.* (Cronbach, 1957, p. 681, italics added)

As the italicized phrase indicates, Cronbach was calling for an increase in designs like the P × E factorials (P = person or organism; E = environmental treatment) you learned about in the previous chapter. He was also calling for a renewed appreciation of the correlational method in general, an outcome that has occurred to some degree in the last 40 years. Aided by the speed and capacity of modern computers, sophisticated correlational procedures such as multiple regression and factor analysis are in widespread use today. However, many experimental psychology textbooks continue the Woodworth tradition of paying little attention to the correlational method, often devoting just a page or two in a chapter on "nonexperimental" methods. This text is an exception, as you're about to discover. Before diving into a description of the nuts and bolts of correlational research, however, you should read Box 9.1, which describes the origins of the correlational procedure in the attempts by Sir Francis Galton to study the inheritance of genius.

Box 9.1

ORIGINS—Galton's Studies of Genius

When you first encountered him in Chapter 1 (p. 13), Sir Francis Galton (1822–1911) was portrayed as a bit of an eccentric (e.g., trying to measure the usefulness of prayer). However, it would be a mistake to dismiss Galton as a crank. He was a pioneer in the empirical study of intelligence, among the first to make a strong case that genius is inherited and not the result of one's upbringing. Along the way, he invented correlations.

Galton was much impressed by Darwin's theory of evolution, especially the idea that individual members of a species vary from each other. Individual variations that are useful for survival are then "naturally selected" and passed on to offspring. Galton believed that intelligence was a trait on which people varied, that it was important for survival, and that it seemed to be inherited much like physical characteristics such as eye color and height. He set out to gather evidence for the idea that intelligence was inherited and produced two books on the subject: *Hereditary Genius* (1869) and *English Men of Science: Their Nature and Nurture* (1874), the latter popularizing the now famous terms "nature" and "nurture." In his books Galton noted the statistical tendency for genius and for skills in specific areas (e.g., chemistry, law) to run in families. He discounted the influence of the environment, however, and declared that genius

Children's heights (Mean = 68.0")

Parents' heights (Mean = 68.1")	63"	64"	65"	66"	67"	68"	69"	70"	71"	72"	73"
72"							1	2	2	2	1
71"				2	4	5	5	4	3	1	
70"	1	2	3	5	8	9	9	8	5	3	
69"	2	3	6	10	12	12	2	10	6	3	
68"	3	7	11	13	14	13	10	7	3	1	
67"	3	6	8	11	11	8	6	3	1		
66"	2	3	4	6	4	3	2				
65"											
Mean height of parents in each column	67.2	67.3	67.4	67.6	67.9	68.2	68.4	68.8	69.1	69.3	

FIGURE 9.1   A table used by Galton to correlate the heights of parents and children—an original scatterplot.

was the result of inheritance. In part, his argument was based on the idea that intelligence was normally distributed in the population. Other traits (e.g., height) known to be influenced by heredity were also normally distributed, so Galton took this statistical fact to be an indication that heredity was involved (Fancher, 1990).

It wasn't until 1888 that Galton solved the problem of how to express the strength of a tendency for a trait like genius to run in families; he expressed his ideas in a paper called "Co-relations and Their Measurement." (cited in Fancher, 1990). First, Galton discovered that he could organize his data into a row and column arrangement like the one in Figure 9.1. The numbers in each cell indicated how many people fell into the categories defined by the row and column headings. Hence, the largest number in those cells indicates that the sample included 14 children who were between 67 and 68 inches tall and whose parents' heights were also between 67 and 68 inches. As you will discover in a few pages, Galton's table is the origin of what are now called "scatterplots."

Second, Galton noticed that while the "co-relations" were imperfect, one regularity occurred quite consistently. Taller than average parents had tall children, but they tended to be not quite as tall as Mom and Dad. Shorter than average parents had short children, but not quite as short. That is, the children's heights tended to drift back to, or regress to, the mean for the population. This "regression to the mean" phenomenon, which you already know can threaten a study's internal validity, is one of Galton's greatest discoveries.

A third observation made by Galton was that a plot of the average of each column of his scatterplot yielded a more or less straight line. This in fact is a type of "regression line," another concept that you'll be encountering shortly. In sum, Galton discovered the main features of a correlational analysis.

Shortly after reading about Galton's work, the young British statistician Karl Pearson continued developing the idea, eventually devising the modern formula for calculating coefficients of correlation. He named it *"r"* for "regression," in honor of Galton's discovery of the regression to the mean phenomenon. Also following Galton's lead, Pearson believed that correlational analysis supported the idea that many traits were inherited because they ran in families. A feature of correlations that you'll be learning about shortly is that drawing conclusions about causality from them, as both Galton and Pearson did, is a hazardous venture.

Correlation and Regression—The Basics

A correlation is said to exist whenever two variables are associated or related to each other in some fashion. This idea is implied by the term itself: "co" for two and "relation" for, well, relation. In a direct or **positive correlation,** the relationship is such that a high score on one variable is associated with a high score on the second variable; similarly, a low score on one relates to a low score on the other. A **negative correlation,** on the other hand, is an inverse relationship. High scores on one variable are associated with low scores on the second variable, and vice versa.

Positive and Negative Correlations

The relationship between study time and grades is a simple example of a positive correlation. If study time, operationalized as the total number of hours per week spent studying, is one variable and grade point average (GPA) ranging from 0.0 to 4.0 is the second, you can easily see the positive correlation between the two in these hypothetical data from eight students:

	Study hours	GPA
Student 1:	42	3.3
Student 2:	23	2.9
Student 3:	31	3.2
Student 4:	35	3.2
Student 5:	16	1.9
Student 6:	26	2.4
Student 7:	39	3.7
Student 8:	19	2.5

Spending a significant amount of time studying (e.g., 42 hours) is associated with a high GPA (3.3), while minimal study time (e.g., 16 hours) is paired with a low GPA (1.9).

An example of negative correlation might be the relationship between goof-off time and GPA. Goof-off time could be operationally defined as the number of hours per week spent in a specific list of activities that might include video game playing, soap opera watching, and playing golf (of course, these same activities could be called "therapy" time). Here's some hypothetical data for another eight students. This time, examine the inverse relationship between the number of hours per week spent goofing off and GPA:

	Goof-off hours	GPA
Student 1:	42	1.8
Student 2:	23	3.0
Student 3:	31	2.2
Student 4:	35	2.9
Student 5:	16	3.7
Student 6:	26	3.0
Student 7:	39	2.4
Student 8:	19	3.4

Notice that in a negative correlation, the variables go in opposite directions. Large amounts of goof-off time (e.g., 42) accompany a low GPA (1.8); less goof-off time (e.g., 16) relates to a higher GPA (3.7).

The strength of a correlation is indicated by the size of a descriptive statistic known as the "coefficient of correlation," which ranges from −1.00 for a perfect negative correlation, through 0.00 for no relationship, to +1.00 for a perfect positive correlation. The most common coefficient is the **Pearson's** r, mentioned in Box 9.1, and named for the British statistician who rivals Sir Ronald Fisher in stature. Pearson's r is calculated for data measured on either an interval or a ratio scale. Other kinds of correlations can be calculated for data measured on other scales. For instance, a correlation coefficient called Spearman's rho (rhymes with "throw") is calculated for ordinal (i.e., rankings) data. Appendix C shows you how to calculate Pearson's r.

Like means and standard deviations, a coefficient of correlation is a descriptive statistic. The inferential analysis for correlations involves determining if a particular correlation is significantly greater than (or less than) zero. That is, in correlational research the null hypothesis (H_0) is that the true value of r is 0 (i.e., no relationship exists); the alternative hypothesis (H_1) is that $r \neq 0$. Rejecting the null hypothesis means deciding that a significant relationship between two variables exists. Appendix C shows you how to determine if a correlation is statistically significant.

Scatterplots

An indication of the strength of a correlation also can be discerned by examining the modern version of Galton's Figure 9.1, what is now called a **scatterplot** or scattergraph; it provides a visual representation of the relationship shown by a correlation. As shown in the examples in Figure 9.2, perfect positive (9.2a) and perfect negative (9.2b) correlations produce points falling on a straight line, while a correlation of zero yields a scatterplot (9.2c) in which the points appear to be randomly distributed on the surface

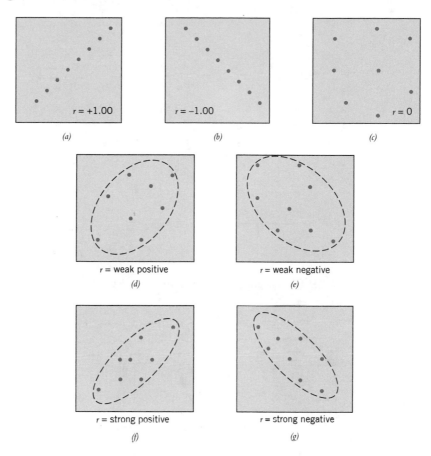

FIGURE 9.2 Varieties of scatterplots.

of the graph. Compared to relatively weak correlations (9.2d and 9.2e), the points bunch closer together for relatively strong ones (9.2f and 9.2g). In general, as any correlation weakens, the points on a scatterplot move further away from the diagonal lines that would connect the points in a perfect correlation of +1.00 or −1.00.

Figure 9.3 shows you how a scatterplot is created from a set of data, and Figure 9.4 shows you the scatterplots for the hypothetical GPA examples. They show a strong positive correlation between study time and GPA and a strong negative one between goof-off time and GPA. The actual correlations are +.88 and −.89, respectively. Your instructor might ask you to verify these Pearson's r's by using the procedures outlined in Appendix C.

Assuming Linearity

So far, the scatterplots you've examined contain points that vary to some degree from the straight line of a perfect correlation of −1.00 or +1.00. Some relationships are not linear, however, and applying Pearson's r to them will fail to identify the nature of the relationship. Figure 9.5 shows a hypothetical example, one of psychol-

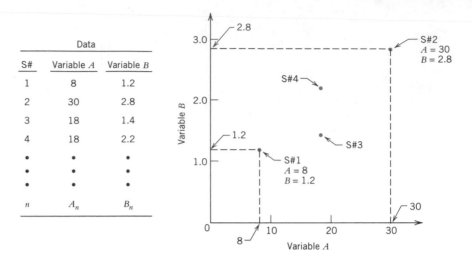

	Data	
S#	Variable A	Variable B
1	8	1.2
2	30	2.8
3	18	1.4
4	18	2.2
•	•	•
•	•	•
•	•	•
n	A_n	B_n

FIGURE 9.3   Creating a scatterplot from a data set.

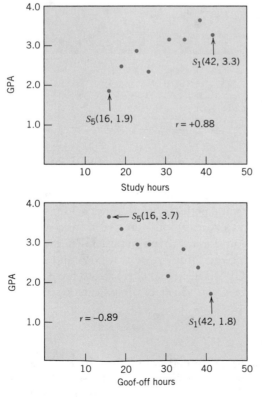

FIGURE 9.4   Scatterplots for some hypothetical GPA data.

ogy's enduring findings: the relationship between arousal and performance. On tasks that are somewhat difficult, performance is good at moderate levels of arousal but suffers if arousal is very low or very high (e.g., Anderson, 1990). At very low levels of arousal the person doesn't have the energy to perform the task, and at very high levels the intense arousal interferes with the efficient processing of information necessary to complete the task. You can see from the scatterplot that points would fall consistently along this curved line, but trying to apply a linear correlational procedure would yield a Pearson's *r* of zero or very close to it. More specialized techniques beyond the scope of this text are needed for analyzing curvilinear relationships like the one in Figure 9.5.

Restricting the Range

When doing a correlational study, it is important to include individuals with a wide range of scores. **Restricting the range** of one (or both) of the variables lowers the correlation, an effect that you can see in Figure 9.6. Suppose you are investigating the relationship between SAT scores and success in college, the latter measured in terms of GPA at end of the freshman year. Figure 9.6a shows what a scatterplot might look like for a sample of 25 students. The correlation is +.70. Suppose, however, that you decide to study this relationship, but only for students who score 1200 or above on the SAT. Figure 9.6b highlights the points on the scatterplot for such students; these points can form their own scatterplot, as shown in Figure 9.6c. If you now examine 9.6a and 9.6c, it is clear that the correlation is lower for 9.6c. In fact, the correlation drops to +.26.

This example has some interesting implications for colleges that decide not to consider students whose combined SAT scores fall below 1200. Studies (e.g., Schrader, 1971) have shown the overall correlation between SAT scores and freshman year grades to be somewhere in the vicinity of +.40, statistically significant but not huge. That correlation is calculated using students throughout the whole range of SAT scores, however. If the range of SAT scores is restricted to those of 1200 or above, the correlation will drop considerably. Procedures exist for "correcting" correlations to account for the restriction problem, but one has to be aware that restricting the range has direct effects on the ability to make predictions. Highly selective schools using an

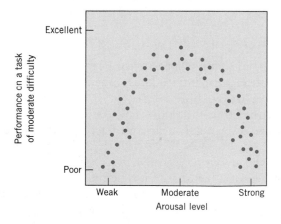

FIGURE 9.5 The curvilinear relationship between arousal level and performance.

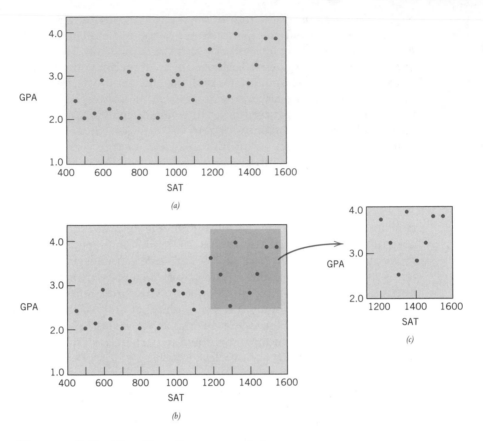

FIGURE 9.6   The effect of a range restriction.

"SAT = 1200" cutoff will certainly be getting a lot of good students, but their ability to predict grades from SAT scores will not be as great as in a school without such a cutoff point. The correlation between SAT and academic success will be higher at the less restrictive school than it will be at the more restrictive school.

Coefficient of Determination—r^2

It is easy to misinterpret the meaning of a particular Pearson's *r*. If it equals +.70, the relationship is a relatively strong one, but students sometimes look at such a correlation and think that the +.70 somehow relates to 70%, and that the correlation means the relationship is true 70% of the time. This is not what a Pearson's *r* means. A better sense of how to interpret the meaning of a correlation is to use what is called the **coefficient of determination (r^2).** It is found by squaring the Pearson's *r*—hence, the coefficient will always be a positive number, regardless of whether the correlation is positive or negative. Technically, it is defined as the portion of variability in one of the variables in the correlation that can be accounted for by variability in the second variable. An example should make this clear.

Suppose you complete a study involving 100 people in which you measure emotional depression and grade point average (GPA) in each of them. You correlate the two variables and find a negative correlation. The more depressed people are, the worse their grades are; conversely, nondepressed people tend to have better grades. Consider two possible correlations that might result from this study, -1.00 and $-.50$. The coefficients of determination will be 1.00 and .25, respectively. To understand what this means, first recognize that the GPAs for the 100 people in the study will probably vary quite a bit, possibly from 0.0 to 4.0. As researchers, we would like to know what produces this variability—why one person gets a 3.8, another a 2.4, and so on. That is, what accounts for individual differences in GPA? There are probably a number of factors in real life—study habits, general intelligence, motivation, emotional stability, ability to pick easy courses, etc. Our hypothetical study has examined one of those factors, emotional stability, as reflected in scores on a test for depression. The r^2 provides us with an indication of how much the variability in GPA can be associated directly with depression. In the first outcome, with an r of -1.00 and an r^2 of 1.00, we could conclude that 100% of the variability in GPA can be accounted for with reference to the variability in the depression scores. That is, we could say that 100% of the difference between the GPAs of 3.8 and 2.4 (and others) could be attributed to depression. This of course would never happen in a real study. In the second case, with an r of $-.50$ and an r^2 of .25, only one-fourth (25%) of the variability in GPA scores can be associated with depression. Presumably, the remaining 75% would be related to other factors, such as the ones listed above. In short, then the coefficient of determination gives us a better indication of the strength of a relationship than does Pearson's r.

One final point. Notice that in a correlation of $+.70$, the coefficient of determination is .49, while a correlation of $+.50$ has an r^2 of .25. Although we might be tempted to think that the relationships aren't all that different, that $+.70$ isn't *that* much bigger than $+.50$, the reality is that the amount of shared variance is almost twice as much in the first case as in the second. That is, a correlation of $+.70$ is *much* stronger than a correlation of $+.50$.

Regression Analysis—Making Predictions

As the above example suggests, a major feature of correlational research is that predictions about behavior can be made when strong correlations exist. If you know that two variables are correlated, then knowing a score on one of the variables enables you to predict a score on the other. You can see how this would work with the GPA example. Knowing of the strong relationship between study time and GPA, if I tell you that someone studies 45 hours per week, you could safely predict a relatively high GPA for that student. Similarly, a high GPA allows a prediction about study time. As you'll see later in the chapter, correlational research provides the foundation for using psychological tests to make predictions. Making predictions on the basis of correlational research is referred to as doing a **regression analysis.**

Figure 9.7 reproduces the scatterplots for (a) study time and GPA and (b) goof-off time and GPA, but this time each plot includes what is called a **regression line.** This line is used for making the predictions and is called a "best-fitting line": it provides the best possible way of summarizing the points on the scatterplot. More pre-

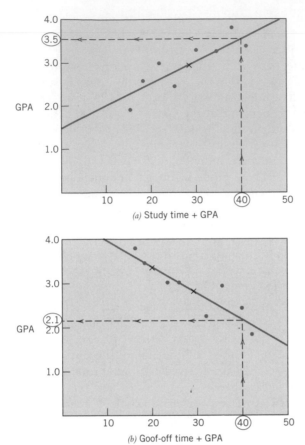

FIGURE 9.7 Scatterplots with regression lines.

cisely, if you took the absolute values of the vertical distances between each point and the line, those distances would be at a minimum.

The formula for the regression line is essentially the same formula you learned in high school for creating a straight line on a graph with X and Y coordinates:

$$Y = a + bX$$

where a is the place where the line crosses the Y-axis (i.e., the Y-intercept) and b is the slope, the line's relative steepness. X is a known value and Y is the value you are trying to predict. The value of b can be calculated knowing (1) the size of the correlation and (2) the standard deviations for the variables being correlated, and a can be calculated knowing (1) the calculated value of b and (2) the mean scores for the variables being correlated. See Appendix C for a specific example of how these values are calculated and fit into the regression equation.

In a regression analysis, the regression equation is used to predict a value for Y (e.g., GPA) based on a given value of X (e.g., study time). Y is sometimes referred to as the **criterion variable** and X as the **predictor variable.** In order to predict with confidence, however, the correlation must be significantly greater than zero. The higher the correlation, the closer the points on the scatterplot will be to the regression line and the more confident you can be in the prediction you make.

Thus, the problem mentioned previously of restricting the range, which generally lowers correlations, also has the effect of reducing the effectiveness of predictions.

From Figure 9.7 you also can see how a regression line aids in making predictions. Given the relationship between study time and GPA, one could ask what GPA could be expected from someone with 40 study hours. As you can see, the process can be visualized by drawing vertical dotted lines up from the X-axis to the regression line, then taking a 90° left turn until the Y-axis is encountered. The value on the Y-axis is the prediction (keep in mind that the confidence you have in the prediction is related to the strength of the correlation). Thus, a study time of 40 hours predicts a GPA of about 3.5, while 40 hours of goof-off time predicts a GPA of just under 2.1. The exact predictions, 3.48 and 2.13, respectively, can be calculated by using the regression formula. See Appendix C again.

You can be certain that some form of regression analysis has occurred in much of the research you hear about on the news or read about in the popular press. For instance, a report about "risk factors for heart attacks" will be describing a study in which a significant correlation between, say, smoking and heart disease allows the prediction that heavy smokers will be more likely to develop coronary problems than nonsmokers. That is, smoking predicts heart disease. Another study describing the "profile of a spouse abuser" might include the idea that such behavior is more likely to occur if the abuser is unemployed. Again, this follows from a correlation between unemployment and the tendency to be abusive and allows a prediction, via regression analysis, of the latter from the former.

One final point about a regression analysis is both procedural and ethical. In general, predictions should be made only for people who fall within the range of scores on which the correlation is based. For example, if a regression equation predicting college success is based on a study using middle-class suburban whites whose scores range from 1000 to 1400, then the equation should not be used to predict success for any applicant not within that population.

Interpreting Correlations

With its ability to predict, then, correlational research gives the researcher a powerful tool. However, great care must be taken in interpreting the results of correlational studies. Specifically, finding a correlation between two variables does not allow the conclusion that one of the variables is causing the other to occur. Unfortunately, a failure to appreciate this fundamental rule makes correlational research the method least understood by the general public. It is not uncommon for news reports to describe correlational research and for the narrative of the report to suggest to the noncritical reader that one variable in the relationship is the cause of the other. To illustrate, there is a considerable body of research indicating that a certain type of baldness is a predictor of heart disease. In one study, for instance (Lotufo, Chae, Ajani, Hennekens, & Manson, 1999), researchers studying more than 22,000 physicians found that coronary heart disease was associated with "vertex" baldness (more so than with frontal baldness or receding hairlines). Most press reports were careful to point out that the link was not a causal one, but the uncritical reader might be led to conclude that going bald is a direct cause of having a heart attack. I don't know if sales of hair transplants increased after the research was reported, but anyone thinking that eliminating their baldness by investing in transplants would save them from a potential heart attack would be falling prey to the classic misinterpretation of correlational research.

If you can see the problem with this line of thinking, then you already have a sense of what is to follow. As you recall from Chapter 1, one of my goals is to help you become a more critical consumer of information. Understanding how to interpret correlational research properly will help you approach that goal because drawing inappropriate conclusions from correlational research occurs quite frequently in popular descriptions of medical and psychological research.

Correlations and Causality

In an experimental study with a manipulated independent variable, we've already seen that cause-and-effect conclusions can be drawn with some degree of confidence. The variable of interest is manipulated, and if all else is held constant, the results can be attributed directly to the independent variable. With correlational research, the "all else is held constant" feature is missing, however, and this lack of control makes it impossible to conclude anything about cause and effect. Let's consider two specific ways in which interpretation problems can occur with correlations. These are referred to as the reversibility or directionality problem and the third variable problem (Neale & Liebert, 1973).

Directionality

If there is a correlation between two variables, A and B, it is possible that A is causing B to occur (A→B), but it also could be that B is causing A to occur (B→A). That the causal relation could occur in either direction is known as the **directionality problem.** The existence of the correlation *by itself* does not allow one to decide about the direction of causality.

Research on the relationship between TV watching and children's aggression typifies the directionality problem. Some of these studies are correlational and take the following general form. Some measure (variable A) of TV watching is made, the number of hours per week perhaps. For the same children, a second measure (variable B) of aggressive behavior is taken. It might be a combined score of teacher ratings of the aggressiveness of those participating in the study. Suppose this study yields a correlation of +.58, which is found to be significantly greater than zero. What can be concluded?

One possibility, of course, is that watching large amounts of TV inevitably exposes the child to a great deal of violence, and we know that children learn by observation; thus, it would follow that a large dose of TV watching causes children to become aggressive. That is, A→B.

But could causality be working in the reverse direction? Could it be that already aggressive children simply like to watch TV more than their nonaggressive peers? Knowing that much of television involves violent programming, perhaps aggressive children choose to watch more of the things that really interest them. In short, perhaps being aggressive causes children to watch more TV violence. That is, B→A.

Solely on the basis of an existing correlation, then, choosing the correct causal direction is not possible. However, there is a way to a deal with the directionality problem to some extent. It derives from the criteria for determining causality first described in Chapter 1. As you recall, research psychologists are generally satisfied with attributing causality between A and B when they occur together, when A precedes B in time, when A causing B makes sense in relation to some theory, and when other explanations for their co-occurrence can be ruled out.

For the TV and aggressiveness study described earlier, all we have is A and B occurring together and the fact that A causing B makes some sense from what is known about observational learning. However, using a procedure called a **cross-lagged panel correlation,** it is possible to increase one's confidence about directionality. In essence, this procedure investigates correlations between variables at several points in time. Hence, it is a type of longitudinal design. The following well-known example illustrates the procedure.

Case Study 19—TV and Aggression

Eron, Huesman, Lefkowitz, and Walder (1972) were interested in the same relationship between TV watching and aggression that I've been using as a hypothetical example. In particular, they measured (a) preference for watching violent television programs and (b) peer ratings of aggressiveness. The subjects were 875 third graders from a rural area of New York State, first studied in 1960; a modest but significant correlation of +.21 between preference for violent TV and aggressiveness was found. What made the study interesting, however, was that Eron's team returned 10 years later, found 427 of the same students (now arbitrarily labeled "13th graders"), and reassessed the same two variables. By measuring the two variables at two points in time, six correlations could be calculated. These correlations, as they occurred in the Eron et al. study, are displayed in Figure 9.8.

Of special interest are the diagonal or "cross-lagged" correlations because they measure the relationships between variables separated in time. If third grade aggressiveness caused a later preference for watching violent TV (B→A), then we would expect a fair-sized correlation between aggressiveness at time 1 and preference at time 2; in fact, the correlation is virtually zero (+.01). On the other hand, if an early preference for viewing violent TV programs led to a later pattern of aggressiveness

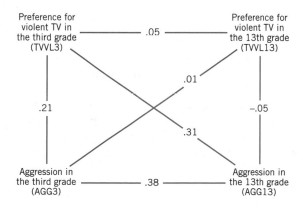

FIGURE 9.8 Results of a cross-lagged panel study of the effects of preference for violent TV programs on later aggression.

(From Eron et al., 1972)

(A→B), then the correlation between preference at time 1 and aggressiveness at time 2 should be substantial. As you can see, this correlation is +.31, not large but significant. Based on this finding, as well as on some other indications in their study, Eron and his colleagues concluded that an early preference for watching violent TV is at least partially the cause of later aggressiveness.

Cross-lagged panel correlations must be interpreted cautiously, however (Rogosa, 1980). For one thing, if you examine the overall pattern of correlations in Figure 9.8, you will notice that the correlation of +.31 may be partially accounted for by the correlations of +.21 and +.38. That is, rather than there being a direct path from 3rd-grade preference to 13th-grade aggression, perhaps the path is an indirect result of the relationship between preference for violent TV and aggression in the 3rd grade and between the two measures of aggression. A child scoring high on preference for violent TV in the 3rd grade might also be aggressive in the 3rd grade and still be aggressive (or even more so) in the 13th grade. Alternatively, it could be that aggressiveness in the 3rd grade produced both (a) a preference for watching violent TV in the 3rd grade and (b) later aggressiveness. Thus, cross-lagged panel correlations help with the directionality dilemma, but problems of interpretation remain. More generally, interpretation difficulties take the form of the third variable problem.

Third Variables

The June 4, 2000, issue of the *New York Times Magazine* contained a playful article entitled "Greens Peace" (Plotz, 2000). In it the author addressed the weighty issue of why some countries seem to be always at war, while others remain relatively peaceful. His answer was golf—countries in which a substantial portion of the population plays golf are less belligerent than countries without golf. As Plotz put it:

> Every peaceful European nation loves golf. But Russia, at war in Chechnya, doesn't hit the links. Non-golf Greece and non-golf Turkey have long warred over non-golf Cyprus. The former Yugoslavia has fragmented into five states. Only peaceful Slovenia swings the sticks. Do India or Pakistan golf? Of course not. Algerians shoot one another; Moroccans next door shoot par. (p. 32)

Although the slogan "make par, not war" (p. 37) certainly has merit, I think you can see the absurdity of the argument that golf causes peace. And it is only slightly more likely that the reverse is true—that peace causes golf. Rather, if there really is a correlation between peace and golf on a national level, and Plotz doesn't present a Pearson's *r*, of course, its existence is an exaggerated example of what researchers call the **third variable problem.** Because correlational research does not attempt to control extraneous variables directly, these variables might provide the explanation for the correlation found. That is, rather than A causing B or B causing A, some unknown third variable, C, might be causing both A and B to happen. "C" is some uncontrolled third variable (or variables—it is often the case that more than one uncontrolled variable lies behind a correlation). Can you think of some third variables that could produce the alleged golf/peace correlation? Economic prosperity perhaps? Highly prosperous countries might be more likely to be peaceful and also have more time for leisure, including golf.

Other examples of third variables are not quite so absurd as the peace/golf one and can easily mislead someone into making an unwarranted causal connection that could have dramatic effects. In Box 9.1, for example, you learned about Galton's and Pearson's belief that a positive correlation between parents and children on some trait proved that heredity was the prime cause of differences in level of intelligence. Both discounted the effects of the environment (e.g., intelligent parents providing a stimulating environment for their children) as the factor underlying the relationship between parents' and children's abilities. Furthermore, both argued that because inheritance was the cause of intelligence, smart people should be encouraged to have a lot of children. In fact, Galton is the founder of the "eugenics" movement, which advocated, among other things, that Great Britain take steps to improve the overall intelligence of its people through selective breeding. As Galton rather crassly put it, just as it is possible "to obtain by careful selection a permanent breed of dogs or horses with peculiar powers of running, ... so it would be quite practical to produce a highly-gifted race of men by judicious marriages during several consecutive generations" (Galton, 1869, cited in Fancher, 1990, p. 228). It isn't difficult to imagine the dark side of a eugenics movement, a recommendation that a group deemed "unfit" or "defective" be prevented from reproducing. Such thoughts occurred to leaders in Germany in the 1930s.

The relationship between watching violent TV programming and children's aggressiveness provides a more modern example of the third variable problem. As we've already seen, it is possible that watching TV violence increases aggression (A→B) but that causality in the opposite direction could also occur (B→A). Already aggressive children might seek out and watch violent programs. The third possibility is that both A and B result from some third variable, C (C→A+B). For instance, perhaps the parents are violent people. They cause their children to be violent by modeling aggressive behavior, and they also cause their children to watch a lot of TV. The children might watch TV in order to "lie low" and avoid contact with parents who are always physically punishing them. Another third variable might be a lack of verbal fluency. Perhaps children are aggressive because they don't argue very effectively, and they also watch a lot of TV as a way of avoiding verbal contact with others.

Sometimes trying to identify third variables is a purely speculative affair. On other occasions, however, one might have reason to suspect that a particular third variable is operating. If so, and if it is possible to measure this third variable, its effects can be evaluated using a procedure called **partial correlation,** which attempts to control for third variables statistically. In effect, it is a post facto (after the fact) attempt to create at least semiequivalent groups. For example, suppose you know that the correlation between reading speed and reading comprehension is high, +.55 perhaps (example from Sprinthall, 2000). Furthermore, you suspect that a third variable, IQ, might be producing this correlation. To complete a partial correlation, you would correlate (a) IQ and reading speed and (b) IQ and reading comprehension. Let's suppose these correlations turn out to be +.70 and +.72, respectively, high enough for you to suspect that IQ might be an influential third variable. Calculating a partial correlation involves incorporating all three of these correlations (see Sprinthall, 2000, for the exact procedure). What results is a partial correlation that measures the relationship between reading speed and reading comprehension, with IQ "partialed out" or "controlled." In this case, the partial correlation is +.10.

TABLE 9.1   *Partial Correlations in Eron, Huesman, Lefkowitz, and Walder's (1972) Study of the Relationship Between a Preference for Watching Violent TV and Aggressive Behavior*

Controlled Variable	Partial Correlation between TVVL3 and AGG13*
None (original correlation)	.31
Third-grade variables	
Peer-rated aggression	.25
Father's occupational status	.31
Child's IQ	.28
Father's aggressiveness	.30
Mother's aggressiveness	.31
Punishment administered	.31
Parents' aspirations for child	.30
Parents' mobility orientation	.31
Hours of television watched	.30
Thirteenth-grade variables	
Father's occupational status	.28
Subject's aspirations	.28
Hours of television watched	.30

* TVVL3 = preference for watching violence on TV in the 3rd grade; AGG13 = level of aggressiveness in the 13th grade.

Source: Adapted from Eron et al. (1972), Table 4.

Thus, when IQ is statistically controlled ("partialed out"), the correlation between speed and comprehension virtually disappears, which means that IQ is indeed an important third variable making a major contribution to the original +.55 correlation between speed and comprehension.

Several partial correlations were calculated in the Eron et al. (1972) study to see if any important third variables might have been responsible for the relatively high correlation (+.31) between 3rd-grade preference for violence and 13th-grade aggressiveness. Table 9.1 shows the results for 12 different potential third variables (called "controlled variables" in the table). As you can see, the partial correlations range from +.25 to +.31, indicating that none of the 12 factors made a significant contribution to the original correlation of +.31. That is, even taking into account these other factors, the correlation between early preference for violent TV programs and later aggressiveness *remained* close to +.31. The analysis strengthened their conclusion "that there is a probable causative influence of watching violent television programs in [the] early formative years on later aggression" (Eron et al., 1972, p. 263).

Caution: Correlational Statistics versus Correlational Research

After reading the chapters on experimental design and this one on correlational research, you might be tempted to assume that if you encounter a Pearson's *r* in the description of a study, then the study must be using a "correlational design." Unfortunately, things are not quite that simple. It is important to make a distinction between the use of correlations as a statistical tool and the use of a correlational design. A Pearson's *r* can be calculated whenever you wish to examine the relationship between any two variables. Although this might occur most frequently in a correlational study, it can also occur in an experimental study, in which the researcher calculates a correlation between the independent variable and the dependent variable. Indeed, the determination of effect size (Chapter 4, Appendix C) amounts to an estimate of the degree of association between independent and dependent variables.

Just as the presence of a Pearson's *r* in the results doesn't necessarily mean that a correlational design has been used, the presence of a *t* test or an ANOVA does not necessarily mean that a strictly experimental design has been used. Consider, for example, a study comparing introverts and extroverts on their level of obedience to authority. One way to perform the study would be to administer a test of introversion and another one of obedience and correlate the two. A second approach would be to administer the introversion test, then select those scoring in the top 25% (i.e., introverted) and bottom 25% (i.e., extroverted) on the test. These subjects could then be placed in an obedience situation and some measure of obedience taken. The obedience scores for the two groups could then be compared with a *t* test or a 1-way ANOVA. Note, however, that these results tell you no more about cause and effect than does the strategy of calculating a Pearson's *r* between the two variables. Thus, the interpretation problems in correlational research exist regardless of how the data are managed in the study.

Finally, you should recognize that the interpretation problems occurring in correlational studies are exactly the same problems that exist in studies described in earlier chapters, in which subject variables were selected as independent variables. The last two chapters described three such designs:

Single-factor, nonequivalent groups designs (both two-level and multilevel)

Factorial nonequivalent groups designs

Factorial P × E designs

Using Correlations

Considering the pitfalls that exist when trying to interpret correlations, combined with the fact that those envied conclusions about cause and effect only can be made from so-called true experiments with manipulated independent variables, why not just do pure experimental studies? That is, why bother with correlational research in the first place?

The Need for Correlational Research

The answer has to do with both practical and ethical considerations. On fairly obvious practical grounds, some important research would not be feasible or may not even be possible as a pure experimental study. Studying gender differences in behavior, differences between age groups, or differences between personality types are major research areas in which it is not possible to randomly assign. A study looking for a correlation between severity of clinical depression and task perseverance has value in its own right even if subjects cannot be randomly assigned to "high-depression" and "low-depression" conditions. As Cronbach put it in his two-disciplines address, the correlational approach "can study what [we have] not learned to control or can never hope to control" (Cronbach, 1957, p. 672). Furthermore, some research is conducted with prediction as the major goal. For example, finding a correlation between certain personality attributes and job success allows personnel managers to predict who will succeed on the job while remaining unconcerned about why the relationship exists.

Secondly, on rather clear ethical grounds, there are some studies that simply cannot be done as experiments with manipulated variables. When the 19th-century French physiologist Paul Broca discovered the brain's speech center, later named for him, he did it by noting a relationship between certain types of speech disorders and the extent of brain damage discovered upon a postmortem examination (Goodwin, 1999). *Experimental* evidence that the disorder was caused by the brain damage would require randomly assigning people to a "brain damage" group, which would have portions of their brain pulverized, or to a safer "control" group. Actually, you would also need a third group that could be called a "sham brain damage" group. They would go through most of the same surgical procedures as the brain damage group, except for the actual brain destruction. I think you can appreciate the difficulty of recruiting human volunteers for this experiment. This is one reason why animals are used as subjects in experimental research investigating the relationship between brain and behavior.

Varieties of Correlational Research

Research using correlational procedures can be found in all areas of psychology. Correlations are especially prevalent in (a) research concerning the development of psychological tests, (b) research in personality and abnormal psychology, and (c) research in the Galton tradition that relates to the nature-nurture issue. These areas all emphasize ways in which people differ from each other. Let's look at some typical research from each of the three.

Case Study 20—Psychological Testing

In Chapter 4 you learned that for a measure to be of value, it must be both reliable and valid. Reliable measures are repeatable measures that are relatively free from measurement error. A measure is valid if it truly measures the trait in question. A reliable and valid measure of intelligence will yield about the same IQ score on two separate occasions and will be a true measure of intellectual ability and not a measure of something else. Research to establish reliability and validity depends heavily on correlations, as the following series of studies shows.

For measuring IQ scores in children, the big two are the Stanford–Binet IQ Test and the Wechsler Intelligence Scale for Children (WISC). Recently, however, a test called the Kaufman Assessment Battery for Children (K•ABC) test has been making inroads (Kaufman & Kaufman, 1983). This test yields a "mental processing" score that is a composite of several subtests for "sequential processing" and "simultaneous processing." These are assumed to be basic mental abilities possessed by the child. In addition, there is a separate "achievement" score to reflect the kind of knowledge derived from school and elsewhere.

The Kaufmans evaluated the reliability of their test in several ways. For example, they used a procedure called **split-half reliability.** This involves taking the items that make up a particular subtest, dividing them in half (e.g., even-numbered vs. odd-numbered items), and correlating the two halves. The correlation should be high if the test is reliable—someone scoring high on one half should score high on the other half as well. A second type of reliability is called **test-retest reliability,** the relationship between two separate administrations of the test. Again, these reliabilities should be high—a reliable test yields consistent results from one testing to another. For the K•ABC, both split-half and test-retest reliabilities were high. What about the test's validity?

One indication of a test's validity is its **criterion validity,** the ability of the test to predict some future event. This validity is determined by correlating scores on the test in question (the K•ABC) with scores on some "criterion." The criterion is typically some other test or measurement that is conceptually related to the test in question. For an IQ test, criterion measures are often scores on tests relating to school performance because IQ tests are designed to predict how well someone will perform in an academic environment. Scores on a valid test should correlate positively with criterion scores.

Numerous validity studies have been carried out with the K•ABC using a wide range of criterion measures of school achievement (Kaufman & Kaufman, 1983). In general, the results are impressive; for instance, the test is known to be correlated with such criterion measures as the Iowa Tests of Basic Skills and the California Achievement Test, both well established as indicators of school success.

Implied in this K•ABC example is the importance of using good (i.e., reliable and valid) tests. After all, decisions that can affect lives often are made at least in part on the basis of these instruments. Children are placed into gifted programs, managers are promoted, college students get into medical school, and psychiatric patients get the correct diagnosis. All of these important decisions are made with the help of psychological tests. Hence, there are ethical issues related to the reliability and validity of these tools. Box 9.2 considers some of them and describes the APA guidelines for the development and use of tests.

Case Study 21—Research in Personality and Abnormal Psychology

The assessment of reliability and validity is also important when developing tests to measure normal and abnormal personality traits. Besides their use during test development, however, correlational procedures are important when investigating individual differences in personality. For example, a study might select a large group of people, give them tests for several different traits, and then correlate the scores. From this type of study, one might learn of a positive correlation between introversion and anxiety (introverts tend to be anxious) or of a negative correlation between introversion and sociability (introverts tend to avoid social contact). An example of this strategy is a study on explanatory style and depression by Seligman et al. (1988).

In Chapter 3, I introduced you to Seligman's work on learned helplessness as an illustration of how research is generated from theory and how theories evolve in the

Box 9.2

ETHICS—APA Guidelines for Psychological Testing

A glance back at Table 2.2 (p. 38) will show you that the 1992 revision of the APA ethics code includes a section called "Evaluation, Assessment, or Intervention." The 10 standards listed there have to do with the development, use, and interpretation of psychological tests. Two standards in particular relate to research issues (American Psychological Association, 1992):

2.02. *Competence and Appropriate Use of Assessments and Interventions*

(a) Psychologists who develop, administer, score, interpret, or use psychological assessment techniques, interviews, tests, or instruments do so in a manner and for purposes that are appropriate in light of the research on or evidence of the usefulness and proper application of the techniques.

2.03. *Test Construction*

Psychologists who develop and conduct research with test and other assessment techniques use scientific procedures and current professional knowledge for test design, standardization, validation, reduction or elimination of bias, and recommendations for use.

From these standards, and from the discussion of reliability and validity, it should be clear that there is considerably more to psychological testing than simply making up a questionnaire that seems to make sense and administering it. Yet that is the typical procedure used in developing most of the pseudoscientific psychological tests you'll find in popular magazines. These tests might appear to be scientific because they include a scoring key ("if you scored between 0 and 25, it means …"), but the scales are essentially meaningless because there's never been any attempt to determine their reliability or validity, or to standardize the test so that a specific score you obtain can be compared to some population data.

These tests are harmless as long as you understand that they aren't to be taken seriously. Armed with the appropriate skeptical attitude, then, you could explore the following:

✓ Has stress got you by the neck? (*Self*, April 2000)

✓ Are you boring? (*Young and Modern*, June/July 1992)

✓ Test yourself: How angry are you? (*Self*, January 1993)

✓ What's your secret sexual personality and his? (*Glamour*, June 2000)

To learn how *real* psychological tests are created and validated, take the tests and measurements course that I'm sure your psychology department offers.

face of various research outcomes. You'll recall that Seligman began with a theory of learned helplessness based on some animal conditioning studies and then revised the theory to take "explanatory style" into account. People who are depressed have a history of learned helplessness, according to Seligman, and their pessimistic explanatory style correlates with depression. The Seligman et al. (1988) study was designed to investigate the relationship between a pessimistic attributional style and the tendency to be emotionally depressed. The investigators also wished to see if "cognitive therapy" could have the dual effect of alleviating the depression and making the explanatory style more positive.

Those with a pessimistic explanatory style who experience a negative outcome of some kind blame themselves for the failure, assume it to be symptomatic of a more general inadequacy, and believe that failure will be the rule and not the exception in their future (Abramson, Seligman, & Teasdale, 1978). If so, it is easy to see how this way of thinking would also be accompanied by a feeling of depression. In Seligman's study, an "Attributional Style Questionnaire" was used to measure explanatory style; depression was measured by means of a well-known instrument called the Beck Depression Inventory. Briefly, what the researchers found was that the severity of depression correlated significantly with a pessimistic explanatory style; this was true before therapy ($r = +.56$), after therapy ($r = +.57$), and 1 year after therapy ($r = +.63$). The correlations remained about the same as the patients were improving in therapy because "[d]uring cognitive therapy, explanatory style and depression changed in lockstep from intake to termination, and as explanatory style became more optimistic, the patient became less depressed" (Seligman et al., 1988, p. 17). That is, as their scores on explanatory style changed after being in therapy, their depression scores showed a corresponding change and, as a result, the correlations stayed about the same. Because cognitive therapy is designed to change the way people think and hence how they explain to themselves what happens to them, the researchers believed their study yielded strong evidence for the idea that an effective way to treat depression is to get people to change the way they think about and interpret the events in their lives.

One of psychology's most famous series of studies is another example of using a correlational strategy to study personality, in this case the personality trait called "achievement motivation." Before reading on, take a look at Box 9.3, which describes a classic study from this tradition, a study suggesting that it might be wise for a culture to ensure that the characters in stories read by children are high achievers.

Case Study 22—The Nature–Nurture Issue

As you learned from Box 9.1, Sir Francis Galton was impressed by the tendency for genius to run in families. Studying family resemblances has become a major research strategy that bears on the issue of how heredity and environment contribute to various traits. The typical procedure is to measure some characteristic for each of many pairs of family members and calculate the correlations between them. Heredity and environmental factors can be evaluated separately by comparing pairs differing in genetic similarity and in the similarity of their home environments. For example, identical twins reared together can be compared with identical twins separated at birth and reared in different environments, thereby keeping genetics constant and varying environmental similarity. Likewise, the

Box 9.3

CLASSIC STUDIES—The Achieving Society

Can you predict the achievement level of an entire society by analyzing the stories told to the children of that society? Yes, according to psychologist David McClelland's 1961 book *The Achieving Society,* which documents an extraordinarily ambitious attempt to extend the results of psychological research on achievement into the realm of historical explanation. Along with colleague John Atkinson, McClelland was a pioneer in the study of achievement motivation, the drive to take on challenges and succeed (McClelland, Atkinson, Clark, & Lowell, 1953). Together, they developed ways of measuring the achievement motive, completed countless studies on the correlates of achievement and the environments conducive to developing the need to achieve (hint: give your children lots of opportunities to be independent), and developed a theory of achievement motivation (Atkinson & Feather, 1966). Furthermore, by elaborating on the "interaction between stable motives that characterize the personality and immediate situational influences, the theory of achievement motivation represent[ed] a step toward conceptual integration of 'the two disciplines of scientific psychology'" (Atkinson & Feather, 1966, p. 5) called for by Cronbach (1957) in his famous APA presidential address.

One way of measuring the need for achievement, or "nAch," is to use the Thematic Apperception Test (TAT), in which subjects look at ambiguous pictures and describe what they see in them (Murray, 1943). For instance, a drawing of a young boy staring at a violin might elicit a story about how he is dreaming of being a classical violinist. Someone writing such a story would get a higher score for nAch than someone who wrote a story about the child's planning to take the violin and whack his sister over the head with it. Presumably the stories people create reflect the underlying motives important to them.

The idea that one could infer motives from stories led McClelland to wonder about the role that children's stories and a culture's myths and fables might have in the developing motives of young people. If these stories are loaded with achievement themes, might not the young children gradually develop the idea that achievement is important? Could it be that the overall level of nAch in a society could be inferred from an interpretation of children's literature, cultural myths, music, and plays? And if children are raised in an environment stressing achievement, might they achieve at a high level as adults?

Such speculation led to McClelland's classic research on achievement in society. He subjected children's literature to the same kind of analysis given TAT stories, then took various measures of societal economic health and correlated the two. What he found was a positive correlation; as achievement themes increased, actual achievement increased. Of particular interest was the fact that actual achievement lagged behind high levels of achievement in literature by about 50 years—just about the time it would take for children exposed to high-achievement literature to be old enough to have their high levels of nAch affect society.

McClelland's ideas have not gone without criticism. Although his research solves the directionality problem in much the same way that a cross-lagged correlational study does, the most obvious problem is the usual one with correlational research: third variables. The relationship between children's literature and later achievement is surely an intriguing one, but historical trends are immensely complicated and susceptible to countless factors. Nonetheless, McClelland's research has become a classic example of trying to extend psychological principles to historical analysis.

environment could be kept more or less constant and the genetics varied by comparing identical twins (genetically the same) reared together and fraternal twins (genetically not the same) reared together. Such research typically demonstrates the joint influence of both nature and nurture, as illustrated in Table 9.2, which summarizes the results from dozens of studies on the origins of intelligence (Bouchard & McGue, 1981). The higher the correlation, the more similar the IQ scores for the pairs involved. Hence the correlation of +.86 for identical twins means that if one twin has a high IQ, the other twin will also have a high IQ. Clearly, the size of the correlation declines as genetic similarity decreases, indicating the importance of heredity for intelligence. The environment is also critical, as indicated by the difference in correlations between identical twins raised together (+.86) and identical twins raised apart (+.72).

Historically, most twin studies have centered on the question of intelligence, but recently there have been a number of studies demonstrating the heritability of personality and temperament traits (Bouchard, Lykken, McGue, Segal, & Tellegen, 1990). Even shyness appears to have some genetic basis. Emde et al. (1992) studied 200 pairs of 14-month-old identical and fraternal twins (raised together) on a number of personality and cognitive factors. One variable was shyness, measured in several ways. First, it was considered to be an element of a general measure of

TABLE 9.2   *Correlations Between IQ Scores for Pairs of Relatives Differing in Genetic Similarity and Home Environment*

	Number of Studies	Number of Pairs	
Identical twins reared together	34	4,672	.86
Identical twins reared apart	3	65	.72
Fraternal twins raised together	41	5,546	.60
Siblings reared together	69	26,473	.47
Siblings reared apart	2	203	.24
Cousins	4	1,176	.15

Note: The data reported are weighted averages of correlations from studies summarized by Bouchard and McGue (1981).

TABLE 9.3   *Correlations Between "Shyness" Scores for Pairs of Identical and Fraternal Twins*

	Pearson's r Value	
Shyness Measure	Identical Twins	Fraternal Twins
Behavioral inhibition	.57	.26
Shyness observations	.70	.45
Parent survey	.38	.03

Source: Adapted from Emde et al. (1992), Table 2.

"behavioral inhibition," which was assessed from videotapes of the infants responding when strangers entered a playroom. Avoiding a stranger while staying close to Mom produced a high score. Shyness was also measured by how the infant reacted to a home visit by the examiner and by the infant's behavior upon encountering the lab. Finally, parents filled out a survey that included a shyness scale. As with other twin studies, the correlations were calculated for identical and fraternal twins. Table 9.3 shows the resulting higher correlations for the twins who were closer genetically, hence supporting the hypothesis of a genetic component for shyness.

Multivariate Analysis

A **bivariate** approach investigates the relationships between any two variables. A **multivariate** approach, on the other hand, examines the relationships between more than two variables (often many more than two). Up to this point in the chapter we've been considering the bivariate case, except for the discussion of partial correlation, which evaluates the effects of third variables on the relationship between two others. Let me briefly introduce two additional popular multivariate procedures—multiple regression and factor analysis.

Multiple Regression

In the case of simple regression, two variables are involved: the predictor variable and the criterion variable. If SAT scores correlate with freshman year GPA, then SAT can be used as a predictor of academic success. However, as you know from firsthand experience, phenomena like "success in college" are more complicated than this. SAT scores might predict success, but what about the influence of other factors like "motivation" or "high school grades" or "ability to avoid physics"?

Multiple regression solves the problem of having more than one predictor of some outcome. In a **multiple regression** study, there is one criterion variable and a minimum of two predictor variables. The analysis enables you to determine not just the fact that these two or more variables combine to predict some criterion, but also the relative strengths of the predictors. These strengths are reflected in the multiple regression formula for raw scores, which is an extension of the formula for simple regression:

$$\text{Simple regression:} \quad Y = a + bX$$
$$\text{Multiple regression:} \quad Y = a + b_1X_1 + b_2X_2 + \ldots b_nX_n$$

where each X is a different predictor variable, Y is the criterion, and the size of the b's reflect the relative importance of each predictor—they are known as "regression weights" (Licht, 1995). A multiple regression analysis will also yield a multiple correlation coefficient (R) and a multiple coefficient of determination (R^2). R is a correlation between the combined predictors and the criterion and R^2 provides an index of the amount of variation in the criterion variable than can be accounted for by the combined predictors. Note the use of upper case letters to differentiate the multivariate R and R^2 from the bivariate Pearson's r and r^2. Their interpretations are similar, however. Both R and r tell you about the strength of a correlation and both R^2 and r^2 tell you about the amount of shared variation.

The advantage of a multiple regression analysis is that when the influences of several predictor variables are combined (especially if the predictors are not highly correlated with each other), prediction improves far beyond the single regression case. High school grades by themselves predict college success, as do SAT scores. Together, however, they predict better than either one by itself (Sprinthall, 2000). To give you an idea of the types of studies using a multiple regression analysis, consider these two examples:

1. A study predicting empathy from two aspects of early childhood experience (Barnett & McCoy, 1989): Empathic students tended to have experienced distressing childhood events that could have made them more sensitive to the trauma of others. The severity of the childhood trauma was weighted more heavily as a predictor of later empathy than was the total number of traumatic events.

2. A study predicting susceptibility to the common cold from negative life events, perceived stress, and negative affect (Cohen, Tyrell, & Smith, 1993): While you might think that getting a cold is the simple result of standing too close to the person who just sneezed all over your lunch, this study demonstrated that getting colds could be predicted from three variables related to stress. The college students most likely to catch colds were those who (a) recently experienced some stressful event(s), (b) were feeling that current demands on them were overwhelming, and (c) described their general emotional state as negative.

Factor Analysis

Another multivariate technique is called **factor analysis.** In this procedure, a large number of variables are measured and correlated with each other. It is then determined whether groups of these variables cluster together to form "factors." A simple example will clarify the idea. Suppose you gave a group of school-age children the following tasks:

a vocabulary test (VOC)

a reading comprehension test (COM)

an analogy test (e.g., doctor is to patient as lawyer is to _____) (ANA)

a geometry test (GEO)

a puzzle completion test (PUZ)

a rotated figures test (ROT)

Pearson's r's could be calculated for all possible pairs of tests, yielding what is called **a correlation matrix.** It might look like this:

	VOC	COM	ANA	GEO	PUZ	ROT
VOC	—	+.76	+.65	−.09	+.02	−.08
COM		—	+.55	+.04	+.01	−.02
ANA			—	−.07	−.08	+.09
GEO				—	+.78	+.49
PUZ					—	+.68
ROT						—

Notice how some of the correlations cluster together (I've circled two clusters). Correlations between vocabulary, reading comprehension, and analogies are all high, as are those between geometry, puzzles, and rotation. Correlations between tests from one cluster and tests from the second cluster are essentially zero. This pattern suggests that the tests are measuring two fundamentally different mental abilities or "factors." We could probably label them "verbal fluency" and "spatial skills."

Factor analysis is a sophisticated statistical tool that identifies factors from sets of intercorrelations. It would undoubtedly yield the same two factors we just arrived at by scanning the matrix. The analysis also determines what are called "factor loadings." These in essence are correlations between each of the tests and each of the identified factors. In the above example, the first three tests would be "heavily loaded" on factor 1 (verbal fluency), and the second three tests would be heavily loaded on factor 2 (spatial skills). Of course, in real research the correlations never cluster together as clearly as in the example I've used, and there is often some debate among researchers about whether the factors identified are truly separate from other factors. Also, there is occasional disagreement over the proper labels for the factors. Factor analysis itself only identifies factors; what they should be called is left to the researcher's judgment.

Factor analysis has been a tool in one of psychology's more enduring debates—whether intelligence is a unitary trait or not. Charles Spearman, who originated factor analysis early in the 20th century, believed that all tests for intelligence had significant loadings on a single factor that he called a general intelligence factor, or *"g."* Furthermore, each test would load heavily on a second factor that would involve a skill specific to the test involved (e.g., math). These secondary or "special" factors he called *"s."* According to his "two-factor" theory, then, performance on IQ tests could be accounted for by the person's general intelligence (*g*) plus that person's special skills (*s*). He believed that *g* was inherited but that the various *s* factors represented learning (Fruchter, 1954).

Other investigators, most notably Louis Thurstone, believed that intelligence was composed of a number of separate factors and that no unitary factor *g* existed. Again on the basis of factor analysis, he believed there existed seven distinctly different factors, which he called "primary mental abilities" (Thurstone, 1938). These were verbal comprehension, word fluency, number skill, spatial skill, memory, perceptual speed, and reasoning.

The question of whether or not intelligence is unitary continues to perplex those who specialize in the measurement of intelligence and is well beyond the scope of this chapter. The important point for our purposes is that factor analysis can yield different outcomes. This is because (a) there are several varieties of factor analytic procedures that, in effect, make different decisions about how high the correlations must be before separate factors are identified and (b) different studies of the issue use different tests of intelligence. Consequently, researchers using alternative techniques and tests produce a range of outcomes. In short, like other statistical techniques, factor analysis is merely a tool; it cannot by itself resolve theoretical issues such as the nature of intelligence.

As you can tell from this brief introduction, correlational procedures contribute substantially to modern research in psychology. They are often necessary when experimental procedures cannot possibly be used, and with the development of some highly sophisticated multivariate procedures, questions of cause and effect can be addressed more directly than in the past, when most correlational research was bivariate in nature.

Much correlational research takes place outside of the laboratory. In the next chapter, we'll look more closely at applied research by outlining the details of several so-called quasi-experimental designs. We'll also look at program evaluation research as a specific example of applied research that is becoming increasingly important for the social service industry and for education.

Chapter Summary

Psychology's Two Disciplines

Along with experimental research, correlational research has been identified as one of psychology's two traditional approaches to science. Whereas experiments manipulate variables directly and observe the effects, correlational studies observe relationships among naturally occurring variables.

Correlation and Regression—the Basics

Two variables are correlated when a reliable relationship exists between them. The relationship is a direct one in a positive correlation and an inverse one in a negative correlation. The strength of the relationship can be inferred from a scatterplot, from the absolute value of the correlation coefficient (e.g., Pearson's *r* for interval and ratio data), and from the coefficient of determination, found by squaring the correlation coefficient. Knowing a correlation allows predictions to be made through a process called regression analysis. If there is a significant correlation between two variables, A and B, then knowing the value of A enables the prediction of B with some probability.

Interpreting Correlations

A significant correlation between variables A and B does not, by itself, allow us to conclude that A causes B. The directionality problem refers to the fact that causality could be in either of two directions, A causing B or B causing A. The directionality problem can be reduced if there is a time lag between the measurement of A and B. The third variable problem refers to the fact that for many correlations, the relationship results from one or some combination of uncontrolled variables that naturally covary with the variables being measured. That is, some third variable might cause changes in both variables A and B. The influence of third variables can be evaluated using a partial correlation procedure.

Using Correlations

Correlational studies are often necessary when experiments cannot be carried out for practical or ethical reasons. The method is frequently used in research evaluating psychological tests (i.e., determining reliability and validity), in research concerning individual differences in personality and psychopathology, and in twin studies and similar procedures for studying the relative contributions of heredity and environment to some trait.

Multivariate Analysis

Bivariate analysis studies the relationship between two variables. Multivariate analysis looks at the interrelationships among more than two variables. Multiple regression predicts some outcome (criterion) on the basis of two or more predictor variables. Factor analysis identifies clusters of factors underlying a large number of relationships.

Chapter Review

Multiple Choice

1. For which of the following correlations is the relationship strongest?
    a. +.81
    b. −.67
    c. −.86
    d. +1.04

2. In correlational studies, extraneous variables are not controlled, resulting in the interpretation problem known as the
    a. directionality problem
    b. regression to the mean problem
    c. range restriction problem
    d. third variable problem

3. A graduate school decides to use a formula for making its acceptance decisions. Into the formula go the candidate's college grades over 4 years, grades in the major, and Graduate Record Examination (GRE) scores. GRE scores are weighed most heavily, then grades in the major. What procedure has been used to develop this formula?
    a. multiple regression
    b. bivariate regression
    c. factor analysis
    d. partial correlation

4. In the 19th century, many people believed that intelligence could be measured by determining brain size. Which of the following is true about this measure?
    a. it would have criterion validity
    b. it would pass the test-retest reliability test
    c. it would be neither reliable nor valid
    d. it would be considered valid but not reliable

5. A cross-lagged panel technique is sometimes used to help solve the _____ problem.
    a. third variable
    b. regression to the mean
    c. negative correlation
    d. directionality

Short Essay

1. What were the essential points made by Cronbach in his "two disciplines" talk?

2. Describe how the shape of a scatterplot changes when comparing (a) positive and negative correlations and (b) strong and weak correlations.

3. What is the coefficient of determination and what does it tell you? Use the example of depression and GPA to illustrate.

4. A researcher finds that people with high self-esteem tend to exercise more than people with low self-esteem. Explain the directionality problem and how it could influence the interpretation of this correlation.

5. A researcher finds that children who play lots of video games also tend to be aggressive with their peers at school. Explain the third variable problem and how it could influence the interpretation of this correlation

6. Use the Eron et al. (1972) study, which found a significant relationship between 3rd-grade TV preferences and 13th-grade aggression, to explain the reason why you would use a partial correlation procedure.

7. Define reliability and describe two ways to assess it.

8. Use the research connected with the K•ABC test to illustrate the meaning of criterion validity.

9. In his famous study of achievement motivation through history, David McClelland concluded that societies should encourage independence training in their children, in order to make them high achievers. Describe the method used by McClelland to arrive at this conclusion.

10. Describe how correlational procedures can be used to examine the nature–nurture issue.

11. Distinguish between bivariate and multivariate analysis and describe the logic behind the use of a multiple regression procedure.

12. Describe the essential logic of factor analysis.

Applications Exercises

Exercise 9.1.—Interpreting Correlations

Each of the following describes the outcome of a hypothetical bivariate correlational study. With both the directionality problem and the third variable problem in mind, describe at least two ways of interpreting each.

1. There is a positive correlation between the level of dominance shown by mothers and the level of shyness shown by children.
2. There is a negative correlation between depression and aerobic fitness level.
3. There is a positive correlation between the number of books found in the home and the college GPAs of the students coming from those homes.
4. Happily married couples tend to have more sex (with each other) than unhappy couples.
5. There is a negative correlation between grades and test anxiety.
6. Seating location in class is correlated with grades—the closer to the front, the higher the grade.

Exercise 9.2.—Scatterplots, Calculating Pearson's *r*, and Regression

Create a scatterplot for the following data. After guessing what the correlation would be from looking at the plot, use the procedures described in Appendix C to calculate the actual Pearson's *r*. Then calculate the coefficient of determination, and write a statement that describes the relationship. Finally, formulate the regression equation and predict the explanatory style of Ed, whose self-esteem is 10; Ned, whose self-esteem is 20; and Fred, whose self-esteem is 30.

1. Variable A = self-esteem: scores range from 0 to 50; higher scores indicate a higher level of self-esteem.
2. Variable B = explanatory style: scores range from 0 to 75; higher scores indicate a negative or pessimistic way of interpreting life's bumps and bruises, and lower scores indicate a positive or optimistic way of interpreting these same outcomes

Subject No.	Variable A	Variable B
1	42	32
2	22	34
3	16	65
4	4	73
5	46	10
6	32	28
7	40	29
8	12	57
9	28	50
10	8	40
11	20	50
12	36	40

Exercise 9.3.—Understanding Scatterplots

Draw scatterplots that would approximately illustrate the following relationships. Write a single statement that summarizes each relationship.

1. A correlation of +.50 between the sequential processing and the simultaneous processing subtests of the K•ABC.

2. A correlation of −.80 between GPA and scores on a test of "soap opera IQ."

3. A correlation of −.02 between intelligence and depression.

4. A correlation of +.90 between tendency to suffer from obsessive–compulsive disorder and love of experimental psychology.

CHAPTER 10

Quasi-Experimental Designs and Applied Research

Preview & Chapter Objectives

In this chapter we will consider applied research in general and program evaluation in particular. The former is a research strategy you first encountered in Chapter 3, when it was contrasted with basic research. You will learn that applied research represents a strong tradition in American experimental psychology and reflects the core American value of usefulness. Program evaluation is the name given to a form of applied research that examines the effectiveness of programs designed to help people in various ways. The chapter also describes several so-called quasi-experimental designs that are frequently encountered in program evaluation/applied research.[1] When you finish this chapter, you should be able to:

---

[1] It is important to note that the pairing of quasi-experimental and applied research in this chapter does not mean that quasi-experimental designs are only found in applied research. Such designs might be more likely to be found in an applied setting, but they can be found in basic research as well. Furthermore, pairing quasi-experimental and applied does not mean to imply that experimental designs are never used in applied research.

- Identify the dual functions of applied research.

- Understand why applied psychology has always been an important element in American psychology.

- Identify the design and ethical problems associated with applied research, especially if that research occurs in a field setting.

- Identify the defining feature of a quasi-experimental design and recognize which designs appearing in earlier chapters were quasi-experimental.

- Describe the features of a nonequivalent control group design and understand why this design is necessarily confounded.

- Understand why matching nonequivalent groups on pretest scores can introduce a regression effect.

- Describe the features of interrupted time series designs and understand how they can be used to evaluate trends.

- Describe the strategies that can be used to complete a needs analysis.

- Understand the purposes and the procedures involved in formative evaluation, summative evaluation, and cost-effectiveness evaluation.

- Identify and describe the special ethical problems that often accompany program evaluation research.

As I mentioned at the very beginning of the text, I would like nothing more than to see you emerge from this methods course with a desire to contribute to our knowledge of behavior by becoming an experimental psychologist. My experience as a teacher in this course tells me that some of you indeed will become involved in research, but that most of you won't. Many of you will become professional psychologists of some kind, however, perhaps working as counselors or personnel specialists or in some other field in which your prime focus will be the delivery of psychological or health-related services (e.g., physical therapy). As such, you will encounter the worlds of applied research and program evaluation. You may discover you will need to be able to do things like:

    ✓ read, comprehend, and critically evaluate some research literature on the effectiveness of a program that your agency is thinking about implementing;

    ✓ help plan a new program by informing (tactfully) those who are completely ignorant of research design about the adequacy of the evaluation portion of their proposal;

    ✓ participate in an agency self-study in preparation for some type of accreditation process; and possibly, because your agency's director found out that you took this course,

    ✓ design and be in charge of a study to evaluate some agency program.

In other words, this chapter is important whether or not you intend to do research in psychology ever again.

Beyond the Laboratory

You first learned about the distinction between basic and applied research in the opening pages of Chapter 3. To review, the essential goal of basic research in psychology is to increase our core knowledge about behavior. The knowledge might eventually have some application, but that possible outcome isn't the prime motivator; knowledge is valued as an end in itself. On the other hand, applied research is designed primarily for the purpose of increasing our knowledge about a particular real-world problem, with an eye toward directly solving that problem. A second distinction between basic and applied research is that while basic research usually takes place within the confines of a laboratory on a college or university campus, applied research normally occurs outside of the academic setting, in clinics, in social service agencies, in jails, and in business settings. There are exceptions, of course—some basic research occurs in the field and some applied research takes place in a lab.

To give you a sense of the variety of applied research, consider these article titles from two prominent applied psychology journals: the *Journal of Applied Psychology* and the *Journal of Experimental Psychology: Applied:*

"Gender and the Relationship Between Perceived Fairness of Pay or Promotion and Job Satisfaction" (Witt & Nye, 1992)

"Visual–Spatial Abilities of Pilots" (Dror, Kosslyn, & Waag, 1993)

"Situation Awareness During Driving: Explicit and Implicit Knowledge in Dynamic Spatial Memory" (Gugerty, 1997)

"Probability and Utility Components of Endangered Species Preservation Programs" (DeKay & McClelland, 1996)

These titles illustrate two features of applied research. First, following from the definition above, the studies clearly focus on easily recognizable problems ranging from job satisfaction to preserving endangered species. Second, the titles demonstrate that while the prime goal of applied research is problem solving (e.g., improving driving), these studies also further our knowledge of basic psychological processes (e.g., spatial memory). Indeed, there is a close connection between basic and applied research, as illustrated by research designed to evaluate what is called "equity theory" (Adams, 1965). The theory's core premise is that when judging the quality of any interaction with another person, we weigh the relative contribution we make with the relative gain that we receive. If the costs and benefits are out of whack, we perceive the situation to be inequitable and are motivated to restore the balance. For example, in a marriage with both partners working full time, the wife might perceive an inequity if most household chores were her responsibility. She would then initiate various procedures (e.g., negotiation) to restore equity.

Most applied research has the dual function of addressing applied problems directly and providing evidence of basic psychological phenomena that influence theory development. Equity, for example, is frequently studied in applied research settings. The study listed above on gender differences in perceived fairness in pay and in promotions deals with an important problem for industry (how to improve job satisfaction), but it also provides some data relevant to broader questions about the adequacy of equity theory. Another illustration of this point comes from the following case study, which evaluated a method for improving eyewitness identification.

Case Study 23—Applied Research

Remember the study involving the Scottish diving club (Chapter 8), which showed that recall is best if learning and recall both occur in the same place (e.g., underwater)? The importance of context for recall, combined with the generally known inaccuracies of eyewitness testimony, led Edward Geiselman and Ronald Fisher to develop a technique called the "cognitive interview." One of its several features is a principle they refer to as "event-interview similarity," in which the interviewer tries to "reinstate in the witness's mind the external (e.g., weather), emotional (e.g., feelings of fear), and cognitive (e.g., relevant thoughts) features that were experienced at the time of the crime" (Fisher, Geiselman, & Amador, 1989, p. 723). In short, the interviewer tries to get the witness to reinstate mentally the context of the event witnessed.

Geiselman and his colleagues had previously demonstrated the technique's effectiveness in the controlled laboratory environment, but they were also interested in evaluating it "outside the friendly confines of the laboratory" (Fisher et al., 1989, p. 724) with "real victims and witnesses of crime" (p. 724). With cooperation from the robbery division of the Miami, Florida, police department, they trained seven detectives in the cognitive interview technique. Compared to the nine officers in a control group, those given the training elicited more reliable (i.e., corroborated with other information) facts during interviews with eyewitnesses. In Figure 10.1 you can see that both groups performed about the same on the pretest, which summarized a 4-month period during which detectives recorded their interviews with witnesses and separate judges scored the interviews for factual content. After the experimental group completed the training, both groups recorded several additional interviews, which were scored in the same fashion. Clearly, those trained to use the cognitive interview were able to elicit more information from witnesses.

In summary, the Fisher et al. (1989) study is an excellent illustration of how applied research can solve real problems while contributing to our knowledge of

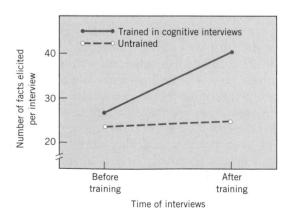

FIGURE 10.1 Effectiveness of the cognitive interview in an applied setting.

(From Fisher et al., 1989)

some fundamental psychological phenomenon. The study shows how a specific interview procedure can improve the efficiency of police work while at the same time providing further evidence for the general importance of context on recall.

Applied Psychology in Historical Context

Because psychology in America developed in an academic setting, you might think that research in psychology traditionally has been biased toward basic research. Not so. From the time psychology emerged as a new discipline in the late 19th century, psychologists in the United States have been interested in applied research. For one thing, institutional pressures in the early 20th century forced psychologists to show how their work could improve society. In order to get a sufficient piece of the academic funding pie at a time when psychology laboratories were brand new entities, psychologists had to show that their ideas could be put to use.

Psychologists trained as researchers, in addition to their prime focus on extending knowledge, often found themselves trying to apply basic research methods to solve problems in areas like education, mental health, child rearing, and, in the case of Walter Miles, sports. Miles was director of the laboratory at Stanford University in the 1920s. Although devoted to basic research throughout most of his career, he nonetheless found himself on the football team's practice field in 1927, as shown in Figure 10.2 (that's Miles in the suit). Stanford's legendary football coach, "Pop" Warner, was known as an innovator, and open to anything that might improve his team's performance. Enter Miles, who built what he called a "multiple chrono-

FIGURE 10.2 Simultaneously testing the reaction times of Stanford football players, circa 1927.

(From Archives of the History of American Psychology, University of Akron, Akron, Ohio)

graph" as a way of simultaneously testing the reaction time of seven football players (Miles, 1928). On a signal that dropped seven golf balls onto a cylinder rotating at a constant speed (one ball per player), the players would charge forward, pushing a board that pulled a string that released a second set of golf balls onto the drum. The balls left marks on the cylinder and, knowing the speed of the rotation and the distance between the marks, Miles was able to calculate the players' reaction times. Miles conducted several studies with his multiple chronograph (e.g., Miles, 1931) and demonstrated that it was a useful tool for selecting the fastest players, but the apparatus never enjoyed widespread use.

A more lasting attempt to apply psychological principles can be found in the first clinic devoted to the treatment of psychologically related problems, founded by Lightner Witmer of the University of Pennsylvania. Witmer was trained as an experimental psychologist in Wundt's laboratory in Leipzig and was an avid experimentalist in the 1890s. At one time (1895) he even advocated that experimentalists secede from the fledgling APA and form their own organization because he felt the APA wasn't scientific enough (Goodwin, 1985). Yet in March 1896, when a schoolteacher brought a young boy with what we would now call a learning disability to Witmer's laboratory, this event marked the origin of American psychology's first clinic (McReynolds, 1987). Witmer became devoted to applying all that was known about mental processes to the treatment of various psychological maladies, especially learning disorders related to school performance.

Psychology's interest in application also can be seen in the mental testing movement. I indicated in the previous chapter that intelligence and personality testing are major industries in America; their roots can be found among the earliest psychologists. For example, James McKeen Cattell, like Witmer a product of Wundt's laboratory, invented the term "mental test" (1890) and developed an extensive (but fatally flawed—see Sokal, 1987) testing program in the 1890s at Columbia patterned after Galton's approach in Great Britain. In the early 1920s, he founded the Psychological Corporation, which exists today as a giant in the psychological testing industry (for example, it publishes all of the Wechsler intelligence tests).

Finally, consider the career of Hugo Münsterberg, arguably the prototype of the applied psychologist in America. Like many of the early psychologists, he was trained as a research psychologist but was renowned as an expert in applying psychological principles to business, to the clinic, and even to the courtroom. He was also one of the more hated men in America at one time, which is why he has been largely ignored in historical accounts of applied psychology until recently. For more on someone who could claim the title of America's first true applied psychologist (even though he was German), read Box 10.1.

Psychologists at the beginning of the 21st century are as interested in application as their predecessors at the beginning of the 20th century were. Besides applying what is known about behavior to the problems facing professional psychologists, they conduct research that fits the previous definition of applied research. That is, they design and carry out studies in order to help create solutions to real-world problems while at the same time contributing to the basic core knowledge of psychological principles. However, applied research projects encounter several difficulties not usually found in the laboratory.

Box 10.1

ORIGINS—Hugo Münsterberg: Applied Psychologist Extraordinaire

That applied psychology is a pivotal force in American psychology is not really surprising. After all, Americans are known for their abiding Yankee pragmatism. "What good is it?" is a sentence that comes naturally to us. Thus, it is surprising that Hugo Münsterberg (1863–1916), a native German, is considered one of the very first prominent applied psychologists in America. When he arrived in this country to run the psychology laboratory at Harvard in 1892, he spoke barely a word of English. Yet, by the time of his death, he had written nearly 20 books in English, and he was an acknowledged pioneer in industrial and forensic psychology and a contributor to clinical psychology.

Münsterberg's *Psychology and Industrial Efficiency,* published in 1913, is sometimes believed to mark the origins of industrial psychology (Goodwin, 1999). It included advice and summaries of research on such topics as the best way to select people for various jobs, the factors that most seriously affect worker productivity, and suggestions about marketing and advertising. He included some of his own research on developing tests for employee selection, using procedures now standard for validating such tools. For example, when asked to develop a selection system by the New England Telephone Company, Münsterberg analyzed the operator's job into the cognitive tasks involved (he identified 14 different ones), developed tests for each, and validated the tests by showing that those who scored highest became the best operators.

Münsterberg was also a pioneer in the area of forensic psychology—applying psychological principles to the law. His *On the Witness Stand,* which first appeared in 1908, includes a fascinating description of the perils of eyewitness testimony, issuing the same cautions that resulted from the experimental work on the subject that began later in the century. Lacking direct experimental evidence of faulty eyewitness memory, he used his knowledge of such things as perceptual illusions to show how unreliable the human observer could be. He also argued that various physiological measures could be useful in detecting lying.

As often happens when an academician ventures into the public spotlight, however, Münsterberg was something of a controversial figure. Citing a study of problem solving in which group judgments were better than individual judgments, but only for male subjects, Münsterberg concluded that juries should not include females. His conclusion was reported widely in the press and earned him the ire that is reflected in this newspaper headline, cited in Hothersall (1990): "Angry at Münsterberg, Suffragists Say Women Fit for Jury."

More controversial was Münsterberg's attempts to portray the people of his native Germany in a favorable light. Unfortunately, he chose to do this in the years leading up to World War I, and his efforts earned him volumes of hate mail and accusations of being a German spy. According to Hothersall (1990), someone even offered Harvard

$10 million to fire him, but backed off when Münsterberg agreed to resign if the man would give $5 million to the university and $5 million to him! When Münsterberg died in 1916, just before the end of the war, he was one of America's villains. The *American Journal of Psychology*, which routinely published long obituaries on psychologists of much lesser light, failed even to mention his death. Consequently, his importance as an early pioneer and promoter of applied psychology was forgotten for years (Landy, 1992).

Design Problems in Applied Research

From what you've already learned in Chapters 2, 5, and 6, you should be able to anticipate most of the material in this section. The problems encountered in applied research include:

✓ *Ethical dilemmas* (Chapter 2). A study conducted in the field may create problems relating to informed consent and privacy. Also, debriefing may not always be possible. Research done in an industrial or corporate setting may include an element of coercion if employees believe their job status depends on whether they volunteer to participate in a study (see Box 10.3 for more on ethics and applied research).

✓ *A trade-off between internal and external validity* (Chapter 5). Because research in applied psychology often takes place in the field, the researcher loses varying degrees of control over the variables operating in the study. Hence the danger of possible confounding reduces the study's internal validity. On the other hand, external validity is often high in applied research because the setting more closely resembles real-life situations and the problems addressed by the research are everyday problems.

✓ *Problems unique to between-subjects designs* (Chapter 6). In applied research it is often impossible to use random assignment to form equivalent groups. Therefore the studies often must compare nonequivalent groups. This, of course, introduces the possibility of reducing internal validity by selection problems or interactions between selection and other threats such as maturation. When matching is used to achieve a degree of equivalence, regression problems can occur (Chapter 5; this chapter, pp. 326–329).

✓ *Problems unique to within-subjects designs* (Chapter 6). It is not always possible to counterbalance properly in applied studies using within-subjects factors. Hence the studies may have uncontrolled sequence effects. Also, attrition can be a problem for studies that extend over a long period of time.

Before going much further in this chapter, you should look back at the appropriate sections of Chapters 2, 5, and 6 and review the ideas I've just mentioned. You also might review the section in Chapter 5 about the kinds of conclusions that can be drawn from manipulated variables and from subject variables.

Quasi-Experimental Designs

Strictly speaking, "true" experimental studies include manipulated independent variables and either equivalent groups for between-subjects designs or appropriate counterbalancing for within-subjects designs. Anything less is quasi-experimental ("almost" experimental). In Chapter 5, the discussion of nonmanipulated variables centered on the use of subject variables as independent variables. In this chapter the emphasis will broaden somewhat. In general, a **quasi-experiment** exists whenever causal conclusions cannot be drawn because there is less than complete control over the variables in the study. Thus far we have seen several examples of designs that could be considered quasi-experimental:

Single-factor nonequivalent groups designs, with two or more levels

Nonequivalent groups factorial designs

P × E factorial designs

All of the correlational designs

In this chapter we will consider two designs typically found in texts on quasi-experimental designs (e.g., Cook & Campbell, 1979): nonequivalent control group designs and interrupted time series designs. Other quasi-experimental designs exist, but these are the two most frequently encountered.

Nonequivalent Control Group Designs

In this type of study the purpose is to evaluate the effectiveness of some treatment program. Those in the program are compared with those in a control group who aren't treated. This design is used when random assignment is not possible, so in addition to the levels of the independent variable, the control group differs in some other way(s) from the treatment group. That is, the groups are not equivalent to each other at the outset of the study. You will recognize this as a specific example of the design labeled a "nonequivalent" groups design in Chapter 7, a type of design comparing nonequal groups, often selected with reference to a subject variable like age, gender, or some personality characteristic. In the case of a **nonequivalent control group design,** the groups are not equal to each other at the start of the study; *in addition,* they experience different events in the study itself. Hence there is a built-in confound that can cloud the interpretation of these studies. Nonetheless, they can be useful for evaluating treatment programs when random assignment is impossible.

Following the scheme first outlined by Campbell and Stanley (1963), equivalent control group design can be symbolized like this:

Experimental group:	O_1	**T**	O_2
Nonequivalent control group:	O_1		O_2

where O_1 and O_2 refer to pretest and posttest observations or measures, respectively, and T refers to the treatment program that is being evaluated. Because the groups might differ on the pretest, the important comparison between the groups is not simply a test for differences on the posttest, but also a comparison of the different amounts of change from pre- to posttest in the two groups. Hence, the statistical comparison is between the change scores (the difference between O_1 and O_2) for each group. Let's make this a bit more concrete.

Suppose the management of an electric fry pan company wants to institute a new flextime work schedule. Workers will continue to work 40 hours per week, but the new schedule allows them to begin and end each day at different times or to put all of their hours into 4 days if they wish to have a 3-day weekend. Management hopes this will increase productivity by improving morale and sets up a quasi-experiment to see if it does. The company owns two plants, one just outside of Pittsburgh and the other near Cleveland. Through a coin toss, the managers decide to make Pittsburgh's plant the experimental group and Cleveland's plant the nonequivalent control group. Thus, the study is quasi-experimental for the obvious reason that workers cannot be randomly assigned to the two plants (imagine the moving costs, legal fees over union grievances, etc.). The independent variable is whether or not flextime is present, and the dependent variable is some measure of productivity. Let's suppose the final design looks like this:

Pittsburgh plant:	pretest:	average productivity for 1 month prior to instituting flextime
	treatment:	flextime instituted for 6 months
	posttest:	average productivity during the 6th full month of flextime
Cleveland plant:	pretest:	average productivity for 1 month prior to instituting flextime in Pittsburgh
	treatment:	none
	posttest:	average productivity during the 6th full month that flextime is in effect in the Pittsburgh plant

Outcomes

Figure 10.3 shows you four different outcomes of this quasi-experiment. All the graphs show improved productivity for the Pittsburgh plant. The question is whether the improvement was due to the program or to some other factor(s). Before reading on, try to determine which of the graphs provides the strongest evidence that introducing flextime increased productivity, and try to identify the threats to internal validity that make it difficult to interpret the other outcomes.

I don't imagine you found it difficult to conclude that in Figure 10.3a, something besides the flextime produced the apparent improvement. This graph makes the importance of some type of control group obvious, even if it has to be a nonequivalent control group. Yes, Pittsburgh's productivity increased, but the same thing happened in Cleveland. Therefore the Pittsburgh increase cannot be attributed to the program, but could have been due to several of the threats to internal validity that you've studied. History and maturation are good possibilities. Perhaps a national

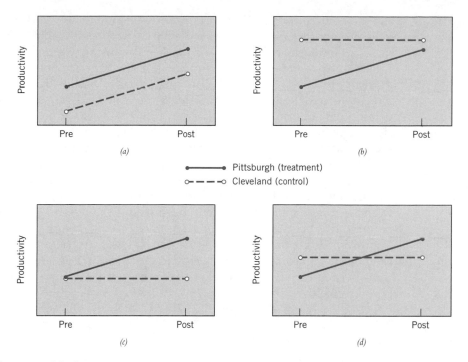

FIGURE 10.3 Hypothetical outcomes of a nonequivalent control group design.

election intervened between pre- and posttest and workers everywhere felt more optimistic, leading to increased productivity. Perhaps workers just showed improvement with increased experience.

Figure 10.3b suggests that productivity in Cleveland was high throughout the study and that in Pittsburgh productivity began at a very low level but improved due to the flextime program. However, there are two dangers here. For one thing, the Cleveland scores might reflect a ceiling effect (see Chapter 8, p. 257). That is, their productivity level is so high to begin with that no further improvement could possibly be shown. If an increase could be seen (i.e., if scores on the Y-axis could go higher), you might see two parallel lines, as in Figure 10.3a. The second problem is that because Pittsburgh started so low, the increase there might be a regression effect rather than a true one.

Figure 10.3c seems at first glance to be the ideal outcome. Both groups start at the same level of productivity, but the group with the program (Pittsburgh) is the only one to improve. This may indeed be the case, and such an outcome generally makes applied researchers happy, but a problem can exist nonetheless. Because of the nonequivalent nature of the two groups, it is conceivable that subject selection could interact with some other influence. That is, some factor such as history or maturation could affect one plant but not the other. For example, it's not hard to imagi~ tion × history problem here—some event affects the Pittsburgh plant b Cleveland plant. Perhaps the knowledge that they are participating in a s vated the Pittsburgh workers (remember Hawthorne?). Perhaps betweer and the posttest the Steelers won a Super Bowl, and because workers in Pittsburgh are such avid sports fans, their general feeling of well-being could improve morale and therefore productivity. The Browns, on the other hand, who never win Super Bowls, are less likely to inspire productivity boosts in the Cleveland plant.

You've probably noted the similarity of Figures 10.3c and Figure 10.1 from the cognitive interview study. Fisher et al. (1989) did not randomly assign detectives to the training and nontraining groups, but they believed the two groups to be roughly equivalent nonetheless, based on a matching procedure using "information gathered in … preliminary interviews and the recommendations of the detectives' commanding officer" (Fisher et al., 1989, p. 724). Hence, they believed that the results shown in Figure 10.1 represented a real training effect and that any selection effects were minimal.

The outcome in Figure 10.3d provides the strongest support for program effectiveness. Here the treatment group begins *below* the control group yet *surpasses* the controls by the end of the study. Regression can be ruled out as causing the improvement because one would expect regression to raise the scores only to the level of the control group, not beyond it. Of course, selection problems and interactions between selection and other factors cannot be excluded completely, but this type of crossover effect is generally considered to be good evidence of program effectiveness (Cook & Campbell, 1979).

Regression and Matching

A special threat to the internal validity of nonequivalent control group designs occurs when there is an attempt to reduce the nonequivalency of diverse groups through a matching procedure. This did not occur in the example we just worked through, but it sometimes occurs in applied research. Matching was described in Chapter 6 as an alternative to random assignment, and it works rather well to create equivalent groups if the independent variable is a manipulated one and participants can be randomly assigned to groups after being paired together on some matching variable (see Chapter 6, pp. 183–187, to review the matching procedure). However, it can be a problem in nonequivalent control group designs when the two groups are sampled from populations that are significantly different from each other on the matching variable. If this occurs, then using a matching procedure can enhance the influence of a **regression effect** and even make it appear that a successful program has failed. Let's look at a hypothetical example.

Suppose you are developing a program to improve the reading skills of disadvantaged youth. You advertise for volunteers to participate in an innovative reading program and select those most in need (i.e., those whose scores will be, on average, very low). To create a control group that controls for socioeconomic class, you recruit additional volunteers from similar neighborhoods in other cities. Your main concern is with equating the two groups for initial reading skill, so you decide to match the two groups on this variable. You administer a reading skills pretest to the volunteers in your target neighborhood and to the potential control group participants, and use the results to form two groups that will have the same average score. Let's say the test has a range from 0 to 50. You decide to select children for the two groups so that the average score is 25 for both groups. The treatment group then gets the program and the control group doesn't; the design is a typical nonequivalent control group design:

Experimental group:	pretest	reading program	posttest
Control group:	pretest	—	posttest

Naturally, you're excited about the prospects of this study because you really believe the reading program is unique and will help a lot of children. Hence you're shocked when these results occur:

Experimental group:	pre = 25	reading program	post = 25
Control group:	pre = 25	—	post = 29

Not only did the program not seem to work, but it appears that it even hindered the development of reading skills—the control group apparently improved! What happened?

A strong possibility here is that regression effects resulting from the matching procedure overwhelmed any possible treatment effect. Remember that the experimental group was formed from those with the greatest need for the program because their skills were so weak. If the reading pretest were given to all children who fall into this category (i.e., this population), the average score might be quite low, say, 17. When using the matching procedure, however, you were forced to select children who scored much higher than the average child from this population of "poor readers." Presumably, at least some of the children in this group scored higher than they normally would have on the pretest because no test is perfectly reliable—some degree of measurement error is likely to occur. Therefore on a posttest, many of these children will score lower simply due to regression to the mean. Let's suppose the program truly was effective and would add an average of 4 points to the reading score. However, if the average regression effect was a loss of 4 points, this would account for the apparent lack of change from pre- to posttest:

$$[25] + [+4] + [-4] = [25]$$

For participants in the control group, just the opposite might have occurred. Maybe their population score was much higher than 25 (35 perhaps). Maybe they were pretty good readers to begin with (i.e., from a different population than the other group). Selecting participants who scored much lower than their population mean, in order to produce pretest scores to match those of the experimental group, could result in a regression effect producing higher posttest scores. For these children, the posttest score would result from the same 4-point regression effect used above. Thus,

$$[25] + [0] + [+4] = [29]$$

Figure 10.4 shows the problem in visual form. Regression and program improvements cancel each other out in the experimental group, while in the control group, regression is the only factor operating, and it pushes the scores toward the high end. In sum, the reading program might actually have been a good idea, but the matching procedure caused a regression effect that masked its effectiveness.[2]

---

[2] Although the practical realities of applied research in the field might prevent it, a better procedure would be to give a large group of children the reading readiness test, match them on the test, and randomly assign them to a reading program group and a control group.

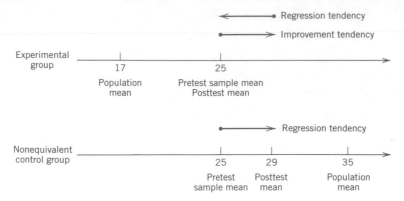

FIGURE 10.4 Hypothetical influences of a regression effect when matching is used with nonequivalent groups.

This type of regression artifact apparently occurred during the first large-scale attempt to evaluate the effectiveness of Head Start, one of the cornerstone programs of President Lyndon Johnson's "Great Society" initiative in the 1960s (Campbell & Erlebacher, 1970). The program originated in 1965 as an ambitious attempt to give underprivileged preschool children a "head start" on school by teaching them various school-related skills and getting their parents involved in the process. By 1990, about 11 million children had participated, and Head Start is now recognized as perhaps the most successful social program run by the federal government (Horn, 1990). Yet in the early 1970s, it was under attack for its "failure" to produce lasting effects, largely on the basis of what has come to be known as the "Westinghouse study" (because the study was funded by a grant to the Westinghouse Learning Corporation and Ohio University), conducted by Victor Cicirelli and his colleagues (1969).

The Westinghouse study documented what it called "fade-out effects"—early gains by children in Head Start programs seemed to fade away by the third grade. The implication, of course, was that perhaps federal dollars were being wasted on ineffective social programs, a point made by President Nixon in an address to Congress, in which he explicitly referred to the Westinghouse study. Consequently, funding for Head Start came under attack during the Nixon years. At the same time, the basis for the criticism, the Westinghouse study, was being assaulted by social scientists.

Because Head Start was well underway when the Westinghouse evaluation project began, children couldn't be randomly assigned to treatment and control groups. Instead, the Westinghouse group selected a group of Head Start children and matched them for cognitive achievement with children who hadn't been through the program. However, in order to match the groups on cognitive achievement, Head Start children selected for the study were those scoring well above the mean for their overall group and control children were those scoring well below the mean for their group. This is precisely the situation just described in the hypothetical case of a program to improve reading skills. Hence the Head Start group's apparent failure to show improvement in the third grade was at least partially the result of a regression artifact caused by the matching procedure (Campbell & Erlebacher, 1970).

In fairness to the Westinghouse group, it should be pointed out that they would have disagreed vehemently with politicians who wished to cut the program. Cicirelli (1984) insisted that the study *"did not conclude that Head Start was a failure"* (p. 915; italics in the original), that more research was necessary, and that "vigorous and intensive approaches to expanding and enriching the program" (p. 916) be undertaken. More recently, Cicirelli (1993) pointed out that a key recommendation of the Westinghouse study was "not to eliminate Head Start but to try harder to make it work, based on encouraging findings from full-year programs" (p. 32).

Nonequivalent control group designs do not always produce the type of controversy that engulfed the Westinghouse study. Consider the following case study of an attempt to improve the self-esteem of Little League baseball players through a training program for coaches.

Case Study 24—A Nonequivalent Control Group Design

Coaches can be significant figures in the lives of young children involved in sports. The effects can be devastating for children whose skills are just developing, if their coach's only goal is to win championships, and anything less than perfect performance produces censure and ridicule. On the other hand, coaches can be marvelous teachers and role models for children in their formative years. Smoll, Smith, Barnett, and Everett (1993) set out to evaluate a training program for coaches aimed at helping them develop the self-esteem of their young athletes. Two weeks before the start of a Little League baseball season, some coaches underwent a program called "Coach Effectiveness Training." The program emphasized several target behaviors that coaches should use—reinforcing effort as well as good performance, providing encouragement and positive instruction after mistakes, and reinforcing team participation and cooperation. The program was evaluated using a nonequivalent control group design. Eight coaches, all from the same league, were in the experimental group. Ten coaches from different leagues were in the control group. Why not make this an experimental design, take a single league, and randomly assign some coaches to each group? Three reasons. First, it made it easier to coordinate the training program. Second, it ensured that the average won-lost records of the teams in each group would be 50%. Third, it ensured "that no leakage of information would occur and that guidelines derived from the program would not be communicated to control coaches" (p. 603). Thus, the two groups were by definition nonequivalent, but the authors also took steps to make them as similar as possible, except for the training. Socioeconomic status was controlled, for instance.

The children being coached by those in the experimental and control groups were evaluated before and after the Little League season. The boys completed a standardized test of self-esteem, and in the posttest they were asked in an interview about their coaches' behaviors (the interviewers were "blind" to whether the boys were in the experimental or control group). Players in the experimental group reported liking their coaches more and liking baseball more. On the measure of self-esteem, there were no overall differences between the two groups of boys, but when Smoll et al. (1993) examined only the boys who scored below the median on the pretest, Figure 10.5 resulted. As you can see, boys with relatively low self-esteem at the start of the season showed a large increase when they were coached by someone from the training program, while boys with coaches from the control group stayed

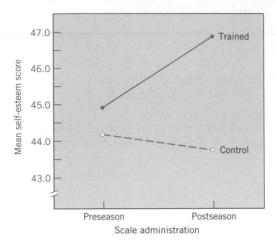

FIGURE 10.5 Changes in self-esteem scores for Little Leaguers before and after the coaches received training about ways to enhance self-esteem.

(From Smoll et al., 1993)

the same (the apparent decline was not significant). If you consider that low–self-esteem boys might be the most easily discouraged by a bad experience in sports, this is a very encouraging outcome. If coaches do the right things, they can make a big difference in the lives of their young players. This is a really nice study.

Nonequivalent control group designs typically include pretests, but that is not always the case. Sometimes they occur when an unforeseen opportunity for research makes pretesting impossible. One such opportunity was the 1989 San Francisco earthquake. To James Wood and Richard Bootzin of the University of Arizona, the event suggested an idea for a study about nightmares, a topic already of interest to them (Wood & Bootzin, 1990). Along with some colleagues from Stanford University (located near the quake's epicenter), they quickly designed a study to see if the experience of such a traumatic event would affect dream content in general and nightmares in particular (Wood, Bootzin, Rosenhan, Nolen-Hoeksema, & Jourden, 1992). By necessity, they used a nonequivalent control group design. As is generally the case with this design, the groups were nonequivalent to begin with (students from two different states); in addition, one group was treated one way (earthquake experience) and the second group was treated differently (no direct earthquake experience).

The experimental group consisted of students from Stanford and from San Jose State University who experienced the earthquake. Nonequivalent controls were college students recruited from the University of Arizona. They did not experience the quake, of course, but they were exposed to the extensive media accounts of it. All participants began keeping a dream log, which was then analyzed for nightmare content and frequency. The results were intriguing. Over the 3 weeks of the study, approximately 40% of those who experienced the quake had at least one nightmare; only 5% of the control subjects did. Of the nightmares experienced by the first group, roughly one-fourth were about earthquakes. Virtually none of the control group's nightmares were about quakes. Furthermore, the frequency of nightmares correlated significantly with how anxious participants reported they were during the time of the earthquake.

Well aware of the interpretation problems that accompany quasi-experimental studies, Wood et al. (1992) recognized the dangers inherent in making comparisons between nonequivalent groups. For instance, lacking any pretest ("pre-quake") information about nightmare frequency for their participants, they couldn't "rule out the possibility that California residents have more nightmares about earthquakes than do Arizona residents even when no earthquake has recently occurred" (p. 222). If one lives in California, perhaps earthquake nightmares are a normal occurrence. However, relying partly on their general expertise in the area of nightmare research, the authors argued that the nightmare frequency was exceptionally high in the California group and was likely to be the result of their recent traumatic experience.

Interrupted Time Series Designs

If Wood and his colleagues could have foreseen San Francisco's earthquake, they might have started collecting nightmare data from their participants for several months leading up to the quake and then for several months after the quake. That would have enabled them to determine (a) if the quake truly increased nightmare experiences for the participants in the quake zone and (b) if the nightmare frequency peaked shortly after the quake and then returned to baseline. Of course, not even talented research psychologists can predict earthquakes, so Wood and his co-workers did the best they could and designed a nonequivalent control group study. If they had been able to take measures for an extended period before and after the event expected to influence behavior, their study would have been called an **interrupted time series design.**

Using the system in Campbell and Stanley (1963) again, the basic time series study can be symbolized like this:

$$O_1 \quad O_2 \quad O_3 \quad O_4 \quad O_5 \quad \text{T} \quad O_6 \quad O_7 \quad O_8 \quad O_9 \quad O_{10}$$

where all the O's represent measures taken before and after T, which is the point where some treatment program is introduced or some event (e.g., an earthquake) occurs. T is the "interruption" in the interrupted time series. Of course, the number of measures taken before and after T will vary from study to study and is not limited to a total of five each. It is also not necessary that the number of pre-interruption and post-interruption points be the same number. As a general rule, the more data points the better, and some experts (e.g., Orwin, 1997) recommend at least *50* pre-interruption data points.

Outcomes

The main advantage of a time series design is that it allows one to evaluate **trends,** predictable patterns of events that occur with the passing of time. For example, suppose you were interested in seeing the effects of a 2-month antismoking campaign on the number of teenage smokers in a community. The program might include some persuasion techniques, peer counseling, showing the teens a smoked-out lung or two, and so on. Assuming that you had a good measure of the smoking behavior, you could take the measure a month before and a month after introducing the program and perhaps get the results in Figure 10.6.

Did the program work? There certainly is a reduction in smoking from pre- to posttest, but it's hard to evaluate it in the absence of a control group. Yet even without a control group, however, it might be possible to see if the campaign worked if

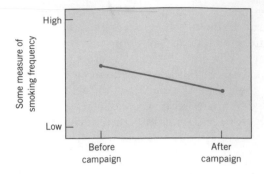

FIGURE 10.6 Incidence of smoking behavior just before and just after a hypothetical antismoking campaign.

not one but several measures were taken both before and after the program was put in place. Consider the possible outcomes in Figure 10.7, which examines the effect of the antismoking campaign by measuring smoking behavior every month for a year before and a year after the program.

Figure 10.7a is a good illustration of how an interrupted time series can identify trends. In this case, the reduction that looked so good in Figure 10.6 is shown to be nothing more than part of a general trend toward reduced smoking among adolescents. This demonstrates an important feature of interrupted time series designs—they can serve to rule out (i.e., falsify, remember?) alternative explanations of an apparent change from pre- to posttest.

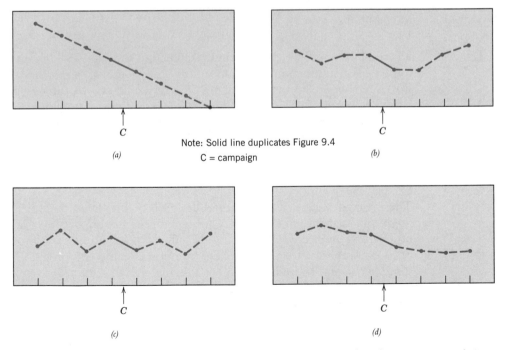

Note: Solid line duplicates Figure 9.4
C = campaign

FIGURE 10.7 Hypothetical antismoking campaign evaluated with an interrupted time series design—several possible outcomes.

Two other outcomes that raise questions about the program's effectiveness are seen in Figures 10.7b and 10.7c. In Figure 10.7b, smoking behavior was fairly steady before the campaign and then dropped, but just briefly. In other words, if the anti-smoking program had any effect at all, it was short-lived. In Figure 10.7c, the decrease after the program was part of another general trend, this time a periodic fluctuation between higher and lower levels of smoking. The ideal outcome is shown in Figure 10.7d. Here the smoking behavior is at a steady and high rate before the program begins, drops after the antismoking program has been put into effect, and remains low for some time afterward. Note also in Figure 10.7d that the relatively steady baseline prior to the campaign enables the researcher to rule out regression effects.

Case Study 25—An Interrupted Time Series Design

An actual example of an outcome like the last one can be found in a study of worker productivity completed at an iron foundry by Wagner, Rubin, and Callahan (1988). They were interested in the effect of instituting an incentive plan in which workers were treated not as individuals but as members of small groups, each responsible for an entire production line. Productivity data were compiled over a period of about 10 years, 4 years prior to introducing the incentive plan and 6 years afterward. As you can see from their time series plot in Figure 10.8, productivity was fairly flat and not very impressive prior to the plan but increased steadily after the plan was implemented.

This study also illustrates how those conducting interrupted time series designs try to deal with potential threats to internal validity. Figure 10.8 certainly appears to

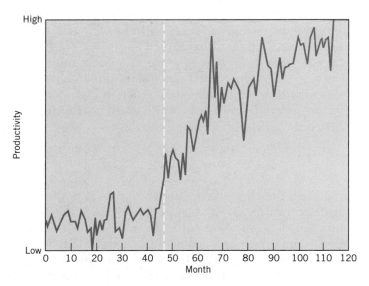

FIGURE 10.8 Interrupted time series design; effect of an incentive plan on worker productivity in an iron foundry.

(From Wagner et al., 1988)

show that the incentive plan worked wonders, but the changes could have been influenced by other factors, including history, instrumentation, and selection. The authors argued that history did not contribute to the change, however, because they carefully examined as many events as they could in the period before and after the change and could find no reason to suspect that some unusual occurrence led to the jump in productivity. In fact, some events that might be expected to hurt productivity (e.g., recession in the automobile industry, which affects sales of iron castings) didn't. The researchers also ruled out instrumentation, which could be a problem if the means of recording worker productivity changed over the years. It didn't. Third, although we normally think of subject selection as being a potential confound only in studies with two or more nonequivalent groups, it can occur in a time series if significant worker turnover occurred during the time of the new plan—the cohort of workers on site prior to the plan then could be different from the group there after the plan went into effect. This didn't happen in Wagner et al.'s study though. In short, designs like this one are susceptible to several threats to internal validity, but these threats often can be ruled out by systematically examining available information, as Wagner and his colleagues did.

Variations on the Basic Time Series Design

Sometimes the conclusions from an interrupted time series design can be strengthened if some type of control comparison can be made. One approach amounts to combining the best features of the nonequivalent control group design (a control group) and the interrupted time series design (long-term trend analysis). The design looks like this:

$$O_1 \quad O_2 \quad O_3 \quad O_4 \quad O_5 \quad \mathbf{T} \quad O_6 \quad O_7 \quad O_8 \quad O_9 \quad O_{10}$$
$$O_1 \quad O_2 \quad O_3 \quad O_4 \quad O_5 \qquad\ O_6 \quad O_7 \quad O_8 \quad O_9 \quad O_{10}$$

If you will look ahead a second to Figure 10.10 in Box 10.2, you will see a classic example of this strategy, a study that evaluated a speeding crackdown in Connecticut by comparing outcomes for that state with data from similar states.

A second strategy for strengthening conclusions from a time series study can be used when a program is to be introduced in different locations at different times, a design labeled an **interrupted time series with switching replications** by Cook and Campbell (1979) and operating like this:

$$O_1 \quad O_2 \quad O_3 \quad \mathbf{T} \quad O_4 \quad O_5 \quad O_6 \quad O_7 \quad O_8 \quad O_9 \quad O_{10}$$
$$O_1 \quad O_2 \quad O_3 \quad O_4 \quad O_5 \quad O_6 \quad O_7 \quad \mathbf{T} \quad O_8 \quad O_9 \quad O_{10}$$

With this procedure, the same treatment or program is put in place in two locations, but separated in time. There is no control group, but the design provides the benefit of a built-in replication. If the outcome pattern in location 2 matches that of location 1, the researchers can be more confident about the generality of the phenomenon being studied. This happened in an unpublished study reported in Cook and Campbell (1979). It was completed in the late 1940s and early 1950s, when televisions were just starting to change our lives. A number of Illinois communities were given licenses for new TV stations, but in 1951 there was a freeze on new licenses that wasn't lifted until 1953. That gave researchers an opportunity to study the impact of new televisions on communities at two different points in time—in the late 1940s, before the freeze, and just after 1953, with the freeze lifted. Hypothesizing that the new inventions would reduce the amount of reading done, researchers studied library circulation data and found support for their concerns about reading. As TVs began infiltrating communities, library circulation dropped, and the pattern was virtually identical during the two times examined.

A third elaboration on an interrupted time series design, again in the absence of a control group, is to measure several dependent variables, some expected to be affected by the "interruption," others not expected to change. This was the strategy used in a study by Stolzenberg and D'Alessio (1997). They wished to examine the effect of a California mandatory jail sentencing law, the so-called "three strikes and you're out" policy, on crime rates. The essence of the policy is that jail sentences occur automatically once a person has been convicted of three serious crimes (felonies). Combining data from California's 10 largest cities, Stolzenberg and D'Alessio examined two types of crime rates (i.e., two dependent variables). They looked at serious crimes, supposed to be reduced by mandatory sentencing, and relatively minor crimes (misdemeanors), not predicted to be affected by the new law. Figure 10.9 shows the results, a good example of the advantages of a time series. If you look just at the curve for serious crimes right after the law was passed, it actually looks like there is a decline, especially when compared to the flat curve for the nonserious crimes. If you look at the serious crime curve as a whole, however, it is clear that any reduction in serious crime is just part of a trend that had been occurring since around 1992. Overall, the researchers found that the three strikes law had no measurable effect on any type of crime.

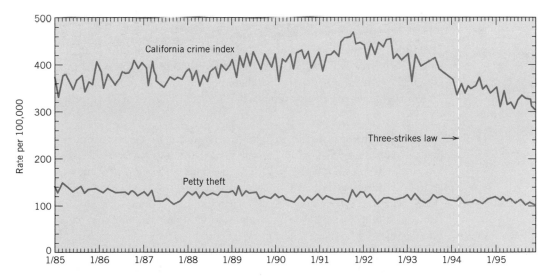

FIGURE 10.9 Interrupted time series using two different dependent measures; the effect of mandatory sentencing on crime rates.

(From Stolzenberg & D'Alessio, 1997)

Program Evaluation

The attempt to assess changes in sentencing laws is just one example of a type of applied research known as **program evaluation.** This research area developed in the 1960s in response to the need to evaluate social programs like Head Start, but it is concerned with much more than just answering the question "Did program X work?" More generally, program evaluation includes (a) procedures for determining if a true need exists for a particular program and who would benefit if the program is implemented, (b) assessments of whether a program is being run according to plan and if not, what changes can be made to facilitate its operation, (c) methods for evaluating program outcomes, and (d) cost analyses to determine if program benefits justify the funds expended. Let's consider each in turn. First, however, you should read Box 10.2, which highlights a paper by Donald Campbell (1969) that is always included at or near the top of the list of the "most important papers in the young history of program evaluation."

Box 10.2

CLASSIC STUDIES—Reforms as Experiments

The 1969 article by Campbell entitled "Reforms as Experiments" is notable for three reasons. First, it argues forcefully that we should have an experimental attitude toward social reform. In the opening sentence, Campbell argued for applying the scientific way of thinking by writing that we should be ready for an experimental approach to social reform, an approach in which we try out new programs designed to cure specific social problems, in which we learn whether or not these programs are effective, and in which we retain, imitate, modify, or discard them on the basis of apparent effectiveness. (p. 409)

Second, Campbell's article describes several studies that have become classics in the field of program evaluation and prototypical examples of designs like the interrupted time series. Perhaps the best-known example is his description of a study to evaluate an effort to reduce speeding in Connecticut (Campbell & Ross, 1968). Following a year (1955) with a record number of traffic fatalities (324), Connecticut Governor Abraham Ribicoff instituted a statewide crackdown on speeding, making the reasonable assumption that speeding and traffic fatalities were correlated. The following year, the number of deaths fell to 284. This statistic was sufficient for Ribicoff to declare that with "the saving of 40 lives in 1956, a reduction of 12.3% from the 1955 … death toll, we can say that the program is definitely worthwhile" (quoted in Campbell, 1969, p. 412). Was it?

I hope you're saying to yourself that other interpretations of the drop are possible. For example, history could be involved; perhaps the weather was better and the roads

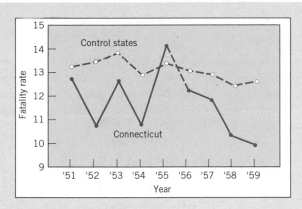

FIGURE 10.10 The Connecticut speeding crackdown, a classic example of an interrupted time series with a nonequivalent control.

(From Campbell, 1969)

were drier in 1956. Even more likely is regression— 324 is the perfect example of an extreme score that would normally be followed by regression to the mean. Indeed, Campbell argued that regression contributed to the Connecticut results, pointing out that "[r]egression artifacts are probably the most recurrent form of self-deception in the experimental social reform literature" (p. 414). Such effects frequently occur in these kinds of studies because interventions like a speeding crackdown often begin right after something especially bad has happened. Purely by chance alone, things are not likely to be as bad the following year.

Was regression all that was involved here? Probably not. By applying an interrupted time series design with a nonequivalent control (nearby states without a crackdown on speeding), Campbell concluded that the crackdown probably did have some effect, even if it was not as dramatic as was believed by the governor. You can see the results for yourself in Figure 10.10.

The third reason the Campbell article is so important is that it gave researchers some insight into the political realities of doing research on socially relevant issues. Politicians often propose programs they believe will be effective, and while they might say they're interested in a thorough evaluation, they tend not to be too appreciative of a negative evaluation. After all, by backing the program, they have a stake in its success and its continuance, especially if the program benefits the politician's home state or district. For this reason, politicians and the administrators hired to run programs seldom push for rigorous evaluation and are willing to settle for favorable research outcomes even if they come from flawed designs. For example, Governor Ribicoff was willing to settle for looking at nothing more than traffic fatalities immediately before and right after the crackdown on speeding.

Campbell recommended an attitude change that would shift the emphasis from stressing the importance of a particular program to acknowledging the importance of the problem. This would lead politicians and administrators alike to think of programs as experimental attempts to solve the problem; different programs would be tried until one was found to work. As Campbell put it in the article's conclusion,

> *Trapped administrators* have so committed themselves in advance to the efficacy of the reform that they cannot afford an honest evaluation.... *Experimental administrators* have justified the reform on the basis of the importance of the problem, not the certainty of their answer, and are committed to going on to other potential solutions if the first one tried fails. They are therefore not threatened by a hard-headed analysis of the reform. (1969, p. 428; italics in the original)

Planning for Programs—Needs Analysis

An agency begins a program because administrators believe a need exists that would be met by the program. How is that need determined? Clearly, more is required than just an administrative decision that a program seems to make sense. An exercise program in a retirement community sounds quite reasonable, but if none of the residents will participate, much time and money will be wasted. Before any project is even planned in any detail, some type of planned needs assessment should be completed.

Needs analysis is a set of procedures for predicting whether a population of sufficient size exists that would benefit from the proposed program, whether the program could solve a clearly defined problem, and whether members of the population would actually use the program. Several systematic methods exist for estimating need, and it is important to rely on at least some of these techniques because it is easy to overestimate need. One reason for caution follows from the **availability heuristic,** first introduced in Chapter 1's discussion about ways of knowing. Events that grab headlines catch our attention and become more "available" to our memory. Because they come so readily to mind, we tend to overestimate how often they occur. All it takes is one or two highly publicized cases of children being abandoned by vacationing parents for a call to be made for new programs to fix this seemingly widespread problem. Also, a need for some new program can be overestimated by those in a position to benefit (i.e., keep their jobs) from the existence of such a program.

As outlined by Posavac and Carey (1997), there are several ways to identify the potential need for a program. These include:

✓ *Census data.* If your proposed program is aimed at the elderly, it's fairly obvious that its success will be minimal if there are very few seniors living in the community. Census data (www.census.gov) can provide basic demographic information about the number of people fitting into various categories. Furthermore, the information is fine-grained enough for you to determine such things as the number of single mothers under the age of 21, the number of people with various disabilities, or the number of elderly people below the poverty line.

In addition to census data, local organizations might have some archival data available. For instance, a corporation thinking of starting a worksite day care center can examine its own files to estimate the number of employees who are working parents of young children. Finally, published research can also provide important information about need. Studies showing long-term decreases in IQ for children raised in impoverished environments provide strong evidence of a need for enrichment programs.

✓ *Surveys of available resources.* There's no reason to begin a "meals on wheels" program if one already exists in the community and is functioning successfully. Thus, one obvious step in a needs analysis is to create an inventory of existing services. It will include a description of who is providing the services, exactly which services are being provided, and an estimate of how many people are receiving the services. You might discover, for example, that an existing meals on wheels program is being run by an agency that is overextended financially and understaffed and, as a result, is meeting no more than 10% of the need. In that case, developing a second program could be worthwhile.

✓ *Surveys of potential users.* A third needs analysis strategy is to administer a survey within the community, either to a broadly representative sample or to a target group identified by census data. Those participating could be asked whether they believe a particular program is needed. More important, the survey may enable the planner to estimate just how many people would actually use the proposed program.

✓ *Key informants, focus groups, and community forums.* A **key informant** is someone in the community who has a great deal of experience and specialized knowledge about the problem at hand that is otherwise unavailable to the researcher (Gilchrist & Williams, 1999). Such persons include community activists, clergy, people who serve on several social service agency boards, and so on. Sometimes they might be too close to a problem to judge it realistically, but in general they are an indispensable source of information. A **focus group** is a small (7–9 typically) group of individuals who respond to a set of open-ended questions about some topic, such as the need for a particular program. They are often used as a follow-up to a community survey, but they also can be used as a means to shape the questions that would appear in a survey. Focus group members tend to be similar to each other in age and in socioeconomic status, presumably to produce a congenial group that will stay on task. Finally, useful information can sometimes emerge from a **community forum,** an open meeting where all members of a community affected by some potential program are invited to come and participate. Key informants, focus groups, and forums can all be useful tools, but the researcher also needs to be careful of weighing too heavily the arguments of an especially articulate (but perhaps nonrepresentative) informant, focus group member, or speaker at a forum.

The past two decades have seen an increased awareness in corporate America that profits are related to worker health. Consequently, companies have begun to develop, implement, and evaluate health care programs for workers. The following case study describes a large-scale example, which began with a thorough analysis of need.

Case Study 26—Assessing Need

The needs analysis project was undertaken by the Du Pont Company prior to starting a program designed to promote healthy behaviors in the workplace (Bertera, 1990). The plan called for implementing a series of changes that would affect over 110,000 employees at 100 worksites. The obvious cost of putting such an ambitious plan into effect made it essential that need be demonstrated clearly.

The Du Pont needs assessment included an analysis of existing data on the frequency of various types of employee illnesses, on employee causes of death, and on the reasons for employee absence and disability over a 15-year period. One unanticipated result was that employees making the least amount of money and performing the lowest-ranking jobs were the highest on all major categories of illness. That finding told the evaluators that this particular subgroup of workers needed special attention.

Additional indicators that the health promotion program was needed came from a survey of existing company programs for enhancing health. The survey revealed a wide range of programs run by the medical staffs at the various Du Pont plants, including programs on weight loss, smoking cessation, stress management, and the like. The programs tended to be one-time lectures or films, however, with minimal follow-up and no systematic evaluation of effectiveness. Employees were also surveyed to determine their knowledge of health-enhancing behaviors, their intention to change things like their eating habits, their self-assessments of whether their own behaviors were health enhancing or not, and their preferences for a range of health programs.

On the basis of all of this information, Du Pont developed a comprehensive series of programs aimed at improving the health of its workers. These included training programs that went far beyond one-shot lectures, including creation of local employee Health Promotion Activity Committees, recognition and award programs for reaching certain health goals, and workplace climate changes (e.g., removing cigarette vending machines). Also, all workers completed a Health Risk Survey. The results generated a Health Risk Appraisal, which became part of their personnel files, and included an individualized plan for promoting healthy behaviors.

Once the needs analysis is complete and the decision is made to proceed, details of the program can be planned and the program begun. Once the program is underway, the second type of evaluation activity begins.

Monitoring Programs—Formative Evaluation

Programs often extend over a considerable period of time. To wait for a year or so before doing a final evaluation of program effectiveness might be nice and clean from a strict methodological point of view, but what if it is clear in the first month that problems exist that could be corrected easily? That is, rather than waiting until the program's completion, why not carefully monitor the progress of the program while it is in progress? This monitoring is called **formative evaluation,** and according to one analysis (Sechrest & Figueredo, 1993), it is the most common form of evaluation activity.

A formative evaluation can include several components. For one thing, it determines if the program is being implemented as planned. For example, suppose a local crisis hotline decides to develop a program aimed at the needs of young children who are home alone after school while their parents are working. One important piece of the implementation plan is to make the hotline's phone number available and well known. A formative evaluation would determine whether the planned ads were placed in the newspapers at appropriate times and whether mass mailings of stickers with the hotline's number went out as planned. Also, a sample of residents could be called and asked if they'd heard of the new hotline for kids. There's no point in trying to evaluate the effectiveness of the program if people don't even know about it.

Another general function of the formative evaluation is to provide clear and continuing data on how the program is being used. Borrowing a term from accounting, evaluators sometimes refer to this procedure as a **program audit.** Just as a corporate auditor might look for inconsistencies between the way inventories are supposed to be managed and the way they are actually managed, the program auditor examines whether the program as described in the agency's literature is the same as the program that is actually being implemented.

A final part of a formative evaluation can be a pilot study. Program implementation and some preliminary outcomes can be assessed on a small scale before extending the program. This happened in the Du Pont study. A pilot program at one of the plants, which showed a significant decline in sick days after implementation of the health promotion program, encouraged program planners and led to an elaboration of the program at other sites (Bertera, 1990).

Evaluating Outcomes—Summative Evaluation

Politically, formative evaluations are less threatening than **summative evaluations,** which are overall assessments of program effectiveness. Formative evaluation is aimed at program improvement and is less likely to call into question the very existence of a program. Summative evaluation, on the other hand, can do just that. If the program isn't effective, why keep it, and by extension, why continue to pay the program's director and staff (see what I mean about "threatening")? As Sechrest and Figueredo (1993) stated:

> Summative evaluation and even the rationale for doing it call into question the very reasons for existence of the organizations involved. Formative evaluation, by contrast, simply responds to the question "How can we be better?" without strongly implying the question "How do [we] know [we] are any good at all?" (p. 661)

Despite this political difficulty, summative evaluations are the core of the evaluation process and are an essential feature of any program funded by the federal government. Any agency wishing to spend tax dollars to develop a program is obligated to show that those dollars are being used effectively.

The actual process of performing summative evaluations involves applying some of the techniques you already know about, especially those having to do with quasi-experimental designs. However, more rigorous experiments with random assignment are possible sometimes, especially when evaluating a program that has more people desiring it than space available. In such a case, random assignment in the form of a lottery (random winners get the program; others get their names on a waiting list) is not only methodologically ideal, it is also the only fair procedure to use.

One problem that sometimes confronts the program evaluator is how to interpret a failure to find significant differences between experimental and control groups. That is, the statistical decision is "fail to reject H_0." Such an outcome can be difficult to interpret. It could be that there just isn't any difference, yet there's always the possibility of a Type II error (see Chapter 4, pp. 138–139) being committed, especially if the measuring tools are not very sensitive or very reliable. The program might indeed have produced some small but important effect, but the analysis failed to discover it.

Although a finding of no difference can be problematic, most researchers believe that such a finding (especially if replicated) contributes important information for decision making, especially in applied research. For instance, someone advocating the continuation of a new program is obligated to show how the program is better than something already in existence. Yet if differences between this new program and one already well established cannot be shown, then it might be wise to discontinue the new program, especially if it is more expensive than the older one. Indeed, as Yeaton and Sechrest (1986) argue, there may be life-and-death issues involved. They cite a study comparing different treatments for breast cancer that varied in the degree of surgical invasiveness. Survival rates for women undergoing minimally invasive procedures were not significantly different from the rates for women subjected to radical mastectomies. Such an outcome is an example of "failing to reject H_0." Should the results be ignored because no significant differences were found? Of course not. If the same outcome occurs with a less traumatic treatment procedure, why take the more radical step? Of course, the confidence one has in decisions made on the basis of finding no difference is directly related to how often such a finding has been replicated. A recommendation to rely on minimal surgical procedures only follows from repeated failure to find a difference between major and minor procedures.

A "failure to reject H_0" decision also can help evaluate claims made by proponents of some new program. Someone claiming that mandatory jail sentences after a third felony will dramatically reduce serious crime, for instance, is obligated to demonstrate such an effect. The time series study of mandatory sentences mentioned above (Stolzenberg & D'Alessio, 1997), which found no effect of the "three strikes" program on crime rate, is an important finding even though it is a finding of "no difference." If replicated, it would raise serious questions about the value of mandatory sentencing.

As implied in these "failure to reject H_0" examples, a finding of no difference has important implications for decision making for reasons having to do with cost, and this brings us to the final type of program evaluation activity.

Weighing Costs—Cost-Effectiveness Analysis

Suppose a researcher is interested in the question of worker health and fitness and is comparing two health-enhancement programs. One includes opportunities for exercising on company time, educational seminars on stress management, and a smoking ban. The second plan is a more comprehensive (and more expensive) program of evaluating each worker and developing an individually tailored fitness program, along with financial incentives for things like reducing blood pressure and cholesterol levels. Both programs are implemented on a trial basis in two plants; a third plant is used as a control group. Hence the design is a nonequivalent control group design with two experimental groups instead of just one. A summative evaluation finds no difference between the two experimental groups in terms of improved worker health, but both show improvements compared to the control group. That is, both health programs work, but the Chevy version works just as well as the Mercedes version. If two programs producing the same outcome differ in cost, why bother with the expensive one?

This corporate fitness example illustrates one type of **cost-effectiveness analysis:** monitoring the actual costs of a program and relating those costs to the effectiveness of the program's outcomes. If two programs with the same goal are equally effective but the first costs half as much as the second, then it is fairly obvious that the first program should be used. A second type of cost analysis takes place during the planning stages for a program. Estimating costs at the outset helps determine whether a program is even feasible and provides a basis for comparison later on between projected costs and actual costs.

A study by Erfurt, Foote, and Heirich (1992) provides an illustration of a cost-effectiveness analysis. They compared several "worksite wellness programs" at four automobile manufacturing plants that differed in cost. One of their findings was that "[t]he addition of a physical fitness facility (Site B) did not produce any incremental benefit in reducing [health] risks, as compared with health education classes (Site A) ..." (p. 5). Because the cost per employee at Site A was $17.68 compared with $39.28 for Site B, it appeared that the fitness facility was either a bad idea (i.e., not worth the money) or not being used properly.

Estimating costs with reference to outcomes can be a complicated process, often requiring the expertise of a specialist in cost accounting. Thus, a detailed discussion of the procedures for relating costs to outcomes is beyond the scope of this chapter, an opinion shared by my wife, who happens to be a cost accountant and finds my rudimentary knowledge amusing. Some of the basic concepts of a cost analysis can be discovered by reading Chapter 11 of Posavac and Carey's (1997) fine introduction to program evaluation.

A Note on Qualitative Analysis

Chapter 3 (p. 75) first introduced the difference between a quantitative analysis (numbers involved) and a qualitative analysis (numbers not so critical). Although much of the analysis that occurs in program evaluation is quantitative in nature, there is a great deal of qualitative analysis as well, especially in the first three of the categories of evaluation just described. Thus, during a needs analysis, quantitative data from a community survey and census data can be combined with in-depth interview information from key informants and focus groups. In formative and summative assessments, quantitative data can be supplemented with a qualitative analysis of interviews with agency workers and clients and with direct observations of the program in action. In short, in program evaluation research, it is seldom a question of whether quantitative or qualitative research is better. Rather, it is more often the case that researchers rely on (and value) both.

As first mentioned in Chapter 5's discussion of external validity, research in psychology is sometimes criticized for avoiding real-world investigations. This chapter on applied research should make it clear that the criticism is without merit. Indeed, concern over application and generalizability of results is not far from the consciousness of all psychologists, even those committed primarily to basic research. It is evident from psychology's history that application is central to American psychology, if for no other reason than the fact that Americans can't help it. Looking for practical applications is as American as apple pie. The next chapter introduces a slightly different tradition in psychological research—an emphasis on the intensive study of individuals. As you will see, just as the roots of applied research can be found among psychology's pioneers, experiments with small N also trace to the beginnings of the discipline. Before moving on to Chapter 11, however, read Box 10.3, which summarizes some of the ethical problems likely to be encountered when doing program evaluation research.

Box 10.3

ETHICS—Evaluation Research and Ethics

Whether evaluating programs that provide services to people, conducting studies in a workplace environment, or evaluating some government service, program evaluation researchers often encounter ethical dilemmas not faced by laboratory psychologists. Some special problems include:

✓ *Informed consent.* People receiving social services are often powerless. When asked to "volunteer" for a study and sign an informed consent form, they may fear that a failure to "sign up" could mean a loss of services. Researchers must take deliberate steps to reassure participants in situations like this.

✓ *Maintaining confidentiality.* In some research, confidentiality can be maintained by gathering behavioral data from participants but not adding any personal identifiers. In other studies, however, it is necessary for the researcher to know who the participants are. For instance, the researcher might need to recontact participants, especially if the study is a longitudinal one, or a researcher might want to know who replied to a survey so that nonrespondents can be recontacted. In such cases, it is important to develop coding systems to protect the identities of participants. Sometimes, participants in longitudinal studies can use aliases, and survey respondents can send back the anonymous survey and a postcard verifying their participation In separate mailings (Sieber, 1998).

✓ *Perceived injustice.* As mentioned in Box 7.2, some people might object to being in a control group because they could be missing out on some potentially beneficial treatment. Although most control group members in program evaluation research receive the prevailing treatment, rather than none at all, control group problems can still happen. For example, "leakage" (see Box 8.2, p. 273) can occur if control group members discover important information about the program being offered to someone else. Their resentment of "special treatment" being given to others can seriously affect the outcome. For example, in a study designed to evaluate some worksite changes in a coal mine, control group miners quickly grew to resent those in the treatment group, who they felt were getting special attention and did not have to work as hard for the same money (Blumberg & Pringle, 1983). The ill will even extended to the researchers. Control group workers believed them to be in league with the mine owner in an attempt to break the union. The study as originally designed had to be discontinued.

✓ *Avoiding conflict with stakeholders.* **Stakeholders** are persons connected with a program with a vested interest in it, including clients, staff, and program directors. Program evaluators need to be aware of and take steps to avoid potential conflicts with various stakeholders. This means being aware of the needs of stakeholders and explicitly addressing them during the planning stages of the evaluation. For example, program evaluators might build to the initial contract some specific statements about how the results will be reported and what the consequences will be for certain types of outcomes (Posavac & Carey, 1985). A clear understanding ahead of time can help transform "trapped" administrators into "experimental" administrators, to use Campbell's terms (Box 10.2).

Chapter Summary

Beyond the Laboratory

The goal of applied research is to shed light on the causes of and solutions to real-world problems. Like basic research, however, its outcomes also contribute to general theories about behavior (e.g., the cognitive interview study contributes to our knowledge of the influence of context on memory). American psychologists have always been interested in applied research, partly because of institutional pressures to show that the "new" psychological science of the late 19th century could be put to good use. Applied research can encounter ethical problems (e.g., with informed consent) and problems with internal validity (e.g., nonequivalent groups), but it is often strong in external validity.

Quasi-Experimental Designs

Research in which participants cannot be randomly assigned to conditions is referred to as quasi-experimental research. Nonequivalent control group designs are one example. They typically compare pretest/posttest changes in a group receiving some treatment with pre/post changes in a control group that has been formed without random assignment. Regression effects can make interpretation difficult when nonequivalent groups are matched on pretest scores. In a time series design, researchers take several measurements both before and after the introduction of some treatment that is being evaluated. Interrupted time series studies enable the researcher to evaluate the effects of trends. Sometimes a nonequivalent control condition, a "switching" replication, or additional dependent measures can be added to the basic time series design.

Program Evaluation

The field of program evaluation is a branch of applied psychology that provides empirical data about the effectiveness of various human service and government programs. Needs analysis studies determine whether a new program should be developed. Census data, surveys, and other community data can help assess need. Formative evaluations determine whether a program is operating according to plan, and summative evaluations assess program outcomes. Cost analyses help determine whether a program's benefits are worth the funds invested. Program evaluation research combines quantitative and qualitative methods.

Chapter Review

Multiple Choice

1. As a general rule, applied research
   a. is more likely to take place outside of the laboratory
   b. is a recent development in the history of American psychology
   c. produces results that are irrelevant for testing general theories of behavior
   d. is synonymous with program evaluation research

2. Which of the following is a problem typically encountered by applied research?
   a. can never get the informed consent of the participants
   b. the results seldom contribute to psychological theory
   c. there is reduced internal validity
   d. the results seldom have external validity

3. In a nonequivalent control group design
   a. it is essential that both groups score the same on the pretest
   b. the results enable the researcher to evaluate linear trends

c.   the key dependent measure is the amount of change between pre- and posttest

d.   selection × history confounds can be ruled out because of the control group

4.   Suppose Ohio decides to implement a child restraint seatbelt law because of a record number of child injuries. Which of the following is true?

a.   the number of injuries will most likely increase in the following year or two, because trends don't reverse overnight

b.   the nonequivalent control design is the best way to evaluate the law's effectiveness

c.   comparison with a similar state that doesn't have the law would help assess potential regression effects

d.   in this situation, qualitative analysis would be superior to quantitative analysis

5.   A family service agency implements a new program for debt counseling. A program evaluator periodically sits in on and assesses a debt counseling session to see if the plan is being followed. What type of program evaluation procedure is this?

a.   needs analysis

b.   summative evaluation

c.   cost analysis

d.   formative evaluation

Short Essay

1.   Use the case study of the cognitive interview as a way of (a) distinguishing basic and applied research and (b) showing that applied research relates to theory development.

2.   Describe two major contributions of Hugo Münsterberg to the early history of applied psychology.

3.   Describe the essential features of a nonequivalent control group design and explain why Figure 10.3c does not necessarily allow one to conclude that the program was a success.

4.   Early program evaluations of Head Start seemed to show that gains made by Head Start children were short-lived; by the third grade, no differences existed between those who had been in the program and those who had not. However, this outcome might have been the result of a regression effect brought about by the matching procedure used to form the groups. Explain.

5.   Describe the case study that evaluated a "coach effectiveness training" program and explain why the researchers decided to use a quasi-experimental instead of an experimental design.

6.   Describe the essential features of an interrupted time series design and three variations on the basic procedure that can strengthen the conclusions drawn from such a design.

7.   Describe two quantitative and two qualitative procedures that can be used when conducting a needs analysis.

8.   Distinguish between formative and summative assessments and explain why agency workers generally prefer the former.

9.   A finding of "no difference" sometimes occurs in program evaluation research. Explain why this is not necessarily a bad thing.

10. Briefly describe the main attributes of the four main types of program evaluation research.

11. Briefly describe the ethical dilemmas that can face those doing program evaluation research.

Applications Exercises

Exercise 10.1.—Identifying Threats to Internal Validity

Threats to internal validity are common in quasi-experimental studies. What follows is a list of some of the threats you've encountered in this chapter and in Chapter 5. For each of the hypothetical experiments that are described, identify which of these threats is most likely to provide a reasonable alternative explanation of the outcome.

Some threats to internal validity:

history	maturation
regression	selection
attrition	selection × history

1.   A college dean is upset about the low percentage of freshmen who return to the college as sophomores. Historically, the rate has been around 75%, but in the academic year just begun, only 60% of last year's freshmen return. The dean puts a tutoring program into effect and then claims credit for its effectiveness when the following year's return rate is 65%.

2.   Two nearby colleges agree to cooperate in evaluating a new computerized instructional system. College A gets the program and college B doesn't. Midway through the study, college B announces that it has filed for bankruptcy. One year later, computer literacy is higher at college A.

3.   Twelve women who volunteer for a home birthing program are compared with a random sample of other pregnant women who undergo normal hospital procedures for childbirth. Women in the first group spend an average of 6 hours in labor, while those in the control group spend an average of 9 hours.

4.   A 6-week program in managing test anxiety is developed and given to a sample of first-semester college students. Their anxiety levels are significantly lower at the conclusion of the program than they were at the start.

5.   A teacher decides to use an innovative teaching technique in which all students will proceed at their own pace throughout the term. The course will have 10 units, and each student goes to unit N after completing unit $N-1$. Once all 10 units have been completed, the course is over and an A has been earned. Of the initial 30 students enrolled in the class, the final grade distribution looks like this:

A: 16   F: 2   W: 12

The instructor considers the new course format an unqualified success.

6. A company decides to introduce a flextime program. It measures productivity for January, then runs the program for 6 months and evaluates productivity during the month of June. Productivity increases.

Exercise 10.2.—Interpreting Nonequivalent Control Group Studies

A wheel bearing manufacturer owns two plants, both in Illinois. She wishes to see if money for health costs can be reduced if a wellness program is instituted. One plant (E) is selected for a year-long experimental program that includes health screening and individually tailored fitness activities. The second plant (C) is the control group. Absentee-due-to-sickness rates, operationally defined as the number of sick days per year per 100 employees, are measured at the beginning and end of the experimental year. What follows are four sets of results. Construct a graph for each and decide which (if any) provide evidence of program effectiveness. For those outcomes not supporting the program's effectiveness, provide an alternative explanation for the experimental group's apparent improvement.

Outcome 1 E: pretest = 125 posttest = 100
            C: pretest = 125 posttest = 140
Outcome 2 E: pretest = 125 posttest = 100
            C: pretest = 100 posttest = 100
Outcome 3 E: pretest = 125 posttest = 100
            C: pretest = 110 posttest = 110
Outcome 4 E: pretest = 125 posttest = 100
            C: pretest = 130 posttest = 105

Exercise 10.3.—Interpreting Time Series Studies

Imagine a time series study evaluating the effects of a helmet law on head injuries among hockey players. Injuries were significantly lower in the year immediately after the law was passed than in the preceding year. Construct three time series graphs, one for each of the following patterns of results.

1. The helmet law worked.
2. The helmet law seemed to work initially, but its effects were short-lived.
3. The helmet law had no effect; the apparent drop was probably just a regression effect.
4. The helmet law didn't really work; the apparent drop seemed to reflect a general trend toward reduced violence in the sport.

Exercise 10.4.—Planning a Needs Assessment

You are the head of a five-person psychology department at a liberal arts university. One day the dean says to you, "Why don't you develop a master's program in counseling psychology?" The college already has an MBA program and another master's program in physical therapy. Because you've read this chapter, you respond that a thorough needs analysis should be done. The dean tells you to go ahead and even approves a modest budget for the project. Describe the factors that would have to be considered before implementing the new degree and explain the techniques you would use to conduct a needs assessment.

11

Small N Designs

Preview & Chapter Objectives

Up to this point in the text, the designs you've encountered typically have tested relatively large groups of participants, specific methodological problems like creating equivalent groups or avoiding sequence effects have been dealt with, mean scores have been calculated, inferential analyses like ANOVA have been completed, and general conclusions about the effects of independent variables have been drawn. In this chapter, however, you will encounter a very different type of study. The designs used are often called "single-subject designs" because the behavior of each research subject is considered individually, but they can also be called "small N designs" because these studies sometimes use several participants. The data for these subjects *might* be combined statistically, but more often the data for the additional individuals are described individually and used for replication purposes. When you finish this chapter, you should be able to:

- Describe several examples of classic studies in psychology's history, all using single individuals or small numbers of participants, with the additional persons used for replication purposes.
- Explain how grouping data from large numbers of participants can yield misleading conclusions about behavior and describe some practical reasons for doing small N research.
- Describe Skinner's basic philosophy about the proper way to conduct research—the experimental analysis of behavior.
- Describe the essential components of any single-subject design.
- Explain the logic of an A–B–A–B withdrawal design.
- Explain the logic of a multiple baseline design and describe three types of multiple baseline procedures.
- Explain the logic of a changing criterion design and relate it to the operant concept of shaping.
- Describe several additional single-subject designs (e.g., alternating treatments design).
- Describe the criticisms that have been directed at small N research in the operant tradition.
- Describe the main purposes of psychophysics research and compare the three most common methods of psychophysics.

The small N strategy is most frequently associated with B. F. Skinner, who you first encountered in Chapter 1. However, it is important to realize that Skinner was not the first to focus on individual subjects. Rather, small N designs have a long history; in fact, the first experimental psychologists used this approach all the time.

Research in Psychology Began with Small N

When psychology emerged as a new science in the second half of the 19th century, statistical analysis was also in its infancy. Galton was just beginning to conceptualize correlations, and inferential techniques like ANOVA did not yet exist. Widespread use of large N designs and inferential statistics occurred only after Fisher's work on the analysis of variance appeared in the 1930s (see Chapter 8, Box 8.3). Before this time, small N ruled.

Some of psychology's pioneers used the smallest N possible—they studied their own behavior or the behavior of a single individual. In Chapter 7 (Box 7.3), you learned about the most famous example of this—Hermann Ebbinghaus's exhaustive study of his own ability to learn and recall lists of nonsense syllables. Another pioneering example is Charles Darwin's study of child development, accomplished by keeping a detailed diary of his own son's childhood. It was published as "A Biographical Sketch of an Infant" in the British journal *Mind* in 1877 (Goodwin, 1999). A third example is Watson and Rayner's infamous Little Albert experiment (1920; see Chapter 2, Box 2.1).

In Wundt's laboratory at Leipzig, small N designs were also the dominant strategy. Students pursuing the doctorate were assigned specific research topics that typically took a year or so to complete. The studies normally involved a very small number of research participants, with the investigator often serving as one of the participants. The additional participants usually were other doctoral students. For instance, the bulk of James McKeen Cattell's dissertation research on reaction time included data from just two people—Cattell and his friend and fellow student Gustav Berger (Sokal, 1981). Clearly, the separation in role (and status) that exists today between Experimenter with a capital E and subject with a small s was not in evidence in those days. In fact, while in the 1890s participants were sometimes called "subjects," they were more likely to be called "observers," a term that suggests a higher status and a more active role than subject. Whether to use the term subject or observer was an issue as late as 1930 (Danziger, 1985).

Pioneer experimental psychologists sometimes crudely summarized data (e.g., reporting means) from several observers, but more often they reported the data for each person participating. A good illustration of this strategy is a study from the laboratory at Clark University completed in the early 1890s. It was a study of something called "facial vision," the ability to detect the presence of nearby objects even when they cannot be seen. At one time, blind people were believed to have developed this as a special sense to compensate for their loss of vision. However, Fletcher B. Dressler (1893) was able to show that the skill had more to do with hearing than with vision.

Figure 11.1 is a picture of the actual experimental setup, one of a series of photos showing research in progress at Clark in 1892. As you can see, a blindfolded person was seated next to a panel made up of four 1-foot squares. From left to right, the squares were either open or filled with (a) wood in a latticed design, (b) wood in a solid panel, or (c) wire screening. The panel hung from the ceiling and could be moved by the experimenter (it's Dressler in the photo) so that each of the squares could be placed next to the subject's face. The task was to identify which surface was next to one's face; the participants were Dressler and two other graduate student colleagues.

Remarkably, all three participants learned to distinguish between pairs of surfaces, as shown in Table 11.1, reproduced from the original article. The data represent the number of right ("R.") or wrong ("W.") responses. For example, when comparing the latticed surface with the solid one, F. B. D. (guess who that was) was correct 69 times and wrong just once when the correct answer was "lattice" and was correct 70 out of 74 times when the correct answer was "solid." Similar results occurred for the other two participants.

Notice that while data for all three participants are presented, there are no summary statistics combining the three data sets. This is because the strategy was to show the phenomenon occurring reliably for each participant, not for the average subject. That is, Dressler tested two additional subjects in order to *replicate* the initial finding twice. This strategy is frequently used today in small N designs.

Do the results of Dressler's study mean that facial vision as a separate sense truly exists? No. As a good research psychologist, Dressler looked for a more parsimonious explanation and for a way to rule out (falsify) the existence of the special facial sense. He found it by making a small procedural change—he plugged everyone's ears. The result was clear: their "power to distinguish [the panels] was lost

FIGURE 11.1 Dressler's apparatus for studying facial vision, 1892.

entirely" (Dressler, 1893, p. 349). Hence facial vision turned out to be the ability to detect slight differences in reflected sound waves.[1]

Studies like the one by Dressler, featuring data from one or just a few participants, can be found throughout the early years of experimental psychology, but large N studies were not completely absent. For example, some could be found in educational psychology and in child study research (Danziger, 1985). Such studies featured empirical questions like "What do elementary school children fear?" and they summarized questionnaire results from hundreds of children (e.g., Hall, 1893). However, as indicated earlier, it wasn't until the 1930s and Sir Ronald Fisher that psychologists began to collect data from large numbers of participants and perform the kinds of descriptive and inferential statistical analyses that are widely used today.

One final example, described in Box 11.1, of an early small N design is worth discussing in some detail. Because the research is an important historical antecedent of B. F. Skinner's work on operant conditioning and foreshadowed the coming of behaviorism when it was completed about 100 years ago, it is deservedly considered

TABLE 11.1   *Data from Dressler's Study of Facial Vision*

Subject	Open and Lattice				Lattice and Solid				Solid and Wire			
	R.	W.	R.	W.	R.	W.	R.	W.	R.	W.	R.	W.
J.A.B.	65	15	59	25	58	2	56	0	45	0	46	2
O.C.	72	47	74	46	33	13	28	14	21	4	14	9
F.B.D.	53	24	58	17	69	1	70	4	73	0	77	2

[1] Given this result, what would you as an experimenter do next? For example, what if you varied the distance between the panels and the subject?

Box 11.1

CLASSIC STUDIES—Cats in Puzzle Boxes

Edward L. Thorndike (1874–1959) had a distinguished career as an educational psychologist. He is best remembered among experimental psychologists for his doctoral dissertation research, however, in which he studied how cats escape from puzzle boxes (Thorndike, 1898). The research is important for several reasons: it shows how psychology's pioneers relied on the detailed study of individual research subjects, it is a good example of how to use parsimonious explanations for behavior, and it is an early example of the kind of research that paved the way for the development of behaviorism, especially the Skinnerian variety.

Studying individual cats

To investigate learning in cats, Thorndike built fifteen puzzle boxes, each with its own unique escape mechanism. Quite by accident, photos of the actual boxes were discovered in the papers of Robert Yerkes by historian John Burnham (1972), and two of them are reproduced in Figure 11.2. Clearly, Thorndike was not a very talented apparatus builder. In fact, his mechanical aptitude was so minimal that he never learned

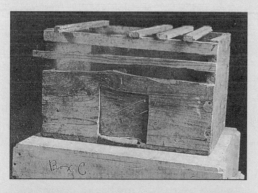

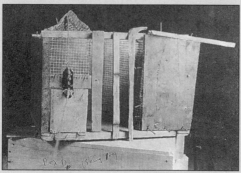

FIGURE 11.2 Two of the puzzle boxes (C and D) built and used by Thorndike in his classic study of cats in puzzle boxes.

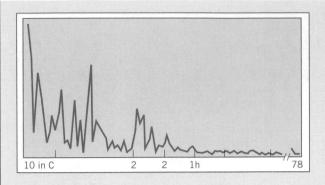

FIGURE 11.3 A record of cat no. 10 learning to escape from Box C.

(From Thorndike, 1911/2000)

how to drive a car (Hothersall, 1990). There is an important lesson here, though: consequential research can be done without highly sophisticated equipment. The quality of the idea for the study is more important than the bells and whistles.

Cats were studied individually, and Thorndike described his results cat by cat. The cats learned to escape from the boxes through a process Thorndike (1911/2000) called "trial and error, with accidental success" (p. 150) and according to what he named the "Law of Effect" (p. 244). The cats' actions were initially random and only occasionally, and by accident, successful. Behaviors that worked tended to be repeated ("stamped in" was the phrase Thorndike used), while unsuccessful behaviors were gradually eliminated ("stamped out"). That is, the "effect" of a successful behavior was to increase the chances of the behavior occurring on the next trial. The progress of one of Thorndike's cats (no. 10, in Box C) can be seen in Figure 11.3.[2]

Using parsimonious explanations

Thorndike's Law of Effect challenged prevailing ideas about the thinking abilities of animals and provided a more parsimonious explanation of problem-solving abilities. He argued that there was no reason to attribute reasoning to animals if their behavior could be explained by a simpler process (i.e., basic trial-and-error learning). Thorndike had little patience with animal researchers who uncritically attributed higher mental processes to animals, an attitude shaped by Lloyd Morgan, whose famous canon of parsimony (see Chapter 3, p. 88) appeared at about this time. Thorndike was familiar with Morgan's work and probably heard the Englishman give an invited address on animal learning while visiting Harvard in 1896 (Jonçich, 1968).

Anticipating Skinner

The final point worth noting about Thorndike's puzzle box research is that it represented an experimental approach to the study of learning that paved the way for other

---

[2] Thorndike did not label the *X*-axis on his graphs, except to note when a significant period of time passed between his otherwise consecutive trials. In Figure 11.3, for example, an unmarked vertical line meant a day, a "2" was 2 days, "1 h." was an hour, and "78" was 78 hours.

> behavioral researchers. It also provided a model for learning that eventually took the form of B. F. Skinner's experimental analysis of behavior, which you will encounter shortly. Skinner (1953) acknowledged his debt to Thorndike by referring to the latter's work as being among "the first attempts to study the changes brought about by the consequences of behavior" (p. 59).

a classic study. It also shows that good science can be done with a meager budget (and minimal talent) for apparatus construction.

Reasons for Small N Designs

Despite the popularity of large N designs in modern psychology, studies using one or just a few subjects have made and continue to make important contributions to our knowledge of behavior. As you will soon discover, these studies cover the entire range from laboratory to field studies and from basic to applied research. There are several reasons why small N designs are used.

Misleading Results from Grouped Data

The process of summarizing data from large groups of individuals sometimes yields results that characterize no single individual who participated in the study. That is, these outcomes can fail to have what has been called **individual-subject validity** (Dermer & Hoch, 1999)—the extent to which a general research result applies to the individual participants in the study. The lack of such validity in large group studies was a central theme in Sidman's *Tactics of Scientific Research* (1960), considered to be the classic text on small N methodology by advocates of the approach. Because group averages disguise individual differences between subjects, Sidman argued, "[g]roup data may often describe a process, or a functional relation, that has no validity for any individual" (p. 274).

More important, Sidman's concern was that averaging data could produce a result supporting theory X when perhaps it shouldn't do so. Consider an example from a concept-learning experiment with young children as participants. They are shown a long series of stimulus pairs and have to guess which is correct. If they make the right choice, they are rewarded. The stimuli are in the form of simple geometric objects; Figure 11.4 shows what the stimulus pairs might be for seven of the trials. The plus signs refer to the stimulus in each pair that will be reinforced (with an M&M perhaps). As you can see, the stimuli vary in shape (triangle or square or circle), color (red or green), and position (left or right). The correct concept in the example is "red," and to accumulate a large pile of M&Ms, the child must learn that shape and position are irrelevant stimulus dimensions. In the language of concept-learning research, color is the "relevant dimension" and red is the "relevant value" on that dimension. The task is considered to be learned when the child reaches some "criterion" score, perhaps 10 consecutive correct choices.

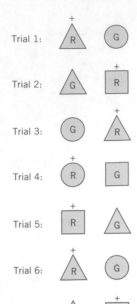

Trial 1:

Trial 2:

Trial 3:

Trial 4:

Trial 5:

Trial 6:

Trial 7:

FIGURE 11.4   Typical stimuli used in a discrimination learning study with children.

An old controversy in the concept-learning literature concerns the manner in which this type of task is learned (Manis, 1971, pp. 64–68). According to "continuity" theory, learning is a gradual process of accumulating "habit strength." Each reinforced trial strengthens the tendency to respond to the relevant dimension and weakens responses to the irrelevant dimensions. A graph of this hypothesized incremental learning process should look something like Figure 11.5a. On the other hand, "noncontinuity" theory holds that subjects actively try out different "hypotheses" about the solution during the early trials. While they search for the correct hypothesis, their performance is at chance level (50%), but once they hit on the correct hypothesis, their performance zooms up to 100% accuracy and stays there. Noncontinuity theory predicts that performance should look more like Figure 11.5b.

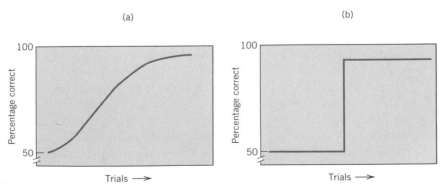

FIGURE 11.5   Concept learning data as predicted by (a) continuity and (b) noncontinuity theory.

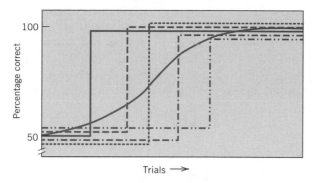

FIGURE 11.6 How grouping data from individual children in a concept-learning experiment can produce a smooth but deceptive curve.

The history of this issue is long and complicated, and general conclusions are subject to many qualifications, but part of the resolution hinges on how the data are handled. If data from many participants are grouped together and plotted, the result indeed often looks something like Figure 11.5a, and continuity theory is supported. However, a picture more like Figure 11.5b, which supports a noncontinuity theory, emerges when one looks more closely at individual performance, especially on difficult tasks (Osler & Trautman, 1961). Examining performance on trials just before a solution is achieved reveals that accuracy is about 50% (e.g., Trabasso, 1963). After criterion, performance is virtually perfect. That is, participants perform at chance level up to the point when they hit on the correct solution; then their performance improves dramatically. So how does the individual performance illustrated in Figure 11.5b end up as Figure 11.5a when the data are summarized?

The key factor is how long it takes each child to hit on the correct solution; some figure it out quickly, others take longer. This situation is portrayed in Figure 11.6. As you can see, a series of individual curves, when combined, could easily yield the smooth curve of Figure 11.5a. This is a clear instance of how grouped data can create an impression that is not confirmed by examining the behavior of individual participants. As a general rule, any researcher using large N designs, especially in research where learning is involved, should examine at least some of the individual data to see if they mirror the grouped data.

Practical Problems with Large N Designs

Small N designs are sometimes necessary because potential participants are rare or difficult to find. This can happen in clinical psychology, for example, when a researcher wants to study people with a rare disorder, or in cognitive psychology, when people with unusual memories are being studied (see Box 12.3, p. 407 for a classic example of such a person). A related problem occurs in some animal research, especially if surgery is involved; the surgical environment is expensive and the procedures are time consuming. The animal colony itself can be difficult to maintain, with costs in these days of animal rights activism including the expense of a security system. In some cases, the species being studied might be hard to obtain, prohibitively expensive, or require long training. For example, the research on teaching sign language to chimpanzees and other apes requires hundreds of hours per animal, and the studies typically extend over many years. In a study teaching sign language to a lowland gorilla (Patterson & Linden, 1981), the ape knew more than 400 different signs at age 10; the study began when the ape was just a year old.

The Experimental Analysis of Behavior

Thus, large N designs may occasionally fail to reflect the behaviors of individuals, and they may not be feasible even if they are desired. However, there are also philosophical reasons for preferring small N designs. Those reasons were articulated best by the most famous advocate of this approach, B. F. Skinner (1904–1990). As you may recall from Chapter 4, Skinner was rated the most eminent contemporary psychologist in a survey of historians and heads of psychology departments (Korn, Davis, & Davis, 1991).

Skinner believed passionately that if psychology was to achieve its goals of predicting and controlling behavior, it must study individual organisms intensively and derive general principles only after the exhaustive study of individual cases. That is, psychology should be an inductive science, reasoning from specific cases to general laws of behavior. Indeed, Skinner once said that the investigator should "study one rat for a thousand hours" rather than "a thousand rats for an hour each, or a hundred rats for ten hours each" (Skinner, 1966, p. 21). The goal is to reduce random variability by achieving precise control over the experimental situation affecting the single subject. As Skinner put it, "I had the clue from Pavlov: control your conditions and you will see order" (1956, p. 223). He called his system the "experimental analysis of behavior," and while you should look elsewhere for a thorough discussion of his ideas (e.g., Skinner, 1953), the essentials are worth mentioning here because they provide the philosophical underpinning for the research designs in applied behavior analysis.

Operant Conditioning

Skinner is best known for his research on **operant conditioning,** a "process in which the frequency of occurrence of a bit of behavior is modified by the consequences of the behavior" (Reynolds, 1968, p. 1). That is, when some behavior occurs in a particular situation, it will be followed by some consequence. If the consequence is positive, the behavior will tend to recur when the individual is in the same situation again. Negative consequences, on the other hand, decrease the future probability of some behavior occurring. If a child's tantrum behavior works (i.e., results in a toy), it will tend to be repeated; if it doesn't, it won't. Note that the definition includes the phrase "frequency of occurrence." Skinner believed that in an experimental analysis of behavior, the only dependent variable worth studying was the **rate of response.** If the goals of psychology are to predict and control behavior, and for Skinner those were the only important

FIGURE 11.7   An operant chamber with cumulative recorder, as used by rats.

ones, then all that matters is whether a behavior occurs or doesn't occur and how frequently it occurs per unit of time.

Thus, for the Skinnerian, the behaviors that characterize our lives are controlled by the environment in which we live. To predict and control behavior, according to Skinner, all that is needed is to be able to "specify three things: (1) the occasion upon which a response occurs, (2) the response itself, and (3) the reinforcing consequences. The interrelationships among them are the 'contingencies of reinforcement'" (Skinner, 1969, p. 7).

In the laboratory, operant conditioning is most often studied using an apparatus called an "operant chamber," or "Skinner box." Figure 11.7 shows a typical one designed for rats. The rat is in the process of pressing the lever protruding from the wall. The positive consequence is that a food pellet will be released into the food cup; the rat will then become more likely to press the bar again. A negative consequence could be a brief jolt of electricity across the floor grid, which would reduce the chances of a future bar press.

Once bar pressing has been established, it can be brought under the environmental control of stimuli such as the light you can see just above the bar. If food pellets follow bar presses only when the light is on, the animal quickly learns a simple discrimination: press when the light is on, but don't bother if the light is off. In Skinner's contingencies of reinforcement language, the light being on in the chamber constitutes the "occasion upon which a response occurs," the "response itself" is the bar press, and the food pellet is the "reinforcing consequence."

The rate of bar pressing is recorded continuously with an apparatus called a **cumulative recorder;** Figure 11.8a shows one in operation. As the paper is fed out at a constant rate of speed, thereby producing time on the *X*-axis, a pen moves

(a)

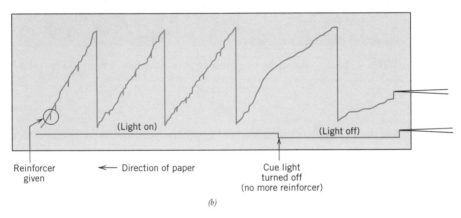

(b)

FIGURE 11.8 (a) The basic operation of a cumulative recorder and (b) a hypothetical cumulative record showing both a high and a low rate of responding.

across the paper by a fixed distance every time the animal presses the bar. When a response is followed by a reinforcer, the pen is programmed to create a short vertical marking line. When the pen reaches the top of the paper, it returns to the baseline to start over. The second pen keeps track of events like the light going on and off. Response rate can be assessed very simply by looking at the slope of the cumulative record. In the cumulative record in Figure 11.8b, the rat is bar pressing very rapidly in the initial portion of the record (perhaps the cue light in the box is on, and it signals that bar pressing produces food) but is hardly pressing at all in the second half (light off, perhaps).

A classic illustration of the operant approach, with its inductive philosophical approach, can be found in the encyclopedic *Schedules of Reinforcement* (Ferster & Skinner, 1957). Its importance to the experimental analysis of behavior is elaborated in Box 11.2. Be sure to read it before you encounter the reinforcement schedules discussed in Case Study 27.

Box 11.2

CLASSIC STUDIES—Schedules of Reinforcement

Schedules of Reinforcement (Ferster & Skinner, 1957) is not a book meant to be read. Rather, it is a book to have on the shelves so that if someone asks you how a "fixed ratio" schedule affects behavior, you can open to the fixed ratio chapter and say, "Here, see for yourself." That is, the 739-page book is more of an "atlas" (Skinner's term) than a summer-reading page turner.

Co-authored with Skinner's student and colleague Charles Ferster, the book is a remarkable achievement, arguably Skinner's most important research contribution, and perhaps the ultimate example of a purely *inductive* approach to science. It is filled with example after example of descriptions and cumulative records that illustrate dozens of different types of reinforcement contingencies. Something of Skinner's work ethic can be seen from his description of the process of compiling the book:

Thousands of hours of data meant thousands of feet of cumulative records.... We worked systematically. We would take a protocol and a batch of cumulative records, dictate an account of the experiment, select illustrative records, and cut and nest them in a few figures. In the end we had more than 1,000 figures, 921 of which went into the book. (Skinner, 1984, p. 109)

The 921 (!) cumulative records in Ferster and Skinner's book showed how behavior was affected by various schedules of reinforcement. A schedule is said to be in effect "[w]henever the environment reinforces some but not all occurrences of a response emitted by the organism" (Reynolds, 1968, p. 59). Few behaviors are reinforced every time they occur, and some behaviors (gambling, for example) are reinforced very infrequently. Yet partial reinforcement produces behaviors that can be very resistant to extinction (gambling again).

As you might recall from the learning chapter of your general psychology textbook, two common types of schedules are called "interval" and "ratio" schedules. On a fixed interval (FI) schedule, for instance, behavior is reinforced only after a certain fixed amount of time has passed. A variable interval (VI) schedule also reinforces behavior after certain amounts of time: the times vary from reinforcer to reinforcer. Ratio schedules depend not on time but on the amount of behavior produced. A fixed ratio (FR) schedule reinforces the individual for producing a certain number of responses. Analogous to the VI schedule, a variable ratio (VR) schedule reinforces after a certain number of responses, but the number keeps changing. Ratio schedules produce relatively high response rates because the amount of reinforcement earned depends on how often the behavior occurs. Interval schedules usually produce low rates of responding, although you will learn of an exception to this in Case Study 27.

The major publication for basic research in operant conditioning is the *Journal of the Experimental Analysis of Behavior*. These titles will give you a sense of what you might encounter there:

"Effects of Fixed and Variable Ratios on Human Behavioral Variability" (Tatham, Wanchisen, & Hineline, 1993)

"Effects of Delayed Reinforcement on Infant Vocalization Rate" (Reeve, Reeve, Brown, Brown, & Poulson, 1992)

"Low-Response-Rate Conditioning History and Fixed-Interval Responding in Rats" (LeFrancois & Metzger, 1993)

Case Study 27—An Experimental Analysis

The third study just listed is an excellent example of the type of basic research encountered in the experimental analysis of behavior. LeFrancois and Metzger (1993) were interested in one of behaviorism's fundamental questions: How does prior conditioning history influence current behavior? All behaviorists believe that knowing one's learning history is essential in order to predict current behavior, but there is disagreement about whether present-day behavior is affected *primarily* by the most recently encountered contingencies of reinforcement or by earlier contingencies. If behavior is adaptive, then one might expect recent contingencies to have the greater effect. However, it could be argued that an especially powerful reinforcement schedule early in life could have effects that carry over to the present day.

LeFrancois and Metzger tested these two possibilities in an operant experiment with six rats. All rats began by being trained to a DRL-20s schedule. "DRL" stands for "differential reinforcement of low rates," and it means that the animals were reinforced for a bar press *only* if it was preceded by 20 seconds during which no bar presses occurred. After the DRL schedule, half of the rats were put on a fixed interval (FI) schedule and half were given a fixed ratio (FR) schedule. Finally, the second group was placed on an FI schedule. Thus the sequence for the two groups was:

1. DRL → FI

2. DRL → FR → FI

That is, all rats wound up on the FI schedule, but some experienced one type of learning history (DRL) and others a different type (DRL, then FR). Would the final schedule, the FI, control the behavior, yielding no differences between the groups, or would prior history affect the behavior? The answer can be seen in Figure 11.9, which compares the cumulative records for one of the rats in each group. Quite clearly, when DRL was followed immediately by FI (Figure 11.9a), the response rate was low during FI. However, when an FR schedule intervened, it dramatically affected the response rate on FI, producing many more responses (Figure 11.9b). Thus, performance on the FI schedule was most influenced by what immediately preceded it. The DRL schedule influenced behavior only if it reflected the animal's *recent* past (first rat). LeFrancois and Metzger (1993) concluded that "the findings underscore the influence of immediately prior conditioning over current responding" (p. 549), an outcome consistent with the idea that animals adapt quickly to changes in the contingencies in their environments.

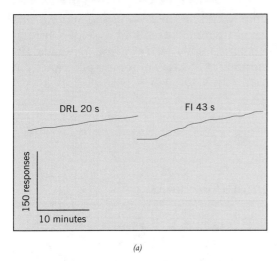

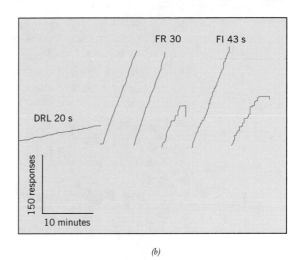

(a)

(b)

FIGURE 11.9   Cumulative records from rats experiencing either (a) DRL→FI or (b) DRL→FR→FI.

(From LeFrancois & Metzger, 1993)

You might be thinking that this experiment sounds a bit like the grouped data experiments you encountered in earlier chapters. However, while there are indeed two groups of three rats in the study, no summary statistics were presented and you will find no inferential statistics in the journal article. Rather, the behavior of each of the six animals was described and six cumulative records were included. This strategy is, of course, identical to the one used by Dressler in the 1890s when he studied facial vision—the phenomenon is demonstrated on a single individual and replicated on others.

Applied Behavior Analysis

As the historian Laurence Smith (1992) has pointed out, a distinction can be made between two broad categories of scientists: those representing the "contemplative ideal" focus on trying to understand the basic causes of events in the natural world and those reflecting the "technological ideal" look for ways to use science to control and change the world. Skinner was firmly in the latter group. Although most of his own research was pure laboratory work, he was always interested in applying the results of an experimental analysis of behavior to real-world problems, and he made important contributions to education, industry, child rearing, and behavior therapy. His ideas even contributed directly to the NASA space program; on at least two space flights, chimpanzees were given complex operant tasks to learn while being sent into space. One psychologist involved in the space project stated that "[e]very technique, schedule, and programming and recording device we used then and subsequently can be traced to [Skinner] or his students" (Rohles, 1992).

Finally, Skinner was not shy about calling for the redesign of society based on operant principles, a recommendation that made him a controversial figure. To some, his prescriptions for improving the world seemed ominous, and he was accused of trying to turn everyone into rats in Skinner boxes. This issue of control is elaborated in Box 11.3, and you should read it carefully and see if you agree with its conclusion before going on to the descriptions of how conditioning principles can be used to solve a variety of applied behavior problems.

Box 11.3

ETHICS—Controlling Human Behavior

In Chapter 1, the goals of psychology were described as description, prediction, explanation, and control. You might have felt a bit uneasy about "control" because it suggests a deliberate attempt to manipulate behavior, perhaps against a person's will. Because of this implication, behaviorists from Watson to Skinner have been accused of seeking dictatorial control via conditioning. For example, when "Cliff's Notes" summarized Skinner's *Walden Two,* a fictional account of a community established on operant principles, it compared the community to Orwell's nightmare world of *1984* (Todd & Morris, 1992). The perception of behaviorist as Big Brother overstates the case but is strengthened when one encounters chapters in Skinner's books with headings like "Designing a Culture" (1953) or superficially reads some of Skinner's statements, usually taken out of context.

The notion that one can and perhaps should act to alter behavior follows from the behaviorist's dictum that much of our behavior is conditioned by our surroundings. If the environment will shape behavior *anyway,* why not ensure that productive behaviors are shaped? This attitude is clearly reflected in two famous quotes. They both imply a more extreme environmentalism than their authors really believed, but each illustrates an almost mischievous willingness to make controversial statements. The first is John Watson's famous claim about child rearing:

> Give me a dozen healthy infants, well-formed and my own specified world to bring them up in and I'll guarantee to take any one at random and train him to become any type of specialist I might select—doctor, lawyer, artist, merchant-chief, and yes, even the beggarman and thief... (1924, p. 82)

The second quote is from Skinner's *Walden Two.* Through the voice of the community's founder and perhaps with Watson's above quote in mind, Skinner wrote:

> "What remains to be done?" he said, his eyes flashing. "Well, what do you say to the design of personalities? Would that interest you? The control of temperament? Give me the specifications, and I'll give you the man!" (1948/1976, p. 274)

For Skinner, the controversy over behavior control was a nonissue. It is not a question of deciding whether to control behavior or not, he believed. Behavior *was* controlled by its consequences, period. Given that basic fact, he believed it followed that some effort should be made to create contingencies that would yield productive rather than nonproductive behaviors. Critics remained unconvinced and asked who would be the person deciding which behaviors should be shaped. Skinner believed his critics were missing the point.

One particular manifestation of the controversy over control exists in the psychology clinic, where the behavioral procedures you are about to study have been quite successful in helping people. One especially controversial procedure has been the use of punishment, including electric shock, to alter the behavior of disturbed children. For example, in a study by Kushner (1970), a severely retarded 7-year-old child (with a mental age of 2) was treated with electric shock for hand biting. The child frequently bled after biting his hand and had suffered serious infections. Attempts to curb the behavior by having him wear boxing gloves or elbow splints failed. The treatment consisted of placing electrodes on the child's thigh and immediately shocking him every time his hand reached his mouth. The result was an almost immediate decline in the behavior that lasted even when the electrodes were removed.

When procedures like this are used in a study evaluating their effectiveness, has the ethical principle of not harming research participants been violated? Defenders of the use of punishment argue that other procedures often don't work with behaviors like self-biting or head banging. As long as appropriate safeguards are in place (e.g., other procedures have been tried unsuccessfully, informed consent from parents or guardians has been obtained), the courts have upheld the use of shock "in extraordinary circumstances such as self-destructive behavior that [is] likely to inflict physical damage" (Kazdin, 1978, p. 352).

Researchers also contend that it is essential to investigate the procedures empirically, even if this means manipulating the level and the frequency of punishment, in order to discover the optimal procedure. This could mean that some children in a study will be punished at a higher level than is later determined necessary to alter the behavior, but the ideal therapy procedure (i.e., minimum punishment that still solves the problem) can never be known until the research is conducted. With the ultimate goal of finding the best way to help these terribly disturbed children, research evaluating the use of punishment seems to be not only justified but essential.

The applications side of the experimental analysis of behavior is sometimes called **applied behavior analysis.** It includes any procedure that uses behavioral, especially operant, principles to solve real-life problems. To get a sense of the range of environments in which these principles are used, consider the following titles from the *Journal of Applied Behavior Analysis:*

"Musical Reinforcement of Practice Behaviors Among Competitive Swimmers" (Hume & Crossman, 1992)

"Analysis of a Simplified Treatment for Stuttering in Children" (Wagaman, Miltenberger, & Arndorfer, 1993)

"A Single-Subject Approach to Evaluating Vehicle Safety Belt Reminders: Back to Basics" (Berry & Geller, 1991)

"Behavioral Treatment of Caffeinism: Reducing Excessive Coffee Drinking" (Foxx & Rubinoff, 1979)

The designs that we'll be examining in the next section are most frequently applied to clinical settings, but as you can see from the above list, the earlier mention of Skinner's applied work, and the designs that follow, operant principles are used in an assortment of circumstances.

Small N Designs in Applied Behavior Analysis

Near the end of their research report on fear conditioning in the Little Albert experiment, Watson and Rayner (1920) described several ways in which the fear might be removed. Although they never tried any of these on Little Albert, the attempt to reduce fear using behavioral methods was made a few years later in a pioneering study by Mary Covey Jones (1924). Taking a 34-month-old boy named Peter who was afraid of rabbits, Jones succeeded in eliminating the fear. Her strategy was to give Peter his favorite food while placing the rabbit at a distance from him and gradually moving the animal closer, a technique similar to modern-day "systematic desensitization" procedures.

Behavioral approaches to therapy did not immediately flourish following Jones's successful treatment of Peter, but they did become popular beginning in the 1950s and especially in the 1960s. The impetus was provided by some additional demonstrations of the effectiveness of procedures based on learning principles, along with a developing skepticism of traditional approaches to therapy, especially those relying on Freudian methods (Eysenck, 1952). In the 1960s, several journals featuring behavioral approaches to therapy appeared, including *Behavior Research and Therapy* (1963) and the *Journal of Applied Behavior Analysis* (1968). From that point on, research began to appear regularly that included designs attempting to demonstrate that a particular method produced a specific behavioral change in a single subject.

Elements of Single-Subject Designs

The essential logic of single-subject designs is quite simple. Because there are usually no control groups in these studies, the behavior of a single individual must be shown to change as a result of the treatment being applied and not as a result of some confounding factor. At a very minimum, this requires three elements. First, the target behavior must be operationally defined. It's not sufficient to say simply that an attempt will be made to reduce a child's disruptive classroom behavior. Rather, the behavior must be precisely defined in terms of easily recorded events, such as speaking out in class while someone else is already speaking, leaving his or her chair without permission, and so on.

The second feature of any single-subject design is to establish a **baseline** level of responding. This means the behavior in question must be observed for a period of time prior to treatment to determine its typical frequency (i.e., normal rate of response, as Skinner would say). It is against this baseline level of responding that the effects of a treatment program can be assessed. The third element is to begin the treatment and continue to monitor the behavior. Congratulations if you've noticed that this sounds just like the logic of the interrupted time series design described in the previous chapter. In both cases, the goal is to be able to evaluate some treatment against an established baseline.

The simplest single-subject design is sometimes referred to as an **A–B design,** with A standing for baseline and B for treatment. The ideal outcome is for the behavior to change when A changes to B. From your knowledge of threats to internal validity, however, I suspect you may be thinking that the A–B design is a weak one. You're right. A change in behavior might be the result of treatment, but it could also result from a variety of confounding factors, including history, maturation, and even regression. To reduce the chances of alternative explanations like these, the withdrawal design was developed.

Withdrawal Designs

If a treatment goes into effect and behavior changes, but the change is due perhaps to maturation, then it is unlikely that the behavior will change back to its original form if the treatment is subsequently removed or withdrawn. However, if the treatment is withdrawn and the behavior does return to its baseline level, then it is likely that the behavior is being affected directly by the treatment and not by maturation. This is the logic behind the use of a **withdrawal design** (sometimes referred to as a "reversal" design), the simplest of which is an **A–B–A design.** As you might guess, this design begins just like the A–B design, but after the treatment has been in effect for a while, it is withdrawn (the second A).

If behavior changes correlate precisely with the introduction and removal of treatment, confidence is increased that the treatment is producing the change. That confidence is further strengthened if reintroducing the treatment brings about another change in behavior. For this reason, researchers prefer an **A–B–A–B design** over the A–B–A design. In effect, the treatment program is evaluated twice. The A–B–A–B design also has the ethical advantage of finishing the experiment with treatment in place. Its ideal outcome is illustrated in Figure 11.10. Note that in order for the treatment to be considered successful, the behavior must return to baseline (or close to it) after the withdrawal, and it must change again when treatment is reinstated. When this result occurs, it is difficult to interpret it in any way other than as the successful application of a treatment program. As an example of how this very common design is actually used, consider the following case study of competitive swimmers.

Case Study 28—An A–B–A–B Design

The study, by Hume and Crossman (1992), was designed to improve the practice behaviors of five 12- to 16-year-old male members of a swim club during "dry-land training periods" (p. 665), those times when the boys were not in the water but were nonetheless supposed to be doing certain things to improve their swimming performance. "Productive" behaviors included things like exercising (e.g., doing sit-ups) or

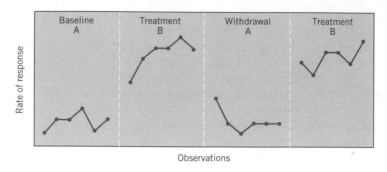

FIGURE 11.10   Ideal outcome of an A–B–A–B withdrawal design.

demonstrating techniques to another swimmer. "Nonproductive" behaviors included inappropriate exercise (e.g., doing handstands), distracting activities (e.g., stealing other swimmers' goggles), and off-task discussions (e.g., about girls). As you might guess, especially considering the age of the boys, the baseline level of non-productive behaviors was quite high and a source of some irritation to the coaches, who apparently forgot about once being 12–16 themselves.

Three trained observers recorded behavior during a baseline period (A) of about a dozen practice sessions (why three?[3]). Then the reinforcement program was introduced (B) for several sessions, withdrawn (A) for several more, and introduced (B) again. Three of the boys were assigned to a "contingent reinforcement" group; the remaining pair were in a "noncontingent reinforcement" group. The reinforcement consisted of playing music, already known to be popular with the boys, during practice time. The three boys in the contingent reinforcement group each had to reach a certain level of productive behavior during their out-of-pool time in order for music to be played (for all five boys) during the immediately following session.

As is customary for small N designs in the operant tradition, the results for each swimmer were presented individually. Figure 11.11 shows you what happened for one of them in the contingent reinforcement group; the program seemed to work quite well for him. During baseline, nonproductive behaviors were dominant for all but one practice session, but this changed quickly during the intervention; productive behaviors were now more frequent. Withdrawing and then reinstating treatment also produced effects consistent with the idea that making music contingent on behavior improved the quality of the practice sessions.

Multiple Baseline Designs

Sometimes a withdrawal design simply isn't feasible. For example, if the treatment program involves teaching a particular skill, that skill will remain learned even if the program is terminated. That is, when the treatment is withdrawn, the behavior will not

---

[3] For an answer, look ahead to Chapter 12's discussion of "interobserver reliability" on p. 393.

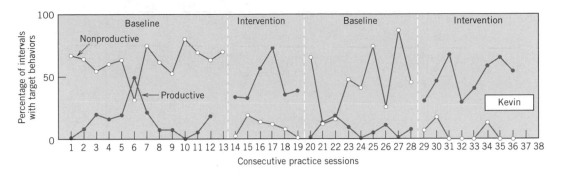

FIGURE 11.11 Data from an A–B–A–B design used by Hume and Crossman (1992) to increase the productivity of swimming practice

return to baseline but will remain high. A withdrawal design may also present ethical problems, especially if the behavior being changed is self-destructive. If the treatment group consists of severely disturbed children who are systematically banging their heads against the wall, and an operant procedure manages to stop the behavior, withdrawing the procedure to see if the head banging resumes may not be justified. Multiple baseline designs solve these types of practical and ethical difficulties.

In a **multiple baseline design,** baseline measures are established and treatment then is introduced *at different times.* There are three varieties. Baselines can be established (a) for the same type of behavior in two or more individuals, (b) for two or more different behaviors within the same individual, or (c) for the same behavior within the same individual, but in two or more different settings. The logic is the same in all cases. Consider, for example, a situation in which the goal is to change three different behaviors in the same individual. The ideal outcome is shown in Figure 11.12, taken from a study by Renne and Creer (1976). They were attempting to train asthmatic children to use a breathing apparatus, and they identified three specific "inappropriate" behaviors that needed to be eliminated in order for the child to operate the device correctly. As you can see, the study begins by establishing the usual baseline for each of the three behaviors. Then treatment is begun for one behavior but not for the other two. If the treatment is effective, it should change the first behavior only. Similarly, when the treatment is extended to behavior 2, it should begin to affect that behavior but not behavior 3. At time 3, the third behavior should change. Hence, the effectiveness of the treatment program is inferred from the fact that as it is introduced at different times, the behavior responds only at that time and not before. On the other hand, if all three, or two of the three, behaviors change after treatment occurs at time 1, then it becomes difficult to attribute the changes directly to the treatment. In the Renne and Creer study, behavior 1 was eye fixation—children had to maintain visual focus on the dial of an air pressure gauge. Doing so kept their heads at a 90° angle to the apparatus. Anything other than 90° was inappropriate. The second behavior was to avoid nostril flaring, an indication that they were breathing through their noses instead of their mouths; and the third was to use a specific type of breathing. Correct behaviors were reinforced by a point system that led to more tangible rewards. As you can see from Figure

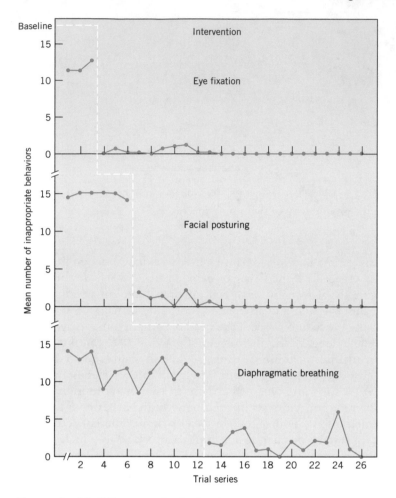

FIGURE 11.12 A multiple baseline design changing three behaviors in the same individual.

(From a study by Renne & Creer, 1976, on training asthmatic children to use a respiration device.)

11.12, both eye fixation and facial posturing responded immediately to the contingencies. Diaphragmatic breathing also responded well, although not as completely (it was the most difficult task of the three).

Multiple baseline studies are among the most frequently encountered in the applied behavior analysis literature. A good example to examine in more detail is a study by Wagaman, Miltenberger, and Arndorfer (1993), who used a multiple baseline design to evaluate a program to help children who stuttered.

Case Study 29—Multiple Baselines Across Subjects

The study illustrates the first type of multiple baseline described above; the goal was to change the same type of behavior in several individuals. In effect, this strategy examines the effect of some treatment program on one individual and then repli-

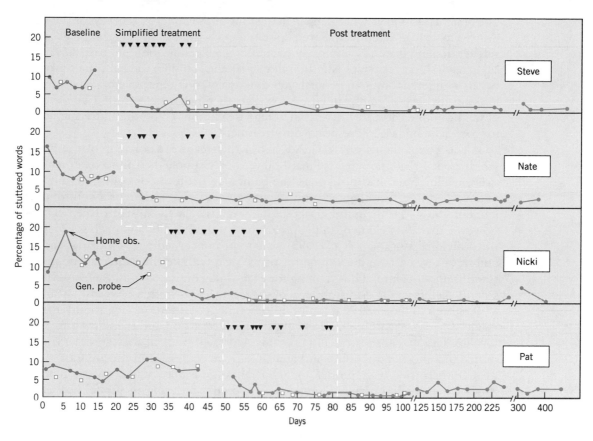

FIGURE 11.13 Decreasing stuttering behaviors in a multiple baseline study by Wagaman, Miltenberger, & Arndorfer (1993).

cates it for several others. The behavior was stuttering, and the individuals were eight school children (six males, two females) ranging in age from 6 to 10. The treatment included a simplified form of a procedure called "regulated breathing," in which the children are taught to improve the way they coordinate speaking and breathing. The children were taught at home; parents were also taught the technique. The program also included elements of social reinforcement (from parents) and awareness training, in which both parents and children were taught to identify quickly every type of speech problem.

This latter feature of the program brings into focus a question that may have occurred to you: How was stuttering defined? Obviously, a program to train full awarness of stuttering must begin with clear operational definitions of the phenomenon. Wagaman et al. (1993) developed specific criteria to identify four categories of stuttering: "(a) word repetitions, (b) part-word repetitions, (c) prolongation of a sound, and (d) blocking or hesitation before the completion of a word" (p. 55). To ensure the reliability of their measures, they tape-recorded all sessions and had multiple raters evaluate the tapes. Agreement among raters was high.

Figure 11.13 shows what happened for four of the children (curves for the other four were virtually identical). Several points are worth nothing. First, as in all single-subject designs, the study begins by establishing a baseline, multiple baselines in this case. Second, as is characteristic of multiple baseline studies, the treatment program began at different times. In general, you can usually spot a multiple baseline study by looking for several graphs piled on top of each other, with a dotted line moving down from one curve to the next in a stepwise fashion. Third, the stuttering behavior for each child clearly responded to treatment.

If you count the tiny arrowheads above the treatment portions of the curves, you'll notice that they aren't equal. "Steve," for example, had nine treatment sessions, while "Nate" had just seven (the names are fictitious, of course). From what you learned in earlier chapters, you might be wondering if there is a control problem here. Shouldn't the number of training sessions be held constant? Keep in mind, however, that a key element in the philosophy of the small N approach is a focus on the individual. Wagaman et al. (1993) were more concerned with ensuring that each child reached a certain level of performance than with keeping the total number of sessions under control. Thus training for each child continued until each child "consistently achieved the criterion level of stuttering (<3% stuttered words)" (p. 57).

Research in the small N tradition is sometimes criticized on the grounds that the results don't generalize beyond the experimental situation and there is a lack of follow-up. The Wagaman et al. (1993) study addressed both of these problems. First, notice that most of the points in Figure 11.13 are circles, but some are squares; one of them is labeled "gen. probe," for "generalization probe." These squares represent times when the researchers assessed the children's stuttering in the school setting. The circles ("home obs.") refer to sessions in the home. Clearly, even though training took place at home, the results generalized to the school. Second, notice that an extensive follow-up (10–13 months) was done for each child, as indicated by the "post treatment" sections of Figure 11.13. Hence, the program not only worked in the short term; its effects lasted.

Changing Criterion Designs

A third major category of single-subject design is called a **changing criterion design** (Hartman & Hall, 1976), a procedure inspired by the operant procedure of **shaping,** in which a behavior is developed by reinforcing gradual approximations to the final, desired behavior. In this design, the target behavior is too difficult for the subject to accomplish all at once; it must be shaped in small increments. The procedure begins by establishing the usual baseline; then a treatment is begun and continued until some initial criterion has been reached. Then the criterion is made increasingly stringent until the final target behavior has been shaped. Health-related behaviors, such as developing exercise or diet programs, are perfect candidates for this type of design. For example, a study by Foxx and Rubinoff (1979) tackled the familiar problem of excessive caffeine consumption. For someone who drinks 15–20 cups of coffee a day, changing immediately to 2–3 cups is probably impossible (are you starting to get a caffeine-withdrawal headache just thinking about it?). Reducing it step by step can be effective, however, especially when there are specific rewards for reaching a series of gradually more demanding criteria. This was the strategy used successfully by Foxx and Rubinoff. In Case Study 30, the changing criterion approach was applied to another common problem, that of improving the physical conditioning of out-of-shape children.

Case Study 30—A Changing Criterion Design

It's no secret that "the battle of the bulge" is a major obsession for Americans. What is particularly troubling is the number of children with weight problems—by some estimates, as many as one in four children are obese (Gleitman, Fridlund, & Riesberg, 1999),[4] and for many of them, a lack of exercise contributes significantly to the problem. In a nice example of a changing criterion design that also incorporated elements of the withdrawal design, DeLuca and Holborn (1992) set out to see if the exercise behaviors of three obese and three nonobese 11-year-old boys could be shaped. All the exercise took place on a stationary bicycle, which was specially programmed to ring bells and flash lights to signal moments when reinforcers had been earned. The study began by establishing the usual baseline. For eight consecutive sessions, each boy was simply told to "exercise as long as you like" (p. 672). After an average baseline level of exercise was established, measured in terms of average cycle revolutions per minute, the first criterion was set at 15% above baseline level. Notice that in line with the small N philosophy of focusing on the individual, the first criterion (as well as all subsequent ones) was set not at the same level for all boys, but at a level that was determined by each boy's starting point.

With the establishment of the first criterion, a variable ratio reinforcement schedule began. The boys were again told to exercise as long as they liked, but now the bell would ring and the light would go on whenever they pedaled at a rate that was, on average, 15% higher than their baseline rate. By getting the bell and light to work, they earned points that could accumulate, allowing them to earn valued prizes (e.g., comic books). After another eight sessions, the criterion increased by another 15%, and then increased once more. This was followed by a three-session withdrawal phase, during which the reinforcement contingencies were temporarily suspended. The study then ended with a return to the criterion level in effect just prior to the withdrawal. Figure 11.14 shows the results for all six boys. Clearly, the level of exercise increased steadily for both the obese and the nonobese boys, with the possible exception of Perry, who missed several sessions (marked by the dashed lines). Just as clear is the fact that the exercise levels dropped off without the reinforcement contingencies in effect (the withdrawal phase is labeled "BL," for baseline, in the graphs). Note that a possible weakness in the study is the absence of any follow-up data. As you might know from your own experiences with exercise programs, it is notoriously difficult to maintain them for any length of time. It would have been nice to find out if the effects of this operant approach were more lasting than is usually the case.

This study illustrates two other points about applied behavior analysis. First, it addresses the question of what constitutes a reinforcer—some boys might be willing to work for comic books, but others might not. To ensure that the boys would be

---

[4] People whose weight is 20% (or more) higher than the average weight for others of their height are said to be obese.

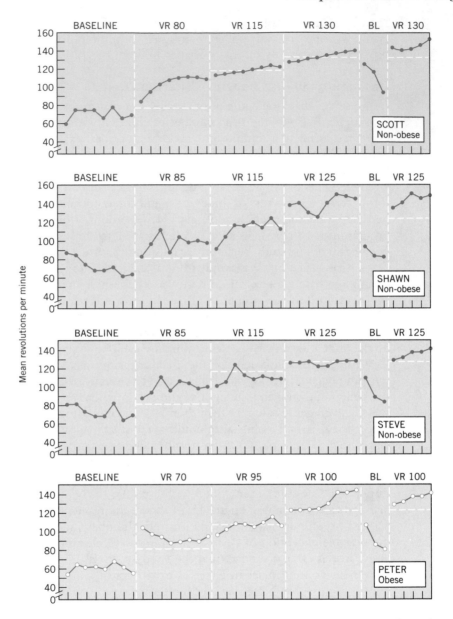

FIGURE 11.14 Data from a changing criterion design to increase the physical conditioning of obese and nonobese 11-year-old boys.

(From DeLuca & Holborn, 1992)

working for outcomes of equal value, DeLuca and Holborn had them complete a "reinforcement survey" at the outset of the study, rating how much they liked certain things on a 10-point scale. Each boy then worked for reinforcers that were highly valued. Second, the researchers directly addressed what applied behavior analysts call **social validity** (Wolf, 1978). This type of validity refers to (a) whether a

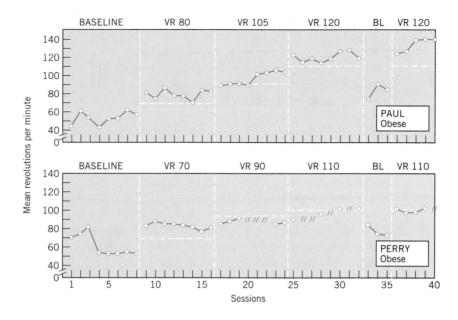

FIGURE 11.14   Continued.

particular applied behavior analysis program has value for improving society, (b) whether its value is perceived as such by the study's participants, and (c) the extent to which the program is actually used by participants (Geller, 1991). DeLuca and Holborn (1992) assessed social validity by having each boy, his parents, and his homeroom and physical education teachers fill out a "social validation question-naire" (p. 673), the results of which they described as "uniformly positive." Other indications of program success were anecdotal—all the boys subsequently partici-pated in track, each of the obese boys convinced his parents to buy him a new bicy-cle during the program, and all the boys seemed distressed when the program ended. As mentioned earlier, however, the results could have been strengthened with a follow-up 6 months or so later.

Other Designs

The A–B–A–B withdrawal, multiple baseline, and changing criterion designs are not the only ones used in applied behavior analysis. Depending on the problem at hand, many researchers combine elements of the main designs, modify the designs slightly, or create a new design. An example of a modification of the A–B–A–B design is called the **A–B–C–B design.** It is often used in situations where the treatment program involves the use of contingent reinforcement. That is, during treatment (B), the target behavior is reinforced immediately after it occurs and reinforcement occurs at no other time. During C, reinforcement is provided, but it is not made contingent on the target behavior. Thus reinforcement is given at both B and C but depends on the behaviors being performed only during B. The design helps to control for placebo effects by demonstrating that the behavior change occurs not just because the subject is pleased about getting reinforcers, happy about being attended to, and so on, but also because of the specific reinforcement contingencies.

Another example of a modified A–B–A–B design is one that is used in evaluating the effectiveness of some drug treatment for a single individual. Several different sequences have been used, but a common one is an **A–A$_1$–B–A$_1$–B design** (e.g., Liberman, Davis, Moon, & Moore 1973). A is the normal baseline, and A$_1$ is a second baseline during which the participant receives a placebo. The real drug is given during B.

A final example of a single-subject design is called the **alternating treatments design,** used when comparing the effectiveness of more than one type of treatment for the same individual. It has become popular because of its ability to evaluate more than a single treatment approach within the same study. After the usual baseline is established, different treatment strategies are alternated several times, usually in random order to reduce any specific sequencing effects that might occur (you'll recognize this as another example of counterbalancing).

Evaluating Single-Subject Designs

The designs we've been considering have been enormously helpful in assessing the effectiveness of operant and other conditioning approaches to behavior change. They all derive from the Skinner/Pavlov dictum that if conditions are precisely controlled, then orderly and predictable behavior will follow. They have been found to be effective in situations ranging from therapeutic behavior change in individuals to community behavior changes in littering. Small N behavioral designs are not without critics, however.

The most frequent complaint concerns external validity, the extent to which results generalize. If a particular form of behavior therapy is found to be effective for a single individual in a specific situation, how do we know the therapy is generally effective for other people with the same problem? Maybe there was something very unusual about the individual who participated in the study. Maybe treatment effects that occur in one setting won't generalize to another.

Advocates reply that generalization is indeed evaluated directly in some studies; the Wagaman et al. (1993) multiple baseline study that helped children overcome stuttering is a good example. Second, although conclusions from single-subject studies are certainly weak if the results aren't replicated, replication and extension are common features of this approach. For instance, the use of "differential attention" to shape behavior (i.e., parents attending to their child's desired behaviors and ignoring undesired behaviors) is now a well-established phenomenon, thanks to dozens of small N studies demonstrating its effectiveness for a variety of behaviors. Considering just the population of young children, for example, Barlow and Hersen (1984) provide a list of 65 studies on the use of differential attention published between 1959 and 1978.

Single-subject designs are also criticized for not using statistical analyses but for relying instead on the mere visual inspection of the data. To some extent, this reflects a philosophical difference between those advocating large and small N designs. Defenders of small N designs argue that conclusions are drawn only when the effects are large enough to be obvious to anyone. It is worth noting, however, that some statistical analyses are beginning to be found in research reports of single-subject designs. For example, borrowing from program evaluation research, some studies have used time series analyses to separate treatment effects from trend effects (Junginger & Head, 1991). Time series analyses also help with the problem of relatively unstable baselines, which can make a visual inspection of a single-subject graph difficult. Statistical analyses have even begun to creep into the *Journal of the Experimental Analysis of Behavior,* traditionally the purest of the pure Skinnerian journals. One operant researcher lamented that in a survey of articles in the 1989 volume of this journal, he found that nearly one-third of the articles used inferential statistics in one form or another and that no more than 10% of the articles included cumulative records (Baron, 1990).

A third criticism of single-subject designs is that they cannot test adequately for interactive effects. As you recall from Chapter 8, one of the attractive features of the factorial design is its ability to identify the interactions between two or more independent variables. Interactive designs for small N studies exist, but they are exceedingly cumbersome. For example, a study by Leitenberg et al. (1968, cited in Barlow & Hersen, 1984) used an A–B–BC–B–A–B–BC–B design to compare two therapy techniques (B and C) plus their combined effect (BC). Notice, however, that technique C never occurred by itself. This required a replication on a second participant, which took the form A–C–BC–C–A–C–BC–C.

One especially interesting interaction that you learned about in Chapter 8 can result from the P × E design, which includes both a subject (P) and a manipulated (E) variable. One type of P × E interaction occurs when the manipulated factor affects one type of person one way but affects others in a different way. The subject variables in P × E designs are, of course, between-subjects variables, but except for some multiple baseline studies, single-subject designs are within-subjects designs. Thus, P × E interactions analogous to the one just described can be found only in single-subject designs through extensive and complicated replications in which it is found that (a) treatment 1 works well with person type 1 but not with person type 2 and (b) treatment 2 works well with person type 2 but not with person type 1.

A final criticism of small N designs in the operant tradition concerns their exclusive reliance on frequency of response as the dependent variable. This approach excludes research using reaction times, whether or not a word is recalled correctly, amount of time spent looking (as in a habituation study), and a number of other dependent variables that shed important light on behavior. Response rate is certainly a crucial variable, but it is difficult to discount the value of the other measures.

Small N designs are by no means confined to operant research and applied behavior analysis. One of psychology's earliest small N research strategies involved studying sensory thresholds using the methods of psychophysics.

Psychophysics

In the opening paragraph of this book, I referred to Wilhelm Wundt's 1874 text as a landmark in establishing psychology as a scientific discipline. Experimental psychology preceded Wundt, however, most obviously in the person of Gustav Fechner (1801–1887), whose 1860 book, *Elements of Psychophysics,* is a classic and is occasionally considered the first real text in experimental psychology. His research established **psychophysics,** the study of the relationship between the physical stimulus and the individual's perception of it.

A detailed description of research in psychophysics is well beyond the scope of this chapter. You can get a thorough dose by taking a course in sensation and perception. Rather, my goals are to provide a brief overview of the type of research found in psychophysics and to show how the research is another example of the small N strategy.

Thresholds

Research in psychophysics concerns two related skills: the ability to detect the presence of a stimulus and the ability to distinguish between slightly different stimuli. The problem of detection originally concerned identifying what Fechner called an **absolute threshold,** the stimulus intensity just sufficient for us to be aware of a stimulus. Every time you take a hearing or a visual acuity test, you are in an experiment about absolute thresholds. More commonly, because it is recognized that absolute thresholds are seldom if ever absolute cutoff points, modern detection research uses what is called "signal detection theory" and takes the form of identifying (a) the factors that affect our ability to detect stimuli, and (b) how the process of deciding whether to say that the stimulus has been detected can be influenced by such individual variables as incentive, attention, and fatigue.

The second type of threshold studied in psychophysics concerns discrimination and is called the **difference threshold,** or "just noticeable difference" (jnd). If you are looking at two lights that differ slightly in intensity but they look identical to you, then a difference threshold has not yet been reached. If the intensity of one of the lights is increased until you now just barely notice a difference, then you've achieved a difference threshold. Difference thresholds can become more finely tuned with practice, as is obvious from the differences between professional piano tuners, wine tasters (and, in the 19th century, wool sorters), and the rest of us.

Methods of Psychophysics

Fechner described three basic psychophysical methods that continue to be used today. To illustrate each, imagine you are taking a hearing test. You are sitting in a soundproof booth wearing earphones, and your instructions are to raise your hand every time you hear a tone. The examiner sounds a tone that you easily hear, then one that is a bit softer, then softer still, until you cannot hear it anymore. After a time you begin to think that you can hear the tone again, then there's one that is a bit louder, then another that's louder still, and so on. The examiner in this case is using the **method of limits,** which alternates what are called "descending" and "ascending" trials. On a descending trial, the first stimulus is well above threshold; subsequent stimuli gradually decrease in intensity until they are no longer detected. On ascending trials, the first stimulus is below threshold, and with subsequent stimuli the intensity is gradually increased. Overall threshold is determined by averaging the intensity level at which the tone is just barely detected during ascending trials and just barely lost on descending trials.

Two other ways of establishing thresholds are the method of constant stimuli and the method of adjustment. In a hearing test using the **method of constant stimuli,** the intensity of a stimulus on any given trial is determined randomly. This procedure avoids some of the guessing and anticipating that can occur with the method of limits. In the **method of adjustment,** the subject controls the stimulus intensity directly and is told to adjust it until the stimulus is just barely detectable or just barely different from a second stimulus.

Finally, operant methods have been used to study thresholds in animals. For instance, discrimination procedures can be used. If an animal can learn to bar press when hearing tone 1 but not to press when hearing tone 2, then it must be able to distinguish between the tones. If it cannot learn the discrimination, it probably cannot tell the difference between the tones.

Psychophysics and Small N

If you think about these methods for a minute, you'll see why psychophysics research almost always uses a small number of participants. First, few participants are required in most psychophysics studies because most people have very similar sensory systems. Because individual differences are so small, results found with just a few participants can be easily generalized to others. As always, of course, replication confirms the verdict.

The second reason for using small N designs in psychophysics relates back to the distinction between within-subjects and between-subjects factors. Establishing thresholds requires the use of a within-subjects design in which each person is exposed to a large number of stimulus intensities. It makes no sense to give one subject stimulus 1, another subject stimulus 2, and so on, and then calculate some average threshold for a large group of people. Rather, thresholds need to be established within single individuals, and they can only be established by taking large numbers of trials over a range of stimuli for a single individual. Thus, rather than taking a few measurements for many individuals, psychophysics researchers take many measurements for just a few individuals. Furthermore, there's no point wasting a participant's time by presenting only one or a few stimuli per person; a single trial takes only a few seconds. Who wants to do a study that requires 5 minutes to set up the equipment, another 5 minutes to instruct the participant, perhaps 10 minutes to debrief the participant, and 30 *seconds* to actually collect data?

A third and related reason why psychophysics research uses small N studies has to do with control. Most threshold research is done under highly controlled laboratory conditions. Thus, on each trial, the data obtained will be less affected by error variance than might be the case, say, in a social psychology experiment on helping behavior. This, of course, is reminiscent of Skinner again: if conditions are controlled, order will follow.

This chapter has introduced you to a tradition of research in psychology that has deep roots and vigorous advocates. It is an approach ideally stuited for some circumstances, such as for studying the effects of reinforcement contingencies on behavior and for determining sensory thresholds. It may be less suited for other situations that may require between-subjects designs or include a wider range of dependent measures. The next chapter completes our survey of methods by examining approaches that are primarily descriptive.

Chapter Summary

Research in Psychology Began with Small N

Before the advent of sophisticated statistical tools, research in psychology featured studies using a single individual or at most a small number of persons, and the experimenter was usually one of them. In studies with more than one participant, the additional subjects served the purpose of replication. That is, their data were presented individually and seldom summarized as an average score for a group.

Reasons for Small N Designs

Modern advocates of research featuring one or just a few participants argue that grouping data can obscure individual performance and can mislead the researcher about the phenomenon being investigated. Second, large numbers of participants may not be available when certain phenomena are studied (e.g., a rare mental disorder). A third argument derives from Skinner's belief that the best way to understand, predict, and control behavior is to study individuals intensively. He argued that if environmental circumstances were controlled sufficiently, predictable behavior would occur and could be measured.

Small N Designs in Applied Behavior Analysis

Applied behavior analysis is the name given to the application of behavioral principles to change human behavior, often in a clinical setting. The designs used are sometimes referred to as single-subject designs. The most common approach is to use some form of withdrawal design in which a baseline measure of behavior is taken before a treatment program is introduced. After a time, the therapy is removed (withdrawn) and then reinstated (A–B–A–B design). Evidence for the effectiveness of the treatment is inferred if the behavior to be changed is immediately affected by these reversals. Other single-subject designs include multiple baseline designs, used when reversals aren't feasible, and changing criterion designs, which gradually shape some target behavior that cannot be achieved immediately.

Psychophysics

In addition to research in the operant tradition, there are other varieties of small N research. The best example is psychophysics, the study of the relationships between the physical stimulus and the perceptual reaction to it. Traditional psychophysics research focused on the identification of absolute and difference thresholds; this work dates from the very beginnings of experimental psychology's history. Fechner first identified three methods that are still used today: the method of limits, the method of constant stimuli, and the method of adjustment. Modern psychophysics, influenced by signal detection theory, examines thresholds in the context of both the observer's basic perceptual abilities and nonperceptual factors such as decision criteria.

Chapter Review

Multiple Choice

1. Which of the following is true about Dressler's study of facial vision?
   a. it shows that grouping the data from several participants can produce a result that does not reflect the behavior of any single individual
   b. it is an early example of a small N design in which the additional participants served the purpose of replication
   c. it is an example of the psychophysics method of limits
   d. it is an exception to the fact that in psychology's early years, small N designs were the rule

2. All of the following are arguments typically made by those in favor of using small N designs *except:*
   a. because of individual differences, inferential statistics are needed to determine if the independent variable is responsible for changes in the dependent variable
   b. sometimes when data from many participants are averaged, the picture that emerges does not reflect the behavior of any single individual
   c. research on relatively rare psychological phenomena may not be possible except by using a small N design
   d. if the precise control of conditions yields orderly behavior, then the emphasis should be on controlling environmental conditions for single organisms rather than on achieving statistical control

3. When is a multiple baseline design preferred over an A–B–A–B design?
   a. when the target behavior cannot be reached all at once
   b. when the goal is to compare two different treatment strategies in the same participant
   c. when withdrawing treatment is not feasible for some reason
   d. when the goal is to study more than a single individual

4. A researcher in an institution for retarded children wishes to develop and evaluate a treatment program that would get the children to make their beds properly each morning. Two approaches are recommended by the staff. One involves a token economy system, in which points can be earned and traded for other reinforcers. The second approach relies on the use of staff attention as a reinforcer, in which bed making is reinforced by giving the child extra attention. To evaluate the relative effectiveness of these strategies, what would be the best design to use?
   a. alternating treatments design
   b. withdrawal design
   c. multiple baseline design
   d. changing criterion design

5. Why is an A–B–A–B design preferred over an A–B–A design?
   a. it isn't; the A–B–A design is more parsimonious because it takes less time
   b. because it includes a withdrawal of treatment

c. because it compares contingent with noncontingent reinforcement
d. because it evaluates the treatment effect twice rather than once

Short Essay

1. Describe Dressler's facial vision study, describe how the results were presented, and explain why he used three participants instead of just one.

2. Explain why Thorndike's research is a good illustration of the principle of parsimony.

3. Use the discrimination learning example to illustrate how grouped data summaries can mask what individual participants are doing in a study.

4. Use the behavior of a rat bar-pressing in a Skinner box to illustrate Skinner's claim that behavior can be predicted and controlled if three main factors are known.

5. What is meant by a schedule of reinforcement? Describe two examples.

6. Skinner's work is said to reflect the "technological ideal." Explain.

7. Describe the three essential elements of every single-subject design.

8. Describe the essential features of a withdrawal design and distinguish between these designs: A–B–A, A–B–A–B, A–B–C–B.

9. Define a multiple baseline design, explain when it is preferred over a withdrawal design, and describe three varieties of it.

10. Use the case study on exercising for obese and nonobese boys as a way of describing the main features of a changing criterion design. Be sure to work the term "shaping" into your answer.

11. Describe any three ways in which single-subject designs have been criticized.

12. Distinguish between absolute and difference thresholds and distinguish between Fechner's three methods for determining thresholds.

Applications Exercises

Exercise 11.1.—Designing Self-Improvement Programs

Design a changing criterion program for one of the following self-improvement projects. For each project, be sure to define the target behavior(s) operationally, identify what you would use as reinforcement, and indicate what each successive criterion would be.

1. Increase productive study time
2. Develop an exercise program
3. Change to healthier eating behaviors
4. Improve time management

Exercise 11.2.—Hypothetical Outcomes of Applied Behavior Analyses

For each of the following, sketch hypothetical graphs in the single subject style that illustrate each of the alternative outcomes.

1. A–B–C–B design:
    a. reinforcement works, but only if it is made contingent on specific behaviors
    b. reinforcement works regardless of whether or not it is made contingent on specific behaviors

2. A–A_1–B–A_1–B design:
    a. the drug worked
    b. cannot tell if the drug worked or not; could have been a placebo effect

3. multiple baseline across three settings:
    a. the treatment program works
    b. cannot discount a history or maturation effect

4. A–B–A–B design
    a. the treatment program works
    b. hard to tell if the program brought about the change or if some other factor such as maturation was responsible

Exercise 11.3.—Depicting the Results of Applied Behavior Analyses

For each of the following descriptions and data sets, prepare a graph in the single-subject style that would accurately portray the results. Write a brief conclusion.

1. An A–B–A–B design was used to reduce the number of interruptions made in class by a child whose behavior was disrupting his second-grade class. During treatment, the teacher was instructed to ignore the child's interruptions and to pay special attention to the child when he was behaving productively (e.g., doing class work). The number of interruptions per 1-hour recording session were as follows:
    a. during first A: 12, 12, 7, 6, 6, 9, 8, 10, 9, 11
    b. during first B: 9, 8, 9, 4, 3, 2, 2, 1, 4, 2
    c. during second A: 4, 5, 10, 6, 12, 10, 10, 10, 12, 9
    d. during second B: 9, 9, 2, 1, 1, 1, 0, 3, 4, 1

2. A multiple baseline across persons design was used to improve the foul shooting percentage of three basketball players during practices. A system was used in which successful shots earned points that could later be used to obtain more substantial reinforcers. Each of the following numbers represents the number of foul shots made for each 50 attempted. The numbers that are underlined are baseline data.

    Player 1: 32, 29, 38, 31, 33, 44, 36, 37, 44, 41, 40, 38, 45, 42, 40, 44
    Player 2: 30, 32, 28, 30, 30, 40, 35, 32, 33, 38, 40, 45, 44, 44, 42, 44
    Player 3: 22, 28, 29, 28, 26, 25, 22, 26, 21, 21, 23, 24, 35, 39, 40, 39

CHAPTER 12

Descriptive Research Methods

Preview & Chapter Objectives

In this final chapter, we will examine methods for doing research in psychology that could collectively be called descriptive. That is, their major purpose is to provide accurate descriptions of the interrelationships among individuals and their environments. They are sometimes the only approach that circumstances permit, and in general, they can be a rich source of hypotheses for further study. They often rely on qualitative analysis of the phenomena being studied, but they can also include sophisticated quantitative analysis. The methods to be considered include observational research, survey research, case studies, and archival research. When you finish this chapter, you should be able to:

- Distinguish between naturalistic and participant observation.
- Articulate the problems that can occur in observational research (e.g., control, bias, reactivity, and ethics) and how researchers address those problems.

- Describe three different types of survey research and list the advantages and disadvantages of each.
- Explain the problems (e.g., social desirability bias, item wording) that can make it difficult to interpret survey data.
- Describe two varieties of case studies and evaluate the adequacy of case study research.
- Describe the essential features of archival research and evaluate this research strategy.

As you can tell from the overall structure of this text, center stage has been occupied by the experimental method. It was the direct focus of attention in Chapters 5 through 8, and the earlier chapters, especially Chapter 3, led up to it. As you recall, the starring role for the experiment derives from its potential to yield cause-and-effect conclusions, at least within the constraints of the way in which research psychologists view causality (see p. 23–24). In the last three chapters, you have encountered methods that some traditionalists might relegate to supporting role status because the conclusions drawn from them are weaker than those drawn from experiments. However, we've seen that while drawing causal conclusions from correlational, quasi-experimental, and small N studies can be problematic, these methods are essential if we are to understand behavior fully. The same can be said about the methods you're about to encounter in this chapter. They each have weaknesses, but they are indispensable members of the cast.

Observational Research

As you know from the discussion of psychology's goals in Chapter 1, behavior cannot be predicted, controlled, or explained unless it is first described accurately. The major purpose of observational research is to contribute this descriptive information; these studies provide in-depth accounts of individuals or groups of individuals as they behave naturally in some specific setting.

Varieties of Observational Research

Observational research with the goal of describing behavior can be classified along two dimensions. First, studies vary in terms of the degree of experimenter involvement with participants. Sometimes the researcher does not interact in any substantial way with the group being observed; at other times the researcher may even become a member of the group being studied. These types of studies are called "naturalistic observation" and "participant observation," respectively. Second, observational researchers impose varying degrees of structure on the setting being observed. This can range from "zero," when the researcher simply enters some environment and observes behavior unobtrusively, to "quite a bit," when the researcher creates a structured setting and observes what occurs in it. Differing degrees of structure can exist in both naturalistic and participant observation studies.

Naturalistic Observation

In a **naturalistic observation** study, an attempt is made to study the behaviors of people or animals as they act in their everyday environments. Settings for naturalistic observation studies range from preschools to the African rain forest, and the subjects observed have included humans of all ages and animals of virtually every species. In some cases, semiartificial environments are sufficiently "natural" for the research to be considered a naturalistic observation. Studying animal behavior in modern zoos, which often simulates the animals' normal environment to a remarkable degree, is an example.

In some naturalistic studies the observer is hidden from those being observed. In a study of sharing behavior among preschoolers, for example, observers may be in the next room, viewing the children through a two-way mirror (the observers can see through it; to the child it appears to be a mirror). In a mall, an observer studying the mating rituals of the suburban adolescent could simply sit on a bench in a strategic location. In other studies, the observer may not be present at all; increasingly, naturalistic observation studies are being conducted with the aid of video recorders. The films are viewed later and scored for the behaviors being investigated.

In naturalistic observations of animals, it is often impossible for the observer to remain hidden—the animals quickly sense the presence of an outsider. Under these circumstances, the observer typically makes no attempt to hide. Rather, it is hoped that after a period of time, the animals will become so habituated to the observer that they will behave normally. This is a strategy borrowed from the field of anthropology, in which field workers spend long periods of time living among native members of remote cultures.

Participant Observation

Occasionally, the researcher will join a group being observed, thus making the study a **participant observation.** Its chief virtue is its power to get the investigator as close to the action as possible. Being a participating member of the group can give the researcher firsthand insights that remain hidden to a more remote observer.

One of psychology's classic studies involved participant observation. In it, a small group of social psychologists joined a religious cult in order to examine the kinds of thinking that characterized its members. In particular, they examined this empirical question: If you publicly prophesize the end of the world and the world fails to end, how do you deal with your failed prophecy? The answer was surprising enough to contribute to the development of one of social psychology's best-known theories—the theory of cognitive dissonance. To learn more about this classic study of what happens when prophecy fails, read Box 12.1.

Evaluating Observational Methods

The researcher using observational methods must be prepared to counter several problems, including the absence of control, the possibilities of observer bias and subject reactivity, and the ethical dilemmas associated with the issues of invasion of privacy and informed consent.

Box 12.1

CLASSIC STUDIES—When Prophecy Fails

One of social psychology's dominant theories in the 1960s and 1970s was the theory of cognitive dissonance, developed by Leon Festinger. In general, it held that when we experience thoughts that contradict each other, we will be uncomfortable (i.e., we will experience cognitive dissonance) and we will be motivated to reduce the dissonance by convincing ourselves that everything is fine. One prediction derived from the theory is that if we exert a tremendous effort in some way and the outcome is not what we initially expected, we will need to convince ourselves that the effort was nonetheless worthwhile. Festinger got the chance to test the prediction after encountering a news story with the following headline (Festinger, Riecken, & Schachter, 1956, p. 30):

Prophecy from Planet. Clarion Call to City: Flee That Flood.

It'll Swamp Us on Dec. 21, Outer Space Tells Suburbanite

The story described how a certain Mrs. Keetch had predicted a flood that would destroy most of North America in late December. How did she know? She believed she was in direct contact with aliens from a planet called Clarion who had been visiting Earth in their flying saucers and had seen fault lines that were about to rupture and open the floodgates. Mrs. Keetch gathered a small group of followers, in effect a religious cult, and they became devoted to convincing the world to repent of their sins before it was too late (and time was running out; the story appeared just 4 months before the predicted catastrophe).

Festinger guessed the flood would not occur, so he became interested in how Mrs. Keetch and the group would react during the aftermath of a failed prophecy. He decided to see firsthand. Over the next several weeks, along with two colleagues and five hired observers, Festinger joined the group as a participant observer. What transpired is described in a delightful book (Festinger et al., 1956) with the same title as this box. There are several points worth noting from a methodological standpoint.

First, recording the data created a number of problems. The observers did not want to reveal their true purpose, so they could hardly take notes during the meetings at Mrs. Keetch's house. Hence, they found it necessary to rely on memory more than they would have liked. The problem was overcome to some degree when they hit on the idea of using the bathroom as a place to write down as much of their narrative data as they could. A second problem was reactivity (look ahead to p. 393). At no point did they believe their true purpose was known to the group, but they were very concerned that their presence strengthened certain of the group's beliefs. Because so many new people seemed to be joining the group over a short period of time, Mrs. Keetch believed (and therefore the group believed) that the mass joining was a "sign from above" that the flood prophecy was correct. Two of the observers were believed by the group to have been "'sent' by the Guardians" (p. 242), the residents of Clarion, and one observer was actually believed to be *from* Clarion. Hence, the participant observers probably strengthened the convictions of Mrs. Keetch's small group, the effects of which are difficult to assess. This reactivity also poses an ethical dilemma. By strengthening the group's convictions, it could be argued that Festinger and his colleagues contributed to their "pathology."

As you know because you're reading this now, the world didn't end that December 21 in the 1950s. It was not the only failed prophecy. Mrs. Keetch also told the group that the Guardians would send a spaceship that would land in her backyard on December 17 to carry them to safety. Of course, the ship didn't arrive and the world didn't end 4 days later. Did the group become discouraged, give up, call Mrs. Keetch insane, and return to their normal lives? No. In fact, most of them became even *more* vigorous in their proselytizing. Apparently, in order to justify their efforts, they convinced themselves that their work had prevented the catastrophe—the group "spread so much light that God had saved the world from destruction" (p. 169). Hence rather than quitting after a prophecy fails, one's commitment can actually be strengthened.

Absence of Control

Some degree of control occurs in observational studies that are structured (see Case Study 32, page 397), but in general, the observational researcher must take what circumstances provide. Because of this lack of control, the conclusions drawn from observational studies must be drawn very carefully. If an observer records that child A picks up a toy and shortly thereafter child B picks up a duplicate of the same toy, does it mean that B is imitating A? Perhaps, but other interpretations are possible, the most obvious one being that the toy is simply attractive. When reading accounts of observational research, you won't encounter sentences like "X caused Y to occur."

On the other hand, observational research can often serve the purpose of falsification, an important strategy for theory testing. An observation consistent with theoretical expectations provides useful inductive support, but an observation that contradicts a theory is even more informative. One contradiction won't disprove a theory, as you recall from Chapter 3, but it can certainly call it into question. For example, an influential theory of animal aggression in the 1960s (Lorenz, 1966) held that fighting between members of the same species was hardly ever fatal to the combatants (except for humans). For years, those studying aggression argued over the reasons why human aggression seemed to be so different from and so much worse than animal aggression. However, explaining the difference presupposes that the difference truly exists; observational research, however, has raised serious questions about the alleged nonfatality of animal aggression. In conflicts over territory among chimpanzees, for example, something analogous to "border wars" has been observed (Goodall, 1978). If a lone chimp from one group encounters several chimps from another group, the lone chimp will almost certainly be attacked and killed. Such a finding raises serious questions about Lorenz's claim that nonhuman aggression is seldom if ever fatal.

FIGURE 12.1 Chimpanzees using tools. An adult female is eating a nut, which she has just cracked with a stone hammer while her son inspects the nut shell. Mother chimpanzees share many of their cracked nuts with their offspring. Through this sharing, mother chimpanzees teach their offspring how to use tools to open nuts.

(From Boesch-Achermann & Boesch, 1993)

In a more recent example, Boesch-Achermann and Boesch (1993) observed several instances of parent chimpanzees teaching their offspring how to use tools (a hammer/anvil operation) to open several varieties of nuts (see Figure 12.1). This is an important finding that questioned earlier beliefs. As the researchers put it:

> Recent critical reviews of animal learning processes have denied that animals have the ability to imitate, but the teaching instances we observed would have no functional role if the chimpanzees did not have an imitative capacity. Many people still consider pedagogy one of the uniquely human attributes; our observations of chimpanzees indicate otherwise. (p. 20)

Despite control difficulties, then, observational research can provide important and useful information. It can call some ideas into question, and it can also be a fruitful source of hypotheses for further study. Hence, the Boesch-Achermann and Boesch study questioned prior claims about the teaching abilities of chimps; it also could lead to further research on the teaching capacities of nonhuman primates. For instance, could chimpanzees in captivity who have learned an operant task teach it to their offspring?

Observer Bias

A second problem for those doing observational research comes in the form of experimenter bias. In Chapter 6 (pp. 201–203), you learned that when experimenters expect certain outcomes to occur, they might act in ways that could bring about such a result. In observational research, **observer bias** means having preconceived ideas about what will be observed and having those ideas color one's observations. For example, consider what might happen if someone is studying aggression in preschoolers and believes from the outset that little boys will be more aggressive than little girls. For that observer, the exact same ambiguous behavior could be scored as aggressive if a boy did it but not aggressive if performed by a girl. Similarly, in an animal study, observers with different beliefs about whether animals can be altruistic might interpret certain ambiguous behaviors differently. Biasing can also occur because observational studies can potentially collect huge amounts of information. Deciding what to observe invariably involves reducing this information to a manageable size, and the choices about what to select and what to omit can be affected by preconceived beliefs.

Biasing effects can be reduced significantly by using good operational definitions and by giving observers some training in identifying the precisely defined target behaviors. When actually making the observations, **behavior checklists** are normally used. These are lists of predefined behaviors that observers are trained to spot. Consider, for example, the care taken in a study that observed the behavior of pizza deliverers, whose driving accident rate is three times the national average. Ludwig and Geller (1997) used a checklist "developed over a decade of driver observations and over 2 years of observing pizza deliverers" (p. 254). Part of the list included observations of driver behavior while turning on a main road from an intersection near the pizza shop. There was a stop sign there, and the behaviors were placed into three categories: a complete stop, a "slow rolling advance," and a "fast rolling advance." Each had its own definition; for instance, the slow rolling advance was defined as when the vehicle moved through the stop sign at "approximately the walking speed of an adult" (p. 255). Observers also recorded oncoming traffic conditions, whether the driver used a directional signal, and whether the driver wore a seat belt.

In addition to defining behaviors with some precision, another way to control for observer bias is to have several observers present and see if their records match. This you might recognize as a form of reliability; in this case it is called **interobserver reliability,** usually measured in terms of the percentage of times that observers agree. Of course, both observers could be biased in exactly the same way, but a combination of checklists, observer training, and agreement among several observers generally controls bias. Bias also can be reduced to the extent that procedures are mechanized. We've already seen that videotaping allows for increased objectivity.

Finally, bias can be reduced by introducing various sampling procedures for systematically selecting a subset of the available information for observation and analysis. For example, a procedure called **time sampling** is sometimes used in observational studies. Rather than trying to maintain a continuous record of everything occurring, behavior is sampled at predefined times and only at those times. These times can be selected according to some rule or they may be randomly selected. Similarly, **event sampling** selects only a specific set of events for observation; others are ignored. These procedures were used in Case Study 31 (p. 395).

Subject Reactivity

Think about all of the things you do in a typical day. Would you do all of them in exactly the same way if you knew you were being observed? Probably not. In all likelihood, you would show **reactivity;** that is, your behavior would be influenced by the knowledge that it was being recorded. Obviously, this problem can occur in observational research and is the reason for the popularity of devices like two-way mirrors. The problem also exists when animals are the subjects of observation and the observers cannot hide. As mentioned earlier, researchers assume that after a period of time the animals will become accustomed to the presence of outsiders, but it is difficult to evaluate the extent to which this occurs.

Reactivity can be reduced by using **unobtrusive measures.** These are any measures taken of behavior, either directly or indirectly, when the subject is unaware of the measurement being made. Direct unobtrusive measures include hidden video or audio recordings or behavior samples collected by hidden observers. Indirect unobtrusive measures record events and outcomes that one assumes have resulted from certain behaviors even though the behaviors themselves have not been observed. Webb, Campbell, Schwartz, Sechrest, and Grove (1981) describe a number of these indirect measures and they can be quite creative. Here's just a sample:

- ✓ contents of trash to study eating and drinking habits
- ✓ accumulation of dust on library books as an indication of usage
- ✓ degree of wear on floor coverings placed in strategic locations to study foot traffic patterns
- ✓ analysis of political bumper stickers in an election year

Ethics

As I am sure you have recognized by now, reducing reactivity inevitably raises the ethical problems of invading privacy and lack of informed consent. Wouldn't you be a bit disturbed to discover that researchers were hiding under the bed in your dorm, keeping track of everything you said and did? Believe it or not, that study has already been done (Henle & Hubbell, 1938), although quite clearly it would not gain IRB approval today.

In Box 3.1 (p. 76), I pointed out that some researchers are hesitant to conduct research in the field because of concerns over privacy rights. However, observational research is generally condoned by the APA's ethics code (1992), provided that certain safeguards are in place. For example, informed consent of participants is not considered essential if behavior is studied in public environments (as opposed to the privacy of one's dorm room), people are not interfered with in any way, and confidentiality is maintained. The standards related to observational research are reprinted in Table 12.1.

Notice that in two places in the table, in Standards 6.12 and 6.13, it is stated that informed consent is not required under certain circumstances for naturalistic observation. But what about participant observations? You might have been concerned about the lack of consent in Festinger's failed prophecy study (Box 12.1). With good reason, Festinger believed that he and his colleagues would never have been able to join the group if normal consent procedures had been followed, but there is some question about whether an IRB would approve such a study today. Participant observation is a common method among those doing qualitative research, and informed consent of the group being observed from within is now routine and its absence requires a strong justification (Taylor & Bogdan, 1998).

To conclude this section on observational research, consider the following two observational studies that illustrate the second dimension described earlier—the degree of structure created by the researcher. The first is purely observational, without any direct intervention on the part of the researchers; the second is more highly structured.

TABLE 12.1 *APA Ethical Code and Observational Research*

In addition to the general guidelines for research, the following standards from the APA's 1992 code of ethics are especially relevant to observational research:

Standard 1.14. Avoiding Harm

Psychologists take reasonable steps to avoid harming their ... research participants ... and to minimize harm where it is foreseeable and unavoidable.

Standard 5.03. Minimizing Intrusions on Privacy

(a) In order to minimize intrusions on privacy, psychologists include in written and oral reports, consultations, and the like, only information germane to the purpose for which the communication was made.

(b) Psychologists discuss confidential information ... or evaluative data concerning research participants ... only for appropriate scientific or professional purposes and only with persons clearly concerned with such matters.

Standard 5.08. Use of Confidential Information for Didactic or Other Purposes

(a) Psychologists do not disclose in their writings, lectures, or other public media, confidential, personally identifiable information concerning their ... research participants ... unless [they have] consented in writing or unless there is other ethical or legal authorization for doing so.

(b) Ordinarily, in such scientific and professional presentations, psychologists disguise confidential information concerning such persons ... so that they are not individually identifiable...

Standard 6.12. Dispensing with Informed Consent

Before determining that planned research (such as research involving only anonymous questionnaires, naturalistic observations, or certain kinds of archival research) does not require the informed consent of research participants, psychologists consider applicable regulations and institutional review board requirements, and they consult with colleagues as appropriate.

Standard 6.13. Informed Consent in Research Filming or Recording

Psychologists obtain informed consent from research participants prior to filming or recording them in any form, unless the research involves simply naturalistic observations in public places and it is not anticipated that the recording will be used in a manner that could cause personal identification or harm.

Source: American Psychological Association (1992).

Case Study 31—Naturalistic Observations of Touching

When males and females are together in public places, they often are observed touching each other. Who is more likely to initiate the touching, males or females? Are there gender differences in the types of touching that occur? Are there age differences in touching? These and other questions were investigated by Hall and Veccia (1990), using naturalistic observations of couples in public places. Their work nicely illustrates the complexities of running a naturalistic observational study.

Hall and Veccia trained five observers to make detailed yet unobtrusive records of mixed-sex and same-sex touching in a variety of public places ranging from airports to subways to malls, all in the Boston area. As in any observational study, they first had to face the problem of operational definitions. What exactly constitutes a touch? When should recording begin and end? Exactly what should be recorded in each observation?

Observers were equipped with a handheld tape recorder for their descriptions and a small timing device that beeped every 10 seconds. To prevent others from hearing these signals (i.e., to remain unobtrusive), observers listened through earphones. The interval between beeps was considered a recording interval, during which several things were observed about a specific couple in view. First, their ages (by decade) were estimated; then it was noted whether or not they were touching at the beginning of the interval, whether touching commenced during the interval, or whether no touching at all occurred. If touching occurred, the body parts involved and the form of touching (e.g., hand-holding) were described. Finally, the person initiating the touch was identified. For mixed-sex pairs, touches were coded as being initiated either by males (MF touch) or females (FM). This was not always possible, especially for touches already in progress at the start of an interval, but interobserver reliability was high (91% agreement).

When the participants being observed were in motion (e.g., moving through a mall), the observers used a time sampling technique to select subject pairs. Once an initial pair was selected and their behavior recorded during a 10-second recording interval, another 10 seconds was allowed to pass before another couple was selected. A form of event sampling was also used; the couple selected after the end of 10 seconds was the one closest to a predefined landmark.

Based on some earlier research, Hall and Veccia thought that in mixed-sex pairs, males would be more likely to initiate touches than females, perhaps because of a gender difference in the need for power or control. To their surprise, they found no differences: MF touches equaled FM touches overall. A closer analysis yielded some interesting outcomes, however. For example, Table 12.2 shows a large age effect. For younger couples, especially those under age 30, MF touches were indeed more frequent. In older couples, however, the reverse was true—the female was more likely to initiate the touch. The effect is open to several interpretations, but one possibility

TABLE 12.2   *Age Differences in Touching in Mixed-Sex Pairs*

Age of dyad	No. of touches		Percent of touches	
	MF	FM	MF	FM
Teens	16	6	73	27
20s	58	46	56	44
30s	28	29	49	51
40+	7	26	21	79

Note: MF = male-initiated touch; FM = female-initiated touch.

Source: Adapted from Hall and Veccia (1990), Table 6.

suggested by Hall and Veccia is that males may feel a greater need to assert power and control in the early stages of a relationship; older couples are more likely to have been in a relationship for a longer time. (Of course, it also could be that in older couples, the FM touching amounts to an elbow to the ribs, resulting from the male's wistful observing of the touching patterns among younger couples.)

Another interesting difference found by Hall and Veccia concerned the form of the touching. Although there were no significant gender differences in touches initiated by the hand, there were differences in touches defined as "arm around" and "arms linked." Males were more likely to use the former and females the latter.

Case Study 32—Observing Altruism in Children

A study by Peterson, Ridley-Johnson, and Carter (1984) is an interesting example of an observational study that adds a structured element to a naturalistic observation. They were interested in helping behavior among school children, a phenomenon that was estimated from prior observations to occur spontaneously no more than once or twice per hour. Because it occurs so infrequently, the researchers decided to create a situation in which helping behavior would be more likely to occur. Thus, one important reason to introduce greater structure into an observational study is to increase the frequency of otherwise rare events.

The structure was created by telling the children they would each have a turn wearing a "supersuit," a "smock of royal blue with a red satin star in the middle of the chest" (Peterson et al., 1984, p. 237). It was fastened with one large button at the back of the neck; pilot testing showed that buttoning it usually required the help of a second person. During free play periods, children took turns wearing the suit, with the order determined by drawing names from a jar. Each child had about 4 minutes to wear the supersuit.

The observations were videotaped, and two observers independently rated the tapes for helping behavior. Interobserver reliability was high: they agreed more than 90% of the time. The coding scheme for defining the behaviors operationally broke them into two general categories: the "donor" behaviors exhibited by potential helpers and the "recipient" behaviors of those wearing the suit. An example of a donor behavior was "*spontaneous helping*—without any direct verbal or physical prompt, the donor offers verbally or physically to fasten the button on the supersuit" (p. 237; italics in the original). An example of a recipient behavior was "*requesting help*—recipient verbally asks for help … or approaches the donor, turns so the button at the back is toward the potential donor, and gestures toward it" (p. 238; italics in the original).

The results? Of 56 opportunities for help, spontaneous helping occurred 32 times and prompted helping occurred 13 times. More interesting, however, was the way in which recipients responded to being helped. Surprisingly, Peterson et al. found that children rarely reinforced others for helping. In fact, "more child recipients actually gave negative consequences (e.g., 'go away' and a shove in response to another child's attempt to help fasten the suit) than positive consequences for helping" (p. 238)! Also, very little reciprocal help (child A helps child B and child B subsequently helps child A) was observed.

Peterson et al. also asked each child to rate the social competence of classmates, and it was determined that most of the helping was done by the most socially competent children. This rating procedure is an example of how an observational study can add elements of other methods. In this case, the added element involved a type of survey, which brings us to that topic.

Survey Research

Survey research is based on the simple idea that if you want to find out what people think about some topic, just ask them. That is, a **survey** is a structured set of questions or statements given to a group of people in order to measure their attitudes, beliefs, values, or tendencies to act. Over the years, people have responded to surveys assessing everything from political preferences to favorite sexual activities.

Unlike most of the methods described in this text, surveying usually requires careful attention to sampling procedures. As you recall from Chapter 4 (and a quick review of the section on sampling, pp. 121–125, is a good idea), researchers sometimes try to estimate a specific feature (e.g., political preference) of a large category of people, a population, based on the data collected from just a small number of people, the sample. In order for survey results to be valid, the sample must reflect the same properties as the population; that is, the sample must be **representative.** Hence, with the survey method, the adequacy of the conclusions drawn depends in part on the quality of the sampling procedures.

Varieties of Survey Methods

There are three major techniques for collecting survey data. Each has its own strengths and weaknesses, both in terms of sampling and otherwise. Survey data are sometimes collected through direct, face-to-face interviews, sometimes through written questionnaires, sometimes through telephone interviews, and occasionally through some combination of the three.

Interviews

You have undoubtedly heard of the Kinsey Report, perhaps the most famous sex survey of all time. Completed in the years following World War II, it resulted from detailed, face-to-face interviews with thousands of men and women and yielded two large books on sexual behavior in America, one for men (Kinsey, Pomeroy, & Martin, 1948) and one for women (Kinsey, Pomeroy, Martin, & Gebhard, 1953). Although you might think that Kinsey's **interview survey** format might have prevented people from describing the intimate details of their sexual attitudes and behaviors, especially considering the historical era in which the studies were done, this apparently did not occur. In fact, conservative postwar America was shocked by the repeated revelations of premarital sex, masturbation, and adultery. The books, although written in dry academic prose and loaded with tables and bar graphs, nonetheless reached best-seller status and made Kinsey a controversial figure. Accused by some of contributing to a moral decline and even of being a Communist, he was regarded by others as a pioneer in the scientific study of an important aspect of human behavior (Christenson, 1971).

The interview format for surveying has the advantages of being comprehensive and of yielding highly detailed information. Even though the interviewer typically asks a standard set of questions, the skilled interviewer is able to elicit considerable information through follow-up questions or probes. Having an interviewer present also reduces the problem of unclear questions; the interviewer can clarify on the spot. Sampling is sometimes a problem because, in many cases, sizable segments of the population may not be included if they refuse to be interviewed, cannot be located, or live in an area the interviewer would prefer to avoid. For example, the poor are often underrepresented in national surveys using the interview format. Interviews can occur in a group format—the focus groups described in Chapter 10 (p. 339) are an example.

Other problems with the interview approach are cost, logistics, and interviewer bias. Interviewers need to be hired and trained, travel expenses can be substantial, and interviews might be restricted to a fairly small geographic area because of the logistical problems of sending interviewers long distances. And despite training, there is always the possibility that interviewer bias can affect the responses given in the face-to-face setting. For example, cross-race bias may exist, resulting in systematic differences between interviews with members of one's own race and members of other races.

The careful researcher will develop a training program to standardize the interview process as much as possible, and sometimes certain types of interviewers may be trained for specific purposes. For example, middle-aged female interviewers may elicit more cooperation in an interview survey of retired women than young male interviewers, who may not even get past the door (van Kammen & Stouthamer-Loeber, 1998)

Written Surveys

The second type of survey format is the paper-and-pencil test or **written survey.** These are found in a number of formats but usually involve asking participants whether they agree or disagree with a series of statements or questions. When questions are asked, they can be either open ended or closed. An **open-ended question** requires a response involving more than just a yes or no answer; participants must provide descriptive information. A **closed question** can be answered with a yes or a no or by choosing a single response from among several alternatives. To illustrate the difference, consider these two ways of asking about school financing:

Open: How do you think we should finance public education?

Closed: Do you think that property taxes should be used to finance public education?

Written surveys with closed questions often use an interval scale for measuring the responses. As you recall from Chapter 4, with an interval scale there is no true zero point, but the intervals between points on the scale are assumed to be equal. The most common type of interval scale used in surveys is the so-called Likert scale (after the person who invented it, Rensis Likert). A typical Likert scale has anywhere from 5 to 9 distinct points on it, with each point reflecting a score on the continuum. For example, on a survey of attitudes toward televised coverage of news, participants might be asked to indicate how much they agree with a series of statements according to a 5-point scale. A sample item might look like this:

> The person anchoring a news show should have at least five years of experience as a professional journalist.

SD D U A SA

Respondents circle the point on the scale that indicates what they believe. "SD" stands for "strongly disagree," "D" for "disagree," "U" for "undecided," and so on. These points could then be converted to a 5-point scale (SD = 1, D = 2, etc.), and scores from several items dealing with the same issue could be combined.

Written surveys can be sent through the mail, as you know because you've probably thrown a few away, or they can be administered in a group setting. Obviously, the percentage of people filling out and handing in the survey will be higher with the latter procedure. Return rate is often a problem for mailed surveys. Return rates of 85% or higher are considered excellent (and rare), 70–85% very good, and 60–70% more or less acceptable (Mangione, 1998). Anything below 60% makes researchers very nervous about whether the data are representative. Another problem with rate of return occurs when those who return surveys differ in some important way from those who don't return them, a problem called **nonresponse bias** (Rogelberg & Luong, 1998). When this happens, drawing a conclusion about a population is risky at best.

The best chance for a decent return rate for a mail survey occurs if (a) the survey is brief, easy to fill out, and includes mostly closed questions, with open-ended questions included only as options, (b) the form starts with relatively interesting questions and leaves the boring items (i.e., demographic information) until the end, (c) before the survey is sent out, participants are notified that a survey is on the way, and that their help will be greatly appreciated, (d) nonresponse triggers follow-up reminders, a second mailing of the survey, and perhaps even a phone request to fill out the form, (e) the entire package is highly professional in appearance, with a cover letter signed by a real person instead of a machine, and (f) the recipient has no reason to think the survey is merely step one in a sales pitch. Return rates can also be improved by including a small gift or token amount of money (Fowler, 1993; Rogelberg & Luong, 1998). With adequate return rates and a well-designed written survey, this method can be more efficient and less expensive than interviews while still yielding valuable data.

Phone Surveying

The third way to conduct a survey is to pick up the phone and call people. You might recall from Chapter 4 that sampling from phone books caused a problem for *Literary Digest's* prediction about the presidential election of 1936; not everyone could afford phones then. Today, however, phones are found in more than 90% of American homes. But what about unlisted numbers? This is a potential problem because, by one estimate, about one-third of all residential phone numbers are not listed in directories (Lavrakas, 1998). The solution is a procedure called "random-digit dialing," in which a simple computer program generates lists of numbers within a region, making it possible for any phone number to be in the sample.

Phone surveying has an obvious advantage in cost over interviews and written surveys. It also combines the efficiency of a mail survey with the personal contact of an interview. A clear advantage over the interview is a logistical one; many more interviews can be completed per unit of time. Furthermore, the phone interviewer is not likely to be assaulted, a problem that sometimes occurs when field interviewers venture into high-crime areas. The downside of phone interviewing is that the surveys must be brief because people can lose patience; this restriction also tends to cut down on open-ended questioning. A related problem is response rate. Although you might think that the response rate would be quite high with phone surveying, this is not the case. For one thing, the large number of two-income families means that phone surveyors reach more answering machines than people during the day. Thus, many calls go unanswered, including repeat calls to the same number. This has led researchers to concentrate their activities during the early evening hours. Unfortunately, this is also the time when telemarketers call with fabulous deals on vinyl siding or "free" vacations to Orlando. Compounding the problem is the fact that many telemarketers, unconcerned with ethics, begin their pitch by making the call sound like a survey. It's not clear how many people have hung up on legitimate researchers, thinking they were hearing just another sales pitch. One technique that legitimate surveyors can use is to precede the call with a brief letter or postcard alerting the respondent that a phone call is on the way ("and please cooperate").

The three techniques of interviewing, giving written surveys, and doing phone surveys are not mutually exclusive. Each can stand alone, of course, but they are often combined. Interviewers might ask some open-ended questions verbally and then ask participants to fill out a written questionnaire; written notice and a preliminary description of a survey might be sent just prior to phone surveying; or phone surveying might follow up on either interviews or written surveys. Each particular research project creates separate demands on the researcher, often requiring a certain amount of creativity in order to achieve the goals of the study. A good example of a combination strategy was a group phone interview conducted by a firm hired by the publisher of this text. On two separate occasions, groups of eight to ten professors using the text's second edition were interviewed in a conference call format about how the book could be improved in its third edition. Although I initially thought the groups were too large for this idea to work, the moderator did a fine job of keeping people on task and working through a set of structured interview questions about the book's strengths and weaknesses and how to improve it. I found both interview transcripts extremely useful—for example, because of the interviews we decided to create the lab manual/study guide that now accompanies the book.

Evaluating Survey Research

Surveys have become an established means of collecting data and have a well-earned reputation for yielding valuable information about human behavior. Nonetheless, four major problems can occur. The first has to do with sampling considerations, as described earlier. Clearly, a biased sample can produce misleading results. The second problem concerns response bias, the most common of which is called a **social**

desirability bias. Sometimes people respond to a survey question in a way that reflects not how they truly feel or what they truly believe, but how they think they should respond. That is, they attempt to create a positive picture of themselves—one that is socially desirable. The social psychology literature has a long history of research showing that the attitudes people express on some issue do not always correlate with their behavior. Thus, the results of survey research have to be interpreted with response bias in mind, and conclusions can be strengthened to the extent that other research provides converging results.

A third major problem in survey research concerns the content of the items contained in the survey. Questions may be ambiguous, as when people are asked whether they agree with statements like this:

Visiting relatives can be fun.

Sometimes survey writers try to include too much in an item, resulting in an item that actually asks for two responses at once. For example, respondents might be asked whether they agree with this statement:

It is wrong for female patrons in bars to swear and to buy drinks for men who are unknown to them.

The responder who agrees with the swearing part but disagrees with the drink-buying part would not know how to answer this question.

Questions may also be in the form of what lawyers call a "leading question." Here are two ways of asking about the Clean Air Act that would almost certainly yield different responses:

Given the importance to future generations of preserving the environment, do you believe the Clean Air Act should be strengthened, weakened, or left alone?

Given the fact that installing scrubbers at utility plants could increase electricity bills by 25%, do you believe the Clean Air Act should be strengthened, weakened, or left alone?

This type of survey bias occurs frequently in the business world, where the intent is to sell a product. In an attempt to outsell McDonald's, for instance, Burger King once reported a survey claiming that about 75% of people surveyed preferred their Whoppers to Big Macs. The key question was phrased this way (Kimmel, 1996, p. 195):

Do you prefer your hamburgers flame-broiled or fried?

Do you see the problem? Naturally, Burger King's "flame-broiled," method sounds more natural and appetizing than McDonald's "fried" method, so perhaps the outcome was not a surprise. However, another surveyor asked the question a different way (Kimmel, 1996, p. 195):

Do you prefer a hamburger that is grilled on a hot stainless steel grill or cooked by passing the raw meat through an open gas flame?

In this case, McDonald's method was preferred by more than half of the respondents, a figure that rose to 85% when the researcher indicated that after encountering the gas flame, the Burger King burgers were reheated in a microwave oven before being served. The moral of the story: it is probably fair to say that skepticism is the best response when businesses report survey results in their advertising. Unfortunately, this situation lends credence to the widely held belief that surveys can be created and manipulated to produce virtually any outcome.

These are just a few examples of the difficulties that occur when creating survey items. For more detailed guidance on the construction of reliable and valid survey items, several excellent guides exist (e.g., Converse & Presser, 1986; Fink, 1995; Fowler, 1993; Patten, 1998). Also, take a look at Appendix B; it provides some useful ideas for creating a good written survey.

A fourth and final problem with surveys is not methodological but ethical and overlaps to a degree with the first three problems. Decisions affecting people's lives are sometimes made with the help of survey data, and if the surveys are flawed in some way, people can be hurt. Although professional psychologists operating within the APA's ethics code are unlikely to use surveys inappropriately, abuses nonetheless can occur. The problem is recognized by the judicial system, which has established a set of standards for the use of survey data in courts of law (Morgan, 1990). The standards amount to this: if you are going to collect and use survey data, do it as a professional psychologist would. That is, be careful about sampling, survey construction, and data analysis. For an interesting and rather disturbing example of how survey methods can be badly misused, read Ethics Box 12.2, which examines the case of a female journalist who was fired from her news anchor job, partly on the basis of a rigged survey.

Box 12.2

ETHICS—Using and Abusing Surveys

In early 1981, station KMBC of Kansas City hired Christine Craft, a news journalist from California, to co-anchor their evening news. Less than a year later, she was demoted from that position. The station claimed incompetence but Ms. Craft sued, arguing that she was hired for her journalistic talent, not her youthful good looks, yet was fired for the latter reason. She won.

On the surface, the station appeared to act prudently, basing their decision not merely on whim but on data collected in a professional survey of viewers. However, this case illustrates not the use of survey research, but its misuse. According to Beisecker (1988), the study had several major flaws.

First, although the use of a survey conveys the impression of objectivity, the research was hopelessly biased from the start. One major problem was that the firm doing the research also served as a paid consultant to the station, and those doing the research already knew what decision the station wanted. The resulting bias was reflected in the wording of a phone survey that was used. One purpose of the survey was to compare Ms. Craft with other local news anchors, yet the questions were stacked against her. For example, she did poorly compared to other anchors on a question regarding which news anchor "knows Kansas City best" (p. 23), which is not surprising when one considers that (a) at the time of the survey Ms. Craft had been with the station for 6 months and the other anchors had all been at their stations at least a year and (b) in her early months with KMBC, Ms. Craft had been vigorously promoted as "a fresh new face from California" (p. 23). Also, very few survey items assessed journalistic ability; rather, much of the survey dealt with questions about attractiveness and appearance (e.g., "Her good looks are a big plus for the newscast she's on," p. 23).

In addition to the bias that characterized the project from the start, there were statistical problems serious enough for Beisecker (1988) to conclude that "the research firm did not employ any recognizable statistical tests or principles of statistical inference to justify its generalizations from the sample data" (p. 25). In other words, while the consultant firm reported simple *descriptive* statistics summarizing the survey results, they did not conduct the proper *inferential* statistics that would allow conclusions about the significance of the results. For example, it was reported that among 25- to 34-year-olds in the survey who were asked which channel's news had declined in quality, 30% said KMBC and 16% said a competing channel, KCMO. Much was made of this "2-1 margin," and it was attributed to the allegedly detrimental effects of Ms. Craft's presence. However, the year before (1980), when Ms. Craft was still in California, the same question on another survey by the *same* firm yielded 26% for KMBC and 15% for KCMO. An inferential analysis surely would have shown no difference between the numbers for the 2 years. Not only was the analysis not done, the consultant/researchers conveniently omitted the 1980 data from the 1981 results.

Clearly, survey research can be done well and its results interpreted meaningfully. In the case of Christine Craft, though, the research was not done in the spirit of Standard 1.06 of the APA's ethics code (American Psychological Association, 1992):

> Psychologists rely on scientifically and professionally derived knowledge when making scientific or professional judgments or when engaging in scholarly or professional endeavors.

As you recall from Chapter 2, discussions about the use of animals as research subjects often generate more heat than light. One approach to understanding how people feel about the issue is to conduct a good survey; that was done in Case Study 33, which follows.

Case Study 33—Surveying Attitudes about Animal Research

In 1996, Plous published two different surveys about animal research, one directed at academic psychologists (Plous, 1996a) and a second directed at undergraduate psychology majors (Plous, 1996b). The latter concerns your peer group, so let's consider it in more detail than the former.

In survey research, the term **sample frame** is normally defined as the complete list of individuals from whom the sample will be drawn. When cluster sampling is used, the sample frame refers to the list of initial clusters chosen. Plous used this sampling procedure; the initial sample frame was a list of 708 colleges and universities taken from a standard college guide. The sample frame excluded very small schools and schools with a religious affiliation. From the list of 708, 50 schools were randomly sampled. Psychology department chairs at these schools were contacted, and 42 schools chose to participate. Some additional sampling within each department was done, and the final results were based on the returns of 1,188 undergraduate psychology majors. The return rate was 58.75%. This was low enough to trigger concerns about representativeness, so Plous examined the sample more closely. For example, government data for 1995 showed that 73.1% of graduating psychology majors were women, and 26.9% were men. This matched Plous's sample almost perfectly—73% female and 27% male.

Students were informed that the survey concerned the use of animals in psychological, not medical, research (while acknowledging some overlap) and animal use in an educational setting. They were then asked a series of closed questions, including the ones in Table 12.3. They were also asked to fill in a table with four columns labeled with different species names (primates, dogs, rats, and pigeons), and three rows labeled in terms of the severity of the experimental procedures used (observation, confinement, but no pain or death, and physical pain and death). For each cell, the students were asked to indicate whether they thought the research would be "usually justified" or "usually unjustified." Because the topic is so controversial, Plous wanted to be sure that the questions would be clear and unbiased. This goal was achieved by doing some pretesting of the items with a separate sample of undergraduate psychology majors.

The results in Table 12.3 show that psychology majors clearly approved the use of animals both for research and for teaching purposes. Over 70% either supported or strongly supported animal research, about two-thirds believed animal research to be necessary for progress to occur in psychology, and while most thought that lab work with animals should not be required of psychology majors, there was majority support for the use of animals in undergraduate instruction. There was concern about pain and suffering, however, with almost unanimous support for protecting the psychological well-being of primates and for required assessments of the amount of pain the animals might experience. Also, on the 3 × 4 grid, there was little support for procedures involving pain and death; this was true for all four species listed.

And what about the other survey, the one sent to academic psychologists (Plous, 1996a)? Interestingly enough, the results were virtually identical. The only notable difference was for item 1. While 71.7% of psychology majors either strongly supported (14.3%) or supported (57.4%) the use of animals in psychological research, support was even stronger among the psychologists—31.4% strongly supported it and 48.6% supported it (i.e., 80% supporting or strongly supporting).

Case Studies

At the beginning of the previous chapter, when pointing out that psychology began with small N designs, I briefly mentioned Darwin's detailed analysis of his son's early years (p. 352). This can be considered an example of a **case study,** defined broadly as an in-depth analysis of a single case. The "case" is usually a person; if so, the method is occasionally referred to as a "case history" because it involves a close analysis of the history of that person's life or a major portion of it. The approach is common in clinical

TABLE 12.3   *Attitudes About Animal Research—A Survey of Psychology Majors*

Here is a sample of the items from the survey by Plous (1996a).

In general, do you *support* or *oppose* the use of animals in psychological research?

Strongly support	14.3%
Support	57.4%
Oppose	13.8%
Strongly oppose	4.7%
Not sure	9.8%

Do you believe that the use of animals in psychological research is necessary for progress in psychology, or not?

Yes	68.4%
No	15.7%
Not sure	15.9%

In general, do you *support* or *oppose* the use of animals in undergraduate psychology courses?

Support	56.9%
Oppose	28.4%
Not sure	14.7%

Do you feel that laboratory work with animals should be a required part of the undergraduate psychology major?

Yes	34.1%
No	54.3%
Not sure	11.6%

Federal regulations protect the "psychological well-being" of primates used in research. Do you *support* or *oppose* the idea of protecting the psychological well-being of primates?

Support	85.1%
Oppose	4.0%
Not sure	10.9%

Before being granted approval to run an experiment, investigators in Great Britain, Canada, and the Netherlands are required to assess the degree of pain animals may experience. Would you *support* or *oppose* a similar requirement in the United States?

Support	85.2%
Oppose	7.0%
Not sure	7.8%

Source: Adapted from Plous (1996a), Table 1.

work, in which the case of someone with a particular disorder is used to illustrate the factors that lead to and influence it and the methods of treatment for it. The most famous practitioner of this type of case study was Sigmund Freud, who built his personality theory on the basis of detailed case examples of his patients.

Case histories have also been completed by experimental psychologists, and one of the best-known examples is Alexander Luria's fascinating account of a man who seemed unable to forget anything. This classic study is detailed in Box 12.3, and if you think that having a nearby perfect memory would solve many of your problems, you'll have second thoughts after reading about "S."

Box 12.3

CLASSIC STUDIES—The Mind of a Mnemonist

Case histories often document lives that are classic examples of particular psychological types. In abnormal psychology, for example, the case history approach is often used to understand the dynamics of specific disorders by detailing individual examples of them. Case histories also can be useful in experimental psychology, however, shedding light on basic psychological phenomena. A classic example of such a history is the one compiled by Alexander Romanovich Luria (1902 – 1977), a Russian physiologist/psychologist famous for his studies of Russian soldiers brain injured during World War II and for his work on the relationship between language and thought (Brennan, 1991).

The case involved one S. V. Sherashevsky, or "S.," as Luria referred to him, whose remarkable memory abilities gave him a career as a stage mnemonist (yes, people actually paid to watch him memorize things) but also caused him considerable distress. The case is summarized in Luria's *The Mind of a Mnemonist* (1968). Luria studied S. for more than 20 years, documenting both the range of S.'s memory and the accompanying problems of his being virtually unable to forget anything. Luria first discovered that there seemed to be no limit on how much information S. could memorize; more astonishing, the information did not seem to decay with the passage of time. He could easily memorize lists of up to 70 numbers and could recall them in either a forward or a reverse order. Also, "he had no difficulty reproducing any lengthy series … whatever, even though these had been presented to him a week, a year, or even many years earlier" (Luria, 1968, p. 12).

This is an unbelievable performance, especially considering that most people cannot recall more than seven or eight items on this type of task and that forgetting is the rule rather that the exception. As a student, you might be wondering what the down side to this could possibly be. After all, it would seem to be a wonderful "problem" to have, especially during final exam week.

Unfortunately, S.'s extraordinary memory skills were accompanied by severe deficits in other cognitive areas. For example, he found it almost impossible to read for comprehension. This was because every word evoked strong visual images from his memory and interfered with the overall organization of the idea conveyed by the sentence. Similarly, he was an ineffective problem solver, found it difficult to plan and organize his life, and was unable to think abstractly. The images that produced his remarkable memory interfered with everything else.

Is S. anything more than an idle curiosity, a bizarre once-in-a-lifetime person who doesn't really tell us anything about ourselves? No. In fact, the case sheds important light on normal memory. In particular, it provides a glimpse into the functional value of the limited capacity of short-term memory. We sometimes curse our inability to recall something we were thinking about just a few minutes before, but the case of S. shows that forgetting allows us to clear the mind of information that might be useless (e.g., there's no reason to memorize most of the phone numbers we look up) and enables us to concentrate our energy on more sophisticated cognitive tasks like reading for comprehension. Because S. couldn't avoid remembering things, he was unable to function at higher cognitive levels.

One final point. It turns out that S. was not a once-in-a-lifetime case. Another person ("VP") with a similarly remarkable memory was studied by the American psychologists Hunt and Love (1972). Oddly enough, VP grew up in a city in present-day Latvia that was just a short distance from the birthplace of Luria's S.

A case study is not limited to the investigation of a single person, however. The term also applies to the analysis of a single event or a single class of events that exemplifies some phenomenon. For example, although the Festinger study of cults was described in Box 12.1 as a famous example of participant observation, the study could also be considered a case study of a cult. Case studies of events are often completed when a rare event or an event of historic importance occurs. For example, researchers have done case studies of how nearby residents reacted to the nuclear accident at Three Mile Island in Pennsylvania in 1979 (Aronson, 1999a) and whether people retained accurate "flashbulb" memories of where they were and what they were doing when President Kennedy was assassinated in 1963 (Yarmen & Bull, 1978).

Case Study 34—Being Hypnotized on Stage

Besides chronicling the effects of rare and extraordinary occurrences, case studies can also investigate common yet intriguing events like staged displays of hypnotism, in which ordinary people seem to be willing to do some very unusual things. Such was the focus of a case study by Crawford, Kitner-Triolo, Clarke, and Olesko (1992). They interviewed 22 college students who had participated on stage during a campus performance by a stage hypnotist in order to study the aftereffects of such an experience. Being hypnotized was enjoyable for most students, but a small minority found it annoying, embarrassing, or even frightening. Somewhat surprising was the finding that a substantial proportion of the group experienced posthypnotic amnesia. Of the 22, eight agreed with the statement "After I left the stage, I could not remember some things I did," and six agreed that "The next day I could not remember some things I did." One participant who was especially disturbed by the amnesia likened it to an alcoholic blackout. Also surprising was the report that five of the 22 believed the hypnotist to have total control over their actions. These levels of amnesia and perceptions of control aren't normally found in follow-up studies of participants in laboratory studies of hypnosis. Hence, this case study yielded important information about the effects of hypnotism that would not have been apparent from more controlled studies.

On the basis of their analysis, Crawford et al. (1992) made several recommendations about on-campus hypnotism shows, including "screening out participants who are in therapy or counseling, correcting misperceptions about hypnosis among the participants before the hypnosis begins, ... removing all amnesia suggestions and reviewing the events at the end of the hypnotic experience, and remaining available afterward for further questions" (p. 666).

Finally, the term "case study" can be used when referring to an especially good example of some phenomenon, which is how I've been using the term since Chapter 4. Beginning there and including the hypnotism example you just read, you've encountered numerous "case studies"—relatively in-depth descriptions of studies that I chose because they seemed to be good illustrations of particular methods or experimental designs.

Evaluating Case Studies

At first glance, it might appear that the description of a single case would not be very informative. External validity is the most obvious weakness—how much can be generalized from a single example? Of course, as is true in all research, confidence in external validity accumulates gradually, as the findings replicate. This can occur with case studies, just as it can with other varieties of research. While it might be difficult to replicate a spectacular event like the 1989 San Francisco earthquake, it isn't difficult to see if the same behavioral effects occur with other kinds of natural disasters.

A second difficulty with the case study is that ample opportunity exists for the biases of the researcher to color the case description. Is it so surprising to find unending discussions of unresolved Oedipal complexes and various other sexually based problems in case histories written by Freudians? To illustrate, during a session using PsycINFO to find research examples for this chapter, I encountered a study called "Ph.D. Envy: A Psychoanalytic Case Study" (Behr, 1992). It described the case of a woman with a "profound and debilitating anxiety around not being able to finish her Ph.D. dissertation.... [Her] contempt for those without Ph.D.s and the intense envy of those who possessed them led to the psychical equivalence of Ph.D. envy and penis envy" (p. 99). Would her case be described differently by a non-Freudian? Almost certainly.

A third problem concerns memory. Because the participants in case histories of individuals are often required to recall events from the past, a whole range of memory problems occurs. As researchers such as Elizabeth Loftus have shown repeatedly, memories for the events of our lives are often distorted by circumstances that intervene between the target event and the later recall of it. Take, for example, a Floridian who experienced the devastating Hurricane Andrew in 1992. If asked to describe the experience as part of a case study a year later, some of the information would undoubtedly be accurate. After all, someone is not likely to forget the roof being blown off the house. However, during the intervening year, the person has (a) experienced the event, (b) seen videos, news stories, TV re-creations, and photographs of the event, (c) listened to countless hurricane stories from friends and neighbors, and (d) probably dreamed of the event a few times. As Loftus and her research team have demonstrated (e.g., Loftus & Hoffman, 1989), our subsequent memories are often "constructions" of the event itself and of these later occurrences. That is, we now have a memory that incorporates many elements, only one of which is the event itself.

Despite the difficulties, case histories can be quite informative. First, because of the level of detail, they can provide insights into behavior that cannot occur in larger N studies that collect limited amounts of data per subject. Luria's study not only details S.'s extraordinary memory capacity, but also shows how it affected other aspects of the poor man's life. Luria's S. also illustrates a second point: some individuals are so rare that a case study approach is the only feasible one. Third, like all descriptive research, case studies can be a useful source of empirical questions for future investigation. As you've seen, Crawford et al. (1992) were surprised that about one-third of the college students participating in the hypnotism show experienced some degree of amnesia for what happened on stage, and almost as many believed the hypnotist to be in complete control. Is there some important personality or cognitive factor that differentiates these students from others? In what ways are posthypnosis and postalcohol amnesia alike and different? Would those students who believed the hypnotist was in control also be more likely to develop learned helplessness than students who felt more in control?

Besides providing hypotheses for further research, case studies, like observational research, can sometimes serve the purpose of falsification. That is, if a strong assertion is made about some psychological phenomenon, a single disconfirming case can raise serious questions about it. You already know about one famous example (Box 3.3, pp. 89–90). Claims made about Clever Hans's math skills were effectively falsified when the case was investigated by the psychologist Pfungst.

A second example comes from the field of parapsychology, which investigates phenomena like extrasensory perception. You've undoubtedly read about "psychics" who claim to have special abilities to read minds, predict the future, and to influence events (e.g., make a spoon bend) through mental power. These claims can be questioned by describing case studies in which a person, usually a professional magician, is able to repeat every phenomenon demonstrated by the psychic, yet makes it clear that nothing but the ordinary deceptions of the professional magician are involved (e.g., Randi, 1982). Defenders of parapsychology may argue that psychics produce their results mentally and magicians produce theirs physically, but the more parsimonious explanation is that both outcomes occur the same way (i.e., physically).

In sum, case studies are susceptible to biases and their results may not generalize easily, but like observational studies they can be useful in generating new research, they can help falsify weak theories, and at times they can be the only way to document an extraordinary person or event.

Archival Research

Researchers sometimes take advantage of information that is already available in order to test hypotheses. When this occurs, the approach is called **archival research,** with the term "archives" referring both to the records themselves and to the places where the records are stored. Archival data range from public information such as census data, court records, genealogical data, corporate annual reports, and patent office records to more private information such as credit histories, health history data, educational records, personal correspondence, and diaries. "Archives" as locations refer to places like university libraries, government offices, and computerized databases. You can begin to get a sense of the topics that can be studied using archival data from the following titles of research articles:

"Perceived Equity, Motivation, and Final-Offer Arbitration in Major League Baseball" (Bretz & Thomas, 1992)

"The Institutionalization of Premarital Cohabitation: Estimates from Marriage License Applications, 1970 and 1980" (Gwaltney-Gibbs, 1986)

"Attributions in the Advice Columns: Actors and Observers, Causes and Reasons" (Schoeneman & Rubanowitz, 1985)

Varieties of Archival Research

Archival research is often a component of a larger research effort that includes other methods. Program evaluation research is a good example. As you recall from Chapter 10, program evaluation research includes needs analysis studies, formative and summative evaluations, and cost analyses. All of these can include archival information. Needs assessments usually examine census data, and both agency records and statistical data from other programs can contribute to evaluations and cost analyses. Furthermore, at least one of the methods you encountered in Chapter 10, the interrupted time series design, usually includes archival information, such as traffic accident data, in order to chart trends.

Sometimes, archival research will require not just the selection and statistical analysis of records, but also a **content analysis** of the information, which can be defined as any systematic examination of materials that organizes qualitative information in terms of predefined categories. Any type of record can be content analyzed; and while most content analyses examine verbal materials like text or interview data, nonverbal material can be analyzed as well. For example, in a study by Brantjes and Bouma (1991), the drawings of patients suffering from Alzheimer's disease were content analyzed, correlated with the degree of mental deterioration, and compared to drawings of non-Alzheimer's participants of the same age.

As with observational research, when checklists of target behaviors are developed ahead of time, it is important to have operationally defined categories of content in mind before beginning a content analysis. It is also a good idea to have more than one person doing the analysis so as to check on the reliability of the content analysis. If possible, in order to avoid any biasing effects, scorers should be blind to the hypothesis being tested.

The effective use of a content analysis of verbal materials is illustrated in a study by Lau and Russell (1980). To investigate how people explain their successes and failures in sports, they examined newspaper accounts of major sporting events for comments by players, coaches, and sportswriters about why they (or the team they were writing about) either won or lost. Explanations were coded into two broad categories, depending on whether a win or a loss was blamed on internal (it was our responsibility entirely) or external (an excuse of some type) factors. In general, they found that winners were more likely to give internal explanations for their success; after losing, there was about an equal proportion of internal and external explanations.

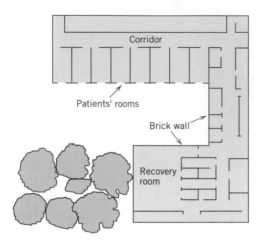

FIGURE 12.2 Floor plan of a hospital used in archival study of recovery from surgery, showing rooms facing either a group of trees or a brick wall.

(From Ulrich, 1984)

Although by their nature archival studies do not allow the direct manipulation of independent variables, they often involve sophisticated attempts to control for potential confounding factors. A clever example of this is a study by Ulrich (1984), who demonstrated that recovery from surgery could be influenced by having a room with a pleasant view of the outside world.

Case Study 35—A Room with a View

One of the more interesting areas of research that has developed in psychology within the past 30 years concerns the relationship between mental and physical well-being. Health psychologists study such problems as the link between stress and illness, the doctor-patient relationship, and, in the case of the Ulrich study, whether such a seemingly minor factor as hospital architecture can affect patient health.

Ulrich examined patient records over a period of about 10 years in a suburban Pennsylvania hospital. He was interested in whether recovery from surgery could be affected by the type of room in which the patient spent postoperative time. In particular, he compared rooms that had windows overlooking a brick wall with rooms having windows that provided a pleasant view of a small group of trees (see Figure 12.2 for a floor diagram). All the rooms were the same size, and in each room the beds were arranged so that patients could easily look out of the window.

Because the study was archival, Ulrich could not randomly assign patients to the rooms, but he did everything possible to make the two groups of patients comparable. First, he only used patients recovering from a common type of gallbladder surgery and omitted those under the age of 20 and over 69. Second, he created two similar groups using a variety of matching variables including age, gender, smoking history, and weight. Thus, he examined records for two groups of patients who were roughly equivalent to each other; the only major difference was the type of view they had out of their windows—bricks or trees.

From the archival records, Ulrich examined the length of postoperative hospitalization, whether and in what amounts patients requested medication for pain and/or anxiety, the frequency of minor complications such as headache or nausea, and nurses' notes about the patients. What he found was a clear advantage for those recovering in a room with a view. They spent an average of one less day in the hospital after surgery (7.96 vs. 8.70), they requested less pain medication, and when they did request it, they asked for lower doses than did patients staring at the bricks. A content analysis of nursing records determined that those looking out on the parklike setting were more likely to elicit positive rather than negative comments from the nurses (but maybe the nurses were affected by the trees too!). The groups did not differ in their requests for antianxiety medication, nor were there differences in minor postoperative complications.

The Ulrich study is one of a growing number that show how physical health can be influenced by myriad nonmedical factors. The study also illustrates how health psychology has become a multidisciplinary field: at the time of the study's publication, Ulrich taught in the Department of *Geography* at the University of Delaware.

Evaluating Archival Research

There are several advantages inherent in archival research. The most obvious one is that the amount of information available in the early 21st century is virtually unlimited and the possibilities for archival research are restricted only by the creativity of the investigator. A second strength is that archival research can converge with the results of laboratory research, thereby increasing external validity. McClelland's research on achievement motivation is an example. The studies that you read about in Box 9.3 used archival information such as children's literature and patent information in different historical eras in order to show that achievement themes in the literature predicted later technological achievement. The results were consistent with other laboratory research on the relationship between the achievement needs of individuals and their achieving behavior. A third advantage is that archival information is nonreactive; because the information already exists, collecting it eliminates the possibility of subject reactivity.

The fact that archival data already exist also creates problems for researchers. Despite the vast amount of data available, some information vital to a researcher may be missing or the available data may not be representative. In the study listed earlier that examined the content of advice columns, for example, Schoeneman and Rubanowitz (1985) had to contend with the fact that what eventually is printed in an advice column is just a small proportion of the letters written to advice columnists. Who can say what factors determine the selection of letters for publication?

A final problem with archival research is the one common to all the strategies described in this chapter—experimenter bias. In archival research, this can take the form of selecting only those records that support one's hypothesis or interpreting content in a way that is biased by one's expectations. The problem can be difficult to avoid completely because the researcher doing archival research is typically faced with much more information than can be used and the information can often be open to several interpretations.

Of course, the judicious researcher can reduce the effects of bias by developing a clear plan ahead of time that includes a carefully worked out procedure, operational definitions for all the pertinent variables, criteria for selecting materials, multiple coders, and so on. In the hospital recovery study, for example, only patients hospitalized between May 1 and October 20 of a given year had their records scrutinized. Why were those months the only ones selected? Because during the rest of the year, there was no foliage on the trees and Ulrich's goal was to compare patients who were looking at brick walls with those looking at fully bloomed and presumably more aesthetically pleasing trees.

In sum, archival studies are an effective way to use information about events that have already occurred and therefore enable the researcher to test hypotheses when variables aren't available for direct experimental manipulation. Considering the vast amount of information out there and its increased availability (e.g., on the Internet), archival research is an approach that promises to become even more visible in the years ahead.

With this chapter on descriptive methods, the cast of characters for the production called "research in psychology" is complete. What remains is a brief epilogue that returns to a theme introduced back in Chapter 1, the excitement of doing research in psychology, and closes with some ideas about how the methods course might have influenced you.

Chapter Summary

Observational Research

The goal of providing accurate qualitative and quantitative descriptions of behavior can be accomplished by using basic observational methods. In naturalistic observation, the observer is separate from those being observed and the subjects of study are either unaware of the observer's presence or habituated to it. The observer becomes an active member of the group being studied in participant observation studies. Observation studies vary in the amount of structure imposed by the researcher. Lack of control, observer bias, and subject reactivity are three methodological problems that accompany observational research. The researcher also must confront the ethical dilemmas of informed consent and invasion of privacy. Observational research, as well as the other forms of descriptive research described in this chapter, can be used to falsify claims about behavior, and are often a useful source of hypotheses for further investigation.

Survey Research

The primary purpose of survey research is to gather descriptive information about people's attitudes, opinions, and self-described behaviors. Surveys can be administered in face-to-face interviews, by means of written questionnaires, or over the phone. Constructing reliable and valid surveys is a major task, and survey data can be affected by the expectations and response biases of those taking the survey. Conclusions drawn from survey research can be invalidated if the group sampled does not reflect the population targeted by the survey.

Case Studies

Case studies are in-depth descriptions and analyses of individual persons or events. Case histories of individuals serve to highlight the backgrounds and current attributes of individuals fitting into defined categories (e.g., those diagnosed as suffering from specific psychological disorders) or to provide a careful analysis of extraordinary individuals. Case histories of events occur when researchers have the opportunity either to collect data about some significant current event (e.g., an earthquake) or to investigate a type of event (e.g., stage hypnotism) that is of interest for some reason.

Archival Research

When a researcher uses information that has already been collected for some other purpose or as part of the public record, the result is called archival research. Archival information is often an essential part of program evaluation research, especially with interrupted time series studies. Archival research projects can be designed to answer empirical questions, but the results are limited by what information is available and there is no guarantee that the data will be representative.

Chapter Review

Multiple Choice

1. Becoming so involved with a group that one loses objectivity is most likely to occur in which type of study?
   a. participant observation of a cult
   b. group survey with an interview format
   c. naturalistic observation of a primate group
   d. case study of a group of social workers

2. In a naturalistic observation, how does one deal with the problem of reactivity?
   a. subjects never know they are being observed
   b. subjects always know they are being observed and give informed consent
   c. observers are hidden or subjects are habituated to the observer's presence
   d. the observer becomes a member of the group

3. The major advantage of interviews over written and phone surveys is that interviews
   a. yield more comprehensive in-depth information
   b. are less expensive
   c. don't experience sampling problems
   d. avoid the problem of bias

4. Which of the following empirical questions would be best answered by using an archival study?
   a. Which species of tropical fish most vigorously defends its territory?
   b. How do most Americans feel about the concept of national health insurance?
   c. Are natural disasters given greater news coverage if they occur in popular tourist locations?
   d. At a movie theater, are overweight patrons more likely to buy the "bucket" of popcorn, while normal-weight patrons buy the "cup" of popcorn?

5. Which of the following is true of the case study as a method?
    a. case studies always involve in-depth studies of individual persons
    b. of the methods discussed in this chapter, the case study comes closest to being able to draw conclusions about cause and effect
    c. it may be the only reasonable choice for dealing with rare individuals
    d. experimenter bias is not likely to be a problem

Short Essay

1. Distinguish between naturalistic and participant observational procedures, both in terms of method and ethics.

2. What is meant by the problem of "reactivity" and how can it be overcome?

3. Give an example to show how observer bias can influence observational research and describe how such bias can be reduced.

4. Describe the advantages and disadvantages of using interviews as a way of doing survey research.

5. If you are conducting a written survey, what can you do to increase the return rate? What is meant by a nonresponse bias?

6. Use the hamburger example to illustrate the dangers of wording biases in survey research.

7. Use the case of the news journalist Christine Craft to illustrate how survey research can be misused.

8. What are the advantages and disadvantages of conducting a survey by phone?

9. What are the two varieties of case studies and what are the strengths and weaknesses of the case study method?

10. In the Ulrich archival study (room with a view), what was the independent variable and what other variables were controlled in order to make the two groups comparable? What was the outcome of the study?

11. Describe the advantages and disadvantages of archival research. What methods encountered in other chapters would be likely to rely on archival data?

Applications Exercises

Exercise 12.1.—Improving Poor Survey Items

The following are several examples of items that could be found on surveys. Some are in the form of closed questions, others in the form of agree/disagree statements. For each item, (a) identify what is wrong and (b) rewrite it so as to solve the problem. Refer to Appendix B for additional help.

1. Have you had an upset stomach lately?

2. Highly prejudiced people are usually hostile and not very smart.

3. In your opinion, how young is the average smoker?

4. Do you agree with most people that violations of seat belt laws should result in harsh penalties?

5. Most doctors have a superior attitude.

6. People who are overweight lack will power and are usually unhappy.

Exercise 12.2.—Defining Behaviors for Observational Research

Imagine that you are in the beginning stages of an observational research study and have to arrive at clear operational definitions for the behaviors you'll be observing. For each of the following hypotheses, operationally define the behaviors to be recorded and describe how you would set up the study (i.e., where you would conduct the study, whether you would create some level of structure, etc.).

1. Men interrupt women more than women interrupt men.

2. In a free play situation, older children play cooperatively but younger children engage in parallel play.

3. In the college library, most students spend less than half of their time actually studying.

4. Teenagers patrolling malls follow clearly defined routes that they repeat at regular intervals.

5. Couples look at each other more when they are dating than when they are married.

6. Dogs are more aggressive within their own territories than outside of them.

Exercise 12.3.—Deciding on Descriptive Methods

For each of the hypotheses listed below, identify the best methodological approach from among the following possibilities. Indicate the reason(s) for your choice. There may be more than one correct answer for some of the items.

> naturalistic observation   written survey   case study
> participant observation   phone survey   archival study
> interview survey

1. Fraternities and sororities represent well-ordered cultures that reward conformity to unwritten norms for behavior.

2. When respondents are given the opportunity and encouragement to explain their opinions on controversial issues, their ideas are usually based on anecdotal evidence.

3. A national sample (2,000 people) is chosen for a consumer survey on preferred snack foods.

4. For a period of 1 month after a highly publicized suicide, there will be an increase in driver fatalities in which the driver is alone in the car and the accident does not involve other drivers.

5. After a near–disastrous landing in which the landing gear failed and passengers had to be evacuated, most of the people who flew on Flight 304 will experience mild to severe anxiety problems that will interfere with sleep.

6. When college students enter the cafeteria, males are more likely to be unaccompanied by other students than females are: this is especially true for the dinner meal.

7. Analysis of the personal ads in newspapers supports the hypothesis from evolutionary psychology that males prefer younger (i.e., more fertile) women, while women prefer older (i.e., more stable, able to support a family) men.

8. As a consequence of altering the content of bird feeders, the proportions of two different species of birds at the feeder will change within three days.

Epilogue

I sincerely hope that your experience in this research methods course has been a positive and successful one. The course can be difficult, and at times tedious, but I believe it is the most important one in the psychology curriculum (history of psychology is a close second). In the letters of recommendation that I write for my students, both for graduate school *and* for jobs, I always look back to how they did in my research methods course, and much of the letter will be framed in terms of the kinds of skills developed in that course. I'd like to close the book by (a) listing those skills, some of which I introduced briefly in Chapter 1, and (b) returning to another theme introduced in Chapter 1, the idea that researchers typically become deeply involved and passionate about their work.

What I Learned in My Research Methods Course

To become a professional psychologist requires an advanced degree, preferably the doctorate, and because graduate study includes a strong dose of research, the undergraduate methods course is an obvious first step to developing the research skills that will be put to use in graduate school. Yet the majority of undergraduate psychology majors won't go on to earn doctorates in psychology, and as a result, students sometimes question the value of the methods course if their goal is to finish college and get a job. If you're in that category, I'd like to convince you that your chances of getting a decent position and of advancing on the job have been improved if you've done well in your methods course. Here's a list of some of the career-enhancing skills you've begun to develop as a result of taking this course. Naturally, if you are heading to graduate school, these skills also apply, and will increase your chances of doing well as you work toward an advanced degree. Here goes:

- Ability to think empirically
  - Framing questions in ways that they can be answered with data
  - Looking for data-based conclusions about behavior
  - Recognizing that conclusions based on data are "working truths," pending further research and replication
  - Using logical thinking in the research context, both inductive and deductive varieties
- Ability to examine claims and information about behavior with a critical eye
  - Being skeptical about unsubstantiated, excessive, and/or simplistic claims

- Looking out for overly strong (i.e., causal) conclusions based only on correlational data
- Looking carefully at graphs to see that they don't provide misleading information
- Looking for alternative and more parsimonious explanations for results being used to support some claim
- Being skeptical about claims based on questionable evidence (e.g., anecdotal data or glowing testimonials, observations affected by bias, results based on an insufficient number of observations)
- Seeing a red flag whenever claims about behavior include the word "prove," as in "listening to Mozart has been proven to increase your child's IQ"
- Ability to read difficult material for comprehension
  - Through text reading and reading of original research articles
- Ability to take a vague problem, give it some structure, and work out a systematic plan to solve it
  - Through direct experience in developing, implementing, and completing an empirical research project
- Ability to search efficiently for important information to help solve problems and organize that information coherently
  - Through experience with PsycINFO and other electronic search tools
- Ability to organize, summarize, and interpret data
  - Through lab reports and data summaries for data collection exercises
  - Through the application of descriptive and inferential statistics to evaluate data collected in labs
- Improved writing
  - Rules for creating APA-format lab report lead writers to be precise and parsimonious with the language
- Improved communication skills
  - Through experience with oral presentations, posters, lab reports
- Improved computer skills
  - Especially computer statistical packages (e.g., SPSS), but possibly presentation software (e.g., PowerPoint), and possibly through packages or websites that present experiments to be completed by students

This is a rather impressive list, but note that I prefaced it by writing that you've *just begun* to develop these skills. To develop them further, as you continue your career as a psychology major with an interest in research, I would suggest the following:

- Seek out opportunities for independent research with your professors. They will be delighted to have you in their labs, and although you might start by doing routine tasks (e.g., data entry), before long you'll be more deeply involved in projects. By the time you graduate, you might even have completed one or two studies that reflect your own research ideas and for which you are the lead researcher.

- Complete an independent research project or a senior thesis, if your school offers such an opportunity.

- Choose electives likely to have laboratory components. These typically include such courses as Learning, Cognitive Psychology, Physiological Psychology, and Sensation/Perception.

- Go to research conferences and present your research (most likely in poster format). At the very least, you should go to an undergraduate research conference or two. These are small conferences especially designed for undergraduates to present their work. They typically last just a day and feature poster sessions, maybe some oral presentations of research, and an invited address by a prominent researcher. Better yet, submit your work to a regional psychology conference such as the Eastern or Midwestern Psychological Association. These are typically three-day conferences that feature lots of good talks by prominent psychologists and opportunities to meet other student researchers. Third, consider going to one of the national conferences, either of the American Psychological Association (August every year) or the American Psychological Society (June every year). These are larger versions of the regional conferences. Be careful about timing, however. In order to present your research at the regional or national conferences just mentioned, you will have to submit your work, or an abstract of your work, sometime in November or December. Hence, it's a good idea to become involved in research no later than the middle of your junior year.

- Work hard to meet the requirements for Psi Chi, the national honor society in psychology (www.psichi.org). Besides enhancing your resume, membership gives you special opportunities for research. Psi Chi sponsors several research awards, and at all of the regional and national meetings just mentioned, Psi Chi sponsors poster sessions for research by members.

- Submit your work to journals that specialize in undergraduate research. The best known is a journal sponsored by Psi Chi, but others exist. You can find a listing of them, with their website addresses, by looking at Psi Chi's website.

- Find a topic of interest and immerse yourself in it thoroughly. That is, develop a passion for research. This brings us to the book's closing section.

A Passion for Research in Psychology (Part II)

Near the end of his long and productive life, the renowned Russian physiologist Ivan Pavlov was asked by a group of students to write a brief article for their student journal on what it takes to be a great scientist. Pavlov wrote that it took three things. The first was to be systematic in the search for knowledge and the second was to be modest and to recognize one's basic ignorance. The third thing, he wrote, "is *passion*. Remember that science demands [your] whole life. And even if you could have two lives, they would not be sufficient. Science calls for tremendous effort and great passion. Be passionate in your work and in your search for truth" (quoted in Babkin, 1949, p. 110; italics added).

In Chapter 1, you briefly met two famous psychologist/scientists, Eleanor Gibson and B. F. Skinner, and you learned something about the excitement that comes from making important discoveries by doing psychological research. I tried to make the point that perhaps the best reason for doing research in psychology is that it is great fun and can be enormously rewarding, despite the occasional frustrations and setbacks and the guarantee of long hours. That lesson is repeated over and over again through the lives of the men and women who are leaders among today's generation of psychological researchers. Two good present-day examples are Elliot Aronson, currently a visiting professor at Standford University, and Elizabeth Loftus of the University of Washington.

Elliot Aronson

Ask psychologists to name the field's most prominent social psychologist, and the name Elliot Aronson (Figure E.1) will be at or near the top of every list. He is known among research psychologists for his long and productive career investigating topics ranging from basic research in prejudice, persuasion, and cognitive dissonance, to applied research in prejudice reduction, condom use, and energy conservation. When the APA recently named him a recipient of their Award for Distinguished Scientific Contributions, the award citation's final sentence read: "Aronson's vision of social psychology as a rigorous science in the service of humanity stands as a beacon for generations of scientists to come" (Award, 1999, p. 873). He is also recognized by many undergraduates who take the social psychology course, because he probably wrote their textbook. Aronson's award-winning (APA's National Media Award in 1973) *Social Animal* (1999a) is now in its eighth edition and going strong. You met him earlier in this book as the creator of the distinction between experimental and mundane realism (Chapter 3, p. 73).

FIGURE E.1.   Elliot Aronson

Aronson had an enviable list of academic mentors. As an undergraduate at Brandeis University, he wandered into an introductory psychology lecture on prejudice by the famous humanistic psychologist Abraham Maslow. The topic caught the attention of Aronson, who had been on the receiving end of the behavioral products of prejudice while growing up as Jewish child in the tough working class town of Revere, Massachusetts. He immediately changed his major to psychology and developed a close relationship with Maslow. Later, after earning a master's degree at Wesleyan College with David McClelland (of achievement motivation fame, see Box 9.3, p. 304), Aronson went west, arriving at Stanford in the same year that Leon Festinger arrived there as a new professor. Festinger was just then developing his famous theory of cognitive dissonance, which you read about briefly in the context of the discussion of participant observation in Chapter 12 (Box 12.1, p. 390). Aronson became Festinger's best-known student and dissonance theory has remained central to his work; Aronson and his students are responsible for most of the theory's elaboration over the years. A major contribution was Aronson's argument, first articulated in 1960, that cognitive dissonance was strongest and had its most pervasive effects whenever some important aspect of the self concept was threatened, as when we do something (e.g. cheat on an exam) that is inconsistent with our firmly held beliefs about ourselves (e.g., I am an honest person)(Aronson, 1999b).

As you recall from Chapter 3, psychological scientists sometimes develop ideas for research from everyday observations and sometimes as a logical deduction from theory. Aronson does both, often deriving research hypotheses from observations that are then fit into the framework of dissonance theory. When asked about the origins of his ideas for research, Aronson will mention both sources: first, "[j]ust being alive in the world and noticing certain things that pique my curiosity," and second, "from theory or restructuring of theory" (Aronson, personal communication, 2000). For example, for a while, he was stymied by how ineffective it was to use rational arguments as a way of convincing intelligent college students to use condoms in the era of AIDS. Then he hit on an idea that followed from an extension of dissonance theory. Assuming that most people don't like to think of themselves as hypocrites (saying one thing, doing another), Aronson developed a series of studies (e.g., Aronson, Fried, & Stone, 1991) in which college students were induced to give public talks urging condom use, and subsequently were confronted with their own failure to use condoms. Feeling hypocritical produced dissonance, which the students reduced by increasing their reported levels of condom use.

Throughout his long career, Aronson's enthusiasm for his science has never wavered. In response to a question about the factors that keep him going as a researcher, he replies simply and elegantly, "Three things: One, I am passionately curious about human social behavior; two, I am excited about trying to find out things that might better the human condition, and finally, doing research is great fun" (Aronson, personal communication, 2000).

Elizabeth Loftus

The work of Elizabeth Loftus (Figure E.2) is a perfect blend of the ideals of basic and applied research, as described in Chapter 3. She has contributed much to our knowledge of the fundamental processes of human memory, while at the same time

FIGURE E.2   Elizabeth Loftus

showing how these principles apply to real-world memory phenomena such as eye-witness memory. Loftus herself identifies this mixture as the most interesting aspect of her work as a research psychologist: "I get to make interesting scientific discover-ies and at the same time apply these and other psychological discoveries to the lives of real people" (Loftus, personal communication, 1993).

Loftus is arguably the world's leading expert on the phenomenon of eyewitness memory, part of her broader interest in the factors affecting long-term memory. As a result of her recognized expertise, she has testified in more than 100 court cases in which eyewitness testimony was a crucial element (Loftus, 1986). As you recall, her research was mentioned briefly in the previous chapter as a caution against relying on the accuracy of case history information when it depends on memory of the dis-tant past. Loftus and her colleagues and research team have completed dozens of studies of the ways in which past memories become distorted by information inter-vening between the time of the event to be recalled and the time of recall. Most of this research has focused on direct eyewitness recall, but in recent years Loftus has taken on the empirical question of whether memories of childhood sexual abuse can be accurate when remembered many years later. She argues that serious distor-tions can and do occur.

Loftus's enthusiasm for her research in memory was sparked near the end of her graduate school career at Stanford. Her doctoral dissertation was a basic research project: "An Analysis of the Structural Variables That Determine Problem-Solving Difficulty on a Computer-Based Teletype." If your eyes glaze over as you read the title, Loftus would not be offended. As the project neared its end, she was also "a bit bored with the whole thing" (Loftus & Ketcham, 1991, p. 5). Luckily, she took a social psychology course from Jon Freedman, who sparked her interest in some of the more practical aspects of memory. As Loftus described it:

In my last six months of graduate school, I spent every free moment in Freedman's lab, setting up the experimental design, running subjects, tabulating the data, and analyzing the results. As the project took shape and [we] realized that we were on to something, that we were actually discovering something new about how the brain works, I began to think of myself as a *research psychologist*. Oh, those were *lovely* words—I could design an experiment, set it up, and follow it through. If felt for the first time that I was a scientist, and I knew with ultimate clarity that it was exactly what I wanted to be doing with my life. (Loftus & Ketcham, 1991, p. 6; first italics in the original; second italics added)

There is a thread that weaves together the work of Gibson and Skinner (as described in Chapter 1) and that of Aronson, Loftus, and other psychological researchers. Pavlov accurately identified this common feature when he exhorted his students to be *passionate* about their work. You can detect this passion if you read carefully the quotes I've chosen, both in Chapter 1 and here. In both the Gibson and Skinner quotes, for example, the concept of beauty appears. For Gibson, the first tentative studies with the visual cliff "worked *beautifully*." When Skinner returned to his jammed pellet dispenser, he found "a *beautiful* curve." Similarly, when Aronson said he is "*passionately* curious" about social behavior, and when Loftus referred to her self-identity as a research psychologist as "*lovely* words," that same intensity of feeling was being expressed.

There are enormous gaps in our knowledge of behavior. Hence, there is ample space available for those with the kind of passion displayed by people like Gibson, Skinner, Aronson, Loftus, and countless other researchers. What could be better than to have a career that is continually exciting and rewarding and helps us to understand the complexities of behavior and mental processes? The invitation is open.

APPENDIX A

Communicating the Results of Research in Psychology

In this appendix, you will learn how to:

- Prepare and write an APA-style laboratory report
- Prepare a professional presentation of your research either as a
  - paper to be read or as a
  - poster to be written and organized

Research Reports, APA Style

You are about to enter the world of the obsessive-compulsive. As you begin to learn about APA-style lab reports, it will seem to you that the criticism of every omitted comma, every word not capitalized when it should be, and every F or t not underlined will be symptomatic of something seriously wrong with your instructor. The format will seem to be impossible to master. Take heart. The rules have an important purpose, and the procedures for preparing a lab report can be learned; furthermore, the APA (1994) publishes an easy-to-use *Publication Manual (PM)* that can answer any of your format questions. With the *PM* by your side, it really isn't necessary to memorize the rules about commas and underlining.

If you don't already own a copy of the *PM* and expect to take some additional courses in psychology, you should obtain one immediately. This appendix will help you learn how to communicate results, but at 368 pages, the manual is the ultimate weapon against a botched report.

There are two main reasons for the rules that dictate a consistent format for reporting the results of empirical research. First, research outcomes accumulate external validity as they are repeated in different labs with different participants and perhaps with slightly varied procedures. In order to replicate a study exactly or to make a systematic variation in some procedure, the reader must know precisely what was done in the original study. If the results of a study are written in a known and predictable format, the replication process is made easier. Second, a consistent format makes the review process more efficient. Thousands of research articles are submitted to dozens of psychological research journals every year. Typically, each article is screened by an editor and then sent to two or three other researchers with expertise in the article's topic. These "peer reviewers" read the article and send the editor a written critique that includes a recommendation about whether the article should be published (most journals reject 70–80% of the articles submitted to them). In the absence of an agreed-upon format, the work of the editor and reviewers would be hopelessly complicated. For the purposes of the methods course you are now taking, having a regular format makes it easier for your instructor to grade your report fairly.

General Guidelines

One of my beliefs is that the only way to learn how to do research in psychology is to actually do some research. The same principle applies to writing. It is a skill like any other and it improves with practice, assuming that one's efforts are followed by feedback of some kind. Hence, the most basic recommendation I can make is for you to write whenever you can and ask others to read what you've written. When writing a lab report, I would suggest that you find someone who has already completed the research methods course *and* earned a decent grade. As you are writing your report, ask this person to read your work and critique it.

Writing Style

The APA-style laboratory report is not the Great American Novel. Therefore, some literary devices that might enhance a creative writing exercise, such as deliberately creating an ambiguity to hold the reader's attention or omitting details to arouse curiosity, are out of place in scientific writing. Rather, one should always strive for perfect clarity and simplicity of expression. This is easier said than done, of course, but despite the grain of truth in Figure A.1, academic writing is not necessarily stuffy and difficult to follow.

Calvin and Hobbes

by Bill Watterson

FIGURE A.1   Academic writing?

All good writing includes correct grammatical usage. Grammatical errors automatically create ambiguity and awkwardness, so your first step in learning to write a lab report is to be sure that you know the basic rules of sentence structure. Numerous English usage guides are available, and the *PM* includes a series of guidelines specifically targeted for the kinds of sentences found in scientific writing. One problem that seems especially common in scientific writing, perhaps out of a desire to sound objective, is a tendency to overuse the passive voice. Whenever possible, use the active voice, which generally adds clarity and simplifies sentences. To illustrate,

Passive: An investigation of sleep deprivation was done by Smith (1992).

Active: Smith (1992) investigated sleep deprivation.

In addition to grammatical problems, beginning writers of APA lab reports often use some common words inappropriately. For example, although the term "significant" generally means important or meaningful, the writer using the term in this fashion in a lab report may mislead the reader. This is because, in a lab report, "significant" implies "statistically significant," which has a technical definition relating to the rejection of H_0. A reader encountering the word in a lab report may assume that the technical definition is being used even if the writer didn't mean it that way. To eliminate ambiguity, never use this term in the lab report except when it clearly refers to statistical significance.

Two other common problems with word usage concern the confusion between "affect" and "effect" and the use of some plural nouns such as "data." These and related problems are elaborated in Tables A.1 and A.2.

Reducing Bias in Language

For years, linguists and psychologists interested in language use have investigated the connections between language and thinking. Although there is much disagreement over the nature of this relationship, there is a consensus that using language in certain ways can reinforce and perpetuate certain concepts, including stereotypes about people. One example that is specifically addressed in the *PM* is language considered

TABLE A. 1   *Effectively Using the Terms "Affect" and "Effect"*

One of the most common errors found in student lab reports is the failure to distinguish between the different meanings for the words "affect" and "effect."

affect as a noun means an emotional state; thus
• Because of the pressure of a rapid presentation rate, subjects showed increased <u>affect</u>.
affect as a verb means to influence; thus
• Increasing the presentation rate <u>affected</u> recall.
effect as a noun means the result of some event; thus
• The <u>effect</u> of increasing the presentation rate was a decline in recall.
effect as a verb means to bring about or accomplish some result; thus
• We <u>effected</u> a change by increasing the presentation rate.

A common error is to use "effect" as a verb when "affect" should be used; thus
   Incorrect: Changing to a fixed ratio schedule <u>effected</u> the rat's behavior.
   Correct: Changing to a fixed ratio schedule <u>affected</u> the rat's behavior.

A second common error is to use "affect" as a noun when "effect" should be used; thus
   Incorrect: Changing to a fixed ratio schedule had a major <u>affect</u> on the rats's behavior
   Correct: Changing to a fixed ratio schedule had a major <u>effect</u> on the rat's behavior

to be sexist because it implies inequalities between males and females. The APA first developed guidelines for nonsexist or "gender-neutral" language in 1977. Authors submitting their manuscripts to an APA journal must use nonsexist language.

   Language that is gender neutral avoids two kinds of problems. The first is known as a "problem of designation." These are instances when terms include only masculine terminology but are supposed to refer to both males and females. The most common example is the use of "man" when "person" is intended, as in "Man has long been

TABLE A.2   *Plurals of Words with Latin or Greek Origins*

The plural forms of many words found in scientific writing derive from their origins in Latin and Greek. A failure to recognize the plural form can lead to a grammatical error of disagreement between noun and verb. The most common example is the word **data**, which refers to more than one piece of information and is the plural of **datum**. Although the term "data" is sometimes found in common usage as a singular noun, the PM (p. 34) suggests that it be used only in the plural form.

   Incorrect: The <u>data was</u> subjected to a content analysis.
   Correct: The <u>data were</u> subjected to a content analysis.
Other examples:

Singular form	Plural form
analys**is**	analys**es**
criteri**on**	criteri**a**
hypothes**is**	hypothes**es**
phenomen**on**	phenomen**a**
stimul**us**	stimul**i**

interested in the causes of mental illness." Some research has shown that even though the intent may be truly nonsexist when using such language, readers often interpret the language in ways that exclude females. For example, a study by Kidd (1971) found that when subjects read sentences using "man" or "his" in a supposedly nonsexist fashion, they perceived the sentences as referring to men 86% of the time.

Here are some examples of sentences with problems of designation, along with suggested corrections. As you will see, the problems can be solved fairly easily by rewording, using plurals, or omitting gender designations altogether. The examples are taken directly from Table 1 of the *PM* (pp. 54–60).

1. The client is usually the best judge of the value of his counseling.

    Better: Clients are usually the best judges of the counseling they receive.

2. Man's search for knowledge...

    Better: The search for knowledge...

3. Research scientists often neglect their wives and children.

    Better: Research scientists often neglect their spouses and children.

In addition to problems of designation, some sexist language shows "problems of evaluation." That is, the terms selected for males and females imply inequality. For example, a writer describing high school athletes may refer to the "men's basketball team" and the "girls' basketball team" (better: "women's basketball team"). Also, using phrases like "typically male" or "typically female" can promote stereotypical thinking, as can using stereotypical descriptors for behaviors that may be identical for males and females (e.g., "ambitious men" but "aggressive women"; "cautious men" but "timid women").

Although the guidelines for gender-neutral language are generally designed to correct problems harmful to women, at least one example addresses an inequality detrimental to men. This occurs when the term "mothering" is used to refer to any behavior involving some kind of supportive interaction between parent and child. Using "mothering" to refer to females and "fathering" to refer to the same behavior in males doesn't work because fathering has a different meaning altogether. The APA recommends that the gender-neutral terms "nurturing" or "parenting" be used here to recognize the fact that males perform these kinds of supportive behaviors also.

Gender bias is not the only form of language bias addressed by the *PM*. The *PM* also urges the writer to be cautious about language bias relating to sexual orientation, racial and ethnic identity, age, and disability. Here are some more examples from Table 1 in the *PM:*

1. The sample consisted of 200 adolescent homosexuals.

    Better: The sample consisted of 100 gay male and 100 lesbian adolescents.

2. We studied Eskimos...

    Better: We studied Inuit from Canada and Aleuts...

---

[1] The term derives from the Latin word *plaga,* meaning a snare or hunting net. The term was eventually applied to the capturing, snaring, or kidnapping of children; thus plagiarism is like "kidnapping" someone's ideas (*Webster's Word Histories,* 1989).

3.   …disabled person.

   Better:…person with a disability.

4.   …depressives

   Better:…people who are depressed.

Academic Honesty

In the section in Chapter 2 on scientific fraud, the discussion centered on the falsification of data, but plagiarism[1] was also mentioned as a serious problem to be avoided, and you probably worked through the plagiarism exercise at the end of the chapter. Standard 6.22 of the 1992 ethics code specifically addresses plagiarism, stating that writers "do not present substantial portions or elements of another's work as their own…" (American Psychological Association, 1992, p. 1609).

The most obvious form of plagiarism is copying information directly from some source without using quotation marks and then failing to cite the source. The principle is clear: don't do this under any circumstance, even if the information has been taken from a web page. A second form of plagiarism is subtler, however, and students may not always realize they are plagiarizing and that a citation is necessary. This occurs when students use their own words for concepts, but the concepts clearly belong to some other person. The Applications Exercise in Chapter 2 focuses specifically on this problem. Any time you use an idea, term, theory, or research finding that seems to belong to another person, be sure to cite that person's work. To avoid plagiarism, then, either use direct quotes and clearly attribute the words to the original source or give credit to the creator of an idea, again by the use of a proper citation. (You'll encounter the APA guidelines for accurately citing sources below.)

Miscellaneous

Although your instructor may have some specific additions to or deletions from the following checklist, the following APA formatting rules are designed to create a document that is physically easy to read.

- ✓   double space the entire manuscript
- ✓   make the margins (top, bottom, and sides) at least one inch (2.54 cm) throughout
- ✓   use a paper clip, not a stapler, to join the pages
- ✓   avoid changing the printing fonts
- ✓   don't print in **boldface** or *italics* (items that would be italicized in a journal article are underlined in the manuscript; see the sample paper)
- ✓   make a photocopy of the manuscript and turn in the original; also, be sure to save the file with your manuscript on it on a disk

Main Sections of the Lab Report

The APA-style lab report describing the outcome of an empirical study includes each of the following elements, in this order:

Title page

Abstract

Introduction

Method

Results

Discussion

References

Following the References section, reports typically include separate pages for author notes, other footnotes (if any), tables, a list of figures, and the figures themselves. In some cases, an appendix (listing the actual stimulus materials, for instance) might be included. What follows is a description of how to prepare each main section of the lab report. As you read, refer to (a) Table A.3, which lists the most common (in my experience) formatting errors occurring in each section and (b) the sample lab report included at the end of this appendix.

Title Page

The title page has a precise format, as you can see from the sample paper. It includes the following elements:

The Manuscript Page Header/Page Number

Found in the upper-right-hand corner, the **manuscript page header** is the first two or three words of the complete title. Five spaces to the right is the number 1, which designates the title page as page 1 of the manuscript. Both the page header and the page number are right-justified (i.e., they are flush with the right-hand margin). Except for pages on which figures (e.g., graphs, diagrams, flow charts) are drawn, *every* page of the manuscript includes the page header and the page number. This helps to identify the manuscript if pages become separated for some reason. Use the Header tool on your word processor to create this.

Running Head

If you examine an article printed in any of the APA journals, you will find that after the first page, the top of every page includes a "header" that is either the author's name (even-numbered pages) or a brief version of the full title (odd-numbered pages). The latter is called the "running head" because it is found in a header to the article and it runs throughout the printed article.

To fit into its assigned location, a running head must be brief, yet sufficiently informative to convey the sense of the title. Thus, the running head is not the same thing as the manuscript page header. The only time they are identical is when the

TABLE A.3   *Top 20 Formatting Errors*

In the title page

1. not including the manuscript page header and page 1
2. not right-justifying the page number
3. nor capitalizing all the letters of the running head
4. capitalizing all the letters of the title
5. capitalizing the "h" in "Running head"

In the abstract

6. typing the word "Abstract" all in caps
7. indenting the first line as in a normal paragraph
8. using more than a single paragraph
9. writing more than 120 words

In the introduction

10. failing to start the section by repeating the exact title
11. starring the section by labeling it "Introduction"
12. making referencing errors

In the method section

13. failing to label the section properly ("Method" is centered between the margins)
14. failing to underline the subheadings (e.g., "Participants")
15 starting the section on a new page instead of continuing immediately after the end of the introduction

In the results section

16. failing to label the section properly
17. failing to use proper abbreviations for statistical concepts like the mean
18. failing to report inferential srarisrical analyses properly

In the discussion section

19. failing to label the section properly
20. making referencing errors

first two or three words of the title just happen to provide a good description of the study's content.

The running head is printed at the top of the title page, just below the manuscript page header and page number, and flush with the left-hand margin. It is limited to 50 characters, which include letters, spaces between words, and punctuation marks. For the hypnotism case study in Chapter 12, which had a running head of 39 characters, the top of the title page of the submitted manuscript looked like this:

Running head: EXPERIENCES ACCOMPANYING STAGE HYPNOSIS

Title/Author/Affiliation

The title of the article, the name of the person writing the paper (or names, for papers with more than one author), and the author's college, university, or other professional affiliation go on the top half of the title page, centered between the left and right margins. The first letters of the primary words in the title are capitalized. Thus, for the hypnotism case study (Crawford, Kitner-Triolo, Clarke, & Olesko, 1992), the title looked like this:

Transient Positive and Negative Experiences Accompanying Stage Hypnosis

Give some thought to the wording of the article's title, which should range from 10 to 12 words. It should give the reader a clear idea of the article's content and preview the variables being investigated. For example, in an experimental study, a common title format is "The effect of X on Y," which enables the reader to identify the independent and dependent variables. Thus, a study entitled "The Effect of Landmarks and North Orientation on Directionality" tells the reader that participants will be performing some kind of direction-finding task for the dependent measure and that two independent variables will be manipulated: whether or not landmarks are present and whether or not participants are told the direction of north.

A second common format is a declarative sentence that summarizes the main result. An example would be "Helping Behavior Depends on Situational Ambiguity and the Empathy Level of Bystanders." This title tells the reader that the study includes a manipulated independent variable, whether or not the situation clearly calls for help, and (probably) a subject variable, whether or not bystanders are empathic individuals.

The APA has specific guidelines about authorship when more than one person is involved in a research project. In general, a person should not be an author unless he or she has made a substantial contribution to the work. Being in on the initial planning, helping to set up the study, collecting some of the data, working on the analysis, and providing feedback to someone else's draft of the article would constitute a substantial contribution. On the other hand, entering all the data into a spreadsheet and coordinating the subject pool would not be a contribution sufficient to warrant authorship. On a paper with more than a single author, the first author (i.e., the name listed first on the title page) should be the person who has done the most work. When students work in projects in groups, it is generally a good idea to have one person be the overall leader of the project, carrying responsibilities sufficient to justify first authorship.

Abstract

This is the first text material to be read in a lab report and the last to be written. It is also the *only* part of the article looked at by many readers, who are forced by the sheer mass of information to read the abstract first in order to determine if the entire article is worth examining in detail. Abstracts are reprinted in full in PsycINFO.

The abstract contains elements of each of the remaining four major sections, and because it cannot exceed 960 total characters and spaces (about 120 words) in a single paragraph, it must be very carefully prepared—every word counts. To save space, numbers are never spelled out in the abstract unless they begin sentences. The abstract's opening statement is perhaps the most informative. It always includes a statement of the problem, and it usually informs the reader about the individuals tested and/or the variables under investigation. Here are some samples of the opening sentences of abstracts, taken from three of the case studies used in Chapter 12.

- To describe sex differences in interpersonal touch, observation was made of 4,500 dyads in their teens and older in public places (Hall & Veccia, 1990, p. 1155)

- Frequency of positive and negative experiences accompanying stage hypnosis was assessed in follow-up interviews with 22 participants of university-sponsored performances (Crawford et al., 1992, p. 663).

- Records on recovery after cholecystectomy of patients in a suburban Pennsylvania hospital between 1972 and 1981 were examined to determine whether assignment to a room with a window view of a natural setting might have restorative influences (Ulrich, 1984, p. 420).

In addition to the meaty opening sentence, an abstract mentions something about the method, briefly summarizes the key results (the second most important sentence), and usually closes with a brief conclusion. The abstract occupies page 2 and only page 2 of the lab report. You should begin a new page when starting the introduction.

Introduction

The introduction thoroughly describes the problem being studied and, by reviewing the pertinent research literature, makes it clear what is known and what is not known about the problem. What is unknown or unclear provides the basis for one or more predictions, and these predictions form the hypotheses for the study. Thus, an introduction includes, normally in this order, a statement of the problem, a review of related research literature, and one or more hypotheses to be tested in the study. In a well-written introduction, the hypotheses are found in the final paragraph and flow naturally from the earlier descriptions of the problem and the review of related research. In a poorly written introduction, the hypotheses just seem to pop out at the end of the section and don't seem to have any rational basis. The introduction's literature review only includes studies directly relevant to the study summarized in the lab report.

The introduction begins page 3 of the manuscript and is the only major section of the lab report that is not headed by an identifying label. Rather than being headed with the label "Introduction," the section begins with the article's full title.

APA Citation Format

When reviewing past research related to the problem at hand, you will need to provide citations for the studies mentioned; the *PM* provides a specific format for this. Sometimes the author's name will be part of the sentence you are writing. If so, the date of publication follows the name and is placed in parentheses. For example:

> In a study by Smith (1990), helping behavior declined as the situation became more ambiguous.

If the author's name is not included in the sentence, the name, a comma, and the date are placed in parentheses. For example:

> In an earlier study (Smith, 1990), helping behavior declined as the situation became more ambiguous.

If a direct quote is used, the page number is included. For example:

> Situational ambiguity occurred when "participants had difficulty determining whether the confederate had fallen onto the live wire" (Smith, 1990, p. 23).

> or

> In the study by Smith (1990), situational ambiguity occurred when "participants had difficulty determining whether the confederate had fallen onto the live wire" (p. 23).

Take careful note of this: every work cited in the introduction (or any other part of the manuscript) must be given a complete listing at the end of the paper. You'll learn how that is accomplished shortly in the description of the "References" section of the report. The *PM* has a thorough guide to citations and can be consulted for virtually any question you may have. Also, you will find the APA's format being used in most of your psychology texts, including this one; hence several models are available to you.

Method

The guiding principle of the method section is that it must be detailed enough for other researchers to read it and be able to replicate the study in their own laboratories. Notice that I've written "Other researchers" and not "anyone else." Thus, you can assume that the reader will have some specialized knowledge of methodology. It is enough to say that participants were matched according to variables X, Y, and Z; explaining matching step by step is not necessary. Similarly, it is enough to describe the type of counterbalancing used (e.g., a 4 × 4 Latin square) without explaining in great detail why such a control procedure is needed or how the square was constructed.

The method section includes several subsections, which vary depending on the particular study. One subsection always occurs, however, and it is labeled "Participants." This normally opens the method section and includes a description of the sample of people or animals participating in the study. The reader of this subsection should be able to determine the general types of persons who participated in the study, some of their demographic features, how many there were, and how they were selected.

The description of participants is usually followed by a subsection called "Apparatus" if laboratory equipment was used or "Materials" if the experimenter used paper-and-pencil materials such as questionnaires or personality tests. Standard equipment usually can be described with reference to the manufacturer and model number. Apparatus created especially for the study should be described in more detail and perhaps drawn (as in the sample study reprinted below). Copyrighted surveys or personality questionnaires can simply be listed with the appropriate reference citation.

A third subsection is called "Procedure" or sometimes "Procedure and Experimental Design." It is the longest portion of the method section. It describes and operationally defines all the variables, discusses the design of the study and all the control features, and reports exactly what happened to the research participants.

Unlike the introduction, the method section does not begin on a new page. It immediately follows the introduction and is labeled with the word "Method," which is centered (refer to the sample paper for the formatting rules for the subsections). This same continuity rule applies to the results and discussion sections.

Results

This section of the report provides a concise yet complete verbal description of the results, along with descriptive and inferential statistics. A typical paragraph in the results section includes a verbal description of some finding, accompanied by the relevant descriptive and inferential statistics supporting the statement. No attempt is made to explain why some prediction succeeded or failed: such interpretation belongs in the discussion section.

A good way to organize the results section is with reference to the sequence of hypotheses in the introduction. For instance, if the introduction ends with three hypotheses, the results section should have a paragraph devoted to each prediction, presented in the same order as in the intro.

Reporting the Data: Statistics

As you recall from Chapter 4, descriptive statistics summarize data and inferential statistics determine whether it is prudent to reject the null hypothesis(es) or not. The most common descriptive statistics reported are means, standard deviations, and correlation coefficients. Typical inferential statistics includes *t* tests, *F* ratios from ANOVAs, and chi square (χ^2) tests. The *PM* also encourages the inclusion of effect size calculations (p. 18). Procedures for calculating all of these are presented in Appendix C. For now, be aware of two things. First, there are standard abbreviations for statistical terms such as the sample mean ($\underline{M}$) and standard deviation ($\underline{SD}$). Second, the general rule in reporting statistics is to put the descriptive statistics before the inferential statistics in any given paragraph. A typical results section might have consecutive sentences like this:

> Subjects given the imagery instructions recalled a mean of 16.5 words ($\underline{SD}$ = 2.3), while those told merely to repeat the words recalled 12.3 words ($\underline{SD}$ = 3.1) on the average. The difference was significant, $\underline{F}$(1, 18) = 12.8, $\underline{p}$ < .01.

The shorthand method for reporting inferential statistics is basically the same for all types of analysis. The test is identified (e.g., $\underline{F}$), the degrees of freedom are listed (1 for the numerator of the F ratio and 18 for the denominator), the calculated value of the test is reported (12.8), and the probability value (e.g., $\underline{p}$ < 01) is indicated. Note that the "F" and "p," as well as the "M" and "SD," are underlined. This indicates that the letters are to be italicized in a published account, but in your paper do not use italics—stick with the underline. This rule also applies in the Reference section for those parts of a cited reference that are to be underlined in your paper, but italicized in the final publication (see below).

Portraying the Data: Tables and Figures

Descriptive statistics, especially in factorial designs, are often complicated enough that a paragraph-length description of them will be impossible to follow. To avoid the problem, data are often presented in tables and/or figures. **Tables** are row and column arrangements that typically present means and standard deviations or sets of correlations. **Figures** can be graphs, diagrams, flow charts, sketches of apparatus, or photos. Each has specific formatting rules, which can be seen in the sample paper.

It is sometimes difficult to decide whether to present the data in either a table or a figure. In general, a table is preferred if it seems important to report the precise mean scores (on a graph the exact scores require some guessing) or if there is so much data that a graph would be hopelessly cluttered. On the other hand, graphs can often illustrate a point dramatically, and they are especially useful for showing an interaction effect in a factorial study. One certainty is that it is inappropriate to present the same data in two ways—both in a table and as a figure. If a graph is used, it can take several forms; the most common are line graphs and bar graphs. As described and illustrated in Chapter 7, line graphs are normally (but not necessarily) used when the variable on the X-axis is continuous; for discrete variables (e.g., gender), bar graphs should be used.

When using tables or figures, it is not sufficient just to present them. In the results section, you must refer the reader to them and point out their important features. Some skill is involved here because you don't want to write a detailed description that points out every aspect of a table or graph. Thus, in a graph showing a serial position curve in a memory experiment, you might encounter a sentence like this:

> Figure 1 shows that recall was quite high for the first few words of the list, poor for middle words, and almost perfect for the final three words.

As you can tell from the sample paper, tables and figures are not placed in the middle of the text description. Rather, they are placed at the end of the report.

Also in the sample paper, notice that the title of the table is included on the same page as the table but the figure titles (called "figure captions") are typed on a page that is separate from the figures themselves. This is not an arbitrary rule designed to lower your grade but follows from the way a manuscript is transformed into a printed journal article. Tables are set in type like any other text, as are the figure captions. The figures themselves, however, are submitted as high-quality photographs and have to be fitted into their appropriate space (this is why the pages of figures don't include manuscript page headers and page numbers). Hence, the figures and their captions are submitted separately. If you have more than one figure, it is not necessary to create a separate figure caption page for each one; simply list all the captions on a single page.

Discussion

This is the final section of the text material and serves to tie the entire report together. It begins by summarizing the main results with reference to the original hypothesis(es) and then proceeds with its major task—interpretation. This evaluation includes relating the results to any theoretical points raised in the introduction and trying to explain failed predictions. The discussion also addresses the problem of alternative explanations of results. As the author of the article, you will decide on the interpretation that seems most reasonable, but sometimes other alternatives could be conceived. You should mention these alternatives and then explain why you think yours is better.

Finally, the discussion includes an important element of any research program: consideration of "what's next?" questions. That is, writers usually make suggestions about what the next study should be, given the outcome of the one just completed. This, of course, is a natural consequence of the fact that research always answers some questions but raises others.

References

Unlike the method, results, and discussion sections, the references section starts on a new page and consists of a list of all the items cited in the lab report. Each item has its first line indented, as in a paragraph indent. The *PM* includes a complete set of rules for virtually every type of citation; here are examples of the most common ones:

1. *A journal article with one author*

   Loftus, E. L. (1986). Ten years in the life of an expert witness. <u>Law and Human Behavior, 10,</u> 241–263.

2. *A journal article with more than one author*

   Hall, J. A., & Veccia, E. M. (1990). More "touching" observations: New insights on men, women, and interpersonal touch. <u>Journal of Personality and Social Psychology, 59,</u> 1155–1162.

3. *A magazine*

   Palmer, J. D. (1982, October). Biorhythm bunkum. <u>Natural History,</u> 90–97.

4. *A book*

   Skinner, B. F. (1953). <u>Science and human behavior.</u> New York: Free Press.

5. *A book that is not a first edition*

   Aronson, E. (1999). <u>The social animal</u> (8th ed.). New York: W. H. Freeman.

6. *A chapter from an edited book*

   Weiss, J. M. (1977). Psychological and behavioral influences on gastrointesti-nal lesions in animal models. In J. D. Maser & M. E. P. Seligman (Eds.), <u>Psychopathology: Experimental models</u> (pp. 232–269). San Francisco: Freeman.

7. *Electronic sources*

Rules for citing references from websites, electronic databases, e-mail, and so on, have been evolving in recent years and are frequently updated. For the most recent set of guidelines, consult the page on APA's website that is dedicated to this topic: www.apa.org/journals/webref.html

One final point, and mistakes are often made here, is that before turning in a lab report, you should check the citations in the body of your paper against the list in the Reference section. Specifically, make sure that (a) every source mentioned in the text of your lab report is given a listing in the Reference section of the paper and (b) every reference listed in the Reference section is cited somewhere in the text of your lab report.

Presentations and Posters

If you're lucky, you may find yourself in a position to present the results of some of your research publicly. This can range from a presentation to other psychology students as part of a course requirement to a more formal presentation at a professional conference. For example, as mentioned in the Epilogue, sessions for undergraduate research are scheduled at national meetings of the APA and the American Psychological Society (APS) and at regional meetings (e.g., that of the Midwestern Psychological Association, or MPA). Also, a number of colleges and universities host conferences specifically for the purpose of presenting undergraduate research.

Tips for Presenting a Paper

Presentations at professional psychology conferences take one of two forms: papers or, more likely, posters. The paper is the more traditional format. In a typical 1-hour session (50 minutes, actually), several researchers will each read a paper describing their work. If this happens to you, here are some recommendations:

1. You will be given a strict time limit—stick to it. A typical limit is 12 minutes, which allows time for four papers in the session. If you take 20–25 minutes, the person who is scheduled to go last in the session will hate you forever.

2. Prepare a one-page handout that a friend can distribute to the audience just as you are being introduced. The handout should include the title of the paper and your name and affiliation, your hypothesis(es), an abbreviated description of the design, the results, usually as a table or graph, and a concise conclusion. Unfortunately, many in the audience will be thinking about what session they are going to attend in the next hour, planning dinner, or rehearsing their own presentation rather than listening carefully to you, so your handout can be an effective way for them to take useful information away with them.

3. If audiovisual equipment is available, take advantage of it. For example, if the room where you give your presentation will have an overhead projector, prepare transparencies that duplicate the tables and graphs in your handout. Then show them at the appropriate spot in your presentation and point out the salient features. If the room has electronic capability, learn how to use Power-Point and deliver your presentation that way.

4. Prepare a normal lab report and then adapt it to the form of a document to be presented orally. This means focusing on the essential points and avoiding picky details. For example, although you should include the model name for some apparatus in the lab report, the generic name (e.g., "operant chamber") is fine for an oral presentation. The listener should be clear about the purpose of your study, the essential elements of design and control, the results, and what your

overall conclusions are. Your presentation should be more conversational than it would be in the more formal lab report.

5. Practice your presentation in front of friends; ideally, have it videotaped; then practice some more. To help with the inevitable anxiety, try to remember that of all the people in the room, you know your project better than anyone.

Tips for Presenting a Poster

Poster sessions have the advantage of allowing the presentation of many more research projects per hour than in a typical paper session and, of course, they eliminate the public-speaking anxiety that accompanies a paper presentation (this could be a disadvantage; learning to speak in public is an important skill). They also increase the chances that you will meet people with research interests similar to yours. At an effective poster session, you will have half a dozen good conversations, get some ideas for interpreting your results differently perhaps, develop some answers to "what next?" questions, and perhaps exchange e-mail addresses.

If you do a poster, you will find yourself in a large room filled with row after row of bulletin boards. On one of these boards, you will arrange a display that enables someone to understand what you have discovered in your research. You will also prepare copies (usually 50) of a brief version of your paper to be given to those who wish to take one. Here are some tips for presenting a good poster:

1. Layout is critically important. Readers of your poster should be able to figure out the essence of what happened in your study in just a minute or two. If their first response is confusion, they will move on to the next poster. Figure A.2 shows you one possible layout, but the particular conference you're attending might have some specific rules, so pay attention to them. For instance, some smaller conferences publish all the abstracts in a booklet given to conference attendees. If so, there's no need for you to include an Abstract page in the poster itself. Instead, start with a section called "Introduction" or "Problem Statement."

2. In general, the layout of your poster should be organized and logical. Readers should be able to determine easily the purpose of your study, the method, the results, and your overall conclusions. Be sure the content of the poster flows easily from left to right. Feel free to use arrows to direct the reader.

3. It should be possible to read and understand your poster from a distance of six feet. Your title should be printed in letters about 1.5″ high and your name and university affiliation a bit smaller. The major headings should be set at about 36 pt, things like figure captions at 24 pt, and text no smaller than 18 pt. Use fonts that are easy to read (e.g., Arial, Geneva, Helvetica). Using color conservatively is OK, but don't overuse it to the point of distraction (e.g., don't create a graph with six different colors in it). Mount each page of your poster on backing that is a consistent color. Poster board makes for a good backing, but construction paper will do. Bring extra pushpins for mounting your poster pages to the bulletin board—conferences supply pins, but there never seem to be enough to go around.

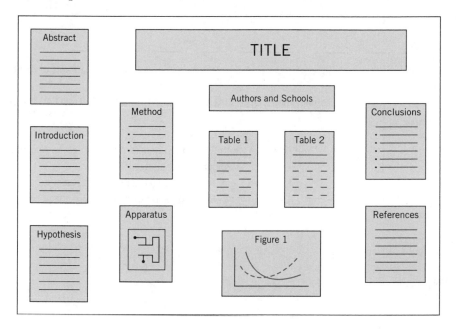

FIGURE A.2   Sample poster layout

4. Less is more—edit to the bare bones. Use bulleted lists instead of long paragraphs. If someone needs more precise detail about some aspect of the study, you'll be there to tell them.

5. The poster is essentially a visual form of presentation, so use graphics liberally. In addition to tables and graphs, feel free to include drawings of apparatus, photos of the research environment, and so on. Every graphic should tell an important part of the story of the research, however.

A Sample Research Report

The following sample report is a revised version of a paper that three of my students authored and delivered to an undergraduate research conference. This report is shorter than and not as sophisticated as the articles you'll find in most journals, but it is closer to the kind of lab report that you will be preparing as you begin to learn APA format, so you should find it helpful.

1. Manuscript page header and page number are placed on the same line, separated by five spaces and with the page number right justified.

2. Manuscript page header: first two or three main words of title.

3. Leftjustified.

4. No cap for "head."

5. All caps; no more than 50 characters, including spaces; unlike the page header, the running head should be somewhat informative about the variables in the study.

6. Title, author(s), and affiliation are centered (your instructor may want you to add the date even though it is not in the APA format; for papers subirutred to APA journals, the date will be on the cover letter sent by the author to the editor).

7. Title should inform the reader about the variables to be encountered in the study.

Effects of North   1   1
2

3
Running head: ORIENTATION, DISTANCE, AND POINTING ACCURACY
4   5

7
The Effects of North Orientation and Target Distance on Accuracy
in Pointing to Geographic Locations
6   Aimee Faso, Theresa Yuncke, and Teresa Kotiman
Wheeling Jesuit University

8. Center.

9. Double space (throughout the entire manuscript).

10. No paragraph indent here.

11. Maximum of 960 characters and spaces here; about 120 words.

8 Abstract 9

10 The ability to point accurately toward fixed geographical targets was investigated in a 2 x 2 x 6 factorial design. Seventy-two participants (36 male and 36 female) tried to locate 6 different targets; 3 of these targets were within walking distance of the 11 psychology laboratory, and the remaining 3 were at least 70 miles from campus. Half of the subjects were oriented to the compass direction of north; half were not. A north orientation facilitated performance for the 3 distant targets but did not significantly improve performance for the 3 nearby targets. No gender differences occurred.

12. Continue to right justiFy the page header and page numbers, but do not right justiFy the text of the article.

13. Do not include the label "Introduction", instead, reproduce the title exactly as it is on the cover page.

14. Begin a new page for the introduction.

15. Opening paragraph introduces the topic area of the research and defines terms (e.g., "cognitive maps").

16. Introduction describes some prior research, but only if it is relevant to your study. Here, the Evans and Pezdek study is described because it introduces the difference between two ways of developing cognitive maps.

17. When a reference like this is within parentheses, the ampersand (&) is used; when the reference is in the flow of a sentence, use the word "and."

Effects of North   3   12

13   The Effects of North Orientation and Target Distance on Accuracy   14
in Pointing to Geographic Locations

15   Cognitive maps are mental representations of spatial
information (Ormrod, Ormrod, Wagner, & McCallin, 1988). They   17
enable us to know where we are in the geographic environment,
and they help us navigate through the environment in order to
move efficiently from point A to point B. Researchers interested in
cognitive mapping have studied such topics as how the elements of
these maps develop (e.g., Cohen, 1985), how they are structured
(e.g., Sholl, 1987), how they are used for navigation (e.g., Kaplan,
1976), and how accurate we are when using them for making
decisions about where things are located. This last topic was the
focus of the experiment described here.

16   Evans and Pezdek (1980) demonstrated that people rely on two
methods of developing cognitive maps. First, they use the results of
direct experience in navigating through the environment. Thus
students become familiar with a campus by moving around in it.
They know, for instance, that to get to the library from the gym, one
takes a left at the campus shop and goes about 200 yards. A
second type of cognitive map knowledge is cartographic: people
study maps. Even if we have never visited Europe, we know that
France is just to the south of England and separated from it by the
English Channel. Of course, some cognitive map knowledge can
result both from direct experience and from studying maps.

Evans and Pezdek (1980) asked volunteers to decide as quickly
as possible if sets of three target locations were in the correct
spatial positions with reference to each other. When the locations
were states, subjects used cartographic information when making

18. The last portion of the introduction describes the study's hypotheses and the basis for them. It isn't enough to say that you expect X to happen; you must make a case for X. This paragraph ends with a specific hypothesis; the sentences leading up to it build the ease for that hypothesis.

19. If two or more works are cited within parentheses, separate them with a semicolon and place them in alphabetical order (with reference to the first author's name in a multiauthored article).

20. Do not begin the method section on a new page; continue to double space throughout.

21. Centered.

22. The method should be described so that another researcher can read the explanation and replicate the study.

Effects of North   4

their decisions. When the target locations were nearby on-campus locations, however, they apparently relied on their direct experience.

18   Our study had two purposes. First, it was designed to measure how accurately individuals could point toward locations that were either nearby or distant. If distant targets (e.g., cities) are learned and thought of with reference to actual maps, then accuracy in pointing to these targets should be improved if people receive some specific cartographic information such as the direction of "north." If nearby targets are learned by moving through the local environment, however, rather than by using maps, then a north orientation might not be very helpful when pointing to them. On this basis, we hypothesized that when pointing at distant geographic targets, accuracy would be improved by giving subjects a north orientation. When pointing at local targets, however, north orientation was not expected to help.

The second purpose of the study was to explore possible gender differences in using cognitive maps. Some studies (e.g., Kozlowski & Bryant, 1977) have failed to find differences between males and females on a cognitive mapping task, but several (e.g.,

19   Herman, Kail, & Siegel, 1979; Ward, Newcombe, & Overton, 1986) have found that males use spatial information more efficiently than females. On this basis, we expected that males might point more accurately to geographic targets than females.

20   Method   21

23   Participants

24   Seventy-two undergraduate volunteers (36 males and 36 females)   22
from a small private university took part in the study. Experimenters

---

23. Subheadings are underlined and placed flush with the left margin; the description follows in paragraph form.

24. If you begin a sentence with a number, the number must be spelled out completely. This sentence could not begin like this: "72 undergraduates…"

25. Figures are usually graphs, but they can also be such things as photographs, maps, or, in this case, a sketch of the apparatus. The actual figures are drawn on separate pages and included at the end of the report.

26. Notice that the order in which the variables are described is maintained through the method and results sections. First gender is described, then orientation, then location.

Effects of North   5

visited freshman- and sophomore-level classes, described the general procedure, and asked for volunteers. No course credit was given. None of the participants were residents of the three distant target cities, but all were familiar with the cities. Participation required approximately 10 minutes. The volunteers were tested individually.

Apparatus

     Participants pointed toward a series of targets by means of a goniometer (see Figure 1), a device used by physical therapists   25
for measuring angles (e.g., at the elbow). One arm of the goniometer was fixed to a board and the second was free to rotate through 360°. This second arm served as a pointer. The experiment took place in a small classroom that had blackout curtains drawn to prevent subjects from seeing anything outside of the building. Participants stood at a lab table with the goniometer lined up so that its fixed arm was pointing either (a) directly toward north or (b) approximately east/northeast. This latter direction was the result of lining up the goniometer so that the board on which it was fixed was flush with the edge of the lab table.

Procedure

26   The study used a 2 × 2 × 6 factorial design. The first factor was the subject variable of gender. The second factor was whether or not participants performed the task while knowing the direction of north. The 36 males and 36 females were randomly assigned to the two levels of this north orientation factor, with the restriction that an equal number of males and females be assigned to each group.

27. Something about debriefing is usually mentioned, but it is not necessary to describe how you conformed to all aspects of the ethics code; it is assumed that you did. Authors submitting articles to APA journals are required include a statement in their cover letter to the editor confirming that the guidelines were followed.

Thus, 18 males and 18 females were given a north orientation; the remaining 18 males and 18 females were not.

The third factor was the within-subjects variable of target location. Six different targets were used. Three were locations that were either on or within walking distance of the campus: the college's front entrance, a local bar, and a money machine. The remaining locations were distant geographical targets that were at least 70 miles from Wheeling: Pittsburgh, Cleveland, and Washington, DC. Target sequence was counterbalanced through the use of a 6×6 Latin square. Participants were randomly assigned to a row of the square, with the restriction that equal numbers of males and females were assigned to each row.

The students were told that they would be given a series of locations, some nearby and some far away, and that they were to move the free arm of the goniometer so that it was pointing directly at each location. Those in the north orientation condition were told that the fixed arm of the goniometer was pointed toward north and they could use it as a reference point. Those in the control condition were told nothing about the orientation of the goniometer.

27   The primary dependent measure was accuracy of pointing. Experimenters determined the correct answers for each location with reference to reliable maps. This made it possible to determine the degree of error for each response. Whether the error was to the "left" or to the "right" of the target was ignored. Thus the error scores ranged from 00 to 1800. Participants were also asked to describe any strategies they used when performing the task.

28. Do nor begin the results section on a new page; continue to double space throughout.

29. Centered.

30. Report descriptive statistics; in this case, some means are reported in the text, others in Table 1, and still others in graph form (Figure 2).

31. Report inferential statistics, in this ease the results of the ANOVA; note that the format for reporting the ANOVA contains these elements:

—the name of the test, underlined: F

—the degrees of freedom, in parentheses: (1,68)

—the calculated value of the F ratio: 24.87

—the chances of making a Type I error, with p underlined: $p < .01$

—note: if the value of F is less than 1, just say so and omit the p value

32. Never place tables in the body of the report. As with figures, place them at the end of the report.

After completing all six trials and describing any strategies they used, subjects were debriefed. Those requesting the final results were sent a brief summary at the conclusion of the study.

Results 29

28   The data were analyzed with a 2 (gender) $\times$ 2 (orientation) $\times$ 6 (target location) analysis of variance, with the level of alpha set at .05. The mean error across all conditions for

30   males was 52.10 and for females it was 46.9˚; the difference was not significant, $F(1, 68) < 1$. A main effect for orientation was

31   found, however ($F(1, 68) = 24.87$, $p < .01$). The average error for those given the north orientation was 33.2˚ ($SD = 12.6$); it was 65.9˚ ($SD = 15.4$) for those in the control group. As shown in

32   Table 1, the overall advantage for those given a north orientation occurred both for males and for females.

There was no overall effect for target location, $F(5, 340) < 1$, but there was a significant interaction between north orientation and target location, $F(5, 340) = 7.91$, $p < .01$. A simple effects analysis of the effect of north orientation for each location found that those given the orientation had less error for all three distant locations ($p < .01$). For the closer targets, there were no differences between those given and those not given a north orientation ($p > .05$) for the first two locations, but the north orientation did facilitate performance for the third close location, a money machine just off campus (p < .05). These effects can be seen in Figure 2.

33. Do nor begin the discussion section on a new page; continue to double space throughout.

34. Centered.

35. Recall from Chapter 8 that when both main effects and interactions occur, the interaction should be interpreted first. Sometimes the interaction is more important than the main effect (this is one of those times).

36. Results don't always come our as nicely as one would like; an outcome with a slight ambiguity calls for further research to determine if the effect is reliable.

37. Concentrate on the main finding and try to interpret what it means by relating it back to what was described in the introduction.

Effects of North   8

Neither the 2-way interaction between gender and location ($F(5, 340) < 1$) nor the 3-way interaction between gender, orientation, and location ($F(5, 340) < 1$) was significant.

33
35

Discussion   34

A significant main effect for north orientation occurred in the study, but the more important result is the interaction between north orientation and location. When pointing to distant targets,

36

subjects clearly were aided by being told the direction of north; when the targets were nearby, a north orientation was not as helpful. However, the fact that the north orientation did provide an advantage for one of the three local targets suggests a need for

37

replication before the interaction can be considered a reliable finding.

This outcome is consistent with the research of Evans and Pezdek (1980) in finding that cognitive mapping includes two types of knowledge. One type of spatial knowledge results from the direct experience of moving to and from nearby locations. Such knowledge is perhaps organized in terms of local landmarks and direction changes with reference to those landmarks ("take a right at the mailroom"). Hence pointing accurately to such targets is not as likely to be aided by reference to compass points. Indeed, when explaining their strategies, several participants visualized the trip from the building where they were being tested to the location in question.

The second type of spatial knowledge is more oriented to the compass and results from our experience with maps, which are always oriented to north. When pointing to these locations, we apparently rely on images of the maps we have studied, an idea

38. This is a good place to show off some what's next?" thinking.

39. There is no need to go into a elaborate explanation about why some prediction failed, especially if there is no immediately obvious way to interpret the result. Something should be said about each hypothesis, however, whether it came out as expected or not.

40. Summarize your conclusions but try to avoid being repetitive.

supported by participants' comments. More than half said that they tried to visualize a map when trying to decide about Pittsburgh, Cleveland, or Washington; none mentioned maps when referring to the nearby locations.

38　In addition to replicating our results, future research might extend the findings by examining the effects of local landmarks on pointing accurately toward nearby targets. Just as the current study found that cartographic information improved performance for distant targets more than for nearby ones, perhaps the opposite result would occur if subjects were given the direction of local landmarks instead of a north orientation. If navigating to nearby targets involves using these landmarks, then pointing accuracy might be improved for them but not for distant targets.

39　No gender differences were found, perhaps due to the nature of the task. Although several studies have found a slight advantage for males, one other study that failed to find a difference between males and females (Kozlowski & Bryant, 1977) also used a "point to X" procedure.

40　In summary, our knowledge of geographic locations results from direct experience in traveling to those places and from a more abstract map knowledge. When asked to point to geographic targets, giving people a north orientation enhances their performance when pointing at targets learned with reference to maps; however, a north orientation does not help people point more accurately to nearby targets that are learned by the experience of visiting them.

41. Begin the references section on a new page.

42. Centered; if you only have a single reference, call this part of the report the "Reference" section.

43. Note the proper formatting: what is underlined; where the commas and periods are; what is capitalized.

44. The first line of a reference is indented with a normal paragraph indent; when the article is printed in a journal, this is convened to a "hanging indent" format, which has the flint line flush to the left margin and subsequent lines indented two or three spaces.

45. Note: Every item in the references section should be mentioned in the paper itself, likewise, every reference cited in the paper should be found in the references section.

Effects of North   10

41   42 References   43

44 Cohen, R. (1985). The development of spatial cognition. Hillsdale, NJ: Erlbaum.

Evans, G. W., & Pezdek, K. (1980). Cognitive mapping: Knowledge of real world distance and location information. Journal of Experimental Psychology: Human Learning and Memory, 6, 13–24.

Herman, J. F., Kail, R. V., & Siegel, A. W. (1979). Cognitive maps of a college campus: A new look at freshman orientation. Bulletin of the Psychonomic Society, 13, 183–186.

45 Kaplan, R. (1976). Way-finding in the natural environment. In G. T. Moore & R. G. Golledge (Eds.), Environmental knowing (pp. 46–57). Stroudsburg, PA: Dowden, Hutchinson, and Ross.

Kozlowski, L. T., & Bryant, K. J. (1977). Sense of direction, spatial orientation, and cognitive maps. Journal of Experimental Psychology: Human Perception and Performance, 3, 590–598.

Ormrod, J. E., Ormrod, R. K., Wagner, E. D., & McCallin, R. C. (1988). Reconceptualizing map learning. American Journal of Psychology, 101, 425–433.

Sholl, J. (1987). Cognitive maps as orienting schemata. Journal of Experimental Psychology: Learning, Memory, and Cognition, 13, 615–628.

Ward, S. L., Newcombe, N., & Overton, W. F. (1986). Turn left at the church, or three miles north: A study of direction giving and sex differences. Environment and Behavior, 18, 192–213.

46. Use a separate page for each table if you have more than one; "Table 1" is not underlined.

47. Continue to include the manuscript page header and the page number on pages with tables.

48. Note underlining and use of horizontal lines to organize the table; never use vertical lines.

49. Statistical symbols (e.g., M, SD, t, r, F) are always underlined.

50. Clarifies dependent measure; notice the underlining.

Effects of North   11   47

46   Table 1

Error Scores as a Function of Gender and Whether North
Orientation Was Given

48

Gender	Orientation	
	With North	Without North
Male		
49 M	30.7	63.2
SD	10.5	22.9
Female		
M	35.7	68.5
SD	19.1	12.8

50   Note. The error score is measured as the difference in degrees between
the correct response and the subject's actual response.

51. Call this "Figure Caption" if your report only has one figure.

52. Center

53. Notice the underline.

54. Carry second line back to left margin.

55. These are the description that will appear beneath the figures if your paper gets published in a journal.

Effects of North   11

51   Figure Captions   52

53   <u>Figure 1</u>. A goniometer. The fixed arm pointed toward north for half   55
54   of the subjects; the arm free to rotate was used for pointing toward
geographic targets.

<u>Figure 2</u>. Amount of error in pointing toward three nearby and three
distant targets, both for those given a north orientation and for
those given no orientation.

56. Do not include the manuscript page header or the page number on pages with figures (in pencil, print "top," "Figure 1," and the page header on the back of this page near the top left edge). Do the same for Figure 2 on the next page.

57. if you have more than one figure, use a separate page for each (all of the figure captions can be placed on single page, though).

56

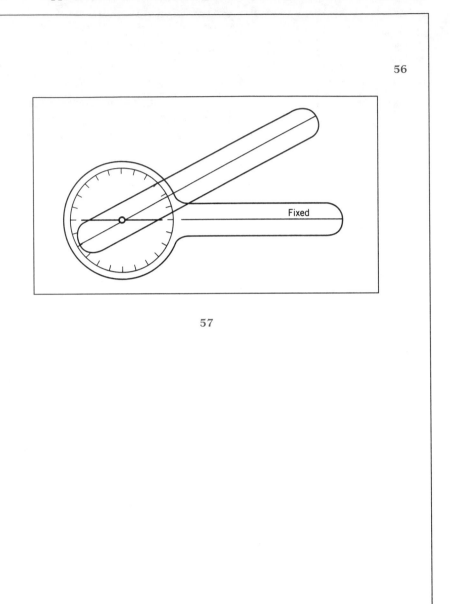

Fixed

57

58. Carefully label the X- and Y-axes.

59. Place an identiFying key so that it fits somewhere below the high point on the X-axis and to the left of the most extreme point on the X-axis.

60. If a numbered axis does nor begin at zero, put in parallel slashes to indicate a break.

61. Why is this a bar graph and not a line graph?

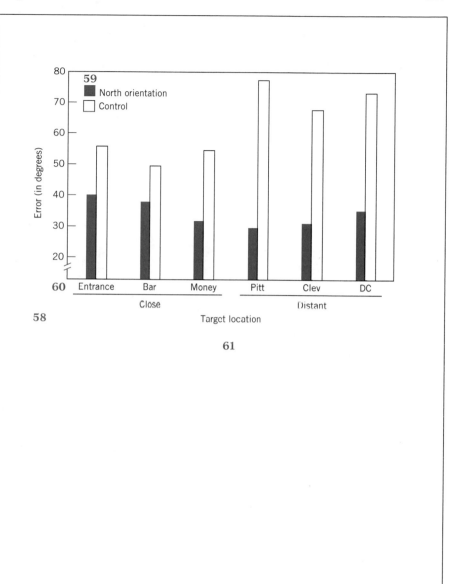

58

61

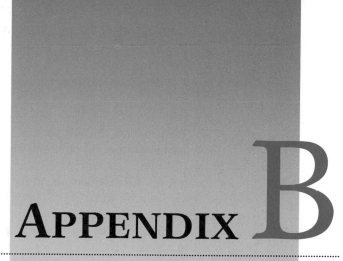

APPENDIX B

Developing Surveys for Research in Psychology

In this appendix, you will learn how to:

- Develop a survey research project
- Construct a good survey instrument to measure:
  - attitudes
  - knowledge and memory
  - demographic information

Survey Research—General Planning Guidelines

As with any research in psychology, survey research begins with empirical questions that develop into hypotheses to be tested by collecting data. For example, in a college or university environment, such questions might include focused, single-issue ones:

✓   Do students feel safe when crossing the campus at night?
✓   Do students eat balanced, nutritious meals?
✓   Are faculty more politically liberal than students?

Or they might be more broad-based:

✓   Are students satisfied with their education at the university?
✓   Considering student behavior as a whole, can it be characterized as health-enhancing or health-inhibiting?

Once empirical questions have been framed, the survey project must be planned carefully. Decisions need to be made about how to conduct the survey—with face-to-face interviews, over the phone, by means of a written questionnaire, or through some combination. See Chapter 12 for the advantages and disadvantages of each. Decisions also need to be made about sampling procedures. Because having a representative sample is important in survey research, some form of probability sampling should be done. As you recall from Chapter 4, this could range from simple random sampling to stratified sampling to cluster sampling. If the population is small (e.g., a small campus) and a list of students is readily available, simple random sampling or stratified sampling might suffice. Stratified sampling should be chosen if some important subgroups, with different proportions in the population, need to be represented precisely within the sample. For example, if the campus happened to be 60% female and 40% male, it might be a good idea to ensure the same female-male proportion in the sample. Similarly, the number of first-year students, sophomores, juniors, and seniors might need to be represented proportionally. For large populations, some form of cluster sampling might be required. From a long list of general education courses being offered in a semester, for example, a sample might be selected and all members in the selected classes surveyed (with their individual consent, of course).

With empirical questions in mind and the form of the survey and sampling procedures decided upon, you are ready to begin thinking about the specific information that you need to accumulate in the survey. For example, if you are interested in studying whether student lifestyles are healthy or unhealthy, you have to compile a list of individual behaviors and attitudes that will be targeted by the survey. You might examine alcohol consumption, eating behavior, sexual practices, smoking behavior, exercise behavior, or some combination of these. With this information identified, it is time to form the survey instrument itself.

Survey Construction

Suppose that you have decided to construct and administer a written survey. This survey normally will be designed to elicit three general types of information. The first concerns respondent attitudes, the second is the level of knowledge held by respondents on some issue or their recall of some information, and the third is demographic information—age, gender, socioeconomic status, and so on.

Attitudes

Attitudes about certain objects or issues are general tendencies to think, feel, and behave. For example, we might hold the attitude that women are treated unfairly in employment situations. This attitude includes a cognitive component that might encompass some of the arguments to support the attitude (e.g., salary differences for males and females in the same job), an emotional component (e.g.,"This is wrong and I'm angry about it") that will vary in strength, and a tendency to behave in ways that are consistent with the cognitive and emotional components (e.g.,"I might sign a petition for salary equity"). Attitudes are frequently measured through the use of surveys. When constructing such a survey, here are some useful guidelines:

1. *Don't reinvent the wheel–use published surveys when possible.* There are hundreds of published surveys in existence. If a good survey already exists, you can avoid the trouble of designing your own by getting permission to use an already published one. Published surveys can be found through PsyclNFO searches. For example, if you happened to be interested in attitudes toward animal research, a search on the topic would undoubtedly identify the Plous study (1996b) that was featured as a case study in Chapter 12. You could then write to Plous, ask for permission to use the survey, and ask for a copy of it. Another good source is the "Test Locator" in the ERIC Clearinghouse on Assessment and Evaluation, which can be found at: http://ericae.net

2. *Use open-ended questions carefully.* Open-ended questions can be useful for eliciting a wide range of responses, including some not even conceived of by the researchers. They can also increase the respondent's sense of control while filling out the survey. Because they can produce such a wide range of responses, however, open-ended questions are difficult to score and can add considerably to the time required to complete the survey. Hence, they should be used sparingly. One good method is to give respondents an opportunity to elaborate on their responses to closed questions. For example, at the end of a set of closed questions, the survey might provide space for the respondents to comment on their answers to any of the items, especially those for which they gave extreme ratings.

   Another good use of open-ended questions is in a pilot study as a way of identifying alternatives for a subsequent questionnaire to be composed of closed items. For example, a common open-ended question is sometimes referred to as the "most important problem" item (Schuman & Presser, 1996). An example might be:

   In your judgment, what are the most important problems facing this university today?

   This question is likely to elicit a variety of responses in a pilot test, and these responses could become the alternatives in a final item that could ask:

   Which of the following is the most important problem facing this university today? (alternatively, rankings of the items could be requested)

   _____ aging professors
   _____ inadequate computer facilities

_____ dictatorial president

_____ poor quality of dormitory rooms

_____ inadequate career advising

(and so on)

    Finally, some survey items can be "partially" open by including a specific checklist, ending it with the category "Other," and allowing respondents to write in their responses.

3.   *Consider using a Likert scale.* As you recall from Chapter 12, a survey using a Likert scale includes a sequence of statements, and the task is to indicate the level of agreement or disagreement with those statements. For example, a statement on a survey about attitudes toward the university's core curriculum program might be phrased like this:

Introductory psychology (PSY 100) is a course that should be required of all students.

The choices on a 5-point Likert scale might read:

_____ strongly agree

_____ agree

_____ undecided (sometimes "neutral" is better)

_____ disgree

_____ strongly disagree

This could be made into a 7-point scale by adding "very strongly agree" and "very strongly disagree." There is no clear advantage to a 5- or a 7- (or more) point scale. A 5-point scale normally provides sufficient discrimination among levels of agreement but might become a de facto 3-point scale in practice, given a tendency for some people to avoid making the choices at each end of the scale. On the other hand, a 7-point scale still yields 5 points if people avoid the extremes, but adding the extra level of discrimination can increase the time it takes to complete the survey. One general rule is to avoid mixing formats. If you decide to use a 5-point Likert scale, use it throughout; don't mix 5- and 7-point scales in the same survey.

    When using a Likert scale, word some of the statements favorably and others unfavorably. In a survey that evaluates teaching, for example, consecutive statements might be phrased like this:

The instructor held my attention during class lectures.

The instructor wrote exams that fairly tested the material covered.

The instructor seemed to be well prepared for class.

The instructor was available for extra help outside of class.

    These items are all worded favorably, so if a student liked the instructor, that student might race through the survey without reading the items carefully and simply agree with everything. Also, some students might have a response bias that social psychologists call "response acquiescence"—a tendency to agree with virtually all statements. To avoid these problems, surveys with Likert scales typically balance favorable and unfavorable statements. This forces respondents to read each item carefully and make item by item decisions (Patten, 1998). For example, the above statements could be presented like this, with two items worded favorably and two unfavorably:

The instructor was seldom able to hold my attention during class lectures.

The instructor wrote exams that fairly tested the material covered.

The instructor often appeared to be unprepared for class.

The instructor was available for extra help outside of class.

4. *Be careful of wording.* Chapter 12 briefly described some examples of the pitfalls here. It is important to avoid ambiguity, leading questions, and bias, and to be sure that two different questions aren't being asked in a single survey item. Here are some additional tips (most examples from Fink, 1995):

✓ Use complete sentences.

poor: Place of residence?

better: What is the name of the city where you currently live?

✓ Avoid most abbreviations.

— USC could be University of Southern California, but it could also be the University of South Carolina

✓ Avoid slang and colloquial expressions.

— they go out of fashion; by the time this book is published, for instance, "information superhighway" will be an overused and outdated expression

✓ Avoid jargon.

— you might know the difference between "formative" and "summative" evaluations (Chapter 10), but most survey respondents won't

✓ Avoid negatively phrased questions.

— negative statements are more difficult to process than positive ones

poor: Do you believe that the university should not have the right to search your dorm room?

better: Should the university have the right to search your dorm room?

— Use balanced items, not those favoring one position or another.

poor: Do you support the use of animals in undergraduate laboratory courses?

better: Do you support or oppose the use of animals in undergraduate laboratory courses?

Knowledge and Memory

The guidelines you've encountered thus far also apply to survey items designed to elicit the respondent's knowledge about some topic or memory of some event. In addition, however, some special problems are encountered when probing someone's knowledge base and/or memory.

1. *Don't ask the impossible of someone's memory.* When asking how often respondents have done certain things, making the interval too long increases the chances of memory errors. For example, on a survey about drinking behavior (assume that the definition of a "drink" has been made clear to the respondent):

    poor: How many drinks did you have in the past month?

    better: How many drinks did you have in the past week?

    Of course, the proper interval will depend on the question being asked. If the activity is a relatively infrequent one (e.g., visiting zoos), a short interval will yield too many scores of zero.

    One way to aid memory problems is to provide lists. In a survey about leisure-time activities, for instance, respondents might be asked to examine the past month and indicate how frequently they have rented a movie, gone on a hike, attended the symphony, and so on.

2. *Use DK alternatives carefully.* When inquiring about what a person knows, there is always the chance that the honest answer will be "I don't know." Hence, survey items that deal with knowledge often include what is called a DK ("Don't know") alternative. Some experts discourage the use of DK alternatives because respondents might overuse them, conservatively choosing DK even if they have some knowledge of the issue at hand. Survey results with a lot of DK answers are not very useful. On the other hand, omitting DK as a choice might force respondents to mentally flip a coin on items about which they are truly ignorant (Schuman & Presser, 1996). One way to include DK choices, while at the same time encouraging respondents to avoid overusing them, is to disguise knowledge questions by prefacing them with such statements as "Using your best guess ..." or "Have you heard or have you read that ..." (examples from Fink, 1995, p. 76). Also, DK alternatives should be used only when it is reasonable to expect that some respondents will have no idea about what the answer might be (Patten, 1998).

Demographic Information

Including demographic information enables the survey researcher to group the results by categories. In the survey on psychology majors' attitudes toward animal research that formed a case study in Chapter 12, for instance, Plous (1996b) asked respondents for demographic information about gender, about whether they planned to apply to graduate school, and about their year in college (e.g., sophomore). This enabled him to determine that females were more likely to be opposed to animal research than males, but that attitudes did not vary systematically as a function of graduate school aspirations or year in college.

It is a good idea to put the questions about demographic information *at the end of the survey.* If you start the survey with them, participants might become bored with the survey and not attend to the key items as well as they should. Also, you should only include demographic categories that are important for the hypotheses you are testing. The more demographic information you include, the longer the survey and the greater the risk that respondents will become bored. And they might become irritated: some requests for demographic information (e.g., income) can be perceived as invasions of privacy, even though respondents will have been assured about confidentiality (Patten, 1998).

When requesting demographic information, here are some guidelines:

✓ When asking about age, ask for date of birth.

✓ When asking for annual income, provide a range to reduce privacy concerns (e.g., $50,000 or less; $50,001–$100,000).

✓ Don't let the alternatives overlap (e.g., as in the income question just used as an example of providing a range).

✓ If making comparisons to other surveys, ask for identical demographic information.

✓ Let the pros do the work—for instance, borrow items from the U.S. Census Bureau (www.census.gov); for example, whereas a novice might include "married, single, divorced, and widowed" under marital status, a pro would recognize the ambiguity in "single" and use the census categories—"married, separated, widowed, divorced, never married" (Patten, 1998, p. 27).

Miscellaneous Tips

1. *Pilot test the survey.* If you are writing your own survey questions, rewrite them at least twice and then have two friends read them for clarity. Pick friends who aren't afraid to tell you that a particular item is awful. Once you believe the survey is reasonably good, do some pilot testing. For example, if you are writing a survey as a project in your research methods class, ask the professor if you can administer it to the class. Then ask your peers to (a) take the survey and (b) criticize it in writing. Then perform a crude item analysis on the results. For example, suppose you have an item like this:

   In the past month, how many times have you smoked marijuana?

   _____ 0–10   _____ 11–20   _____ 21–30

   and every person chooses "0–10." This tells you that the categories are too inclusive. A revision might include more alternatives, including "0" as a separate category.

2. *Work hard on the introduction.* In a mailed survey, this will be a cover letter that explains the purpose of the study, ensures the respondent of confidentiality, and does everything possible to encourage the respondent to fill out the survey. Within the survey itself, there may be one opening set of instructions or several sets that introduce various portions of the survey. These too must be carefully worded. They must be crystal clear while at the same time (a) not being overly long and (b) not insulting to the respondent's intelligence.

3. *Work hard on the survey's visual appeal.* Making the survey look professional will encourage the respondent to believe that you are serious about the research and that the research has merit. For example, there should be clearly perceived spaces between the end of one item and the start of another, no typographical errors, and high-quality production (i.e., don't use a poor-quality duplicating machine).

4. *Be careful about the order of questions.* If you have questions that some respondents might find objectionable (e.g., frequency of alcohol or drug use, sexual activities), put them near the end of the survey. If you start with them, respondents might stop right away; if they are at the end, respondents have already invested some time and may be more willing to finish the survey. Start the survey with questions that are not especially personal and are both easy to answer and interesting. Cluster items on the same general topic in the same place on the survey.

5. *Provide a reward for responding.* I once filled out a survey about the kinds of features I look for in a social psychology text mainly because it earned me a $5 gift certificate to a Barnes & Noble bookstore. You might not be able to afford such a reward, but you might consider some creative ways to increase the response rate. It could be something as simple as a pen that is included as part of the survey or as elaborate as an entry into a drawing for a relatively large prize. In his survey of psychology majors about animal research, for example, Plous (1996b) gave away a laser printer to a psychology department and, through a lottery, $500 to one of the students who responded (he also had a big National Science Foundation grant).

6. *Finally, remember research ethics.* Follow your school's IRB policies carefully, prepare an informed consent form if necessary (the cover letter might serve this purpose), take deliberate steps to ensure confidentiality, and be sure to give your participants the opportunity to learn about the results of the survey.

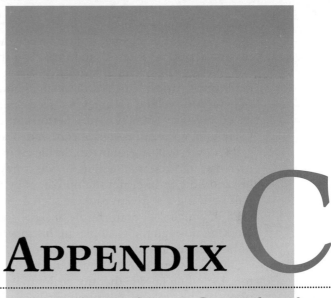

APPENDIX C

Using Statistics

In this appendix, you will learn how to:

- Assess the degree of relationship between two variables by calculating the most common coefficient of correlation, Pearson's *r*
- Perform a simple regression analysis
- Calculate two varieties of the chi-square (X^2) test ("chi" rhymes with "pie"), an inferential test for nominal data
- Calculate an inferential test for ordinal data, the Mann-Whitney *U* test
- Calculate the most common inferential analyses for interval and ratio data
  - *t* test
  - analysis of variance

Making Intelligent Use of Statistics

Deciding on the proper statistical analysis is an essential skill for the psychological researcher. You already know part of the process from the descriptions in Chapters 4, 7, 8, and 9. Chapter 4 introduced you to the different scales of measurement (nominal, ordinal, interval, and ratio) and the basic distinction between descriptive and inferential statistics. It also showed you how to calculate some of the common descriptive statistics, such as mean and standard deviation, and introduced the logic of hypothesis testing. Chapters 4, 7, and 8 introduced the use of *t* tests and the analysis of variance (ANOVA) for performing inferential analyses of experiments. In Chapter 9, correlation coefficients were described.

Here you will learn how to decide among the various types of analyses for your own data and research designs, how to carry out some of the more common analyses, and how to interpret the outcomes by referring to statistical tables. Ideally, you will be using a software package such as Statistical Package for the Social Sciences (SPSS), which will perform the analyses for the projects you'll be doing; however, working through the examples in this appendix can give you a better understanding of how these procedures are actually done.

The decisions about which statistical analyses to perform depend on several factors, including (a) whether the goal is to examine an association or make a comparison, (b) the scale of measurement being used, (c) certain aspects of the research design, such as whether an independent variable is tested between or within subjects, and, in some cases, (d) sample size.

When the purpose of the analysis is to determine the degree of relationship between any two measured variables, some form of correlation coefficient will be calculated. The most common is Pearson's *r*, which is used whenever the data are measured on either interval or ratio scales. If an ordinal scale is used, you must calculate a Spearman's rho, symbolized r_s; it will give you a measure of the degree of relationship between two sets of ordinal rankings. A measure of association also exists for nominal data (the contingency coefficient, *C*). See below for an example of Pearson's *r*. Consult a statistics text for instructions about how to perform r_s and *C*.

When the analysis is designed to compare two or more conditions of a study to see if *differences* exist between or among them, a number of inferential procedures exist. The examples below illustrate several of the most common tests: chi-square (X^2), Mann-Whitney *U*, the *t* test and the analysis of variance (ANOVA). The X^2 test is used with nominal data and the Mann-Whitney *U* test is used for ordinal data. The *t* test and ANOVA both require that data be measured on either an interval or a ratio scale.

Assessing Relationships

Example 1. Pearson's *r*

When both variables are measured on either an interval or a ratio scale, the relationship between them can be calculated by using Pearson's *r*. For example, suppose a researcher is interested in determining the relationship between the amount of goof-off time that a student accumulates and the student's GPA. GPA ranges from 0.0 to 4.0, and goof-off time is the number of hours spent per week in several specifically defined activities (e.g., soap opera watching). The data for eight students (same as on page 274 of Chapter 9) are as follows:

Student #	Goof-Off Hrs Variable X	X^2	G.P.A. Variable Y	Y^2	X times Y
1	42	1764	1.8	3.24	75.6
2	23	529	3.0	9.00	69.0
3	31	961	2.2	4.84	68.2
4	35	1225	2.9	8.41	101.5
5	16	256	3.7	13.69	59.2
6	26	676	3.0	9.00	78.0
7	39	1521	2.4	5.76	93.6
8	19	361	3.4	11.56	64.6
sum	231	7293	22.4	65.50	609.7

Formula for Pearson's *r:*

$$ r = \frac{N\Sigma XY - \Sigma X \Sigma Y}{\sqrt{\left[N\Sigma X^2 - \left(\Sigma X\right)^2 \right]\left[N\Sigma Y^2 - \left(\Sigma Y\right)^2 \right]}} $$

Step 1. *Calculate Each Element*

$$ N\Sigma XY = (8)(609.7) = 4877.6 $$
$$ \Sigma X \Sigma Y = (231)(22.4) = 5174.4 $$
$$ N\Sigma X^2 = (8)(7293) = 58344 $$
$$ (\Sigma X)^2 = (231)(231) = 53361 $$
$$ N\Sigma Y^2 = (8)(65.5) = 524 $$
$$ (\Sigma Y)^2 = (22.4)(22.4) = 501.76 $$

Step 2. *Fit Elements into the Formula for r and Solve*

$$ r = \frac{4877.6 - 5174.4}{\sqrt{\left[58344 - 53361 \right]\left[524 - 501.76 \right]}} $$

$$ r = \frac{-296.8}{\sqrt{\left[4983 \right]\left[22.24 \right]}} $$

$$ r = \frac{-296.8}{\sqrt{\left[110821.9 \right]}} = \frac{-296.8}{332.9} = -.89 $$

Step 3.   *Determine if the Calculated r is Significant (i.e., different from zero)*
This is accomplished by examining Table D.2 in Appendix D, which lists "critical values" *(cv)* for *r*. To use the table, first determine the degrees of freedom *(df)*. In the case of Pearson's *r*, $df = N - 2$, where *N* refers to the number of pairs of scores. In our example, then, $df = 8 - 2 = 6$. In the table at the line for $df = 6$, you'll find two critical values, one for a significance level of .05 *(cv* = .707) and one for .01 *(cv* = .834). If the calculated value is *equal to or greater than* the critical value, then you may reject the null hypothesis that $r = 0$. That is, you can conclude that the correlation is statistically significant. In our case, the −.89 is significant at the .01 level because it exceeds the *cv* of .834. Thus, the probability is a very small .01 (1 in 100) that the obtained correlation of −.89 occurred by chance. Of course, whether the correlation is positive or negative doesn't matter; it is the absolute value of the calculated correlation that counts.

If you examine Table D.2 carefully, you will notice a basic fact about correlations. If you have just a few pairs (as in the above example), the correlation has to be quite high before it can be considered significant. It is fairly easy to arrive at a relatively high correlation purely by chance when there are only a few pairs. On the other hand, if there are a large number of pairs of scores, correlations that seem quite low can nonetheless be significant.

Example 2. Regression Analysis

In Chapter 9 you learned that correlations enable predictions to be made, using a procedure called a "regression analysis." The analysis yields a regression line, and this line in turn provides the basis for the predictions. Here's how it works with the example just completed about the relationship between goof-off time and GPA. Formula for a regression line:

$$Y = a + bX$$

$$a = \text{the } Y\text{-intercept}$$
$$b = \text{the slope of the line}$$
$$X = \text{a known value}$$
$$Y = \text{the value you are trying to predict}$$

Step 1.   *Calculate Each Element*

$$b = r\frac{s_y}{s_x}$$

$r = $ Pearson's $r = -.89$

$s = $ standard deviation (see Table 4.4, pp. 130–131 for calculations)

$$s_y = 0.63$$
$$s_x = 9.43$$

$$b = -.89\,\frac{.63}{9.43} = (-.89)(.07) = -.06$$

$$a = \bar{Y} - b\bar{X}$$

$$\bar{Y} = \text{mean score for } Y = 2.80$$
$$\bar{X} = \text{mean score for } X = 28.88$$
$$a = 2.80 - (-.06)\,(28.88) = 4.53$$

Step 2. *Insert Values for the Y-Intercept and Slope into the Regression formula*

$$Y = a + bX = 4.53 + (-.06)X$$
$$= 4.53 - .06X$$

Step 3. *Use the Formula for Predictions*

If Pat has 40 goof-off hours, what is his predicted GPA?

$$Y = 4.53 - .06X$$
$$= 4.53 - (.06)(40)$$
$$= 4.53 - 2.40$$
$$= 2.13$$

If Pat has 20 goof-off hours, what is her predicted GPA?

$$Y = 4.53 - .06X$$
$$= 4.53 - (.06)(20)$$
$$= 4.53 - 1.20$$
$$= 3.33$$

Assessing Differences

Example 3. χ^2—Goodness of Fit

When data are reported in terms of the number of times certain events fall into clearly defined categories, a nominal scale of measurement is being used. To determine if the frequencies of these events reveal a systematic pattern, or are merely the result of chance, requires an inferential test for nominal data. Chi-square (χ^2) is such a test, certainly the most common statistical procedure used for nominal data. There are two varieties of χ^2, depending on whether one or more samples are used. The one-sample case is sometimes called "χ^2 goodness of fit" because it assesses whether the frequencies obtained in a study deviate from frequencies that would be expected either by chance or according to some predicted model.

As an example, suppose students suspect that their professor's multiple-choice tests are biased in terms of how often each of five alternatives is the correct answer. That is, it seems to them that alternatives b, c, and d are correct more frequently than alternatives a or e. The professor is concerned and decides to evaluate all the previous semester's multiple-choice tests. The number of times that each alternative is chosen is counted. If no bias is operating, the number of times that each alternative is correct should be about the same. Thus, the null hypothesis is that all the expected frequencies will be the same. There are 400 multiple-choice items in the sample, so the expected frequency *(E)* for each alternative is equal to 400/5 or 80. The actual frequencies are:

Alternative a: 62

Alternative b: 85

Alternative c: 78

Alternative d: 111

Alternative e: 64

    [Total: 400]

Formula for χ^2—goodness of fit:

$$\chi^2 = \Sigma \frac{(O - E)^2}{E}$$

Step 1.   *Calculate Each Element*

$$O - E: \quad 62 - 80 = -18$$
$$85 - 80 = +5$$
$$78 - 80 = -2$$
$$111 - 80 = +31$$
$$64 - 80 = -16$$

$$(O - E)^2: \qquad (-18)^2 = 324$$
$$(+5)^2 = 25$$
$$(-2)^2 = 4$$
$$(+31)^2 = 961$$
$$(-16)^2 = 256$$

Step 2.   *Fit Elements into the Formula for χ^2 and Solve*

$$\chi^2 = \Sigma \frac{(O - E)^2}{E}$$

$$= \frac{324}{80} + \frac{25}{80} + \frac{4}{80} + \frac{961}{80} + \frac{256}{80}$$
$$= 4.05 + .31 + .05 + 12.01 + 3.20$$
$$= 19.62$$

Step 3.   *Determine if the Calculated χ^2 is Significant*

Table D.3 in Appendix D lists "critical values" for χ^2. The degrees of freedom for a one sample χ^2 is equal to the number of categories minus 1, or 4 (5 − 1 = 4) in this particular case. In the table at the line for *df* = 4, you'll find two critical values, one for a significance level of .05 (*cv* = 9.49) and one for .01 (*cv* = 13.28). The calculated value exceeds both; hence, χ^2 is significant at the .01 level. The professor would conclude that some bias does exist in the distribution of multiple choice alternatives; alternatives a and c indeed seem to be underused.

Example 4. χ^2—Two Samples

For research in psychology, χ^2 is most frequently used when more than one sample of frequencies exists. The most common case is when two different groups of subjects are used and each group is placed into two or more categories, depending on the topic of interest. For example, suppose a researcher wanted to know if there are gender differences in the choice of certain majors. The application forms of incoming students are examined (i.e., an archival procedure) to determine the number of males and females choosing psychology, biology, and math. The following table, called a "contingency table," shows the results:

	Psychology	Biology	Math	Row Totals
Males	13	17	20	50
Females	24	16	10	50
Column Totals	37	33	30	100

The null hypothesis is that no gender differences exist in the choice of major. To test the null hypothesis for these frequency data, χ^2 is calculated: Formula for χ^2—two samples:

$$\chi^2 = \Sigma \frac{(O-E)^2}{E}$$

Step 1. Calculate Expected Frequencies (E)

$$E = [(\text{row total}).(\text{column total})]/\text{grand total}$$

- for the cell "males preferring psychology" (m,p):

$$E_{m,p} = [(50)(37)]/100 = 1850/100 = 18.5$$

- for the remaining cells:

$$E_{m,b} = [(50)(33)]/100 = 1650/100 = 16.5$$
$$E_{m,m} = [(50)(30)]/100 = 1500/100 = 15.0$$
$$E_{f,p} = [(50)(37)]/100 = 1850/100 = 18.5$$
$$E_{f,b} = [(50)(33)]/100 = 1650/100 = 16.5$$
$$E_{f,m} = [(50)(30)]/100 = 1550/100 = 15.0$$

Step 2. *Calculate* $(O - E)^2$ *for Each Cell*

$$(O - E)^2: m,p \rightarrow (13 - 18.5)^2 = 30.25$$
$$m,b \rightarrow (17 - 16.5)^2 = .25$$

$$m,m \rightarrow (20 - 15.0)^2 = 25.00$$
$$f,p \rightarrow (24 - 18.5)^2 = 30.25$$
$$f,b \rightarrow (16 - 16.5)^2 = .25$$
$$f,m \rightarrow (10 - 15.0)^2 = 25.00$$

Step 3. *Fit Elements into the Formula for χ^2 and Solve*

$$\chi^2 = \Sigma \frac{(O - E)^2}{E}$$

$$= \frac{30.25}{18.5} + \frac{.25}{16.5} + \frac{25.00}{15.0} + \frac{30.25}{18.5} + \frac{.25}{16.5} + \frac{25.00}{15.0}$$

$$= 1.64 + .02 + 1.67 + 1.64 + .02 + 1.67$$

$$= 6.66$$

Step 4. *Determine if the Calculated χ^2 is Significant*

The degrees of freedom for a two sample χ^2 is equal to:

$$(\# \text{ rows} - 1)(\# \text{ columns} - 1) = (3 - 1)(2 - 1) = 2$$

In Table D.3 at the line for $df = 2$, the critical values are 5.99 (.05 significance level) and 9.21 (.01 level). The calculated value of 6.66 exceeds the first but not the second; hence χ^2 is significant at the .05 level but not at the .01 level. Gender differences did seem to occur in the choice of major: significantly more females than males expressed interest in majoring in psychology, the opposite was true for match, and males and females showed about equal preference for biology.

Example 5. Mann-Whitney *U* test

The Mann-Whitney *U* test is just one example of a class of inferential tests used when the data are presented in the form of rankings (i.e., ordinal scale of measurement) or converted to ranks. In the latter case, ratio or interval data are collected in the study, but *t* tests or ANOVAs cannot be used. This occurs because in order to use these tests, certain assumptions need to be met. For example, the data to be analyzed by a *t* test or ANOVA should at least approximate a normal distribution, and the variances for the different conditions should be approximately equal to each other. Sometimes, however, the data might be severely skewed or the variances might be quite different. This often occurs with small sample sizes. In such cases, researchers will turn to a category of tests called "nonparametric tests." The Mann-Whitney *U* is an example of one such test, to be used in a study involving independent groups.[1]

---

[1] Thus the Mann–Whitney *U* test is the nonparametric alternative to a *t* test for independent groups. Other nonparametric tests exist as alternatives to the *t* test for dependent groups and for the various ANOVA procedures.

Consider a study in which behavior therapy is being evaluated as a technique to reduce snake phobias. The researcher recruits 14 snake-phobic persons and randomly assigns them to a therapy group and a waiting list control group. After therapy, an interval scale test for snake avoidance is given. Scores range from 1 to 25, with high scores indicating high fear of snakes. Here are the scores for the two groups:

Therapy	WL Control
4	20
7	17
1	3
12	15
2	7
2	12
9	18

Both sets of scores appear to be skewed, the variance is much higher for the second group (45.97) than for the first (17.22), and sample size is small. Consequently, the researcher decides to use the Mann-Whitney U test instead of a t test for independent groups.

Step 1. *Convert the Data to Rankings*

This means taking all 14 participants, lining up their scores from lowest to highest, and then converting the scores to ranks. Note what happens to tied scores (take a mean of ranks). The numbers in boldface are the scores for those in the Therapy group.

score: **1** **2** 2 3 **4** **7** 7**9** **12** 12 15 17 18 20
rank: 1 2.5 2.5 4 5 6.5 6.5 8 9.5 9.5 11 12 13 14

Step 2. *Add Up the Ranks for Each Group*

Therapy	WL Control
1	4
2.5	6.5
2.5	9.5
5	11
6.5	12
8	13
9.5	14
$\Sigma R_1 = 35$	$\Sigma R_2 = 70$

Step 3. *Apply the Formula for the Mann-Whitney U Test to Each Group*

For the Therapy group (group 1):

$$U_1 = (N_1)(N_2) + \frac{N_1(N_1 + 1)}{2} - \Sigma R_1$$

$$U_1 = (7)(7) + \frac{7\,(8)}{2} - 35 = 49 + 28 - 35 = \mathbf{42}$$

For the Control group (group 2):

$$U_2 = (N_1)(N_2) + \frac{N_2(N_2 + 1)}{2} - \Sigma R_2$$

$$U_2 = (7)(7) + \frac{7\,(8)}{2} - 68.5 = 49 + 28 - 70 = \mathbf{7}$$

Step 4. *Determine If the Calculated* U *Is Significant*

Table D.4 lists the critical values for evaluating a Mann-Whitney U test. The critical values are found at the intersection points of the sample sizes for the two groups N_1 and N_2. As you can see when N_1 and N_2 are both equal to 7, a 2-tailed test is used, the cv for an alpha level of .05 is 8; at the .01 level, the $cv = 4$. To evaluate the calculated value of U, first take the lowest value of the two. That is, consider the 7 and ignore the 42. If the calculated value of this lower U is *less than* or equal to the value in the table, then the null hypothesis can be rejected and it can be concluded that there is a significant difference in rankings between the two groups. In our case, the difference is significant at the .05 but not the .01 level (the calculated 7 is less than 8, but not less than 4). The research conclusion is that the therapy worked—participants in that group showed a much lower level of snake phobia than the control group.

Example 6. *t* Test—Independent Groups

In studies with a single independent variable and just two levels, the difference between the two sets of scores is often assessed with a *t* test. As you recall from Chapter 7, there are two basic varieties, depending on whether the two sets of scores derive from independent groups of subjects or not. Independent groups occur when subjects are randomly assigned or when a subject variable such as gender or age is used. Such designs call for a *t* test for independent groups. A *t* test for dependent groups (sometimes referred to as "correlated" groups) is used when the same subjects serve in both conditions or when the two different groups of subjects are related in some way, either through a matching procedure (see Example 7) or some natural matching, as happens when parents are compared with children. Here's a simple way to calculate a *t* test for independent groups. It uses the variance, which you recall from Chapter 4 is an important measure of the variability in a set of scores; taking the square root of it yields the standard deviation. Refer back to Table 4.4 (pp. 130–131) for the details. In essence, the *t* test for independent groups compares the differences between groups with the variance within each group. It is hoped that differences between the groups will be large, while the variability within each group will be small.

Suppose a researcher is doing a simple memory experiment in which two groups of subjects are formed through random assignment. One group studies a list of 25 words at a presentation rate of 2 seconds per item; the rate for the other group is 4 seconds per item. Here are the numbers of words recalled by the five participants in each group:

Subject no.	2 sec/item (X_1)	Subject no.	4 sec/item (X_2)
1	14	6	18
2	11	7	23
3	12	8	19
4	17	9	17
5	13	10	22
sum	67		99
n	5		5
mean	13.4		19.8
standard deviation	2.3		2.6
variance	5.3		6.7

The *t* test divides the differences between the two means obtained in the study by the "standard error of the difference," an estimate of how much the means should vary on the basis of chance or error. The researcher hopes for a large numerator and a small denominator and therefore a large value for *t*; when this happens the actual differences between the means are likely to be larger than those expected by chance.

The formula for the *t* test for independent groups:

$$t = \frac{\overline{X}_1 - \overline{X}_2}{\sqrt{\left[\frac{(n_1 - 1)s_1^2 + (n_2 - 1)s_2^2}{n_1 + n_2 - 2} \right]\left[\frac{1}{n_1} + \frac{1}{n_2} \right]}}$$

Step 1. *Calculate Each Element*

$$t = \frac{\overline{X}_1 - \overline{X}_2}{\sqrt{\left[\frac{(n_1 - 1)s_1^2 + (n_2 - 1)s_2^2}{n_1 + n_2 - 2} \right]\left[\frac{1}{n_1} + \frac{1}{n_2} \right]}}$$

$$t = \frac{13.4 - 19.8}{\sqrt{\left[\frac{(5 - 1)5.3 + (5 - 1)6.7}{5 + 5 - 2} \right]\left[\frac{1}{5} + \frac{1}{5} \right]}}$$

$$t = \frac{-6.4}{\sqrt{\left[\frac{21.2 + 26.8}{8} \right][.2 + .5]}}$$

$$t = \frac{6.4}{\sqrt{[(6)(.4)]}} = -\frac{6.4}{1.55}$$

$$t = -4.13$$

Step 2. *Fit Elements into the Formula for t and Solve*

Step 3. *Determine if the Calculated t is Significant*

The degrees of freedom for a *t* test for independent groups is equal to:

$$(n_1 + n_2 - 2) = (5 + 5 - 2) = 8$$

Table D.5 lists the critical values for assessing the outcome of the *t* test. On the line for *df* = 8, the critical values are 2.31 (.05 significance level) and 3.36 (.01 level). The calculated value of 4.13 exceeds both (the minus sign doesn't matter); hence *t* is significant at the .01 level. It would be reasonable for the researcher to reject the null hypothesis and conclude that recall performance differed for subjects given different presentation rates.

Step 4. *Estimate Effect Size*

As you recall from Chapter 4 (p. 140), researchers usually examine not just whether the differences between means are statistically significant, but also the relative size of the effect that has been obtained. In a *t* test, effect size is the amount of variability in the dependent variable that can be accounted for or attributed to the independent variable (Cohen, 1988). Several estimates of effect size exist, and a common one is Cohen's *d*. It is calculated by taking the difference between the means and dividing by an estimate of the population standard deviation for both groups combined:

$$d = \frac{\overline{X}_1 - \overline{X}_2}{s}$$

The estimated population standard deviation is found by adding together the variances for the two groups and taking the square root of the result. Thus,

$$s = \sqrt{5.3 + 6.7} = \sqrt{12} = 3.46$$

Effect size then becomes

$$d = \frac{13.4 - 19.8}{3.46} = -1.85$$

What does this mean? According to general guidelines suggested by Cohen (cited in Spatz, 1997), effect sizes can be classified as small (about .2), medium (about .5), and large (about .8). By these standards, 1.85 is a very large effect (the negative sign can be ignored; it merely indicates which mean appeared first in the numerator). Hence, doubling the presentation rate, from 2 to 4 seconds per item, had a major influence on recall performance in this example.

Note: effect size analyses can be carried out for the second type of *t* test, which you are about to encounter, as well as for the various ANOVAs. Consult a statistics text for the specific procedures.

Example 7. *t* Test–Dependent Groups

As mentioned above, the *t* test for dependent groups is used for matched groups and repeated-measures designs when the independent variable has two levels. Each pair of scores will be related to some degree because each pair comes from (a) subjects who are similar to each other in some way or (b) the same subjects. Like the *t* test for independent groups, the one for dependent groups relates the actual difference between the means to the variability within each condition. The procedure includes calculating the correlation between the two sets of scores and working it into the formula for the *t* test. The following example accomplishes the same thing with a simpler raw-score formula that allows for a direct calculation of *t* without first calculating a Pearson's *r*.

Suppose a researcher uses a matched groups design to compare two ways of teaching computer literacy: a self-paced approach versus straight lecture. The 10 students in each group have been matched for previous GPA and general verbal intelligence. Thus, subject pair 1 (below) refers to two individuals with about the same GPA and intelligence. The dependent measure is a test score that can reach a maximum of 35. Here are the data, along with the preliminaries to the analysis, calculating *D* and D_2 for each paired set of scores.

Subject Pairs	Self-Paced	Lecture	D	D²
1	26	18	8	64
2	31	22	9	81
3	26	21	5	25
4	28	20	8	64
5	22	17	5	25
6	22	15	7	49
7	23	21	2	4
8	29	20	9	81
9	24	19	5	25
10	24	23	1	1
sum	255	196	59	419
N = 10				
mean	**25.5**	**19.6**		

The formula for the t test for dependent groups:

$$t = \frac{\Sigma D}{\sqrt{\left[\dfrac{N\Sigma D^2 - (\Sigma D)^2}{N-1}\right]}}$$

Step 1. *Calculate Each Element*

$$\Sigma D = 8 + 9 + \ldots 1 = 59$$
$$(\Sigma D)^2 = (59)^2 = 3481$$
$$\Sigma D^2 = 64 + 81 + \ldots 1 = 419$$

Step 2.   *Fit Elements into the Formula for* t *and Solve*

$$t = \frac{\Sigma D}{\sqrt{\left[\dfrac{N\Sigma D^2 - (\Sigma D)^2}{N-1}\right]}}$$

$$t = \frac{59}{\sqrt{\left[\dfrac{(10)(419) - 3481}{9}\right]}}$$

$$t = \frac{59}{\sqrt{\left[\dfrac{709}{9}\right]}} = \frac{59}{\sqrt{78.8}} = \frac{59}{8.9}$$

$$t = 6.63$$

Step 3.   *Determine if the Calculated* t *is Significant*

The degrees of freedom for a *t* test for dependent groups is equal to the number of pairs of scores minus 1; in this case $df = 10 - 1 = 9$. Use Table D.5 again. On the line for $df = 9$, the critical values are 2.26 (.05 significance level) and 3.25 (.01 level). The calculated value of 6.63 exceeds both; hence, *t* is significant at the .01 level. It appears that the self-paced strategy worked better than the traditional lecture approach.

Example 8. 1-Way ANOVA—Independent Groups

A *t* test works fine when two conditions are being compared, but most experiments compare more than two conditions.[2] They might include a single independent variable with more than two levels, or they might include more than one independent variable (i.e., a factorial design). Consider first the case of a single independent variable with multiple levels. If the data are measured on an interval or ratio scale, then the 1-way ANOVA is the analysis of choice (*note:* 1-way = 1 independent variable, 2-way = 2 such variables, and so on).

   As an example, consider a study in which three different groups of animals are taught a complex maze. The independent variable is the delay of reinforcement that occurs when they reach the goal box. Group 1 rats are reinforced immediately upon reaching the goal. Those in group 2 are reinforced 5 seconds after they reach the goal, and for those in group 3, reinforcement is delayed by 10 seconds. The dependent measure is the number of trials it takes the animals to learn the maze, with learning defined as two consecutive errorless trials.

---

[2] Recall from Chapter 7 (pp. 238–239) that when there are more than two conditions, calculating multiple *t* tests is not a good idea because it increases the odds of making a Type I error. Also, if there is a single independent variable with two levels, a 1-way ANOVA will produce the same outcome as a *t* test. Indeed, the *t* test can be considered a special case of the analysis of variance.

Five rats are randomly assigned to each condition. Hence, there are three distinct groups, and the proper analysis is a 1-way ANOVA for independent groups. Here are the results, along with some basic summary statistics.

		Group X_1	Group X_2	Group X_3	
Subject #	No Delay	Subject #	5-sec Delay	Subject #	10-sec Delay
1	12	6	19	11	21
2	15	7	17	12	25
3	13	8	22	13	20
4	10	9	24	14	19
5	16	10	20	15	23
ΣX	66		102		108
(ΣX^2)	4356		10404		11664
n	5		5		5
$\overline{X}$	**13.2**		**20.4**		**21.6**
ΣX^2	894		2110		2356

The analysis of variance calculates a statistic called the "F ratio." In the 1-way ANOVA for independent groups, basic formula for F divides the "mean square between groups" by the "mean square within groups" (also called the "mean square error"). In essence, this comparison between the variability between conditions and the variability within each condition is the same comparison made with the t test. The ANOVA formulas might seem rather daunting to you at first, but you'll find that there is a certain rhythm to them and that you will catch on quickly (really).

The formula for the F ratio in a 1-way ANOVA for independent groups is

$$F = \frac{MS_{BG}}{MS_{WG}} \text{ or } F = \frac{MS_{BG}}{MS_e}$$

Step 1. *Calculate Sums of Squares*

$$\text{total SS} = \left(\Sigma X_1^2 + \Sigma X_2^2 + \Sigma X_3^2\right) - \frac{\left(\Sigma X_1 + \Sigma X_2 + \Sigma X_3\right)^2}{N}$$

$$= \left(894 + 2110 + 2356\right) - \frac{\left(66 + 102 + 108\right)^2}{15}$$

$$= 5360 + 5078.4 = 281.6$$

$$SS_{BG} = \frac{\left(\Sigma X_1^2\right)}{n_1} + \frac{\left(\Sigma X_2^2\right)}{n_2} + \frac{\left(\Sigma X_3^2\right)}{n_3} - \frac{\left(\Sigma X_1 + \Sigma X_2 + \Sigma X_3\right)^2}{N}$$

$$= \frac{4356}{5} + \frac{10404}{5} + \frac{11664}{5} - \frac{\left(66 + 102 + 108\right)^2}{15}$$

$$= \left[871.2 + 2080.8 + 2332.8\right] - 5078.4$$

$$= 5284.8 - 5078.4 = 206.4$$

$$\text{total SS} = SS_{BG} + SS_{WG}$$
$$281.6 = 206.4 + SS_{WG}$$
$$SS_{WG} = 281.6 - 206.4 = 75.2$$

Step 2. *Calculate Degrees of Freedom*

$$\text{total } df = (N - 1) = (15 - 1) = 14$$
$$df_{BG} = (\text{\# of conditions}) - 1 = 3 - 1 = 2$$
$$df_{WG} = (n_1 - 1) + (n_2 - 1) + (n_3 - 1)$$
$$= (5 - 1) + (5 - 1) + (5 - 1) = 12$$

Step 3. *Calculate Mean Square Values (i.e., Variances)*

$$MS_{BG} = SS_{BG}/df_{BG}$$
$$= 206.4/2 = 103.2$$
$$MS_{WG} = SS_{WG}/df_{WG}$$
$$= 75.2/12 = 6.3$$

(*Note:* the MS_{WG} is also known as the "error term" or MS_e)

Step 4. *Fit Mean Squares into the Formula for F and Solve*

$$F = \frac{MS_{BG}}{MS_{WG}}$$
$$= \frac{103.2}{6.3} = 16.5$$

Step 5. *Construct an ANOVA Source Table*

The essential components of the analysis of variance can be summarized in what is called a source table. It includes a listing of the sources of variance found in the study and for each source, the sums of squares, degrees of freedom, and mean square values; the *F* value is also included. For the maze study a source table would look like this:

Source	SS	df	MS	F
Amount of delay	206.4	2	103.2	16.5
Error	75.2	12	6.3	

Step 6. *Determine if the Calculated F is Significant*

Table D.6 lists the critical values for assessing the outcome of the *F* test. The table is read by reading across the top of the table until you reach the correct *df* value for the numerator of the *F* ratio (2 in our example), then reading down until you reach the *df* value for the denominator of the *F* ratio (i.e., until you reach the values for $df = 12$). The critical values are 3.89 (.05 significance level) and 6.93 (.01 level). The calculated value of 16.5 exceeds both; thus, *F* is significant at the .01 level. It would be reasonable for the researcher to reject the null hypothesis and conclude that some differences exist between the three groups.

Step 7.   *Perform Subsequent Analyses*

When a 1-way analysis like the one just completed yields a significant effect, the question of the exact location of that effect remains unresolved. To solve the problem requires additional testing of each of the pairs of means (13.2 vs. 20.4, 13.2 vs. 21.6, and 20.4 vs. 21.6), using one of several tests that have been developed for the purpose. For example, using a test called the "Tukey HSD (stands for "honesty significant difference") test" is frequently used. The formula, when sample size is the same for all the levels of the independent variable, is

$$HSD = \frac{\bar{X}_1 - \bar{X}_2}{S_{\bar{X}}}$$

where $S_{\bar{X}} = \sqrt{MS_{wg}/n_1} = \sqrt{6.3/5} = 1.12$

In this study, three different HSD calculations can be made:

Comparing the 0 and the 5-second delay: $HSD = \dfrac{13.2 - 20.4}{1.12} = -6.43$

Comparing the 0 and the 10-second delay: $HSD = \dfrac{13.2 - 21.6}{1.12} = -7.50$

Comparing the 5- and the 10-second delay: $HSD = \dfrac{20.4 - 21.6}{1.12} = -1.07$

To determine which of these comparisons yields significant differences requires consulting a table for "studentized ranges," which can be found in most advanced statistics texts. Critical values are read with reference to the number of levels of the independent variable and the degrees of freedom for the within-groups (error) variance (MS_{wg}). For this case, the outcome would be that the first two comparisons are significant, while the third is not. Thus, the research conclusion would be that some reinforcement delay retards the learning process, but that whether the delay is 5 or 10 seconds doesn't seem to matter.

Example 9. 1-Way ANOVA—Repeated Measures

Although the basic calculations are similar, the ANOVA is slightly different when the design is a within-subjects or repeated-measures design. Because each subject serves in all of the study's conditions, there is a reduced amount of variance between the conditions. You can see why if you return for a second to the discussion of between- and within-subjects factors at the beginning of Chapter 6. In the golf ball example, you learned that when using a within-subjects design, the differences in distance between golf ball 1 and golf ball 2 cannot be attributed to individual differences because the same individuals are hitting both balls. As you will see from the following calculations, the mean square for the error term is lessened because it does not include variance attributed to individual differences between the participants in the study. This variance is called "subject variance," and it is calculated separately from the error term and in effect is removed from the error term.

Although the repeated-measures ANOVA is designed for the within-subjects design, it is also used in between-subjects designs when matching is used to create related groups of subjects. This is because in a matched-groups design the matching procedure reduces the variability between the individuals assigned to the different conditions. It is not reduced as much as in the repeated-measures design, of course, but it is lowered enough to warrant using the repeated-measures ANOVA.

As an example of a repeated-measures ANOVA, consider a hypothetical longitudinal study examining the effect of age on logical thinking. Using a test of logic that yields scores ranging from 0 (bad) to 50 (good), a researcher compares the performance of seven individuals at three different times. The first assessment is at their 30th birthday. Their abilities are reassessed at age 45 and again at age 60. Here are the results, along with some basic summary statistics (including row totals).

Subject #	X_1 Age 30	X_2 Age 45	X_3 Age 60	ΣSs	ΣSs^2
1	32	27	25	84	7056
2	43	44	40	127	16129
3	23	27	18	68	4624
4	30	25	20	75	5625
5	45	41	37	123	15129
6	29	31	23	83	6889
7	19	23	15	57	3249
ΣX	221	218	178		
n	7	7	7		
$\overline{X}$	**31.6**	**31.1**	**25.4**		
ΣX^2	7529	7190	5072		
$\Sigma\Sigma Ss^2$				58701	

The formula for the F ratio in a 1-way ANOVA for repeated measures:

$$F = \frac{MS_{BC}}{MS_e}$$

where MS_{BC} refers to the mean square "between conditions"

Step 1.   *Calculate Sums of Squares*

$$\text{total SS} = \left(\Sigma X_1^2 + \Sigma X_2^2 + \Sigma X_3^2\right) - \frac{\left(\Sigma X_1 + \Sigma X_2 + \Sigma X_3\right)^2}{N}$$

$$= 7529 + 7190 + 5072 - \frac{\left(221 + 218 + 178\right)^2}{21}$$

$$= 19791 - 18128 = 1663$$

$$SS_{BG} = \frac{(\Sigma X_1)^2}{n_1} + \frac{(\Sigma X_2)^2}{n_2} + \frac{(\Sigma X_3)^2}{n_3} - \frac{(\Sigma X_1 + \Sigma X_2 + \Sigma X_3)^2}{N}$$

$$= \frac{(221)^2}{7} + \frac{(218)^2}{7} + \frac{(178)^2}{7} - \frac{(221 + 218 + 178)^2}{21}$$

$$= [6997.3 + 6789.1 + 4526.3] - 18128$$

$$= 19567 - 18128 = 1439$$

$$\text{total } SS = SS_{BG} + SS_{\text{subjects}} + SS_e$$

$$1663 = 164.7 + 1439 + SS_e$$

$$SS_e = 1663 - 164.7 - 1439 = 59.3$$

Step 2. *Calculate Degrees of Freedom*

$$\text{total } df = (N - 1) = (21 - 1) = 20$$

$$df_{BC} = (\# \text{ of conditions}) - 1 = 3 - 1 = 2$$

$$df_{\text{subjects}} = (\# \text{ of subjects}) - 1 = 7 - 1 = 6$$

$$df_e = (df_{BC})\,(df_{\text{subjects}})$$

$$= (2)(6) = 12$$

Step 3. *Calculate Mean Square Values*

$$MS_{BC} = SS_{BC}/df_{BC}$$

$$= 164.7/2 = 82.4$$

$$MS_e = SS_e/df_e$$

$$= 59.3/12 = 4.9$$

(*Note:* the *MS* and *F* ratio for "subjects" ordinarily is not calculated)

Step 4. *Fit Mean Squares into the Formula for* F *and Solve*

$$F = \frac{MS_{BC}}{MS_e}$$

$$= \frac{82.4}{4.9} = 16.8$$

Step 5. *Construct an ANOVA Source Table*

The source table for a repeated measures ANOVA adds a line for "subjects" and it would look like this for the study on aging and logic:

Source	SS	df	MS	F
Age	164.7	2	82.4	16.8
Subjects	1439	6	—	—
Error	59.3	12	4.9	

Step 6. *Determine if the Calculated F Is Significant*

Refer to Table D.6 again for the critical values for assessing the outcome of the *F* test. Because the degrees of freedom happen to be the same as in the 1-way ANOVA for independent groups, the critical values are also the same: 3.89 (.05 significance level) and 6.93 (.01 level). The calculated value of 16.8 exceeds both; *F* is significant at the .01 level. The null hypothesis of no age differences can be rejected.

Step 7. *Perform Subsequent Analyses*

As in the earlier example, finding a significant *F* by itself doesn't tell you where the true differences lie. Subsequent testing is again required; by examining the means (31.6, 31.1, and 25.4) you can probably guess the outcome of this hypothetical study on age differences in logic ability.

Example 10. 2-Way ANOVA—Independent Groups

A 2-way ANOVA is used for a factorial design with two independent variables. If both variables are between-subjects variables and subjects are randomly assigned to conditions, the appropriate analysis is an independent groups ANOVA. If both variables are testing within subjects, an analysis similar to the 1-way ANOVA for repeated measures is completed. Finally, if the design is a mixed one, involving both within-subjects and between-subjects factors, the analysis combines elements of an independent groups ANOVA and a repeated-measures ANOVA. The following example is of the simplest case, a 2 × 2 ANOVA for independent groups. For details about other factorial ANOVAs, consult an advanced text in statistics.

To assess the effects of program content and level of anger on aggressive behavior, a researcher uses a 2 × 2 independent groups factorial design and randomly assigns five third-grade boys to each of the following conditions:

1. Violent content/subjects angered.
2. Violent content/subjects not angered.
3. Nonviolent content/subjects angered.
4. Nonviolent content/subjects not angered.

After experiencing one of these four conditions, each boy is given the opportunity to be aggressive. Assume a reliable and valid measure is used and it yields a score from 0 to 25, with higher numbers indicating greater aggression. For the following data, film content is factor *A*, with violent films being level A_1 and nonviolent films being A_2. Factor *B* is whether or not the boys were made angry; for level B_1, they were angered and for level B_2 they were not.

	B_1 (angry)	B_2 (not angry)	
	22	16	
	23	18	
	12	19	
A_1	19	19	
(violent)	22	13	
	$\Sigma X_{A1B1} = 98$	$\Sigma X_{A1B2} = 85$	$\Sigma X_{A1} = 183$
	$n_{A1B1} = 5$	$n_{A1B2} = 5$	$n_{A1} = 10$
	$\overline{X}_{A1B1} = \mathbf{19.6}$	$\overline{X}_{A1B2} = \mathbf{17.0}$	$\overline{X}_{A1} = \mathbf{18.3}$
	$\Sigma X^2_{A1B1} = 2002$	$\Sigma X^2_{A1B2} = 1470$	$\Sigma X^2_{A1} = 3473$
	14	10	
	13	12	
	20	15	
A_2	15	11	
(nonviolent)	17	9	
	$\Sigma X_{A2B1} = 79$	$\Sigma X_{A2B2} = 57$	$\Sigma X_{A2} = 136$
	$n_{A2B1} = 5$	$n_{A2B2} = 5$	$n_{A2} = 10$
	$\overline{X}_{A2B1} = \mathbf{15.6}$	$\overline{X}_{A2B2} = \mathbf{11.4}$	$\overline{X}_{A2} = \mathbf{13.6}$
	$\Sigma X^2_{A2B1} = 1279$	$\Sigma X^2_{A2B2} = 671$	$\Sigma X^2_{A2} = 1950$
	$\Sigma X_{B1} = 177$	$\Sigma X_{B2} = 147$	$\Sigma X_T = 319$
	$n_{B1} = 10$	$n_{B2} = 10$	$N = 20$
	$\overline{X}_{B1} = \mathbf{17.1}$	$\overline{X}_{B2} = \mathbf{14.2}$	
	$\Sigma X^2_{B1} = 3281$	$\Sigma X^2_{B2} = 2141$	$\Sigma X^2_T = 5423$

In a 2-way ANOVA, three separate F ratios are calculated, one for each of the two main effects and one for the interaction:

Main effect for factor A   *Main effect for factor B*   *Main effect for interaction*

$$F = \frac{MS_A}{MS_e}$$ $$F = \frac{MS_B}{MS_e}$$ $$F = \frac{MS_{A \times B}}{MS_e}$$

Step 1. *Calculate Sums of Squares*

$$\text{total SS} = \Sigma X_T^2 - \left(\frac{\Sigma X_T}{N}\right)^2$$

$$= 5423 - \frac{(319)^2}{20}$$

$$= 5423 - 5088.1 = 334.9$$

$$SS_A = \frac{(\Sigma X_{A1})^2}{n_{A1}} + \frac{(\Sigma X_{A2})^2}{n_{A2}} - \frac{(\Sigma X_T)^2}{N}$$

$$= \frac{(183)^2}{10} + \frac{(136)^2}{10} - 5088.1$$

$$= \left[3348.9 + 1849.6\right] - 5088.1$$

$$= 110.4$$

$$SS_B = \frac{(\Sigma X_{B1})^2}{n_{B1}} + \frac{(\Sigma X_{B2})^2}{n_{B2}} - \frac{(\Sigma X_T)^2}{N}$$

$$= \frac{(177)^2}{10} + \frac{(142)^2}{10} - 5088.1$$

$$= \left[3132.9 + 2016.4\right] - 5088.1$$

$$= 61.2$$

$$SS_{A \times B} = \frac{(\Sigma X_{A1B1})^2}{n_{A1B1}} + \frac{(\Sigma X_{A1B2})^2}{n_{A1B2}} + \frac{(\Sigma X_{A2B1})^2}{n_{A2B1}} + \frac{(\Sigma X_{A2B2})^2}{n_{A2B2}} - \frac{(\Sigma X_T)^2}{N}$$

$$- SS_A - SS_B$$

$$= \frac{(98)^2}{5} + \frac{(85)^2}{5} + \frac{(79)^2}{5} + \frac{(57)^2}{5} - 5088.1 - 110.4 - 61.2$$

$$= \left[1920.8 + 1445.0 + 1248.2 + 64938\right] - 5088.1 - 110.4 - 61.2$$

$$= 4.1$$

$$\text{total SS} = SS_A + SS_B + SS_{A \times B} + SS_e$$

$$334.9 = 110.4 + 61.2 + 4.1 + SS_e$$

$$SS_e = 334.9 - \left(110.4 + 61.2 + 4.1\right)$$

$$= 159.2$$

Step 2. *Calculate Degrees of Freedom*

$$\text{total } df = (N - 1) = (20 - 1) = 19$$

$$df_A = (\text{\# of levels of A}) - 1 = 2 - 1 = 1$$

$$df_B = (\text{\# of levels of B}) - 1 = 2 - 1 = 1$$
$$df_{A\times B} = (df_A)(df_B) = (1)(1) = 1$$
$$df_e = (n_{A1B1} - 1) + (n_{A1B2} - 1) + (n_{A2B1} - 1) + (n_{A2B2} - 1)$$
$$= (5 - 1) + (5 - 1) + (5 - 1) + (5 - 1) = 16$$

Step 3. *Calculate Mean Square Values*

$$MS_A = SS_A/df_A$$
$$= 110.4/1 = 110.4$$
$$MS_B = SS_B/df_B$$
$$= 61.2/1 = 61.2$$
$$MS_{A\times B} = SS_{A\times B}/df_{A\times B}$$
$$= 4.1/1 = 4.1$$
$$MS_e = SS_e/df_e$$
$$= 159.2/16 = 9.9$$

Step 4. *Fit Mean Squares into the Formula for* F *and Solve*

Main effect for factor A	*Main effect for factor B*	*Main effect for interaction*
$F = \dfrac{110.4}{9.9}$	$F = \dfrac{61.2}{9.9}$	$F = \dfrac{4.1}{9.9}$
$^- 11.2$	$= 6.2$	$-.41$

Step 5. *Construct an ANOVA Source Table*

The source table for a 2-way ANOVA for independent groups would look like this for the study on the effects of program content and anger on aggression:

Source	SS	df	MS	F
Content (A)	110.4	1	110.4	11.2
Anger (B)	61.2	1	61.2	6.2
Interaction (A × B)	4.1	1	4.1	.4
Error	159.2	16	9.9	

Step 6. *Determine if the Calculated* F *Values Are Significant*

Refer again to Table D.6. This time the degrees of freedom for all three F values are 1 for the numerator and 16 for the denominator. The critical values are 4.49 (.05 significance level) and 8.53 (.01 level). From the calculated values of F, it can be concluded that the study resulted in two main effects and no interaction. The main effect for factor A is significant ($p < .01$), as is the main effect for B ($p < .05$). The main effect for A means that the overall level of aggression when violent films are seen ($\overline{X}_{A1} = 18.3$) is greater than when nonviolent films are seen ($\overline{X}_{A2} = 13.6$). The effect for B means that aggression is higher when subjects are angered ($\overline{X}_{B1} = 17.7$) than when this doesn't happen ($\overline{X}_{B2} = 14.2$).

Step 7. *Perform Subsequent Analyses*

As described in Chapter 7, subsequent testing in a factorial ANOVA can take two forms. If there is a significant main effect for a factor with more than two levels, then pairwise comparisons of the overall means would be done, perhaps using Tukey's HSD test again. If a significant interaction occurred, simple effects testing could be done. In the aggression example, neither of these situations occurs and no subsequent testing is needed.

APPENDIX D

Statistical Tables

In this appendix you will find tables for statistical decision making. The tables are:

TABLE D.1   *Random numbers*

03 47 43 73 86	36 96 47 36 61	46 98 63 71 62	33 26 16 80 45	60 11 14 10 95
97 74 24 67 62	42 81 14 57 20	42 53 32 37 32	27 07 36 07 51	24 51 79 89 73
16 76 62 27 66	56 50 26 71 07	32 90 79 78 53	13 55 38 58 59	88 97 54 14 10
12 56 85 99 26	96 96 68 27 31	05 03 72 93 15	57 12 10 14 21	88 26 49 81 76
55 59 56 35 64	38 54 82 46 22	31 62 43 09 90	06 18 44 32 53	23 83 01 30 30
16 22 77 94 39	49 54 43 54 82	17 37 93 23 78	87 35 20 96 43	84 26 34 91 64
84 42 17 53 31	57 24 55 06 88	77 04 74 47 67	21 76 33 50 25	83 92 12 06 76
63 01 63 78 59	16 95 55 67 19	98 10 50 71 75	12 86 73 58 07	44 39 52 38 79
33 21 12 34 29	78 64 56 07 82	52 42 07 44 38	15 51 00 13 42	99 66 02 79 54
57 60 86 32 44	09 47 27 96 54	49 17 46 09 62	90 52 84 77 27	08 02 73 43 28
18 18 07 92 46	44 17 16 58 09	79 83 86 19 62	06 76 50 03 10	55 23 64 05 05
26 62 38 97 75	84 16 07 44 99	83 11 46 32 24	20 14 85 88 45	10 93 72 88 71
23 42 40 64 74	82 97 77 77 81	07 45 32 14 08	32 98 94 07 72	93 85 79 10 75
52 36 28 19 95	50 92 26 11 97	00 56 76 31 38	80 22 02 53 53	86 60 42 04 53
37 85 94 35 12	83 39 50 08 30	42 34 07 96 88	54 42 06 87 98	35 85 29 48 39
70 29 17 12 13	40 33 20 38 26	13 89 51 03 74	17 76 37 13 04	07 74 21 19 30
56 62 18 37 35	96 83 50 87 75	97 12 25 93 47	70 33 24 03 54	97 77 46 44 80
99 49 57 22 77	88 42 95 45 72	16 64 36 16 00	04 43 18 66 79	94 77 24 21 90
16 08 15 04 72	33 27 14 34 09	45 59 34 68 49	12 72 07 34 45	99 27 72 95 14
31 16 93 32 43	50 27 89 87 19	20 15 37 00 49	52 85 66 60 44	38 68 88 11 80
68 34 30 13 70	55 74 30 77 40	44 22 78 84 26	04 33 46 09 52	68 07 97 06 57
74 57 25 65 76	59 29 97 68 60	71 91 38 67 54	13 58 18 24 76	15 54 55 95 52
27 42 37 86 53	48 55 90 65 72	96 57 69 36 10	96 46 92 42 45	97 60 49 04 91
00 39 68 29 61	66 37 32 20 30	77 84 57 03 29	10 45 65 04 26	11 04 96 67 24
29 94 98 94 24	68 49 69 10 82	53 75 91 93 30	34 25 20 57 27	40 48 73 51 92
16 90 82 66 59	83 62 64 11 12	67 19 00 71 74	60 47 21 29 68	02 02 37 03 31
11 27 94 75 06	06 09 19 74 66	02 94 37 34 02	76 70 90 30 86	38 45 94 30 38
35 24 10 16 20	33 32 51 26 38	79 78 45 04 91	16 92 53 56 16	02 75 50 95 98
38 23 16 86 38	42 38 97 01 50	87 75 66 81 41	40 01 74 91 62	48 51 84 08 32
31 96 25 91 47	96 44 33 49 13	34 86 82 53 91	00 52 43 48 85	27 55 26 89 62

TABLE **D**.1   *(continued)*

66 67 40 67 14	64 05 71 95 86	11 05 65 09 68	76 83 20 37 90	57 16 00 11 66
14 90 84 45 11	75 73 88 05 90	52 27 41 14 86	22 98 12 22 08	07 52 74 95 80
68 05 51 18 00	33 96 02 75 19	07 60 62 93 55	59 33 82 43 90	49 37 38 44 59
20 46 78 73 90	97 51 40 14 02	04 02 33 31 08	39 54 16 49 36	47 95 93 13 30
64 19 58 97 79	15 06 15 93 20	01 90 10 75 06	40 78 78 89 62	02 67 74 17 33
05 26 93 70 60	22 35 85 15 13	92 03 51 59 77	59 56 78 06 83	52 91 05 70 74
07 97 10 88 23	09 98 42 99 64	61 71 62 99 15	06 51 29 16 93	58 05 77 09 51
68 71 86 85 85	54 87 66 47 54	73 32 08 11 12	44 95 92 63 16	29 56 24 29 48
26 99 61 65 53	58 37 78 80 70	42 10 50 67 42	32 17 55 85 74	94 44 67 16 94
14 65 52 68 75	87 59 36 22 41	26 78 63 06 55	13 08 27 01 50	15 29 39 39 43
05 26 93 70 60	22 35 85 15 13	92 03 51 59 77	59 56 78 06 83	52 91 05 70 74
07 97 10 88 23	09 93 42 99 64	61 71 62 99 15	06 51 29 16 93	58 05 77 09 51
68 71 86 85 85	54 87 66 47 54	73 32 08 11 12	44 95 92 63 16	29 56 24 29 48
26 99 61 65 53	58 37 78 80 70	42 10 50 67 42	32 17 55 85 74	94 44 67 16 94
14 65 52 68 75	87 59 36 22 41	26 78 63 06 55	13 08 27 01 50	15 29 39 39 43
17 53 77 58 71	71 41 61 50 72	12 41 94 96 26	44 95 27 36 99	02 96 74 30 83
90 26 59 21 19	23 52 23 33 12	96 93 02 18 39	07 02 18 36 07	25 99 32 70 23
41 23 52 55 99	31 04 49 69 96	10 47 48 45 88	13 41 43 89 20	97 17 14 49 17
60 20 50 81 69	31 99 73 68 68	35 81 33 03 76	24 30 12 48 60	18 99 10 72 34
91 25 38 05 90	94 58 28 41 36	45 37 59 03 09	90 35 57 29 12	82 62 54 65 60
34 50 57 74 37	98 80 33 00 91	09 77 93 19 82	74 94 80 04 04	45 07 31 66 49
85 22 04 39 43	73 81 53 94 79	33 62 46 86 28	08 31 54 46 31	53 94 13 38 47
09 79 13 77 48	73 82 97 22 21	05 03 27 24 83	72 89 44 05 60	35 80 39 94 88
88 75 80 18 14	22 95 75 42 49	39 32 82 22 49	02 48 07 70 37	16 04 61 67 87
90 96 23 70 00	39 00 03 06 90	55 85 78 38 36	94 37 30 69 32	90 89 00 76 33

Source: Fisher, R. A., & Yates, F. (1963). Statistical tables for biological, agricultural, and medical research (6th ed.). Table XXXIII. Edinburgh: Oliver & Boyd.

TABLE **D.2** *Critical Values for Pearson's* r

df	.05	.01	df	.05	.01
	Alpha (α) Level			Alpha (α) Level	
1	.997	1.00	16	.468	.590
2	.950	.990	17	.456	.575
3	.878	.959	18	.444	.561
4	.811	.917	19	.433	.549
5	.755	.875	20	.423	.537
6	.707	.834	25	.381	.487
7	.666	.798	30	.349	.449
8	.634	.767	35	.325	.418
9	.602	.735	40	.304	.393
10	.576	.708	45	.288	.372
11	.553	.694	50	.273	.354
12	.532	.661	60	.250	.325
13	.514	.641	70	.232	.302
14	.497	.623	80	.217	.283
15	.482	.606	90	.205	.267
			100	.195	.254

Source: Fisher, R. A., & Yates, F. (1963). *Statistical tables for biological, agricultural, and medical research* (6th ed.). Table VII. Edinburgh: Oliver & Boyd.

TABLE **D.3** *Critical Values for Chi-Square (X^2)*

df	.05	.01	df	.05	.01
	Alpha (α) Level			Alpha (α) Level	
1	3.84	6.64	16	26.30	32.00
2	5.99	9.21	17	27.59	33.41
3	7.82	11.34	18	28.87	34.80
4	9.49	13.28	19	30.14	36.19
5	11.07	15.09	20	31.41	37.57
6	12.59	16.81	21	32.67	38.93
7	14.07	18.48	22	33.92	40.29
8	15.51	20.09	23	35.17	41.64
9	16.92	21.67	24	36.42	42.98
10	18.31	23.21	25	37.65	44.31
11	19.68	24.72	26	38.88	45.64
12	21.03	26.22	27	40.11	46.96
13	22.36	27.69	28	41.34	48.28
14	23.68	29.14	29	42.56	49.59
15	25.00	30.58	30	43.77	50.89

Source: Fisher, R. A., & Yates, F. (1963). *Statistical tables for biological, agricultural, and medical research* (6th ed.). Table IV. Edinburgh: Oliver & Boyd.

TABLE D.4 *Critical values for the Mann-Whitney U test*[*]

One-tailed test
α = .01 (lightface)
α = .005 (boldface)

Two-tailed test
α = .02 (lightface)
α = .01 (boldface)

N_2 \ N_1	1	2	3	4	5	6	7	8	9	10	11	12	13	14	15	16	17	18	19	20
1	—	—	—	—	—	—	—	—	—	—	—	—	—	—	—	—	—	—	—	—
2	—	—	—	—	—	—	—	—	—	—	—	—	0	0	0	0	0	0	1	1
	—	—	—	—	—	—	—	—	—	—	—	—	—	—	—	—	—	—	**0**	**0**
3	—	—	—	—	—	—	0	0	1	1	1	2	2	2	3	3	4	4	4	5
	—	—	—	—	—	—	—	—	**0**	**0**	**0**	**1**	**1**	**1**	**2**	**2**	**2**	**2**	**3**	**3**
4	—	—	—	—	0	1	1	2	3	3	4	5	5	6	7	7	8	9	9	10
	—	—	—	—	—	**0**	**0**	**1**	**1**	**2**	**2**	**3**	**3**	**4**	**5**	**5**	**6**	**6**	**7**	**8**
5	—	—	—	0	1	2	3	4	5	6	7	8	9	10	11	12	13	14	15	16
	—	—	—	—	**0**	**1**	**1**	**2**	**3**	**4**	**5**	**6**	**7**	**7**	**8**	**9**	**10**	**11**	**12**	**13**
6	—	—	—	1	2	3	4	6	7	8	9	11	12	13	15	16	18	19	20	22
	—	—	—	**0**	**1**	**2**	**3**	**4**	**5**	**6**	**7**	**9**	**10**	**11**	**12**	**13**	**15**	**16**	**17**	**18**
7	—	—	0	1	3	4	6	7	9	11	12	14	16	17	19	21	23	24	26	28
	—	—	—	**0**	**1**	**3**	**4**	**6**	**7**	**9**	**10**	**12**	**13**	**15**	**16**	**18**	**19**	**21**	**22**	**24**
8	—	—	0	2	4	6	7	9	11	13	15	17	20	22	24	26	28	30	32	34
	—	—	—	**1**	**2**	**4**	**6**	**7**	**9**	**11**	**13**	**15**	**17**	**18**	**20**	**22**	**24**	**26**	**29**	**30**
9	—	—	1	3	5	7	9	11	14	16	18	21	23	26	28	31	33	36	38	40
	—	—	**0**	**1**	**3**	**5**	**7**	**9**	**11**	**13**	**16**	**18**	**20**	**22**	**24**	**27**	**29**	**31**	**33**	**36**
10	—	—	1	3	6	8	11	13	16	19	22	24	27	30	33	36	38	41	44	47
	—	—	**0**	**2**	**4**	**6**	**9**	**11**	**13**	**16**	**18**	**21**	**24**	**26**	**29**	**31**	**34**	**37**	**39**	**42**
11	—	—	1	4	7	9	12	15	18	22	25	28	31	34	37	41	44	47	50	53
	—	—	**0**	**2**	**5**	**7**	**10**	**13**	**16**	**18**	**21**	**24**	**27**	**30**	**33**	**36**	**39**	**42**	**45**	**48**
12	—	—	2	5	8	11	14	17	21	24	28	31	35	38	42	46	49	53	56	60
	—	—	**1**	**3**	**6**	**9**	**12**	**15**	**18**	**21**	**24**	**27**	**31**	**34**	**37**	**41**	**44**	**47**	**51**	**54**
13	—	0	2	5	9	12	16	20	23	27	31	35	39	43	47	51	55	59	63	67
	—	—	**1**	**3**	**7**	**10**	**13**	**17**	**20**	**24**	**27**	**31**	**34**	**38**	**42**	**45**	**49**	**53**	**56**	**60**
14	—	0	2	6	10	13	17	22	26	30	34	38	43	47	51	56	60	65	69	73
	—	—	**1**	**4**	**7**	**11**	**15**	**18**	**22**	**26**	**30**	**34**	**38**	**42**	**46**	**50**	**54**	**58**	**63**	**67**
15	—	0	3	7	11	15	19	24	28	33	37	42	47	51	56	61	66	70	75	80
	—	—	**2**	**5**	**8**	**12**	**16**	**20**	**24**	**29**	**33**	**37**	**42**	**46**	**51**	**55**	**60**	**64**	**69**	**73**
16	—	0	3	7	12	16	21	26	31	36	41	46	51	56	61	66	71	76	82	87
	—	—	**2**	**5**	**9**	**13**	**18**	**22**	**27**	**31**	**36**	**41**	**45**	**50**	**55**	**60**	**65**	**70**	**74**	**79**
17	—	0	4	8	13	18	23	28	33	38	44	49	55	60	66	71	77	82	88	93
	—	—	**2**	**6**	**10**	**15**	**19**	**24**	**29**	**34**	**39**	**44**	**49**	**54**	**60**	**65**	**70**	**75**	**81**	**86**
18	—	0	4	9	14	19	24	30	36	41	47	53	59	65	70	76	82	88	94	100
	—	—	**2**	**6**	**11**	**16**	**21**	**26**	**31**	**37**	**42**	**47**	**53**	**58**	**64**	**70**	**75**	**81**	**87**	**92**
19	—	1	4	9	15	20	26	32	38	44	50	56	63	69	75	82	88	94	101	107
	—	**0**	**3**	**7**	**12**	**17**	**22**	**28**	**33**	**39**	**45**	**51**	**56**	**63**	**69**	**74**	**81**	**87**	**93**	**99**
20	—	1	5	10	16	22	28	34	40	47	53	60	67	73	80	87	93	100	107	114
	—	**0**	**3**	**8**	**13**	**18**	**24**	**30**	**36**	**42**	**48**	**54**	**60**	**67**	**73**	**79**	**86**	**92**	**99**	**105**

[*] To be significant the *U* obtained from data must be equal to or **less than** the value shown in the table. Dashes in the body of the table indicate that no decision is possible at the stated level of significance.

Source: Kirk, R. E. (1984). *Elementary Statistics.* Belmont, CA: Brooks/Cole..

TABLE D.4   (continued)

One-tailed test
α = .01 (lightface)
α = .005 (boldface)

Two-tailed test
α = .10 (lightface)
α = .05 (boldface)

N_2 \ N_1	1	2	3	4	5	6	7	8	9	10	11	12	13	14	15	16	17	18	19	20
1	−	−	−	−	−	−	−	−	−	−	−	−	−	−	−	−	−	−	0	0
2	−	−	−	−	0	0	0	1	1	1	1	2	2	2	3	3	3	4	4	4
					−	−	−	**0**	**0**	**0**	**0**	**1**	**1**	**1**	**1**	**1**	**2**	**2**	**2**	**2**
3	−	−	0	0	1	2	2	3	3	4	5	5	6	7	7	8	9	9	10	11
	−	−	−	−	**0**	**1**	**1**	**2**	**2**	**3**	**3**	**4**	**4**	**5**	**5**	**6**	**6**	**7**	**7**	**8**
4	−	−	0	1	2	3	4	5	6	7	8	9	10	11	12	14	15	16	17	18
	−	−	−	**0**	**1**	**2**	**3**	**4**	**4**	**5**	**6**	**7**	**8**	**9**	**10**	**11**	**11**	**12**	**13**	**13**
5	−	0	1	2	4	5	6	8	9	11	12	13	15	16	18	19	20	22	23	25
	−	−	**0**	**1**	**2**	**3**	**5**	**6**	**7**	**8**	**9**	**11**	**12**	**13**	**14**	**15**	**17**	**18**	**19**	**20**
6	−	0	2	3	5	7	8	10	12	14	16	17	19	21	23	25	26	28	30	32
	−	−	**1**	**2**	**3**	**5**	**6**	**8**	**10**	**11**	**13**	**14**	**16**	**17**	**19**	**21**	**22**	**24**	**25**	**27**
7	−	0	2	4	6	8	11	13	15	17	19	21	24	26	28	30	33	35	37	39
	−	−	**1**	**3**	**5**	**6**	**8**	**10**	**12**	**14**	**16**	**18**	**20**	**22**	**24**	**26**	**28**	**30**	**32**	**34**
8	−	1	3	5	8	10	13	15	18	20	23	26	28	31	33	36	39	41	44	47
	−	**0**	**2**	**4**	**6**	**8**	**10**	**13**	**15**	**17**	**19**	**22**	**24**	**26**	**29**	**31**	**34**	**36**	**38**	**41**
9	−	1	3	6	9	12	15	18	21	24	27	30	33	36	39	42	45	48	51	54
	−	**0**	**2**	**4**	**7**	**10**	**12**	**15**	**17**	**20**	**23**	**26**	**28**	**31**	**34**	**37**	**39**	**42**	**45**	**48**
10	−	1	4	7	11	14	17	20	24	27	31	34	37	41	44	48	51	55	58	62
	−	**0**	**3**	**5**	**8**	**11**	**14**	**17**	**20**	**23**	**26**	**29**	**33**	**36**	**39**	**42**	**45**	**48**	**52**	**55**
11	−	1	5	8	12	16	19	23	27	31	34	38	42	46	50	54	57	61	65	69
	−	**0**	**3**	**6**	**9**	**13**	**16**	**19**	**23**	**26**	**30**	**33**	**37**	**40**	**44**	**47**	**51**	**55**	**58**	**62**
12	−	2	5	9	13	17	21	26	30	34	38	42	47	51	55	60	64	68	72	77
	−	**1**	**4**	**7**	**11**	**14**	**18**	**22**	**26**	**29**	**33**	**37**	**41**	**45**	**49**	**53**	**57**	**61**	**65**	**69**
13	−	2	6	10	15	19	24	28	33	37	42	47	51	56	61	65	70	75	80	84
	−	**1**	**4**	**8**	**12**	**16**	**20**	**24**	**28**	**33**	**37**	**41**	**45**	**50**	**54**	**59**	**63**	**67**	**72**	**76**
14	−	2	7	11	16	21	26	31	36	41	46	51	56	61	66	71	77	82	87	92
	−	**1**	**5**	**9**	**13**	**17**	**22**	**26**	**31**	**36**	**40**	**45**	**50**	**55**	**59**	**64**	**67**	**74**	**78**	**83**
15	−	3	7	12	18	23	28	33	39	44	50	55	61	66	72	77	83	88	94	100
	−	**1**	**5**	**10**	**14**	**19**	**24**	**29**	**34**	**39**	**44**	**49**	**54**	**59**	**64**	**70**	**75**	**80**	**85**	**90**
16	−	3	8	14	19	25	30	36	42	48	54	60	65	71	77	83	89	95	101	107
	−	**1**	**6**	**11**	**15**	**21**	**26**	**31**	**37**	**42**	**47**	**53**	**59**	**64**	**70**	**75**	**81**	**86**	**92**	**98**
17	−	3	9	15	20	26	33	39	45	51	57	64	70	77	83	89	96	102	109	115
	−	**2**	**6**	**11**	**17**	**22**	**28**	**34**	**39**	**45**	**51**	**57**	**63**	**67**	**75**	**81**	**87**	**93**	**99**	**105**
18	−	4	9	16	22	28	35	41	48	55	61	68	75	82	88	95	102	109	116	123
	−	**2**	**7**	**12**	**18**	**24**	**30**	**36**	**42**	**48**	**55**	**61**	**67**	**74**	**80**	**86**	**93**	**99**	**106**	**112**
19	0	4	10	17	23	30	37	44	51	58	65	72	80	87	94	101	109	116	123	130
	−	**2**	**7**	**13**	**19**	**25**	**32**	**38**	**45**	**52**	**58**	**65**	**72**	**78**	**85**	**92**	**99**	**106**	**113**	**119**
20	0	4	11	18	25	32	39	47	54	62	69	77	84	92	100	107	115	123	130	138
	−	**2**	**8**	**13**	**20**	**27**	**34**	**41**	**48**	**55**	**62**	**69**	**76**	**83**	**90**	**98**	**105**	**112**	**119**	**127**

TABLE D.5   *Critical Values for the* t
Distribution (two-tailed test)

	Alpha (α) Level			Alpha (α) Level	
df	.05	.01	df	.05	.01
1	12.71	63.66	18	2.10	2.88
2	4.30	9.93	19	2.09	2.86
3	3.18	5.84	20	2.09	2.85
4	2.78	4.60	21	2.08	2.83
5	2.57	4.03	22	2.07	2.82
6	2.45	3.71	23	2.07	2.81
7	2.37	3.50	24	2.06	2.80
8	2.31	3.36	25	2.06	2.79
9	2.26	3.25	26	2.06	2.78
10	2.23	3.17	27	2.05	2.77
11	2.20	3.11	28	2.05	2.76
12	2.18	3.06	29	2.05	2.76
13	2.16	3.01	30	2.04	2.75
14	2.15	2.98	40	2.02	2.70
15	2.13	2.95	60	2.00	2.66
16	2.12	2.92	120	1.98	2.62
17	2.11	2.90	∞	1.96	2.58

Source: Fisher, R. A., & Yates, F. (1963). *Statistical tables for biological, agricultural, and medical research* (6th ed.). Table III. Edinburgh: Oliver & Boyd.

TABLE D.6   *Critical Values for the F Distribution*

	Degrees of Freedom (numerator)								
	1	2	3	4	5	6	7	8	9
1	161.4	199.5	215.7	224.6	230.0	234.0	236.8	238.9	240.5
	4052.40	**4999.5**	**5403**	**5625**	**5764**	**5859**	**5928**	**5981**	**6022**
2	18.51	19.00	19.16	19.25	19.30	19.33	19.35	19.37	19.38
	98.50	**99.00**	**99.17**	**99.25**	**99.30**	**99.33**	**99.36**	**99.37**	**99.39**
3	10.31	9.55	9.28	9.12	9.01	8.94	8.89	8.85	8.81
	34.12	**30.82**	**29.46**	**28.71**	**28.24**	**27.91**	**27.67**	**27.49**	**27.35**
4	7.71	6.94	6.59	6.39	6.26	6.16	6.09	6.04	6.00
	21.20	**18.00**	**16.69**	**15.98**	**15.52**	**15.21**	**14.98**	**14.80**	**16.66**
5	6.61	5.79	5.41	5.19	5.05	4.95	4.88	4.82	4.77
	16.26	**13.27**	**12.06**	**11.39**	**10.97**	**10.67**	**10.46**	**10.29**	**10.16**
6	5.99	5.14	4.76	4.53	4.39	4.28	4.21	4.15	4.10
	13.75	**10.92**	**9.78**	**9.15**	**8.75**	**8.47**	**8.26**	**8.10**	**7.98**
7	5.59	4.74	4.35	4.12	3.97	3.87	3.79	3.73	3.68
	12.25	**9.55**	**8.45**	**7.85**	**7.46**	**7.19**	**6.99**	**6.84**	**6.72**
8	5.32	4.46	4.07	3.84	3.69	3.58	3.50	3.44	3.39
	11.26	**8.65**	**7.59**	**7.01**	**6.63**	**6.37**	**6.18**	**6.03**	**5.91**
9	5.12	4.26	3.86	3.63	3.48	3.37	3.29	3.23	3.18
	10.56	**8.02**	**6.99**	**6.42**	**6.06**	**5.80**	**5.61**	**5.47**	**5.35**
10	4.96	4.10	3.29	3.48	3.33	3.22	3.14	3.07	3.02
	10.04	**7.56**	**6.55**	**5.99**	**5.46**	**5.39**	**5.20**	**5.06**	**4.94**
11	4.84	3.98	3.24	3.36	3.20	3.09	3.01	2.95	2.90
	9.65	**7.21**	**6.22**	**5.67**	**5.32**	**5.07**	**4.89**	**4.74**	**4.63**
12	4.75	3.89	3.20	3.26	3.11	3.00	2.91	2.85	2.80
	9.33	**6.93**	**5.95**	**5.41**	**5.06**	**4.82**	**4.64**	**4.50**	**4.39**
13	4.67	3.81	3.16	3.18	3.03	2.92	2.83	2.77	2.71
	9.07	**6.70**	**5.74**	**5.21**	**4.86**	**4.62**	**4.44**	**4.30**	**4.19**
14	4.60	3.74	3.13	3.11	2.96	2.85	2.76	2.70	2.65
	8.86	**6.51**	**5.56**	**5.04**	**4.69**	**4.46**	**4.28**	**4.14**	**4.03**
15	4.54	3.68	3.29	3.06	2.90	2.79	2.71	2.64	2.59
	8.68	**6.36**	**5.42**	**4.89**	**4.56**	**4.32**	**4.14**	**4.00**	**3.89**
16	4.49	3.63	3.24	3.01	2.85	2.74	2.66	2.59	2.54
	8.53	**6.23**	**5.29**	**4.77**	**4.44**	**4.20**	**4.03**	**3.89**	**3.78**
17	4.45	3.59	3.20	2.96	2.81	2.70	2.61	2.55	2.49
	8.40	**6.11**	**5.18**	**4.67**	**4.34**	**4.10**	**3.93**	**3.79**	**3.68**
18	4.41	3.55	3.16	2.93	2.77	2.66	2.58	2.51	2.46
	8.29	**6.01**	**5.09**	**4.58**	**4.25**	**4.01**	**3.84**	**3.71**	**3.60**
19	4.38	3.52	3.13	2.90	2.74	2.63	2.54	2.48	2.42
	8.18	**5.93**	**5.01**	**4.50**	**4.17**	**3.94**	**3.77**	**3.63**	**3.52**

Source: Pearson, E. S., & Hartley, H. O. (1966). Biometrika tables for statisticians (Vol. 1, 3rd ed.). London Cambridge University Press.

Note: In normal print are critical values for alpha = .05.
 In boldface are critical values for alpha = .01.

TABLE D.6   *Critical Values for the F Distribution (continued)*

			Degrees of Freedom (numerator)						
10	12	15	20	24	30	40	60	120	∞
241.9	243.9	245.9	248.0	249.1	250.1	251.1	252.2	252.3	254.6
6056.90	**6106**	**6157**	**6209**	**6235**	**6261**	**6287**	**6313**	**6339**	**6366**
19.40	19.41	19.43	19.45	19.45	19.46	19.47	19.48	19.49	19.50
99.40	**99.42**	**99.43**	**99.45**	**99.46**	**99.47**	**99.47**	**99.48**	**99.49**	**99.50**
8.79	8.74	8.70	8.66	8.64	8.62	8.59	8.57	8.55	8.53
27.23	**27.05**	**26.87**	**26.69**	**26.60**	**26.50**	**26.41**	**26.32**	**26.22**	**26.13**
5.96	5.91	5.86	5.80	5.77	5.75	5.72	5.69	5.66	5.63
14.55	**14.37**	**14.20**	**14.02**	**13.93**	**13.84**	**13.75**	**13.65**	**13.56**	**13.46**
4.74	4.68	4.62	4.56	4.53	4.50	4.46	4.43	4.40	4.36
10.05	**9.89**	**9.72**	**9.55**	**9.47**	**9.50**	**9.29**	**9.20**	**9.11**	**9.02**
4.06	4.00	3.94	3.87	3.84	3.81	3.77	3.74	3.70	3.67
7.87	**7.72**	**7.56**	**7.40**	**7.31**	**7.23**	**7.14**	**7.06**	**6.97**	**6.88**
3.64	3.57	3.51	3.44	3.41	3.38	3.34	3.30	3.27	3.23
6.62	**6.47**	**6.31**	**6.16**	**6.07**	**5.99**	**5.91**	**5.82**	**5.74**	**5.65**
3.35	3.28	3.22	3.15	3.12	3.08	3.04	3.01	2.97	2.93
5.81	**5.67**	**5.52**	**5.36**	**5.28**	**5.20**	**5.12**	**5.03**	**4.95**	**4.86**
3.14	3.07	3.01	2.94	2.90	2.86	2.83	2.79	2.75	2.71
5.26	**5.11**	**4.96**	**4.81**	**4.73**	**4.65**	**4.57**	**4.48**	**4.40**	**4.31**
2.98	2.91	2.85	2.77	2.74	2.70	2.66	2.62	2.58	2.54
4.85	**4.71**	**4.56**	**4.81**	**4.33**	**4.25**	**4.17**	**4.08**	**4.00**	**3.91**
2.85	2.79	2.72	2.65	2.61	2.57	2.53	2.49	2.45	2.40
4.54	**4.40**	**4.25**	**4.10**	**4.02**	**3.94**	**3.85**	**3.78**	**3.69**	**3.60**
2.75	2.69	2.62	2.54	2.51	2.47	2.43	2.38	2.34	2.30
4.30	**4.16**	**4.01**	**3.86**	**3.78**	**3.70**	**3.62**	**3.54**	**3.45**	**3.36**
2.67	2.60	2.53	2.46	2.42	2.38	2.34	2.30	2.25	2.21
4.10	**3.96**	**3.82**	**3.66**	**3.59**	**3.51**	**3.43**	**3.34**	**3.25**	**3.17**
2.60	2.53	2.46	2.39	2.35	2.31	2.27	2.22	2.18	2.13
3.94	**3.80**	**3.66**	**3.51**	**3.43**	**3.35**	**3.27**	**3.18**	**3.09**	**3.00**
2.54	2.54	2.40	2.33	2.29	2.25	2.20	2.16	2.11	2.07
3.80	**3.67**	**3.52**	**3.37**	**3.29**	**3.21**	**3.13**	**3.05**	**2.96**	**2.87**
2.49	2.42	2.35	2.28	2.24	2.19	2.15	2.11	2.06	2.01
3.69	**3.55**	**3.41**	**3.26**	**3.18**	**3.10**	**3.02**	**2.93**	**2.84**	**2.75**
2.45	2.38	2.31	2.23	2.19	2.15	2.10	2.06	2.01	1.96
3.59	**3.46**	**3.31**	**3.16**	**3.08**	**3.00**	**2.92**	**2.83**	**2.75**	**2.65**
2.41	2.34	2.27	2.19	2.15	2.11	2.06	2.02	1.97	1.92
3.51	**3.37**	**3.23**	**3.08**	**3.00**	**2.92**	**2.84**	**2.75**	**2.66**	**2.57**
2.38	2.31	2.23	2.16	2.11	2.07	2.03	1.98	1.93	1.88
3.43	**3.30**	**3.15**	**3.00**	**2.92**	**2.84**	**2.76**	**2.67**	**2.58**	**2.49**

TABLE D.6   *(continued)*

	Degrees of Freedom (numerator)								
	1	2	3	4	5	6	7	8	9
20	4.35	3.49	3.10	2.87	2.71	2.60	2.51	2.45	2.39
	8.10	**5.85**	**4.94**	**4.43**	**4.10**	**3.87**	**3.70**	**3.56**	**3.46**
21	4.32	3.47	3.07	2.84	2.68	2.57	2.49	2.42	2.37
	8.02	**5.78**	**4.87**	**4.37**	**4.04**	**3.81**	**3.64**	**3.51**	**3.40**
22	4.30	3.44	3.05	2.82	2.66	2.55	2.46	2.40	2.34
	7.95	**5.72**	**4.82**	**4.31**	**3.99**	**3.76**	**3.59**	**3.45**	**3.35**
23	4.28	3.42	3.03	2.80	2.64	2.53	2.44	2.37	2.32
	7.88	**5.66**	**4.76**	**4.26**	**3.94**	**3.71**	**3.54**	**3.41**	**3.30**
24	4.26	3.40	3.01	2.78	2.62	2.51	2.42	2.36	2.30
	7.82	**5.61**	**4.72**	**4.22**	**3.90**	**3.67**	**3.50**	**3.36**	**3.26**
25	4.24	3.39	2.99	2.76	2.60	2.49	2.40	2.34	2.28
	7.77	**5.57**	**4.99**	**4.18**	**3.85**	**3.63**	**3.46**	**3.32**	**3.22**
26	4.23	3.37	2.98	2.74	2.59	2.47	2.39	2.32	2.27
	7.72	**5.53**	**4.98**	**4.14**	**3.82**	**3.59**	**3.42**	**3.29**	**3.18**
27	4.21	3.35	2.96	2.73	2.57	2.46	2.37	2.31	2.25
	7.68	**5.49**	**4.60**	**4.11**	**3.78**	**3.56**	**3.39**	**3.26**	**3.15**
28	4.20	3.34	2.95	2.71	2.56	2.45	2.36	2.29	2.24
	7.64	**5.45**	**4.57**	**4.07**	**3.75**	**3.53**	**3.36**	**3.23**	**3.12**
29	4.18	3.33	2.93	2.70	2.55	2.43	2.35	2.28	2.22
	7.60	**5.42**	**4.54**	**4.04**	**3.73**	**3.50**	**3.33**	**3.20**	**3.09**
30	4.17	3.32	2.92	2.69	2.53	2.42	2.33	2.27	2.21
	7.56	**5.39**	**4.51**	**4.02**	**3.70**	**3.47**	**3.30**	**3.17**	**3.07**
40	4.08	3.23	2.84	2.61	2.45	2.34	2.25	2.18	2.12
	7.31	**5.18**	**4.31**	**3.83**	**3.51**	**3.29**	**3.12**	**2.99**	**2.89**
60	4.00	3.15	2.76	2.53	2.37	2.25	2.17	2.10	2.04
	7.08	**4.98**	**4.13**	**3.65**	**3.34**	**3.12**	**2.95**	**2.82**	**2.72**
120	3.92	3.07	2.68	2.45	2.29	2.17	2.09	2.02	1.96
	6.85	**4.79**	**3.95**	**3.48**	**3.17**	**2.96**	**2.79**	**2.66**	**2.56**
∞	3.84	3.00	2.60	2.37	2.21	2.10	2.01	1.94	1.88
	6.63	**4.61**	**3.78**	**3.32**	**3.02**	**2.80**	**2.64**	**2.51**	**2.41**

Degrees of Freedom (denominator)

TABLE D.6   *(continued)*

		Degrees of Freedom (numerator)							
10	12	15	20	24	30	40	60	120	∞
2.35	2.28	2.20	2.12	2.08	2.04	1.99	1.95	1.90	1.84
3.37	**3.23**	**3.09**	**2.94**	**2.86**	**2.78**	**2.69**	**2.61**	**2.52**	**2.42**
2.32	2.25	2.18	2.10	2.05	2.01	1.96	1.92	1.87	1.81
3.31	**3.17**	**3.03**	**2.88**	**2.80**	**2.72**	**2.64**	**2.55**	**2.46**	**2.36**
2.30	2.23	2.15	2.07	2.03	1.98	1.94	1.89	1.84	1.78
3.26	**3.12**	**2.98**	**2.83**	**2.75**	**2.67**	**2.58**	**2.50**	**2.40**	**2.31**
2.27	2.20	2.13	2.05	2.01	1.96	1.91	1.86	1.81	1.76
3.21	**3.07**	**2.93**	**2.78**	**2.70**	**2.62**	**2.54**	**2.45**	**2.35**	**2.26**
2.25	2.18	2.11	2.03	1.98	1.94	1.89	1.84	1.79	1.73
3.17	**3.03**	**2.89**	**2.74**	**2.66**	**2.58**	**2.49**	**2.40**	**2.31**	**2.21**
2.24	2.16	2.09	2.01	1.96	1.92	1.87	1.82	1.77	1.71
3.13	**2.99**	**2.85**	**2.70**	**2.62**	**2.54**	**2.45**	**2.36**	**2.27**	**2.17**
2.22	2.15	2.07	1.99	1.95	1.90	1.85	1.80	1.75	1.69
3.09	**2.96**	**2.81**	**2.66**	**2.58**	**2.50**	**2.42**	**2.33**	**2.23**	**2.13**
2.20	2.13	2.06	1.97	1.93	1.88	1.84	1.79	1.73	1.67
3.06	**2.93**	**2.78**	**2.63**	**2.55**	**2.47**	**2.38**	**2.29**	**2.20**	**2.10**
2.19	2.12	2.04	1.96	1.91	1.87	1.82	1.77	1.71	1.65
3.03	**2.90**	**2.75**	**2.60**	**2.52**	**2.44**	**2.35**	**2.26**	**2.17**	**2.06**
2.18	2.10	2.03	1.94	1.90	1.85	1.81	1.75	1.70	1.64
3.00	**2.87**	**2.73**	**2.57**	**2.49**	**2.41**	**2.33**	**2.23**	**2.14**	**2.03**
2.16	2.09	2.01	1.93	1.89	1.84	1.79	1.74	1.68	1.62
2.98	**2.84**	**2.70**	**2.55**	**2.47**	**2.39**	**2.30**	**2.21**	**2.11**	**2.01**
2.08	2.00	1.92	1.84	1.79	1.74	1.69	1.64	1.58	1.51
2.80	**2.66**	**2.52**	**2.37**	**2.29**	**2.20**	**2.11**	**2.02**	**1.92**	**1.80**
1.99	1.92	1.84	1.75	1.70	1.65	1.59	1.53	1.47	1.39
2.63	**2.50**	**2.35**	**2.20**	**2.12**	**2.03**	**1.94**	**1.84**	**1.73**	**1.60**
1.91	1.83	1.75	1.66	1.61	1.55	1.50	1.43	1.35	1.25
2.47	**2.34**	**2.19**	**2.03**	**1.95**	**1.86**	**1.76**	**1.66**	**1.53**	**1.38**
1.83	1.74	1.67	1.57	1.52	1.46	1.39	1.32	1.22	1.00
2.32	**2.18**	**2.04**	**1.88**	**1.79**	**1.70**	**1.59**	**1.47**	**1.32**	**1.00**

APPENDIX E

Answers to End-of-Chapter Reviews

This appendix provides feedback for the end-of-chapter multiple choice items and for selected applications exercises. For the multiple choice items, the relevant chapter pages are in parentheses. In the Instructor's Manual, your instructor has a complete set of answers to the Applications Exercises.

Chapter 1. Scientific Thinking in Psychology

Multiple Choice:
1. c (10)   2. a (7)   3. d (24)   4. b (22)   5. b (8)

Applications Exercises:

1.1. Asking Empirical Questions

　1. Is God dead?

　　Possible empirical question: To what extent do people of different religious faiths believe in a personal God who is directly involved in their day-to-day lives?

3. Are humans naturally good?

   Possible empirical question: Will people be less likely to donate to charity if they believe their donations will be anonymous?

5. What is beauty?

   Possible empirical question: Do 20-year-old men differ from 40-year-old men in terms of how they define beauty in a woman?

Chapter 2.   Ethics in Psychological Research

Multiple Choice:
1. b (34)   2. c (49)   3. d (44)   4. a (59)   5. c (61)

Applications Exercises:

2.1.   Thinking Scientifically About Deception

    1.   One possible study could examine attitudes toward research and toward psychologists held by students who had been through experiments that either included deception or did not. In addition to the measure of attitudes, students could be asked to rank psychologists, among a number of other professions, on a scale of "trustworthiness."

2.2.   Recognizing Ethical Problems

    1.   This study could be a problem for Standards 6.08 (unwitting participants could possibly sue for privacy invasions and even bring criminal charges of harassment or criminal trespass—see Box 3.1), 6.11 (lack of informed consent; not told they could discontinue participant), 6.15 (deception — the study might impose too high a level of "unpleasant emotional experience"), 6.17 (minimizing invasiveness). To defend the study to an IRB, the researcher would stress that it is important to understand how stress affects physiological systems, that the experience was not significantly different from what can happen in any men's room, that proper debriefing would be done, that confidentiality would be maintained, and that the data would not be used without the person's permission.

Chapter 3.   Developing Ideas for Research in Psychology

Multiple Choice:
1. c (73)   2. b (77)   3. c (84)   4. c (93)   5. a (94)

Applications Exercises:

3.1.   What's Next?

Milgram study: One variation could be to bring the victim into the same room with the teacher. By making the suffering more salient, the hypothesis would be that the level of obedience would decline (Milgram did this, by the way, and the level of obedience did indeed decline somewhat).

3.2. Creating Operational Definitions

1. Frustration could be operationally defined as (a) blood pressure elevated 20% above the baseline level for a person, or (b) amount of time spent pushing against a blockade keeping a child from a desired toy.

3. Anxiety could be operationally defined as (a) level of muscle tension in the shoulders, or (b) a person's self-rating of anxiety just before an exam begins, on a scale from 1 to 10.

Chapter 4. Measurement, Sampling, and Data Analysis

Multiple Choice:
1. c (111)   2. b (112)   3. b (114)   4. b (124)   5. d (117)

Applications Exercises:
4.2. Scales of Measurement

1. categories are being used—this is nominal

3. rank order is ordinal

5. nominal, assuming the study is set up so that what is measured is whether people help or not (i.e., two categories); could be ratio, though, if the amount of time it takes for someone to help is measured.

4.3. H_0, H_1, Type I errors, and Type II errors

1. H_0: male and female participants are equally able to detect deception H_1: females will be better able to detect deception than males (rationale—reading facial expressions of emotion is not a "guy thing")

Type I error: females outperform males, when in fact there are no true differences in the ability to judge deception

Type II error: no differences are found in the study, but in fact, females are superior to males in judging deception

Chapter 5. Introduction to Experimental Research

Multiple Choice:
1. b (160)   2. d (166)   3. a (151)   4. d (157)   5. d (165)

Applications Exercises:
5.1. Identifying Variables

1. There are two independent variables. The first is class; its levels are freshmen and seniors; it is a subject variable. The second is building location; its levels are central and peripheral; it is a manipulated variable. There are also two dependent variables, confidence ratings (interval scale) and pointing accuracy (ratio scale).

3. There is one manipulated independent variable, which could be called "tone-food sequencing." Its three levels are (a) tone on and off, then food, (b) tone on, then food, and (c) food, then tone. There are two dependent variables: how long it takes for saliva to begin, and how much saliva accumulates. Both are ratio.

5.2. Spot the Confound(s)

1. The independent variable is driver type (four levels, one for each type of driver) and the dependent variable is the distance traveled by a struck golf ball. Confounds are club sequence (the golfers shouldn't all hit the clubs in the same order) and golf course hole (some holes might lend themselves to longer distances, if, for instance, they are downwind).

Levels of IV	EV1	EV2	DV
Club 1	first to be hit	first hole	distance
Club 2	second to be hit	second hole	distance
Club 3	third to be hit	third hole	distance
Club 4	fourth to be hit	fourth hole	distance

3. The independent variable is memorization strategy (or a similar label), with two levels, imagery and rote repetition. Confounds are word type (should all be either concrete or abstract) and presentation mode (should all be either visual or auditory). The dependent variable is the number of words recalled.

Levels of IV	EV1	EV2	DV
imagery	concrete nouns	visual	recall
rote repetition	abstract nouns	auditory	recall

5.3. Operational Definitions (Again)

1. The independent variable is situational ambiguity and in a helping behavior study it could be manipulated by staging an emergency (e.g., a person slumped against a wall groaning) and manipulating the level of lighting with perhaps three levels: bright, medium, and dim. These could be operationally defined in terms of some physical measure of brightness. The dependent variable would be helping, and could be operationally defined as occurring whenever a passerby stops and verbally offers aid.

Chapter 6.   Control Problems in Experimental Research

Multiple Choice:
1. d (180)   2. c (183)   3. c (183)   4. a (196)   5. b (201)

Applications Exercises:

6.1. Between-Subject or Within-Subject?

1. The study would need both young and old animals, a between-subject variable. For each group, some animals would have their visual cortex damaged and others wouldn't, another between-subjects variable.

3. The study would involve comparing the repeated exposure procedure with some other procedure or with the absence of a procedure (control group). In either case, this is a between-subjects situation.

5. This study compares problem solving when done in groups or when done alone. It could be done as a between-subjects variable, but a within-subjects approach would also be fine and might even be preferable, allowing direct comparisons within a specific person of whether problem solving works better in a group or not.

Chapter 7. Experimental Design I: Single-Factor Designs

Multiple Choice:
1. c (229)   2. d (218)   3. c (217)   4. b (227)   5. a (231)

Applications Exercises:

7.1. Identifying Designs

1. The independent variable is whether or not a person has bulimia; it is a between-subjects variable and a subject variable. The dependent variable is the choice of the body size drawing. The design is: single-factor, 2-level, nonequivalent groups.

3. The independent variable is size of the gratification delay; it is a between-subjects manipulated variable. The dependent variable is how long they continue doing the puzzle. The design is: single-factor, multi-level, independent groups.

7.2. Outcomes

1. The independent variable is a discrete variable (type of group in the study), so a bar graph should be used.

Outcome A. Marijuana impairs recall, while subject expectations about marijuana have no effect on recall.

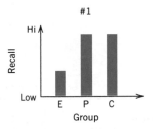

Outcome B. Marijuana impairs recall, but subject expectations about marijuana also reduce recall performance.

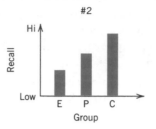

Outcome C. The apparently adverse effect of marijuana on recall can be attributed entirely to placebo effects.

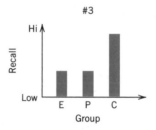

3.   The independent variable is a continuous variable (time delay of reinforcement), so a line graph is preferred (a bar graph could be used, however).

Outcome A. Reinforcement delay hinders learning.

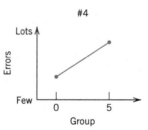

Outcome B. Reinforcement delay has no effect no learning.

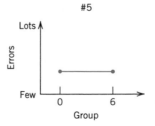

Chapter 8.   Experimental Design II: Factorial Designs

Multiple Choice:
1. c (251)   2. d (270)   3. c (246)   4. b (262)   5. d (263)

Applications Exercises:

8.1. Identifying Designs

1. Independent variable #1: personality type (A, B, intermediate) (between; subject)

    Independent variable #2: cognitive task (video game, no video game) (between; manipulated)

    Dependent variable: accuracy in estimating the passage of 2 minutes

    Design: 2 × 3 P × E Factorial

3. Independent variable #1: skin location (10 locations) (within; manipulated)

    Independent variable #2: visual capacity (blind; sighted) (between; subject)

    Independent variable #3: time of testing (morning; evening) (between; manipulated)

    Dependent variable: threshold judgments

    Design: 2 × 2 × 10 P × E Mixed Factorial

5. Independent variable #1: stimulus color (color; b/w) (within; manipulated)

    Independent variable #2: stimulus distance (10′; 20′) (within; manipulated)

    Dependent variable: error score

    Design: 2 × 2 Repeated Measures Factorial

Chapter 9.   Correlational Research

Multiple Choice:

1. c (285)   2. d (296)   3. a (306)   4. b (301)   5. d (294)

Applications Exercises:

9.1. Interpreting Correlations

1. It could be that dominant mothers never allow their children to develop independence and they become shy as a result (A→B). However, it could also be that naturally shy children cause their mothers to take more control of the relationship (B→A).

3. It could be that all the books in the home were read by the children, making them smarter and therefore better students (A→B). It could be that the third variable of parental attitudes toward learning led to (a) lots of books in the home, and (b) reinforcement for their children being good students (C→A&B).

9.3. Understanding Scatterplots

1. The Pearson's *r* of +.50 is relatively strong, indicating some similarity in cognitive function between sequential and simultaneous processing.

3. This correlation indicates that there is no relationship at all between being intelligent and being depressed.

Chapter 10.   Quasi-Experimental Designs and Applied Research

Multiple Choice:
1. a (317)   2. c (322)   3. c (323)   4. c (336)   5. d (340)

Applications Exercises:

10.1.   Identifying Threats to Internal Validity

1.   Without a control group, there are several alternative explanations. Because the 60% is way below the norm of 75% (i.e., an extreme score), regression would be the most likely threat. History and selection are two other possibilities, but maturation is less likely because two different groups of students would be involved in the study.

3.   This is most likely a selection problem. The women who volunteer are possibly different in some significant way (e.g., more willing to try new things) than the women selected randomly.

5.   Thirty students started the course but only 18 finished it. The problem is attrition, resulting in a group at the end of the course that is systematically different (e.g., more persevering) than those who started the course. This course format might not be effective for the student who needs more direct guidance.

Chapter 11.   Small N Designs

Multiple Choice:
1. b (353)   2. a (357)   3. c (370)   4. a (378)   5. d (369)

Applications Exercises:

11.2.   Hypothetical Outcomes of Applied Behavior Analysis

1.   A–B–C–B

   a.   reinforcement works, but only if it is made contingent on specific behaviors

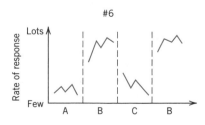

    b.   reinforcement works regardless of whether it is made contingent on specific behaviors

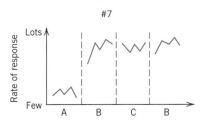

Chapter 12.   Descriptive Research Methods

Multiple Choice:
1. a (390)   2. c (393)   3. a (398)   4. c (410)   5. c (409)

Applications Exercises:

12.1.   Improving Poor Survey Items

    1.   Have you had an upset stomach lately?

        a.   "Upset stomach" could be described more precisely, but the major problem is the lack of precision in the "lately;" does it mean within the past week? Month?

        b.   After telling the test taker to define an upset stomach as "nauseous to the point where you think you might vomit but you don't," the item could read: Have you had an upset stomach in the last week? If so, how often?

    3.   In your opinion, how young is the average cigarette smoker?

        a.   The "how young" could bias the person toward giving a younger age and some people might even misinterpret the question as a question about when people first start smoking.

        b.   Better: In your opinion, what is the average age of a typical cigarette smoker?

12.3.   Deciding on Descriptive Methods

    1.   Because these organizations tend to be private, participant observation would be more revealing than naturalistic observation, but gaining entry to the group could be a problem. In depth interviews in a qualitative study might be effective.

    3.   Sample size is too large for interviews, so a written survey, or possibly a phone survey, would be the way to go.

    5.   This is a case study that would probably include in–depth interviews with the passengers.

Glossary

A priori method A way of knowing proposed by Peirce in which a person develops a belief by reasoning and reaching agreement with others who are convinced of the merits of the reasoned argument.

A–A$_1$–B–A$_1$–B A small N design for evaluating placebo effects; A$_1$ is a condition in the sequence in which a placebo treatment is given.

A–B design A small N design in which a baseline period (A) is followed by a treatment period (B).

A–B–A design A small N design in which a baseline period (A) is followed by a treatment period (B) followed by a period in which the treatment is reversed or withdrawn (second A).

A–B–A–B design Like an A–B–A design except that a second treatment period is established (second B).

A–B–C–B design A small N design that compares contingent reinforcement (B) with non-contingent reinforcement (C); allows the researcher to separate the effects of reinforcers and contingency.

Absolute threshold Stimulus intensity sufficient for the participant to detect the presence of a stimulus.

Alpha level The probability of making a Type I error; the significance level.

Alternating treatments design A small N design that compares, in the same study and for the same participant(s), two or more separate forms of treatment for changing some behavior.

Alternative hypothesis The researcher's hypothesis about the outcome of a study (H$_1$).

Anecdotal evidence Evidence from a single case that illustrates a phenomenon; when relied on exclusively, as in pseudoscience, faulty conclusions easily can be drawn.

ANOVA Short for **AN**alysis **Of VA**riance, the most common inferential statistical tool for analyzing the results of experiments when dependent variables are measured on interval or ratio scales.

Applied behavior analysis Research using various methods to evaluate the effectiveness of various conditioning procedures in bringing about changes in the rate of response of some behavior.

Applied research Research with the goal of trying to solve some immediate real-life problem.

Archival research A descriptive method in which already existing records are examined to test some research hypothesis.

Assent To give assent is to say "yes." In the SRCD code of ethics for research with children, assent refers to the willingness on the part of the child to participate in the study.

Asymmetric transfer Occurs when one sequence produces a transfer effect that is different from that produced by another counterbalanced sequence.

ATI design Aptitude by treatment interaction design; form of P × E factorial design found in educational research, the goal of which is to examine possible interactions between an aptitude variable (person factor) and a treatment variable (environmental factor).

Attrition A threat to the internal validity of a study; occurs when participants fail to complete a study, usually but not necessarily in longitudinal studies; those finishing the study may not be equivalent to those who started it.

Authority A way of knowing proposed by Peirce in which a person develops a belief by agreeing with someone perceived to be an expert.

Availability heuristic Social cognition bias in which vivid or memorable events lead people to overestimate the frequency of occurrence of these events.

Baseline   The initial stage of a small N design, in which the behavior to be changed is monitored to determine its normal rate of response.

Basic research   Research with the goal of describing, predicting, and explaining fundamental principles of behavior.

Behavior checklists   Lists of behaviors with predefined operational definitions that researchers are trained to use in an observational study.

Belief perseverance   Unwillingness to consider any evidence that contradicts a strongly held view; similar to Peirce's principle of tenacity.

Between-subjects design   Any experimental design in which different groups of participants serve in the different conditions of the study.

Biased sample   A sample that is not representative of the population.

Bivariate analysis   Any statistical analysis investigating the relationship between two variables.

Block randomization   A procedure used to accomplish random assignment and ensure an equal number of subjects in each condition; ensures that each condition of the study has a subject randomly assigned to it before any condition has a subject assigned to it again; also used in within-subjects design as a counterbalancing procedure to ensure that when subjects are tested in each condition more than once, they experience each condition once before experiencing it again.

Carryover effect   Form of sequence effect in which systematic changes in performance occur as a result of completing a sequence of conditions rather than a different sequence.

Case study   A descriptive method in which an in-depth analysis is made of either a single individual, a single rare event, or an event that clearly exemplifies some phenomenon.

Ceiling effect   Occurs when scores on two or more conditions are at or near the maximum possible for the scale being used, giving the impression that no differences exist between the conditions.

Changing criterion design   A small N design in which the criterion for receiving reinforcement begins at a modest level and becomes more stringent as the study progresses; used to shape behavior.

Closed question   A type of question found on surveys that can be answered with a "yes" or a "no" or by marking a point on some scale.

Cluster sample   A probability sample that randomly selects clusters of people having some feature in common (e.g., students taking history courses) and tests all people within the selected cluster (e.g., all students in three of the nine history courses available).

Coefficient of correlation   See Pearson's r

Coefficient of determination   For two correlated factors, the proportion of variance in one factor that can be attributed to the second factor; found by squaring Pearson's r.

Cohort effect   A cohort is a group of people born at the same time; cohort effects can reduce the internal validity of cross-sectional studies because differences between groups could result from the effects of growing up in different historical eras.

Community forum   In program evaluation research, a meeting open to community members to discuss the need for, or the operation of, some program.

Complete counterbalancing   Occurs when all possible orders of conditions are used in a within-subjects design.

Confirmation bias   Social cognition bias in which events that confirm a strongly held belief are more readily perceived and remembered; disconfirming events are ignored or forgotten.

Confound   Any extraneous variable that covaries with the independent variable and could provide an alternative explanation of the results.

Construct   A hypothetical factor (e.g., hunger) that cannot be observed directly but is inferred from certain behaviors (e.g., eating) and assumed to follow from certain circumstances (e.g., 24 hours without food).

Construct validity   In measurement, it occurs when the measure being used accurately assesses some hypothetical construct; also refers to whether the construct itself is valid; in research, refers to whether the operational definitions used for independent and dependent variables are valid.

Content analysis A procedure used in descriptive research to categorize systematically the content of the behavior (often verbal behavior) being recorded.

Continuous variable Variable for which an infinite number of values potentially exists (e.g., a drug's dosage level).

Control A goal of science in which basic principles discovered through scientific methods are applied in order to solve problems.

Control group A group not given a treatment that is being evaluated in a study; provides a means of comparison.

Convenience sample A nonprobability sample in which the researcher requests volunteers from a group of people who meet the general requirements of the study (e.g., teenagers); used in most psychological research, except when specific estimates of population values need to be made.

Converging operations Occurs when the results of several studies, each defining its terms with slightly different operational definitions, nonetheless converge on the same general conclusion.

Correlation See Positive correlation and Negative correlation

Correlation matrix A table that summarizes a series of correlations among several variables.

Cost-effectiveness analysis Form of evaluation that assesses program outcomes in terms of the costs involved in developing, running, and completing the program.

Counterbalancing For a within-subjects variable, any procedure designed to control for sequence effects.

Creative thinking A process of making an innovative connection between seemingly unrelated ideas or events.

Criterion validity Form of validity in which a psychological measure is able to predict some future behavior or is meaningfully related to some other measure.

Criterion variable In a regression analysis, this is the variable that is being predicted from the predictor variable (e.g., college grades are predicted from SAT scores).

Critical incidents Method used by ethics committees that surveys psychologists and asks for examples of unethical behavior by professional psychologists.

Cross-lagged panel correlation Refers to a type of correlational research designed to deal with the directionality problem; if variables X and Y are measured at two different times and if X precedes Y, then X might cause Y but Y cannot cause X.

Cross-sectional study In developmental psychology, a design in which age is the independent variable and different groups of people are tested; each group is of a different age.

Cumulative recorder Apparatus for recording the subject's cumulative rate of response in operant conditioning studies.

Data-driven Belief of research psychologists that conclusions about behavior should be supported by data collected scientifically.

Debriefing A postexperimental session in which the experimenter explains the study's purpose, reduces any discomfort felt by participants, and answers any questions posed by participants.

Deception A research strategy in which participants are not told of all the details of an experiment at its outset; used for the purpose of avoiding demand characteristics.

Deduction Reasoning from the general to the specific; in science, used when deriving research hypotheses from theories.

Dehoaxing That portion of debriefing in which the true purpose of the study is explained to participants.

Demand characteristic Any feature of the experimental design or procedure that increases the chances that participants will detect the true purpose of the study.

Dependent variable Behavior measured as the outcome of an experiment.

Description A goal of psychological science in which behaviors are accurately classified or sequences of environmental stimuli and behavioral events are accurately listed.

Descriptive statistics Provide a summary of the main features of a set of data collected from a sample of participants.

Desensitizing That portion of debriefing in which the experimenter tries to reduce any distress felt by participants as a result of their research experience.

Determinism An assumption made by scientists that all events have causes.

Difference threshold Occurs when stimulus 1 is just noticeably different from stimulus 2.

Directionality problem In correlational research, this refers to the fact that for a correlation between variables X and Y, it is possible that X is causing Y, but it is also possible that Y is causing X; the correlation alone provides no basis for deciding between the two alternatives.

Discoverability An assumption made by scientists that the causes of events can be discovered by applying scientific methods.

Discrete variable Variable in which each level represents a distinct category that is qualitatively different from another category (e.g., males and females).

Double blind A control procedure designed to reduce bias; neither the participant nor the person conducting the experimental session knows which condition of the study is being tested; often used in studies evaluating drug effects.

Ecological validity Said to exist when research studies psychological phenomena in everyday situations (e.g., memory for where we put our keys).

Effect size Amount of influence that one variable has on another; the amount of variance in the dependent variable that can be attributed to the independent variable.

Effort justification After expending a large amount of time or effort to obtain some goal, people giving the effort feel pressured to convince themselves that the effort was worthwhile, even if the resulting outcome is less positive than originally thought.

Empirical question A question that can be answered by making objective observations.

Empiricism A way of knowing that relies on direct observation or experience.

Equivalent groups Groups of participants in a between-subjects design that are essentialy equal to each other in all ways except for the different levels of the independent variable.

Error variance Nonsystematic variability in a set of scores due to random factors or individual differences.

Ethics A set of principles prescribing behaviors that are morally correct.

Evaluation apprehension A form of anxiety experienced by participants that leads them to behave so as to be evaluated positively by the experimenter.

Event sampling A procedure in observational research in which only certain types of behaviors occurring under precisely defined conditions are sampled.

Experiment A research procedure in which some factor is varied, all else is held constant, and some result is measured.

Experimental group In a study with an identified control group, the experimental group is given the treatment being tested.

Experimental realism Refers to how deeply involved the participants become in the experiment; considered to be more important than mundane realism.

Experimenter bias Occurs when an experimenter's expectations about a study affect its outcome.

Explanation A goal of science in which the causes of events are sought.

Extension Replicating part of a prior study but adding some additional features (e.g., additional levels of the independent variable).

External validity The extent to which the findings of a study generalize to other populations, other settings, and other times.

Extraneous variable Any uncontrolled factor that is not of interest to the researcher but could affect the results.

Face validity Occurs when a measure appears to be a reasonable measure of some trait (e.g., as a measure of intelligence, problem solving has more face validity than hat size).

Factor analysis   A multivariate analysis in which a large number of variables are intercorrelated; variables that correlate highly with each other form "factors."

Factorial design   Any experimental design with more than one independent variable.

Factorial matrix   A row and column arrangement that characterizes a factorial design and shows the independent variables, the levels of each independent variable, and the total number of conditions (cells) in the study.

Falsification   Research strategy advocated by Popper that emphasizes putting theories to the test by trying to disprove or falsify them.

Falsifying data   Manufacturing or altering data in order to bring about a desired result.

Field experiment   An experiment that is conducted outside of the laboratory; a narrower term than field research.

Field research   Research that occurs in any location other than a scientific laboratory.

Figures   In a lab report or description of research, these are graphs, diagrams, flow charts, sketches of apparatus, or photos.

Focus group   A small and relatively homogeneous group brought together for the purpose of participating in a group interview on some topic or, in program evaluation research, to discuss the need for or the operation of a program.

Formative evaluation   Form of program evaluation that monitors the functioning of a program while it is operating to determine if it is functioning as planned.

Frequency distribution   A table that records the number of times that each score in a set of scores occurs.

Good subject role   A form of participant bias in which participants try to guess the experimenter's hypothesis and then behave in such a way as to confirm it.

Hawthorne effect   Name often given to a form of participant bias in which behavior is influenced by the mere knowledge that the participant is in an experiment and is therefore of some importance to the experimenter.

Histogram   Graph of a frequency distribution in bar form.

History   A threat to the internal validity of a study; occurs when some historical event that could affect participants occurs between the beginning of a study and its end.

Hypothesis   An educated guess about a relationship between variables that is then tested empirically.

Independent groups design   A between-subjects design that uses a manipulated independent variable and has at least two groups of participants; subjects are randomly assigned to the groups.

Independent variable   The factor of interest to the researcher; it can be directly manipulated by the experimenter (e.g., creating different levels of anxiety in subjects) or participants can be selected by virtue of their possessing certain attributes (e.g., selecting two groups who differ in the normal levels of anxiousness).

Individual-subject validity   the extent to which the general outcome of a research study characterizes the behavior of the individual participants in the study.

Induction   Reasoning from the specific to the general; in science, used when the results of specific research studies are used to support or refute a theory.

Inferential statistics   Used to draw conclusions about the broader population on the basis of a study using just a sample of that population.

Informed consent   The idea that persons should be given sufficient information about a study in order to make their decision to participate as a research subject an informed and voluntary one.

Institutional Review Board (IRB)   University committee responsible for evaluating whether research proposals provide adequate protection of the rights of participants; must exist for any college or university receiving federal funds for research.

Instructional variable   Type of independent variable in which participants are given different sets of instructions about how to perform (e.g., given a list of stimuli, various groups might be told to process them in different ways).

Instrumentation   A threat to the internal validity of a study; occurs when the measuring instrument changes from pretest to posttest (e.g., because of their experience with the instrument, experimenters might use it differently from pretest to posttest).

Interaction   In a factorial design, occurs when the effect of one independent variable depends on the level of another independent variable.

Internal validity   The extent to which a study is free from methodological flaws, especially confounding factors.

Interobserver reliability   The degree of agreement between two or more observers of the same event.

Interrupted time series design   Quasi-experimental design in which a program or treatment is evaluated by measuring performance several times prior to the institution of the program and several times after the program has been put into effect.

Interrupted time series with switching replications   A time series design in which the program is replicated at a different location and at a different time.

Interval scale   Measurement scale in which numbers refer to quantities and intervals are assumed to be of equal size; a score of zero is just one of many points on the scale and does not denote the absence of the phenomenon being measured.

Interview survey   A survey method in which the researcher interviews the participant face-to-face; allows for more in-depth surveying (e.g., follow-up questions and clarifications).

Introspection   Method used in the early years of psychological science in which a subject would complete some task and then describe the events occurring in consciousness while performing the task.

IRB   see Institutional Review Board.

Key informant   In program evaluation research, a community member with special knowledge about the needs of a community.

Laboratory research   Research that occurs within the controlled confines of the scientific laboratory.

Latin square   Form of partial counterbalancing in which each condition of the study occurs equally often in each sequential position and each condition precedes and follows each other condition exactly one time.

Laws   Regular, predictable relationships between events.

Leakage   A tendency for people who have participated in a research study to inform future participants about the true purpose of the study.

Longitudinal study   In developmental psychology, a design in which age is the independent variable and the same group of people are tested repeatedly at different ages.

Main effect   Refers to whether or not statistically significant differences exist between the levels of an independent variable in a factorial design.

Manipulation check   In debriefing, a procedure to determine if subjects were aware of a deception experiment's true purpose; also refers to any procedure that determines if systematic manipulations have the intended effect on participants.

Matched groups design   A between-subjects design that uses a manipulated independent variable and has at least two groups of participants; subjects are matched on some variable assumed to affect the outcome before being randomly assigned to the groups.

Matching   A procedure for creating equivalent groups in which participants are measured on some factor (a "matching variable") expected to correlate with the dependent variable; groups are then formed by taking participants who score at the same level on the matching variable and randomly assigning them to groups.

Matching variable   Any variable selected for matching participants in a matched groups study.

Maturation   A threat to the internal validity of a study; occurs when participants change from the beginning to the end of the study simply as a result of maturational changes within them and not as a result of some independent variable.

Mean   The arithmetic average of a data set, found by adding the scores and dividing by the total number of scores in the set.

Measurement error   Produced by any factor that introduces inaccuracies into the measurement of some variable.

Measurement scales   Ways of assigning numbers to events; see nominal, ordinal, interval, and ratio scales.

Median   The middle score of a data set; an equal number of scores are both above and below the median.

Median location   The place in the sequence of scores where the median lies.

Method of adjustment   Psychophysics method in which the subject adjusts the stimulus intensity until the stimulus is just barely detected or differences between two stimuli are just noticeably different.

Method of constant stimuli   Psychophysics method in which stimulus intensities, either individually (absolute threshold) or in pairs (difference threshold), are presented in a random order.

Method of limits   Psychophysics method that alternates ascending and descending series of stimuli; on ascending trials, the stimulus begins below threshold and is intensified until detected; on descending trials, the stimulus begins well above threshold and is decreased until it is no longer detected.

Mixed factorial design   A factorial design with at least one between-subjects factor and one within-subjects factor.

Mode   The most frequently appearing score in a data set.

Multiple baseline design   A small N design in which treatment is introduced at staggered intervals when trying to alter (a) the behavior of more than one individual, (b) more than one behavior in the same individual, or (c) the behavior of an individual in more than one setting.

Multiple regression   A multivariate analysis that includes a criterion variable and two or more predictor variables; the predictors will have different weights.

Multivariate analysis   Any statistical analysis investigating the relationships among more than two variables.

Mundane realism   Refers to how closely the experiment mirrors real-life experiences; considered to be less important than experimental realism.

Naturalistic observation   Descriptive research method in which the behavior of people or animals is studied as it occurs in its everyday natural environment.

Needs analysis   Form of program evaluation that occurs before a program begins and determines whether the program is needed.

Negative correlation   A relationship between variables X and Y such that a high score for X is associated with a low score for Y and a low score for X is associated with a high score for Y.

Nominal scale   Measurement scale in which the numbers have no quantitative value, but rather serve to identify categories into which events can be placed.

Nonequivalent control group design   Quasi-experimental design in which participants cannot be randomly assigned to the experimental and control groups.

Nonequivalent groups design   A between-subjects design with at least two groups of participants that uses a subject variable or that creates groups that are nonequivalent.

Nonlinear effect   Any outcome that does not form a straight line when graphed; can occur only when the independent variable has more than two levels.

Nonresponse bias   Occurs in survey research when those who return surveys differ in some systematic fashion (e.g., political attitudes) from those who don't respond to the surveys.

Normal curve   A theoretical frequency distribution for a population; a bell-shaped curve.

Null hypothesis   The assumption that no real difference exists between treatment conditions in an experiment or that no significant relationship exists in a correlational study (H_0).

Objectivity   Said to exist when observations can be verified by more than one observer.

Observer bias   Can occur when preconceived ideas held by the researcher affect the nature of the observations made.

Open-ended question A type of question found on surveys that requires more than a "yes" or "no" answer.

Operant conditioning Form of learning in which behavior is modified by its consequences; a positive consequence strengthens the behavior immediately preceding it, and a negative consequence weakens the behavior immediately preceding it.

Operational definitions A definition of a concept or variable in terms of precisely described operations, measures, or procedures.

Operationism Philosophy of science approach proposed by Bridgman that held that all scientific concepts should be defined in terms of a set of operations to be performed.

Order effect See Sequence effect.

Ordinal scale Measurement scale in which assigned numbers stand for relative standing or ranking.

Parsimonious A theory that includes the minimum number of constructs and assumptions in order to explain and predict some phenomenon adequately.

Partial correlation A multivariate statistical procedure for evaluating the effects of third variables; if the correlation between X and Y remains high, even after some third factor Z has been "partialed out," then Z can be eliminated as a third variable.

Partial counterbalancing Occurs when a subset of all possible orders of conditions is used in a within-subjects design (e.g., a random sample of the population of all possible orders could be selected).

Partial replication Repeats a portion of some prior research; usually completed as part of a study that extends the results of the initial research.

Participant See Research participant.

Participant bias Can occur when the behavior of participants is influenced by their beliefs about how they are supposed to behave in a study.

Participant observation Descriptive research method in which the behavior of people is studied as it occurs in its everyday natural environment and the researcher becomes a part of the group being observed.

Participant pool Group of students asked to participate in research as part of an introductory course requirement; historically referred to as a "subject pool."

Pearson's *r* Measure of the size of a correlation between two variables; ranges from a perfect negative correlation of -1.00 to a perfect positive correlation of $+1.00$; if $r = 0$ then no relationship exists between the variables.

Phone survey A survey method in which the researcher asks questions over the phone.

Pilot study During the initial stages of research it is common for some data to be collected; problems spotted in this trial stage enable the researcher to refine the procedures and prevent the full-scale study from being flawed methodologically.

Placebo control group Control group in which some participants believe they are receiving the experimental treatment, but they are not.

Plagiarism Deliberately taking the ideas of someone and claiming them as one's own.

Population All the members of an identifiable group.

Positive correlation A relationship between variables X and Y such that a high score for X is associated with a high score for Y and a low score for X is associated with a low score for Y.

Posttest A measurement given to participants at the conclusion of a study after they have experienced a treatment or been in a control group; comparisons are made with pretest scores to determine if change occurred.

Power The probability of rejecting H_0 when it is false; affected by alpha, effect size, and sample size.

Predictions A goal of psychological science in which statements about the future occurrence of some behavioral event are made, usually with some probability.

Predictor variable In a regression analysis, the variable used to predict the criterion variable (e.g., SAT scores are used to predict college grades).

Pretest A measurement given to participants at the outset of a study, prior to their being given a treatment (or not treated when subjects are in a control group).

Productivity With reference to theory, this refers to the amount of research that is generated to test a theory. Theories that lead to a great deal of research are considered productive.

Program audit An examination of whether a program is being implemented as planned; a type of formative evaluation.

Program evaluation A form of applied research that includes a number of research activities designed to evaluate programs from planning to completion.

Programs of research Series of interrelated studies in which the outcome of one study leads naturally to another.

Progressive effect In a within-subjects design, any sequence effect in which the accumulated effects are assumed to be the same from trial to trial (e.g., fatigue).

Pseudoscience A field of inquiry that attempts to associate with true science, relies exclusively on selective anecdotal evidence, and is deliberately too vague to be adequately tested.

Psychophysics One of experimental psychology's original areas of research; investigates the relationship between physical stimuli and the perception of those stimuli; studies thresholds.

P × E factorial design A factorial design with at least one subject factor (P = person variable) and one manipulated factor (E = environmental variable).

Qualitative research A category of research activity characterized by a narrative analysis of information collected in the study; can include case studies, observational research, and interview research.

Quantitative research A category of research in which results are presented as numbers, typically in the form of descriptive and inferential statistics.

Quasi-experiment Occurs whenever causal conclusions about the effect of an independent variable cannot be drawn because there is incomplete control over the variables in the study.

Random assignment The most common procedure for creating equivalent groups in a between-subjects design; each individual volunteering for the study has an equal probability of being assigned to any one of the groups in the study.

Range In a set of scores, the difference between the score with the largest value and the one with the smallest value.

Rate of response The favored dependent variable of researchers working in the Skinnerian tradition; refers to how frequently a behavior occurs per unit of time.

Ratio scale Measurement scale in which numbers refers to quantities and intervals are assumed to be of equal size; a score of zero denotes the absence of the phenomenon being measured.

Reactivity Occurs when participants' behavior is influenced by the knowledge that they are being observed.

Regression analysis In correlational research, knowing the size of a correlation and a value for variable X, it is possible to predict a value for variable Y; this process occurs through a regression analysis.

Regression line Summarizes the points of a scatterplot and provides the means for making predictions.

Regression to the mean If a score on a test is extremely high or low, a second score taken will be closer to the mean score; can be a threat to the internal validity of a study if a pretest score is extreme and the posttest score changes in the direction of the mean.

Reliability The extent to which measures of the same phenomenon are consistent and repeatable; measures high in reliability will contain a minimum of measurement error.

Repeated-measures design Another name for a within-subjects design; participants are tested in each of the experiment's conditions.

Replication To repeat an experiment; exact replications are rare, occurring primarily when the results of some prior study are suspected to be erroneous.

Representative sample   A sample with characteristics that match those same attributes as they exist in the population.

Research participant   Any person who takes part in and contributes data to a research study in psychology.

Research team   A group of researchers (professors and students) working together on the same research problem.

Restricting the range   Occurs in a correlational study when only a limited range of scores for one or both of the variables is used; range restrictions tend to lower correlations.

Reverse counterbalancing   Occurs in a within-subjects design when participants are tested more than once per condition; subjects experience one sequence, then a second with the order reversed from the first (e.g., A–B–C–C–B–A).

Sample   Some portion or subset of a population.

Sample frame   List of individuals from whom the sample will be drawn; with cluster sampling, a list of groups from which a sample of groups will be selected.

Scatterplot   A graph depicting the relationship shown by a correlation.

Science   A way of knowing characterized by the attempt to apply objective, empirical methods when searching for the causes of natural events.

Self-selection problem   In surveys, when the sample is composed of only those who voluntarily choose to respond, the result can be a biased sample.

Sequence effect   Can occur in a within-subjects design when the experience of participating in one of the conditions of the study influences performance in subsequent conditions (see Progressive effect and Carryover effect).

Serendipity   The process of making an accidental discovery; finding X when searching for Y.

Shaping   Operant procedure for developing a new behavior that underlies the changing criterion design; behaviors are reinforced as they become progressively close to final desired behavior.

Simple random sample   A probability sample in which each member of the population has an equal chance of being selected as a member of the sample.

Single-factor design   Any experimental design with a single independent variable.

Single-factor multilevel designs   Any design with a single independent variable and more than two levels of the independent variable.

Situational variable   Type of independent variable in which subjects encounter different environmental circumstances (e.g., large vs. small rooms in a crowding study).

Social desirability bias   A type of response bias in survey research; occurs when people respond to a question by trying to put themselves in a favorable light.

Social validity   The extent to which an applied behavior analysis program has the potential to improve society, whether its value is perceived by the study's participants, and whether participants actually use the program.

Split-half reliability   A form of reliability in which one-half of the items (e.g., the even-numbered items) on a test are correlated with the remaining items.

Stakeholders   In program evaluation research, persons connected with a program who have a vested interest in it; includes clients, staff, and program directors.

Standard deviation   A measure of the average deviation of a set of scores from the mean score; the square root of the variance.

Statistical conclusion validity   Said to exist when the researcher uses statistical analysis properly and draws the appropriate conclusions from the analysis.

Statistical determinism   An assumption made by research psychologists that behavioral events can be predicted with a probability greater than chance.

Stem and leaf display   A method of displaying a data set that combines the features of a frequency distribution table and a histogram into one display.

Stratified sample   A probability sample that is random, with the restriction that important subgroups are proportionately represented in the sample.

Subject Name traditionally used to refer to a human or animal research participant; humans volunteering for research are now referred to as research participants, while nonhuman animals are still typically referred to as subjects.

Subject selection effect A threat to the internal validity of a study; occurs when those participating in a study cannot be assigned randomly to groups; hence the groups are nonequivalent.

Subject variable A type of independent variable that is selected rather than manipulated by the experimenter; refers to an already existing attribute of the individuals chosen for the study (e.g., gender)

Summative evaluation Form of program evaluation completed at the close of a program that attempts to determine its effectiveness in solving the problem for which it was planned.

Survey A descriptive method in which participants are asked a series of questions or respond to a series of statements about some topic.

Systematic variance Variability that can be attributed to some identifiable source, either the systematic variation of the independent variable or the uncontrolled variation of a confound.

t **test for dependent groups** An inferential statistical analysis used when comparing two groups in either a matched groups design or a repeated-measures design.

t **test for independent groups** An inferential statistical analysis used when comparing two groups in either an independent groups design or a nonequivalent groups design.

Tables In a research report, these are summaries of data or descriptions of research design that are laid out in a row and column arrangement.

Task variable Type of independent variable in which participants are given different types of tasks to perform (e.g., mazes that differ in level of difficulty).

Tenacity A way of knowing proposed by Peirce in which a person maintains a biased view and refuses to alter it in the face of contradictory data.

Test–retest reliability A form of reliability in which a test is administered on two separate occasions and the correlation between them is calculated.

Testing A threat to the internal validity of a study; occurs when the fact of taking a pretest influences posttest scores, perhaps by sensitizing participants to the purpose of a study.

Theory A set of statements that summarizes and organizes existing information about some phenomenon, provides an explanation for the phenomenon, and serves as a basis for making predictions to be tested empirically.

Third variable problem Refers to the problem of drawing causal conclusions in correlational research; third variables are any uncontrolled factors that could underline a correlation between variables X and Y.

Time sampling A procedure in observational research in which behavior is sampled only during predefined times (e.g., every 10 minutes).

Time series design See Interrupted time series design

Trends Predictable patterns of events that occur over a period of time; evaluated in time series studies.

Type I error Rejecting the null hypothesis when it is true; finding a statistically significant effect when no true effect exists.

Type II error Failing to reject the null hypothesis when it is false; failing to find a statistically significant effect when the effect truly exists.

Unobtrusive measures Any measure of behavior that can be recorded without participants knowing that their behavior has been observed.

Validity In general, the extent to which a measure of X truly measures X and not Y (e.g., a valid measure of intelligence measures intelligence and not something else).

Variance A measure of the average squared deviation of a set of scores from the mean score; the standard deviation squared.

Waiting list control group Control group in which participants aren't yet receiving treatment but will eventually; used to ensure that those in the experimental and control groups are similar (e.g., all seeking treatment for the same problem).

Withdrawal design Any small N design in which a treatment is in place for a time and is then removed to determine if the rate of behavior returns to baseline.

Within-subjects design Any experimental design in which the same participants serve in each of the different conditions of the study; also called a "repeated-measures design."

Written survey A survey method in which the researcher creates a written questionnaire that is filled out by participants.

Yoked control group Control group in which the treatment given a member of the control group is matched exactly with the treatment given a member of the experimental group.

References

ABRAMOVITZ, C. V., ABRAMOVITZ, S. I., ROBACK, H. B., & JACKSON, M. C. (1974). Differential effectiveness of directive and nondirective group therapies as a function of client internal-external control. *Journal of Consulting and Clinical Psychology, 14,* 849–853.

ABRAMSON, L. Y., SELIGMAN, M. E. P., & TEASDALE, J. D. (1978). Learned helplessness in humans: A critique and reformulation. *Journal of Abnormal Psychology, 87,* 49–74.

ADAIR, J. G. (1973). *The human subject: The social psychology of the psychological experiment.* Boston: Little, Brown.

ADAMS, J. S. (1965). Inequity in social exchange. In L. Berkowitz (Ed.), *Advances in experimental social psychology* (pp. 267–299). New York: Academic Press.

ADLER, T. (1992, September). Debate: Control groups—bad for cancer patients? *APA Monitor, 23,* 34.

ADLER, T. (1992, November). Trashing a laboratory is now a federal offense. *APA Monitor, 23,* 14.

American Heritage Dictionary. (1971). New York: American Heritage.

American Psychological Association. (1953). *Ethical standards of psychologists.* Washington, DC: Author.

American Psychological Association. (1973). *Ethical principles in the conduct of research with human participants.* Washington, DC: Author.

American Psychological Association. (1982). *Ethical principles in the conduct of research with human participants.* Washington, DC: Author.

American Psychological Association. (1985). *Guidelines for ethical conduct in the care and use of animals.* Washington, DC: Author.

American Psychological Association. (1992). Ethical principles of psychologists and code of conduct. *American Psychologist, 47,* 1597–1611.

American Psychological Association. (1994). *Publication manual of the American Psychological Association* (4th ed.). Washington, DC: Author.

ANDERSON, C. A., LEPPER, M. R., & ROSS, L. (1980). Perseverance of social beliefs: The role of explanation in the persistence of discredited information. *Journal of Personality and Social Psychology, 39,* 1037–1049.

ANDERSON, C. A., LINDSAY, J. J., & BUSHMAN, B. J. (1999). Research in the psychological laboratory: Truth or triviality? *Current Directions in Psychological Science, 8,* 3–9.

ANDERSON, J. E. (1926). Proceedings of the thirty-fourth annual meeting of the American Psychological Association. *Psychological Bulletin, 23,* 113–174.

ANDERSON, K. J. (1990). Arousal and the inverted-U hypothesis: A critique of Neiss's "reconceptualizing arousal." *Psychological Bulletin, 107,* 96–100.

Animal rights activity increases: Threats made against behavioral scientists. (1997, January/February). *Science Agenda, 10(1),* 1, 4.

Anonymous Advertisement. (1881, October). *Phrenological Journal, 73,* old series, 3–4.

ARONSON, E. (1999a). *The social animal* (8th ed.). New York: W. H. Freeman.

ARONSON, E. (1999b). Dissonance, hypocrisy, and the self-concept. In E. Harmon-Jones & J. Mills (Eds.), *Cognitive dissonance: Progress on a pivotal theory in social psychology* (pp. 103–126). Washington, DC: American Psychological Association.

ARONSON, E., FRIED, C., & STONE, J. (1991). Overcoming denial and increasing the intention to use condoms through the induction of hypocrisy. *American Journal of Public Health, 81,* 1636–1638.

ASCH, S. (1956). Studies of independence and conformity: A minority of one against a unanimous majority. *Psychological Monographs, 70,* (Whole No. 416).

ATKINSON, J. W., & FEATHER, N. T. (1966). *A theory of achievement motivation.* New York: Wiley.

Award for distinguished scientific contributions: Eliot Aronson (1999). *American Psychologist, 54,* 873–884.

BABKIN, B. P. (1949). *Pavlov: A biography.* Chicago: University of Chicago Press.

BAHRICK, H. P. (1984). Semantic memory content in permastore: 50 years of memory for Spanish learned in school. *Journal of Experimental Psychology: General, 113,* 1–29.

BAKAN, D. (1966). The influence of phrenology on American psychology. *Journal of the History of the Behavioral Sciences, 2,* 200–220.

BAKEMAN, R., & BROWNLEE, J. R. (1980). The strategic use of parallel play: A sequential analysis. *Child Development, 51,* 873–878.

BANDURA, A., ROSS, D., & ROSS, S. A. (1963). Imitation of film-mediated aggressive models. *Journal of Abnormal and Social Psychology, 66,* 3–11.

BARBER, T. X. (1976). *Pitfalls in human research.* New York: Pergamon Press.

BARLOW, D. H., & HERSEN, M. (1984). *Single case experimental designs: Strategies for studying behavior change* (2nd ed.). New York: Pergamon Press.

BARNETT, M. A., & McCOY, S. J. (1989). The relation of distressful childhood experiences and empathy in college undergraduates. *Journal of Genetic Psychology, 150,* 417–426.

BARON, A. (1990). Experimental designs. *The Behavior Analyst, 13,* 167–171.

BAUMRIND, D. (1964). Some thoughts on ethics of research: After reading Milgram's "Behavioral study of obedience." *American Psychologist, 19,* 421–423.

BAUMRIND, D. (1985). Research using intentional deception: Ethical issues revisited. *American Psychologist, 40,* 165–174.

BAVELAS, J. B. (1978). *Personality: Current theory and research.* Monterey, CA: Brooks/Cole.

BEAUCHAMP, T. L., & CHILDRESS, J. F. (1979). *Principles of biomedical ethics.* New York: Oxford University Press.

BEHR, W. A. (1992). Ph.D. envy: A psychoanalytic case study. *Clinical Social Work Journal, 20,* 99–113.

BEISECKER, T. (1988). Misusing survey research data: How not to justify demoting Christine Craft. *Forensic Reports, 1,* 15–33.

BENEDICT, J., & STOLOFF, M. (1991). Animal laboratory facilities at ``America's Best'' undergraduate colleges. *American Psychologist, 46,* 535–536.

BENJAMIN, L. T. JR., CAVELL, T. A., & SHALLENBERGER, W. R. (1984). Staying with initial answers on objective tests: Is it a myth?. *Teaching of Psychology, 11,* 133–141.

BERRY, T. D., & GELLER, E. S. (1991). A single-subject approach to evaluating vehicle safety belt reminders: Back to basics. *Journal of Applied Behavior Analysis, 24,* 13–22.

BERTERA, R. L. (1990). Planning and implementing health promotion in the workplace: A case study of the Du Pont Company experience. *Health Education Quarterly, 17,* 307–327.

BEYERSTEIN, B. (1993, JULY). Subliminal self-help tapes: Promises, promises... *Rational Enquirer, 6(1).*

BLAGROVE, M. (1996). Effects of length of sleep deprivation on interrogative suggestibility. *Journal of Experimental Psychology: Applied, 2,* 48–59.

BLAKEMORE, C., & COOPER, G. F. (1970). Development of the brain depends on the visual environment. *Nature, 228,* 477–478.

BLUMBERG, M., & PRINGLE, C. D. (1983). How control groups can cause loss of control in action research: The case of Rushton coal mine. *Journal of Applied Behavioral Science, 19,* 409–425.

BOESCH-ACHERMANN, H., & BOESCH, C. (1993). Tool use in wild chimpanzees: New light from dark forests. *Current Directions in Psychological Science, 2,* 18–21.

BOORSTIN, D. J. (1985). *The discoverers.* New York: Vintage Books.

BORING, E. G. (1950). *A history of experimental psychology* (2nd ed.). Englewood Cliffs, NJ: Prentice-Hall.

BOUCHARD, T. J., LYKKEN, D. T., McGUE, M., SEGAL, N. L., & TELLEGEN, A. (1990). Sources of human psychological differences: The Minnesota study of twins reared apart. *Science, 250,* 223–228.

BOUCHARD, T. J., & McGUE, M. (1981). Familial studies of intelligence: A review. *Science, 212,* 1055–1059.

BRADY, J.V. (1958, April). Ulcers in "executive" monkeys. *Scientific American, 199,* 95–100.

BRADY, J. V., PORTER, R. W., CONRAD, D. G., & MASON, J. W. (1958). Avoidance behavior and the development of gastroduodenal ulcers. *Journal of the Experimental Analysis of Behavior, 1,* 69–72.

BRAMEL, D., & FRIEND, R. (1981). Hawthorne, the myth of the docile worker, and class bias in psychology. *American Psychologist, 36,* 867–878.

BRANSFORD, J. D., & JOHNSON, M. K. (1972). Contextual prerequisites for understanding: Some investigations of comprehension and recall. *Journal of Verbal Learning and Verbal Behavior, 11,* 717–726.

BRANTJES, M., & BOUMA, A. (1991). Qualitative analysis of the drawings of Alzheimer's patients. *The Clinical Neuropsychologist, 5,* 41–52.

BRENNAN, J. F. (1991). *History and systems of psychology.* Englewood Cliffs, NJ: Prentice-Hall.

BRETZ, R. D., JR., & THOMAS, S. L. (1992). Perceived equity, motivation, and final-offer arbitration in major league baseball. *Journal of Applied Psychology, 77,* 280–287.

BRIDGMAN, P. W. (1927). *The logic of modern physics.* New York: Macmillan.

BROADBENT, D. E. (1958). *Perception and communication.* New York: Pergamon Press.

BROWN, M. F. (1992). Does a cognitive map guide choices in the radial-arm maze? *Journal of Experimental Psychology: Animal Behavior Processes, 18,* 56–66.

BRYAN, J. H., & TEST, M. A. (1967). Models and helping: Naturalistic studies in aiding behavior. *Journal of Personality and Social Psychology, 6,* 400–407.

BURKS, B. S., JENSEN, D. W., & TERMAN, L. (1930). *Genetic studies of genius, Vol. 3. The promise of youth: Follow-up studies of a thousand gifted children.* Stanford, CA: Stanford University Press.

BURNHAM, J. C. (1972). Thorndike's puzzle boxes. *Journal of the History of the Behavioral Sciences, 8,* 159–167.

BURTON, A. M., WILSON, S., COWAN, M., & BRUCE, V. (1999). Face recognition in poor-quality video: Evidence from security surveillance. *Psychological Science, 10,* 243–248.

BYRNE, G. (1988, October 7). Breuning pleads guilty. *Science, 242,* 27–28.

CAMPBELL, D. T. (1969). Reforms as experiments. *American Psychologist, 24,* 409–429.

CAMPBELL, D. T., & ERLEBACHER, A. (1970). How regression artifacts in quasi-experimental evaluations can mistakenly make compensatory education look harmful. In J. Hellmuth (Ed.), *Compensatory education: A national debate* (pp. 185–210). New York: Brunner-Mazel.

CAMPBELL, D. T., & ROSS, H. L. (1968). The Connecticut crackdown on speeding: Time series data in quasi-experimental analysis. *Law and Society Review, 3,* 33–53.

CAMPBELL, D. T., & STANLEY, J. C. (1963). *Experimental and quasi-experimental designs for research.* Chicago: Rand-McNally.

CARNAP, R. (1966). *An introduction to the philosophy of science.* New York: Basic Books.

CARELLO, C., ANDERSON, K. L., & KUNKLER-PECK, A. J. (1998). Perception of object length by sound. *Psychological Science, 9,* 211–214.

CARR, H. A., & WATSON, J. B. (1908). Orientation in the white rat. *Journal of Comparative Neurology and Psychology, 18,* 27–44.

CATTELL, J. M. (1890). Mental tests and measurements. *Mind, 15,* 373–380.

CATTELL, J. M. (1895). Proceedings of the third annual meeting of the American Psychological Association. *Psychological Review, 2,* 149–172.

CHRISTENSEN, L. (1988). Deception in psychological research: When is its use justified? *Personality and Social Psychology Bulletin, 14,* 664–675.

CHRISTENSON, C. V. (1971). *Kinsey: A biography.* Bloomington: Indiana University Press.

CICIRELLI, V. G. (1984). The misinterpretation of the Westinghouse study: A reply to Zigler and Berman. *American Psychologist, 39,* 915–916.

CICIRELLI, V. G. (1993). Head Start evaluation. *APS Observer, 6(1),* 32.

CICIRELLI, V. G., COOPER, W. H., & GRANGER, R. L. (1969). The impact of Head Start: An evaluation of the effects of Head Start on children's cognitive and affective development. *Westinghouse Learning Corporation, OEO Contract B89–4536.*

COHEN, J. (1988). *Statistical power analysis for the behavioral sciences* (2nd ed.). Hillsdale, NJ: Lawrence Erlbaum Associates.

COHEN, S., TYRELL, D. A., & SMITH, A. P. (1993). Negative life events, perceived stress, negative affect, and susceptibility to the common cold. *Journal of Personality and Social Psychology, 64,* 131–140.

COILE, D. C., & MILLER, N. E. (1984). How radical animal activists try to mislead humane people. *American Psychologist, 39,* 700–701.

CONVERSE, J. M., & PRESSER, S. (1986). *Survey questions: Hand crafting the standardized questionnaire.* Newbury Park, CA: Sage.

COOK, T. D., & CAMPBELL, D. T. (1979). *Quasi-experimental design and analysis issues for field settings.* Chicago: Rand-McNally.

COULTER, X. (1986). Academic value of research participation by undergraduates. *American Psychologist, 41,* 317.

CRAWFORD, H. J., KITNER-TRIOLO, M., CLARKE, S. W., & OLESKO, B. (1992). Transient positive and negative experiences accompanying stage hypnosis. *Journal of Abnormal Psychology, 101,* 663–667.

CRONBACH, L. J. (1957). The two disciplines of scientific psychology. *American Psychologist, 12,* 671–684.

CRONBACH, L. J., HASTORF, A. H., HILGARD, E. R., & MACCOBY, E. E. (1990). Robert R. Sears (1908–1989). *American Psychologist, 45,* 663–664.

DALLENBACH, K. M. (1913). The measurement of attention. *American Journal of Psychology, 24,* 465–507.

DANZIGER, K. (1985). The origins of the psychological experiment as a social institution. *American Psychologist, 40,* 133–140.

DARLEY, J. M., & LATANE, B. (1968). Bystander intervention in emergencies: Diffusion of responsibility. *Journal of Personality and Social Psychology, 8,* 377–383.

DEKAY, M. L., & MCCLELLAND, G. H. (1996). Probability and utility components of endangered species preservation programs. *Journal of Experimental Psychology: Applied, 2,* 60–83.

DELUCA, R.V., & HOLBORN, S.W. (1992). Effects of a variable-ratio schedule with changing criteria on exercise in obese and nonobese boys. *Journal of Applied Behavior Analysis, 25,* 671–679.

Department of Health and Human Services. (1983). Federal regulations for the protection of human research subjects. In L. A. Peplau, D. O. Sears, S. E. Taylor, & J. L. Freedman (Eds.), *Readings in social psychology* (2nd ed.). Englewood Cliffs, NJ: Prentice-Hall.

DERMER, M. L., & HOCH, T. A. (1999). Improving descriptions of single-subject experiments in research texts written for undergraduates. *Psychological Record, 49,* 49–66.

DEWSBURY, D. A. (1990). Early interactions between animal psychologists and animal activists and the founding of the APA committee on precautions in animal experimentation. *American Psychologist, 45,* 315–327.

DIENER, E., & CRANDALL, R. (1978). *Ethics in social and behavioral research.* Chicago: The University of Chicago Press.

DOMJAN, M., & PURDY, J. E. (1995). Animal research in psychology: More than meets the eye of the general psychology student. *American Psychologist, 50,* 496–503.

DONNERSTEIN, E. (1980). Aggressive erotica and violence against women. *Journal of Personality and Social Psychology, 39,* 269–277.

DRESSLER, F. B. (1893). On the pressure sense of the drum of the ear and "facial-vision." *American Journal of Psychology, 5,* 344–350.

DROR, I. E., KOSSLYN, S. M., & WAAG, W. L. (1993). Visual-spatial abilities of pilots. *Journal of Applied Psychology, 78,* 763–773.

DUTTON, D. G., & ARON, A. P. (1974). Some evidence for heightened sexual attraction under conditions of high anxiety. *Journal of Personality and Social Psychology, 30,* 510–517.

EBBINGHAUS, H. (1964). *Memory: A contribution to experimental psychology* (H. A. Ruger & C. A. Bussenius, Trans.). New York: Dover. (Original work published 1885).

EGELAND, B. (1975). Effects of errorless training on teaching children to discriminate letters of the alphabet. *Journal of Applied Psychology, 60,* 533–536.

EKMAN, P. (1985). *Telling lies: Clues to deceit in the marketplace, politics, and marriage.* New York: W. W. Norton.

ELKINS, I. J., CROMWELL, R. L., & ASARNOW, R. F. (1992). Span of apprehension in schizophrenic patients as a function of distractor masking and laterality. *Journal of Abnormal Psychology, 101,* 53–60.

ELMES, D. G., KANTOWITZ, B. H., & ROEDIGER, H. L., III. (1992). *Research methods in psychology* (4th ed.). St. Paul, MN: West.

EMDE, R. N., PLOMIN, R., ROBINSON, J., CORLEY, R., DEFRIES, J., FULKER, D. W., REZNICK, J. S., CAMPOS, J., KAGAN, J., & ZAHN-WAXLER, C. (1992). Temperament, emotion, and cognition at fourteen months: The MacArthur longitudinal twin study. *Child Development, 63,* 1437–1455.

ERFURT, J. C., FOOTE, A., & HEIRICH, M. A. (1992). The cost-effectiveness of worksite wellness programs for hypertension control, weight loss, smoking cessation, and exercise. *Personnel Psychology, 45,* 5–27.

ERON, L. D., HUESMAN, L. R., LEFKOWITZ, M. M., & WALDER, L. O. (1972). Does television violence cause aggression? *American Psychologist, 27,* 253–263.

EYSENCK, H. J. (1952). The effects of psychotherapy: An evaluation. *Journal of Consulting Psychology, 16,* 319–324.

FADEN, R. R., & BEAUCHAMP, T. L. (1986). *A history and theory of informed consent.* New York: Oxford University Press.

FANCHER, R. E. (1990). *Pioneers of psychology* (2nd ed.). New York: W. W. Norton.

FECHNER, G. (1966). *Elements of psychophysics* (H. E. Adler, Trans.). New York: Holt. (Original work published 1860).

FEINBERG, J. (1974). The rights of animals and unborn generations. In W. T. Blackstone (Ed.), *Philosophy and environmental crisis* (pp. 43–68). Athens: University of Georgia Press.

FERNALD, D. (1984). *The Hans legacy.* Hillsdale, NJ: Erlbaum.

FERSTER, C. B., & SKINNER, B. F. (1957). *Schedules of reinforcement.* Englewood Cliffs, NJ: Prentice-Hall.

FESTINGER, L. (1999). Reflections on cognitive dissonance: 30 years later. In E. Harmon-Jones & J. Mills (Eds.), *Cognitive dissonance: Progress on a pivotal theory in social psychology* (pp. 381–385). Washington, DC: American Psychological Association.

FESTINGER, L., RIECKEN, H. W., & SCHACHTER, S. (1956). *When prophecy fails.* Minneapolis: University of Minnesota Press.

FINK, A. (1995). *How to ask survey questions.* Thousand Oaks, CA: Sage.

FISCHMAN, M. W. (2000). Informed consent. In B. D. Sales & S. Folkman (Eds.), *Ethics in research with human participants* (pp. 35–48). Washington, DC: American Psychological Association.

FISHER, R. A. (1925). *Statistical methods for research workers.* London: Oliver & Boyd.

FISHER, R. A. (1951). *The design of experiments* (6th ed.). New York: Hafner. (Original work published 1935).

FISHER, R. A., & YATES, F. (1963). *Statistical tables for biological, agricultural, and medical research* (6th ed.). Edinburgh: Oliver & Boyd.

FISHER, C. B., & FRYBERG, D. (1994). Participant partners: College students weight the costs and benefits of deceptive research. *American Psychologist, 49,* 417–427.

FISHER, R. P., GEISELMAN, R. E., & AMADOR, M. (1989). Field test of the cognitive interview: Enhancing the recollection of actual victims and witnesses of crime. *Journal of Applied Psychology, 74,* 722–727.

FLOURENS, P. (1978). Phrenology examined (C. D. Meigs, Trans.). In D. N. Robinson (Ed.), *Significant contributions to the history of psychology.* Series E. Volume II. Washington, DC: University Publications of America. (Original work published 1846).

FOLKMAN, S. (2000). Privacy and confidentiality. In B. D. Sales & S. Folkman (Eds.), *Ethics in research with human participants* (pp. 49–57). Washington, DC: American Psychological Association.

FORREST, D. W. (1974). *Francis Galton: The life and work of a Victorian genius.* New York: Taplinger.

FOWLER, F. J., JR. (1993). *Survey research methods* (2nd ed.). Newbury Park, CA: Sage.

FOXX, R. M., & RUBINOFF, A. (1979). Behavioral treatment of caffeinism: Reducing excessive coffee drinking. *Journal of Applied Behavior Analysis, 12,* 335–344.

FRAYSSE, J. C., & DESPRELS-FRAYSSE A. (1990). The influence of experimenter attitude on the performance of children of different cognitive ability levels. *Journal of Genetic Psychology, 151,* 169–179.

FRIEDMAN, H, S., TUCKER, J. S., SCHWARTZ, J. E., TOMLINSON-KEASEY, C., MARTIN, L. R., WINGARD, D. L., & CRIQUI, M. H. (1995). Psychological and behavioral predictors of longevity: The aging and death of the "Termites." *American Psychologist, 50,* 69–78.

FRIEDMAN, M., & ROSENMAN, R. H. (1974). *Type A behavior and your heart.* New York: Knopf.

FRUCHTER, B. (1954). *Introduction to factor analysis.* Princeton, NJ: D. Van Nostrand.

FULERO, S. M., & KIRKLAND, J. (1992, August). *A survey of student opinions on animal research.* Poster presented at the annual meeting of the American Psychological Association, Washington, DC.

GALLUP, G. G., & BECKSTEAD, J. W. (1988). Attitudes toward animal research. *American Psychologist, 43,* 74–76.

GALLUP, G. G., & EDDY, T. J. (1990). Animal facilities survey. *American Psychologist, 45,* 400–401.

GALLUP, G. G., & SUAREZ, S. D. (1985a). Animal research versus the care and maintenance of pets: The names have been changed but the results remain the same. *American Psychologist, 40,* 968.

GALLUP, G. G., & SUAREZ, S. D. (1985b). Alternatives to the use of animals in psychological research. *American Psychologist, 40,* 1104–1111.

GALTON, F. (1872). Statistical inquiries into the efficacy of prayer. *Fortnightly Review, 12,* 125–135.

GALTON, F. (1883). *An inquiry into human faculty and its development.* London: MacMillan.

GARDNER, G. T. (1978). Effects of federal human subjects regulations on data obtained in environmental stressor research. *Journal of Personality and Social Psychology, 36,* 628–634.

GELLER, E. S. (1991). Editor's introduction: Where's the validity in social validity? *Journal of Applied Behavior Analysis, Monograph #ns5,* 1–6.

GIBSON, E. J. (1980). Eleanor J. Gibson. In G. Lindsey (Ed.), *A history of psychology in autobiography. Volume 7* (pp. 239–271). San Francisco: W. H. Freeman.

GIBSON, E. J., & WALK, R. D. (1960). The "visual cliff." *Scientific American, 202,* 64–71.

GILCHRIST, V. J., & WILLIAMS, R. L. (1999). Key informant interviews. In B. F. Crabtree & W. L. Miller (Eds.), *Doing qualitative research* (2nd ed., pp. 71–88). Thousand Oaks, CA: Sage.

GILLESPIE, R. (1988). The Hawthorne experiments and the politics of experimentation. In J. G. Morawski (Ed.), *The rise of experimentation in American psychology* (pp. 114–137). New Haven, CT: Yale University Press.

GILLIGAN, C. (1982). *In a different voice: Psychological theory and women's development.* Cambridge, MA: Harvard University Press.

GLEITMAN, H., FRIDLUND, A. J., & RIESBERG, D. (1999). *Psychology* (5th ed.). New York: W. W. Norton.

GODDEN, D. R., & BADDELEY, A. D. (1975). Context-dependent memory in two natural environments: On land and under water. *British Journal of Psychology, 66,* 325–331.

GOODALL, J. (1978). Chimp killings: Is it the man in them? *Science News, 113,* 276.

GOODWIN, C. J. (1985). On the origins of Titchener's Experimentalists. *Journal of the History of the Behavioral Sciences, 21,* 383–389.

GOODWIN, C. J. (1999). *A history of modern psychology.* New York: Wiley.

GREEN, B. F. (1992). Exposé or smear? The Burt affair. *Psychological Science, 3,* 328–331.

GREENBERG, M. S. (1967). Role playing: An alternative to deception. *Journal of Personality and Social Psychology, 7,* 152–157.

GREENWALD, A. G., SPANGENBERG, E. R., PRATKANIS, A. R., & ESKENAZI, J. (1991). Double-blind tests of subliminal self-help audiotapes. *Psychological Science, 2,* 119–122.

GRISSETT, N. I., & NORVELL, N. K. (1992). Perceived social support, social skills, and quality of relationships in bulimic women. *Journal of Consulting and Clinical Psychology, 60,* 293–299.

GROSE, P. (1994). *Gentleman spy: The life of Allen Dulles.* Boston: Houghton-Mifflin.

GUGERTY, L. J. (1997). Situation awareness during driving: Explicit and implicit knowledge in dynamic spatial memory. *Journal of Experimental Psychology: Applied, 3,* 42–66.

GUNTER, B., BERRY, C., & CLIFFORD, B. R. (1981). Proactive interference effects with television news items: Further evidence. *Journal of Experimental Psychology: Human Learning and Memory, 7,* 480–487.

GWALTNEY-GIBBS, P. A. (1986). The institutionalization of premarital cohabitation: Estimates from marriage license applications, 1970 and 1980. *Journal of Marriage and the Family, 48,* 423–434.

HALL, G. S. (1893). *The contents of children's minds on entering school.* New York: Kellogg.

HALL, J. A., & VECCIA, E. M. (1990). More "touching" observations: New insights on men, women, and interpersonal touch. *Journal of Personality and Social Psychology, 59,* 1155–1162.

HARRIS, B. (1979). Whatever happened to little Albert? *American Psychologist, 34,* 151–160.

HARTMAN, D. P., & HALL, R. V. (1976). The changing criterion design. *Journal of Applied Behavior Analysis, 9,* 527–532.

HENLE, M., & HUBBELL, M. B. (1938). "Egocentricity" in adult conversation. *Journal of Social Psychology, 9,* 227–234.

HILGARD, E. R. (Ed.). (1978). *American psychology in historical perspective.* Washington, DC: American Psychological Association.

HILGARD, E. R. (1987). *Psychology in America: A historical survey.* San Diego, CA: Harcourt Brace Jovanovich.

HILGARTNER, S. (1990). Research fraud, misconduct, and the IRB. *IRB: A Review of Human Subjects Research, 12,* 1–4.

HITE, S. (1987). *Women and love.* New York: Knopf.

HOBBS, N. (1948). The development of a code of ethics for psychology. *American Psychologist, 3,* 80–84.

HOLAHAN, C. K., SEARS, R. R., & CRONBACH, L. J. (1987). *The gifted group in midlife.* Stanford, CA: Stanford University Press.

HOLDEN, C. (1987, March 27). NIMH finds a case of "serious misconduct." *Science, 235,* 1566–1577.

HOLMES, D. S. (1976a). Debriefing after psychological experiments. I. Effectiveness of postdeception dehoaxing. *American Psychologist, 31,* 858–867.

HOLMES, D. S. (1976b). Debriefing after psychological experiments. II. Effectiveness of postexperimental desensitizing. *American Psychologist, 31,* 868–875.

HOLMES, D. S., MCGILLEY, B. M., & HOUSTON, B. K. (1984). Task-related arousal and Type A and Type B persons: Levels of challenge and response specificity. *Journal of Personality and Social Psychology, 46,* 1322–1327.

HORN, J. L. (1990, October). Psychology can help kids get a Head Start. *APA Monitor, 22,* 3.

HOTHERSALL, D. (1990). *History of psychology* (2nd ed.). New York: McGraw-Hill.

HOWELL, D. C. (1997). *Statistical methods for psychology* (4th ed.). Belmont, CA: Duxbury Press.

HUBEL, D. H. (1988). *Eye, brain, and vision.* New York: Scientific American Library.

HUBEL, D. H., & WIESEL, T. N. (1959). Receptive fields of single neurons in the cat's striate cortex. *Journal of Physiology, 148,* 574–591.

HUFF, D. (1954). *How to lie with statistics.* New York: W. W. Norton.

HULL, D. B. (1996). Animal use in undergraduate psychology programs. *Teaching of Psychology, 23,* 171–174.

HUME, K. M., & CROSSMAN, J. (1992). Musical reinforcement of practice behaviors among competitive swimmers. *Journal of Applied Behavior Analysis, 25,* 665–670.

HUNT, E., & LOVE, T. (1972). How good can memory be? In A. W. Melton & E. Martin (Eds.), *Coding processes in human memory* (pp. 237–260). Washington, DC: V. H. Winston.

JENKINS, J. G., & DALLENBACH, K. M. (1924). Minor studies from the psychological laboratory of Cornell University: Oblivescence during sleep and waking. *American Journal of Psychology, 35,* 605–612.

JONCICH, G. (1968). *The sane positivist: A biography of Edward L. Thorndike.* Middletown, CT: Wesleyan University Press.

JONES, J. H. (1981). *Bad blood: The Tuskegee syphilis experiment.* New York: Free Press.

JONES, M. C. (1924). A laboratory study of fear: The case of Peter. *Pedagogical Seminary, 31,* 308–315.

JORDAN, N. C., HUTTENLOCHER, J., & LEVINE, S. C. (1992). Differential calculation abilities in young children from middle- and low-income families. *Developmental Psychology, 28,* 644–653.

JUNGINGER, J., & HEAD, S. (1991). Time series analyses of obsessional behavior and mood during self-imposed delay and responsive prevention. *Behavior Research and Therapy, 29,* 521–530.

KAUFMAN, A. S., & KAUFMAN, N. L. (1983). *KABC: Kaufman Assessment Battery for Children. Interpretive manual.* Circle Pines, MN: American Guidance Service.

KAZDIN, A. E. (1978). *History of behavior modification: Experimental foundations of contemporary research.* Baltimore: University Park Press.

KELTNER, D., ELLSWORTH, P. C., & EDWARDS, K. (1993). Beyond simple pessimism: Effects of sadness and anger on social perception. *Journal of Personality and Social Psychology, 64,* 740–752.

KENDALL, M. G. (1970). Ronald Aylmer Fisher, 1890–1962. In E. S. Pearson & M. G. Kendall (Eds.), *Studies in the history of statistics and probability.* London: Charles Griffin.

KENT, D. (1994). Interview with APS president-elect Richard F. Thompson. *APS Observer, 7, 4, 10.*

KEY, W. B. (1973). *Subliminal seduction.* Englewood Cliffs, NJ: Signet.

KIDD, V. (1971). A study of the images produced through the use of the male pronoun as the generic. *Moments in Contemporary Rhetoric and Communication, 1,* 25–30.

KIM, K., & SPELKE, E. S. (1992). Infants' sensitivity to effects of gravity on visible object motion. *Journal of Experimental Psychology: Human Perception and Performance, 18,* 385–393.

KIMMEL, A. J. (1996). *Ethical issues in behavioral research: A survey.* Cambridge, MA: Blackwell.

KINSEY, A. C., POMEROY, W. B., & MARTIN, C. E. (1948). *Sexual behavior in the human male.* Philadelphia: W. B. Saunders.

KINSEY, A. C., POMEROY, W. B., MARTIN, C. E., & GEBHARD, P. H. (1953). *Sexual behavior in the human female.* Philadelphia: W. B. Saunders.

KIRK, R. E. (1968). *Experimental design: Procedures for the behavioral sciences.* Belmont, CA: Brooks/Cole.

KITAYAMA, S., MARKUS, H. R., MATSUMOTO, H., & NORASAKKUNKIT, V. (1997). Individual and collective processes in the construction of the self: Self-enhancement in the United States and self-criticism in Japan. *Journal of Personality and Social Psychology, 72,* 1245–1267.

KNEPPER, W., OBRZUT, J. E., & COPELAND, E. P. (1983). Emotional and social problem-solving thinking in gifted and average elementary school children. *Journal of Genetic Psychology, 142,* 25–30.

KOHLBERG, L. (1963). Development of children's orientation towards a moral order. *Vita Humana, 6,* 11–36.

KOHN, A. (1986). *False prophets: Fraud and error in science and medicine.* Oxford: Basil Blackwell.

KOLATA, G. B. (1986). What does it mean to be random? *Science, 231,* 1068–1070.

KORN, J. H. (1988). Students' roles, rights, and responsibilities as research participants. *Teaching of Psychology, 15,* 74–78.

KORN, J. H., DAVIS, R., & DAVIS, S. F. (1991). Historians' and chairpersons' judgments of eminence among psychologists. *American Psychologist, 46,* 789–792.

KOSSLYN, S. M., BALL, T. M., & REISER, B. J. (1978). Visual images preserve metric spatial information: Evidence from studies of image scanning. *Journal of Experimental Psychology: Human Perception and Performance, 4,* 47–60.

KRANTZ, D. L. (1969). The Baldwin-Titchener controversy: A case study in the functioning and malfunctioning of schools. In D. L. Krantz (Ed.), *Schools of psychology: A symposium* (pp. 1–19). New York: Appleton-Century-Crofts.

KRUPAT, E. (1975). Conversation with John Darley. In E. Krupat (Ed.), *Psychology is social: Readings and conversations in social psychology.* Glenview, IL: Scott, Foresman.

KRUTA, V. (1972). Marie-Jean-Pierre Flourens. In C. C. Gillespie (Ed.), *Dictionary of scientific biography* (Vol. V). New York: Scribner's.

KUHN, T. S. (1970). The function of dogma in scientific research. In B. A. Brody (Ed.), *Readings in the philosophy of science* (pp. 356–373). Englewood Cliffs, NJ: Prentice-Hall.

KUSHNER, M. (1970). Faradic aversive controls in clinical practice. In C. Neuringer & J. L. Michael (Eds.), *Behavior modification in clinical practice.* New York: Appleton-Century-Crofts.

LANDRUM, E. R., & CHASTAIN, G. (1999). Subject pool policies in undergraduate-only departments: Results from a nationwide survey. In G. Chastain & E. R. Landrum (Eds.), *Protecting human subjects: Department subject pools and Institutional Review Boards* (pp. 25–42). Washington, DC: American Psychological Association.

LANDY, F. J. (1992). Hugo Münsterberg: Victim or visionary? *Journal of Applied Psychology, 77,* 787–802.

LANGER, E. J., & RODIN, J. (1976). The effects of choice and enhanced personal responsibility for the aged: A field experiment in an institutional setting. *Journal of Personality and Social Psychology, 34,* 191–198.

LAU, R. R., & RUSSELL, D. (1980). Attributions in the sports pages. *Journal of Personality and Social Psychology, 39,* 29–38.

LAVRAKAS, P. J. (1998). Methods for sampling and interviewing in telephone surveys. In L. Bickman & D. J. Rog (Eds.), *Handbook of applied social research methods* (pp. 429–472). Thousand Oaks, CA: Sage.

LEAK, G. K. (1981). Student perception of coercion and value from participation in psychological research. *Teaching of Psychology, 8,* 147–149.

LEE, D. N., & ARONSON, E. (1974). Visual proprioceptive control of standing in human infants. *Perception and Psychophysics, 15,* 529–532.

LEFRANCOIS, J. R., & METZGER, B. (1993). Low-response-rate conditioning history and fixed-interval responding in rats. *Journal of the Experimental Analysis of Behavior, 59,* 543–549.

LIBERMAN, R. P., DAVIS, J., MOON, W., & MOORE, J. (1973). Research design for analyzing drug–environment–behavior interactions. *Journal of Nervous and Mental Disease, 156,* 432–439.

LICHT, M. M. (1995). Multiple regression and correlation. In L. G. Grimm & P. R. Yarnold (Eds.), *Reading and understanding multivariate statistics* (pp. 19–64). Washington, DC: American Psychological Association.

LOFTUS, E. F. (1979). *Eyewitness testimony.* Cambridge, MA: Harvard University Press.

LOFTUS, E. F. (1986). Ten years in the life of an expert witness. *Law and Human Behavior, 10,* 241–263.

LOFTUS, E. F., & HOFFMAN, H. G. (1989). Misinformation and memory: The creation of new memories. *Journal of Experimental Psychology: General, 118,* 100–104.

LOFTUS, E. F., & KETCHAM, K. (1991). *Witness for the defense: The accused, the eyewitness, and the expert who puts memory on trial.* New York: St. Martin's Press.

LOFTUS, E. F., & PALMER, J. C. (1974). Reconstruction of automobile destruction: An example of the interaction between language and memory. *Journal of Verbal Learning and Verbal Behavior, 13,* 585–589.

LORENZ, K. (1966). *On aggression.* New York: Harcourt Brace Jovanovich.

LOTUFO, P. A., CHAE, C. U., AJANI, U. A., HENNEKENS, C. H., & MANSON, J. E. (1999). Male pattern baldness and coronary heart disease: The physician's health study. *Archives of Internal Medicine, 160,* 165–171.

LUDWIG, T. D., & GELLER, E. S. (1997). Assigned versus participative goal setting and response generalization: Managing injury control among professional pizza deliverers. *Journal of Applied Psychology, 82,* 253–261.

LURIA, A. R. (1968). *The mind of a mnemonist.* New York: Basic Books.

MACLEOD, C. M. (1992). The Stroop task: The "gold standard" of attentional measures. *Journal of Experimental Psychology: General, 121,* 12–14.

MANGIONE, T. W. (1998). Mail surveys. In L. Bickman & D. J. Rog (Eds.), *Handbook of applied social research methods* (pp. 399–427). Thousand Oaks, CA: Sage.

MANIS, M. (1971). *An introduction to cognitive psychology.* Belmont, CA: Brooks/Cole.

MARCEL, A., J. (1983). Conscious and unconscious perception: Experiments on visual masking and word recognition. *Cognitive Psychology, 15,* 197–237.

MAREAN, G. C., WERNER, L. A., & KUHL, P. K. (1992). Vowel categorization by very young infants. *Developmental Psychology, 28,* 396–405.

MCCLELLAND, D. C. (1961). *The achieving society.* Princeton, NJ: Van Nostrand.

MCCLELLAND, D. C., ATKINSON, J. W., CLARKE, R. A., & LOWELL, E. L. (1953). *The achievement motive.* New York: Appleton-Century-Crofts.

MCREYNOLDS, P. (1987). Lightner Witmer: Little-known founder of clinical psychology. *American Psychologist, 42,* 849–858.

MERIKLE, P. M., & SKANES, H. E. (1992). Subliminal self-help audiotapes: A search for placebo effects. *Journal of Applied Psychology, 77,* 772–776.

MIDDLEMIST, R. D., KNOWLES, E. W., & MATTER, C. F. (1976). Personal space invasions in the lavatory: Suggestive evidence for arousal. *Journal of Personality and Social Psychology, 33,* 541–546.

MILES, W. R. (1928). Studies in physical exertion I: A multiple chronograph for measuring groups of men. *American Physical Education Review, 33,* 379–387.

MILES, W. R. (1930). On the history of research with rats and mazes: A collection of notes. *Journal of General Psychology, 3,* 324–337.

MILES, W. R. (1931). Studies in physical exertion II: Individual and group reaction time in football charging. *Research Quarterly, 2(3),* 5–13.

MILES, W. R. (1933). Age and human ability. *Psychological Review, 40,* 99–123.

MILGRAM, S. (1963). Behavioral study of obedience. *Journal of Abnormal and Social Psychology, 67,* 371–378.

MILGRAM, S. (1974). *Obedience to authority: An experimental view.* New York: Harper & Row.

MILLER, A. G. (1972). Role playing: An alternative to deception? *American Psychologist, 27,* 623–636.

MILLER, N. (1985). The value of behavioral research on animals. *American Psychologist, 40,* 423–440.

MILLER, W. R., & DiPILATO, M. (1983). Treatment of nightmares via relaxation and desensitization: A controlled evaluation. *Journal of Consulting and Clinical Psychology, 51,* 870–877.

MINTON, H. L. (1987). Lewis M. Terman and mental testing: In search of the democratic ideal. In M. M. Sokal (Ed.), *Psychological testing and American society. 1890–1930* (pp. 95–112). New Brunswick, NJ: Rutgers University Press.

MINTON, H. L. (1988). Charting life history: Lewis M. Terman's study of the gifted. In J. G. Morawski (Ed.), *The rise of experimentation in American psychology* (pp. 138–162). New Haven, CT: Yale University Press.

MISCHEL, W. (1981). *Introduction to personality* (3rd ed.). New York: Holt, Rinehart, & Winston.

MORGAN, C. L. (1903). *Introduction to comparative psychology.* London: Walter Scott.

MORGAN, F. W. (1990). Judicial standards for survey research: An update and guidelines. *Journal of Marketing, 54,* 59–70.

MOSES, S. (1991, July). Animal research issues affect students. *APA Monitor, 22,* 47–48.

MOWRER, O. H., & MOWRER, W. M. (1938). Enuresis—a method for its study and treatment. *American Journal of Orthopsychiatry, 8,* 436–459.

MURRAY, H. A. (1943). *Thematic apperception test.* Cambridge, MA: Harvard University Press.

MYERS, D. G. (1990). *Social psychology* (3rd ed). New York: McGraw-Hill.

MYERS, D. G. (1992). *Psychology* (3rd ed.). New York: Worth.

NEALE, J. M., & LIEBERT, R. M. (1973). *Science and behavior: An introduction to methods of research.* Englewood Cliffs, NJ: Prentice-Hall.

NEISSER, U. (1963). Decision-time without reaction-time. *American Journal of Psychology, 76,* 376–385.

NEISSER, U. (1976). *Cognition and reality.* San Francisco: W. H. Freeman.

NEISSER, U. (1981). John Dean's memory: A case study. *Cognition, 9,* 1–22.

NORCROSS, J. C., HANYCH, J. M., & TERRANOVA, R. D. (1996). Graduate study in psychology: 1992–1993. *American Psychologist, 51,* 631–643.

O'Donnell, J. M. (1985). *The origins of behaviorism: American psychology, 1870–1920.* New York: New York University Press.

Orne, M. T. (1962). On the social psychology of the psychology experiment: With particular reference to demand characteristics and their implications. *American Psychologist, 17,* 776–783.

Orne, M. T., & Scheibe, K. E. (1964). The contribution of nondeprivation factors in the production of sensory deprivation effects. *Journal of Abnormal and Social Psychology, 68,* 3–12.

Orwin, R. G. (1997). Twenty-one years old and counting: The interrupted time series comes of age. In E. Chelimsky & W. R. Shadish (Eds.), *Evaluation for the 21st century* (pp. 443–465). Thousand Oaks, CA: Sage.

Osler, S. F., & Trautman, G. E. (1961). Concept attainment II: Effect of stimulus complexity upon concept attainment at two levels of intelligence. *Journal of Experimental Psychology, 62,* 9–13.

Overmier, J. B., & Leaf, R. C. (1965). Effects of discriminative Pavlovian fear conditioning upon previously or subsequently acquired avoidance responding. *Journal of Comparative and Physiological Psychology, 60,* 213–218.

Parson, H. M. (1974). What happened at Hawthorne? *Science, 183,* 922–932.

Patten, M. L. (1998). *Questionnaire research: A practical guide.* Los Angeles: Pryczak.

Patterson, F. G., & Linden, E. (1981). *The education of Koko.* New York: Holt, Rinehart, & Winston.

Pearson, E. S., & Hartley, H. O. (1966). *Biometrika tables for statisticians* (Vol. 1, 3rd ed.). London: Cambridge University Press.

Peck, F. S. (1978). *The road less traveled.* New York: Simon & Schuster.

Peterson, C., Maier, S. F., & Seligman, M. E. P. (1993). *Learned helplessness: A theory for the age of personal control.* New York: Oxford University Press.

Peterson, L., Ridley-Johnson, R., & Carter, C. (1984). The supersuit: An example of structured naturalistic observation of children's altruism. *Journal of General Psychology, 110,* 235–241.

Plous, S. (1996a). Attitudes toward the use of animals in psychological research and education: Results from a national survey of psychologists. *American Psychologist, 51,* 1167–1180.

Plous, S. (1996b). Attitudes toward the use of animals in psychological research and education: Results from a national survey of psychology majors. *Psychological Science, 7,* 352–358.

Popper, K. R. (1959). *The logic of scientific discovery.* New York: Basic Books.

Porsolt, R. D., LePichon, M., & Jalfre, M. (1977). Depression: A new animal model sensitive to antidepressant treatments. *Nature, 266,* 730–732.

Posavac, E. J., & Carey, R. G. (1997). *Program evaluation: Methods and case studies* (5th ed.). Englewood Cliffs, NJ: Prentice-Hall.

Poulton, E. C. (1982). Influential companions: Effects of one strategy on another in the within-subjects designs of cognitive psychology. *Psychological Bulletin, 91,* 673–690.

Pratkanis, A. R., Eskenazi, J., & Greenwald, A. G. (1994). What you expect is what you believe (but not necessarily what you get): A test of the effectiveness of subliminal self-help audiotapes. *Basic and Applied Social Psychology, 15,* 251–276.

Randi, J. (1982). *Flim flam! Psychics, ESP, unicorns, and other delusions.* Buffalo, NY: Prometheus Books.

Rauscher, F. W., Shaw, G. L., & Key, K. N. (1993). Music and spatial task performance. *Nature, 365,* 611.

Reeve, L., Reeve, K. F., Brown, A. K., Brown, J. L., & Poulson, C. L. (1992). Effects of delayed reinforcement on infant vocalization rate. *Journal of the Experimental Analysis of Behavior, 58,* 1–8.

Renne, C. M., & Creer, T. L. (1976). Training children with asthma to use inhalation therapy equipment. *Journal of Applied Behavior Analysis, 9,* 1–11.

Reynolds, G. S. (1968). *A primer of operant conditioning.* Glenview, IL: Scott, Foresman.

Reynolds, R. I. (1992). Recognition of expertise in chess players. *American Journal of Psychology, 105,* 409–415.

Riskind, J. H., & Maddux, J. E. (1993). Loomingness, helplessness, and fearfulness: An integration of harm-looming and self-efficacy models of fear. *Journal of Social and Clinical Psychology, 12,* 73–89.

ROCKEFELLER, J. D. IV. (1994). *Is military research hazardous to veterans' health? Lessons spanning half a century: A report examining biological experimentation on U.S. military* [on-line]. www.trufax.org/trans/roc00.html

RODIN, J., & LANGER, E. J. (1977). Long-term effects of a control-relevant intervention with the institutionalized aged. *Journal of Personality and Social Psychology, 35,* 897–902.

ROGELBERG, S. G., & LUONG, A. (1998). Nonresponse to mailed surveys: A review and guide. *Current Directions in Psychological Science, 7,* 60–65.

ROGOSA, D. (1980). A critique of cross-legged correlation. *Psychological Bulletin, 88,* 245–258.

ROHLES, F. H., JR. (1992). Orbital bar pressing: A historical note on Skinner and the chimpanzees in space. *American Psychologist, 47,* 1531–1533.

ROMANES, G. J. (1886). *Animal intelligence.* New York: D. Appleton.

ROSENBERG, M. J. (1969). The conditions and consequences of evaluation apprehension. In R. Rosenthal & R. L. Rosnow (Eds.), *Artifact in behavioral research* (pp. 280–349). New York: Academic Press.

ROSENTHAL, R. (1966). *Experimenter effects in behavioral research.* New York: Appleton-Century-Crofts.

ROSENTHAL, R. (1994). Science and ethics in conducting, analyzing, and reporting psychological research. *Psychological Science, 5,* 127–133.

ROSENTHAL, R., & FODE, K. L. (1963a). Three experiments in experimenter bias. *Psychological Reports, 12,* 491–511.

ROSENTHAL, R., & FODE, K. L. (1963b). The effect of experimenter bias on the performance of the albino rat. *Behavioral Science, 8,* 183–189.

ROSENTHAL, R., & ROSNOW, R. L. (1991). *Essentials of behavioral research: Methods and data analysis* (2nd ed.). New York: McGraw-Hill.

ROSNOW, R. L., GOODSTADT, B. E., SULS, J. M., & GITTER, A. G. (1973). More on the social psychology of the experiment: When compliance turns to self-defense. *Journal of Personality and Social Psychology, 27,* 337–343.

RUCCI, A. J., & TWENEY, R. D. (1980). Analysis of variance and the "second discipline" of scientific psychology: A historical account. *Psychological Bulletin, 87,* 166–184.

SAMELSON, F. (1992). Rescuing the reputation of Sir Cyril [Burt]. *Journal of the History of the Behavioral Sciences, 28,* 221–233.

SANFORD, E. C. (1910, August 8). *Letter to E. B. Titchener.* Ithaca, NY: Titchener Papers, Cornell University.

SANFORD, E. C. (1914). Psychic research in the animal field: Der Kluge Hans and the Elberfeld horses. *American Journal of Psychology, 25,* 3–31.

SCHACHTER, S. (1959). *The psychology of affiliation.* Stanford, CA: Stanford University Press.

SCHAIE, K. W. (1983). The Seattle longitudinal study: A 21 year exploration of psychometric intelligence in adulthood. In K. W. Schaie (Ed.), *Longitudinal studies of adult psychological development.* New York: Guilford Press.

SCHAIE, K. W. (1988). Ageism in psychological research. *American Psychologist, 43,* 179–183.

SCHNEIDER, W., & BJORKLUND, D. F. (1992). Expertise, aptitude, and strategic remembering. *Child Development, 63,* 461–473.

SCHNEIRLA, T. C. (1929). Learning and orientation in ants. *Comparative Psychology Monographs, 6 (No. 4).*

SCHOENEMAN, T. J., & RUBANOWITZ, D. E. (1985). Attributions in the advice columns: Actors and observers, causes and reasons. *Personality and Social Psychology Bulletin, 11,* 315–325.

SCHRADER, W. B. (1971). The predictive validity of the College Board Admissions tests. In W. H. Angoff (Ed.), *The College Board Admission Testing Program.* New York: College Entrance Examination Board.

SCHUMAN, H., & PRESSER, S. (1996). *Questions and answers in attitude surveys: Experiments on question form, wording, and content.* Thousand Oaks, CA: Sage.

SCOTT-JONES, D. (2000). Recruitment of research participants. In B. D. Sales & S. Folkman (Eds.), *Ethics in research with human participants* (pp. 27–34). Washington, DC: American Psychological Association.

SCRIPTURE, E. W. (1895). *Thinking, feeling, doing.* Meadville, PA: Chautauqua-Century Press.

SEARS, D. O. (1986). College sophomores in the laboratory: Influences of a narrow data base on psychology's view of human nature. *Journal of Personality and Social Psychology, 51,* 515–530.

SECHREST, L., & FIGUEREDO, A. J. (1993). Program evaluation. In L. W. Porter & M. R. Rosenzweig (Eds.), *Annual review of psychology. Volume 44* (pp. 645–674). Palo Alto, CA: Annual Reviews.

SELIGMAN, M. E. P. (1975). *Helplessness: On depression, development, and death.* San Francisco: W. H. Freeman.

SELIGMAN, M. E. P., CASTELLON, C., CACCIOLA, J., SCHULMAN, P., LUBORSKY, L., OLLOVE, M., & DOWNING, R. (1988). Explanatory style change during cognitive therapy for unipolar depression. *Journal of Abnormal Psychology, 97,* 13–18.

SELIGMAN, M. E. P., & MAIER, S. F. (1967). Failure to escape traumatic shock. *Journal of Experimental Psychology, 74,* 1–9.

SELIGMAN, M. E. P., & SCHULMAN, P. (1986). Explanatory style as a predictor of productivity and quitting among life insurance agents. *Journal of Personality and Social Psychology, 50,* 832–838.

SHELDON, W. H. (1940). *The varieties of human physique: An introduction to constitutional psychology.* New York: Harper & Row.

SHELDON, W. H. (1942). *The varieties of temperament: A psychology of constitutional differences.* New York: Harper & Row.

SHEPARD, R. N., & METZLER, J. (1971). Mental rotation of three-dimensional objects. *Science, 171,* 701–703.

SHERROD, D. R., HAGE, J. N., HALPERN, P. L., & MOORE, B. S. (1977). Effects of personal causation and perceived control on responses to an environment: The more control, the better. *Journal of Personality and Social Psychology, 13,* 14.

SHUTE, V. J. (1994). Learners and instruction: What's good for the goose may not be good for the gander. *Psychological Science Agenda, 7(3),* 8–9, 16.

SIDMAN, M. (1960). *Tactics of scientific research.* New York: Basic Books.

SIEBER, J. E. (1994). Will the new code help researchers to be more ethical? *American Psychologist, 25,* 369–375.

SIEBER, J. E. (1998). Planning ethically responsible research. In L. Bickman & D. J. Rog (Eds.), *Handbook of applied social research methods* (pp. 127–156). Thousand Oaks, CA: Sage.

SIEBER, J. E., & SAKS, M. J. (1989). A census of subject pool characteristics. *American Psychologist, 44,* 1053–1061.

SIGALL, H., & OSTROVE, N. (1975). Beautiful but dangerous: Effects of offender attractiveness and nature of the crime on juridic judgment. *Journal of Personality and Social Psychology, 31,* 410–414.

SILVERMAN, I. (1975). Nonreactive methods and the law. *American Psychologist, 30,* 764–769.

SINGER, P. (1975). *Animal liberation.* New York: Avon.

SKINNER, B. F. (1953). *Science and human behavior.* New York: Free Press.

SKINNER, B. F. (1956). A case history in scientific method. *American Psychologist, 12,* 221–233.

SKINNER, B. F. (1966). Operant behavior. In W. K. Honig (Ed.), *Operant behavior: Areas of research and application* (pp. 12–32). New York: Appleton-Century-Crofts.

SKINNER, B. F. (1969). *Contingencies of reinforcement.* Englewood Cliffs, NJ: Prentice-Hall.

SKINNER, B. F. (1976). *Walden Two.* New York: Macmillan. (Original work published 1948).

SKINNER, B. F. (1979). *The shaping of a behaviorist.* New York: New York University Press.

SKINNER, B. F. (1984). *A matter of consequences.* New York: New York University Press.

SMALL, W. S. (1900). An experimental study of the mental processes of the rat. *American Journal of Psychology, 11,* 80–100.

SMITH, L. D. (1992). On prediction and control: B. F. Skinner and the technological ideal of science. *American Psychologist, 47,* 216–223.

SMITH, S., & SECHREST, L. (1991). Treatment of aptitude × treatment interactions. *Journal of Consulting and Clinical Psychology, 59,* 233–244.

SMITH, S. S., & RICHARDSON, D. (1983). Amelioration of deception and harm in psychological research: The important role of debriefing. *Journal of Personality and Social Psychology, 44,* 1075–1082.

SMOLL, F. L., SMITH, R. E., BARNETT, N. P., & EVERETT, J. J. (1993). Enhancement of children's self-esteem through social support training for youth sport coaches. *Journal of Applied Psychology, 78,* 602–610.

Society for Research in Child Development. (1996). Ethical standards for research with children. *SRCD Directory of Members, 337–339.*

SOKAL, M. M. (Ed.) (1981). *An education in psychology: James McKeen Cattell's journal and letters from Germany and England, 1880–1888.* Cambridge, MA: MIT Press.

SOKAL, M. M. (1987). James McKeen Cattell and mental anthropometry: Nineteenth-century science and reform and the origins of psychological testing. In M. M. Sokal (Ed.), *Psychological testing and American society, 1890–1930* (pp. 21–45). New Brunswick, NJ: Rutgers University Press.

SOKAL, M. M. (1992). Origins and early years of the American Psychological Association, 1890–1906. *American Psychologist, 47,* 111–122.

SOLOMON, R. L. (1949). An extension of control group design. *Psychological Bulletin, 46,* 137–150.

SPATZ, C. (1997). *Basic statistics: Tales of distributions* (6th ed.). Pacific Grove, CA: Brooks/Cole.

SPELKE, E. S. (1985). Preferential looking methods as tools for the study of cognition in infancy. In G. Gottlieb & N. Krasnegor (Eds.), *Measurement of audition and vision in the first year of postnatal life* (pp. 323–363). Norwood, NJ: Ablex.

SPRINTHALL, R. C. (2000). *Basic statistical analysis* (6th ed.). Boston: Allyn & Bacon.

SPURZHEIM, J. G. (1978). Outlines of phrenology. In D. N. Robinson (Ed.), *Significant contributions to the history of psychology.* Series E. Volume II. Washington, DC: University Publications of America. (Original work published 1832).

STEELE, K. M., BALL, T. N., & RUNK, R. (1997). Listening to Mozart does not enhance backwards digit span performance. *Perceptual and Motor Skills, 84,* 1179–1184.

STERNBERG, R. J., & GRIGORENKO, E. L. (1999). A smelly 113° in the shade (Or, why we do field research). *APS Observer, 12(8),* 10–11, 20–21.

STERNBERG, R. J., POWELL, C., McGRANE, P., & GRANTHAM-McGREGOR, S. (1997). Effects of a parasitic infection on cognitive functioning. *Journal of Experimental Psychology: Applied, 3,* 67–76.

STOLZENBERG, L., & D'ALESSIO, S. J. (1997). "Three strikes and you're out": The impact of California's new mandatory sentencing law on serious crime rates. *Crime and Delinquency, 43,* 457–470.

STROOP, J. R. (1992). Studies of interference in serial verbal reactions. *Journal of Experimental Psychology: General, 121,* 15–23. (Original work published 1935).

SULLIVAN, D. S., & DEIKER, T. E. (1973). Subject-experimenter perceptions of ethical issues in human research. *American Psychologist, 28,* 587–591.

TATHAM, T. A., WANCHISEN, B. A., & HINELINE, P. N. (1993). Effects of fixed and variable ratios on human behavioral variability. *Journal of the Experimental Analysis of Behavior, 59,* 349–359.

TAYLOR, D. W., GARNER, W. R., & HUNT, H. F. (1959). Education for research in psychology. *American Psychologist, 14,* 167–179.

TAYLOR, S. J., & BOGDAN, R. (1998). *Introduction to qualitative methods: A guide and resource* (3rd ed.). New York: Wiley.

TERMAN, L. M. (1925). *Genetic studies of genius, Vol. 1. Mental and physical traits of a thousand gifted children.* Stanford, CA: Stanford University Press.

TERMAN, L. M., & ODEN, M. H. (1947). *Genetic studies of genius, Vol. 4. The gifted child grows up: Twenty-five years' follow-up of a superior group.* Stanford, CA: Stanford University Press.

TERMAN, L. M., & ODEN, M. H. (1959). *Genetic studies of genius, Vol. 5. The gifted group at mid-life: Thirty-five years' follow-up of the superior child.* Stanford, CA: Stanford University Press.

TERRACE, H. (1963). Discrimination learning with and without ``errors.'' *Journal of the Experimental Analysis of Behavior, 6,* 1–27.

THOMAS, E. (1995). *The very best men.* New York: Simon & Schuster.

THORNDIKE, E. L. (1898). Animal intelligence: An experimental study of the associative processes in animals. *Psychological Review Monographs, 2 (No. 8).*

THORNDIKE, E. L. (2000). *Animal intelligence: Experimental studies.* New Brunswick, NJ: Transaction Publishers. (Original work published 1911).

THURSTONE, L. L. (1938). Primary mental abilities. *Psychometric Monographs, No. 1.* Chicago: University of Chicago Press.

TITCHENER, E. B. (1916). *A textbook of psychology.* New York: MacMillan. (Original work published 1909).

TODD, J. T., & MORRIS, E. K. (1992). Case histories in the great power of steady misrepresentation. *American Psychologist, 47,* 1441–1453.

TOLMAN, E. C. (1959). Principles of purposive behavior. In S. Koch (Ed.), *Psychology: A study of a science: Volume 2. General systematic formulations, learning, and special processes* (pp. 92–157). New York: McGraw-Hill.

TOLMAN, E. C., TRYON, R. C., & JEFFRIES, L. A. (1929). A self-recording maze with an automatic delivery table. *University of California Publications in Psychology, 4,* 99–112.

TOMAS, V. (Ed.). (1957). *Charles S. Peirce: Essays in the philosophy of science.* New York: Liberal Arts Press.

TOMLINSON-KEASEY, C. (1990). The working lives of Terman's gifted women. In H. Y. Grossman & N. L. Chester, (Eds.), *The experience and meaning of work in women's lives* (pp. 213–239). Hillsdale, NJ: Lawrence Erlbaum.

TRABASSO, T. (1963). Stimulus emphasis and all-or-none learning in concept identification. *Journal of Experimental Psychology, 65,* 398–406.

TRIANDIS, H. C. (1995). *Individualism and collectivism.* Boulder, CO: Westview Press.

TRYON, R. C. (1929). The genetics of learning ability in rats: Preliminary report. *University of California Publications in Psychology, 4,* 71–89.

TUKEY, J. W. (1977). *Exploratory data analysis.* Reading, MA: Addison-Wesley.

TULVING, E. (1966). Subjective organization and the effects of repetition in multi-trial free recall. *Journal of Verbal Learning and Verbal Behavior, 5,* 195–197.

TVERSKY, A., & KAHNEMAN, D. (1973). Availability: A heuristic for judging frequency and probability. *Cognitive Psychology, 5,* 207–232.

TWENEY, R. D. (1987). Programmatic research in experimental psychology: E. B. Titchener's laboratory investigations, 1891–1927. In M. G. Asch & W. R. Woodward (Eds.), *Psychology in twentieth-century thought and society* (pp. 34–57). New York: Cambridge University Press.

ULRICH, R. S. (1984). View through a window may influence recovery from surgery. *Science, 224,* 420–421.

VAN KAMMEN, W. B., & STOUTHAMER-LOEBER, M. (1998). Practice aspects of interview data collection and data management. In L. Bickman & D. J. Rog (Eds.), *Handbook of applied social research methods* (pp. 375–397). Thousand Oaks, CA: Sage.

WAGAMAN, J. R., MILTENBERGER, R. G., & ARNDORFER, R. E. (1993). Analysis of a simplified treatment for stuttering in children. *Journal of Applied Behavior Analysis, 26,* 53–61.

WAGNER, J. A., III, RUBIN, P. A., & CALLAHAN, T. J. (1988). Incentive payment and nonmanagerial productivity: An interrupted time series analysis of magnitude and trend. *Organizational Behavior and Human Decision Processes, 42,* 47–74.

WALKER, A. J. (1996). Couples watching television: Gender, power, and the remote control. *Journal of Marriage and the Family, 58,* 813–823.

WASON, P. C., & JOHNSON-LAIRD, P. N. (1972). *Psychology of reasoning: Structure and content.* Cambridge, MA: Harvard University Press.

WATSON, J. B. (1907). Kinesthetic and organic sensations: Their role in the reactions of the white rat to the maze. *Psychological Review Monograph Supplements, 8 (No. 33).*

WATSON, J. B. (1924). *Behaviorism.* New York: W. W. Norton.

WATSON, J. B. (1928). *Psychological care of infant and child.* New York: W. W. Norton.

WATSON, J. B., & RAYNER, R. (1920). Conditioned emotional reactions. *Journal of Experimental Psychology, 3,* 1–14.

WEBB, E. J., CAMPBELL, D. T., SCHWARTZ, R. D., SECHREST, L., & GROVE, J. B. (1981). *Nonreactive measures in the social sciences* (2nd ed.). Boston: Houghton Mifflin.

Webster's word histories. (1989). Springfield, MA: Merriam-Webster.

WEISS, J. M. (1968). Effects of coping response on stress. *Journal of Comparative and Physiological Psychology, 65,* 251–260.

WEISS, J. M. (1977). Psychological and behavioral influences on gastrointestinal lesions in animal models. In J. D. Maser & M. E. P. Seligman (Eds.), *Psychopathology: Experimental models.* San Francisco: W. H. Freeman.

WICKENS, D. D., BORN, D. G., & ALLEN, C. K. (1963). Proactive inhibition and item similarity in short-term memory. *Journal of Verbal Learning and Verbal Behavior, 2,* 440–445.

WINSTON, R. S. (1990). Robert Sessions Woodworth and the "Columbia Bible": How the psychological experiment was redefined. *American Journal of Psychology, 103,* 391–401.

WITT, L. A., & NYE, L. G. (1992). Gender and the relationship between perceived fairness of pay or promotion and job satisfaction. *Journal of Applied Psychology, 77,* 910–917.

WOLF, M. M. (1978). Social validity: The case for subjective measurement, or how behavior analysis is finding its heart. *Journal of Applied Behavior Analysis, 11,* 203–214.

WOLLEN, K. A., WEBER, A., & LOWRY, D. H. (1972). Bizarreness versus interaction of images

as determinants of learning. *Cognitive Psychology, 3,* 518–523.

WOOD, J. M., & BOOTZIN, R. R. (1990). The prevalence of nightmares and their independence from anxiety. *Journal of Abnormal Psychology, 99,* 64–68.

WOOD, J. M., BOOTZIN, R. R., ROSENHAN, D., NOLEN-HOEKSEMA, S., & JOURDEN, F. (1992). Effects of the 1989 San Francisco earthquake and content of nightmares. *Journal of Abnormal Psychology, 101,* 219–224.

WOODWORTH, R. S. (1938). *Experimental psychology.* New York: Henry Holt.

WORD, C. O., ZANNA, M. P., & COOPER, J. (1974). The nonverbal mediation of self-fulfilling prophecies in interracial interaction. *Journal of Experimental Social Psychology, 10,* 109–120.

WUNDT, W. (1904). *Principles of physiological psychology* (5th ed.) (E. B. Titchener, Trans.). New York: MacMillan. (Original work published 1874).

YARMEN, A. D., & BULL, M. P. (1978). Where were you when President Kennedy was assassinated? *Bulletin of the Psychonomic Society, 11,* 133–135.

YEATON, W. H., & SECHREST, L. (1986). Use and misuse of no-difference findings in eliminating threats to validity. *Evaluation Review, 10,* 836–852.

ZEIGARNIK, B. (1967). On finished and unfinished tasks. In W. D. Ellis (Ed.), *A source book of Gestalt psychology* (pp. 300–314). London: Routledge and Kegan Paul. (Original work published 1927).

Name Index

Subject Index

Photo Credits

Chapter 1 Figure 1.1: © 1998 by Sidney Harris. Figure 1.2: Granger Collection. Figure 1.3: Courtesy George Bush Presidential Library & Museum. Figure 1.4: UPI/Corbis-Bettmann.

Chapter 2 Figure 2.1: From *Psychological Care of Infant and Child* by John B. Watson. Copyright 1928 by W. W. Norton & Company. Reprinted by permission of W. W. Norton & Company, Inc. Figure 2.2: © 1965 by Stanley Milgram. From the film, *Obedience,* distributed by the New York University Film Library. Figure 2.4: From *Journal of Zoophily,* 1907.

Chapter 3 Figure 3.3: John de Visser/Masterfile. Figure 3.4: From *Clever Hans, The Horse of Mr. Von Osten* by Oskar Pfungst, 1965; published by Holt, Rinehart and Winston, Inc. Figure 3.5a: Georg Gerster/Photo Researchers.

Chapter 4 Figure 4.3: Courtesy Clark University Archives. Figure 4.4: DILBERT reprinted by permission of United Feature Syndicate, Inc. Figure 4.5: © 1998 by Sidney Harris.

Chapter 7 Figure 7.4: Courtesy Dr. David N. Lee, Department of Psychology, University of Edinburgh, Scotland. Figure 7.6: Donald Reilly © 1993 from The New Yorker Collection. All Rights Reserved.

Chapter 10 Figure 10.2: Courtesy Archives of the History of American Psychology, University of Akron, Akron, Ohio.

Chapter 11 Figure 11.1: Courtesy Clark University Archives. Figure 11.2: Courtesy Robert Mearns Yerkes Papers, Manuscripts and Archives, Yale University Library. Figure 11.7: Sybil Shelton/Monkmeyer Press Photo. Figure 11.8: Courtesy Gerbrands Corporation.

Chapter 12 Figure 12.1: Courtesy Ch. Boesch/Zoological Institute of the University of Basel, Switzerland.

Epilogue Page 422: Photo by Don Harris, courtesy of Public Information Office, University of California, Santa Cruz. Page 424: Courtesy Elizabeth Loftus, University of Washington.

Appendix Page 429: © 1993 Bill Watterson/Universal Press Syndicate.

Text and Illustration Credits

Chapter 1   Pages 3 and 4: Myers, D. G., *Social Psychology, 3rd ed.* Copyright © 1990, p. 393, Worth Publishers. Reprinted with permission of McGraw-Hill. Page 24: Tolman, E. C., *Principles of Purposive Behavior.* Koch, S. (Ed.), p. 152. Copyright © McGraw-Hill, 1959.

Chapter 2   Pages 40, 43, 51–52, 61, and 62: Copyright © 1992 by the American Psychological Association. Reprinted by permission. Page 53: Sullivan, D. S., and Deicker, T. E., *American Psychologist, 48,* p. 589. Copyright © 1973 by the American Psychological Association. Reprinted by permission.

Chapter 3   Pages 81 and 82: From Hubel, D. H., *Eye, Brain, and Vision.* Copyright © 1988 by Scientific American Library. Reprinted with permission of W. H. Freeman and Company. Page 80: Krupat, E. (Ed.), *"Conversation with John Darley."* From *Psychology is Social: Readings and Conversations in Social Psychology,* pp. 255–263. Copyright © 1975. Reprinted by permission of HarperCollins College Publishers. Page 83: Seligman, M. E. P., *Helplessness: On Depression, Development and Death.* Copyright © 1975 by Martin E. P. Seligman. Reprinted with permission of W. H. Freeman and Company. Page 98, Figure 3.6: Reprinted with permission from *Thesaurus of Psychological Index Terms,* American Psychological Association, all rights reserved. Copyright © 1994.

Chapter 4   Page 109, Figure 4.1: From Kim, K., and Spelke, E. S., Infant's sensitivity to effects of gravity on visual motion (pp. 385–393). *JEP: Human Perception and Performance, 18(2).* Copyright © 1992. Reprinted with permission from the American Psychological Association. Page 110, Figure 4.2: From Shepard, R. N., & Metzler, J., Figure 1, Vol. 171, 1971, *Science,* page 702. Copyright © 1971 by the AAAS. Page 115: Excerpt from *Introduction to Personality,* Third Edition, by Walter Mischel. Copyright © 1981 by Holt, Rinehart, and Winston, Inc., reprinted by permission of the publisher. Table 4.2: Adapted from *The Psychology of Affiliation,* by Stanley Schachter with the permission of the publishers, Stanford University Press. Copyright © 1959 by the Board of Trustees of the Leland Stanford Junior University.

Chapter 5   Figure 5.1: From Bandura, A., Ross, D., and Ross, S. A., Imitation of film-mediated aggressive models (pp. 3–11). *Journal of Abnormal and Social Psychology, 66.* Copyright © 1963 by the American Psychological Association. Adapted by permission.

Chapter 6   Figure 6.2: From Carello, C., Anderson, K. L., & Kunkler-Peek, A. J., Perception of object length by sound (pp. 211–214). *Psychological Science, 9.* Copyright © 1998 by Blackwell Publishers. Reprinted by permission.

Chapter 7   Figure 7.2, page 217: From Blakemore, C., and Cooper, G. F., *Nature, 228,* p. 478. Copyright © 1970 by H. Holt-Macmillan. Reprinted by permission. Figure 7.3: From Stroop, J. R., Studies of interference in serial verbal reactions (reprint of 1935 article) (pp. 15–23). *JEP: General, 121(1).* Copyright © 1992 by the American Psychological Association. Reprinted by permission. Figure 7.7: From *Psychopathology: Experimental Models* by Seligman and Maser. Copyright © 1977, Martin E. P. Seligman and Jack Maser. Reprinted with permission of W. H. Freeman and Company. Page 223; Figure 7.11; Table 7.2: From Bransford, J. D., and Johnson, M. K., Contextual prerequisites for understanding (pp. 717–726). *Journal of Verbal Learning and Verbal Behavior, 11.* Copyright © 1972 by Academic Press.

Chapter 8 Figure 8.1: From Wollen et al., 1972, Bizarreness versus interaction of images as determinants of learning (pp. 518–523). *Cognitive Psychology, 3.* Copyright © 1972 by Academic Press. Reprinted by permission. Page 254: From Godden, D. R., and Baddeley, A. D., Context-dependent memory in two natural environments: On land and under water. *British Journal of Psychology, 66,* 325–331, adaptation of Table 1. Copyright © 1975 by the British Psychological Society. Figure 8.4: From Keltner, D., Ellsworth, P. C., and Edwards, K., Beyond simple pessimism: Effects of sadness (pp. 740–752). *Journal of Personality and Social Psychology, 64(5).* Copyright © 1993 by the American Psychological Association. Reprinted by permission. Figure 8.9: From Gunter et al., 1981, Proactive interference effects with television (pp. 480–487). *JEP: Human Learning and Memory, 7(6).* Copyright © 1981 by the American Psychological Association. Adapted by permission. Figure 8.11: From Holmes, D. S., McGilley, B. M., and Houston, B. K., 1984, Task-related arousal of Type A and Type B persons (pp. 1322–1327). *Journal of Personality and Social Psychology, 46(6).* Copyright © 1984 by the American Psychological Association. Reprinted by permission.

Chapter 9 Figure 9.1: From Fancher, R. E., *Pioneers of Psychology (2nd Ed.),* p. 231. Copyright © 1990 by W. W. Norton & Co. Figure 9.8 and Table 9.1: From Eron, L. D. et al., Does television violence cause aggression? (pp. 253–263). *American Psychological, 27.* Copyright © 1972 by the American Psychological Association. Reprinted by permission. Page 302: From APA, Standards 2.02 (a. only), 2.03. Ethical Principles of Psychologists and Code of Conduct. Copyright © 1992 by the American Psychological Association. Reprinted by permission. Table 9.2: From Bouchard, T. J., and McGue, M., Familial studies of intelligence: A review (pp. 1055–1059). *Science, 212.* Copyright © 1981 by the American Association for the Advancement of Science. Adapted by permission. Table 9.3: From Emde, R. N. et al., 1992, Temperament, emotion, and cognition at fourteen months (pp. 1437–1455). *Child Development, 63.* Copyright © 1992 by the Society for Research in Child Development, Inc. Adapted by permission of the University of Chicago Press.

Chapter 10 Figure 10.1: From Fisher et al., Field test of the cognitive interview (pp. 722–727). *Journal of Applied Psychology, 74(5).* Copyright © 1989 by the American Psychological Association. Adapted by permission. Page 341: From Sechrest, L., and Figueredo, A. J. 1993, Program evaluation. Reproduced with permission, from the *Annual Review of Psychology, Volume 44,* © 1993, by Annual Reviews, Inc. Figure 10.8: From Wagner, J. A. et al., 1968, Incentive payment and nonmarginal productivity (pp. 47–74). *Organizational Behavior and Human Decision Processes, 42.* Copyright © 1988 by Academic Press. Reprinted by permission. Pages 337 and 338: From Campbell, D. T., Reforms as experiments (pp. 409–429). *American Psychologist, 24.*

Copyright © 1969 by the American Psychological Association. Reprinted by permission.

Chapter 11   Page 363: From Skinner, B. F., *A Matter of Consequences.* Copyright © 1984 by New York University Press. Reprinted by permission. Page 366: Watson, J. B., 1924, Behaviorism. Copyright © 1924 by W. W. Norton & Co. Reprinted by permission. Figure 11.11: From Hume, K. M., and Crossman, J., Musical reinforcement of practice behaviors (pp. 665–670). *Journal of Applied Behavior Analysis, 25.* Copyright © 1992 by the University of Kansas. Reprinted by permission. Figure 11.13: From Wagaman, J. R., Miltenberger, R. G., and Arndorfer, R. E., Analysis of simplified treatment for stuttering in children (pp. 53–61). *Journal of Applied Analysis, 26.* Copyright © 1993 by the University of Kansas. Reprinted by permission.

Chapter 12   Page 392: From Boesch-Acherman, H., and Boesch, C., Tool use in wild chimpanzees (pp. 18–21). *Current Directions in Psychological Science, 2.* Copyright © 1993. Reprinted with permission of Cambridge University Press. Table 12.1 from APA, Standards 1.14, 5.03, 5.08, 6.12, 6.13. Ethical Principles of Psychologists and Code of Conduct. Copyright © 1992 by the American Psychological Association. Reprinted by permission. Table 12.2: From Hall, J. A., and Veccia, E. M., More "touching" observations: New insights (pp. 1155–1162). *Journal of Personality and Social Psychology, 59(6).* Copyright © 1990 by the American Psychological Association. Reprinted by permission. Page 404: From APA, Standard 1.06. Ethical Principles of Psychologists and Code of Conduct. Copyright © 1992 by the American Psychological Association. Reprinted by permission. Figure 12.2: From Ulrich, R. S., 1984, View through a window may influence recovery from surgery (pp. 420–421). *Science, 224.* Copyright © 1984 by the American Association for the Advancement of Science. Reprinted by permission.

Appendix A   Page 431: From APA, Guidelines for nonsexist language. *Publication Manual.* Copyright 1983 by the American Psychological Association. Reprinted by permission.

Appendix D   Tables on pages 498–500: From Pearson, E. S., and Hartley, H. O., *Biometrika Tables for Statisticians, Vol. 1, 3rd Ed.* Copyright 1966 by Cambridge University Press. Reprinted by permission.